Christmas,
1994

To Marilyn —
A tender of
roses.
Bud

THE ULTIMATE
ROSE BOOK

THE ULTIMATE

1,500 roses—antique, modern
(including miniature), and wild—all shown
in color and selected for their beauty, fragrance,
and enduring popularity

HARRY N. ABRAMS, INC.,
PUBLISHERS

ROSE BOOK

by Stirling Macoboy

Foreword by
Patricia Stemler Wiley

CONTENTS

Features

*To the memories of Alison Madden, Elaine Miller and
Valerie Swane — the rose loving ladies who encouraged
my enthusiasm for the queen of flowers.*

FOREWORD

Book writing is a complex art and Stirling Macoboy reveals his mastery of it again and again. During the last quarter of a century he has produced many magnificent volumes devoted to the world of flowers.

This time the rose comes to his exclusive attention as he guides us on a tour through the fragrant world of this loveliest of blooms. The author's photographic skills transport us all over the globe as he captures the enduring beauty of the rose and provides a splendid visual display of every variety listed.

Stirling's easy and humorous style illuminates a text that is both highly readable and full of fascinating detail. His mastery of the field masks skilful preparation and creates a monumental work to be admired and referred to often. Whatever your favorite rose, you are likely to find all the facts about it here, and more besides. You may discover the romance behind some of the names, and the seductive power of the rose in history.

With the exception of certain Wild Roses and some modern Miniatures, roses of every type are arranged here in a single alphabetical sequence ensuring that the information is easily accessible. This A–Z arrangement of the contents is punctuated with a number of small colorful features in which the rose is revealed at many times in her history.

This is a book to reach for time after time—to admire for its beauty, to read at leisure and to open for specific information. For those in search of the ultimate rose book, here at the end of the rainbow is the treasure they have been seeking.

Patricia Stemler Wiley
Roses of Yesterday
and Today, Inc.
Watsonville
California USA

Sure, and may there be a road before you and it bordered with roses, the likes of which have ne'er been smelt or seen before, for the warm fine color and the great sweetness that is on them.

An Irish Blessing

I sometimes think that never blows so re[d]
The Rose as where some buried Caesa[r]

OMAR KHAYYAM
(TRANSLATED BY EDWARD FITZGERALD 1809–83)

INTRODUCTION

Above the doors of the fourteenth-century chapter house at York Minster is a Latin inscription, placed there by a traveller from Italy: 'As the rose is the flower of flowers, so this is the building of buildings!'

Indeed, the flower of flowers! Other flowers are admired, sometimes very ardently, but the rose is our favorite. In Persian (and in Sanskrit, the Latin of the East) the very word for rose serves for all other flowers too, as though they were but pale imitations of its beauty. In any language, a poet who compares the beloved's lips to the rose is understood to be implying perfection.

Why is the rose singled out, of all the world's beautiful flowers? A glance at the photographs in this book will give part of the answer: roses are very beautiful and they come in such variety that whether one's taste inclines to the subtle, the flamboyant or the delicate, there is a rose to [suit]. A photograph, of course, cannot show one of the rose's greatest [assets], its perfume. This is also familiar distilled into rose water. Attar, the essential oil from roses, was long believed to be a remedy for all sorts of maladies. Bring fragrance and beauty together and you have something irresistible.

All this would raise any flower to pre-eminence, but what about the thorny branches? Perhaps they are the rose's final grace, the flaw that saves it from that too-great perfection that we mortals can only admire, but not really love.

In these pages, I have tried to give a portrait of the rose as it really is, focusing my camera not so much on the dolled-up beauties of the flower shows as on real roses (over 1500 of them) growing in sunshine and in rain, just opening their petals and at the end of their beauty; sometimes coming in for a close look, sometimes standing back to see the bushes in the garden. I have grouped the Wild Roses—not all of them by any means, but those which seem to me the loveliest—together at the beginning, and rather than segregate the Old and Modern Garden Roses into their artificial classes I have preferred to allow them to display their charms together. This means that Albas may vie with Cluster-flowered Roses (formerly known as Floribundas), Ramblers mingle with Large-flowered Roses (formerly known as Hybrid Teas), and roses which are available in every catalogue rub shoulders with some that seem to have disappeared but whose beauty was too irresistible to be left out, all in one single alphabetical sequence. The Miniatures have also been collected separately, so that they may not be overshadowed by their larger cousins.

Every so often, the parade is interrupted by some aspect of the history and romance of the rose, or by glimpses of the people who, down the ages, have loved and cherished the flower of flowers.

Stirling Macoboy
Neutral Bay NSW Australia

THE CLASSIFICATION OF ROSES

The rose may rank with the lily as the oldest of cultivated flowers. Unlike the chaste lily, however, which has only recently consented to the gardener's desire that her species intermarry, the rose is a wanton, only too happy to accept another's pollen and bring forth new forms and colors to tease and delight her admirers. No wonder the ancients dedicated the rose to Venus!

This profligacy has two consequences for those who would get to know the rose. First, the wild species are very variable indeed, and the status of those in our gardens is apt to be uncertain from the all too common hybrids masquerading as species. Second, the rose has become the flower most hybridized and 'improved' by gardeners, so that the number of garden varieties on the nursery lists runs into the thousands, and more are being added all the time. This is no exaggeration. One American digest of available roses gave not far short of 10 000 names in 1990.

Rose-fanciers had tried since the beginning of the nineteenth century to bring order to the bewildering multitude by enlisting each garden rose under the banner of the species to which it seemed to have the most affinity. As the ever more complex hybrids grew less and less like any Wild Rose, rosarians then started to place them with some regard for their ancestry, in classes with names like Hybrid Tea, Bourbon, Climbing Floribunda and the like. There were over thirty of these classes.

Confusing as this system was to the uninitiated, the rose world clung to it until 1979, when the World Federation of Rose Societies finally adopted a simplified classification, into which a rose is fitted not by its supposed ancestors, but by the characters that it displays as a garden plant.

The system divides the thousands of named roses into three broad groups:

1. Wild Roses, which include both the truly wild species and those garden forms that are inseparably associated with them;

2. Old Garden Roses, which are those groups of horticultural origin that were already established prior to the year 1867, when 'La France' was seen to be the first of what, with hindsight, we now see as the Modern Garden Roses; and

3. Modern Garden Roses, the predominant roses of today and still, unlike the Old Garden Roses, in active development by hybridists.

If ever a picture were worth a thousand words, it is here. The diagram on the facing page shows how the three broad groups are themselves subdivided.

Rosa laevigata, *the Cherokee Rose, a vigorous climbing Wild Rose.*

Rosa gallica *'Officinalis', the Apothecary's Rose, an Old Garden Rose.*

'Granada', one of the most richly scented of the Modern Garden Roses.

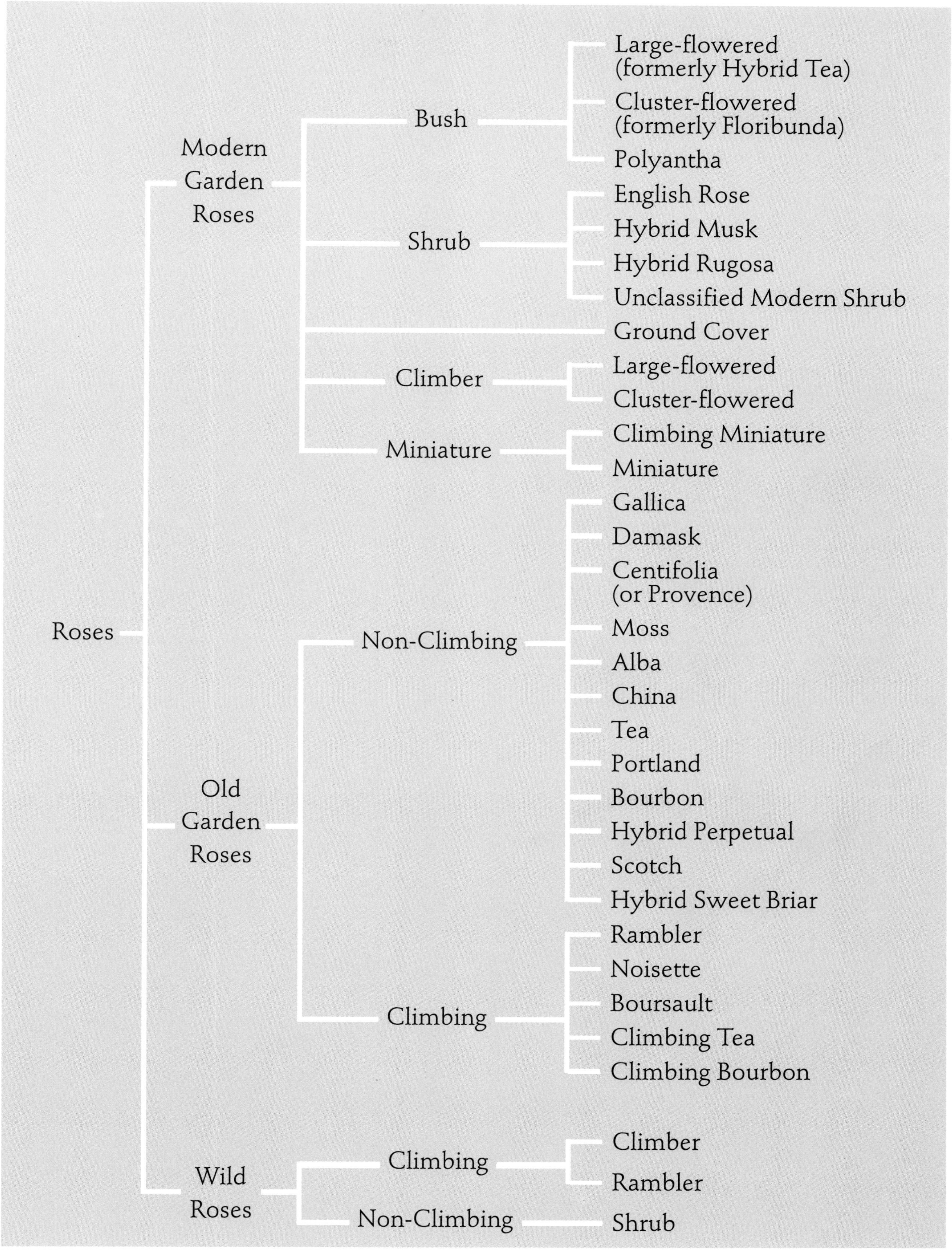

Roses
- Modern Garden Roses
  - Bush
    - Large-flowered (formerly Hybrid Tea)
    - Cluster-flowered (formerly Floribunda)
    - Polyantha
  - Shrub
    - English Rose
    - Hybrid Musk
    - Hybrid Rugosa
    - Unclassified Modern Shrub
  - Ground Cover
  - Climber
    - Large-flowered
    - Cluster-flowered
  - Miniature
    - Climbing Miniature
    - Miniature
- Old Garden Roses
  - Non-Climbing
    - Gallica
    - Damask
    - Centifolia (or Provence)
    - Moss
    - Alba
    - China
    - Tea
    - Portland
    - Bourbon
    - Hybrid Perpetual
    - Scotch
    - Hybrid Sweet Briar
  - Climbing
    - Rambler
    - Noisette
    - Boursault
    - Climbing Tea
    - Climbing Bourbon
- Wild Roses
  - Climbing
    - Climber
    - Rambler
  - Non-Climbing
    - Shrub

GUIDE TO THE ENTRIES

The more than 1500 roses depicted inside this book are presented in three series, and within each series the roses are listed in alphabetical order.

First come the Wild Roses, not all of them by any means, but a representative selection of the botanically important and horticulturally desirable. I have not blinded the reader with science by giving the botanical section to which each genus belongs. In any case, botanists are scarcely unanimous on how to classify the Wild Roses, the most recent revision of the genus having been published in 1820. I have contented myself with noting whether each rose behaves in the garden as a Shrub, Climber, or Rambler.

The Modern and Old Garden Roses follow the Wild Roses and they make up the great bulk of the entries. They have not been separated into their classes. Here, Gallicas vie in beauty with Large-flowered Bush Roses, Teas with Cluster-flowered Roses, in one alphabetical sequence.

The entries for the Miniatures follow, and the reason for grouping them all together is simply so that their diminutive scale will not be either overwhelmed by or confused among the larger roses.

Each rose has its classification alongside its name. Below that will be its codename, if it has one. In this book it often begins with two or three capitalised letters. This is the International Codename, given by the raiser. The capitalised letters are usually the first three of his or her firm's name. The idea is that if every catalogue, magazine or rose-book writer quotes the codename, rose-lovers, and the bureaucrats who administer Plant Patent and Plant Variety copyright laws will recognize just which rose is being talked about. There is no need to use codenames in conversation, and many are deliberately unpronounceable anyway.

Below the codename, if it has one, will be found other names by which the rose is known, if it has any. A large number of roses have multiple names, and deciding to which to give precedence is one of the minor headaches of writing a book like this. Usually, I have gone with the name registered with the American Rose Society's International Registration Authority. Sometimes I have exercised author's privilege and preferred the name used by the raiser, one which is less confusingly similar to that of another rose, or simply the most euphonious or romantic. If you are seeking a favorite rose and cannot find it, look it up in the index: it may be here under an alias.

The entry for each rose gives a description of the flower and foliage and names the breeder and gives the date of breeding. If known, the history of the rose is also supplied. If the rose varies from the norm for its class in habit, cultivation requirements or disease proneness or resistance, this is mentioned. The parentage of the rose follows, given in the standard form (seed parent × pollen parent). Where there are brackets, they indicate that the parent was an unnamed seedling from that cross. The time of flowering—spring, summer, or repeat flowering—is then given, and finally the fragrance of the rose is noted, if applicable.

The term, 'repeat flowering', needs some explanation. Just about all wild roses (*Rosa rugosa* is an exception) flower only in spring or early summer, on laterals grown from the main shoots of the previous year. At some unknown date, Chinese gardeners persuaded the garden forms of *R. chinensis* to have second, third, and even fourth cycles of growth and flower, so that the flowering season was extended until the chill of approaching winter put a stop to it. Despite what catalogues say, roses do not flower 'continuously' or 'perpetually'. There is always a gap between one cycle of bloom and the next. That is why the rosarians of the world prefer 'repeat flowering' or the French word, *remontant*, 'to arise again'. Lovers of irises and day lilies, who have recently performed the same magic with their favorites as the Chinese did a long time ago on the rose, have also adopted this terminology.

'Heritage', a repeat flowering rose with a lovely fragrance.

WILD ROSES

BOTANICAL NAME	***Rosa farreri persetosa***	Shrub	CLASS OF ROSE
SYNONYM	*R. elegantula* 'Persetosa', 'Threepenny Bit Rose'		

DESCRIPTION, HISTORY	One of the most unusual of roses, on account of the contrast between the size of the shrub and the minute daintiness of both foliage and soft pink flowers, *R. farreri persetosa* was discovered by that great plant hunter Reginald Farrer in 1915. It likes a cool moist spot. The very small, pale green ferny leaves color nicely in autumn, or fall, and the tiny hips are orange. *Persetosa* describes the innumerable bristles on the stems.
FLOWERING TIME	*Summer flowering*
FRAGRANCE (where applicable)	*Fragrant*

MODERN AND OLD GARDEN ROSES

CULTIVAR NAME	**'Amber Queen'**	Cluster-flowered	CLASS OF ROSE
CODENAME	HARoony		
SYNONYM	'Prinz Eugen von Savoyen'		

DESCRIPTION, HISTORY, BREEDER AND YEAR OF INTRODUCTION	Clear amber-yellow, 'Amber Queen' has the reputation of being one of the most generous with its flowers of all Modern Garden Roses. The flowers are medium sized, shapely and scented, their warm color being complemented by dark, maroon-tinted foliage. The bushes are low in growth, an increasingly popular feature. The raiser says that it is ideal as a standard. It was raised by Jack Harkness and introduced in England in 1984. It won the AARS award in 1988, the year of its introduction to the United States.
PARENTAGE	'Southampton' × 'Typhoon'
FLOWERING TIME	*Repeat flowering*
FRAGRANCE (where applicable)	*Fragrant*

MINIATURE ROSES

CULTIVAR NAME	**'Dorola'**	Miniature	CLASS OF ROSE
CODE NAME	MACshana		

SYNONYM	'Benson & Hedges Special'
DESCRIPTION, HISTORY, BREEDER AND YEAR OF INTRODUCTION	Sam McGredy had already named a Large-flowered Rose 'Benson & Hedges Special' and, to save confusion between the two, the IRA registered the Miniature as 'Dorola'. Under either of its names, this is one of the best yellow Miniatures. Foliage is dark and glossy. It was introduced in 1962.
PARENTAGE	'Minuetto' × 'New Day'
FLOWERING TIME	*Repeat flowering*
FRAGRANCE (where applicable)	*Fragrant*

WILD ROSES

O, my luve's like a red red rose
That's newly sprung in June
O, my luve's like a melodie
That's sweetly played in tune

ROBERT BURNS
1759–96

The rose is a flower of the northern hemisphere, none ever having crossed the equator without the assistance of a gardener. But there are few countries without a Wild Rose or two to call their own, growing, usually, on the edge of woodland and pasture, where they make use of their thorns to scramble up and over other plants, in the same way as their cousin the blackberry does. The total number is somewhere between 150 and 200; that it is not possible to give a more precise figure is due to the inherent variability of most rose species and their habit of interbreeding promiscuously both in gardens and in the wild.

Indeed, Linnaeus, the father of modern botany, and a man who decreed back in the mid-eighteenth century that science should call the rose by its Roman name *Rosa* rather than the Greek *Rhodon* complained that 'the determination of species of rose is unusually difficult, and he who has seen only a few has less trouble than one who has examined many'. It is still difficult for the gardener, who, used to the idea that every bush of, say, 'Queen Elizabeth', will be recognizably the same, can find it confusing that two apparently quite different Wild Roses might belong to the same species. That a Wild Rose might not be a true species at all but a natural hybrid, as *Rosa alba* seems to be, or even an ancient garden rose that has 'gone wild', as is apparently the case with *R. foetida,* only muddies the water further.

A revision of the genus is sorely needed, to sort matters out. It is astonishing that the most recent revision with any real claim to being comprehensive was published as long ago as 1820! Do not be too hard on the botanists, for it is a daunting task. It will be necessary to re-examine the Wild Roses of the world—in the wild, for many a scientific name has been founded on cultivated plants of doubtful origin—and there is the difficulty that the heartland of the rose is central Asia, encompassing such countries as Afghanistan, Iran, the far western provinces of China and the southern republics of the old Soviet Union, countries where politics have not hitherto made life very easy for visiting botanists.

In the meantime, botanists class the Wild Roses in several 'sections', the most commonly recognized arrangement being that devised in 1949 by the American botanist Alfred Rehder, who proposed ten. The most important are: the Pimpinellifoliae, encompassing the Burnet Rose (*R. pimpinellifolia*) and most of the yellow-flowered Wild Roses such as *R. xanthina, R. ecae,* and *R. foetida;* the Gallicanae, whose chief representative is *R. gallica,* father of the Gallicas, Damasks, and Centifolias of gardens; the Chinenses, a small group of confused botany but nevertheless of supreme horticultural importance, as it is from *R. chinensis* and *R. gigantea* that practically all our repeat-flowering Modern Garden Roses descend; the Cinnamomae, taking its name from the horticulturally unimportant *R. majalis (R. cinnamomea)* but including such noteworthy species as *R. rugosa* and *R. moyesii;* the Synstylae, which includes all the Himalayan Musk Roses and *R. multiflora* and *R. wichuraiana;* and the Carolinae, all of whose members are American.

To try to fit the garden roses into the system, as some recent books have done, is simply fatuous, as they almost always have ancestry from several sections, and in any case, even with the Wild Roses, surely the gardener is more interested in their beauty than in botanical minutiae?

I certainly am. In selecting among the Wild Roses for inclusion in this book, my sole criterion has been their beauty and garden-worthiness, and the only classification I have imposed upon them is to note whether they behave as Shrubs or Climbers in the garden. The botanist might dispute that some, such as the yellow Banksia Rose, are not truly Wild Roses, but all are worth growing and can be found in the catalogues of the many nurseries that specialize in them. Without further ado, here they are.

Rosa acicularis
Shrub
Arctic Rose, Circumpolar Rose

This rose is unique among Wild Roses in occurring right around the northern hemisphere, in the far north of Europe, Asia and North America. No other species hops the continents like this. *Acicularis,* which means 'needled', describes the thin, sharp spines which cover the stems. A low shrub, it is garden-worthy for its bright pink flowers, which appear very early in the spring, and for its extreme hardiness. Foliage is mid-green.

Spring flowering
Fragrant

▲ *Rosa acicularis*

Rosa arvensis
Rambler
Field Rose

Native to Western and Southern Europe, including the British Isles, this is one of the few roses in the region which does not belong to the *R. canina* group. The sweetly scented summer flowers make it likely that this species, not *R. moschata* from Persia, was the famous 'Musk Rose' of Shakespeare, Milton and Keats. The long trailing stems with their dark green leaves can cover hedges and embankments, even in light shade.

Summer flowering

Rosa banksiae lutea
Rambler
Lady Banks's Rose, Banksian Rose, Banksia Rose

Although this double pale yellow form is the best known in gardens, it is the single white form (*R. banksiae normalis*) of the Lady Banks's Rose that is found wild in central China, and it was the fragrant double white that was brought from Canton to Kew by William Kerr in 1807 and named in honor of Sir Joseph Banks's wife, Dorothea. Preferring a warm sunny climate, *R. banksiae* is one of the most rampant of all climbing roses. With small dark evergreen foliage, it makes a curtain of blossom in mid-spring.

Spring flowering
Fragrant

Rosa beggeriana
Shrub

Not among the better-known species in gardens, *R. beggeriana* is native over a large area of Central Asia, from Iran and Afghanistan to some of the old Soviet Republics and Western China. It makes a large spreading bush with slightly greyish foliage and carries its small pure white flowers over a long season. The deep red or purple hips (hardly bigger than peas) follow soon after.

Summer flowering
Fragrant

Rosa blanda
Shrub
Labrador Rose, Meadow Rose, Smooth Rose

The English gardener-botanist William Aiton (one of the designers of the Kew

▲ *Rosa beggeriana*
◀ *Rosa arvensis*

▲ *Rosa banksiae normalis*
▼ *Rosa banksiae lutea*

Gardens) named this species, then newly brought from North America, in 1773. The name he chose is Latin for 'charming', 'gentle' or 'alluring'. It grows wild in the cold north-east regions of North America, and is notable for its hardiness, thornlessness and very early flowering. Foliage is mid-green.

Spring flowering

▶ *Rosa banksiae lutea*
▼ *Rosa blanda*

▲ *Rosa californica*
◄ *Rosa bracteata*

▲ *Rosa canina* Adelaide form

Rosa bracteata   Climber
Macartney Rose

Quite unlike other roses, the Macartney Rose is distinguished by its dense deep green mass of evergreen foliage, its fierce thorns and its large, pure white flowers. A shrubby, vigorous climber, it is best suited to warm climates. *R. bracteata*, said to be the only rose quite immune to black spot, owes its English name to Lord Macartney, English ambassador to its native China in 1793, and its Latin one to the leafy bracts surrounding the flowers.

Repeat flowering
Fragrant

Rosa brunonii   Rambler
Himalayan Musk Rose

Often confused with the true Musk Rose (*R. moschata*), *R. brunonii* found its way to Europe from its native Himalayas only in 1822. By the turn of the century it was widely accepted as the Musk Rose. It is distinct, however, in its much greater vigor, its grey-green foliage and its summer flowering, when it will cover a large tree with masses of richly scented white flowers.

Summer flowering
Fragrant

▼ *Rosa brunonii*

Rosa californica   Shrub
Californian Rose

The Californian Rose is also claimed by Washington and Oregon, and reaches over the Canadian border into British Columbia also. Though the double form (*R. californica plena*) is commonest in the garden, the Wild Rose is garden-worthy too, for its neat bush with mid-green foliage and sprays of lilac-pink flowers in summer, with a few odd ones to follow.

Summer flowering
Fragrant

Rosa canina   Shrub
Dog Rose, Dog Briar, Briar Rose

This species and its close relatives are the Wild Roses of Britain and Western Europe. Often used as an understock, it has gone wild elsewhere. The form illustrated is one often seen in Australia and known as the Adelaide form. A large

▲ *Rosa californica plena*
► *Rosa carolina*

prickly shrub with red hips following pale pink spring flowers, it is thought to be one of the ancestors of the Alba rose.

Spring flowering

Rosa carolina   Climber
R. humilis, R. parvifolia, Pasture Rose

One of the common Wild Roses of the eastern United States and Canada, this is a freely suckering species, making dense low thickets. A late flowerer, it is a useful landscaping subject and is one of the commonest American species in the garden. The foliage is light green. The flowers, mostly borne singly, vary in color from pale pink to cerise, and are followed by glossy hips in brilliant red.

Summer flowering

Rosa chinensis   Climber
R. indica, China Rose

Not many Westerners have seen the wild form of *R. chinensis*—it grows in the remote mountains of Western China—but it is the most important wild species. All our repeat-blooming Modern Garden Roses are hybrids of it. The anonymous Chinese garden form is pictured here, an everblooming bush with red flowers. It will just have to stand in for the wild form. The wild forms are reputed to be moderate climbers, with red flowers that go deeper as they age. Foliage is glossy.

Repeat flowering

▲ *Rosa chinensis*
▼ *Rosa davidii elongata*

Rosa davidii elongata   Shrub
Père David's Rose

Discovered in 1869 in the mountains of Western China by the French missionary and naturalist for whom it is named, *R. davidii* was not introduced to the West until Ernest Wilson sent seed in 1903. The elegant sprays of bright pink flowers appear in summer, and are followed by some of the finest displays of scarlet hips to be seen on any rose. It makes an open bush 3 metres (10 feet) tall with light green leaves.

Summer flowering

Rosa ecae 'Helen Knight'   Shrub

'Helen Knight' is probably the best clone of this very pretty Wild Rose from Afghanistan. The curious scientific name honors Eleanor Carmichael Aitchison (ECA), the wife of the British soldier-botanist who discovered it in 1879. Widespread in Central Asia, it needs a dry climate, and makes a dainty bush adorned in early spring with multitudes of small flowers in dazzling deep yellow. The very dainty fern-like foliage is purple tinted when young. In cool climates, consider growing the magnificent hybrid 'Golden Chersonese'.

Spring flowering

Rosa engelmannii   Shrub
Arkansas Rose

There is a great deal of confusion among botanists over *R. engelmannii*. Strictly speaking, the rose collected last century by Dr Engelmann in Colorado is a form of the widespread *R. acicularis*, and *R. arkansana* has sometimes impersonated it in British gardens. Be that as it may, the pretty pink rose with mid-green leaves in the picture bore the label *R. engelmannii* at the Royal Botanic Gardens, Kew, and it is included as a minor contribution to the debate.

Summer flowering

Rosa farreri persetosa   Shrub
R. elegantula 'Persetosa', 'Threepenny Bit Rose'

One of the most unusual of roses, on account of the contrast between the size of the shrub and the minute daintiness of foliage and soft pink flowers, *R. farreri persetosa* was discovered in 1915 by the great plant hunter Reginald Farrer. It likes a cool moist spot. The very small, pale green ferny leaves color nicely in autumn, or fall, and the tiny hips are orange. *Persetosa* describes the innumerable bristles on the stems.

Summer flowering
Fragrant

Rosa filipes   Rambler
Himalayan Musk Rose

'Kiftsgate' is the clone usually encountered of this giant-growing Rambler from Western China, whose Latin name alludes to the flower stalks, as fine as thread. It takes time to establish, and will then grow far and wide, foaming with millions of intoxicatingly scented white flowers in spring and carrying glistening hips far into winter. Foliage is dark green. Cool climates are preferred.

Late-spring flowering
Fragrant

▲ *Rosa filipes* 'Kiftsgate'
◄ *Rosa engelmannii*

▲ *Rosa farreri persetosa*
◄ *Rosa ecae* 'Helen Knight'

Rosa foetida   Shrub
R. lutea, Austrian Briar, Persian Briar, Nasturtium Rose, Rose Capucine

The Austrian Briar comes to us in two versions: the Austrian Yellow (*R. foetida lutea*), its flowers all gold, and the Austrian Copper (*R. foetida bicolor*) in vivid orange-red and gold, which frequently sports back to yellow. Despite the name, they come not from Austria but from the Middle East. No plant is more dazzling, but the dull green leaves are rather susceptible to black spot. In the 1890s, Joseph Pernet-Ducher finally succeeded

▲ *Rosa foetida lutea*
▼ *Rosa foetida bicolor*

in marrying them both to garden roses; the yellows and oranges of today owe their colors to *R. foetida*.

Summer flowering
Fragrant

Rosa foliolosa 'Anne Endt' Shrub

'Anne Endt' is a selected form of a very graceful species from Oklahoma and Arkansas, making a luxuriant, almost thornless bush with lush bright green foliage (*foliolosa*, given by Thomas Nuttall, means 'leafy') which colors brightly in autumn, or fall. The large carmine flowers appear late and then continue, a few at a time, until the autumn, or fall, when there are round, deep pink hips to be seen.

Late-summer flowering
Fragrant

Rosa forrestiana Shrub
Forrest's Rose

This beautiful species from Western China was introduced in 1918 by the Scottish plant hunter George Forrest (better known for his rhododendrons). It grows to about 2 metres (6 feet) tall, wreathing its arching branches with clusters of pale to deep pink flowers in late spring. Each bunch wears a distinctive collar of bright green bracts, which persist to set off the bright red, flask-shaped hips. Foliage is mid-green.

Summer flowering

Rosa gallica Shrub
R. rubra, French Rose

The wild *R. gallica* is the progenitor of the Gallicas of gardens and their descendants; it does indeed grow in France, but also in much of the rest of southern Europe. It varies, but this one (*R. gallica officinalis*) in the collection of California's Descanso gardens is typical of the wild forms. It is a neat, suckering bush with rough, mid-green leaves and single pink, fragrant blooms. *Rosa gallica* 'Versicolor' is the striped version.

Summer flowering
Fragrant

▲ *Rosa forrestiana*
▼ *Rosa foliolosa* 'Anne Endt'

Rosa gigantea Climber
R. odorata gigantea, Giant Climbing Rose

Everything about this rose justifies the name: the enormous length of the branches, the great drooping mid-green, semi-glossy leaves, and the 14 centimetre (5¹/₂ inch) flowers, in white, palest yellow or pale pink, with their silky,

▲ *Rosa gigantea*

▲ *Rosa gallica officinalis*
▼ *Rosa gallica* 'Versicolor'

▲ *Rosa giraldii*

reflexed petals. It has passed these qualities on to its descendants, the Tea Roses, thought to have been created by long-ago Chinese gardeners from this species and *R. chinensis*. A native of the jungles of Burma and Southern China, it is shy of the slightest frost.

Late-spring flowering
Fragrant

Rosa giraldii
Shrub
Chinese Mountain Rose
The mountains of Western and Central China are the heartland of the rose, but were one of the last regions of the world to be explored by Western botanists. It was not until the late nineteenth century that species such as *R. giraldii* were introduced to gardens. Not, perhaps, outstanding, it is still a pretty plant about 2 metres (6 feet) tall, weeping in habit, with fine mid-green foliage and pink flowers in late spring.

Late-spring flowering

Rosa glauca
Shrub
R. rubrifolia, *R. ferruginea*, Red-leafed Rose
This enchanting shrub from Central Europe is one of the most popular of species roses in gardens, mainly due to the color and grace of its leaves, which are purple in youth and grey, touched with plum, at maturity. The pink flowers and dark red hips play a distinctly secondary role. It grows head-high and has no thorns.

Summer flowering

Rosa helenae
Rambler
Helen Wilson's Musk Rose
The great plant explorer Ernest Wilson named this beautiful rose, discovered by him in Central China, in honor of his wife. Tragically, they were both killed in a car accident shortly after his return to America. It is one of the most garden-worthy of the Himalayan Musk Roses, bearing great bunches of deliciously scented creamy white blooms in late spring, followed by the finest display of hips of any of the group. Foliage is dark green and semi-glossy.

Summer flowering
Fragrant

Rosa hemisphaerica
Shrub
R. sulfurea, *R. glaucophylla*, Sulphur Rose, Yellow Provence Rose
For many years, this was the only double yellow rose, so European gardeners put up with its cantankerousness in the hope that it might consent to open a bloom or two. It really is only a success in warm dry climates like that of its native Iran. The bush is slender and almost thornless, the leaves distinctly grey. The wild, single-flowered form is known as *R. hemisphaerica rapinii*.

Summer flowering
Fragrant

▲ *Rosa hugonis*

▲ *Rosa helenae*
▼ *Rosa hemisphaerica*

Rosa hugonis
Shrub
Father Hugo's Rose, Golden Rose of China
This beautiful yellow Shrub Rose caused quite a stir in 1899 when it was sent to Britain from Central China by missionary Father Hugh Scallon. Its flowers, borne in spring along arching branches, and the ferny pale green foliage are very pretty. It is not an easy rose to grow, and you are more likely these days to see one of its hybrids, such as 'Cantabrigiensis', 'Headleyensis' or 'Canary Bird'.

Spring flowering
Fragrant

◄ *Rosa glauca* ▼

▲ *Rosa laevigata*
► *Rosa longicuspis*

Rosa laevigata Climber
R. sinica alba, Cherokee Rose

The State Flower of Georgia, USA, is one of the very earliest roses to bloom in spring, its white flowers shining against the dark green, evergreen foliage, each leaf of which has only three leaflets. It is native to China, but botanists have debated whether it is also American ever since 1803, when André Michaux found it growing apparently wild in the lands of the Cherokee Indians. A beautiful (if thorny) rose for mild climates only. *R. laevigata rosea,* Pink Cherokee, is not as rampant as the white form.

Spring flowering

Rosa longicuspis Rambler
R. mulliganii, R. lucens, R. yunnanensis, Himalaya Rose

The most manageable of the Himalayan Musk Roses in gardens, *R. longicuspis* has almost evergreen foliage with shiny dark green leaflets almost 10 centimetres (4 inches) long. The young shoots are an attractive reddish color, but it is the scent of the flowers that leaves the most lasting impression—fruity, like ripe bananas! The white flowers appear in midsummer. It was introduced to cultivation early this century.

Summer flowering
Fragrant

flowers in late spring are followed by hips rather like those of its relative *R. moyesii* but even larger. It is a true Himalayan, growing at altitudes of 4000 metres (13 000 feet).

Late-spring flowering
Fragrant

Rosa majalis Shrub
R. cinnamomea, Cinnamon Rose, Rose of May

The old herbalists smelt cinnamon in the bark, though no one else ever has. In any case the name *R. majalis* (originally reserved for the double-flowered garden forms) has superseded *R. cinnamomea.* Native to Europe, it is a species of more interest to botanists than to gardeners, despite its pungent scent and very early flowering in spring. Foliage is a dull green.

Early-spring flowering
Fragrant

▲ *Rosa laevigata*
▼ *Rosa laevigata rosea*

▲ *Rosa macrophylla*
► *Rosa majalis*

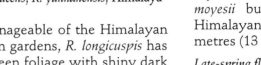

Rosa macrophylla Shrub
Large-leafed Rose

There are roses with larger leaves, but they were unknown when *R. macrophylla* was first discovered in China in 1817. A huge, open-growing shrub, it is almost thornless and has mid-green, matt foliage on purple stems. Elegant pink

Rosa moschata Climber
Musk Rose

The Musk Rose of the old botanists is a short climber, notable mainly for its musky fragrance and for its habit of not producing its clusters of white flowers

▲ *Rosa multibracteata*
◄ *Rosa moschata*
► *Rosa nitida*

until after all other roses have bloomed. Its origin is unknown, though it was always said to have come from Persia. About 100 years ago its name began to be attached to a usurper, *R. brunonii,* the Himalayan Musk Rose. Indeed, it almost vanished until Graham Thomas rediscovered it in the early 1960s. It is an important ancestor of Modern Garden Roses.

Late-summer flowering
Fragrant

Rosa moyesii   Shrub

R. moyesii was named in honor of the Reverend J. Moyes, a friend of E. H. Wilson who introduced it from Western China in 1903. It is one of the most desirable of Wild Roses by virtue of the

unique glowing red of the flowers and the truly magnificent hips. It is, however, a gaunt and ungainly shrub and many people prefer such selected garden forms as 'Geranium' to the wild plant. Foliage is greyish green. Pink-flowered versions are sometimes called *R. holodonta.*

Summer flowering
Fragrant

Rosa multibracteata   Shrub
Many-bracted Rose

This Shrub Rose from Sichuan is noteworthy for the airy grace of its growth. The finely cut pale green leaves and clear pink flowers are set off by the pale green bracts that adorn the flower clusters and give the species its name. *R. multibracteata* has played an unheralded part in the breeding of Modern Garden Roses, being an ancestor of 'Super Star' and 'Floradora', and a parent of 'Queen Elizabeth'.

Repeat flowering
Fragrant

Rosa multiflora   Rambler
R. polyantha

Garden forms of *R. multiflora* with double and colored flowers of Chinese and Japanese origin had been arriving in Europe since about 1800, but it was not until 1862 that the wild species was introduced from Japan. It is a most important parent, not only to a host of

Ramblers but also to the dwarf polyanthas (and through them the Cluster-flowered Roses). It would hardly be seen in gardens today except for its popularity as an understock. The small, single flowers are creamy white and come in clusters against pale, lime-green leaves.

Summer flowering
Fragrant

Rosa nitida   Shrub

This neat, low-growing shrub from America earns its name *(nitida* means 'shining') for its highly polished leaves. Gardeners also admire its delicately scented rose-pink flowers and its red hips, which gleam among bronze foliage in the autumn, or fall. Naturally growing in the swamps of eastern Canada and New England, it is one of the few roses that will endure poor drainage.

Summer flowering
Fragrant

Rosa palustris   Shrub
Marsh Rose

Palustris is Latin for 'swamp loving' and this pretty rose from eastern North America lives up to its name, preferring moist, boggy ground. It is garden-worthy for its light, bright pink flowers, and the

▼ *Rosa palustris*

▲ *Rosa moyesii*
► *Rosa multiflora*
▼ *Rosa moyesii* 'Geranium'

subtle autumn, or fall, color. It grows about 2 metres (6 feet) tall, suckering freely to form thickets.

Summer flowering

Rosa pendulina   Shrub
R. alpina, Alpine Rose

Native to Central and Southern Europe, the Alpine Rose is not very often seen in gardens. It should be, for it is a pretty, thornless shrub, adorning its trailing branches in spring with plum-red flowers. The young leaves are reddish too, maturing to dark green. It is thought to be the progenitor of the thornless Boursault Roses, though some botanists give the credit to *R. blanda*.

Summer flowering

Rosa persica   Shrub
Hulthemia persica, R. berberidifolia, Barberry Rose

Distinct from all other roses by lacking stipules, the leafy bits at the bases of the leaves, by its undivided leaves and by its prickly hips, *R. persica* is usually given a genus of its own, *Hulthemia*. Its flowers are unique too—bright yellow with red blotches at the base of the petals. It is intractable in cultivation, and you are far

▲ *Rosa pimpinellifolia*
◄ *Rosa pendulina*
► *Rosa primula*

more likely to see its hybrid by an unknown rose, ×*Hulthemosa hardii*, than *R. persica* itself. Indeed it is ×*H. hardii* which is pictured here.

Summer flowering

Rosa pimpinellifolia   Shrub
R. spinossissima, Wild Scotch Rose, Burnet Rose

The Scotch Rose is now correctly the 'burnet-leafed rose' *(pimpinellifolia)*, but many botanists still call it *spinossissima*, the 'thorniest rose'. It deserves that name, for the neat little bushes are completely covered, down to the smallest twigs, in sharp spines. The small, scented flowers appear in spring, and may be yellow, white or pink. There are several double-flowered garden forms, known as Scotch Roses, and in recent years the species has been much used by hybridists to create lusty Shrub Roses. Foliage is ferny and greyish green.

Spring flowering
Fragrant

Rosa pisocarpa   Shrub

The botanical name means the 'pea-fruited rose', which would be a good English name for it too, as it describes the size of the little red hips exactly. A relatively prickle-free shrub, it grows about 2 metres (6 feet) tall and has pink flowers.

It comes from western North America, from California into British Columbia. The flowers come in clusters of up to five. Foliage is dark green and gives an attractive autumn, or fall, display.

Summer flowering

Rosa primula   Shrub
Incense Rose

Rather like *R. hugonis* at first sight, though with rather paler yellow flowers, *R. primula* scores over its rather temperamental rival with the intense aroma of its fern-like, mid-green leaves, the strongest scent from the foliage of any rose. It is easier to grow too, though like most of the Middle Eastern roses it is happiest in a warm, dry climate. The name, that of the primrose, is obvious enough from the color of the blooms, but is a piece of botanical naughtiness.

Spring flowering
Fragrant

Rosa roxburghii   Shrub
R. microphylla, Chestnut Rose, Burr Rose

The double-flowered Chestnut Rose (*R. roxburghii plena*) is an old Chinese garden

◄ ×*Hulthemosa hardii*
► *Rosa roxburghii normalis*
▼ *Rosa pisocarpa*

plant, and was introduced to the West by Dr Roxburgh of the Calcutta Botanic Garden, before the wild, single-flowered form, known as *R. roxburghii normalis*. It is distinct from other roses in its flaking bark and prickly, chestnut-like hips, and makes an attractive garden shrub with ferny, greyish green leaves. Flowers appear early in spring, with the odd one to follow all season.

Early-spring flowering
Fragrant

Rosa rubiginosa   Shrub
R. eglanteria, Sweet Briar, Eglantine
Rather similar to its close relative the Dog Rose (*R. canina*), and, like it, something of a pest. The Sweet Briar is im-

mediately distinguished by the delicious, apple-like fragrance of its dark green leaves. It makes a lanky shrub about 2 metres (6 feet) tall, with pink flowers in late spring and red hips in autumn, or fall. Like the Dog Rose, it is native over most of Europe. There are several Old Garden hybrids. 'Lord Penzance' is the best known.

Late-spring flowering
Fragrant

Rosa rugosa   Shrub
Ramanas Rose, Japanese Rose, Hedgehog Rose
There are quite a few forms and hybrids of *R. rugosa* among the garden roses. Here we have the wild species, which comes from China and Japan, where it grows by the sea shore, spreading widely from suckers. It flowers in shades of pink or white and it is one of the few Wild Roses to be repeat flowering. The red hips are rich in vitamin C. The foliage is bright green and quilted. *R. rugosa alba* has large pure white flowers.

Repeat flowering
Fragrant

Rosa sericea pteracantha   Shrub
R. omeiensis pteracantha, Maltese Cross Rose
The white flowers of this large, ferny-leafed Shrub Rose from China are unique in having only four petals. Lovely as they are, the flowers are rather fleeting and you are most likely to encounter the form *R. pteracantha* ('rose with winged thorns') in gardens. Its thorns are extraordinary. On young shoots they are scarlet and almost transparent. Prune them well to encourage many new growths, as on old branches the thorns go grey and ordinary.

Spring flowering
Fragrant

Rosa setigera   Climber
R. rubifolia, Prairie Rose
The Prairie Rose is related to the Musk Roses—*R. moschata, R. multiflora, R. filipes* et al.—but is the only one to come from

America and to have pink flowers. A shrubby sort of climber, with bright green foliage, it carries its bunches of mid-pink flowers quite late in the season. Interestingly, each plant is likely to have flowers fertile in the stamens or the stigmas, not in both. Several hybrids, now rarely seen, were raised in the United States in the 1840s.

Summer flowering

Rosa setipoda   Shrub
Chinese Sweet Briar
R. setipoda is much more elegant than the Sweet Briar, in its arching growth, in its ferny, pleasantly scented, mid-green leaves, in its perfectly symmetrical pink flowers and in its bunches of flagon-shaped hips. It resembles *R. rubiginosa* in

variety *R. stellata mirifica*, which grows, among other places, around the rim of the Grand Canyon. It makes a low shrub, with bright green foliage, and glossy-petalled flowers in bright mauve-pink. Red hips usually follow.

Summer flowering
Fragrant

▲ *Rosa sweginzowii*

Rosa sweginzowii   Shrub

Sometimes called the 'pink moyesii', *R. sweginzowii* suffers from comparison with its flamboyant red-flowered relative, but it is, in fact, a better garden plant. Its clear pink flowers are very lovely; its hips, which ripen earlier, equally fine. Foliage is mid-green. That it was introduced from Western China by E. H. Wilson should be sufficient guarantee of its beauty. Do not overlook it.

Summer flowering
Fragrant

Rosa tomentosa   Shrub
Downy Rose

Do not confuse this rose with its relative *R. villosa* (both have names meaning 'downy' or 'fuzzy'). *R. tomentosa* is the larger grower, its foliage less grey, and the flowers a brasher pink. It is also a less compact and bushy plant. It is, however, a variable species, and sometimes it is hard to tell it apart from *R. canina*. The downiness on the leaves that gives it its name is not always very obvious.

Summer flowering
Fragrant

Rosa virginiana   Shrub
R. lucida, Virginian Rose

This native of eastern United States is one of the most beautiful flowering shrubs. Tall, yet compact in habit, it will make a thicket if you grow it on its own roots. The bright pink flowers appear late over a long season, the red hips are first rate and then there is a really fine display of autumn, or fall, colors. Young leaves are dark green and very glossy.

Summer flowering
Fragrant

Rosa webbiana   Shrub
Tibetan Rose

The closely related *R. sertata*, also from the Himalayas, often impersonates the Tibetan Rose in gardens, for they are similar in beauty and grace. Both flower in late spring, adorning arching, purplish green branches with sprays of pale pink flowers, following them up with decorative hips. Elegant is the word for them.

Late-spring flowering
Fragrant

▲ *Rosa tomentosa*
▼ *Rosa virginiana*

the scent of its leaves. The fragrance is more pine-like, however. A native of Hobei province in China, it was introduced by E. H. Wilson in 1901.

Summer flowering
Fragrant

Rosa sinowilsonii   Climber
R. longicuspis var. *sinowilsonii*

The name honors the great plant explorer E. H. Wilson, nicknamed 'Chinese' Wilson. He found this rose on the sacred Mount Omei in Sichuan. It is notable for its splendid leaves, which are huge, dark green and glossy, often tinted with red on their undersurfaces. The flowers, in great big bunches, are scented like orange blossom. It is very tender, however, and only a success in mild climates.

Summer flowering
Fragrant

Rosa stellata mirifica   Shrub
Hesperrhodos stellatus mirificus, R. mirifica,
Sacramento Rose

The rare, strange and beautiful *R. stellata*, the Gooseberry-leafed Rose from New Mexico and California, is temperamental in gardens, and you usually see the

▲ *Rosa sinowilsonii*
▼ *Rosa stellata mirifica*

Rosa willmottiae — Shrub
Miss Willmott's Rose

Ellen Willmott of Warley Place was the author of *The Genus Rosa*, and a legendary Edwardian English gardener. It is appropriate that the Chinese Wild Rose dedicated to her should be of delicate, feminine beauty. It grows considerably wider than tall, with thin twigs, small greyish green leaves, lilac-pink flowers in summer and small, pear-shaped hips in autumn, or fall.

Summer flowering
Fragrant

▲ *Rosa webbiana*

Rosa woodsii fendleri — Shrub
Sierra Nevada Rose

R. woodsii grows in the west of the United States, but is not at all common in gardens, this variety from California and places east being more garden-worthy. *R. woodsii fendleri* makes a very bushy, head-high plant, well clad with soft greyish green leaves which show off the mauve-pink flowers, crowded in clusters on short twigs. The brown-red hips are small, but abundant enough to be decorative.

Summer flowering

▲ *Rosa willmottiae*

▲ *Rosa woodsii fendleri*
▼ *Rosa xanthina* 'Canary Bird'

Rosa xanthina — Shrub

R. xanthina comes from China and, as has happened often with Chinese plants, the name was originally given to a double-flowered garden form. When the popular 'Canary Bird' was introduced in 1907, it was thought then to be the wild form, *R. xanthina spontanea*. It now appears that it is a hybrid of European garden origin. The true wild *R. xanthina* is the flower in the picture. It is a tallish shrub, with mid-green leaves, covered in spring with scented, bright yellow flowers.

Spring flowering
Fragrant

◄ *Rosa xanthina spontanea*

MODERN AND OLD GARDEN ROSES

THE **MODERN GARDEN ROSES** are the group of roses that appeared after 1867, the cut-off date being the introduction of 'La France', regarded as the first of the Large-flowered Roses. They account for most of the roses grown today, both in the number of plants sold and the number of cultivars available, and are divided into Bush, Shrub, Ground Cover, Miniature and Climbing Roses.

The Bush Roses are the most important. They are the roses most people choose when they want to add just a few roses to the garden, and they supply virtually all the rose blooms found in florists' shops. Their great virtue is their repeat flowering: with proper care a Bush Rose can be expected to flower on and off from the end of spring until late autumn, or fall. Their great fault is the gawky ugliness of the stiffly upright and thorny bushes, which is not enhanced by the pruning and trimming needed to ensure plentiful flowers. Out of bloom they offer no attraction to the eye. In cold climates, where they grow waist-high and you look down on the flowers, they are acceptable, but in a mild climate where they often grow head high or taller, one is only too aware of the thorny stems.

Planting lower growing plants in front for camouflage can help. Another suggestion, not without merit, is to relegate them to an out-of-the-way part of your garden, and enjoy them mainly as cut flowers.

Bush Roses are divided into Large-flowered, Cluster-flowered and Polyantha. The Large-flowered Roses (Hybrid Teas to the traditionally minded) are grown for the beauty of the individual flowers, borne singly or at most in threes or fours. Whether they have only five or as many as seventy petals (thirty is about the norm), they are expected to display a classic form, the petals slowly unfurling from a high, conical centre. They are at their best when about two-thirds open, the full-blown flowers often not quite fulfilling the promise of the sculptured buds. American hybridists tend to favor slimmer flowers, the British and Europeans those of more buxom build. Most cultivars have flowers which range in size from 11 to 15 centimetres (4½ to 6 inches), but there are occasional giants that can touch 18 centimetres (7 inches). These tend to be shy with their blooms. Height varies with soil, climate and pruning, but in most places 'average' implies a bush of 1.0–1.5 metres (3–5 feet) tall. Fragrance ranges from odor-free to overwhelming.

The Cluster-flowered Roses (previously known as Floribundas) are grown for the massed effect of their clusters of bloom, each cluster bearing from five or so to as many as thirty flowers, with solitary flowers only on the weaker shoots. The individual blooms range from about 6 centimetres (2½ inches) to as large as 14 centimetres (5½ inches). As a general rule, the larger the flower, the smaller the cluster. The shape of each bloom is less important than that the cluster as a whole be nicely arranged, with the flowers not bunched tight but given sufficient room to expand unhampered. Some of the newer Cluster-flowered Roses approach the Large-flowered Rose ideal, others are just open and flat; still others are quartered and ruffled, in the Old Garden Rose style. The range of colors is perhaps the widest of any group, but most are deficient in scent.

You can expect a Cluster-flowered Rose to be a little shorter and bushier in growth than a Large-flowered Rose, and often healthier, though both very tall and very dwarf cultivars (called 'Patio Roses' in some catalogues) exist. Cluster-flowered Roses come into bloom a week or so later than the Large-flowered Roses.

There is no reason not to mix the Large-flowered and Cluster-flowered Roses in the same bed, as long as you take the heights of your chosen cultivars into account.

American catalogues sometimes use the term 'Grandiflora' to designate Bush Roses that seem to blend the characters of both the Large-flowered and Cluster-flowered Roses with taller growth than either. The prototype is the exceptionally tall 'Queen Elizabeth'. The rest of the world has found the distinction otiose, and this book follows suit, classing each 'Grandiflora' with either the Large-flowered or the Cluster-flowered Roses as seems most appropriate.

The Polyanthas are Bush Roses too, but are distinct by their very dwarf growth and tiny flowers—one of 5 centimetres (2 inches) is very large for the group—carried in clusters of up to a hundred blooms. Popular in the 1920s, they are not much loved today. They derive their cluster-flowering habit from *Rosa multiflora*, and, crossed with the Large-flowered Roses, gave rise to the earliest Cluster-flowered Roses, which were called Hybrid Polyanthas for a while, and then Floribundas.

Though a dictionary will tell you that 'bush' and 'shrub' mean the same thing, Shrub Roses are a different group, usually growing larger and less stiffly than the Bush Roses. As such they are less suitable for grow-

ing in beds in a formal rose garden. Again they are a mixed bag; some, like 'Scarlet Fire' or 'Frühlingsgold', spring flowering only; others, most of them, repeat flowering. Some are really just overgrown Cluster-flowered Roses. You will find many of the Shrub Roses described as 'Park Roses', 'Landscape Roses', 'Amenity Roses' or some such, according to the whims of the raisers' marketing people. These are not, however, official or recognized groups.

A new group, mostly from the British raiser David Austin, seeks to unite the perfume, full-petalled flowers and relative elegance of growth of the Old Garden Roses with modern colors and repeat flowering. Called English Roses, they have become the height of fashion, but it is still too early to see what their long-term impact will be.

The Hybrid Musks, a small group raised in England in the 1920s, are more arching in growth and can be trained as pillars or pruned harder to grow more like Cluster-flowered Roses.

The Hybrid Rugosas are splendid large shrubs of solid, bushy growth, well clad with wrinkled light green leaves and quite disease-proof. They vary in growth, but are mostly about 2 metres (6 feet) high and as much wide, with fiercely armed branches making a thicket of growth that makes all other roses look flimsy. Pruning is easy: a rough trim and the removal of obviously dead wood is sufficient.

Shrub Roses can deliver the whole range of colors and scents. Many are exceptionally tough, resistant to extreme cold, and easy to grow. The various Ground Cover Roses that are coming from various raisers are of mixed breeding, some being bred from the Japanese-raised Climbing Miniature 'Nozomi', others from various Ramblers. Their performance seems to be less than their promise; so far not many are sufficiently dense or evergreen to really suppress weeds, one of the first duties one asks of a ground-cover plant.

Climbing Roses are something of an assortment. First there are the climbing sports from the Bush Roses, both Large and Cluster-flowered, whose blooms are usually identical to the bush cultivars from which they sprang, and whose names, prefixed by the word 'Climbing', they still bear. Examples include 'Climbing Iceberg' and 'Climbing Double Delight'. They are not always reliably repeat flowering, however, and you should check this point when buying them. They are apt to be rather stiff in growth. Then there are what are called the natural climbers, bred to climb. Some are only spring flowering like 'Lawrence Johnston' and 'Black Boy', though most of the newer cultivars repeat to a greater or lesser extent. They tend to be less vigorous than the climbing sports, and many of the more restrained are excellent pillar roses for training on verandah posts or the like to create pillars of bloom. The flowers may be either Large-flowered or Cluster-flowered in style, and fragrant or not. Just about the full range of colors is available. The 'Kordesii Climbers', mostly raised by Wilhelm Kordes and named for German cities, are a distinct group of pillar roses noted for their continuity of bloom and extreme resistance to disease and cold, which they inherit from *R. wichuraiana* and *R. rugosa*.

The Miniature Roses have been segregated to their own section in this book, mainly to avoid confusing the reader with their scale. An introduction to the Miniature Roses is given on pages 424–5, so no more will be said of them here.

OLD GARDEN ROSES

Sometimes called 'Heritage Roses', these are the groups that were established in gardens prior to the advent of the first Large-flowered Bush Roses (then called Hybrid Teas) in the early 1870s. Long dismissed as mere historical relics, they now have many ardent admirers, for like antique furniture they retain their beauty. Nostalgia for what we like to think of as more gracious days is only a part of their attraction. Their floral style is quite different from that of the Moderns. While a Large-flowered Rose is most admired when the petals are still unscrolling from the bud, a typical Old Garden Rose shows its full beauty when it opens wide, a saucer or a goblet filled with petals. In the finest cultivars the petals are arranged in the fashion called 'quartered'. In fragrance they are unsurpassed, not only by the Modern Garden Roses but by few other flowers.

The official classification divides the Old Garden Roses according to whether they are Climbing or Non-Climbing, but perhaps the more important question is whether they be spring flowering only or repeat flowering. The leading group of summer-flowering Non-Climbing Old Garden Roses are all cousins of the central European *Rosa gallica*, and might be informally called the Old French Roses; they include the Gallica, Damask, Centifolia (Provence), Moss and Alba Roses. Most of the surviving cultivars were raised in France, and they are the roses particularly associated with the memory of the tragic Joséphine de Beauharnais, Napoleon's first empress. They are mostly twiggy shrubs with small sharp prickles, matt, suede-textured leaves, and flowers similar in size (rarely larger) to the Cluster-flowered Roses in threes and fives in summer. Alas, mildew often follows, but it does seem not to impair their vigor very much. Planting them in the company of later flowering perennials will help mask any late season dowdiness.

The Gallicas, once simply known as the French Roses, are the neatest and most compact growers, their almost thornless branches rarely rising to more than a metre (3 feet) or so, and displaying the abundant flowers well above the leaves. The colors are usually in rich tones, pink through purple, with many cultivars going in for such bizarre stripes and blends that they were nicknamed the 'Mad Gallicas' in the old days. Fragrance is rarely less than intense.

The Damask Roses, so-called because they were said to have originated in Damascus, are very thorny, growing to about 1.5 metres (5 feet) or so, and very lax in growth. Colors are softer, in pinks and white, and fragrance invariably strong and sweet. It is a Damask Rose that is grown in Bulgaria to make the legendary Attar of Roses. A small sub-group, the Autumn Damasks, are sparingly repeat flowering.

About the same size as the Damasks, but 'lax' to the point of floppiness (a strategically placed stake or two will be useful), the Centifolia ('Hundred-petalled') Roses bear full-petalled, nodding blooms of soft colors and wonderful rich scent. Called 'Cabbage Roses' for their globular form, the flowers are not very large, 10 centimetres (4 inches) or so, and the smaller varieties would be more fittingly compared to the Brussels sprout. The drooping leaves are rounded and soft, pale green. They are also called Provence Roses.

The Moss Roses originally arose as variants of the Centifolias, and the older varieties differ from them only in the resinous, perfumed 'moss' that grows on the outside of their buds. Later Mosses are derived from the Damasks as well and some of them are sparingly repeat flowering. The Victorians adored them, and they feature on many embroideries, valentines, teacups and the like. Recently, mossy Miniature Roses have been raised, but they conform more to the Miniature than the old Moss Rose in most characteristics.

The Alba Roses are not only white, as their name implies, but come also in delicate shades of pink. The tallest of the Old Garden Roses, they make densely twiggy bushes up to 2.5 metres (8 feet) tall and need only light pruning as the old wood will continue to flower for years. Foliage is normally distinctly greyish in tone, the leaflets singly toothed, as distinct from the double toothing of most roses, and fragrance is sweet. Many regard them as the most refined and elegant of the Old Garden Roses.

In both Modern and Old Garden Roses, the repeat-flowering habit is a gift from the China and Tea Roses. These were Chinese garden roses of some antiquity that were introduced at the end of the eighteenth century to European gardens, where further cultivars were created from the original imports. Both are descended from the elusive *R. chinensis*, so it is not surprising that they are as alike as sisters.

The Chinas, thought to be pure *R. chinensis*, are dainty, slim-wooded bushes, with scattered hooked prickles, finely pointed leaves often tinted red in youth, and clusters of smallish flowers, red or pink, which rarely give much fragrance. The crimson varieties, recognized by some authorities as a distinct group, bear sprays of silver-dollar-sized flowers of a dark, pure shade unknown in European roses. They tend to be quite low bushes, rarely as high as a metre (3 feet). They are all very similar and there is a great deal of confusion over their names. 'Crimson Cerise' is one example of the group. The pink ones can grow to 2 metres (6 feet) in the warm winter climates they enjoy.

The Tea Roses (tea scented) are larger, more heavily wooded bushes, with broader, smooth leaves and large, 12 centimetres (4 inches) or more, flowers, nodding on weak flower stalks. They are shapely in the modern style, the buds long and the petals reflexing, and deliciously fragrant. However, any resemblance to the scent of tea escapes most people. They are said to show their *R. gigantea* ancestry in their long petals, generally in pale shades of pink, salmon and yellow with many blends. Unlike the Chinas, which usually darken as they age, the Teas fade in the sun. They are even more tender than the Chinas, growing best in the subtropical climates where most Modern Garden Roses sulk. In Britain and much of the United States they are greenhouse plants, cosseted by the heirs of those Victorian rosarians who thought them the most beautiful and elegant roses in the world. Several cultivars have climbing sports. All Teas should be pruned very lightly.

The Bourbon Roses bear fragrant blooms of European-style quartered form and colors (no yellow) on bushes like tallish Chinas or shrubby Teas, the leaves smooth and the flowers sometimes nodding like Teas.

The Portland Roses are in appearance repeat-flowering Gallicas, with smoother leaves that usually sit up close beneath the flowers, like ruffs.

The Hybrid Perpetuals blend all the various strains to make large bushes with large flowers, sometimes huge and cabbage-like, and usually splendidly fragrant. The name 'Perpetual' is a little optimistic as many are very shy indeed in autumn, or fall. The French 'Hybrides Remontants' would meet modern truth-in-advertising laws better. Hybrid Perpetuals need more water and fertilizer than Modern Bush Roses do, and are more limited in color range: white, pink and crimson.

A minor group of spring bloomers are the Scotch (or Burnet) Roses, derived from *R. pimpinellifolia* and popular in Scotland in the early years of the nineteenth century, when hundreds were listed. The few survivors make dense, prickly little bushes, less than a metre (3 feet) tall and slowly spreading by suckers. The leaves and flowers are all petite, and there are often distinctive black hips and plum- and russet-toned autumn, or fall, foliage.

A yet smaller group are the Hybrid Sweet Briars (or 'Penzance Briars') derived from *R. eglanteria*.

The Climbing Old Garden Roses are comprised of Rambler, Noisette, Boursault, Climbing Tea and Climbing Bourbon Roses.

Ramblers, with their long, very limber shoots and clusters of small blooms, are summer flowering only. Although some authorities divide the Ramblers into different groups, such as Ayrshire Ramblers, Multiflora Ramblers, Wichuraiana Ramblers and Sempervirens Ramblers, according to their ancestry, for our purposes in this book we simply classify them as Ramblers.

The Noisette Roses were originally a group of shrubby Climbers, with pink or cream clustered flowers, raised from the Chinas and the European Musk Rose, *R. moschata*. Later they became so intermarried with the Climbing Teas as to be virtually indistinguishable from them, in shades of cream and pale yellow.

The Boursaults were originally raised in the early nineteenth century under the auspices of the celebrated French rosarian whose name they bear. They are supposed to be crosses of *R. pendulina* with the garden roses of the day, but some modern experts think it was *R. blanda* that gave them their most important characteristics, their early bloom and freedom from thorns. Scent is only mild and none repeats. Few are grown today.

The Climbing Teas are mostly sports from Bush varieties, but a few are climbers from birth. They share the beauty and tenderness of their Bush fellows, and most repeat bloom very well.

There were a few varieties of Bourbon Roses that were climbing. These were known as Climbing Bourbons. Of these only 'Zéphyrine Drouhin' and 'Blairii No. 2' are well known today.

peach-pink and yellow. The colors, however, tend to be very pale in warm climates. It has mid-green foliage and the stems are quite thorny. Raised in 1985 by David Austin, it is named for one of the great pioneers of the Industrial Revolution, whose ironworks stood not far from where Mr Austin's nursery is located.

'Aloha' × 'Yellow Cushion'
Repeat flowering
Fragrant

▲ 'Ace of Hearts'
◄ 'A Feuilles de Chanvre'
▼ 'Abraham Darby'

'A Feuilles de Chanvre'   Alba

Rosa cannabina, 'Hemp-leaved Rose'
An ancient Alba that was long thought to be extinct, the 'Hemp-leaved Rose' has reappeared. It is a charming rose, with sprays of scented white flowers and long, narrow, greyish leaves that give it its name. The plant is on the small side for an Alba, a metre (3 feet) or so is as tall as you will see it. The origins of this rare rose are lost in the mists of time.

Parentage unknown
Summer flowering
Fragrant

'Abraham Darby'   English Rose

AUScot
'Abraham Darby' grows into a large, arching shrub, or, with encouragement, a modest climber, and it bears large, cupped, sweetly fragrant blooms in

'Adélaïde d'Orléans' — Rambler

The flowers are very pretty, palest pink with deeper touches, and they are scented. The clusters of blooms tend to nod from the branches, which makes this very dainty and rather restrained Rambler a good choice for a pergola. The foliage is matt green and persists virtually all year in a mild climate. It is mildew resistant. It was raised in 1826 by M. Jacques, who named it in homage to Adélaïde, the daughter of his employer, the Duke of Orléans, who went on to become King Louis Phillipe of France.

Probably *Rosa sempervirens* × unknown garden rose
Summer flowering
Fragrant

◀ 'Adam Messerich'

'Ace of Hearts' — Large-flowered
KORred
'Asso di Cuori', 'Toque Rouge'

The crimson flowers are full, shapely and of good size, and the plant is satisfactorily bushy. Foliage is dark green and it is a good rose for cutting. This 1981 Reimer Kordes introduction, however, has never been widely popular, perhaps because its fragrance is regarded as only moderate.

Parentage undisclosed
Repeat flowering
Fragrant

'Adam Messerich' — Bourbon

A late (1920) addition to the Bourbon group, 'Adam Messerich' could pass for a vigorous Cluster-flowered Rose with its upright, almost thornless branches and its clusters of medium-sized, raspberry-pink flowers, which are not overstuffed with petals. The flowers are richly fragrant. Some extra manure and water after the first flowering will be needed to ensure a generous follow-up, as there are not quite as many repeat-flowering genes as in a Modern Garden Rose. The foliage is a glossy, leaden green. The parentage is something of a cocktail, mixed by Peter Lambert of Trier in Germany.

'Frau Oberhofgärtner Singer' × ('Louise Odier' seedling × 'Louis Phillipe')
Repeat flowering
Fragrant

▲ 'Adélaïde d'Orléans'
▼ 'Adolph Horstmann'

'Adolph Horstmann' — Large-flowered

Deep amber-yellow, with some red and orange flushes in warm weather, the elegantly formed flowers of 'Adolph Horstmann' are large and long-lasting, but only slightly scented. Foliage is copper tinted when young, maturing to a pleasing glossy green. The bush is upright and of average height. 'Adolph Horstmann' has become popular with florists because of its long stem and lovely color, but it is a good garden rose too. The name honors a friend and colleague of the breeder, Reimer Kordes, who introduced it in 1971.

'Königin der Rosen' × 'Dr A. J. Verhage'
Repeat flowering

'Aenne Burda'   Large-flowered

'Aenne Burda' has big flowers which are variable in color. Those photographed by the author were a deep coral pink, but the raiser insists that they ought to be blood red. The foliage is a glossy green. 'Aenne Burda' came from Reimer Kordes in 1973.

Parentage undisclosed

▼ 'Aenne Burda'

'Afterglow'   Large-flowered

There have been two roses of this name, one from Britain's E. B. LeGrice in 1938 which is a paler colored sport of 'Mrs Sam McGredy', and one from Joseph Hill in 1930. It is this earlier one that is depicted here, a bushy plant bearing fragrant, deep pink blooms in small clusters. They open a shade or two paler, then touches of coral become evident, like the fading clouds after sunset. A popular rose in its day, it appears to survive only in collections like that of the Portland rose gardens, where it was photographed.

Parentage unknown
Repeat flowering
Fragrant

▲ 'Afterglow'
◀ 'Agathe'

'Agathe'   Gallica
'Pope Pius IX'

This plant is rather taller than the Gallica norm, with arching branches and somewhat greyish leaves. The flowers are on the small side and not especially shapely, but they are an attractive pink with washes and tones of mauve and violet, and sweetly fragrant. Not much is known about this rose, which is thought, like 'Empress Joséphine', to be related to *Rosa cinnamomea*. Agathe was the heroine of Weber's immensely popular opera of 1821, *Der Freischütz*, and several roses were named after her around that time.

Parentage unknown
Summer flowering
Fragrant

'Agathe Incarnata' Gallica

The soft pink color is unusually clear and even in tone for a Gallica. The flowers, usually borne in small clusters, are beautifully quartered and richly perfumed. The bush is about average Gallica in height, 1.5 metres (5 feet) or so, with downy foliage. The branches are very thorny, which leads some admirers of 'Agathe Incarnata' to see the influence of the Damask Rose in her breeding. 'Agathe Incarnata' was probably introduced around the same time as 'Agathe'.

Parentage unknown
Summer flowering
Fragrant

'Agnes' Hybrid Rugosa

Raised by Saunders of Ottawa in 1922, 'Agnes' is the result of a search for a yellow rose hardy enough for Canadian winters. It is certainly able to take the cold. Gardeners in much milder climates should admire it too for its big ruffled blooms, which blend shades of yellow and amber and exhale a rich fragrance. It is sparing with its repeat flowering. The plant is less bushy and solid than is common with Rugosas, but is still attractive in its arching branches and bright green leaves. It is occasionally subject to black spot. There is a huge display of flowers in spring, with scattered blossoms thereafter.

Rosa rugosa × 'Persian Yellow'
Repeat flowering
Fragrant

'Alain' Cluster-flowered

The bright red, smallish flowers show golden stamens and come in large clusters. They are only slightly fragrant, but long-lasting in water. The bush is compact, with glossy foliage. For many years regarded as one of the very best red Cluster-flowered Roses, 'Alain' is still a sound, easy-to-grow variety. Its only fault is a tendency to be a little slow with its repeat bloom. It is quite uncommon today. Raised by Francis Meilland in 1948, it was named for his young son, who also grew up to be a successful breeder of roses.

('Guinée' × 'Wilhelm') × 'Orange Triumph'
Repeat flowering

▲ 'Agathe Incarnata' ▼ 'Agnes'

▶ 'Alain'

'Alain Blanchard' — Gallica

Striped roses are not particularly uncommon, especially among the 'Mad Gallicas' (a nickname that some of the more bizarrely striped Gallica cultivars earned in the old days). Here is one that is *spotted,* in two shades of crimson! The whole combination takes on a purple cast as the flowers age, well set off by golden stamens. The effect is much more attractive and subtle than it sounds. The plant is compact and upright, with rather dull green foliage which is sometimes subject to mildew. It is said to have been raised by J.-P. Vibert of Angers and introduced in 1839, but some suspect it may be older.

Parentage unknown
Summer flowering
Fragrant

▲ 'Alain Blanchard'
▼ 'Albertine'

'Albéric Barbier' — Rambler

When this rose came out in 1900 the catalogues were fond of describing it as 'yellow, fading to cream', but this was wishful thinking. In fact the flowers are

▲ 'Albéric Barbier'

cream, fading rapidly to white. 'Albéric Barbier' is as pretty a white rose to clad a house or a long fence as any. The flowers are of Cluster-flowered Rose size. The foliage is dark green and glossy, a fitting setting for the fragrant flowers which appear early in great profusion. It is a very hardy rose for a rough spot. It is mildew resistant and very good for city gardens. It was raised by Barbier & Co. of Orléans.

Rosa luciae × 'Shirley Hibberd'
Repeat flowering
Fragrant

'Albertine'   Climber

One of the most popular of all the Climbing Roses, 'Albertine' bears masses of salmon-pink blooms, richly scented, informal in shape, and paling as they age. The foliage is glossy, red-tinted when young, and the vigorous branches are plentifully endowed with hooked prickles. There is only one flowering, over several weeks, but with luck you might be able to see an autumn, or fall, flower or two. Mildew will probably strike, but not hard enough to impair the strength of the plant. This rose was very popular in the 1920s and 1930s. It was raised by Barbier & Co. of Orléans and introduced in 1921.

Rosa wichuraiana × 'Mrs A. R. Waddell'
Summer flowering
Fragrant

▲ 'Alchymist'
▶ 'Alec's Red'

'Alchymist'   Large-flowered
'Alchemist'

If the old alchemists made gold as beautiful as this they were happy indeed! Full and quartered in the old style, the flowers are deep yellow, overlaid with buff and peach, and strongly scented. Foliage is mid-green, glossy, and red-tinted when young; the wood is thorny and the plant of medium vigor. It is a good rose for a trellis or tall pillar. This rose is tolerant of cold weather. It was raised by Wilhelm Kordes and introduced in 1956.

'Golden Glow' × Hybrid Sweet Briar seedling
Summer flowering
Fragrant

'Alec Rose'   Cluster-flowered

The bush is tall and upright, with the flowers large, elegantly formed, and a pleasing light red, though with rarely more than half-a-dozen flowers in the cluster. In the United States 'Alec Rose' would probably be called a 'Grandiflora', a term now out of date. There is little scent. This rose has glossy green foliage. Sir Alec Rose won fame by

▲ 'Alec Rose'

sailing around the world, and Sam McGredy commemorated the event with this rose in 1969. It is no longer as popular as it used to be.

'Hassan' × 'John Church'
Repeat flowering

'Alec's Red'   Large-flowered
CORed

The plump buds give promise of a much deeper color than the full-petalled flowers of 'Alec's Red' deliver. They are rarely stronger than cherry

'Alexandra' **Cluster-flowered**
KORbaxand
'Kordes Rose'
'Alexandra' has beautifully formed flowers which are deep yellow in color and shaded with amber and pink. They are exquisite against the glossy foliage. The rose shown here was photographed at the famous Portland Rose Gardens at Portland, Oregon, USA, where the climate seems ideal for it. Alas, 'Alexandra' seems only to appear in German nursery catalogues. 'Alexandra' was introduced

▲ 'Alexandre Girault'
◄ 'Alexander'

red. They do, however, hold their color well, without either fading or 'blueing', and they are strongly fragrant. The bush is of average height, with mid-green foliage. 'Alec's Red' is at its best in a cool climate. It was raised in Scotland by Alexander Cocker of Aberdeen and was introduced in 1970, after winning the RNRS President's Trophy.

'Dame de Coeur' × 'Fragrant Cloud'
Repeat flowering
Fragrant

'Alexander' Cluster-flowered
HARlex
'Alexandra'
Outshining even its parent 'Super Star' in color, 'Alexander' is also notable for the vigor of its growth; indeed the bushes are so much larger than average it is sometimes classed as a Shrub Rose. The flowers open to a good size from elegantly turned buds, with the edges of the petals often being scalloped.

'Alexander' does not have much scent. In cool climates it is a fine rose for the back of the border. It was introduced in 1972 by Jack Harkness, who named it in honor of Earl Alexander of Tunis.

'Super Star' × ('Ann Elizabeth' × 'Allgold')
Repeat flowering

▲ 'Alika'
◄ 'Alexandra'

in 1973 by Reimer Kordes, who has not divulged the parentage. Do not confuse it with the 'Alexander' which has 'Alexandra' as a synonym, or with the pale yellow Tea Rose 'Alexandra', introduced in 1900.

Parentage undisclosed
Repeat flowering

'Alexandre Girault' — Rambler

One of the most admired, and most often photographed, features of any of the world's beautiful rose gardens is the great trellis that forms the centrepiece of the Roseraie de l'Haÿ near Paris. It is completely covered with eighty plants of this rose. On seeing its performance there, you would think the rose-lovers of the world would be clamoring to have the vivid carmine flowers, lightened with a touch of gold at the petal bases, of 'Alexandre Girault' in their own gardens. Yet for many years, this glossy leafed, easily grown rose, disappeared from catalogues. Now it is becoming available again. It was introduced by Barbier & Co. in 1909.

Rosa wichuraiana × 'Papa Gontier'
Summer flowering
Fragrant

'Alika' — Gallica
Rosa gallica grandiflora

For a Gallica, 'Alika' does have large flowers, though at only 10 centimetres (4 inches) or so they are hardly enormous by modern standards. They are, however, a clear light crimson without any purple, and softly scented. 'Alika' has rough, dull green leaves. It is notable for its extreme resistance to cold, which is not surprising, for it seems that it originated in St Petersburg (just when is not known), from where it was introduced to the West in 1906. Kordes has used it as a parent, giving us among other things the remarkable Shrub Rose, 'Scarlet Fire'.

Parentage unknown
Summer flowering
Fragrant

'Alister Stella Gray' — Noisette
'Golden Rambler'

The flowers are of Cluster-flowered Rose size and open from perfect buds to old-style quarterings. They are rich yellow, with a touch of apricot in the centre, paler at the circumference, and

deliciously fragrant. The plant is quite shrubby, with distinctive zig-zag shoots, but is best trained as a climber. It usually takes some time to get going. Flowers come throughout the season, in small clusters at first and then in much larger ones on the strong late summer growth. Alister Stella Gray was presumably a relative of the raiser, Alexander Hill Gray of Bath. William Paul & Sons introduced his rose for him in 1894, and soon discovered it does best in a mild climate.

Parentage unknown
Repeat flowering
Fragrant

'Alleluia' — Large-flowered
DELatur
'Hallelujah'

Deep velvety red with the reverse of the petals white, the flowers are large,

▲ 'Alister Stella Gray'
▼ 'Allen Chandler'

▲ 'Alleluia'

nicely formed, and last well when cut, but they are only slightly scented. The foliage is deep green and glossy. This is a good rose for warm, dry climates. It was introduced in 1980 by Georges Delbard of France.

(['Impeccable' × 'Papa Meilland'] × ['Glory of Rome' × 'Impeccable']) × 'Corrida'
Repeat flowering

'Allen Chandler' — Climber

Restrained enough for a pillar or a small house, 'Allen Chandler' displays large, warm crimson flowers, beautifully shaped, although not endowed with many petals. The foliage is a handsome mid-green and is usually resistant to mildew. There are many flowers to come after the first lavish display. This is a fine rose, its only fault being its lack of strong perfume. It should not be forgotten. It was raised by Mr Chandler, an American rose-lover, and introduced in 1923.

'Hugh Dickson' × unknown
Repeat flowering
Fragrant

'Allgold' — Cluster-flowered

Introduced in 1955 by the English hybridist E. B. LeGrice, 'Allgold' is one of the main landmarks in rose-breeding. Never before had there been a yellow Cluster-flowered Rose of such rich,

unfading color, and none of its predecessors was anything like as reliable and generous in its performance. These days, its semi-double flowers could seem a trifle ordinary against some of the larger and more double newcomers, but it remains one of the best of its class. The dark, glossy green foliage is unusually resistant to black spot. Prune one or two branches hard each year to keep the plants bushy.

'Goldilocks' × 'Ellinor LeGrice'
Repeat flowering

▲ 'Allspice'
◄ 'Allgold'

'Allspice' Large-flowered

'Allspice' is not extremely fragrant, but still pleasantly so. The books say it smells of honey and tea, but this does not seem obvious. 'Allspice' is a tall bush which bears long buds that open to wide, ruffled flowers medium yellow in color. Foliage is mid-green. 'Allspice' was raised by David Armstrong, from the Californian nurseries of that name, in 1977. David Armstrong has been responsible for the breeding of a number of fine roses.

'Buccaneer' × 'Peace'
Repeat flowering
Fragrant

'Aloha' — Climber

This is a very popular rose. Usually borne in small clusters, the medium-sized flowers of 'Aloha' are well furnished with petals, in two-tone pink flushed with salmon, and pleasantly fragrant. Foliage is dark and leathery. The growth is hardly rampant, so grow it on a pillar or prune it a little harder to make a large shrub. Almost continuously flowering, 'Aloha' was bred by Gene Boerner and was introduced by Jackson & Perkins in 1949.

'Mercédes Gallart' × 'New Dawn'
Repeat flowering
Fragrant

'Alpine Sunset' — Large-flowered

Richly tinted with sunset colors of peach-yellow, pink and apricot when young, the very large and shapely flowers pass to more delicate tints with maturity. They are strongly scented, and come in reasonable profusion on a shorter than average bushy plant with mid-green foliage and very thorny branches. A fine rose for the show bench, it was raised by English hybridists Cants of Colchester and introduced in 1974. British gardeners admire the resistance of the flowers to wet weather.

'Dr A. J. Verhage' × 'Grandpa Dickson'
Repeat flowering
Fragrant

'Altaica' — Climber
Rosa spinossissima altaica, R. pimpinellifolia 'Grandiflora'

This is indeed a form of the Scotch or Burnet Rose, *R. pimpinellifolia,* and is said to grow wild in the Altai Mountains of Siberia. In gardens it has to be propagated by buddings or cuttings so it is best thought of as a garden rose rather than a Wild Rose. It is slightly bigger in all its parts—growth, foliage and cream five-petalled flowers—than the typical wild Scotch Roses, which makes it a more desirable garden plant. As one would expect from its origin, it is happiest in a cool climate. Its extreme hardiness has commended it to hybridists, and some lovely, sturdy Shrub Roses have descended from it, most notably 'Frühlingsmorgen'.

Parentage unknown
Spring flowering
Fragrant

▲ 'Altaica'

▲ 'Alpine Sunset'
◄ 'Aloha'

THE ROSE IN ANTIQUITY

The Greek poet Sappho, in the fifth century BC described the rose as 'the Queen of Flowers'. Every writer on roses has to bring in that quotation somewhere. However, a search of complete modern translations of Sappho, most of whose poems only survive in fragments, yielded no mention of roses, royal or otherwise, among all the lyrics in praise of her lady friend's lips. The Greeks certainly did grow and admire the flower, wearing garlands of roses on festive occasions and anointing themselves with rose-scented oil after the bath, and other poets like Anacreon refer to its beauty and fragrance. What the roses themselves were, it is hard to say now, and when they appear in Greek art they are apt to be so stylized that they are unrecognizable.

One gets the impression that the Greeks were not great gardeners. Theophrastus, writing in about 300 BC recommends that rosebushes be pruned by setting them on fire! The Romans were far more garden-conscious. Gentlemen like Pliny not only took a personal interest in the work of their gardeners but wrote with pride about it in their letters. There was a flourishing trade in cut roses, not only for making perfume and for cookery (rose-flavored wine was so popular and expensive that recipes for faking it survive) but for adorning the dinner table and for decorating the house.

Nero is said to have spent millions on roses for a single banquet. The praetor Verres was accused by Cicero of reclining on cushions stuffed with rose petals paid for by the taxpayers. The ultra-decadent boy-Emperor Elegabalus once showered so many roses over his dinner-guests that several of them suffocated. Such carryings-on, which aroused the spleen of the satirists, and later of the Christians, were no more typical of Roman life than the antics of the Hollywood glitterati are of life today. The ordinary Roman enjoyed roses for themselves, giving bunches of blooms as presents (as we do today) and placing red and white roses on the graves of their ancestors (a custom that has led to the widely held modern superstition that it is unlucky to put red and white roses in the same vase). They also gave them pride of place in their gardens, as excavations at Pompeii and the great villa at Fishbourne in Sussex have shown.

The Romans grew their roses well by all accounts. Pliny's directions on how to grow roses could be followed successfully today. Archaeologists are uncertain whether the Romans had greenhouses comparable to ours, but they had mastered the art of forcing roses to bloom out of season; the poet Martial chides the Egyptian gardeners for sending winter roses to Rome when the Romans already grew their own.

◀ *The Getty garden, as accurate a reconstruction of a wealthy Roman garden as scholarship can make it. The white rose growing over the pergola is* Rosa moschata, *the Musk Rose, a native of the Eastern Roman Empire.*

▼ *A coin of Rhodes, bearing the image of a rose. The Greek word for rose is* rhodon. *Whether the flower took its name from the island or vice versa no one knows, but it is said that the rose gardens of Rhodes were so extensive that the scent of their millions of flowers could be smelt miles out to sea.*

► 'The Roses of Heliogabulus', the famous banquet as imagined in the nineteenth century by Sir Lawrence Alma Tadema. The rose became so associated with such excesses in the minds of the early Christian Fathers that for centuries they refused to allow rose blooms in churches. Eventually the flower of Venus found a new patron in the Virgin Mary.

▼ Pliny the elder, one of the 'noblest Romans of them all' who found time from politics and literature to write a treatise on gardening. He perished in the eruption of Vesuvius which destroyed Pompeii, a town famous for its roses.

► The tradition of the 'ceiling rose', usually carved in plaster, originates in a Roman myth. It seems that Cupid, in return for hushing up some scandal about his mother Venus, presented a rose to Harpocrates, the God of Silence, who was so taken by it that he promised the confidentiality of conversations taking place sub rosa ('under the rose') would always be respected.

Most of the varieties that the Greeks and the Romans grew seem to have been lost (it is pretty certain that their *Rosa centifolia*, the rose of a hundred petals, was not the same as ours), with one possible exception. Pliny describes 'the Rose of Miletus' as having semi-double, light red flowers, whose fragrance increases when the petals are dried, though it is not especially scented in the garden. The description exactly fits the rose we now know as *Rosa gallica officinalis*, the Red Rose of Lancaster, and it is a tantalizing thought that we can still grow and enjoy the very same rose that crowned the heads of Roman revellers, that garlanded the sacrificial oxen of the temples, and whose beauty was consecrated to the Goddess of Love herself, Aphrodite, or Venus as the Romans knew her.

◄ Rosa gallica officinalis, *thought to have come down to us unchanged from the gardens of ancient Rome, here growing in the reconstructed Roman Garden at the Getty Museum in Los Angeles.*

▲ 'Ambassador'
◄ 'Altissimo'

'Altissimo'   Climber
DELmur

This name is optimistic. 'Altissimo' means 'highest', but this very popular rose is only a moderately vigorous climber. It bears its large, almost single flowers throughout the season; they are scentless, but much admired for their brilliant scarlet color, which holds without turning magenta. Foliage is dark and leathery. It is customary to describe this rose as a red 'Mermaid', but there is not much resemblance. Keep 'Altissimo' right away from red brick walls; the colors clash. It was introduced by Georges Delbard of France in 1966.

'Ténor' × unknown
Repeat flowering

'Amanda'   Cluster-flowered
BEEsian

Fat buds open to clear yellow, medium-sized flowers in large, well-spaced clusters. There is a little fragrance, and the bush is compact, a little on the short side perhaps, with pale green leaves. It grows well in England, where it was first introduced by the Chester firm Bees Ltd (now Sealand Nurseries) in 1979. The Miniature Rose, 'Red Ace' (AmRUda) is also called 'Amanda' in some catalogues. Do not confuse them!

'Arthur Bell' × 'Zambra'
Repeat flowering

'Ambassador'   Large-flowered
MEInutzan

The beautifully formed flowers are pale orange shot with yellow in their youth, fading to apricot with age, and are well up to exhibition size. They are borne on long stems for cutting on a taller than average bush with dark leaves. Do not confuse this rose, bred by Meilland and introduced in 1979, with the 1930 American Large-flowered Rose of the same name. That had smaller flowers in a blend of apricot and coral-pink, and unlike our present 'Ambassador' was very fragrant.

Unnamed seedling × 'Whisky Mac'
Repeat flowering

'Amber Queen'   Cluster-flowered
HARoony
'Prinz Eugen von Savoyen'

Clear amber-yellow, 'Amber Queen' has the reputation of being one of the most generous with its flowers of all Modern Garden Roses. The flowers are medium sized, shapely and scented, their warm color being complemented by dark, maroon-tinted foliage. The bushes are low in growth, an increasingly popular feature. The raiser says that it is ideal as a standard. It was raised by Jack Harkness and introduced in England in 1984. It won the AARS award in 1988, the year of its introduction in the United States.

'Southampton' × 'Typhoon'
Repeat flowering
Fragrant

◄ 'Amanda'

▲ 'Amber Queen'

▲ 'American Heritage'

'America' Climber

Glowing salmon, the reverses of the petals a trifle paler, the shapely flowers of 'America' tend to bloom in clusters. With disbudding they can be large enough for the show bench, and they are nicely fragrant. 'America' has glossy green leaves. Hard pruning will keep 'America' as a shrub, at least in cool climates, but it is not a rose for hot, humid summers. Raised by Bill Warriner, it was introduced by Jackson & Perkins in 1976, the year of the American Bicentennial, and won the AARS award. It is in fact the third rose to bear the name. The previous two were a pale pink Large-flowered Rose of 1912 and a pink Rambler of 1915.

'Fragrant Cloud' × 'Tradition'
Repeat flowering
Fragrant

'American Beauty' Hybrid Perpetual
'Madame Ferdinand Jamin'

In fact, 'Madame Ferdinand Jamin' is the original name, bestowed on it by M. Lédéchaux in 1875. It was not until ten years later that it was introduced to the United States as 'American Beauty'. It dominated the flower shops of the United States for half a century and it has become the official flower of the District of Columbia. The flowers are very full and are deep pink to almost red in color. Foliage is dull green. It tends to be susceptible to mildew. It is an awkward rose in the garden, being gawky in growth and not very free in the autumn, or fall, unless conditions are ideal. Grow it for history's sake.

Parentage unknown
Repeat flowering
Fragrant

'American Heritage' Large-flowered
LAMlam

The pale salmon-pink that suffuses the cream and ivory of the long buds gradually takes over completely as the large, high-centred flowers of 'American Heritage' mature. They appear charming at all stages. There is little scent, unfortunately. Foliage is large and dark green and the bushes tall, though not so tall (or quite so easily grown) as its parent 'Queen Elizabeth'. 'American Heritage' won the AARS award for 1966 for its raiser, Dr Walter Lammerts.

'Queen Elizabeth' × 'Yellow Perfection'
Repeat flowering

▼ 'America'

▶ 'American Beauty'

'American Pillar' Rambler

The short flowering season of 'American Pillar' and its susceptibility to mildew are leading gardeners to reject it in favor of one of the newer repeat flowering Climbers. In its season it

makes a colorful display with big clusters of small, single flowers, carmine with white centres. Though more-or-less scentless, they last well when cut. Foliage is leathery and glossy. The plant is really a bit too vigorous for a pillar; plant it on the house or over a pergola. It is best in cold climates and flowers in late summer only. The patriotic raiser was Dr Walter Van Fleet of Glenn Dale, Maryland, who introduced it in 1902. It does have native American blood.

(Rosa wichuraiana × *R. setigera)* × a red Hybrid Perpetual
Summer flowering

'American Pride'   Large-flowered

Lack of scent always seems a more serious fault in red roses than in those of other colors, but if 'American Pride' can be forgiven its almost complete scentlessness it is in fact a rather good red rose. The color is dark yet lively, and the flowers are well formed, with the central petals ruffled in the open bloom. The plant is a little taller than average with dark, matt green foliage, and it flowers very freely. It was bred by Bill Warriner for Jackson & Perkins, who introduced it in 1978.

Parentage undisclosed
Repeat flowering

'Ami des Jardins'   Cluster-flowered

This is a pleasing garden rose, its orange-red color clear and not turning magenta with age. The plant grows to average height and has good foliage. It has little scent, unfortunately. Despite its French name, and the fact that it seems nowadays only to be grown in France, this is actually a German rose, bred by Kordes. Because the name was

▲ 'American Pillar'
◄ 'Ami des Jardins'

never registered, its ancestors and date of introduction are unknown.

Parentage unknown
Repeat flowering

'Amiga Mia'   Modern Shrub

'Amiga Mia' is more like an unusually vigorous, bushy Bush Rose, and pruned like one will stand about a metre (3 feet) tall. The flowers are large, graceful, and borne either single or in clusters of half a dozen. They are a delicate shell-pink and very fragrant. The leaves are dark green. 'Amiga Mia' is a creation of Dr Griffith Buck of Iowa State University, whose rose-breeding aimed at the creation of very cold-resistant and disease-resistant, but still lovely, roses. This 1979 introduction was named in affectionate tribute to the late Dorothy Stemler, the great American rose-grower of California.

'Queen Elizabeth' × 'Prairie Princess'
Repeat flowering
Fragrant

◄ 'Amiga Mia'

▲ 'American Pride'
▶ 'Amsterdam'

'Amsterdam' Cluster-flowered
'HAVam'

The foliage of 'Amsterdam', which is dark mahogany when it is young, retains its dusky tone even in maturity. This makes the orange-red of the flowers seem still more fiery. For this reason it stands out among the many Cluster-flowered Roses in this color. It is a good, healthy rose for the garden and for cutting. It was introduced in 1972 by Ted Verschuren of the Netherlands.

'Europeana' × 'Parkdirektor Riggers'
Repeat flowering

'Ann Elizabeth' Cluster-flowered

A tall grower which with light pruning could almost be a Shrub Rose, 'Ann Elizabeth' bears its open flowers in graceful sprays. They are a gentle color, rose-pink with just a hint of coral, and are set off by dark green foliage which is bronze early in its growth. Albert Norman, the raiser, apparently did not declare the parentage, but we do know that the name honors his granddaughter. It was introduced in 1962.

Parentage undisclosed
Repeat flowering

'Angel Face' Cluster-flowered

This is a pretty rose, with 8 centimetre (3 inch) flowers ruffled and flounced in shades of mauve and rose. It is much less ethereal than most modern mauve roses and it is well-scented too. The leaves are dark green. However, it is one of those roses that needs the best of care if it is to be an asset to the garden. Give it fertile soil, keep it well watered, and have a spray gun handy as it is susceptible to black spot. 'Angel Face' won the AARS award for 1969, for Herbert Swim and Ollie Weeks.

('Circus' × 'Lavender Pinocchio') × 'Sterling Silver'
Repeat flowering
Fragrant

▲ 'Angel Face'

'Anisley Dickson' Cluster-flowered
DICkimono
'München Kindl', 'Dicky'

'Anisley Dickson' is a good example of a Cluster-flowered Rose of the Large-flowered type. In other words, its coral-pink flowers are as shapely as a Large-flowered Rose, but borne in sprays. There is not a great deal of scent, but the plant is bushy, of average height, and has abundant glossy mid-green foliage. It was raised by Ireland's Patrick Dickson in 1983 and named for his wife. It won the RNRS's President's Trophy in 1984 for the best new rose.

'Coventry Cathedral' × 'Memento'
Repeat flowering

▲ 'Ann Elizabeth'
◄ 'Anisley Dickson'
▼ 'Anna Marie de Montravel'

'Anna Marie de Montravel' — Polyantha

This rose makes a dainty bush, with red stems and bright green leaves, crowned with clusters of exquisitely shaped little white roses. Its fragrance resembles that of lily of the valley. Certainly one of the first, and perhaps one of the prettiest, of the Polyantha Roses, 'Anna Marie de Montravel' was introduced by the French nursery of Rambeaux & Digreux in 1880.

Rambler × 'Madame de Tartas'
Repeat flowering
Fragrant

▶ 'Anna Zinkeisen'
▼ 'Anna Olivier'

'Anna Olivier' — Tea

From its introduction, by Claude Ducher of Lyon, in 1872 until the advent of the more brilliantly toned salmon and yellow Large-flowered Roses of the 1920s, 'Anna Olivier' was one of the most popular garden roses. It is still as beautiful as ever, its flowers delicately blending cream, buff and pale pink, its fragrance still pleasing, its plant still free and reliable. The leaves are olive-green. Of course, it has the usual Tea Rose inability to cope with severe cold, but it is one of the hardier Teas and is well worth a favored spot in the garden.

Parentage unknown
Repeat flowering
Fragrant

'Anna Zinkeisen' — Shrub
HARquhling

This is a very pretty, not too large shrub, spreading in growth and well furnished with light green leaves. It bears smallish, many-petalled flowers in clusters on and off all season. They open pale yellow and fade to ivory.

Anna Zinkeisen was a Suffolk painter whose designs for the ballet were widely admired. Jack Harkness bred this rose and introduced it in 1983. Although reticent about its origins he has hinted that *R. pimpinellifolia* is in its background.

Unnamed seedling × 'Frank Naylor'
Repeat flowering

'Anne Letts' — Large-flowered

Clear pale pink, but paler still on the petal reverse, the large and perfectly formed flowers are pleasantly fragrant. Foliage is glossy, medium green, and

▲ 'Anne Letts'
▼ 'Anne Marie Trechslin'

the rather spiny bushes are a little shorter than average. Needing both good cultivation and fine weather to give of its best, this is not a rose for the ordinary gardener, but the enthusiast will find its flowers unbeatable on the show bench. It was introduced in 1954 by the breeder, a Mr Letts, who apparently named it for his wife.

'Peace' × 'Charles Gregory'
Repeat flowering
Fragrant

'Anne Marie Trechslin' — Large-flowered
MEIfour
'Anne Marie'

One world authority inexplicably only describes 'Anne Marie Trechslin' as simply 'deep pink'. Actually it is a

blend of pink and apricot, heavily over-laid with copper-red. The flowers are shapely and very fragrant, though the bush is sometimes a little shy of pro-ducing many of them. Foliage is a glossy green. This is the sort of rose to appeal to an artist, and indeed Mlle Trechslin is one of the foremost painters of rose portraits, having illus-trated several books. The rose was named in her honor in 1968 and was raised by Meilland.

'Sutter's Gold' × ('Demain' × 'Peace')
Repeat flowering
Fragrant

'Antigua' Large-flowered

The flowers of this attractive rose are large, full, and high centred, opening from plump buds. They blend several shades of apricot, sometimes with a suggestion of pink, and look well against the dark leathery foliage. They are not especially fragrant. Growth is upright, a shade taller than average. Bred by Bill Warriner, it was introduced by Jackson & Perkins in 1974. Despite receiving a gold medal at the Geneva Trial Grounds, it has never found much favor outside the United States.

'South Seas' × 'Golden Masterpiece'
Repeat flowering

'Antique Silk' Large-flowered
KORampa
'Champagner', 'Champagne'

Florists are likely to call this delightful, very long-stemmed rose 'Champagne', though the International Registration Authority prefers 'Antique Silk' to avoid confusion with Bob Lindquist's Hybrid Tea 'Champagne', which came

out in 1960. Either name suits the deli-cate, off-white of the flowers per-fectly. They are not large, but they are most perfectly shaped, and, unusually for a greenhouse rose, they are scented. The flowers are exceptionally long-lasting, making them good for cutting. The leaves are medium green. It does quite well in the garden too.

Reimer Kordes scored a real hit with it in 1982.

'Anabell' × unnamed seedling
Repeat flowering
Fragrant

▲ 'Antique Silk'
◀ 'Antigua'
▼ 'Antonia Ridge'

'Antonia Ridge' — Large-flowered
MEIparadon

The large, high-centred flowers hold their bright red color well but they are only slightly fragrant. Foliage is medium green. The growth is good, though it will do best in a warm climate. Meilland introduced it in 1976. Miss Antonia Ridge was the author of the best selling book, *For Love of a Rose,* about the Meillands and their roses.

('Chrysler Imperial' × 'Karl Herbst') × unnamed seedling
Repeat flowering

'Anvil Sparks' — Large-flowered
'Ambossfunken'

Bizarrely striped in fiery shades of orange-red, carmine, apricot, and yellow, the flowers of 'Anvil Sparks' are large, opening wide from shapely buds. They are lightly scented and carried on long straight stems that are ideal for cutting. Unfortunately the glossy dark foliage is susceptible to black spot. 'Anvil Sparks' is a sport of 'Signora Piero Puricelli', also pictured in this book, which occurred in the garden of a Herr Meyer in Germany. It was introduced by Kordes in 1961.

Sport from 'Signora Piero Puricelli'
Repeat flowering
Fragrant

'Aotearoa' — Large-flowered
MACgenev
'New Zealand'

This very promising rose has enormous flowers that are long-budded, shapely and richly fragrant; their soft pink color is delightful; and the glossy-leafed bush is strong and healthy. *Aotearoa,* meaning 'Land of the Long White Cloud', is the Maori name for

New Zealand, and was bestowed on the rose in honor of that country's sesquicentenary year in 1990. Sam McGredy must have great faith in his creation, as he is on record as saying that new pink roses are the most difficult for the hybridist to sell, the color lacking novelty.

'Harmonie' × 'Auckland Metro'
Repeat flowering
Fragrant

'Apolline' — China

A small, dainty bush with neat green foliage, bearing small candy-pink flowers for most of the season, 'Apolline' is sometimes classed as a

▲ 'Anvil Sparks'
◄ 'Aotearoa'

▲ 'Apolline'
► 'Apricot Nectar'

Bourbon. Most gardeners will be content to leave the argument over classification to the experts and just enjoy her beauty. If you can find her that is: she is one of those Old Garden Roses that is still only grown by a very few specialist nurseries. The name is the feminine of Apollo, the Greek god of light, prophecy and healing, and was a popular girl's name in the France of the First Empire. Eugène Verdier gave it to this rose in 1848.

'Pierre St-Cyr' × unknown
Repeat flowering

'Apricot Nectar' — Cluster-flowered

It is surprising that 'Apricot Nectar' was not classed as a 'Grandiflora' in the United States where it was bred. It is a tall-growing plant, and the flowers are very large for a Cluster-flowered Rose. They are too large for the rather tight clusters, in fact. Some

▲ 'Apricot Queen'

thinning of the buds is usually called for so that the remaining flowers can each expand in freedom. That is the only fault of 'Apricot Nectar'. The cupped flowers are very attractive in their peach and apricot tonings, their elegant form and their sweet fragrance. The glossy dark-leafed bush is quite disease-resistant. It was raised by Eugene Boerner of Jackson & Perkins in 1965 and won the AARS award in that same year.

Unnamed seedling × 'Spartan'
Repeat flowering
Fragrant

'Apricot Queen' Large-flowered
Blending salmon-pink with apricot, the large flowers of 'Apricot Queen' are full and ruffled, with forty-five petals, though not quite of show-bench form. They are moderately scented of tea, and are borne abundantly on a sturdy bush with dull green foliage. Bred by Fred Howard of Howard & Smith in California, 'Apricot Queen' was introduced in 1940, winning the AARS award in 1941. Despite its age, it remains an excellent garden rose, particularly in climates plagued by humid summers.

'Mrs J. D. Eisele' × 'Los Angeles'
Repeat flowering
Fragrant

'Aquarius' Large-flowered
ARMaq
Blending icecream-pink and candy-pink, these high-centred flowers are medium sized, often coming in clusters, which may be thinned to increase the size of the bloom. Scent is only slight, but the flowers are borne in profusion on a taller than average bush with leathery, olive-green foliage. They last very well in water. Bred by David L. Armstrong and introduced by Armstrong Nurseries in 1971, 'Aquarius' won the AARS award that year. It is still, deservedly, very popular.

('Charlotte Armstrong' × 'Contrast') × ('Fandango' × ['World's Fair' × 'Floradora'])
Repeat flowering

'Archduke Charles'   China

This rose should have been photographed in a great bunch to show it properly, for no two flowers are quite alike. Basically, they are pale pink, but this becomes overlaid with deeper pink and even crimson in the sun, the color intensifying as the blooms age. They are of Cluster-flowered Rose size, sweetly fragrant, and borne all season on a compact, twiggy bush. The foliage is small and dark green. 'Archduke Charles' came from M. Laffay some time in the late 1830s. The Archduke Charles was the father of the Emperor Franz Joseph, the longest serving ruler in European history.

Parentage unknown
Repeat flowering
Fragrant

▲ 'Archduke Charles'
▼ 'Aquarius'

'Ards Beauty'   Cluster-flowered
DICjoy

This has proved a very good yellow rose, with scented flowers borne very freely on a compact, glossy dark-leafed bush. 'Ards Beauty' took its raiser by surprise when it won the RNRS President's Trophy for the best new rose of 1983. At the time Patrick Dickson had only fifteen plants in stock, having not yet decided whether to introduce it. So, with rose-lovers clamoring for it, it could not be introduced until 1986. It

▲ 'Ards Beauty'

was named in honor of Mr Dickson's home town in County Down.

('Eurorose' × 'Whisky Mac') × 'Bright Smile'
Repeat flowering
Fragrant

'Arethusa'   China

The bush is on the large side for a China Rose, but 'Arethusa' still retains much of the China Rose daintiness in its slender stems and dark shiny foliage. Like most of its class it is in flower throughout the season. The color of the flowers varies with the time of year. Sometimes it is more yellow, at others more apricot. The flowers are moderately full and are arranged in small sprays. Foliage is small and dark green. 'Arethusa' is a relatively new China, having been introduced only in 1903 by William Paul. Arethusa was the goddess of fountains to the ancient Greeks and, as such, no doubt a regular visitor to gardens.

Parentage unknown
Repeat flowering

▲ 'Arethusa'

'Arianna' Large-flowered
MEIdali

Rose-pink suffused with salmon, the flowers of 'Arianna' may be a little loosely formed for the exhibition bench, but they are fragrant, and borne with amazing freedom for a rose so large. The foliage is matt green, and the rather open bushes are of average height. It likes a warm climate. A good garden rose, 'Arianna' was raised by Marie-Louisette Meilland and introduced in 1968. It is especially fine in the autumn, or fall.

'Charlotte Armstrong' × ('Peace' × 'Michèle Meilland')
Repeat flowering
Fragrant

▲ 'Arnoldiana'
◄ 'Arianna'

'Arnoldiana' Hybrid Rugosa
'The Arnold Rose'

The books disagree on the date and parentage of this rose, which was apparently introduced (or at least named) by the Arnold Arboretum in Massachusetts just before World War I. This rose is a large, upright bush with mid-green, rather crinkly foliage and clusters of smallish, bright crimson semi-double flowers in spring, with a few later blooms to follow. It is fragrant, hardy and easy to grow, though not in the first rank for the beauty of its flowers. It is a minor piece of rose history.

Rosa rugosa × unknown Bourbon Rose
Spring flowering
Fragrant

'Arrillaga' Hybrid Perpetual

The flowers are enormous, but they are saved from blowsy vulgarity by their perfect form and the tenderness

of their soft pink color. And they are fragrant too. Foliage is matt green. As the plant is in scale with the blooms, growing tall and wide, plant it at the back of the bed. It is a reliable autumn, or fall, performer, as good as most Large-flowered Roses in this respect, but it is happiest in a mild climate. 'Arrillaga' is a rather late Hybrid Perpetual, having been introduced only in 1929 by a gentleman named Schoener.

(*Rosa centifolia* × 'Mrs John Laing') × 'Frau Karl Druschki'
Repeat flowering
Fragrant

▼ 'Arrillaga'

'Arthur Bell' Cluster-flowered

As shapely as most Large-flowered Roses, and nearly as large, the sweetly scented flowers of 'Arthur Bell' start out deep golden yellow but pale to primrose and cream almost as soon as they are fully blown. Some people find this a major fault, others think the contrast of the two tones of yellow charming, but everyone is in agreement that 'Arthur Bell' is one of the easiest yellow roses to grow, especially in a cool climate. The bushes are on the tall side and the foliage large, dark and heavily veined. Raised by Sam McGredy, it made its debut in 1965. Arthur Bell was the maker of the Scotch whisky that bears his name.

'Cläre Grammerstorf' × 'Piccadilly'
Repeat flowering
Fragrant

▲ 'Arthur de Sansal'
◀ 'Arthur Bell'

'Arthur de Sansal'   Portland

It is just the coincidence of alphabetical priority, but 'Arthur de Sansal' does make a good introduction to the Portland Roses. It is like a Gallica in its quartered flowers, in its rich red and purple tonings and its fragrance, but it has the China Rose's ability to flower repeatedly through the season. It also displays characteristic short footstalks, so that the flowers seem to sit among their leaves, like camellias. As with most of its group, the plant is bushy and compact, a desirable trait for modern gardens. Foliage is matt green and can be susceptible to mildew. 'Arthur de Sansal' really is a Hybrid Perpetual by its parentage. M. Cochet who introduced it in 1855 claimed it as a hybrid of 'Géant des Batailles'.

Possibly 'Géant des Batailles' ×
unknown
Repeat flowering
Fragrant

'Astral'   Large-flowered

'Astral' has elegantly shaped large flowers in a rich carmine pink color. The flowers are sweetly fragrant. It has glossy dark green foliage. This rose should have been a hit, but hardly anyone seems to grow it. Its parentage was beyond reproach. It was bred and introduced by Bees of Colchester in 1976.

'Super Star' × 'Pink Favourite'
Repeat flowering
Fragrant

◀ 'Astral'

'Auckland Metro'
Large-flowered

MACbupal

Palest pink to almost white, the flowers are of unusual formation for a Large-flowered Rose. 'Camellia like' the catalogues say, and that is a fair description. The petals are arranged with perfect symmetry, the inner ones smaller than the outer to give an almost flat flower. Scent is excellent (in this regard it is uncamellia like) and the bushy, lower than average plant is well covered in shiny, dark green leaves. It flowers almost as freely as a Cluster-flowered Rose. 'Auckland Metro' is known as 'Precious Michelle' in Australia, in memory of the young lady who is also commemorated by 'Michelle Joy', and was introduced in 1987 by Sam McGredy.

'Sexy Rexy' × (unnamed seedling × 'Ferry Porsche')
Repeat flowering
Fragrant

▲ 'Auckland Metro'
▼ 'Augustine Guinnoisseau'

'Audie Murphy'
Large-flowered

Very long buds open to wide, loose flowers of a velvety but brilliant light red. There are usually three or four together on long stems and they are outstanding for cutting. Scent, though not especially strong, is spicy, and the plant is above average in vigor, with bronze-green foliage when young. It likes a warm humid climate. 'Audie Murphy' bears beautifully colored flowers in great abundance throughout the season. It was bred by Dr Walter Lammerts and introduced in 1957. Lying about his age, Audie Murphy was accepted in the forces at a tender age; soon he was America's most decorated war hero, and later he became a much-admired movie star.

'Charlotte Armstrong' × 'Grand Duchesse Charlotte'
Repeat flowering
Fragrant

▲ 'Audie Murphy'

'Augustine Guinnoisseau'
Large-flowered

'White La France'

The nickname says it all: 'Augustine Guinnoisseau' does closely resemble the famous 'La France' except that its flowers are blush-white and have rather fewer petals. They are beautifully scented. This is a rose that needs the greatest of care if it is to give of its exquisite best. Even then, the plant will be on the small side. Also, it dislikes wet weather. It is indeed a descendant of 'La France', although whether a sport or a seedling that took after its parent the authorities seem unable to decide. It was introduced in 1889 by M. Guinnoisseau.

Parentage in dispute
Repeat flowering
Fragrant

'Australian Bicentennial'   Large-flowered
'The Australian Bicentennial Rose'

Introduced in 1988 as part of that year's celebrations of the two hundredth anniversary of European settlement in Australia, 'Australian Bicentennial' enjoys a modest local reputation as a reliable rose, its matt, dark green leaves usually free from the mildew that is the curse of so many roses of its color. It was raised by Victoria's R. J. Bell, an amateur hybridist who can feel proud of its good shape, rich color and fine perfume; but whether it is sufficiently distinctive to attract attention internationally remains to be seen. So far the world has not taken much notice.

Parentage undisclosed
Repeat flowering
Fragrant

▲ 'Australian Bicentennial'

'Autumn Delight'   Hybrid Musk

'Autumn Delight' makes a compact bush like that of a large Cluster-flowered Rose. The almost thornless branches are nicely clad with leathery foliage, and they bear clusters of almost single cream flowers with maroon stamens and fine fragrance. In the autumn, or fall, the flowers are deeper in tone and the sprays of flowers huge—a real delight. This is one of the lesser known of the Reverend Mr Pemberton's Hybrid Musks, raised in 1933.

Parentage unknown
Repeat flowering
Fragrant

▲ 'Autumn'
► 'Autumn Delight'

'Autumn'   Large-flowered

Blending rich tones of burnt orange, red and gold, these flowers are large, full and fragrant. The colors soften with age, but the compact bushes flower abundantly in the spring; it is a pity to have to report that this rose is not generous with its flowers in the autumn, or fall. The foliage is dark green and glossy, but watch it for black spot. Raised by L. B. Coddrington of New Jersey, 'Autumn' was introduced in 1928. It is a sister-seedling of the same raiser's better known 'President Herbert Hoover', also pictured in this book.

'Sensation' × 'Souvenir de Claudius Pernet'
Repeat flowering
Fragrant

'Aviateur Blériot'
Rambler

Pale Tea Rose yellow, fading almost to white, the small flowers are slightly scented and borne in big clusters in summer, rather late in the rose season. It has glossy dark green foliage. For many years it has been popular as a weeping standard, for the sake of its color, but it is not otherwise seen now except where a 'period piece' Edwardian garden is maintained. There is rarely any repeat bloom. The rose, which appeared in 1910 was raised by a M. Fauque. It was named for Louis Blériot, the first man to make an international aeroplane flight, from Calais to Dover in 1909.

Rosa wichuraiana × 'William Allen Richardson'
Summer flowering
Fragrant

'Avignon'
Cluster-flowered

'Avignon' seems on the verge of dropping out of the catalogues, which is a pity, as it is an attractive rose. Its flowers are nicely shaped, not overly large, about 6 centimetres (2½ inches) or so, and carried in well-spaced clusters on a dark-leafed, tallish bush. They are a pleasing shade of cool yellow, which holds well. It was raised by Cants of Colchester and introduced in 1974.

'Allgold' × 'Zambra'
Repeat flowering

'Avon'
Large-flowered

Ovoid buds open to shapely flowers, not overstuffed with petals, which hold their rich crimson color very well, without fading to purple. Fragrance is intense. The bush is of average height

◄ 'Avignon'

and well clothed with matt, mid-green foliage. It is outstanding in warm climates, but where summers are cool and damp, mildew can be a problem. Bred by Dennison Morey, 'Avon' was introduced by Jackson & Perkins in 1961.

'Nocturne' × 'Chrysler Imperial'
Repeat flowering
Intensely fragrant

▲ 'Avon'
◄ 'Aviateur Blériot'

'Aztec'
Large-flowered

Terracotta to brick-red, 'Aztec' was one of the first Large-flowered Roses in this color range. It is still worth a look, as it is a strong and healthy, if somewhat sprawling, bush, with clean olive-green leaves that tone well with the flowers. The blooms themselves are only moderately fragrant, but they are of fine exhibition form. If the sprays of buds it often produces are thinned to singletons, the blooms can be very large. Try

it as a standard and the blooms will nod closer to eye level. Introduced in 1957 by Armstrong Nurseries, 'Aztec' was raised by Herbert Swim.

'Charlotte Armstrong' × unnamed seedling
Repeat flowering

'Azure Sea'
Large-flowered

AROlala

The word 'Azure' is mere wishful thinking for this rose. It actually blends mauve with varying amounts of pink. The blooms are nicely shaped though only lightly scented. Foliage is dark matt green, and growth is upright. Like most mauve Large-flowered Roses it needs good cultivation to give its best, and the color is richest in the autumn, or fall. It was raised by Jack Christensen and introduced by Armstrong Nurseries in 1983.

('Angel Face' × 'First Prize') × 'Lady X'
Repeat flowering

▲ 'Azure Sea'
▼ 'Aztec'

'Baby Blaze'
'Lunds Jubiläum'

Cluster-flowered

Against the coral and apricot tonings of so many of the newer Cluster-flowered Roses, the cherry-red and white-eyed flowers of 'Baby Blaze' look rather old-fashioned, which probably accounts for its lack of popularity. It is a very generous giver of color, the large clusters coming in abundance on a tough, easy-to-grow, compact plant notable for its resistance to cold. It has some fragrance too. Lund is a city in Sweden, celebrating its 1000th anniversary about the time (1950) Wilhelm Kordes raised the rose. The American name was given by Jackson & Perkins for a fancied resemblance to their very popular climber, 'Blaze'.

'Minna Kordes' × 'Hamburg'
Repeat flowering
Fragrant

◀ 'Baby Faurax'   ▲ 'Baby Blaze'
▼ 'Baccarà'

'Baby Faurax'

Polyantha

'Baby Faurax' is thought to be a dwarf sport of the Rambler 'Veilchenblau', which carries some of the most convincing bluish tones in the world of roses. While the blooms of 'Veilchenblau' are most variable in their color, 'Baby Faurax' is much more consistently amethyst. It is a dwarf in an already dwarf group, rarely growing more than 30 centimetres (12 inches) high. Foliage is a dull mid-green. The dainty flowers are quite fragrant. It was introduced by Leonard Lille of Lyon in 1924. The name was given in honor of a Belgian nursery.

Parentage unknown
Repeat flowering
Fragrant

'Baccarà'   Large-flowered
MEIger
'Baccarat'

For many years 'Baccarà' was the supreme flower-shop rose; you hardly saw a florist's window without a bunch of its mid-sized, shapely scarlet flowers on their unbelievably long stems; the foliage is dark green and leathery. Francis Meilland made a fortune from it, but it was never much of a garden rose, even in warm climates. Now it has been superseded by such varieties as 'Mercedes' and 'Gabriella', which are more economical to grow, but people still ask for it by name. Meilland introduced it in 1954. There is no scent to speak of.

'Happiness' × 'Independence'
Repeat flowering

'Bahia'   Cluster-flowered

The vermilion tone of 'Bahia' is made softer by an overtone of old rose, which looks very much better than it sounds against the dark green foliage. The blooms are of pleasantly informal, ruffled shape. Alas, their color is not very stable: as they age the pink takes over and then fades, and the spent flowers do not drop cleanly. But if you are prepared to clean it up every few days (and keep a spray gun handy in case of black spot), 'Bahia' is a good, tall-growing rose. Good enough to have won the 1974 AARS award for its raiser, Dr Walter Lammerts. The foliage is dark green, glossy and leathery.

'Rumba' × 'Super Star'
Repeat flowering
Fragrant

'Bajazzo'   Large-flowered

Velvety blood-red with sharply contrasting white reverses to the petals, these flowers are very large, shapely, and beautifully fragrant, an unusual quality in a bicolored rose. The foliage is mid-green, the bush upright. This is one for the rose enthusiast only as it does not usually produce its handsome flowers freely enough for a good display in the garden. It was raised by Reimer Kordes of Holstein and introduced in 1961.

Parentage undisclosed
Repeat flowering
Fragrant

▲ 'Bahia'   ▼ 'Bajazzo'

'Ballerina'
Hybrid Musk

Although 'Ballerina' is officially classed as a Hybrid Musk, it is really more like an overgrown Polyantha in its big clusters of little flowers and its lack of perfume. Perhaps it should be classed as a Modern Shrub Rose, as it has many admirers for its compact habit (to just under 1.5 meters [5 feet] high and wide), its freedom from temperament (it is one of the easiest of all roses to grow) and the extraordinary freedom and continuity with which it bears its pretty single flowers, soft pink with white around the stamens. The mid-green foliage is exceptionally healthy and disease-resistant. It was introduced by J. A. Bentall in 1937; its parentage is unrecorded.

Parentage undisclosed
Repeat flowering

◄ 'Ballerina'
▼ 'Bantry Bay'

'Bantry Bay'
Large-flowered Climber

The bright rose-pink flowers are shapely in the bud, opening rather loosely and showing a paler centre. They are only slightly fragrant, but are borne freely throughout the season. The plant is moderately vigorous and rather shrubby in habit, with very glossy leaves and the virtue of not usually becoming bare of foliage low down. Raised by Sam McGredy and named for the famed Irish beauty spot, 'Bantry Bay' was introduced in 1967.

'New Dawn' × 'Korona'
Repeat flowering

'Baron de Wassenaer'
Moss

The buds are not conspicuously mossy, and the light crimson flowers are not very distinctive, but they are scented, and the plant is one of the strongest and most reliable of the Mosses. For this reason it is popular with nurseries,

▲ 'Baron de Wassenaer'

appearing in most selections of Old Garden Roses, and it can make a pleasing show in the garden. Foliage is a matt mid-green. Eugène Verdier named the rose for the musician Baron de Wassenaer in 1854.

Parentage unknown
Summer flowering
Fragrant

▲ 'Baron Girod de l'Ain'

'Baron Girod de l'Ain'   Hybrid Perpetual
'Royal Mondain'

'Baron Girod de l'Ain' is a most distinctive rose, its medium-sized flowers dark red with a fine piping of white around the petal edges and strongly fragrant. It is a sport from the plain crimson 'Eugène Fürst' (also well worth a look), introduced by a gentleman named Reverchon in 1897. The bush is tall, a little leggy (peg it down) and needs good soil to give as good a show of flowers in autumn, or fall, as in summer. Foliage is dull green. The only rose that could be confused with it is 'Roger Lambelin', even more strikingly patterned, but apt to be a sickly grower.

Sport from 'Eugène Fürst'
Repeat flowering
Fragrant

'Baron von Bonstetten'   Hybrid Perpetual
'Baron de Bonstetten'

For all Robbie Burns's delight in 'a red, red rose', really pure dark red roses only arrived after his time, with the red Hybrid Perpetuals. 'Baron von Bonstetten' is as sumptuous as any of them, its flowers large, velvety and intensely fragrant. Foliage is dull green. The bush is more compact than most Hybrid Perpetuals, but needs watching against mildew and, unless given the best of everything, is apt to be shy with its autumn, or fall, flowers. Our rose was named in memory of Charles Victor von Bonstetten, an early nineteenth century philosopher. It was introduced in 1871 by a M. Liabaud who raised it from two most important parents.

'Général Jacqueminot' × 'Géant des Batailles'
Repeat flowering
Fragrant

'Baronne Edmond de Rothschild'   Large-flowered
MELgriso

This is one of the more subtly toned bicolors, deep pink, with an undertone of mauve, and white. The flowers are large, high centred, and very fragrant. Foliage is bright green and glossy, and the bushes are rather taller than the average. Sometimes it is a little shy with its flowers. Growers should keep an eye out for black spot. Do not confuse it with the older Hybrid Perpetual 'Baroness Rothschild', introduced in 1868. 'Baronne Edmond de Rothschild' came along from the Meillands exactly a hundred years later. Baron Edmond de Rothschild is famous for his Exbury Hybrid Rhododendrons.

('Baccará' × 'Crimson King') × 'Peace'
Repeat flowering
Fragrant

'Baronne Henriette de Snoy'   Tea
'Baroness Henriette de Snoy'

It is surprising that this aristocratic beauty is not better known, for it is one of the most cold-tolerant of the Teas, and its sumptuous flowers are strongly fragrant. They are usually a blend of pale pink and cream, but sometimes the 'Baroness' touches up her peaches-and-cream complexion with carmine, as though she were in a party mood. The plant is tall and inclined to be leggy, but that is a fault which gentle pruning will do much to correct. The foliage is glossy green. 'Baroness Henriette de Snoy' was raised by A. Bernaix in 1897.

'Gloire de Dijon' × 'Madame Lombard'
Repeat flowering
Fragrant

▼ 'Baronne Edmond de Rothschild'

◄ 'Baron von Bonstetten'
▼ 'Baronne Henriette de Snoy'

'Baronne Prévost'
Hybrid Perpetual

Raised in 1842, 'Baronne Prévost' is one of the earliest Hybrid Perpetuals, and remains one of the most popular, free-flowering all season. Its blooms have the perfect Old Garden Rose quartered form in rose-pink with shadings of lilac. They are of good size too, and powerfully fragrant. Foliage is matt

▲ 'Basildon Bond'
◄ 'Baronne Prévost'
► 'Bassino'

green. It is a great survivor; plants over a century old have been reported in South Africa where it was much used for hedging in the old days (it is rather thorny). Like all roses, it rewards the gardener's care. It was raised by M. Desprez of Yèbles in France. It is unlikely that the Baroness Prévost here honored was connected with the rather disreputable eighteenth century novelist the Abbé Prévost.

Parentage unknown
Repeat flowering
Fragrant

'Basildon Bond'
Large-flowered

HARjosine

Deep apricot yellow, the shapely buds of 'Basildon Bond' open to loosely informal flowers, sweetly fragrant and set against deep olive-green foliage with plum-tinted young shoots. The bush is about average in height, its wood prickly. It was raised by Jack

Harkness and introduced in 1983. It is surprising that this attractive rose has found so little favor outside Britain.

('Sabine' × 'Circus') × ('Yellow Cushion' × 'Glory of Ceylon')
Repeat flowering
Fragrant

'Bassino'
Ground Cover

KORmixal
'Suffolk'

Seen a cluster at a time, the small, single flowers of 'Bassino' may look distinctly old hat and unexciting; but when the prostrate bush reaches its full spread of a metre (3 feet) or so and covers itself in brilliant red, the effect is striking indeed. The color seems all the more brilliant for the white centres to the flowers, and it holds without fading or going 'blue' no matter what the weather. Introduced in 1988 by Reimer Kordes, this is one of the toughest and

most useful of the new ground-covering roses. Flowering all season, it would make a pretty weeping standard. There is a slightly larger version, also by Kordes, called 'Royal Bassino'.

Parentage undisclosed
Repeat flowering

glossy dark leaves and wiry stems. 'Beauté Inconstante' (and there's a subtly evocative French name for you!) was introduced by Joseph Pernet-Ducher in 1892.

Parentage unknown
Repeat flowering
Fragrant

'Beautiful Britain'   Cluster-flowered
DICfire

The name is not quite as patriotic as it sounds: the rose was sponsored by the Keep Britain Tidy organisation. The raiser describes it as 'tomato-red' but it is usually a distinctly orange-red. There is little scent, but the individual flowers are small replicas of exhibition roses, and come in good sprays on an upright bush. Foliage is a glossy medium green. 'Beautiful Britain' was raised in Northern Ireland by Patrick Dickson, and introduced in 1983. It is a very popular rose in the United Kingdom.

'Red Planet' × 'Eurorose'
Repeat flowering

'Beauté'   Large-flowered

Beauty is the birthright of all roses, and it may seem presumptuous to single out one rose above all others to bear her name, but 'Beauté' is worthy of the compliment. Few roses have such blooms that hold their form until they drop. The foliage is large and dark, dull green, the perfect setting for the huge and exquisite flowers, all apricot and cream. The bushes are apt to be on the low side, though not at all sparing with their flowers! The scent, though not strong, is pleasant. Raised by the remarkable French amateur rose-breeder Charles Mallerin, 'Beauté' was introduced in 1954.

'Madame Joseph Perraud' × unnamed seedling
Repeat flowering
Fragrant

▲ 'Beauté'
► 'Bella Rosa'
▼ 'Beauté Inconstante'

'Beauté Inconstante'   Tea

It used to be a rosarian's *bon mot* not many years ago that this was one of the most beautiful of roses, provided you were not too fussy about advance

knowledge of the color. Indeed, no two flowers are ever the same, though they usually fall in the salmon-pink to cerise range. It can be pale and blushing or almost scarlet, but it is always fragrant. It is an average Tea Rose bush, with

'Bella Rosa'   Cluster-flowered
KORwunder
'Toynbee Hall'

Under the omnibus term 'Patio Roses' the nursery industry is grouping a range of types, all of which have in common short growth, suitable for edging a patio or growing in largish pots. Some are just overgrown Miniatures, but 'Bella Rosa' is the sort of rose the breeders ought to be aiming for. Short and spreading in growth, it

has dark green polished foliage. The flowers are normal Cluster-flowered Rose sized, and very pretty in their perfect form and candy-icing-pink, sometimes quite pale but at others a shade deeper. Having only slight scent is the only demerit. It was raised by Reimer Kordes and introduced in 1982. He has also introduced a sport, 'White Bella Rosa'.

Unnamed seedling × 'Träumeri'
Repeat flowering

'Belle de Crécy' Gallica

The legend that this rose, which Beverley Nichols once called 'the most feminine flower in the world', was named for Mme de Pompadour has, alas, been shown to be untrue; but that scarcely spoils the beauty of these blooms. They are perfectly formed in the Old French style, sweetly fragrant, and in the most beautiful blends of pink, mauve and violet. 'Belle de Crécy' looks best in the garden if two or three are planted in a tight clump and given the best of treatment. The rather small, rough leaves are dark green. 'Belle de Crécy' was raised by a M. Roeser of Crécy-en-Brie, and introduced some time in the late 1820s.

Parentage unknown
Summer flowering
Fragrant

'Belle Isis' Gallica

In the early nineteenth century there was a craze for all things Egyptian. One of the minor manifestations of this was the naming of this charming rose for the Egyptian goddess of love, wisdom and beauty. Some modern enthusiasts speculate that 'Belle Isis' is descended from *Rosa arvensis*, albeit very distantly. They cite foliage, unusually bright green for a Gallica; the scent of the flowers, said to resemble myrrh; and especially the color of the flowers. This is pale salmon-pink, a shade unique among the Old French Roses. This is all rather academic; for most of us, 'Belle Isis' is a typical Gallica, its growth compact, its flowers scented and shapely. It is an excellent garden rose. It was introduced by Parmentier about 1845.

Parentage undisclosed
Summer flowering
Fragrant

▲ 'Beautiful Britain'
► 'Belle de Crécy'
▼ 'Belle Isis'

'Belle Poitevine' — Hybrid Rugosa

One of the smaller growing Hybrid Rugosas, usually less than 2 metres (6 feet) high and wide, 'Belle Poitevine' bears elegant, loosely double blooms in mid-pink, often flushed with mauve and sometimes entirely mauve. The cream stamens show the cool tones of the petals off to perfection, and the bush is typical Rugosa: strong, spiny and with lush, disease-proof foliage. It repeats its bloom very well. It was introduced by Bruant of Angers in 1894.

Parentage unknown
Repeat flowering
Fragrant

'Belle Portugaise' — Large-flowered Climber
'Belle of Portugal'

Like most of the hybrids of *Rosa gigantea,* this splendid rose is rather tender, and only at its best in mild climates. It has long been popular in California for its ease of growth, its great vigor and its lavish display in early summer, before most roses have started. The flowers are not especially scented, but they are very pretty, long-budded and silky, tinted in pale pink and peach. They appear over several weeks. The slightly drooping foliage is olive-green. 'Belle Portugaise' was raised in Portugal by Senhor Cayeux in 1903.

R. gigantea × 'Reine Marie Henriette'
Summer flowering

▲ 'Belle Poitevine'
▼ 'Belle Portugaise'

▶ 'Bengale Centfeuilles'
▼ 'Belle Story'

'Belle Story' — English Rose
AUSelle

Introduced by David Austin in 1984 and named for one of the first nursing sisters who joined the Royal Navy in 1864, 'Belle Story' has large, peony-like flowers in delicate tones of peach-pink. The bush is strong and branching, like a larger edition of its grandparent 'Iceberg', and the foliage is a semi-glossy mid-green.

('Chaucer' × 'Parade') × ('The Prioress' × 'Iceberg')
Summer flowering
Fragrant

'Bellona' — Cluster-flowered
KORilona

Essentially a greenhouse rose for the cut-flower trade, 'Bellona' has medium-sized flowers in small clusters on very long stems. They are exceedingly shapely, open slowly, and retain their deep yellow color, against glossy green foliage, until they drop, but there is not much fragrance. In the garden it needs a warm and sunny spot to flower well. There are plenty of better yellow garden roses! It was raised by Reimer Kordes and introduced in 1976. 'Bellona' was the Roman goddess of war, whose priests marched in procession on state occasions, blowing golden trumpets as they went.

'New Day' × 'Minigold'
Repeat flowering

'Bengale Centfeuilles' — China

The name translates as the Hundred-petalled China, not to be confused with *Rosa centifolia* (the 'hundred-petalled rose')! The French name 'Bengale' for the China Roses arises from the circumstance of the first ones to reach European gardens having travelled via the Botanic Gardens in Calcutta. They are in fact of Chinese stock. This is one of the oldest of them, the reference books giving it a date of 1804, and it could well be a Chinese cultivar. It is a very pretty rose, dainty in growth, its many-petalled blooms a blend of soft pinks, deeper in hot weather, paler in cool. It flowers for months. Foliage is a glossy green, plum-tinted when young.

Parentage unknown
Repeat flowering

'Bengale Cérise' China

This rose is paler than most of the Crimson China Roses. The small flowers are cherry-red rather than crimson, but otherwise it conforms to the class. The foliage is dark green, with plum tints when young. Like most of the Chinas it does not like the cold. It was introduced in the late nineteenth century. It would be a nice choice for tucking in among larger growing Old French Roses, to give flowers when they are over.

Parentage unknown
Repeat flowering

▲ 'Bengale Cérise'
▼ 'Bellona'

'Benjamin Franklin' Large-flowered

The color is often described as 'dawn-pink', which is apt as it is lit with gold and apricot. The bush is strong with leathery, dark green foliage. Exhibitors might complain about shortage of petals, but really its only demerit is that it has only a very light perfume. The raiser was Gordon Von Abrams, the year 1969.

Parentage undisclosed
Repeat flowering

▲ 'Benjamin Franklin'

'Bennett's Seedling' — Rambler
'Thoresbyana'

Loosely double and sweetly scented of musk, the flowers are clear white and borne in small and large clusters in summer. The foliage is dark, and the rampant stems often show the purple tone which characterizes the Ayrshire Rambler Roses. (No one knows how they got that name; they are derived from the British native *Rosa arvensis,* and it is thought that the first varieties may have originated in Scotland. They have the unusual characteristic of flowering well in shade.) 'Bennett's Seedling' was raised in 1840 by a Mr Bennett, the gardener to Lord Manners at Thoresby in Nottinghamshire.

Seedling of *R. arvensis*
Summer flowering
Fragrant

▲ *'Benson and Hedges Gold'*
▼ *'Benvenuto'*
► *'Berlin'*
◄ *'Bennett's Seedling'*

'Benson & Hedges Gold' — Large-flowered
MACgem

Sam McGredy IV combined forces with John Mattock of Oxford to introduce 'Benson & Hedges Gold' in a strong commercial drive. It is a cross between 'Yellow Pages' and a seedling from 'Arthur Bell' and 'Cynthia Brooke'— three beautiful golden roses in one. On a dense bushy plant, with leathery green foliage, ovoid buds open to medium-sized bright yellow blooms, sometimes with a flush of red. Like other newish yellow roses, this 1979 introduction is fragrant. One cannot help wonder about its future if the present authoritarian trend against the faintest suggestion of tobacco advertising continues!

'Yellow Pages' × ('Arthur Bell' × 'Cynthia Brooke')
Repeat flowering
Fragrant

'Benvenuto' — Cluster-flowered Climber
MEIelpa

Bright red flowers are borne in huge clusters on this moderately vigorous (and immoderately thorny) plant with glossy dark foliage. It flowers through the season, but one seldom sees it smothered in bloom: it just produces a few clusters at a time. There is little scent. *Benvenuto* means 'welcome' in

Italian. It was also the Christian name of the great Renaissance goldsmith Cellini. The rose was introduced by Meillands in 1967.

('Alain' × 'Guinée') × 'Cocktail'
Repeat flowering

'Berlin' Modern Shrub

Although classed as a Shrub Rose, 'Berlin' is like an exceptionally strong-growing Cluster-flowered Rose. The foliage is broad and glossy, the wood dark and armed with red thorns, and the almost-single flowers, borne in large trusses, open to a brilliant scarlet. They pale almost at once to cerise. The two tones together create a very brilliant effect. There is little scent, but the flowers are exceptionally resistant to bad weather. 'Berlin' was raised by Wilhelm Kordes in 1949. It is one of a series of so-called 'Park Roses' named in honor of German cities.

'Eva' × 'Peace'
Repeat flowering

'Bernina' Cluster-flowered

Bernina are one of the world's better known makers of sewing machines, and no doubt they are delighted with this 'Patio Rose', whose compact light green bushes are embroidered all over with scented flowers. Pure white, they are individually of perfect form, the petals reflexing very neatly. This rose came from the Dutch firm of de Ruiter in 1988.

Parentage undisclosed
Repeat flowering
Fragrant

'Better Homes and Gardens' Large-flowered

Rose-pink with ivory reverse, the bi-colored flowers of this celebrity are not very large, but they are of pleasing high-centred form and mildly fragrant. The bush is a shade above average in height, and well-clad with dark foliage. It is a pleasing rose, though perhaps not an especially distinguished one, although its parentage is aristocratic. It

▲ *'Better Homes and Gardens'*

was raised in 1976 by Bill Warriner for Jackson & Perkins, and the name was given to honor one of the world's largest selling magazines.

'Super Star' × 'Peace'
Repeat flowering

'Betty Prior' Cluster-flowered

For many years one of the most popular of all roses in the United States, and by no means out of favor there even now, 'Betty Prior' is in fact an English-bred rose, introduced by D. Prior & Son in 1935. At first sight you might wonder what the fuss is about, the flowers are just pink, single, and not especially fragrant. They are a very pleasant shade and come in graceful

▲ *'Betty Prior'*
◀ *'Bernina'*

clusters against dull mid-green foliage. Most importantly, the plant will grow anywhere, resisting cold, heat, disease and unskilled gardeners, to give abundant flowers right through the season. Who could deny it its place?

'Kirsten Poulsen' × unnamed seedling
Repeat flowering
Fragrant

'Bewitched'
Large-flowered

Clear pink, often with a suggestion of salmon, the high-centred flowers of 'Bewitched' are well-scented and very long lasting. This is an outstanding rose for a warm climate, holding its color in midsummer heat when so many roses become fleeting ghosts of themselves. 'Bewitched' does not have the iron constitution of its parent 'Queen Elizabeth', but it scores for softer color and strong fragrance. It has glossy green foliage. A worthy winner of the AARS award in 1967 (the year of its introduction), 'Bewitched' was raised by Dr Walter Lammerts in California.

'Queen Elizabeth' × 'Tawny Gold'
Repeat flowering
Fragrant

'Bhim'
Large-flowered

The most widely planted, and desired, new roses are generally bred and marketed by the big nurseries of Europe and the United States, yet unpublicized roses from elsewhere might turn out to be equally interesting—like 'Bhim', for instance, from India. The camellia-like flatness of its form is unusual; its mid-red color is attractive; and it seems to be a healthy bush, very free with its flowers. It has dark semi-glossy foliage. It is only available in India.

Parentage undisclosed
Repeat flowering

▲ 'Bewitched'
▼ 'Bhim'

'Bienvenu'
Large-flowered

Despite its French name, this rose was bred in America. It is fairly typical of the so-called 'Grandiflora' class, with large, high-centred flowers borne in small clusters, on a taller than average bush. Unusually for a rose of its burnt orange color, it is very fragrant. Raised by Herbert Swim and O. L. Weeks and introduced in 1969, 'Bienvenu' seems to have got lost in the crowd of orange-red roses of the 1970s and '80s; it is rarely catalogued today. Do not confuse it with 'Benvenuto', a Large-flowered Climber also depicted in this book.

'Camelot' × ('Montezuma' × 'War Dance')
Repeat flowering
Fragrant

'Big Ben' Large-flowered

It is not known how this rose, which came from the English firm Gandy's Roses in 1964, looks in a warm climate, but in the cool summer of Vancouver, where it was photographed, it looked outstanding. The blooms were of perfect form, velvety crimson, and very fragrant indeed, as one would expect from a child of 'Ena Harkness' and 'Charles Mallerin'. Foliage is mid-green. 'Big Ben' is the great bell of the Houses of Parliament in London.

'Ena Harkness' × 'Charles Mallerin'
Repeat flowering
Fragrant

▲ 'Big Purple'
▶ 'Bing Crosby'
◀ 'Bienvenu'

'Big Purple' Large-flowered
'Stevens' Big Purple', 'Nuit d'Orient'

This 1986 introduction comes from New Zealand, but not from the hand of Sam McGredy. It was raised in 1986 by Pat Stevens, long-time Secretary of the New Zealand Rose Society. Its name describes it exactly: the blooms are big, full-bodied and purple. However the color does vary: in hot weather the flowers incline towards crimson, and they never reach the deep intensity of such Old Garden Roses as 'Cardinal de Richelieu'. Love or hate the color, this is an outstanding rose, vigorous, free and intensely fragrant. Foliage is very dark green and leathery.

'Purple Splendour' × unnamed seedling
Repeat flowering
Fragrant

'Bing Crosby' Large-flowered

Like many roses that straddle the boundary between red and orange, 'Bing Crosby' varies in tone with the soil and weather. Sometimes almost pure deep orange, at others it is definitely red. Foliage is slightly wrinkled and red in its youth, maturing to olive-green. This magnificent bloom is happiest in a warm climate—certainly it has never found favor in Europe, despite winning the AARS award in 1981, the year of its introduction. It was bred by O. L. Weeks.

Unnamed seedling × 'First Prize'
Repeat flowering

◀ 'Big Ben'
▶ 'Bishop Darlington'

'Bishop Darlington' Hybrid Musk

'Bishop Darlington' is an American Hybrid Musk, introduced by Captain G. C. Thomas in 1926. It conforms to expectations for the class, being a fine arching bush about 2 metres (6 feet) tall with sprays of 8 centimetre (3 inch) flowers, shapely in their coral-pink buds and loosely informal in their open blooms in blush and cream. They are borne throughout the season and have the classic musk scent. Foliage is softly bronzed. Captain Thomas's namesake rose is well worth a look too.

'Aviateur Blériot' × 'Moonlight'
Repeat flowering
Fragrant

'Black Boy' — Large-flowered Climber

Striking easily from cuttings and almost indestructible once established, 'Black Boy' has been popular in Australian gardens for so long that its name is apt to be attached to almost any dark red rose, climbing or not, whose real name has been forgotten! The flowers are in the 'decorative' Large-flowered Rose style, sweetly fragrant, and dark crimson, though they are not usually dark enough to be called 'black'. They are produced freely (it seems on every twig), on a vigorous plant with dull green, slightly olive-toned foliage. Autumn, or fall, flowers are very rare. 'Black Boy' was introduced by the Australian rosarian Alister Clark in 1919.

'Étoile de France' × 'Bardou Job'
Summer flowering
Fragrant

▶ 'Black Garnet'
▼ 'Black Boy'

'Black Garnet' — Large-flowered

Very dark red, almost black, the flowers of this unusual rose are medium sized, usually borne in threes, and of high-centred form. Most disappointingly, they are practically without fragrance. The plant is bushy, with lead-green foliage. Raised by O. L. Weeks in 1980, 'Black Garnet', while

well regarded in the United States, has found little favor elsewhere. It inherits from its parents a tendency to mildew in cool climates like those of Britain and northern Europe.

'Mister Lincoln' × 'Mexicana'
Repeat flowering

'Black Prince' — Hybrid Perpetual

The name refers to the color, which can indeed be dark as dark, with a sheen like black velvet. In hot weather it is apt to be just crimson. It grows well enough, though it is a bit prone to mildew. Grow it for the sake of its gorgeous individual flowers (fragrant, of course) rather than its contribution to the garden. Foliage is dull green. Edward the Black Prince was the son of Edward III of England and the much-admired victor of Poitiers in 1356. William Paul bestowed this name on the rose in 1866.

Parentage unknown
Repeat flowering
Fragrant

▲ 'Black Prince'

'Blanc Double de Coubert' — Hybrid Rugosa

The raiser, Cochet-Cochet, claimed that the 1891 'Blanc Double de Coubert' ('Double White of Coubert') was a cross between *Rosa rugosa* and the Tea Rose 'Sombreuil', but few authorities have believed him; it looks to be pure-bred *R. rugosa*. The bush is a little less bushy and vigorous than the wild types, but it is still a handsome plant with the characteristic spines

and tough, brilliant green leaves. It bears clusters of ruffled flowers all season; they are touched with pink in the bud, but open glistening white. Alas, rain rots them, and in wet conditions the bushes have to be groomed to keep them presentable. There are no hips.

R. rugosa × 'Sombreuil'
Repeat flowering
Fragrant

◄ 'Blanc Double de Coubert'
▼ 'Blairii No. 2'

'Blairii No. 2' Climbing Bourbon

Mr Blair's second seedling, which along with 'No. 1' came out in 1845, is being recognized as a most desirable climbing rose for an arch or a wall, its flowers being of good size and fragrance, lovely in their blending of blush with richer pink. Its only fault is that it flowers very sparingly after its lavish first crop. Mr Blair did not reveal the parentage. By the way, 'No. 1' is still around. Most people do not think it as good as 'No. 2'.

Possibly 'Parkes' Yellow' × unknown
Summer flowering
Fragrant

last well in water, and are scented as well. An excellent rose for a formal bed, 'Blessings' was introduced in 1967 by the British rose-grower Walter Gregory.

'Queen Elizabeth' × unnamed seedling
Repeat flowering
Fragrant

'Bloomfield Courage' Rambler

This rose has been popular for some years as a weeping standard, both for its dark red color and its occasional repeat bloom, but there is no reason why it cannot be grown on a fence too. The flowers are small and single, with a touch of white at the centre, and they come in large clusters. They are scentless, and the foliage, as is usual with the small-flowered Wichuraiana Ramblers, is glossy but undistinguished. It makes a vigorous plant. The name honors the place of residence of the raiser, Captain George S. Thomas (there was a series of 'Bloomfield' roses), who has not recorded the parentage. 'Bloomfield Courage' was introduced in 1925.

Parentage undisclosed
Summer flowering

'Blaze' Large-flowered

For many years 'Blaze' was the most popular climbing rose, at least in America. Gardeners loved its bright, blood-red color, its willingness to grow just about anywhere, and its resistance to mildew. The flowers are middle-sized and come in clusters and the foliage is mid-green. The only fault was a reluctance to repeat bloom. But in 1950 Jackson & Perkins discovered a more continuously blooming clone. Originally called 'Blaze Superior', it has usurped the original in the catalogues, and dropped (usually) the 'Superior' from its name. The original was bred by a Mr Kallay of Painesville, Ohio, and it was introduced by Jackson & Perkins in 1932.

'Paul's Scarlet Climber' × 'Grüss an Teplitz'
Repeat flowering

'Blessings' Cluster-flowered Climber

Pink with a distinct overtone of salmon, the shapely flowers of 'Blessings' are scarcely large enough for exhibition, but they are borne in great profusion, often in small clusters, on a compact bush with dark foliage. They

▲ 'Blaze'
► 'Blessings'
▼ 'Bloomfield Courage'

THE ROSE AND CHRISTIANITY

With the disintegration of the Roman Empire, Western Europe entered the Dark Ages. The name suggests centuries of misery. It was a time when people were reduced to little more than beasts cowering in their hovels, shivering in fear that the barbarian warlords who went rampaging about the country, only too eager to indulge in rapine and pillage, would seize their pitiful possessions and the meagre crops

ignorant and narrow-minded to a degree that would have scandalized a self-respecting pagan (and did scandalize the Muslims), but they were a force for peace and stability in the world, and among the civilized arts that the monasteries kept alive was horticulture.

The larger monasteries had gardens on a scale that a Roman gentleman would have admired— and as the centuries progressed and the monks grew richer, that he would have envied—and in them the rose held pride of place. At first the prelates frowned. Was this not the flower of Venus, featured at decadent and sinful Roman parties? One can imagine the monkish gardeners pleading its cause, citing the usefulness of the rose in medicine and the deliciousness of rose-hip pies.

Marks of divine favor were soon forthcoming. Did not the martyred Saint Dorothy send roses from Heaven to her grieving fiancé Theophilus? (What was good enough for God should be good enough for His servants, surely?) And was it not true (as could be read in many learned books) that the

◄ Rosa pendulina, *the thornless rose, is featured in this painting on vellum by eighteenth-century painter Georg Dionysius Ehret. One of the mystical titles of the Virgin Mary was 'The Rose without Thorns'.*

▼ *'A garden enclosed is my sister, my spouse.' The writer of the Song of Solomon expresses beautifully the feeling of intimacy that a walled garden can evoke.*

that they had eked from the soil with their bare hands. Naturally, gardening, and with it the love of roses, vanished.

Were the times so very awful? True, imported luxuries vanished from the shops and few people thought it worthwhile to build marble palaces. With the dissolution of the imperial civil service, there were no bureaucrats to record the politics of the day, leading the frustrated historians of the future to call the ages 'dark' for lack of records. Yet the soils of Europe were as fertile as ever; the rain still fell; and the sun still shone. Indeed, the times are thought to have been a period of exceptionally benign climate, and it is not fanciful to suggest that the ordinary people enjoyed a standard of living not all that much worse than that of the early colonists in America a thousand or so years later. Roses still grew at the cottage door; lovers still gave flowers to each other; and people still took roses to decorate their churches on holy days.

There was also a new power in the world, the Christian Church. No doubt many of its prelates, priests and monks were

prickly stems of the rose had the honor of furnishing the Crown of Thorns, and that its flowers are red due to their having been stained by the blood of Christ?

Christ was a carpenter and a shepherd, and, it would seem, not all that interested in gardening. His mother, on the other hand, appeared to be very fond of roses, having bestowed them on such favored saints as Bernard and Dominic. To this day Her devotees offer Her their rosaries. The custom of counting one's prayers on a chain of beads apparently originated in the Middle East, but the idea of comparing a set of prayers to a garland or garden of roses is very much a product of the Christian Middle Ages. What woman, after all, can resist a bunch of roses?

As the Chinese say, differences of religion and politics may divide humankind, but the love of flowers unites us all.

◀ *The Madonna was often depicted with a vase of roses by her side. In this painting by Matthias Grünewald they are no doubt included for symbolic reasons, but we can enjoy them also simply for their beauty and fragrance. These are no generic roses, but clearly* Rosa gallica officinalis.

▼ *Saint Elizabeth of Hungary is one of several saints associated with the rose. It seems that she had been forbidden by her husband to distribute food to the needy. One day, he caught her out, but when she unfolded her apron, the bread she had been carrying was miraculously transformed into roses. This terracotta by Andrea Della Robbia records the miracle, which so shamed her husband that he then devoted his great wealth to charity.*

▲ *Monastic gardens grew roses in the company of other flowers and healing herbs, a tradition followed in this modern Canadian garden where climbing roses form a backdrop to beds filled with angelica, mint and thyme.*

'Bloomfield Dainty' — Hybrid Musk

Some people report that as the canary-yellow, five-petalled flowers of 'Bloomfield Dainty' age, they pass to peach-pink; more often though it is just a straight yellow, with perhaps the merest touches of peach. The 5 centimetre (2 inch) flowers, borne in small

▲ 'Bloomfield Dainty'
▶ 'Blossomtime'

clusters all along the arching branches, are fragrant of musk, and dainty indeed. Foliage is a glossy green. The plant is not dainty, however, being a stalwart arching shrub reaching 2 metres (6 feet) or more. It flowers repeatedly. Raised in 1924 by Captain Thomas, it inherits its pollen parent's preference for a warm climate.

'Danäe' × 'Madame Edouard Herriot'
Repeat flowering
Fragrant

'Bloomin' Easy' — Cluster-flowered
AROtrusim
'Blooming Easy'

With bright red flowers all season long on a tall bush well-furnished with glossy leaves, 'Bloomin' Easy' lives up to its name. Like 'Simplicity', of which it is, more or less, a red version, it is claimed by the raisers to be exceptionally easy to grow, needing little protection from disease and only rough and ready pruning. There is a need for the easy-care rose for parks and lazy gardeners, and several raisers are working on them. 'Bloomin' Easy' is Jack Christensen's contribution, and was introduced in 1988.

'Trumpeter' × 'Simplicity'
Repeat flowering

▶ 'Bloomin' Easy'

'Blossomtime' — Large-flowered Climber

Introduced in 1951 by an American called O'Neil who does not seem to have any other roses to his account, 'Blossomtime' was one of the first of the repeat-flowering Climbers to be raised from 'New Dawn'. It remains one of the best of them, with its clusters of shapely flowers in two shades of pink, and is reminiscent of one of the older Large-flowered Roses. Of pillar rose vigor, it makes a great display in early summer, with scattered flowers for the rest of the season. The fragrance is delightful, the foliage mid-green and resistant to mildew.

'New Dawn' × unnamed Large-flowered Rose
Repeat flowering
Fragrant

'Blue Boy' — Modern Shrub

In 1958, Wilhelm Kordes announced two Modern Shrub Roses, 'Black Boy' and 'Blue Boy'. 'Black Boy' seems to have dropped out (do not confuse it with the popular Alister Clark Climber of the same name), but 'Blue Boy' is worth a second look, despite it being non-repeat flowering. It is only a small shrub, but the flowers can be very striking. Fairly large and shapely in the modern style, they blend rich crimsons and violets, which look very well against the greyish leaves; and they are fragrant.

'Louis Gimard' × 'Independence'
Summer flowering
Fragrant

'Blue Moon' — Large-flowered
'Mainzer Fastnacht', 'Sissi'

The blooms are a cold, pale lilac shade, sometimes warmed with a little pink. They are only moderate in size, though well formed and very sweetly scented. The petals are thin and the foliage dull green. The plant is tall. Flower arrangers enjoy the long slender stems, which are fairly free of thorns. Much the most popular of the 'blue' roses, both for its perfume and its willingness to grow and flower freely, 'Blue Moon' was introduced by the Tantau Company in 1964.

'Sterling Silver' × unnamed seedling
Repeat flowering
Fragrant

'Blue Nile' — Large-flowered
DELnible
'Nil Bleu'

The buds of 'Blue Nile' are long and elegant, opening to nicely formed flowers with more substance to the petals than most 'blue' roses. The flowers are strongly fragrant, and a clear mauve in color. Growth is good, the plants on the tall side, with dull green foliage. Bred by Georges Delbard of Paris, 'Blue Nile' was introduced in 1981.

('Holstein' × 'Bayadère') × ('Prélude' × 'Saint-Exupéry')
Repeat flowering
Fragrant

▲ 'Blue Boy'
▶ 'Blue Moon'
▼ 'Blue Nile'

'Blue River'
KORsicht

Large-flowered

Lilac, flushed at the petal edges with a deeper mauve which passes to rose-pink in old age, 'Blue River' may lack the ethereal touch of so many mauve roses, but its stronger colors are more telling in the garden. It flowers quite freely on an average-sized bush with shiny mid-green foliage. The richly fragrant flowers are very long lasting when cut. They are of fine form, but early disbudding will be called for to have them large enough for the show bench. It was introduced by Reimer Kordes in 1984.

'Blue Moon' × 'Zorina'
Repeat flowering
Fragrant

'Blush Boursault'
'Calypso'

Boursault

The now almost forgotten Boursault Roses take their name from an influential rosarian of Napoleon's time. It was said that his approval of a new variety guaranteed its popularity, and he particularly liked this small group of thornless climbing roses. M. Boursault's original rose was red. The illustrated 'Blush Boursault' is a pale pink version. The very large, prettily blowsy flowers are not very fragrant, and they do not like wet weather, tending to ball, but they come very early in the season (one flowering only) and the plant later performs the unusual trick (for a rose) of giving a display of autumn, or fall, leaves. For the rest of the time the foliage is dark green and the bush is practically evergreen.

Parentage unknown
Summer flowering

▲ 'Blue River'
▼ 'Blush Boursault'

'Blush Damask' — Damask

'Blush Damask' is one of the most commonly seen Old Garden Roses surviving in vanished gardens and old cemeteries in Australia and South Africa. Dating from 1759, it is a great survivor. Few roses are easier to grow, and in season the bushy plant is well covered in small clusters of blooms in rose-pink. The color is a bit deep in tone to give it the title 'Blush' today, but it is much the same color as the 'Old Blush' China, another great survivor. Sweetly fragrant, 'Blush Damask' has two faults: its season of bloom is rather short (there is no repeat) and the spent flowers tend to cling to the bushes. Dead heading is called for.

Parentage unknown
Summer flowering
Fragrant

'Blush Rambler' — Rambler

The pale pink flowers open wide to show their stamens, and come in large sprays. They are not at all large, but are refreshingly fragrant. The foliage is light green, scarcely glossy, and the flexible branches are almost thornless. Vigorous in growth, this is a pretty cottage-garden flower. It was raised by B. R. Cant & Sons in 1903.

'Crimson Rambler' × 'The Garland'
Summer flowering
Fragrant

◄ 'Blush Noisette'
▼ 'Blush Rambler'

▲ 'Blush Damask'

'Blush Noisette' — Noisette

Rosa × noisettiana, 'Rosier de Phillipe Noisette'
Grow this rose for its history, certainly, but be prepared to be charmed by the pale pink flowers, borne freely for most of the season on an almost thornless plant, and by the intensity of its fragrance. Foliage is a leathery mid-green. Raised in about 1815, in Charleston, South Carolina, by Phillipe Noisette, a French nurseryman resident there, 'Blush Noisette' is a hybrid of *R. moschata* and a China Rose that came from the garden of John Champney, a local rice grower. It attracted admiration as the first frost-hardy, repeat flowering climber, and has proved an important parent for other roses.

'Champney's Pink Cluster' × unknown
Repeat flowering
Fragrant

'Bobbie James'   Rambler

Its ancestry is unknown—speculation links it to both *Rosa brunonii* and *R. multiflora*. This is one of the best choices if you want a really vigorous double white climbing rose. Effectively, it is a double-flowered version of one of the Himalayan Musks, and, like them, it will smother a large house or a sizeable tree with glossy green foliage and, in early summer, clouds of deliciously fragrant blossoms. Introduced in 1960 by Graham Thomas, it was named in honor of the Honorable Robert James and his wonderful garden, St Nicholas in Yorkshire.

Parentage unknown
Summer flowering
Fragrant

▲ 'Bobby Charlton'

'Bon Silène'   Tea

Not one of the more famous Tea Roses, 'Bon Silène' is still desirable. If the open flowers are a little 'thin', the buds are long and elegant, the fragrance strong, and the color a clear deep pink against rather glossy green foliage. Lack of hardiness probably accounts for its lack of popularity. Those who garden in mild climates will not find this a drawback. Created by M. Eugene Hardy at the Luxembourg Gardens in Paris, it was introduced in about 1837.

Parentage unknown
Repeat flowering
Fragrant

▲ 'Bon Silène'

'Bonfire Night'   Cluster-flowered

The fiery blend of red, yellow and orange in this rose certainly merits the name, 'Bonfire Night'. The clusters of medium-sized flowers do not give much scent, but they do show up well against dark matt foliage. Do not confuse 'Bonfire Night', which was raised by Sam McGredy in 1971, with 'Bonfire', a red Rambler of 1928, which is rarely seen nowadays.

'Tiki' × 'Variety Club'
Repeat flowering

▲ 'Bobbie James'
► 'Bonfire Night'

'Bobby Charlton'   Large-flowered

Deep pink, with a paler shade on the petal reverses, the flowers of 'Bobby Charlton' are very large and of perfect form with a strong spicy fragrance. They don't come in any great number and though the bush is healthy and the foliage dark green, this is really a plant for the exhibitor rather than for garden display. Bred by the Gareth Fryer Nursery in Cheshire, 'Bobby Charlton' was introduced in 1974. The Baden-Baden gold medal of 1976 and the Portland gold medal of 1981 are among its awards. It is named for an English football hero who captained a winning World Cup side.

'Royal Highness' × 'Prima Ballerina'
Repeat flowering
Fragrant

▲ 'Bonica '82'   ▼ 'Bonn'

'Bonica '82'
Cluster-flowered

MEIdomonac
'Bonica'

You can just call it 'Bonica'—most catalogues do—but the full title avoids any confusion should anyone remember Meilland's 1958 Floribunda 'Bonica'. It was scarlet; our current rose is salmon-pink. What won 'Bonica '82' the 1987 AARS award is its extraordinary lavishness with flowers for months on end and for the ease with which it can be grown. The foliage is a glossy green. Meilland, the raisers, call it a 'Landscape Rose', claiming it to be virtually immune to disease and needing no regular pruning. They introduced it in 1982.

Rosa sempervirens × 'Mademoiselle Marthe Caron') × 'Picasso'
Repeat flowering

'Bonn'
Modern Shrub

Another of Wilhelm Kordes's Park Roses, designed to make a bright display with minimum care, 'Bonn' makes a head-high bush with leathery green leaves and sprays of fragrant ruffled flowers, which are scarlet fading to strong pink, sometimes with a wash of magenta. While the early flowers should be removed to encourage continuity of flowering, the later ones can be allowed to make red hips. It was introduced in 1950. Bonn was the capital of West Germany during the period of the division of the country.

'Hamburg' × 'Independence'
Repeat flowering
Fragrant

'Bonnie Hamilton'   Cluster-flowered

For all its merits, 'Bonnie Hamilton' has not achieved wide popularity, perhaps because it is only happy in the British climate where it was bred, and perhaps its lack of fragrance has told against it. In Britain it seems a desirable rose, its flowers shapely, like small Large-flowered Roses, its clusters nicely spaced, and its orange-to-red colors bright without being shrill. The plant appears to be strong and healthy and the foliage is a pleasant dark green. It was introduced in 1976 by Alec Cocker of Aberdeen.

'Anne Cocker' × 'Allgold'
Repeat flowering

'Bonnie Scotland'   Large-flowered

Deep rose-pink, almost red, the flowers of 'Bonnie Scotland' are large and shapely. They are strongly fragrant too, a quality insisted on by the raiser, whose nursery in Aberdeen sells only fragrant cultivars. The bush is upright and the leaves glossy green. This attractive rose, which performs best in a cool climate, was introduced by Anderson's Roses in 1976.

'Wendy Cussons' × 'Percy Thrower'
Repeat flowering
Fragrant

▼ 'Bonnie Hamilton'

▲ 'Bonsoir'
◄ 'Bonnie Scotland'

'Bonsoir'   Cluster-flowered

Palest peach-pink, deeper in the heart of the flower, and sweetly fragrant, the beautifully shaped blooms of 'Bonsoir' usually come in threes. The exhibitor will want to disbud in order to show them at their full size, but in the garden they can be left to develop naturally. The bush is a little below average in height, very thorny, with fine dark foliage, but it is sometimes rather shy with its flowers, and their beauty is easily ruined by a spell of wet weather. This rose-lover's rose was raised by Dickson's in 1968.

Unnamed seedling × unnamed seedling
Repeat flowering
Fragrant

'Borderer'   Cluster-flowered

With the rose industry getting quite excited over the novelty of dwarf-growing Cluster-flowered Roses, there is a certain mischievous pleasure in noting that 'Borderer' has been around since 1918! The bush is very compact, less than 0.5 metre (20 inches) tall, with very glossy, dark green leaves, and smothers itself with rose-pink flowers, ruffled and faintly scented, for months on end. 'Borderer' was raised by Australian hybridist Alister Clark. The name is Australian English. By a 'border', Australians mean the low planting that edges a flower bed, not the grand array of the English herbaceous border.

'Jersey Beauty' × unknown
Repeat flowering

'Botzaris'   Damask

Lovers of Old Garden Roses are used to finding phrases like 'raiser, date and parentage unknown' in books and catalogues. 'Botzaris' is not quite such a foundling, as the date 1856 seems pretty well established for it, even though the name of the raiser has been forgotten. The light green bush is much neater in habit than most Damasks, a sign, it is thought, of Alba ancestry; and the creamy white flowers, opening from red-tinged buds are of perfect symmetry and sweet fragrance.

Parentage unknown
Summer flowering
Fragrant

▲ 'Botzaris'
▼ 'Boule de Nanteuil'

'Bordure Rose'   Cluster-flowered

'Strawberry Ice', 'Happy Anniversary'
The flowers are only semi-double, the better to show off the attractive effect of the wide rose-pink border to the cream petals. They are medium-sized, and carried in well-spaced clusters on a compact, dark-foliaged bush. Whichever of its three names you find it under, this is a pretty garden rose, and long lasting in the vase too. Even the raiser, Georges Delbard, admits that it is quite scentless. It won the Baden-Baden gold medal in 1973 and was introduced in 1975. The name 'Bordure Rose' is to be preferred as it is both descriptive and the original name bestowed by the raiser.

Unnamed seedling × 'Fashion'
Repeat flowering

'Boule de Nanteuil'   Gallica

'Comte Boula de Nanteuil'
In its heyday, 'Boule de Nanteuil' was one of the most popular of roses. Just about every writer in the early days of Queen Victoria's reign recommended it enthusiastically. Then it fell into an obscurity from which it has only very recently been rescued. Now rose-lovers can once again admire its perfect quartering, rich yet soft colors—cerise pink (usually washed over with violet) against olive-green, suede-textured leaves—and sweet fragrance. The plant is compact and robust. This is thought to be another of M. Roeser's creations from the early 1830s, but no one is sure.

Parentage unknown
Summer flowering
Fragrant

'Boule de Neige'   Bourbon

There are some lovers of the Old Garden Roses who consider 'Boule de Neige' to be the most perfect white rose ever raised. Each bloom is as regular and symmetrical as a camellia, its heart warmed with a hint of ivory; then the flowers reflex into perfect snow white globes, just like snowballs (which is what 'Boule de Neige' means). No snowball, however, ever smelt like this; it is very fragrant. The dark green foliage sets the flowers off perfectly, but you

▲ 'Borderer'
▼ 'Bordure Rose'

▲ 'Boule de Neige'

may need to watch for black spot. Good cultivation will ensure a fine autumn, or fall, display. It was introduced by Francis Lacharme in 1867.

'Blanche Lafitte' × 'Sappho'
Repeat flowering
Fragrant

'Bourbon Queen' — Bourbon
'Souvenir de la Princesse de Lamballe', 'Reine des Iles Bourbon', 'Queen of Bourbons'
Named for the supposedly lesbian confidante of Queen Marie Antoinette who was torn to pieces by the mob

▶ 'Brandenburg'
▼ 'Bradley Craig'

in revolutionary Paris, this lovely medium-sized mallow-pink rose was introduced in 1835 by M. Mauget of Orléans. Do not expect many of the crinkle-petalled scented roses after the first flowering, though there will be some. The bush is on the tall side, its branches lax enough to allow it to be trained either as a shrub or as a short climber, and foliage is dull green.

Parentage unknown
Summer flowering
Fragrant

'Bradley Craig' — Cluster-flowered
MACstewar
There are many orange-red Cluster-flowered Roses, often looking rather alike, but their masses of bright color makes them popular, especially in the grey climate of northern Europe. 'Bradley Craig' is a recent entrant in the field, from New Zealand's Sam McGredy. It makes a compact bush with polished leaves, tinted red in their youth, and medium-sized semi-double flowers in good clusters. They hold their color well, without fading or turning blue.

Parentage undisclosed
Repeat flowering

▲ 'Bourbon Queen'

'Brandenburg' — Large-flowered
The deep salmon-red petals are a shade deeper on the reverse and about forty of them build up into a big exhibition-style flower. There is little scent. Stems are long and the olive-green foliage is glossy. This rose is not very free with its blooms, and it has rather lost favor in recent years. It is happiest in a warm climate. 'Brandenburg' was raised by Riemer Kordes and introduced by Sam McGredy in 1965.

('Spartan' × 'Prima Ballerina') × 'Karl Herbst'
Repeat flowering

and glossy with plum tints when young. Its constitution is not very robust—not an uncommon fault among bicolors—and it is prone to black spot in humid climates. Where it does well, though, it is as dazzling a rose as any. Raised by Sam McGredy, it was introduced in 1968.

'Kordes Perfecta' × 'Piccadilly'
Repeat flowering

◄ 'Brandy'
► 'Bridal White'
▼ 'Bridal Pink'

'Brandy' Large-flowered

The deep apricot color softens a little as the flowers open. They are rather loosely formed, with about twenty-five petals, but have a pleasing fruity fragrance and are borne freely on a bush of average height. The leaves are large and glossy, but with a susceptibility to black spot. 'Brandy' won the AARS award in 1982 for its unusual color and fragrance, and has had many admirers since it was launched by Swim & Christensen in 1981.

'First Prize' × 'Dr A. J. Verhage'
Repeat flowering
Fragrant

'Brasilia' Large-flowered

Framing scarlet and gold, the bicolored flowers are full and nicely formed though lacking in scent. The bush is upright and the foliage is mid-green

▲ 'Brasilia'

'Bridal Pink' Cluster-flowered

It is unusual for a bride to wear pink at her first wedding, but many brides choose to carry pink roses. In America, they will almost certainly be 'Bridal Pink', one of that country's leading cut-flower roses. It is less popular in Europe, where its soft candy-pink is less favored than the coral tones of roses such as 'Sonia'. It has dark green foliage. It is not a good rose out of the glasshouse, except in warm climates. It was raised in 1967 by Eugene Boerner for Jackson & Perkins. There is a little scent.

'Summertime' seedling × 'Spartan' seedling
Repeat flowering
Fragrant

'Bridal White' Cluster-flowered

'Bridal White', introduced by Jackson & Perkins in 1970, is a sport of their very successful cut-flower rose 'Bridal Pink'. It is a similar rose except for its creamy white color, and it seems that it has also acquired quite a few more petals along the way. Like 'Bridal Pink' it is

only worth growing in the garden in the mildest climates, but the blooms are very long lasting.

Sport from 'Bridal Pink'
Repeat flowering
Fragrant

'Brigadoon' Large-flowered
JACpal

Every so often a new rose comes along that everyone instantly falls in love with. 'Brigadoon', the 1992 AARS winner, is like that. The huge blooms are of most perfect shape, softly fragrant, and irresistible in the way they blend softest pink, cream and coral. The foliage is a handsome dark olive-green, and the bush is a good grower. It looks to be another winner for Bill Warriner, recently retired as Director of Research for Jackson & Perkins.

'Pristine' × unnamed seedling
Repeat flowering
Fragrant

▲ 'Brigadoon'

THE ROSE IN ISLAM

'The Mahomedans,' the Abbé Belmont wrote, back in 1896, 'so venerate the rose, as having been born from the sweat of the Prophet's brow, that, should they chance to find a rose lying on the ground they hasten to gather it up; and, having kissed it respectfully, insert it in some gap in a wall, to protect it from defilement.'

Whether or not the custom still holds, it is certainly true that roses have been long admired in Islam's heartlands. Centuries before the Prophet, the rose was a mystical symbol to the Persian fire worshippers. The Middle East is rich in Wild Roses, among them forms of *Rosa gallica, R. damascena, R. moschata* (it is said) and *R. foetida*, ancestor of virtually all our modern yellow roses. This is the home of the yellow roses—*R. ecae, R. xanthina, R. persica* as well as *R. foetida*—and the Faithful (or at least the Abbé Belmont) like to tell of the story that their origin involved the Prophet also.

It seems that Mohammed's favorite wife, Aisha, fell in love with a young Persian while her husband was away waging holy war. The distressed Prophet sought the advice of the Angel Gabriel, who told him to ask Aisha to throw something into the pool in the centre of the Medina marketplace. If it remained unchanged, it would prove her fidelity. The next day, he met her there. At his request, she laughingly tossed in a bunch of red roses. Unhappy miracle! They emerged the color of gold, the first yellow roses ever seen. To this day the pool is the refuge of unhappy husbands.

Let not such stories lead us into the common Western picture, fuelled by centuries of rivalry and conflict, of the adherents of Islam as a superstitious and rustic lot. Even the Crusaders, primed by Christian propaganda, were dazzled by the civilization and learning of those they had come to fight. Baghdad, seat of the Califs, was the most brilliant city in the world in its day—a centre of science (most of what the Renaissance learned of Greek and Roman botany and medicine came from the Arabs) and its gardens were famous. Baghdad indeed means 'the garden city', and in the shadow of its domes grew roses, studied by botanists and celebrated by poets. The Califs were mighty warriors, as Islamic sovereigns were expected to be, but in their portraits they are often shown enjoying the fragrance of a rose—a convention that became universal in Islam, from Spain to Turkey to India.

It is the Persian poets, however, that are most familiar to us in the West: Sa'adi, Ha'afiz and, thanks to Edward Fitzgerald's excellent translation of *The Rubaiyat*, Omar Khayyám. All sang the praises of the rose, loved above all flowers (the Persian *gul* means 'a rose', but describes all other flowers too). Sa'adi's most famous volume of poems is called *Gulistan*, 'The Rose Garden'. 'The Rose may

▲ *The theme of the nightingale and the rose is a favorite one with Islamic poets and was taken up by Oscar Wilde in a famous short story. This depiction in lacquer comes from Kashmir.*

◄ *The Damask Rose 'Omar Khayyám', grown from the seed of the rose growing on the poet's grave.*

▲ It was a convention throughout Islam to portray a ruler or other notable smelling a rose, as in this portrait of the Indian Emperor Shah Jahan. The image suggested that these mighty warriors also cultivated the arts of peace.

▲ The heartlands of Islam are also the home of yellow roses. Introduced to Britain in 1837, 'Persian Yellow' is apparently an old garden plant in Iran. From it descend practically all of our yellow Modern Garden Roses.

◄ 'I sometimes think that never blows so red the rose as where some buried Caesar bled.' (Omar Khayyám, translated by Edward Fitzgerald.) The rose is 'Charles Mallerin'.

flower for four or five days, but my verses will blossom forever.' The old theme of the rose as a symbol of love appears again in Ha'afiz—his 'a pair of rosy lips' has become a cliché—and in Omar Khayyám, who celebrates the specially Persian association of the rose and the nightingale. 'Still the nightingale sings to the rose/In high piping Pehlevi, "Wine, wine, red wine"/Her sallow lips to incarnadine.' Music, wine and the rose: but this is more than mere sensuousness—it is a meditation on the shortness of life and how fleeting is happiness.

Omar wished, like the Emperor Babur of India, to be buried in a garden, 'where the North Wind could scatter rose petals on his grave'. His grave is still there at Nashipur, a place of pilgrimage for his admirers, and on it a rose still grows. From it, at the end of the nineteenth century, a hip was taken to England, and a rosebush grown from it to plant in a Surrey churchyard, on the grave of his translator. This rose from Fitzgerald's grave has been propagated and named 'Omar Khayyám'. It turns out to be a Damask, with the typical soft pink flowers and sweet fragrance. Now, when the resurgence of militant Islam has focused anxious eyes on the Middle East, it may bloom in all our gardens to remind us, in East and West alike, that there are things more enduring and important than politics and religious differences.

'Britannia' Polyantha

The name suggests an English raiser, but it may also be a Dutch or Belgian rose, as most of the Polyanthas were named for the British market. Unfortunately, 'Britannia' has vanished completely, not only from the catalogues but also from the reference books. In the face of competition from shapely, fragrant Cluster-flowered Roses, even patriotism was not enough to keep people admiring its little single cerise flowers with their startling white eyes. Foliage is dull green.

Parentage unknown
Repeat flowering

'Bright Beauty' Large-flowered

Georges Delbard is one of France's leading rose-breeders, with a penchant for excellent cut-flower varieties, and is usually one of the most conscientious about registering his new roses, often giving their ancestry unto the third and fourth generations. This time he seems to have slipped up. 'Bright Beauty', introduced in 1986, remains an orphan. It is a beautiful one, though, with large, beautifully formed flowers in brilliant coral, and glossy, healthy leaves. It does very well in warm climates.

Parentage undisclosed
Repeat flowering

▲ 'Bright Beauty'
▶ 'Bright Melody'
▼ 'Britannia'

'Bright Melody' Modern Shrub

'Bright Melody' is one of those roses that can be described as a light shade of red or a deep pink depending on one's point of view. Fairly large and of loose Large-flowered Rose form, the blooms are carried singly or in bunches of up to ten on an upright plant. The leaves are medium to large and olive-green. Like just about all of Griffith Buck's creations, it is easy to grow and flowers right through the season. It was introduced in 1984.

'Carefree Beauty' × ('Herz As' × 'Cuthbert Grant')
Repeat flowering

'Broadway' Large-flowered
BURway

Where the sun strikes the yellow petals it brushes them heavily with bright pink. When the outer petals are heavily flushed and the centre still yellow the effect is very striking and theatrical indeed. The blooms are not especially large, but nicely scented. The bush is upright, maybe a trifle taller than average, and its foliage is dark green. 'Broadway' won the 1986 AARS award for its grower, Anthony Perry. It was introduced by Co-operative Rose Growers in Tyler, Texas, which is a major centre of rose nurseries.

('First Prize' × 'Gold Glow') × 'Sutter's Gold'
Repeat flowering
Fragrant

'Brown Velvet' Cluster-flowered
MACultra
'Colourbreak'

'A new color break!' the old-time rose catalogues used to say whenever a rose appeared that was faintly unusual. It is one of those catch-phrases worn-out from overuse. But the color of 'Brown Velvet' *is* something out of the ordinary, a combination of dark orange and brown, much richer and brighter than it might sound. The bush is upright and the growth is unusually strong for a novel color. 'Color breaks' are usually associated with sickly plants. The dark green foliage is glossy. Scent is only slight. Raised by Sam McGredy in New Zealand, it was introduced in 1975 and won the New Zealand gold medal in 1979.

'Mary Sumner' × 'Kapai'
Repeat flowering

▲ 'Broadway'
▼ 'Brown Velvet'

'Buccaneer' — Large-flowered

Deep buttercup yellow, the ovoid buds of 'Buccaneer' open to loose informal flowers of a slightly paler shade, the blossoms tending to come in small clusters. The dull, grey-green foliage is unusually resistant to disease, making 'Buccaneer' one of the most reliable of yellow roses. Its height allows it to be grown as a Shrub Rose, or at the back of the bed with others of similar stature like 'Alexander', 'Queen Elizabeth' or 'President Hoover'. It was raised by Herbert Swim and introduced by Armstrongs in 1952 and won the Geneva gold medal in the same year.

'Geheimrat Duisberg' × ('Max Krause' × 'Captain Thomas')
Repeat flowering
Fragrant

'Buff Beauty' — Hybrid Musk

The Reverend Mr Pemberton would surely have chosen to dedicate this most delicious of Hybrid Musks to some lovely goddess. It did not come out until 1939, thirteen years after his death, and is credited to Anne Bentall, the widow of his gardener. One of those roses that everyone loves, its habit is pleasing and graceful with branches that arch beneath the weight of the clusters of blooms. Each flower is filled with muddled petals and sweet fragrance, the color varying with the seasons from straw yellow to apricot, but always charming and distinctive. Foliage is dark green and handsome.

Possibly 'William Allen Richardson' × unknown
Repeat flowering
Fragrant

◄ 'Buccaneer'

▲ 'Bullata'

'Bullata' — Centifolia

Rosa centifolia bullata, 'Rose à Feuilles de Laitue', Lettuce-leafed Rose

Back in the days of the Empress Joséphine, gardeners treasured several forms of *R. centifolia* distinguished by their unusual leaves: the 'celery-leafed', the 'peach-leafed' and others. This one, the 'lettuce-leafed', is apparently the only survivor today. Its leaves really are quite splendid: very large, all puckered and quilted ('bullate' in botanese), and richly tinted with pink like a Mignonette lettuce. They give the bush an air of luxuriance that makes it more decorative in the garden than *R. centifolia* itself. The flowers are almost exactly the same in their full-petalled form, sweet pink color and delicious fragrance.

Sport from *R. centifolia*
Summer flowering
Fragrant

'Burnaby' — Large-flowered

'Golden Heart'

Cream, often deeper in the centre, but paling almost to white in hot weather, the flowers of 'Burnaby' are sometimes very large indeed, which has made them a great favorite with rose-show addicts for many years. However, 'Burnaby' is less successful as a garden rose. Despite the handsome dark green foliage, the plants are leggy and often shy with their blooms, especially in the autumn, or fall. Wet weather upsets the flowers a great deal. Although it was introduced in 1954, 'Burnaby' remains a classic exhibition rose to this day. It was bred by the Canadian breeder Gordon Eddie.

'Phyllis Gold' × 'President Herbert Hoover'
Repeat flowering

'Burnett Pink Tea' — Tea

Every botanic garden that collects old roses acquires a few that have survived in local gardens, their names forgotten but their beauty too great to allow them to be lost forever. Here is one such from the Huntington Gardens in California, a charming and fragrant blush-pink Tea with handsome glossy foliage. No doubt when the Huntington people are satisfied as to its true identity ('Burnett Pink Tea' is only a nickname) they will reintroduce it to commerce. It should find a ready welcome. It is a very good rose.

Parentage unknown
Repeat flowering
Fragrant

▲ 'Burnaby'
◄ 'Buff Beauty'
► 'Burnett Pink Tea'

▲ 'Burning Love'
► 'Busy Lizzie'

'Burning Love' Large-flowered
'Brennende Liebe', 'Amour Ardent'
This might be classed with the Cluster-flowered Roses, as its blooms usually come in small bunches. The Americans would call it a 'Grandiflora'. The color is bright scarlet-red, and the glossy-leafed bush is of average height and bushy. There is little scent, but this rather neglected rose is still an excellent variety for making a splash of bright color in a formal bed. It won the Baden-Baden gold medal in 1954 and was introduced in 1956 by Mathias Tantau of Germany.

'Fanal' × 'Crimson Glory'
Repeat flowering

'Busy Lizzie' Cluster-flowered
HARbusy
The buds look as though the open flowers will be a much deeper pink than they actually are. They are not very double, however the clusters are well arranged to show each flower off to advantage, and they have a vague fragrance. This rose was very much favored in England for its soft color and bushy, flower-covered plants. Foliage is mid-green. It appears now to be disappearing from the catalogues, presumably to make way for newer varieties whose plant patents are still in force. 'Busy Lizzie' was introduced by Jack Harkness in 1971.

('Pink Parfait' × 'Masquerade') × 'Dearest'
Repeat flowering

'Butterfly Wings'
Cluster-flowered

One flower in a catalogue photograph does not do justice to this rose. You have to see a bush full of the delicate, almost single flowers to appreciate their subtle tones of cream and pale pink, admirably played up by the large, pale green foliage. 'Butterfly Wings' is scented too, but it has come and virtually gone from the catalogues in only a short time. It was introduced in 1976, having been raised by an amateur rosarian, W. D. Gobbee, in a suburban London garden. It is the child of aristocratic parents.

'Dainty Maid' × 'Peace'
Repeat flowering
Fragrant

▶ 'Calocarpa'
▼ 'Butterfly Wings'

'Calocarpa'
Hybrid Rugosa

Rosa × calocarpa, 'André'

The name is mock-classical Greek for 'beautiful fruit'. It is certainly appropriate, for 'Calocarpa' does give an abundant crop of typical, globular *R. rugosa* hips in the autumn, or fall. Raised by Bruant in 1895, it is effectively pure *R. rugosa,* slightly smaller in growth than usual, with single flowers in rose pink, without the usual Rugosa undertone of magenta. Like most of the tribe, it gives a display of yellow autumn, or fall, foliage to go with its attractive hips. The mid-green foliage is slightly wrinkled.

R. rugosa × unknown China Rose
Repeat flowering
Fragrant

'Camaieux'
Gallica

This is one of the few Gallicas that needs cosseting, for it is a rather small, weak bush except in the best of conditions. It is worth a bit of trouble for the sake of the extraordinary flowers.

▲ 'Camaieux'

Loosely double and very fragrant, they are striped in a constantly changing blend of tones—now pink and white, now violet and blush-pink, now almost pink and grey. Foliage is dull green and rough to touch. The name, which is unpronounceable to an English-speaking tongue, comes from interior decorating. A fabric is said to be *en camaieu* if it is decorated with motifs in a single color on a blending or contrasting ground. 'Camaieux' is thought to have come from M. Vibert in 1830 or thereabouts.

Parentage unknown
Spring flowering
Fragrant

'Camelot'
Large-flowered

Borne both singly and in clusters, the flowers of 'Camelot' are of medium size, in a cupped formation. Their color is an unfading coral-pink, strong rather than delicate, and they have a

pleasing spicy fragrance. The plant is taller than average with heavy glossy foliage. 'Camelot', which won the AARS award in 1964, is an excellent rose both for garden display and for cutting. It was raised by Herbert Swim and O. L. Weeks and introduced by the Conard-Pyle Company of Pennsylvania in 1964. Its name reminds us of the idealism that blossomed during the days of President Kennedy.

'Queen Elizabeth' × 'Circus'
Repeat flowering
Fragrant

'Camphill Glory'   Large-flowered
HARkreme

Pale yellow and pink, the flowers are large and of high-centred exhibition form. Scent is only slight. The foliage is matt green and the very prickly bush is dense and of average height. Raised by Jack Harkness in 1982, 'Camphill Glory' has not been widely grown outside Britain, but there it is much admired for the ability of its delicately colored flowers to stand up to wet weather. The name honors the Camphill Village Trust, a charitable body dedicated to easing the miseries of the mentally handicapped.

'Elizabeth Harkness' × 'Kordes Perfecta'
Repeat flowering

▲ 'Camelot'
▼ 'Camphill Glory'

'Can Can'   Large-flowered
LEGglow

There are two roses of this name. One is a greenhouse variety in orange-red introduced in 1969 by the E. G. Hill Company in the United States. The other one, which is illustrated here, is a coral-salmon Large-flowered Rose raised by E. B. LeGrice in England in 1982. It is not a straight coral, the flowers being suffused with gold towards their bases. It is very well perfumed, which will, perhaps, compensate the frustrated exhibitor for the rather loose structure of the flowers. The bush is good, with glossy foliage.

'Just Joey' × ('Superior' × 'Mischief')
Repeat flowering
Fragrant

'Canadian Centennial'   Cluster-flowered

'Canadian Centennial' is in fact an American rose, having been raised by Eugene Boerner in 1965 and introduced by Jackson & Perkins to celebrate the 100th birthday of the Dominion of Canada in 1967. But these days there does not seem to be even a patriotic

▲ 'Canadian Centennial'

'Canadian White Star'
'Dr Wolfgang Pöschl'

Large-flowered

Long buds open to large, shapely flowers of glistening white, the sharply reflexing petals giving the bloom a starry outline. Scent is only slight. Foliage is glossy and dark green, on a plant that is average in height. A fine rose for cool climates, and well regarded in the United States and Canada, 'Canadian White Star' is not often seen elsewhere. It was raised by George Mander of Coquitlam, British Columbia, in 1980.

'Blanche Mallerin' × 'Pascali'
Repeat flowering

'Canary'
TANcary

Large-flowered

The IRA prefers to use the codename TANcary to avoid confusion between this 1972 rose from Mathias Tantau and Dickson's 1929 Large-flowered Rose also called 'Canary'. Tantau has not revealed the parents of his 'Canary', but it is a safe guess that it descends from 'Super Star', as it is effectively a yellow version of it, with similar vigorous growth and olive-green foliage, which is plum tinted in its youth. The medium-sized blooms are alike, too, except that they are bright, deep yellow, becoming flushed with coral as they open. Fragrance is moderate. Dickson's rose, a clear yellow, deserved the name more.

Parentage undisclosed
Repeat flowering

Canadian nursery offering it. Let us remember it as a pleasing, orange-red Cluster-flowered Rose, with glossy foliage and some fragrance.

'Pinocchio' seedling × 'Spartan'
Repeat flowering
Fragrant

▲ 'Canadian White Star'
► 'Canary'
▼ 'Can Can'

'Candia'

MEIbiranda

Large-flowered

'Candia' made its debut at the Chelsea Flower Show in 1982, where it was photographed, but Meilland the raisers did not get around to introducing it until 1987. Now it seems to be available only in Canada, Israel and (of all places!) Argentina. Such are the ins and outs of the marketing of a new rose. One cannot help wondering whether the rest of us are missing out on something pretty good: if 'Candia' can do well in cold Canada and warm dry Israel, it should do well just about anywhere. The flowers are superb in shape

▲ 'Candy Stripe'

and color. It does not have a great deal of fragrance. The foliage is large and dark green.

Parentage unknown
Repeat flowering

'Candy Stripe' Large-flowered

The deep rose-pink buds of 'Candy Stripe' are boldly slashed with blush-white, and open rather quickly as large, intensely fragrant flowers. Growth is slightly above average in height, the leaves matt green. The flowers are carried on long stems for cutting and this is the best way to enjoy this rose, as its bizarre tulip-like stripes are apt to look a bit restless in the garden. 'Candy Stripe' was introduced by the Conard-Pyle Company in 1963.

Sport from 'Pink Peace'
Repeat flowering
Fragrant

'Cantabrigiensis' Modern Shrub

Rosa pteragonis cantabrigiensis

Spring-time visitors to the garden of the late Vita Sackville-West, at Sissinghurst Castle in Kent, are always taken by the beauty of this tall Shrub Rose, its single pale yellow blooms and dainty light green foliage shining against the mellow brick walls. It is possibly one of the loveliest of the spring-flowering Shrubs. Introduced in around 1935, it apparently originated at the Cambridge Botanic Garden in England, with credit being usually given to the pioneer in the study of the genetics of the rose, Dr C. C. Hurst.

Probably *R. hugonis* × *R. sericea*
Spring flowering
Fragrant

▶ 'Cappa Magna'
▼ 'Canterbury'

▲ 'Cantabrigiensis'
▼ 'Candia'

'Canterbury' English Rose

This 1969 introduction from David Austin is not one of the more robust of his English Roses, being more like a smallish Bush Rose in habit than a Shrub, but the flowers are lovely—large, fragrant and a glowing warm pink in color. They are not quite single, having about eight petals, but are still most elegant against the dark green foliage. The ancient cathedral city of Canterbury was the goal of Chaucer's pilgrims, commemorated by several Austin roses.

'Monique' × ('Constance Spry' × unnamed seedling)
Repeat flowering
Fragrant

'Cappa Magna' Cluster-flowered

Compare the flowers of this rose with those of 'Altissimo', one of the most popular of modern Climbers (see p. 48). They are almost identical in their five petals and flaming red color. The flowers are borne in large clusters and the foliage is glossy and dark green. 'Cappa Magna' is really a Bush version of 'Altissimo', and indeed, it came from the same raiser, Georges Delbard of Paris. He raised it from the same parent, a red Climber called 'Ténor' and released it along with 'Altissimo' in 1966. Yet 'Altissimo' has become one of the most highly praised of Modern Garden Roses, and no one has ever taken much notice of 'Cappa Magna'.

'Ténor' × unknown
Repeat flowering

'Caprice' — Large-flowered
'Lady Eve Price'

Brilliant pink and yellow, the ovoid buds of 'Caprice' open rather quickly as informally decorative flowers, only slightly fragrant, and fading with age. The plant is average in height and foliage is glossy. A favorite bedding rose of the 1950s, much admired in Britain for the way its flowers stand up to the rain, it is sometimes liable to black spot where summers are hot and humid. There is a climbing version with a good reputation for continuous bloom. It was bred by Francis Meilland, who has since found it useful for further breeding, and it was introduced in 1948.

'Peace' × 'Fantastique'
Repeat flowering

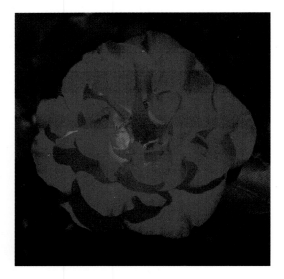

'Captain Harry Stebbings' — Large-flowered

Deep pink, almost red, the flowers of 'Captain Harry Stebbings' are very large and shapely. Their perfume is very strong and fruity and the foliage is dark green and glossy. To judge by its

▲ 'Caprice'
▼ 'Captain Harry Stebbings'

performance in Portland, Oregon, where it was photographed, it appears a desirable exhibition rose. It is difficult to say how it would perform elsewhere. The raiser, Captain Stebbings of Santa Rosa, California, certainly seems to have faith in it, for he named it after himself! It was introduced in 1980.

Sport from unnamed seedling
Repeat flowering
Fragrant

'Captain Hayward' — Large-flowered Climber

'Captain Hayward' is so very vigorous that it is best trained as a pillar rose on a tripod or even on a verandah post, which it will adorn in early summer with great cabbage-like flowers, cerise-pink and fragrant. Unfortunately there are rarely any more to follow; but there will be fat orange hips to admire. Foliage is a strong green. The Bush form was released by the English farmer-turned-rose-breeder Henry Bennett in 1893. William Paul brought out a climbing sport in 1908. Although nurseries refer to this rose as 'Captain Hayward' rather than 'Captain Hayward, Climbing', the latter name would probably be more correct.

Seedling from 'Triomphe de l'Exposition'
Repeat flowering
Fragrant

'Captain Thomas' — Modern Shrub

A rather loose and lax Shrub Rose, 'Captain Thomas' can be trained as a climbing or pillar rose. As such it will display good-sized flowers, over a long period in late summer, though its autum, or fall, flowering is a bit sparse. The flowers are single and pale yellow. The foliage is glossy. It was raised by George Thomas of California and named for the raiser by Armstrong Nurseries, who introduced it in 1938. It has been much used as a parent of yellow roses passing on its great vigor and health.

'Bloomfield Completeness' × 'Attraction'
Repeat flowering

▲ 'Captain Hayward'
▼ 'Captain Thomas'

'Cara Mia'
Large-flowered

DANina

'Dearest One', 'Maja Mauser', 'Natacha'

For a rose seen in relatively few gardens, it has a lot of names. This reflects the popularity of 'Cara Mia' in the greenhouses of cut-flower growers. In the greenhouse, it is a lavish producer of long-stemmed velvet-red blooms against dark green foliage. In the garden it is prone to sulk, except in a warm climate—like that of Australia or California. G. K. McDaniel introduced it in 1969. Would that he had endowed it with more fragrance.

Parentage undisclosed
Repeat flowering

'Carabella'
Cluster-flowered

When this rose came out in 1960 it was almost completely ignored. But fashions change, and 'Carabella' now has a growing circle of admirers for the Wild Rose simplicity of its ivory and blush flowers, fragrant and borne in immense sprays throughout the season. (Leave the late ones to ripen decorative hips.) The plant is larger than average for a

Cluster-flowered Rose. Signs of disease on its glossy light green leaves are very rare, even in a humid climate where fungi flourish. It was raised by Frank Riethmuller of Sydney. He named it in affectionate tribute to a member of the New South Wales Rose Society.

Parentage unknown
Repeat flowering
Fragrant

'Caramba'
Large-flowered

TANca

The bicolored flowers, bright scarlet-red and cream, are large and shapely, though scentless. Growth is about average, and the foliage is mid-green and glossy. It may need protection from black spot: roses of this coloring often inherit the problem from *Rosa foetida bicolor* along with its striking flowers. 'Caramba' was introduced in 1966 by Mathias Tantau.

Parentage undisclosed
Repeat flowering

◄ 'Cara Mia'
▼ 'Cardinal de Richelieu'

'Cardinal de Richelieu'
Gallica

'Rose Van Sian'

When the buds first show color, 'Cardinal de Richelieu' looks as though it will be pink, but as the fluffy pompoms open they take on the most wonderful shades of violet and grape-purple. They are beautifully fragrant. The bush is tall for a Gallica (about head high) with smooth mid-green leaves that possibly betray non-Gallica blood. The name

◄ 'Carabella'
► 'Cardinal Hume'

▲ 'Caramba'

honors the great seventeenth century French statesman, but the rose dates from two hundred years after his death, being raised in 1840. Rose historians argue as to whether the credit should go to M. Laffay of Bellevue, France, or to a Dutchman by the name of Van Sian.

Parentage unknown
Summer flowering
Fragrant

'Cardinal Hume'
Modern Shrub

HARregale

One of the most popular of the Old Garden Roses is the richly purple Gallica 'Cardinal de Richelieu', and it seemed appropriate to Jack Harkness that when he raised a Modern Garden Rose of similar coloring that it be named in honor of a modern prelate, Basil Cardinal Hume, Archbishop of Westminster. 'Cardinal Hume' is not a big shrub, the spreading bushes being only about a metre (3 feet) tall, but it is well furnished with purple-tinted leaves and bears its beautiful purple lightly scented double flowers all season. Introduced in 1984, it is of complex pedigree.

([Unnamed seedling × {'Orange Sensation' × 'Allgold'}] × *Rosa californica*) × 'Frank Naylor'
Repeat flowering
Fragrant

'Careless Love' Large-flowered

The globular flowers are deep cerise-pink, splashed and striped with white, and are intensely fragrant. Growth is bushy and the foliage leaden green, but 'Careless Love', a sport of 'Red Radiance', seems not to have inherited its parent's iron-strong constitution. It was introduced in 1955 by Golden State Nurseries in California. 'Radiance', pale pink, and its sport 'Red Radiance' are rarely seen today, but for fifty years after 'Radiance' came out in 1904, they were widely cherished, especially in America, for their extreme hardiness and sweet perfume.

Sport from 'Red Radiance'
Repeat flowering
Fragrant

'Carla' Large-flowered

Thirty years is a long time for a Modern Garden Rose to hold its public, but it seems strange that 'Carla', introduced by de Ruiter in 1963, should have vanished almost completely from the catalogues except in Australia and France. Perhaps it is just that it prefers a warm, dryish climate. In both places it is still regarded as one of the very best

▲ 'Carla'
◄ 'Careless Love'

pale pink roses, its color warmed with salmon, its flowers shapely and only softly fragrant, but long-lasting, and its bush sturdy and healthy. Foliage is dark green with plum tints in the young growth. It comes of good breeding.

'Queen Elizabeth' × 'Sweet Repose'
Repeat flowering
Fragrant

▲ 'Carrousel'
► 'Catalonia'

'Carrousel' Large-flowered

Clear crimson, the long buds open to loosely decorative flowers which hold their fine color well and are pleasingly fragrant. The plant is a shade taller than average, and the foliage dark and leathery. It needs watching for mildew in cool climates, but is still a very attractive garden rose where summers are sunny. The flowers last very well when cut. 'Carrousel' was raised by Carl Duerhsen in 1950, at the very time that America and the

rest of the world were humming the tunes from the Rodgers and Hammerstein musical, *Carousel*.

Seedling from 'Margy'
Repeat flowering
Fragrant

▲ 'Casanova'

'Casanova' Large-flowered

The straw-yellow flowers are often blushed with pale pink. They are large, sometimes huge, and nicely formed, but the petals are rather thin—they 'lack substance'. The blooms are consequently easily damaged in wet weather and apt to open quickly in hot. Fragrance is good, and the tall bushes are well clad with large, dark leaves. Raised in Northern Ireland by Sam McGredy, 'Casanova' was introduced in 1964.

'Queen Elizabeth' × 'Kordes Perfecta'
Repeat flowering
Fragrant

'Catalonia' Large-flowered

Globular and short petalled, the flowers are remarkable for their warm, brilliant colors of orange, crimson and gold, and

called 'The Bride'. It is the original, however, raised by Jean-Baptiste Guillot in 1869, that remains popular.

Parentage unknown
Repeat flowering
Fragrant

▲ 'Catherine Mermet'
◄ 'Catherine Deneuve'
▼ 'Cayenne'

for their sweet fragrance. They last very well when cut. The bush is of average height and the glossy foliage is prone to black spot except in dry-summer climates where the disease rarely strikes. Raised by Pedro Dot of Barcelona, 'Catalonia' was introduced in 1933. Some fifty years later Señor Dot's son Simon reused the name for a new rose. Hopefully, nurseries and rose gardens will not confuse the two.

'Jean Forestier' × unnamed seedling
Repeat flowering
Fragrant

'Catherine Deneuve' Large-flowered
MEIpraserpi

Long buds open to wide, ruffled flowers, not full enough for exhibition but very pretty and sweetly fragrant. They vary a little in color, the basic coral tone being sometimes shaded with yellow or pink. The dark foliage sets the flowers off very well. Growth is average, the flowers freely borne on

long stems for cutting. Named for the well-known and beautiful French actress, 'Catherine Deneuve' was introduced in 1981 by Meilland.

Parentage undisclosed
Repeat flowering
Fragrant

'Catherine Mermet' Tea

The perfect form, delicate color, and sweet fragrance of 'Catherine Mermet' made it the darling of nineteenth-century florists, who grew it by the thousand in their greenhouses, though it was much less often seen in gardens. The superstition that a good greenhouse rose will not do well in the garden is unfounded here, for this is in fact a first-rate rose for the garden, at least in sunny climates where rain does not spoil the blooms. They are a most beautiful shade of warm light pink, fading as they age. Foliage is dark green. There is a sport, 'Bridesmaid', which is said to hold its color better. There is a white one also,

'Cayenne' Large-flowered

Ovoid buds open to large exhibition flowers in deep burnt orange. They are only slightly scented. Growth is upright and the foliage dark green, russet when young. Raised by American hybridist Bill Warriner and introduced by Jackson & Perkins in 1966, 'Cayenne' seems to have disappeared from the catalogues.

'South Seas' × unnamed seedling
Repeat flowering

'Cécile Brünner'   China

'The Sweetheart Rose', 'Mignon',
'Mademoiselle' (or Madame) Cécile Brünner'

This is one of the best loved of roses, but also one of the most mysterious. How so? Everyone knows its fragrant little blush-pink flowers, unfolding from the most exquisite shapely buds against mid-green, small leaves. Its origin is well documented: 'Cécile Brünner' was introduced in 1881 by Joseph Pernet-Ducher, having been bred by his mother-in-law. The trouble is that there are two roses that are called 'Cécile Brünner': Ducher's original, a petite bush less than a metre (3 feet) tall, with its flowers in small clusters; and an interloper, virtually identical in leaf and flower, but growing four times the size. It bears its flowers in huge airy sprays, often with a hundred flowers in them. This used to be called 'Bloomfield Abundance', but it seems the rightful holder of that name is extinct. How the larger version came to usurp the name 'Cécile Brünner' is unknown. Look carefully at the buds to see which version you have (or are getting): the 'spray-bearing' type often extends one

of its sepals out like a green flag beyond the petals, the original 'Cécile Brünner' never does. Then choose according to the size of plant you want. In both of its incarnations, 'Cécile Brünner' is a delight and one of the easiest of roses to grow, flowering well all season. It needs little pruning. There is also a vigorous climbing sport of 'Cécile Brünner'. It usually does not repeat its lavish spring flowering.

Unnamed Polyantha Rose × 'Souvenir
d'un Ami' or 'Madame de Tartas'
(authorities disagree)
Repeat flowering
Fragrant

'Cécile Brünner, Climbing'   China

'Fiteni's Rose'

The much loved 'Sweetheart Rose' is just as lovely in its climbing version, which originated in California in 1894. Forgive it its lack of repeat-flowering for the sake of its great vigor and the lavishness with which it blooms in early summer. Do not be surprised if the flowers are a trifle darker and larger than on the bush. They are still

exquisite. The foliage is the same as the parent's.

Sport from 'Cécile Brünner'
Summer flowering
Fragrant

▲ 'Climbing Cécile Brünner'
▼ 'Cécile Brünner'

'Céleste'
'Celestial'   Alba

Bleu Céleste is the sky-blue enamel found on Sèvres porcelain. The rose 'Céleste' is not blue, however! Celestial or 'heavenly', certainly, and if you decide this is the most beautiful pink rose there is you will find yourself in very good company. The flowers are not very double, but they are exquisitely formed at all stages of their life; and they are an especially delicate clear shade of pink. Naturally, being an Alba Rose, they are sweetly fragrant, and the finely cut greyish foliage sets them off to perfection. The bush is bushy and upright, usually about head high.

Parentage unknown
Summer flowering only
Fragrant

'Céline'
       Bourbon

This rose was photographed at the Roseraie de l'Haÿ. The blooms are large, full of petals and fragrant, the color is a delightful soft, medium pink, and the smooth leaves are broad and handsome. The Roseraie attributes it to Laffont, 1825. However, some American experts are convinced that 'Céline' and 'Fantin-Latour' are one and the same, the variety having been popular in the 1860s as an understock, hence its survival, unlabelled, in old gardens. Look at the pictures of both. What do you think?

Parentage unknown
Summer flowering
Fragrant

'Céline Forestier'
       Noisette

Like most roses which derive their yellow color from the yellow Tea Roses, 'Céline Forestier' is happiest in climates with mild winters. In cold cli-

▲ 'Céline'
◀ 'Céleste'

mates it needs a sheltered wall. In any case it is likely to be slow to get started. The flowers are very fine—large, quartered in the old style, pale Tea Rose yellow with notes of peach, and intensely fragrant. They are borne right through the season, on a plant that is happiest with minimal pruning. Foliage is mid-green. The raiser was a M. Trouillard of Angers. This is his best known rose, raised in 1842.

Parentage unknown
Repeat flowering
Fragrant

'Cels Multiflora'
       China

You may not find this rose except in specialist collections, but it is worthy of note. The smallish flowers are a delicate blend of pale pink and apricot and softly scented. It is a little taller and heavier in leaf than most Chinas; for this reason, some authorities suspect that it has Tea Rose blood. Like most of the Teas it is a little on the tender side. Foliage is a glossy green. Little is known about its origin. M. F. Cels was a leading Paris nurseryman in Napoleon's time, and perhaps he had a hand in its introduction. 'Multiflora' in this case just praises its freedom of flowering, as there is no blood of *Rosa multiflora* in this rose.

Parentage unknown
Repeat flowering
Fragrant

▲ 'Cels Multiflora'
◀ 'Céline Forestier'

'Celsiana' — Damask

The name honors a prominent Paris nurseryman, M. F. Cels, who is said to have introduced this rose from Holland. Despite the confident date of 1750 in some books, it is best regarded as just 'late eighteenth century' in period. It would be a lovely rose to adorn a Georgian house, its loosely silky, intensely fragrant flowers being elegant indeed. They open soft pink, quickly paling almost to white. The plant is characteristic of the Damasks, being on the tall side, with arching branches and smooth, soft, greyish green, slightly fragrant leaves.

Parentage unknown
Summer flowering
Fragrant

'Centenaire de Lourdes' — Cluster-flowered
DELge
'Mrs Jones'

The soft salmon-pink flowers are only slightly scented, but they are prettily shaped and borne in great abundance. The bush is compact and tidy, with lush, dark green foliage. Despite its reputation for disliking heavy frost, which is unusual for a Cluster-flowered Rose, 'Centenaire de Lourdes' deserves much more popularity than it has received. Perhaps the name, commemorating the visions of St Bernadette in 1858, puts Protestant English-speaking gardeners off. It came from Georges Delbard in 1958.

'Frau Karl Druschki' × unnamed seedling
Repeat flowering

'Centifolia' — Centifolia
Rosa × centifolia, 'Rose des Peintres', 'Provence Rose', 'Cabbage Rose'

This, the original of the Centifolia group, is the full, globular, soft pink rose that features in so many antique flower paintings (hence the French name, which means 'Painters' Rose'), and on old china and chintz. The artists do not exaggerate its beauty, but they could hardly convey the wonderful sweetness

▲ 'Century Two'
◄ 'Celsiana'

of its perfume! Indeed, it has for many years been grown in the south of France to supply the perfume industry there with attar of roses. In the garden, it makes a tallish, rather floppy bush all the better for a discreet stake or two so that it does not collapse under the weight of its luxuriant flowers. The broad leaves are a velvety mid-green. It flourishes best in good rich soil.

Parentage unknown
Summer flowering
Fragrant

'Century Two' — Large-flowered

The strong pink flowers are of medium size, opening from long buds, and are fragrant. They last very well both on the bush and in the vase. The bush is average in height, with dull green, leathery leaves. 'Century Two' inherits much of its freedom and continuity of flower from 'Duet' (one of its parents);

▲ 'Centifolia'

◄ 'Centenaire de Lourdes'
▼ 'Cerise Bouquet'

it is at its best in a sunny climate. It was raised by David Armstrong and introduced by Armstrong Nurseries in 1971.

'Charlotte Armstrong' × 'Duet'
Repeat flowering
Fragrant

'Cerise Bouquet'   Modern Shrub

This early summer flowering shrub rose is sheer delight, covering itself in its season with bouquets of semi-double, cerise blooms the size of a Cluster-flowered Rose. The flowers are sweetly fragrant, and the large shrub has the graceful, arching growth of its parent, the rare *Rosa multibracteata*. The dainty foliage is dark green. It is credited to Wilhelm Kordes in 1958, but he is on record as saying that it is not his, but one of Mathias Tantau's early *R. multibracteata* crosses in the line that led to 'Super Star'.

R. multibracteata × 'Crimson Glory'
Summer flowering only
Fragrant

'Chablis'   Large-flowered

White overlaid with cream in the centre, the flowers are fairly large and of fine exhibition form, with a slight scent. The color, however, lacks the undertone of green that one looks for in white wine, especially in a chablis of fine vintage. The plant is of average height, and the foliage a slightly grey tone of matt green that shows the flowers off very nicely. The raiser and introducer was Ollie Weeks of California, and the year of vintage was 1984.

Unnamed seedling × 'Louisiana'
Repeat flowering

▲ 'Chablis'
▶ 'Champion of the World'

'Champion'   Large-flowered

Blending cream, yellow and salmon-pink, the huge flowers are of perfect exhibition form and well scented too. The bush is shorter than average, the foliage light green. Unfortunately it is

also susceptible to black spot. For such an enormous rose, 'Champion' flowers quite freely, but not really enough to make it a good garden rose. This is another one for the show-bench. Raised by Gareth Fryer of Fryer's Nurseries in Cheshire, it was introduced in 1976.

'Grandpa Dickson' × 'Whisky Mac'
Repeat flowering
Fragrant

'Champion of the World'   Bourbon
'Mrs de Graw'

This is a pretty rose, with refined flowers in a pleasing shade of rose-pink suffused with lilac. They are fragrant, and are borne on and off through the rose season on a sprawling bush which grows to the size of a Large-flowered Rose. Foliage is mid-green. Sometimes classed as a Hybrid Perpetual, it was raised in 1894 by a Mr Woodhouse, who was evidently quite proud of it.

'Hermosa' × 'Magna Charta'
Repeat flowering
Fragrant

▲ 'Champs-Elysées'
◀ 'Champion'

'Champs-Elysées'   Large-flowered
MEIcarl

Shapely buds open fully to lightly scented flowers, too informal for exhibition but of a beautiful warm crimson, rich yet bright. The blooms are very effective in the garden against their dull green leaves. The bush is of average height, and it flowers particularly well in the autumn, or fall. Despite its dislike of wet weather, 'Champs-Elysées' has long been well regarded as a garden rose. Sharing the name of the most glamorous Parisian Avenue, 'Champs-Elysées' is French-bred, by the house of Meilland in 1957.

'Monique' × 'Happiness'
Repeat flowering

'Chanelle'   Cluster-flowered

It is often said that 'Chanelle' is virtually unique among Modern Garden Roses in being immune to black spot. It has other charms too. The flowers are scented, prettily shaped and delicate in their pastel shades of apricot and peach, with the occasional touch of coral; the foliage is glossy and the plant is strong

▲ 'Chanelle'

and compact. The only demerit is that the stems are rather thorny. It was raised in 1959 by Sam McGredy in Northern Ireland and won the Madrid gold medal in the same year.

'Ma Perkins' × ('Fashion' × 'Mrs William Sprott')
Repeat flowering
Fragrant

'Chapeau de Napoléon'   Moss
'Crested Moss', *Rosa centifolia cristata*
Legend has it that the 'Crested Moss' was found growing in a crack in a convent wall in Switzerland, in 1820 (a little after Napoleon's heyday), but the resemblance between the cockaded, mossy buds and the Emperor's tricorne hat is undeniable. The warm pink, globular flowers are almost exactly like those of *R. centifolia muscosa* or the 'Common Moss' and just as fragrant. Similarly, the growth is rather floppy and the broad, coarsely toothed foliage is a flat green. It is the unique and beautiful buds that give this rose its irresistible charm.

Parentage unknown
Summer flowering
Fragrant

'Charisma'   Cluster-flowered
This 1978 AARS winner is a splendid plant, bushy and well clad with very glossy dark, maroon-tinted foliage which grows right up into the clusters of smallish flowers, the better to show off their dazzling colors—scarlet and gold, passing to solid scarlet as the blooms mature. It certainly makes a colorful display, but there is one fault (apart from an almost total lack of fragrance): the spent flowers do not fall cleanly, and you have to pick them off

▲ 'Charisma'
▼ 'Chapeau de Napoléon'

or they spoil the effect. 'Charisma' was introduced by the E. G. Hill Company of Indiana in 1977.

'Gemini' × 'Zorina'
Repeat flowering

'Charles Austin'   English Rose
A rather upright grower to about 1.5 metres (5 feet), 'Charles Austin' bears medium-sized blooms in apricot and yellow, with a bit of pink sometimes thrown in. Nicely formed in the old style, it is fragrant too. Foliage is mid-green. It does repeat its bloom, but even the raiser, David Austin, admits that it needs encouraging with a trimming and some fertiliser after the first crop for the repeat to be generous. It is one of the earlier English Roses, raised in 1973.

'Chaucer' × 'Aloha'
Repeat flowering
Fragrant

'Charles de Gaulle'   Large-flowered
MEIlanein
'Katherine Mansfield'
Warm lilac in color, the flowers are large, shapely and very fragrant. It is regarded by some rosarians as the best

▲ 'Charles de Gaulle'
▼ 'Charles Austin'

of the mauve Large-flowered Roses, but does best in a dry climate. Foliage is dull green. It was raised in France in 1974 by Marie-Louisette Meilland from two unnamed seedlings. Most of the world knows it as 'Charles de Gaulle', in memory of the great French statesman—but New Zealand rosarians prefer to honor one of their own heroes, the writer Katherine Mansfield.

('Blue Moon' × 'Prélude') × ('Independence' × 'Caprice')
Repeat flowering
Fragrant

'Charles de Mills'   Gallica
'Bizarre Triomphant'

Instantly recognisable in its flat, symmetrical form (not quartered but more like a carnation) and its gorgeous crimson, maroon and purple colors, this is one of the best garden roses among the old-timers. Foliage is parsley green. The almost thornless bush virtually smothers itself with flowers every year, and does not need cosseting to make it do so. Its only fault is lack of fragrance, although some refined souls also find 'Charles de Mills' a bit vulgar in his exuberance. No one knows who the gentleman was, or even if his is the original name for the rose, whose origins are uncertain.

Parentage unknown
Summer flowering

'Charles Dickens'   Cluster-flowered

Not surprisingly, novelist Charles Dickens had a rose named after him during his lifetime, a red Hybrid Perpetual. It seems to have been forgotten after his death, and it fell to Sam McGredy to make good the omission in 1970 with this very attractive two-tone pink Cluster-flowered Rose. Faintly scented, the flowers are carried in neat sprays and open to show off golden stamens. The plant is a little below average height and has leathery foliage.

▼ 'Charles Dickens'

▲ 'Charles de Mills'

It flowers early and continues late. The great novelist was the son of a mere naval clerk. His rose is of royal descent.

'Paddy McGredy' × 'Elizabeth of Glamis'
Repeat flowering

'Charles Lefèbvre'   Hybrid Perpetual
'Marguerite Bressac', 'Paul Jamain'

At their best, the flowers of 'Charles Lefèbvre' can be magnificent—rich red, huge and shapely, and fragrant too. Hot weather is inclined to rob it of its depth of color. It was one of the most popular Hybrid Perpetuals for very many years, and is still worth a second look. The bush is upright, relatively thornless, and usually gives a good autumn, or fall, display. The rather light green foliage may need to be protected from both mildew and rust. Bred by François Lacharme, it was introduced in 1861.

'Général Jacqueminot' × 'Victor Verdier'
Repeat flowering
Fragrant

'Charles Mallerin'   Large-flowered

Of all the deep velvet-red, almost black roses, 'Charles Mallerin' has the most sensational flowers, opening huge and ruffled from long, elegant buds. They hold their gorgeous color without fading or 'blueing' until the petals drop, and they are intensely fragrant as well. Foliage is leaden green. Plant it at the back of the bed, prune lightly, and be lavish with water and fertilizer. Raised by Francis Meilland in 1947, it is named in honor of his teacher, the retired engineer who was himself the raiser of many beautiful roses.

('Glory of Rome' × 'Congo') × 'Tassin'
Repeat flowering
Fragrant

▲ 'Charles Mallerin'

'Charles Rennie Mackintosh'   English Rose
AUSren

An arching shrub to a little over 1.5 metres (5 feet), this 1988 David Austin creation bears largish, beautifully old-fashioned flowers in soft pink with strong undertones of lilac. They are sweetly scented. Foliage is mid-green. Charles Rennie Mackintosh was the great Scottish architect of the turn of the century, whose buildings are a powerful reason for visiting Glasgow.

Parentage undisclosed
Repeat flowering
Fragrant

▲ 'Charles Lefèbvre'
▼ 'Charles Rennie Mackintosh'

seems a pity that it has lost popularity except in Germany. It was raised in that country by Mathias Tantau in 1965.

'Prima Ballerina' × 'Montezuma'
Repeat flowering
Fragrant

◀ 'Charleston'
▼ 'Climbing Château de Clos Vougeot'

'Charleston' — Cluster-flowered
MEIridge

The bright colors suggested the Roaring Twenties to the raiser, hence the name. Of all the yellow-turning-red Cluster-flowered Roses it is probably still the brightest, there being little of the intermediate pink tones that dull the contrast between today's and yesterday's flowers in so many of the others. Foliage is a leathery dark green. But it is only a rose for gardens where fungus diseases are no problem. There is a climbing form, which seems a bit more resistant. 'Charleston' was introduced by Alain Meilland in 1963.

'Masquerade' × ('Radar' × 'Caprice')
Repeat flowering

▶ 'Charm of Paris'
▼ 'Charlotte Armstrong'

'Charlotte Armstrong' — Large-flowered

There is scarcely an American rose in our gardens today that does not descend from 'Charlotte Armstrong'. She is desirable for her elegant buds and big ruffled flowers, stained brilliant cerise, and also for her strong constitution. The leaves are a leathery matt green. Lack of scent is her only fault, but many of her descendants are strongly fragrant—'Sutter's Gold', 'Tiffany', 'Double Delight' and 'Papa Meilland' among others. 'Charlotte Armstrong' was raised by Dr Walter Lammerts and introduced in 1940. An AARS award followed in 1941. The lady whose name she bears was the mother of the founder of Armstrong Nurseries.

'Soeur Thérèse' × 'Crimson Glory'
Repeat flowering

'Charm of Paris' — Large-flowered
'Pariser Charme'

Shapely buds open to become medium-to-large flowers, salmon-pink, sweetly fragrant, and usually carried in clusters. 'Charm of Paris' has indeed sometimes been catalogued as a Cluster-flowered Rose. Growth is a trifle lower than average, the foliage deep green but not glossy. The flower stems are a little weak, so that the flowers tend to hang their heads in the rain, but otherwise this is a pleasing garden rose, and it

'Château de Clos Vougeot, Climbing' — Large-flowered Climber

The original bush version, raised by Pernet-Ducher in 1908, has always been admired for its wonderful deep maroon-crimson color and its sweet fragrance, but even in its heyday it was criticized for its spindly, none too vigorous growth. If you want to enjoy it today (and the ruffled, informal flowers can be stunning), grow it as a Climber. It will prove to be of pillar-rose vigor, and usually give at least a few blooms after the main summer flowering. Watch out for mildew on the dark matt green leaves. The name honors one of the legendary wines of Burgundy, as rich and fragrant as the rose. This climbing version was introduced by Morse in 1920.

Parentage undisclosed
Repeat flowering
Fragrant

'Chaucer' — English Rose

David Austin, the raiser, has expressed his surprise that 'Chaucer' should be repeat-flowering, as neither of its parents is. Perhaps there are repeat-flowering ancestors lurking unknown on the family tree. However, 'Chaucer' makes a compact, very thorny bush to about a metre (3 feet), and bears its full-petalled soft pink flowers all season against medium green foliage. One might think of it as a Cluster-flowered Rose with Bourbon Rose flowers. It is scented, and came out in 1970.

Unnamed seedling × 'Constance Spry'
Repeat flowering
Fragrant

▲ 'Chaucer'
▼ 'Cherish'

'Cherish' Cluster-flowered

The flowers are a salmon-pink and are shapely if not very fragrant. They are borne in good-sized, nicely spaced clusters on a low-growing, dark-foliaged bush. It was raised by Bill Warriner of Jackson & Perkins. Like its mother it is a long-lasting cut flower. The name might fall less strangely on the ear when one knows that it is one of a trio of Jackson & Perkins roses that won the AARS award in 1980: 'Love', 'Honour', and 'Cherish'.

'Bridal Pink' × 'Matador'
Repeat flowering

▲ 'Cherry Brandy'

'Cherry Brandy' Large-flowered

The cherry brandy we drink is usually deep cerise in color, nothing at all like this Large-flowered Rose, whose flowers are a blend of coral-pink and orange. Large, high centred and quite fragrant, they are borne on a tall bush with dark olive-green foliage. Mathias Tantau, who raised 'Cherry Brandy' in 1965, has reused the name, as 'Cherry Brandy 85', for a 1985 introduction whose codename is TANryrandy. From its official description it seems very similar except that it is scentless.

Parentage undisclosed
Repeat flowering
Fragrant

'Cherry Gold' Cluster-flowered
AROtigny

Sometimes a breeder will send a new rose for trial to one of his overseas agents who finds it does better for him than at home. Such is the case with this 1986 introduction from Armstrong Nurseries, which is grown in Australia but not at home in the United States. It makes a bright display in the garden with its yellow and red flowers, borne in small clusters on a rather low-growing glossy-leafed plant. Look for it under its international codename: it's hard to say if it will be known elsewhere (other than Australia) as 'Cherry Gold'.

'Gingersnap' × 'Young Quinn'
Repeat flowering

▼ 'Cherry Gold'

'Cheshire Life' — Large-flowered

Bright and unfading orange-red, the flowers of 'Cheshire Life' are shapely, medium to large in size and stand up unusually well to wet weather. They are only faintly scented. The bush is a little lower than average, densely covered with dark green leaves, which are reddish when young. It is well regarded in Britain as a bedding rose, but it has not found wide acceptance elsewhere. Perhaps the name is against it—'Cheshire Life' does not suggest much to a gardener unfamiliar with the English insurance company that sponsored the rose. It was raised by Gareth Fryer and introduced in 1972.

'Prima Ballerina' × 'Princess Michiko'
Repeat flowering

◀ 'Cherry-Vanilla'
▼ 'Cheshire Life'

'Cherry-Vanilla' — Large-flowered
ARMilla

A softly colored blend of icecream-pinks and cream, the flowers of 'Cherry-Vanilla' are of good size and fairly fragrant. The bush is taller than average, with glossy foliage. The flowers tend to appear in small clusters, and 'Cherry-Vanilla' is thus classi-fied as a 'Grandiflora' in the United States, where it was raised by David Armstrong of Armstrong Nurseries in 1973. It is happiest in a warm climate, where, with disbudding, the flowers can be enormous.

'Buccaneer' × 'El Capitan'
Repeat flowering
Fragrant

'Chester' — Cluster-flowered

This is another fairly recent rose (it came out in 1976) that has lost the spotlight. It is possibly unknown in Australia, but it has always looked good in England, with its golden yellow petals and matching stamens and glossy leaves. It does pale a little with age, but not excessively, and it seems to be disease-resistant. One wonders about its lack of popularity—perhaps 'Chester' just never got the right publicity. It was raised by Bees Limited (now Sealand Nurseries) and named for the ancient cathedral city where they have their offices.

'Arthur Bell' × 'Zambra'
Repeat flowering

◀ 'Chester'

'Chevy Chase' — Rambler

One of the most attractive characteristics of the Chinese *Rosa soulieana* is its grey leaves, but they are not much in evidence in 'Chevy Chase', whose leaves are a more conventional green. The flowers are clear crimson, carried in bunches, and the growth is strong and usually free from mildew. Though not repeat flowering, this is an outstanding Rambler, and it ought to be better known. It was introduced in America by Hansen in 1939, rather late in the period when Ramblers were fashionable, and before the present popularity of Chevy Chase the actor. Both he and the rose take their names from the same town in Michigan.

R. soulieana × 'Eblouissant'
Summer flowering
Fragrant

▲ 'Chianti'

'Chicago Peace' — Large-flowered

Discovered in the United States, in Chicago, this is a sport of the universally admired 'Peace', and identical to its parent except for greatly enriched coloring—a blend of carmine and coral-pinks with gold. Some people prefer it to the parent. Others say it misses the delicate touch of 'Peace' and the way the flowers fade to dull pink and cream almost as soon as they are fully open does not please everyone. To each his taste! Like 'Peace', the glossy leaves can suffer from black spot where summers are hot and humid. Found by a gardener named Johnston, 'Chicago Peace' was introduced by the Conard-Pyle Company in 1962 after winning the Portland gold medal in 1961.

Sport from 'Peace'
Repeat flowering
Fragrant

▲ 'Chevy Chase'
▶ 'Chicago Peace'

'Chianti' — English Rose

Although 'Chianti' is officially repeat-flowering, do not count on it. But it is still worth a long look, as it is a strong, bushy shrub, with good-sized blooms, shapely and scented in the old style against dark green foliage. The color is as intense a wine-red as any Old Garden Rose. It was introduced by David Austin in 1967 who was possibly hoping for a red equivalent of his sensationally successful 'Constance Spry'. Although 'Chianti' has never been as popular, its admirers think it is just as good.

'Tuscany' × 'Dusky Maiden'
Summer flowering
Fragrant

'China Doll' · Cluster-flowered

Pretty as they are, the rose-pink flowers of 'China Doll' are not all that unusual. What makes this rose great is the way it blooms in such profusion. You would not think a rosebush only 30 centimetres (1 foot) or so tall could give so many flowers of reasonable size—to 6 centimetres (2½ inches)—and in clusters of up to fifteen. Foliage is a glossy mid-green. Treat it well, and use it closely spaced as an edging plant to taller flowers, as a diminutive standard, or as a charming pot-plant. Dr Walter Lammerts introduced it in 1946.

'Mrs Dudley Fulton' × 'Tom Thumb'
Repeat flowering

'Chinatown' · Cluster-flowered
'Ville de Chine'

Enormously vigorous, 'Chinatown' is best treated as a Shrub Rose 2 metres (6 feet) or so tall. It is apt to sulk if you prune it hard and try to force it into an ordinary rose bed. Its leaves are distinctive—light green, very large and healthy too. Some feel they are a bit coarse for the mid-size flowers, which are frilly and carried in bold clusters, but if you plant it among other plants this will not be so noticeable. The color? The imperial yellow of the Chinese emperors. It was raised in Denmark by Niels Poulsen and introduced in 1963, after winning the gold medal of the NRS in 1962.

'Columbine' × 'Cläre Grammerstorf'
Repeat flowering
Fragrant

'Chivalry' · Large-flowered
MACpow

Scarlet and gold, the flowers are large and nicely shaped, but even the raiser does not claim fragrance for them. The plant is a bit taller than average, with dark glossy leaves, bronze-tinted when young. The flowers often come in clus-

◀ 'China Doll'
▼ 'Chinatown'

ters, but with disbudding they can be fit for the show bench. 'Chivalry' was introduced by Sam McGredy in New Zealand in 1977. It has the reputation of being one of the most reliable bi-colored roses for cold climates.

'Peer Gynt' × 'Brasilia'
Repeat flowering

▲ 'Chivalry'
▼ 'Christian Dior'

'Christian Dior' · Large-flowered
MEllie

Stylish in its perfect form, in its glowing blood-red color, in its presentation on long, plum-colored, almost thornless stems, 'Christian Dior' is appropriately named for the great Parisian couturier. Alas, the flowers are scentless. The mid-green, elegantly cut foliage has to be protected from mildew and black spot, so it is primarily a rose for the exhibitor, though if you can keep it healthy it will flower quite freely. Raised by Francis Meilland it was introduced in Europe in 1958 and won the Geneva gold medal that year. It was not introduced in the United States until 1962, where it won the AARS award.

('Independence' × 'Happiness') × ('Peace' × 'Happiness')
Repeat flowering

'Chrysler Imperial'
Large-flowered

Deep rich crimson with a sheen like velvet, the flowers of 'Chrysler Imperial' are beautifully high centred and nicely fragrant, against matt green foliage. This rose created a sensation when it came out in 1952 (winning the AARS award), and it remains an excellent choice for gardens in warm climates. Cold is apt to cause the flowers to 'blue' and the plant to snuffle with mildew. 'Chrysler Imperial' was raised by Dr Walter Lammerts. Germain's, the introducers, wanted to call it 'Chrysler', but the car-makers objected to the use of their trademark, so 'Chrysler Imperial' it became.

'Charlotte Armstrong' × 'Mirandy'
Repeat flowering
Fragrant

'Circus'
Cluster-flowered

This is one of the classic Cluster-flowered Roses, but also one of the best reasons for buying your roses from a reputable grower! For there are two strains of 'Circus' about: the original, a neat bush with semi-glossy dark green leaves and perfectly arranged clusters of ruffled flowers, at first buff-yellow, turning pink and coral-red as they develop; and an impostor, vigorous to the point of legginess, with colorless flowers that often do not open properly. Insist on getting Herbert Swim's 1956 original. Fragrance is slight. There is also a deeper-colored sport with more petals, 'Circus Parade'.

'Fandango' × 'Pinocchio'
Repeat flowering
Fragrant

'Circus Parade'
Cluster-flowered

This is a sport from 'Circus' with deeper toned and more double flowers, against dark foliage, and a better buy if you are at all uncertain of getting the original, good strain of 'Circus' from your nursery. 'Circus Parade', however, lacks some of the subtlety of color of the original. For all its gaiety, 'Circus Parade' is not very fragrant. It came from a man with a great gardener's name, F. B. Begonia, and was introduced by Armstrong Nurseries in 1963.

Sport from 'Circus'
Repeat flowering

▲ 'Chrysler Imperial'
▶ 'Circus Parade'
▼ 'Circus'

'City of Auckland'
MACtane   Large-flowered

A blend of old gold and orange, sometimes with a bit of pink thrown in, these flowers are large, pleasingly shaped, and very fragrant. The plant is average in height, with medium green leaves. Raised by Irish Sam McGredy and named for his adopted home town, 'City of Auckland' was introduced in 1981. Although it is a popular rose in New Zealand, and McGredy's have used it for further breeding, it has not been much grown elsewhere.

'Benson & Hedges Gold' × 'Whisky Mac'
Repeat flowering
Fragrant

'City of Belfast'
MACci   Cluster-flowered

The flowers are, individually, quite prettily shaped, with ruffled petals. They are orange-red, deepening and dulling with age. But the effect that matters is that of the huge trusses of bloom, borne very freely on average-height bushes with dark leaves. It is hasty to repeat its bloom and if the rather overwhelming color fits your garden, it is a fine, showy garden rose. The name 'City of Belfast' commemorates the establishment of the Rose Trial Ground there. The rose was introduced by Sam McGredy in 1968. It won medals from the RNRS and New Zealand in 1967, Belfast in 1970 and The Hague in 1976.

'Evelyn Fison' × ('Circus' × 'Korona')
Repeat flowering

'City of Leeds'
                            Cluster-flowered

Though it is more or less scentless, 'City of Leeds' can be a fine choice for creating a splash of strong coral-pink in the garden. The flowers are borne freely in large clusters on a dark-leafed, not too tall plant. Individually they are medium sized and nicely shaped, and hold their color without turning magenta. They need good weather to look their best, however, and are inclined to get marked by heavy rain and bleached by hot sun. Definitely a rose for favored climates! It was introduced in 1966, by Sam McGredy in Northern Ireland.

'Evelyn Fison' × ('Spartan' × 'Schweizergrüss')
Repeat flowering

▼ 'City of Leeds'

▲ 'City of Auckland'
▼ 'City of Belfast'

'City of York'
Large-flowered Climber

'Direktor Benschop'

Appropriately, the flowers are creamy white, informally shapely, and pleasingly fragrant. They are as big as a large Cluster-flowered Rose and tend to come in clusters. The foliage is very

glossy, and the vigorous branches easily trained, but there are no repeat flowers. It was introduced in 1946 by Mathias Tantau. It does not seem to have inherited 'Dorothy Perkins' susceptibility to mildew.

'Professor Gnau' × 'Dorothy Perkins'
Summer flowering
Fragrant

'Clair Matin'
Cluster-flowered Climber

MEImont

This Cluster-flowered Rose is on the borderline between Shrub and Climber; either way it is a pretty rose, the plum-colored young foliage maturing to dark bronze-green and making a pleasing setting for sprays of small flowers, pale pink when they open but blushing to a deeper salmon-pink in the sun. There is a Musk Rose scent; indeed had it been introduced in the 1920s instead of in 1960, 'Clair Matin' might have been classed as a Hybrid Musk. It was raised by Marie-Louisette Meilland.

'Fashion' × (['Independence' × 'Orange Triumph'] × 'Phyllis Bide')
Repeat flowering
Fragrant

'Claire Jacquier'
Noisette

One of the most vigorous of repeat-flowering climbers, 'Claire Jacquier' is quite capable of smothering the facade of a two-storey house with its dark

green leaves, which it will spangle with clusters of flowers in the spring and intermittently afterwards. The peachy yellow of the buds has faded almost to cream by the time the blooms are fully open so the effect is subtle rather than dazzling. The fragrance is lovely. It was introduced by A. Bernaix of Lyon in 1888.

Probably *Rosa multiflora* × unknown yellow Tea Rose
Repeat flowering
Fragrant

◄ 'City of York'
▼ 'Claire Jacquier'

▲ 'Claire Rose'
▼ 'Clair Matin'

'Claire Rose'
English Rose

AUSlight

Not overall—it grows to about 1.2 metres (4 feet)—'Claire Rose' is rather like a bushy Large-flowered Rose in its upright growth and large, light green leaves. The flowers are lovely, of good size, well filled with symmetrically arranged petals, and fragrant. They open blush-pink, paling almost to white when they are fully blown. Alas, like so many delicately colored roses, they are easily damaged by rain. It was introduced by David Austin in 1986. As the name honors his daughter, this is probably one of his own favorites.

'Charles Austin' × 'Iceberg' seedling
Repeat flowering
Fragrant

'Class Act' — Cluster-flowered
JACare

The creamy white flowers are almost like Large-flowered Roses in shape and substance and the foliage is dark and unusually resistant to mildew. It does not have much in the way of perfume, though. A most promising new rose; 'classy' describes it well. It was raised by Bill Warriner for Jackson & Perkins and won the 1989 AARS Award.

Parentage undisclosed
Repeat flowering

'Cleo' — Large-flowered
BEEbop

Soft pink with a hint of coral at the centre, the high centred flowers of 'Cleo' are of good size, but they are only slightly fragrant. The red prickled bush is shorter than average, but well furnished with light green foliage. It is well-liked in Britain both as a garden and a show rose. 'Cleo' seems happiest in cool climates. It was introduced by the old Chester firm Bees Ltd, now called Sealand Nurseries, in 1981. Do not confuse it with 'Cleopatra'!

'Kordes Perfecta' × 'Prima Ballerina'
Repeat flowering

▲ 'Class Act'
► 'Cleopatra'
▼ 'Cleo'

'Cleopatra' — Large-flowered
'Kleopatra'

Of good size and fine exhibition form, the flowers of 'Cleopatra' display a regal combination of cerise, scarlet and gold, but they are not very fragrant. The plant is bushy, a little below average in height and the leaves are dark and glossy. Unfortunately they are liable to black spot, and the wood is very soft. For all the splendor of its flowers, 'Cleopatra' has lost favor to more recent, easier-to-grow bicolors.

Introduced in 1955 by Wilhelm Kordes, there is also a sport, 'Curiosity'. It differs in the most unusual feature of having variegated foliage.

('Walter Bentley' × 'Condesa de Sástago') × 'Spek's Yellow'
Repeat flowering

'Cocktail' — Cluster-flowered
MEImick

The single flowers of 'Cocktail' appear in such profusion as to almost hide the foliage. When they first open they are scarlet with gold at the centre, but age turns them crimson. Foliage is often red tinged even at maturity, and

the stems are heavily prickled. You can grow 'Cocktail' as a climber, on a pillar, or prune it hard to make a moderate-sized shrub. There is nothing quite like it, and it is a pity that Meilland, the raisers, reused the name in the 1970s for a yellow and red, rather ordinary Large-flowered Rose. The original came out in 1957.

('Independence' × 'Orange Triumph') × 'Phyllis Bide'
Repeat flowering

▲ 'Cocktail'
▼ 'Cocorico'

'Cocorico'   Cluster-flowered

The current fashion for having Cluster-flowered Roses bear miniature exhibition-type flowers has led to the eclipse of some of the very attractive, almost-single roses like this one. This is a pity, as the wide open flowers showing their stamens are very well suited to being displayed in bunches. 'Cocorico' is a lovely shade of scarlet red, brilliant without being strident, and the bushy plant, a little taller than average, is very free with its flowers. Their brightness and grace compensates for the lack of scent. Foliage is a glossy bright green. It was raised

by Francis Meilland and introduced in 1951. An English-speaking rooster says 'cockadoodle-doo', but a French one *cocorico*!

'Alain' × 'Orange Triumph'
Repeat flowering
Fragrant

▲ 'Color Magic'
▼ 'Columbia'

'Color Magic'   Large-flowered

The flowers are large and of symmetrical form, and only lightly fragrant. What is special about them is the way they blend just about every shade of pink, from blush to carmine, in the one flower. The color is richest where the petals are exposed to the sun, so the blend varies with the position of the flower. The plant itself is about average in height, with handsome deep green foliage. Despite its AARS award in 1978, the year of its introduction, 'Color Magic' strongly prefers to be grown in warm climates. It was raised by Bill Warriner for Jackson & Perkins.

Unnamed seedling × 'Spellbinder'
Repeat flowering

'Columbia'   Large-flowered

Rose-pink and sweetly fragrant, the flowers of 'Columbia' are large and full of petals. They come with long stems on an average-sized bush clothed in dark, leaden green foliage. They are very long-lasting when cut. Raised by E. G. Hill and introduced in 1916, 'Columbia' was for many years one of the most popular roses in the United States, both in gardens and in the greenhouses of the cut-flower growers. It has produced a long series of sports, of which the best known are the deep pink 'Briarcliff' and its sport, the crimson (and scentless) 'Better Times'.

'Ophelia' × 'Mrs George Shawyer'
Repeat flowering
Fragrant

'Columbine'
Cluster-flowered

The cream-to-yellow and pink flowers are rather like miniature editions of 'Peace', but carried in sprays of up to half a dozen or so, and the glossy-leafed bush is upright, a shade taller than average. It is happiest in a cool climate. When Denmark's Svend Poulsen introduced it in 1956, 'Columbine' created something of a sensation. It was one of the first Cluster-flowered Roses to have flowers of such perfect exhibition form.

'Danish Gold' × 'Frensham'
Repeat flowering
Fragrant

▲ 'Comanche'
▼ 'Columbine'

'Comanche'
Large-flowered

There have been several attempts to re-create 'Queen Elizabeth' in red, and perhaps 'Comanche' comes closest to the ideal, though it is orange-red rather than crimson. Otherwise it is remarkably like 'Queen Elizabeth' in the size and shape of the largish flowers and its very tall, easily grown bush, and it is a surprise that it is not bred from. Scent is only slight. Foliage is olive-green. It was raised by Swim and Weeks and won an AARS award in 1969.

'Spartan' × ('Carrousel' × 'Happiness')
Repeat flowering

'Command Performance'
Large-flowered

'Pure enchantment in the garden,' said the catalogues when this Bob Lindquist creation was introduced in 1970. The AARS judges thought so too, giving it their award in 1971. Gardeners in humid-summer areas are less enchanted, as there it gets mildew badly. Where it performs well, however, it remains a fine rose, producing many long, elegant buds which open to starry flowers of brilliant orange-red. Foliage is leathery.

'Super Star' × 'Hawaii'
Repeat flowering

'Common Moss'
Moss

Rosa centifolia muscosa, 'Communis', 'Mousseau Ancien'

'Common' because it was found in almost every cottage garden, the 'Common Moss' is a rose of uncommon beauty. Indeed, many people hold it to

▲ 'Command Performance'
▼ 'Common Moss'

be the most beautiful of the Moss Roses. It is a sport from *R. centifolia* and almost exactly like it in growth and foliage, adding to the luminous pink medium-size flowers the charm of 'mossy' sepals, whose resinous scent adds a note to the sweet fragrance of the petals. If you stroke the buds gently, the 'moss' will leave its scent on your fingers. Foliage is soft green.

Sport from *R. centifolia*
Summer flowering
Fragrant

'Complicata' Gallica

One of the loveliest of single roses, 'Complicata' is hardly a typical Gallica, being a great, rambling bush, quite capable of clambering 3 metres (10 feet) into other shrubs and cascading over them with its shining pink flowers against clear green leaves. It is rather deficient in scent, and rather too straggly to grow on its own. The best way to grow it is to plant it in a mixed shrubbery where it can grow as it pleases, with only mild discipline at pruning time. 'Pruning time' in this case means after flowering, as the hips are nothing special. The name does not mean 'complex' but 'folded together'—there is a distinct pleat in each petal.

Parentage unknown
Summer flowering

'Comte de Chambord' Portland

Gracefully scrolled buds open to 10 centimetre (4 inch) wide flowers in the old French style—flat, sometimes quartered, and filled with petals. They are rose-pink, usually tinged with lilac, and strongly, sweetly fragrant. The bush is about as tall as a modern bedding rose, with lettuce-green leaves, and flowers on and off throughout the season. Introduced in 1860 by Moreau and Robert of Angers, 'Comte de Chambord' is the most popular of the Portland Roses, younger brothers to the Hybrid Perpetuals, and as charming an Old Garden Rose as any. Its name honors the sad and romantic grandson of Charles X who refused the crown of France and died in exile.

Parentage unknown
Repeat flowering
Fragrant

'Comtesse de Murinais' Moss

At head height, 'Comtesse de Murinais' is one of the tallest of the Moss Roses, with light green leaves, and beautiful, shapely flowers, tinted with blush in the bud but opening to clear milk-white. They are strongly perfumed. The 'moss' is lush and hard to the

touch. This probably indicates that it has 'Quatre Saisons Blanc Mousseux' in its breeding, though it is summer flowering only. It was raised by M. Vibert and introduced in 1843—triumphantly, as it was the first white Moss Rose to be raised from seed and thus completely new.

Parentage unknown
Summer flowering
Fragrant

▲ 'Complicata'
◄ 'Comte de Chambord'
▼ 'Comtesse de Murinais'

'Comtesse du Cayla' — China

The long buds open to loosely formed, nodding flowers of flame shot with yellow, fading rapidly to shrimp-pink. They have a pleasing tea fragrance. The young foliage is intensely purpled, the dark tone lasting long enough to set off the flowers. The bush is the size of a Cluster-flowered Rose and the flowers are borne repeatedly. One of the hardiest of the Chinas, despite its evident Tea blood, 'Comtesse du Cayla' was raised by Pierre Guillot and introduced in 1902.

Parentage unknown
Repeat flowering
Fragrant

▲ 'Comtesse du Cayla'
▶ 'Comtesse Riza du Parc'
▼ 'Comtesse Vandal'

'Comtesse Riza du Parc' — Tea

Like so many of the Teas, 'Comtesse Riza du Parc' varies a little in its coloring, from mid-pink to carmine, but it is always lovely. The flowers are fragrant and borne in abundance against dark green leaves on a sturdy plant. It is a

splendid rose for an old-fashioned garden. It was raised by Joseph Schwartz of Lyon and introduced in 1876.

'Duchesse de Brabant' × unknown
Repeat flowering
Fragrant

'Comtesse Vandal' — Large-flowered

Legend has it that, in 1929 or '30, the Countess Vandal was presenting a young rose-breeder with his prize, a cushion beautifully embroidered with a design of roses. 'Ah, Mr Leenders,' she said, 'surely no real rose could surpass a work of art like this!' 'Within two years, Madame,' came the reply, 'I shall create such a rose—and it shall bear your name!' In 1932, 'Comtesse Vandal' appeared, to be greeted as 'the most artistic bloom in rosedom'. The scented flowers in shades of pink and coral are as elegant as ever against dark green leaves. There is also a climbing form.

('Ophelia' × 'Mrs Aaron Ward') × 'Souvenir de Claudius Pernet'
Repeat flowering
Fragrant

'Confetti' — Cluster-flowered
AROjechs

The name suggests something tiny in pastel colors, but the flowers of 'Confetti' are brilliant in yellow and orange, gradually turning orange-red as the sun has its way with them. They are of normal Cluster-flowered Rose size, 6–8 centimetres (2½–3 inches) or so. They come, usually, in rather small clusters, sprinkled over a glossy, dark-leafed bush. 'Confetti' was raised by Herb Swim and Jack Christensen and introduced in 1980. Like most descendants of 'Zorina' it is an excellent, long-stemmed cut flower.

'Jack o'Lantern' × 'Zorina'
Repeat flowering

'Confidence'   Large-flowered

Pale, luminous pink, shot with yellow, the flowers of 'Confidence' are large, shapely and sweetly fragrant. The plants are average in height, perhaps a little less, and the foliage is dark green and leathery. 'Confidence' is happiest in a dry climate, as its flowers do not stand up at all well to rain. They open most freely if it is only pruned lightly. Raised by Francis Meilland, it was introduced in 1951.

'Peace' × 'Michèle Meilland'
Repeat flowering
Fragrant

'Conqueror's Gold'   Cluster-flowered

'Conqueror's Gold' came out in 1986, the 900th anniversary of the Domesday Book, which records a survey carried out at the request of William the Conqueror. This rose was named to commemorate that occasion. Its raiser, Jack Harkness, explains that its gold and red flowers suggest the book's yellow parchment pages and rubricated (highlighted in vermilion) text; but the red ink spreads all over the pages as the flowers age. Still, it is an attractive, colorful rose, the flowers large and shapely in small clusters, and the foliage richly green and glossy on a tallish bush. One might wish for more fragrance though.

'Amy Brown' × 'Judy Garland'
Repeat flowering

▲ 'Confidence'
▼ 'Conqueror's Gold'

▲ 'Conrad Ferdinand Meyer'
◄ 'Confetti'

'Conrad Ferdinand Meyer'   Hybrid Rugosa

The Swiss novelist and poet was widely admired for the aristocratic purity of his German, and his rose (introduced by Doctor Franz Müller of Weingarten in 1899) can produce flowers worthy of him. At their best they are very large and shapely, richly fragrant, in that very pleasing color rosarians call 'silver pink'. The bush is immensely tall, strong and thorny, and the foliage is a rather pale green. Give it its head at the back of the garden and do not try to discipline it too much. 'Conrad Ferdinand Meyer' can be sensational all season, but you must protect it from rust.

Rosa rugosa × 'Gloire de Dijon'
Repeat flowering
Fragrant

'Constance Spry'   English Rose

Forgive it its single season of bloom; this is one of the most beautiful of roses. It makes a very large shrub, its rather floppy branches best supported on a tripod or even trained as a climber. The broad dark leaves are handsome, the flowers magnificent. They are huge 12 centimetre (5 inch) versions of the globular cabbage roses that you see on old chintzes and china, but not in the least blowsy. Richly fragrant, they are an exceptionally clear shade of pink, and after the great early summer show there are hips for the autumn, or fall. Introduced by David Austin in 1961 at the beginning of his career, it commemorates the great flower arranger Constance Spry, an ardent lover of the Old Garden Roses.

'Belle Isis' × 'Dainty Maid'
Summer flowering
Fragrant

'Contempo'   Cluster-flowered

The flowers are 10 centimetres (4 inches) or more across, and but for their coming in clusters of half a dozen or more, might be mistaken for decorative Large-flowered Roses. They open slowly, so the contrast between the coral upper surface of the petals and the yellow underside is effective for quite a while. In cooler weather they soften to salmon-pink and cream. Indeed, this is a rose which is at its best in hot weather. The leaves are a glossy dark green. Perhaps the rather leggy habit has cost it admirers, for it is not seen all that often. It is an Armstrong Nurseries introduction of 1971.

'Spartan' × ('Goldilocks' × 'Fandango' × 'Pinocchio')
Repeat flowering

'Contrast'   Large-flowered

Salmon-pink, often shaded deeper, and cream on the reverse, the flowers of this aptly named rose are nicely formed but not often very large. They are mod-

▲ 'Constance Spry'
▶ 'Contrast'
▼ 'Contempo'

erately fragrant, and borne on a tallish bush with glossy, mid-green leaves. A popular rose in its day, and the parent of some fine seedlings, 'Contrast' is scarcely to be found in modern catalogues. It was raised by Fred Howard and introduced in 1937.

Unnamed seedling × 'Talisman'
Repeat flowering
Fragrant

'Coppélia 76'
MEIgurami   Cluster-flowered

Meillands, the raisers, never registered this rose with the International Registration Authority so nothing is known about its family. However, it is a very strong, tall grower with glossy leaves and smallish clusters of large, informal flowers in a rich, salmon-accented pink and it is a very easy rose to grow. It came out in 1976, and must not be confused with an earlier 'Coppélia', a red and yellow Large-flowered Rose raised by Francis Meilland in 1953.

Parentage undisclosed
Repeat flowering

'Copper Pot'
DICpe   Cluster-flowered

'Copper' describes the color rather well, though in cool weather the shapely flowers can be more salmon-pink than orange. They are nicely scented, borne in clusters, and last well when cut. The leaves are glossy, on a tall bush which usually gives its best blooms in autumn. One of the older roses in this color range, it is by no means outdated

▲ 'Cornelia'
◄ 'Coppélia 76'

yet, though you may have to watch it for fungus attacks. Patrick Dickson introduced 'Copper Pot' in 1968.

'Spek's Yellow' × unknown
Repeat flowering

'Cordula'
KORtri   Cluster-flowered

'Cordula' might almost be regarded as an orange-red version of 'China Doll', and could be used in the same way—as a low border to taller flowers or as a pot-plant. Use it carefully though, because it is a rather strident color, intensified by the toning mahogany-tinted leaves. It is not very widely available; perhaps a catchier name would have helped. It was raised by Reimer Kordes and introduced in 1972.

'Europeana' × 'Marlena'
Repeat flowering

'Cornelia'
       Hybrid Musk

One of the best-loved of Joseph Pemberton's Hybrid Musks, 'Cornelia' is also one of his last, being introduced in 1925. The color of the flowers varies: sometimes soft, peachy pink, at others flushed with coral and much richer in effect. The flowers are small and borne in flattish sprays. They are always very fragrant, with the real scent of musk, and the bush is tall and graceful. With pruning, it can be held to about 1.5 metres (5 feet), but it is flexible enough to train as a short pillar rose. Sometimes the blooms come in enormous clusters, two or three of which would fill the largest vase. Foliage is nicely bronze tinted, glossy and leathery.

Parentage unknown
Repeat flowering
Fragrant

▲ 'Cordula'
◄ 'Copper Pot'

THE FRAGRANCE OF ROSES

The fragrance of the rose has always been one of the main qualities that has drawn us to the flower. The Persian poet Ha'afiz speaks of his being 'lured in to the garden by the scent of roses', where he found comfort from the fever of unrequited love; and the Greeks believed that Eros carelessly spilt some of the nectar of the gods on a rose. The flower has retained its sweet perfume ever since.

If he did, he must have been careless with several vintages, for the rose offers not just one perfume but many. Think of the pure soft sweetness of the Damasks and Centifolias; of the warmer fragrance of the Teas, which does vaguely resemble that of a fresh packet of China tea; of the sharper, more piercing scents of such Modern Garden Roses as 'Fragrant Cloud' or 'Double Delight'. Then there is the intense musk-like fragrance of some of the Ramblers, such as *Rosa filipes*, *R. moschata* and *R. multiflora*. Their scent is exhaled, not by the petals as occurs in other roses, but by the stamens. A note of musk can be detected in the scent of many of their descendants, such as the Hybrid Musk Roses and Cluster-flowered Roses like 'Elizabeth of Glamis'. The scents of roses are as varied as their colors. It is a shame we cannot photograph them!

Unfortunately, there are too many roses Eros seems to have missed, and 'They do not smell like they used to!' is one of the commonest remarks when the subject is roses. Even allowing for the elusiveness of scent, which varies with the weather, the time of day, the age of the flower and the sensitivity of one's nose (smoking notoriously blunts the sense of smell), this does seem to be true. There are relatively few of the Modern Garden Roses that can give the rich fragrance that is the birthright of the Old French Roses.

After denying the obvious for many years, hybridists are now actively seeking to improve things, but they are not finding the process easy at all.

For one thing, fragrance appears to be what students of genetics call a 'recessive character', which makes it difficult for a hybridist to plan for. Crossing two fragrant parents is as likely as not to result in a brood of scentless seedlings, and a rose which is itself scentless may yet be able to give the gift to its children and grandchildren. 'Charlotte Armstrong', parent of 'Sutter's Gold', 'Tiffany' and 'Mojave', and grandmother to 'Chrysler Imperial', 'Mister Lincoln', and 'Double Delight', is one such, and 'Dr A. J. Verhage' another. The family trees of fragrant Large-flowered Roses will often show the names of the same few roses: some examples are 'Ophelia', 'Crimson Glory', 'Signora' and, further back, 'Lady Mary Fitzwilliam'. Indeed, it was the

▲ 'Crimson Glory' is not only intensely fragrant itself but has proved able to transmit fragrance to generations of descendants among the Large-flowered and Cluster-flowered Roses.

◀ Show people a beautiful rose, and their first act will be to sample its perfume.

belief of Wilhelm Kordes that 'Lady Mary' was the most potent of all donors of perfume that led to the revival of this almost-extinct old variety.

The business is complicated by the fact that breeders are usually looking for other things as well as perfume. For a new rose to be successful it must score highly for shape, color, vigor, disease-resistance and what have you, and not all these desirable characteristics appear to be compatible with rich fragrance. The priceless gift of repeated flowering, for instance, comes from the China Rose, which is only mildly fragrant at its best, and many of its early crosses with the old European roses were scarcely fragrant. 'Where has the perfume gone?' is a question that has been asked for a while! Tough, long-lasting petals seem less able to release their scent than those more delicate, which is why the cast-iron varieties you find in the florist's tend to give only the vague smell that all growing plants have. The search for new colors has not helped any either. Some think it fortunate that the 'Persian Yellow' proved unable to transmit its heavy odor along with its golden color, but as a rule, there has to be a suffusion of red on the petals of a yellow rose if there is to be scent as well. ('Sutter's Gold' is an example; 'Friesia' is an exception.) The earlier orange-red varieties tended to scentlessness, but there are fragrant ones coming forward—'Dolly Parton' and the duller-toned 'Fragrant Cloud' are as strong and sweet as any of the dark reds and rich pinks with which fragrance is traditionally associated.

The best spur towards the restoration of fragrance is for the rose-buying public to insist on it. The hybridists are working on the problem, but when a scent-less rose can sell as well as one with fragrance, the temptation to put it on the market will still be there. If only they would resist it!

▲ *Not all fragrant roses are universally admired. The name* Rosa foetida *means 'the stinking rose'. Some people agree; others simply find the odor a trifle heavy, like some medicinal lotion. The admixture of the genes of* R. foetida *in the Modern Garden Roses is no doubt responsible for the rather sharp scents of many.*

◀ *'Baronne Prévost'. The flat, quartered flowers characteristic of the Old Garden Roses are far more efficient at releasing their fragrance than the long, fewer-petalled buds of the Modern Garden Roses.*

▶ *The Ramblers of the Synstylae group of species are often blessed with remarkable fruity fragrance. Unlike all other roses, the fragrance comes from the stamens rather than the petals. This one is* Rosa filipes.

◀ *'Silver Jubilee' has been hailed as the finest Large-flowered Rose since 'Peace'. It endows its descendants with great health and vigor, but, alas, it seems unable to give outstanding fragrance.*

▲ 'Coronado'

'Coronado' Large-flowered

Deep shocking pink and gold, the bi-colored flowers of 'Coronado' are too loosely formed for exhibition, but they are very large and pleasantly fragrant. Foliage is a glossy green. Despite the disdain in which it is held by exhibitors, 'Coronado' has a reputation for being one of the easiest of bicolors to grow, and it seems a pity that it is not as widely available as it used to be. It was raised by Gordon von Abrams and introduced in 1960. Francisco Vásquez de Coronado was one of the more colorful figures in Spanish colonial history, and is much remembered in the American South-West.

('Multnomah' × 'Peace') × ('Multnomah' × 'Peace')
Repeat flowering
Fragrant

'Coronet' Cluster-flowered

This velvet-red, rather large-flowered Cluster-flowered Rose never received a great deal of publicity when it came out in 1957, and now it appears to have dropped out of the catalogues. It suffers from the demerit of no fragrance and a certain slowness in repeating its bloom, but the flowers are shapely, the plant is tall and the foliage is a pleasant dark green, despite an occasional indulgence in mildew. 'Coronet', was raised by the Dutch firm of de Ruiter.

'Independence' × 'Red Wonder'
Repeat flowering

▲ 'Corso'
► 'Coup de Foudre'
▼ 'Coronet'

'Corso' Large-flowered

Orange, usually blended with yellow and sometimes touched with salmon-pink, the flowers of 'Corso' are fairly large and of exhibition form, though its scent is only faint. The bush is tall, with dark and glossy foliage, which is not always as disease-free as it ought to be. This is a rose for cool climates; it sulks in a humid summer. It is an exceptionally fine rose for cutting. It was raised by Alexander Cocker and introduced in 1976.

'Anne Cocker' × 'Dr A. J. Verhage'
Repeat flowering

'Coup de Foudre' Cluster-flowered

'Coup de Foudre' means a 'flash of lightning', which well describes the impact of the dazzling flowers, informally ruffled and carried in well-spaced trusses against bronze-green foliage. The plant is tall, sometimes inclined to legginess. The attrition rate among the orange-red Cluster-flowered Roses is perhaps the highest in any group, as hybridists bring on a constant stream of new ones to jostle older, but often still worthy, varieties from the catalogues. This rose is a good example: it now seems to retain favor only in New Zealand. It was raised by the French firm of Hémeray-Aubert and introduced in 1956.

('Peace' × 'Independence') × 'Oiseau de Feu'
Repeat flowering

'Coupe d'Hébé' Bourbon

This is one of those lax roses that can be trained as a pillar, and most of its admirers find it performs best that way. It can also be pegged down in the Victorian manner. Either way, the flowers will be sumptuous, full of soft pink petals and fragrance against glossy green foliage. Alas, there is only one crop per year, with a very occasional flower in

autumn, or fall. Hebe, goddess of youth, was the cupbearer to the gods.

Bourbon hybrid × China hybrid
Summer flowering
Fragrant

▲ 'Coupe d'Hébé'
► 'Coventry Cathedral'
▼ 'Courvoisier'

'Courvoisier'   Cluster-flowered
MACsee

Rich Tea Rose yellow with flushes of apricot at its heart, 'Courvoisier' bears many of its flowers only singly or in small clusters against dark green, glossy foliage. Perhaps this is a fault in the garden: one would like larger clusters for more color. The plant is on the tall side, performing best in cool weather. It is wont to take a rest in midsummer heat. The name commemorates a leading brand of cognac, and it was raised in Northern Ireland by Sam McGredy and introduced in 1970. The parentage is a source, so it is said, of some merriment to the lady for whom one of those roses is named!

'Elizabeth of Glamis' × 'Casanova'
Repeat flowering
Fragrant

'Coventry Cathedral'   Cluster-flowered
'Cathedral', 'Houston'

'Coventry Cathedral' is very variable in color: sometimes vividly orange-red, sometimes almost salmon-pink. It is not at all uncommon for the older flowers to fade almost to white while retaining a rim of coral around each ruffled, almost transparent petal. The clusters are borne on short stalks, so that the flowers sit among the glossy leaves making it a very pretty garden plant. But 'Coventry Cathedral' is definitely a rose for cool climates. It is odd that it won the AARS award, as that usually implies that the winner will do well everywhere. 'Coventry Cathedral' was raised in cool Northern Ireland by Sam McGredy and introduced in 1975.

'Little Darling' × ('Goldilocks' × 'Irish Mist')
Repeat flowering

'Crackerjack'   Cluster-flowered
POUlcrack

A new Cluster-flowered Rose from Poulsen's is always an event: after all, the firm invented the class back in the 1920s. 'Crackerjack', registered in 1989 but still not yet widely distributed, looks to be a winner. The flowers are loose and informal, the kind that looks so well displayed in large clusters, and their color is dazzling, a blend of orange and coral against very dark green, bronze-tinted foliage. The plant looks to be healthy, compact and lavish with its blooms.

Parentage undisclosed
Repeat flowering

'Cream Delight'   Large-flowered
DUGcream
'Darling', 'Suncredel'

This is a sport of 'Sonia' (also known as 'Sweet Promise') and resembles it in its rather tall growth, its dull green foliage and in its exceptionally long-lasting flowers, which are only of medium size but borne on very long (if prickly) stems. Only the color is different—a very pale creamy pink, sometimes with a note of apricot. Like 'Sonia' it is primarily a rose for those who grow cut roses in greenhouses, but it does well in the open garden too, preferably in a position where hot sun is not able to bleach the flowers. Discovered by Frank B. Schumann, 'Cream Delight' was introduced in 1983.

Sport from 'Sonia'
Repeat flowering

▲ 'Cream Delight'
▼ 'Crackerjack'

'Crépuscule
Noisette

Aptly named for the twilight, the flowers are a blend of burnished gold and salmon, the amount of pink varying with the time of year. Informal in shape, the flowers are deliciously scented, and they are produced right through the season, particularly in a mild climate. The glossy, dark-leafed plant is virtually thornless, and can either be allowed to grow as a large sprawling shrub or trained as a moderately vigorous climber. Raised by Dubreuil and introduced in 1904, 'Crépuscule' is probably more widely admired now than when it was new, when it would have seemed a little tame beside the new-fangled roses from M. Pernet-Ducher, such as 'Soleil d'Or' and 'Madame Eduard Herriot'.

Parentage undisclosed
Repeat flowering
Fragrant

'Cressida'
English Rose

The flowers blend shades of apricot and pink and the many petals fill the flowers to overflowing, like a silk rose from an Edwardian hat. Hat roses, however, do not have a scent like this! 'Cressida' is a very tall grower, with large, dark green leaves and many thorns, and is perhaps best trained as a moderately vigorous climber. It flowers, on and off, all season. 'Cressida' is a David Austin introduction of 1983, named, like so many of his roses, for a Shakespearian character, the beloved of Troilus.

'Conrad Ferdinand Meyer' × unknown
Repeat flowering
Fragrant

▲ 'Cressida'
◄ 'Crépuscule'
▼ 'Crested Jewel'

'Crested Jewel'
Moss

Here is a new 'old' rose, raised by Ralph Moore in California in 1971. It has sprays of deep pink flowers with the sepals crested and mossy, like those of its parent 'Chapeau de Napoléon', but not nearly so fragrant. 'Crested Jewel' is in fact a step towards a mossy Cluster-flowered Rose, but there is a way to go yet—it flowers only in summer. Its mother, 'Little Darling', contributes dark green, rather glossy foliage. The plant is sturdy and compact.

'Little Darling' × 'Chapeau de Napoleon'
Summer-flowering
Fragrant

'Crimson Glory' — Large-flowered

When it was unveiled in 1935, 'Crimson Glory' was hailed as the finest red rose, ever. Alas, its constitution has deteriorated. These days it needs coddling to keep the mildew at bay. But the deep, velvety color and the ravishing perfume remain, and, happily, the climbing sport still gives a good account of itself. Give it a little shade from the midday sun and the color will be richer and clearer, and prune only very gently. Raised by Wilhelm Kordes, 'Crimson Glory' has been a most important parent; you will find it appears in the pedigree of most of the best recent roses.

'Katherine Kordes' seedling ×
'W. E. Chaplin'
Repeat flowering
Fragrant

▲ 'Crimson Glory'
▼ 'Crimson Tide'

'Crimson Tide' — Large-flowered
MACmota

Bright, medium to deep crimson, the flowers are large and of good exhibition form, but they are only slightly scented. This is a major fault in a red rose, and perhaps the reason why this one has not won great popularity. One would expect that where it grows well,

exhibitors, at any rate, would welcome it, as the plant is upright in habit, and the dark, leathery foliage is handsome. It was raised in New Zealand by Sam McGredy, and all he has told us about its ancestry is that it came from a cross between two unnamed seedlings.

Unnamed seedling × unnamed seedling
Repeat flowering

'Crimson Wave' — Cluster-flowered
MEIperator
'Imperator'

A softer red than is usual among the Cluster-flowered Roses, which tend to go in for orange-red or dark sultry tones, 'Crimson Wave' displays good-sized clusters against dark, matt green foliage. All of which might sound a bit dull, but it is a very effective rose. 'Imperator' is the name preferred by Meilland, the raiser, but it is as 'Crimson Wave' that it is officially registered. It was introduced in 1971.

'Zambra' × ('Sarabande' × ['Goldilocks' × 'Fashion'])
Repeat flowering
Fragrant

'Cymbeline' — English Rose
AUSlean

For a lover of subtle colors, this is one of the most rewarding of David Austin's English Roses. Tones of grey and café-au-lait flood its basic pale pink. Its flowers are quite large, silky and informal and its growth arching and graceful. It has a strong fragrance and is continuous in its bloom. Foliage is medium green. It was introduced in 1982. Cymbeline, a legendary king of Britain, is the title role of one of Shakespeare's last plays, about faithfulness in love.

Unnamed seedling × 'Lilian Austin'
Repeat flowering
Fragrant

◄ 'Crimson Wave'
▼ 'Cynthia'

'Cynthia' — Large-flowered
WARdrosa
'Chanterelle'

Large, sometimes very large, the high-centred flowers of 'Cynthia' are shimmering deep pink and fragrant. They come on a tall bush with light green, matt foliage, which is not always as free from mildew as one would like. A very attractive rose, not for some reason seen very often, 'Cynthia' was raised in 1975 by master-breeder Bill Warriner, and introduced by Jackson & Perkins. Its name honors Dr Cynthia Westcott, a well-known American rosarian. Do not confuse it with an earlier 'Cynthia', introduced in 1934, which had orange-red flowers.

Unnamed seedling × 'Bob Hope'
Repeat flowering
Fragrant

◄ 'Cymbeline'

'Cynthia Brooke'
Large-flowered

The somewhat globular flowers blend varying amounts of gold and salmon-pink, usually with more gold than in the picture. They have a fruity fragrance. The plant is a little larger growing than average, with few thorns and leathery foliage. It is inclined to sulk in a humid climate, but in its native Britain it was for long regarded as one of the best garden roses, and still has many admirers. Bred by the Irish firm of McGredy in 1942, 'Cynthia Brooke' was named for a friend of the McGredy family.

'Le Progrès' × ('Madame Mélanie Soupert' × 'Le Progrès')
Repeat flowering
Fragrant

'Dagmar Späth'
Cluster-flowered

'White Lafayette', 'Frau Dagmar Späth'
'Dagmar Späth (pronounced 'Shpeit') is a sport of 'Joseph Guy', one of the earliest Hybrid Polyanthas, as they were then known. Raised in France in 1921, 'Joseph Guy' is really only a period piece now, but 'Dagmar Späth' is still well worth a place in the garden for her snowy white flowers, blushed in the bud, borne in huge clusters over dark, matt foliage. But she needs a warm, dry climate or there will be mildew problems. She was discovered in 1931 by Wirtz & Eicke.

Sport from 'Joseph Guy'
Repeat flowering

'D'Aguesseau'
Gallica

While this rose can be the most vivid red, albeit clouded with purple, it is often just as it is here: a deep pink, shaded with deeper tones in the centre. But either way it is an attractive rose, the flowers shapely and fairly scented, the matt green foliage luxuriant. Henri d'Aguesseau, Chancellor of France, is best remembered for his reforms of French law in the early eighteenth century, but it is more likely that our rose was named after his grandson, the Marquis d'Aguesseau, whose death occurred in 1826, three years after Vibert introduced the rose to gardeners.

Parentage unknown
Summer flowering
Fragrant

▲ 'Cynthia Brooke'
◀ 'Dagmar Späth'

flowers are exquisite—five wide petals, pale soft pink, with maroon stamens at their centre and fragrant too. The plant is on the tall side, with matt green foliage. Prune it lightly and the flowers will be borne abundantly, in small sprays on long stems. There is also a desirable climbing sport. Raised by W. E. B. Archer & Daughter, a firm in Kent, it was introduced in 1926.

'Ophelia' × 'K of K'
Repeat flowering
Fragrant

◄ 'D'Aguesseau'
▼ 'Dairy Maid'

▲ 'Daily Sketch'

'Daily Sketch'   Cluster-flowered
MACai

'Plum and silver', ran the catalogues when Sam McGredy introduced this rose in 1961, '"Daily Sketch" marks a great advance in Floribundas!' And so it did, for it was one of the first to carry exhibition-style flowers in bunches. It is far too tall for a massed bed, and the plum invades the silver as the flower ages so that it does not die very gracefully. On the merit side though, the young flowers can be very handsome indeed; there is scent; and it is an excellent rose for cutting. Foliage is dark and glossy. It was named to honor (and publicize) the British newspaper.

'Ma Perkins' × 'Grand Gala'
Repeat flowering
Fragrant

'Dainty Bess'   Large-flowered
In the 1920s there was something of a vogue for single Large-flowered Roses, but with the advent of the Cluster-flowered Roses it passed, leaving only 'Dainty Bess' with a wide circle of admirers. She deserves them, for her

▲ 'Dainty Bess'

'Dairy Maid'   Cluster-flowered
The late Edmund Burton LeGrice was notable among hybridists for his love of single roses, and his single (or almost so) Cluster-flowered Roses are all roses of great charm, as well as being strong, healthy growers. 'Dairy Maid' is one of the last in the series, introduced in 1957. The cream flowers are enhanced by golden stamens, and the clusters are well spaced, showing each flower off beautifully. The foliage is dark and there is a sweet fragrance. Cut the sprays young, and they will open indoors to a richer color than in the sun.

('Poulsen's Pink' × 'Ellinor LeGrice') × 'Mrs Pierre S. Dupont'
Repeat flowering
Fragrant

'Dallas Gold'
Large-flowered

From its name, one would expect 'Dallas Gold' to be of Texan origin. It was in fact raised by Joseph Winchell in California. However, it was introduced in 1987 by the Texas firm of Kimbrew-Walter, rose-growers of Grand Salinas. This rose has dark green foliage and elegant blooms of deepest gold, touched with cerise.

Parentage undisclosed
Repeat flowering

▲ 'Dallas Gold'
► 'Danse des Sylphes'
▼ 'Dame Edith Helen'

'Dame Edith Helen'
Large-flowered

Cool rose-pink, huge, perfectly formed, and gloriously fragrant, 'Dame Edith Helen' was *the* exhibition rose during the 1920s, '30s, and '40s, and legend has it that until well into the '50s the

Bundaberg (Queensland) Rose Show confined it to a class of its own to give other varieties a chance. But (except in Bundaberg) it was never much of a garden rose, the glossy green bushes flowering sparely and the blooms only showing their best in the autumn, or fall. Now it is a period piece for the rose-lover prepared to coddle it, for it has lost its former vigor. It was raised by Dickson's in 1926—unfortunately the record of its parentage is lost—and named for the then Marchioness of Londonderry.

Parentage unknown
Repeat flowering
Fragrant

'Dame of Sark'
Cluster-flowered

Although there is a plethora of yellow, red, and orange Cluster-flowered Roses, this one is distinct both for the clarity of its colors and its bushy growth. Its decided preference for a cool climate is against it, and so is its lack of perfume, not that fragrance is notable among this color group. Foliage

is dark green. 'Dame of Sark' was raised by Jack Harkness and introduced in 1976. It makes a very colorful display in a small formal garden belonging to the grand lady for whom it was named, the feudal ruler of the semi-independent Isle of Sark in the Channel Islands.

('Pink Parfait' × 'Masquerade') × 'Tabler's Choice'
Repeat flowering

'Danse des Sylphes'
Cluster-flowered

Mallerin probably intended this rose as an improvement on its parent 'Danse du Feu'. The flowers are a trifle larger and more neatly formed, and although the color has less orange and more red, it holds better so that the effect in the garden is brighter. On the other hand, it is not nearly so free with its later flowers, and this has kept it from achieving the popularity of 'Danse du Feu'. Foliage is glossy green. 'Danse des Sylphes', whose name comes from the well-known ballet to Chopin's music, *Les Sylphides*, was raised by Charles Mallerin and introduced in 1960.

'Danse du Feu' × ('Independence' × 'Peace')
Repeat flowering

'Dapple Dawn'
English Rose

Most of David Austin's English Roses have full-petalled flowers in the Old Garden Rose manner. 'Dapple Dawn', however, like 'Red Coat', from which it is a sport, has single flowers, quite large, and borne in small sprays. They are pale

◄ 'Dame of Sark'
▼ 'Dapple Dawn'

pink, prettily veined and flushed deeper, and are borne all season. Indeed David Austin claims this 1983 introduction to be one of the most continuously flowering of all Shrub Roses. Foliage is mid-green. It can be pruned to Bush Rose size, or left to grow to about head height with only light trimming. There is little scent; the point is the translucent delicacy of the flowers.

Sport from 'Red Coat'
Repeat flowering

'De Meaux'   Centifolia

Rosa centifolia pomponia

Rose historians have been arguing for two hundred years over the origin of this little charmer, which is in effect a miniature version of *Rosa centifolia*. Let us leave them to their speculations and just enjoy the scented pink pompoms, borne in late spring on a twiggy plant a metre (3 feet) or so tall, set off by their soft, pale green leaves. There is a white version, pink in the hearts of the flowers. The name may have something to do with a gentleman called Dominique Seguier, who died in 1637 and was bishop of Meaux in France.

Parentage unknown
Summer flowering
Fragrant

'Dearest'   Cluster-flowered

'Dearest' was, deservedly, the most popular pink Cluster-flowered Rose for years. In cool climates the blooms are more delicate in color, medium sized, well-shaped and fragrant, the bush compact, but you need to keep an eye out for black spot, and shelter the flowers from rain. In warmer climates

the color changes to a strong salmon-pink, almost coral. Foliage is a glossy green. 'Dearest' was raised by Dickson's in Northern Ireland and introduced in 1960.

Unnamed seedling × 'Spartan'
Repeat flowering
Fragrant

'Débutante'   Rambler

'Débutante' looks very like 'Dorothy Perkins', but it has qualities that many rosarians consider to be superior—the color is paler and more delicate; the flowers are scented (though not powerfully); and, above all, the glossy green foliage is usually free from mildew. Yet it is 'Dorothy Perkins' that everyone knows and plants. 'Débutante' was raised by the American rosarian M. H. Walsh and introduced in 1902.

Rosa wichuraiana × 'Baroness Rothschild'
Summer flowering

▲ 'Deep Purple'
▼ 'De Meaux'

▲ 'Débutante'
▼ 'Dearest'

'Deep Purple'   Large-flowered

The name exaggerates: the flowers are really a strong magenta pink. They are shapely, however, with thirty-eight petals, carried in nicely spaced sprays, and are nicely fragrant. They tend to open flat, but they are very long lasting as cut flowers. The bush is on the tall side but bushy. The foliage is dark green and glossy. 'Deep Purple' was raised in 1980 by Reimer Kordes in Germany. It is grown both in California and in India, which suggests a preference for a warm climate. It would prove a good greenhouse rose, judging by the parentage.

'Zorina' × 'Silver Star'
Repeat flowering
Fragrant

THE ROSE IN THE RENAISSANCE

Let us leave arguments about the origins of the Renaissance and whether it left Christendom really any happier than it had been in the Middle Ages to the historians; we are concerned with the rose.

It cannot be said that, with the rediscovery of the 'learning of antiquity' during the Renaissance, men rediscovered the rose also, for it had never been lost. Nor can it be said that it was grown for new reasons, as roses have always been grown for their fragrance, for their uses in medicine (mostly imaginary) and for their beauty. The social changes of the times, however, meant that the pleasures of gardening became less exclusively the preserve of the Church, and the new spirit of scientific enquiry led people to study and classify their plants more scientifically than before.

In the thirteenth century, Albert the Great of Cologne had noted only three kinds of roses: red, white and the eglantine, under which name he seems to have lumped all the wild roses of Germany. By the sixteenth century, the Englishman John Gerard in his *Herball* described no less than nineteen, including varieties newly arrived from Holland and Italy; the wild roses of America were not far behind.

Although artificial hybridizing was not properly understood until the end of the nineteenth century, new varieties were being raised in increasing numbers. Renaissance artists, now seeking to depict things as they saw them and not just for their symbolic value, began to include in their paintings roses that we can put names to. We see Gallicas, Damasks and Albas, and sometimes even a yellow rose or two. But most painters still only included the rose as a decorative adjunct in paintings with titles such as *The Birth of Venus* or *The Madonna and Child*. It was not until the Dutch flower painters arose in the seventeenth century that roses became the subject in their own right.

The painters' favorite was *Rosa centifolia*, which the English called prosaically the Cabbage Rose but the French, *La Rose des Peintres* (the 'Rose of the Painters'). The Romans had a rose called *centifolia*, the 'Rose of a Hundred Petals', but it seems that the rose of the painters (which we still cherish for its beauty and perfume) was a new creation.

▲ *Here is the famous quarrel in the Temple Garden between the Yorkists and Lancastrians, from an engraving that hung in many Victorian houses. The famous scene is pure fiction, created by Shakespeare to develop the plot of his King Henry VI, though it is true that the two sides took the red and the white rose as their badges. Hence the romantic name 'the Wars of the Roses'.*

▲ *A detail from an eighteenth-century French Provincial armoire, the whole of whose decoration consists of naturalistically carved roses and birds. Sometimes pieces like this were painted in lifelike colors, which have mellowed to great delicacy over time, but it is just as common to see them simply varnished to show the beauty of the wood and the fineness of the carving.*

▶ Rose centifolia *is still known in France as 'La Rose des Peintres', the artists' rose. If you see a large, full-petalled pink rose in an Old Master's flower painting, it will almost certainly be this one.*

Compared with the neat Gallicas and Albas, its full-petalled blooms were positively voluptuous, and from the end of the seventeenth century onwards you see it everywhere: carved on furniture; garlanded over arches and cornices (Sir Christopher Wren was especially fond of them and some splendid examples adorn St Paul's Cathedral); woven into carpets; printed on chintz; and being clutched to the bosoms of aristocratic ladies in portraits by Largillière and Boucher.

The rose is a very simple and reliable flower to grow. Hence, the conditions for a phenomenon like the Dutch 'tulipomania' of the 1630s never existed, though nurserymen with a desirable new variety have always asked a premium price for it. There has never been a novel like *The Black Tulip* written about a rose. Writers have contented themselves, by and large, with introducing it in lyric poetry or as a universally known metaphor for youth and beauty. Such are the fifty-odd references by Shakespeare to the flower. Most tragic is Othello's line as he wavers between his jealous rage and his love for Desdemona: 'When I have plucked the rose, I cannot give it vital life again/it must needs wither; I'll smell it on the tree.'

Roses have long been borne in heraldry. Rose-lovers are fond of stating that the red rose of Lancaster was *Rosa gallica officinalis* and the white one of York *R. alba maxima*. However, as other European families bore roses of green, blue or black—to say nothing of griffins, mermaids and unicorns—we should not take the depictions of the heralds as necessarily lifelike! With the end of the wars, the Tudor kings symbolised the new-found unity of the land by the half red and half white Tudor rose,

perhaps the best known of all heraldic symbols. This was another fantasy of the time. It has now come to life in such modern cultivars as 'Double Delight'.

With Europe in what we would now call an expansionist mood, people began to travel further than ever before. Where travel goes, trade follows, and empire follows that. It depends on where your ancestors came from whether you regard the imperialism of the eighteenth and nineteenth centuries as a good thing, but to it we owe the Modern Garden Rose, for it was along the sea-lanes of empire that the repeat-flowering roses of China arrived in England and in France, there to marry with the old European roses.

◄ *Cherubs, cupids, putti, whatever you might call them, plump children are a major theme in renaissance and baroque art, carrying coats of arms, presenting the Madonna with a glass of water, or, like this one, simply holding up a wall bracket on which a vase of flowers might be displayed. The garland of roses not only serves modesty, it smooths the transition between the half-length figure and the scrolls of the bracket itself.*

▼ *The most famous rose in heraldry is the Tudor Rose, the royal badge of England. With its red outer and white inner petals, it was a purely imaginary creation. Today, 'Double Delight' shows that nature does sometimes imitate art!*

◄ *Queen Marie Antoinette of France, from a portrait by L. C. Clay. Although not greatly interested in plants or gardening, she did start Redouté on his career as the 'Raphael of the Rose' by appointing him her flower-painter-in-ordinary.*

'Deep Secret'
Large-flowered
'Mildred Scheel'

The intensely fragrant blooms are not especially large, but they are shapely and a most beautiful deep velvety red. The flowers appear fairly continuously throughout the summer. The plant is bushy, with dark and glossy foliage which is said to be more resistant to mildew than is usual among dark red roses. The plant will also tolerate poor soils. Well thought of in Britain, 'Deep Secret' is not often seen elsewhere. It was introduced in 1977 in Germany. Its raiser, Mathias Tantau, has not revealed the parentage.

Parentage undisclosed
Repeat flowering
Fragrant

'Déesse'
Large-flowered
'Goddess'

The long, pointed buds are white with only a blush of pink. Then as the flowers expand in the sunshine, they become flushed with pink, which deepens to carmine by the time the flower is full-blown. There is little scent, but the bush is tall and strong, the foliage dark and glossy. Raised by Jean Gaujard and introduced in 1957, 'Déesse' never found many devotees, despite its novel coloring. Most gardeners now seem to prefer 'Double Delight' which has an even more vivid contrast of red and white and a stronger fragrance.

'Peace' × unnamed seedling
Repeat flowering

'Desprez à Fleur Jaune'
Noisette
'Jaune Desprez'

Compared to the brilliant Modern Garden Roses bred from the 'Persian Yellow' the flowers of this rose are closer to cream. The yellow is very pale, though often shot with suggestions of peach and apricot. The blooms, on slender footstalks, are of Tea Rose shape and warm fragrance. Foliage is pale green. In its day this rose was regarded as one of the most powerfully scented of all. The large, climbing plant is lavish with flowers from the beginning to the end of the season. It was introduced by Desprez in 1830.

'Blush Noisette' × 'Park's Yellow China'
Repeat flowering
Fragrant

▲ 'Deep Secret'
▼ 'Delicata'

'Delicata'
Hybrid Rugosa

Raised by the American rosarian Mr Cooling in 1898, 'Delicata' certainly has flowers of great delicacy, wide, semi-double, ruffled and in a lovely shade of soft lilac-pink against tough, light green foliage. Alas, the plant is delicate, rarely showing the Hybrid Rugosa bushiness or ease of growth, and needs, unlike virtually all its tribe, to be pampered to be seen at its best. Even then it is a small bush, and it has the unfortunate reputation of being very difficult to propagate. It is one for the enthusiast only.

Parentage unknown
Repeat flowering
Fragrant

▲ 'Déesse'
▼ 'Desprez à Fleur Jaune'

'Deuil de Paul Fontaine' Moss

This rose was described as 'very vigorous' when it was introduced in 1873. This is no longer true. It needs the best of care to do well, and never makes a big bush. But the flowers are extraordinary: large for an Old Garden Rose,

▲ 'Deuil de Paul Fontaine'
► 'Devoniensis'

they blend dark tones of crimson, purple and maroon, all overlaid with a blackish sheen and set off with a bit of reddish 'moss'. If you can make it happy, it will flower recurrently. The sombre colors suit the name, which means 'Mourning for Paul Fontaine'.

Parentage unknown
Repeat flowering

'Devoniensis' Tea
'The Magnolia Rose'

This famous Old Garden Rose is usually seen in its climbing version nowadays. It is not overly vigorous, is well furnished with light green leaves (but few thorns) and comes into bloom early in the season. It is rarely without at least a few of its softly fragrant blossoms, which blend cream and palest peach-pink. They are open quartered in the old style, from long buds, and their scent is reminiscent of *Magnolia virginiana*. 'Devoniensis' is one of the first notable roses to be raised by a man named Foster from Devon. He introduced it in 1841. The climbing sport came out in 1858.

Parentage unknown
Repeat flowering
Fragrant

'Diamond Jubilee' Large-flowered

The color varies with the season—now Tea Rose yellow, now cream, now almost apricot, now faintly blushed with pink—but the perfect form and sweet fragrance are constant. The olive-green leaves, copper-brown when young, set the flowers off perfectly.

The bush is of ideal habit, compact and eager to send up new shoots from the base. There is no rose more beautiful than this, but it must have a sunny climate. If it rains the flowers are ruined. Raised by Eugene Boerner, 'Diamond Jubilee' was introduced by Jackson & Perkins in 1947, the year in which they celebrated sixty years of growing roses. It won the AARS award in 1948.

'Maréchal Niel' × 'Feu Pernet Ducher'
Repeat flowering
Fragrant

'Die Welt' Large-flowered
DieKOR
'The World', 'The World Rose'

Large and high centred, the flowers of 'Die Welt' blend orange, salmon and yellow. They become paler as they open and have little fragrance, but they can be large and shapely enough for exhibition, and come on long stems for cutting. The bush is very tall and the foliage glossy. Named for a well-known German magazine, 'Die Welt' does best in cool climates. It was raised by Reimer Kordes and introduced in 1976.

Unnamed seedling × 'Peer Gynt'
Repeat flowering

▲ 'Diamond Jubilee'
▼ 'Die Welt'

'Dioressence' — Cluster-flowered
DELdiore

The scent of 'Dioressence', which was named for Dior's expensive perfume, is delicious. The flowers are large and carried in small clusters on a tallish plant, hence it is sometimes included in the otiose classification 'Grandiflora'. 'Dioressence' is a pleasing shade of mauve, a touch deeper and less ethereal than most, and it is surprising that it is not more widely grown. Foliage is large, mid-green and semi-glossy. It comes from Georges Delbard, the French raiser of greenhouse roses and was introduced in 1984.

(['Holstein' × 'Bayadère'] × 'Prélude') × unnamed seedling
Repeat flowering
Fragrant

'Disco Dancer' — Cluster-flowered
DICinfra

The flowers are only semi-double, with about ten or twelve petals, but the way each petal holds itself apart from the others is graceful and charming, and allows the sunlight full play with the festive orange-red color. The plant is upright, average in height, and has dark foliage, and is said to be very resistant to disease. There is no scent to speak of. Patrick Dickson, who introduced it in 1984, must feel very proud.

'Coventry Cathedral' × 'Memento'
Repeat flowering

◀ 'Disco Dancer'

'Distinction' — Cluster-flowered

This is a rose-pink sport of 'Joseph Guy'. Being a rose for a warm climate, it is a great easy-to-grow rose for making a mass of color. Foliage is rich green and glossy. If you were planting a garden to go with a 1920s or '30s house, you could do worse than to include a bed of 'Distinction' and 'Dagmar Späth', a white sport of 'Joseph Guy'. 'Distinction' was discovered in France by M. Turbat in 1927. You may have to search for it now.

Sport from 'Joseph Guy'
Repeat flowering

▲ 'Distinction'
◀ 'Dioressence'

'Dr Darley' — Large-flowered
HARposter

Strong, bright pink, large, with thirty-five petals, and lightly scented, 'Dr Darley' does not seem to have made much of an impact outside Britain, where it was bred. Perhaps this is only because the color lacks novelty—there are so many rose-pink roses. In Britain it is a desirable garden rose, its plants vigorous and the dark foliage healthy. It was raised by Jack Harkness and introduced in 1982. Dr William Darley was a country GP, who courageously continued to care for the sick after being himself crippled by polio.

'Red Planet' × ('Carina' × 'Pascali')
Repeat flowering

'Doctor Grill' — Tea

'Rose shaded coppery' is the official description. Usually 'Doctor Grill' is a blend of delicate pink and peach, sometimes with a suffusion of salmon. The flowers are beautifully formed and well endowed with the characteristic Tea fragrance, and freely borne on a strong, average-sized bush with dark foliage. It is best not pruned too hard. One of the best of the Tea Roses for the garden, it was raised in 1886 by a M. Bonnaire.

'Ophirie' × 'Souvenir de Victor Hugo'
Repeat flowering
Fragrant

▲ 'Doctor Grill'
▼ 'Dr Darley'

'Dr J. H. Nicolas' — Large-flowered Climber

Quite restrained in vigor, this rose bears large, exhibition-type flowers in soft rose-pink. They tend to come in threes and are sweetly fragrant. Disbudding will bring the flowers to full size. The plant may not make the sheet of color in the garden that some of the newer climbers do, but it flowers well both in spring and autumn, or fall, against dark green and leathery foliage. Jean Henri Nicolas was a remarkable Frenchman, Chevalier of the Legion of Honour, member of the Académie Française and Director of Research at Jackson & Perkins, who introduced this rose in his memory in 1940.

'Charles P. Kilham' × 'George Arends'
Repeat flowering
Fragrant

'Dolce Vita' — Large-flowered

DELdal

Salmon-pink, sometimes tending to coral, at other times more rose-pink in tone, the flowers are large and high centred, of exhibition form but not especially fragrant. The upright, dark-foliaged plant usually develops long flower stems, making this a fine rose for cutting. The color shows up prettily under artificial light. Despite not receiving much publicity, this rose has found many admirers and, although it has an Italian name (celebrating the 'good life'), it was raised in France, in 1971, by Georges Delbard.

'Voeux de Bonheur' × ('Chic Parisien' × ['Michèle Meilland' × 'Madame Joseph Perraud'])
Repeat flowering

'Dolly' — Cluster-flowered

POUlvision
'Springs 75'

There is a certain amount of confusion over this rose, which seems to be sold under both its names, as a Cluster-flowered Rose and also as a Shrub Rose. Perhaps it is just that it is a rather tall and vigorous grower, and the catalogues make up their own minds about how to promote it. The 'Dolly' that I photographed in New Zealand a couple of years ago is a pretty rose, in medium pink with darker shadings; its flowers are mid-sized and neatly shaped and its foliage is dark green, glossy and healthy. It came from the Danish breeder Niels Poulsen in 1975.

('Nordia' × 'Queen Elizabeth') × (unnamed seedling × 'Mischief')
Repeat flowering

◄ 'Dr J. H. Nicolas'
▲ 'Dolly'
▼ 'Dolce Vita'

▲ 'Dolly Parton'

'Dolly Parton' — Large-flowered

Buxom buds open to very large, high-centred flowers in luminous oranged-red, long-lasting and, unusually for a rose of this color, deliciously fragrant. The leaves, bronze-red when young, mature to semi-glossy, bronze-green and are of medium size. The plant is tall and bushy, performing best in warm climates. Named for the voluptuous and talented country-and-western singer, 'Dolly Parton' was raised in California by Joseph Winchel and introduced in 1983.

'Fragrant Cloud' × 'Oklahoma'
Repeat flowering
Fragrant

'Doris Tysterman' Large-flowered

The tangerine-orange flowers are not very large nor are they very fragrant, but they are nicely formed, and come on long stems for cutting. The plant is of average height, with dark bronze-green, glossy foliage. Despite its need for protection against mildew, 'Doris Tysterman', which was named for the raiser's wife, is a well-liked bedding rose in Britain, where it was raised by W. E. Tysterman of the Wisbech Plant Farm in Cambridgeshire, who introduced it in 1975.

'Peer Gynt' × unnamed seedling
Repeat flowering

▲ 'Doris Tysterman'   ▼ 'Dorothy Anderson'

'Dorothy Anderson' Large-flowered

The buds tend to come in clusters and if these are drastically thinned the reward will be huge exhibition flowers in a lovely shade of clear pink. It is only slightly scented, and the color fades badly with age. Despite its freedom of flower it is really only for the exhibitor. The bush is of average height, with mid-green foliage, sometimes afflicted with mildew. Exhibitors being as fickle as the rest of us, 'Dorothy Anderson' is rarely seen now. She was introduced in 1949 by McGredy's.

'Sam McGredy' × 'George Dickson'
Repeat flowering

'Dorothy Perkins'

Rambler

This is one of the best known of all roses. Everyone loves its cascades of small candy-pink pompoms, borne for about three weeks late in the rose season. Pretty as they are, the flowers are only mildly fragrant, and even by flowering time the foliage is usually white with mildew. If they escape, the small leaves are dark green and glossy. But mildew or no, it is a great survivor, flourishing in neglected gardens and layering itself where the canes touch ground, like a blackberry. Dorothy Per-kins in real life was the young daughter of Charles H. Perkins, founder of Jackson & Perkins, who introduced her rose in 1902.

Rosa wichuraiana × 'Madame Gabriel Luizet'
Summer flowering

'Dortmund' Cluster-flowered Climber

Individually the flowers are not all that exciting—single, only mildly fragrant, and red with a white zone at the centre. But en masse they make as eye-catching a display as anyone could want and they are borne freely all through the season. The plant is healthy, with very glossy dark leaves, and of a manageable size: rampant enough for a small pergola, restrained enough for a pillar. One of a series of Climbers raised by Wilhelm Kordes and named after German cities, 'Dortmund' was introduced in 1955.

Unnamed seedling × *Rosa kordesii*
Repeat flowering

▲ 'Double Delight'
◄ 'Dorothy Perkins'

'Double Delight' Large-flowered

Where sun strikes them, the ivory petals of 'Double Delight' stain crimson, in a variable pattern that is always striking. Too striking for some refined tastes, who find the contrast gaudy. The flowers are not especially large, but they are nicely formed and very fragrant. The bush is luxuriant, with matt olive-green foliage, red tinted when young, but it is not very long-lived. In cool climates there is much trouble with mildew; however, 'Double Delight' was voted best in the world by the World Rose Convention in 1986. On its introduction in 1977 it won the AARS award for its breeders, Herbert Swim and O. L. Weeks.

'Granada' × 'Garden Party'
Repeat flowering
Fragrant

'Dublin Bay' Large-flowered Climber
MACdub

A rather stiff, shrubby plant which takes its time to cover its allotted space, 'Dublin Bay' has flowers that are rather like smallish Large-flowered Roses, usually in small clusters. They are a pleasing blood-red and fragrant. The foliage is dark and glossy, and the repeat-flowering is very good. Raised by Sam McGredy, it was introduced in 1969.

'Bantry Bay' × 'Altissimo'
Repeat flowering
Fragrant

▲ 'Dortmund'
▼ 'Dublin Bay'

'Duc de Fitzjames' — Centifolia

The bush is typical Centifolia, tall and rather floppy, with lush leaves. The flowers are beautifully quartered and a soft lilac-rose in color. They come in clusters, and are fragrant. History appears to have taken little notice of M. le Duc de Fitzjames, but his rose gives him a kind of immortality. It was introduced in the 1880s.

Parentage unknown
Summer flowering
Fragrant

▲ 'Duc de Fitzjames'
▼ 'Duc de Guiche'

'Duc de Guiche' — Gallica
'Senat Romain'

Crimson, verging towards magenta and veined with purple, these intensely fragrant flowers are models of perfection in the Old Garden Rose style, their petals most beautifully reflexed and their centres quartered around a green heart. Foliage is dark green and rough. The plant is inclined to sprawl; careful pruning and maybe the assistance of a dahlia stake are needed. Nothing is known about the Duc de Guiche, but there is still a Duc de Guise, a scion of the royal house of Lorraine. Perhaps M. Prevost's catalogue suffered a misprint back in 1835.

Parentage unknown
Summer flowering
Fragrant

'Duchess of Portland' — Portland
'Paestana', 'Scarlet Four Seasons', 'The Portland Rose'

'Scarlet' is an exaggeration. The abundant flowers are carmine-red, opening to show golden stamens. They are fragrant, but not especially so. The neat, Gallica-like bush, which has bright green foliage, will, if it is treated generously, flower a second time in the autumn, or fall. This is a rose of great historic importance, being one of the first fruits of the marriage of the Old French Roses and the China Rose, and giving its name to the Portland class. Its origin and how it came to be associated with the Duchess of Portland, one of the eighteenth century's great amateurs of botany, remain a mystery.

Parentage unknown
Repeat flowering
Fragrant

'Duchesse d'Angoulême' — Gallica
'The Wax Rose'

With its somewhat lax growth, smooth foliage, and sprays of nodding flowers, this cannot be described as a typical Gallica. It is a very desirable one though, with its blush-pink petals, so fine they are almost transparent, and its delightful fragrance. It was a favorite rose for growing as a standard in the old days. For all its laxity the plant is even in its growth, and only very lightly armed with thorns. Marie-Thérèse Charlotte, Duchesse d'Angoulême, was the daughter of Louis XVI and Marie Antoinette. Having survived the Revolution, she remained a leading royalist during the Empire, dying a widow in exile in 1851. Vibert is thought to have christened his rose in her honor in 1835.

Parentage unknown
Summer flowering
Fragrant

▲ 'Duchess of Portland'
▼ 'Duchesse d'Angoulême'

'Duchesse d'Auerstädt' Noisette

A moderately vigorous Climbing Rose, 'Duchesse d'Auerstädt' has fine, broad foliage and large ruffled and scented flowers in blends of yellow, peach and apricot. It is never garish, but always rich. It was raised by Pierre Bernaix in 1888 and it descends from 'Rêve d'Or',

▶ 'Duchesse de Parme'
▼ 'Duchesse d'Auerstädt'

but whether as a seedling or a sport the history books disagree. It is only moderately repeat-flowering and is reasonably hardy, though, like most roses descended from the Tea Roses, it is happiest in a warm climate.

Possibly sport from 'Rêve d'Or'
Repeat flowering
Fragrant

'Duchesse de Brabant' Tea

'Comtesse de Labarthe', 'Countess Bertha', 'Comtesse Ouwaroff', 'Shell'

In Australia this is one of the best-selling roses of any type; and no wonder, for in that mild climate it is a very easy rose to grow. The plants are on the tall side, with neat glossy mid-green foliage, and bear their intensely fragrant flowers with great freedom.

▲ 'Duchesse de Brabant'
▶ 'Duchesse de Montebello'

The buds can be so long that they look almost like tulips. Despite its royal name—the Duke of Brabant was a prince of Belgium—this was the favorite rose of President Theodore Roosevelt, who often wore it in his buttonhole. The raiser's name was Bernède. He was not Belgian but French, and the year was 1857.

Parentage unknown
Repeat flowering
Fragrant

'Duchesse de Montebello' Gallica

There is some doubt about whether the rose we grow as 'Duchesse de Montebello' is indeed the one raised by Laffay in about 1838. That was classed a Hybrid China. The 'Duchesse de Montebello' pictured betrays no sign of China ancestry in its matt, greyish foliage or its summer-only flowering season. One of the taller Gallicas, it makes arching sprays of delightful, shapely blooms in pale pink of a softness and clarity unusual among the Gallicas. A delightfully feminine rose, with a soft, feminine perfume.

Parentage unknown
Summer flowering
Fragrant

'Duchesse de Parme' Moss

The history of this most attractive Moss Rose is hard to trace, but Napoleon's second wife Marie-Louise became Duchess of Parma in 1814, and held the title until her death in 1847. Possibly the rose dates from some time in those years. The flowers are large and shapely in the old style, opening from well-mossed buds, and fragrant. They are lilac in color, with shades of pink and parma violet. The bush is, like so many mosses, lax in habit, with broad, coarsely toothed, bright green foliage.

Parentage unknown
Summer flowering
Fragrant

'Duet'
Large-flowered

Salmon-pink, flushed with rose and backed with orange-red, the flowers of 'Duet' are not especially large or shapely; nor are they fragrant. What is remarkable about them is the extraordinary profusion in which they appear, on a compact, bronze-green bush. There are few roses easier to grow or better able to keep up a show of color in the garden, and the flowers last well in water, their rather unsubtle colors flattered by artificial light. Raised by Herbert Swim, 'Duet' won the AARS award in 1961, the year following its introduction.

'Fandango' × 'Roundelay'
Repeat flowering

'Duftbella'
Cluster-flowered

This rose was probably raised as a greenhouse rose, as ordinary gardeners seem unaware of it. The name 'Duftbella' seems to be a combination of German and Italian for 'fragrant' and 'beautiful'. Although these terms should describe all roses, this one certainly is strongly fragrant, and the velvet-red flowers are shapely and long-stemmed. They do tend to come in rather skimpy clusters though. Foliage is a leathery green. It was raised in Germany by Karl Herzel and introduced in 1973.

'Fragrant Cloud' × ('Monique' × 'Mardi Gras')
Repeat flowering
Fragrant

'Duftgold'
Large-flowered

TANdugoft
'Fragrant Gold'

The name 'Fragrant Gold', a literal translation of the German, is appropriate, as this is one of the most strongly scented of the yellow roses. Its flowers are shapely in the bud, opening quickly to rather loose full blooms, and the rich color holds without fading too much. The bush is on the short side, well clothed in dark green foliage. An attractive garden rose rather than a prize winner at shows, it was raised by Mathias Tantau in 1981.

Parentage undisclosed
Repeat flowering
Fragrant

▲ 'Duet'
► 'Duftgold'
▼ 'Duftbella'

'Duke of Edinburgh'   Hybrid Perpetual

This rose is a fairly typical red Hybrid Perpetual. It is dark and velvety at its best, but needs the best of care to have it so. The flowers are scented, the bush compact. Foliage is matt green and rather prone to mildew. Raised by William Paul and introduced in 1868, 'Duke of Edinburgh' was named, not for the present Duke (who was not born until 1921) but for Alfred, Duke of Edinburgh, son of Queen Victoria, father of Queen Marie of Romania.

'Général Jacqueminot' × unknown
Repeat flowering
Fragrant

▲ 'Duke of Edinburgh'
◄ 'Duke of Teck'
► 'Duke of Windsor'

'Duke of Teck'   Hybrid Perpetual

Deep pink, fragrant and very vigorous, 'Duke of Teck' is a rather pleasant rose for the garden. Foliage is matt green and needs protection from mildew should the weather be dry. Though it never seems to have topped the popularity charts, it is one of those Old Garden Roses that still retains its coterie of admirers. It was raised by William Paul in 1880 and was named for the father of Princess May, a great lover of roses, who later became Queen Mary.

'Duke of Edinburgh' × unknown
Repeat flowering
Fragrant

'Duke of Windsor'   Large-flowered
'Herzog von Windsor'

Large, shapely, with twenty-seven petals, and fragrant, the flowers are a lustrous coral-orange, much like 'Super Star', but the plant is much more compact. Indeed, although a very vigorous rose, it is lower growing than most Large-flowered Roses and should be planted at the front of a mixed bed. The foliage is dark, dull green, russet in its youth, and the branches are thorny. Good cultivation is called for, along with an alert eye for rust, but this is a worthy rose to honor the former king (Edward VIII), a keen gardener and lover of roses all his life. It was raised by Mathais Tantau in 1969.

'Prima Ballerina' × unnamed seedling
Repeat flowering
Fragrant

'Dundee Rambler' — Rambler

This rose is not unlike 'Bennett's Seedling' except that the compact, double white flowers that come in large clusters have more petals, and the growth is said to be a little bushier. It is fragrant too, though not nearly so strongly. Foliage is mid-green and matt. 'Dundee Rambler' was raised by a Mr Martin, who lived in a house called 'Rose Angle' and raised seedling roses. The parentage of this one, named for his home town, and even the date when he raised it, are long forgotten.

Parentage unknown
Spring flowering
Fragrant

▲ 'Dundee Rambler'
▼ 'Dupontii'

'Dupontii' — Gallica

Rosa × dupontii

Believed to be a cross between *R. gallica* and *R. moschata*, 'Dupontii' is named for André Dupont, director of the Luxembourg Gardens in Paris, so it is a safe guess that it was raised there, in about 1817. It makes a 2 metre (6 feet) high and wide bush, well filled with greyish leaves and, in summer only, large single flowers in palest, palest pink. A bush covered in virginal blossoms is an enchanting sight, but it needs regular thinning out of the oldest wood or it will be all twigs and few flowers.

Probably *R. gallica × R. moschata*
Summer flowering
Fragrant

▲ 'Dupuy Jamain'
▼ 'Dusky Maiden'

'Dupuy Jamain' — Hybrid Perpetual

The flowers are large, well perfumed, full and shapely, in that very common color (among roses) which decorators call 'American Beauty'—on the borderline between pink and red. The bush is upright with smooth wood and grey-green foliage. This is one of the more truly 'perpetual' of the Hybrid Perpetuals, and a very desirable garden rose. 'Dupuy Jamain' (sometimes corrupted to 'Deputy Jamain') came from the French raiser Jamain in 1868.

Parentage unknown
Repeat flowering
Fragrant

'Dusky Maiden' — Cluster-flowered

The flowers of this lovely, sweetly scented rose are almost single, their golden stamens lighting up the deep velvet crimson of the eight or so petals, and are carried in large trusses on a fairly compact bush with leaden green foliage. Although vigorous, you might have to keep an eye out for mildew. Like other roses in E. B. LeGrice's series of single Cluster-flowered Roses, 'Dusky Maiden' is one to delight the connoisseur. It was introduced by him in 1947.

('Daily Mail Scented' × 'Etoile de Hollande') × 'Else Poulsen'
Repeat flowering
Fragrant

'Dutch Gold' — Large-flowered

Deep yellow, sometimes with touches of orange, the flowers of 'Dutch Gold' are fragrant, though not exceptionally so. What is remarkable about them is their enormous size. For a rose so large, it is quite free with its blooming on an upright bush with handsome dark leaves. Popular in Europe, it is at its best in a cool climate. Dutch gold, a substitute for real gold leaf, tends to be brassier in color than the real thing. Our rose, however, is named to celebrate its winning of the gold medal at The Hague Rose Trials in 1978. It was introduced in that year by the Wisbech Plant Company.

'Peer Gynt' × 'Whisky Mac'
Repeat flowering
Fragrant

▼ 'Dutch Gold'

'Earth Song' — Large-flowered

Now classed with the Large-flowered Roses (ex-'Grandiflora'), the lovely 'Earth Song' was raised in 1975 at Iowa State University by their horticulturist Griffith Buck, whose maiden rose it may have been. The rose is noted for its rosy red, cup-shaped blooms that open from long, pointed buds, set off against glossy leathery foliage. Many of the twenty-eight petals have an irregular, fluted form. Plants of 'Earth Song' are of strong, bushy habit.

'Music Maker' × 'Prairie Star'
Repeat flowering
Fragrant

▲ 'Easlea's Golden Rambler'

'Easlea's Golden Rambler' — Large-flowered Climber

When a raiser puts his own name on a rose you can be sure he is proud of it. Walter Easlea, an Essex nurseryman, had every right to be proud of this 1923 creation. It is not really a Rambler, which implies a small-flowered rose, but its branches are a lot less stiff than most Large-flowered Climbers. The foliage is distinctive and handsome, a rich olive-green and leathery, and the flowers, which come in one great show early in the season, are glorious: large, fragrant, full of petals, and a lovely clear shade of yellow, occasionally lightly touched with red.

Parentage unknown
Summer flowering
Fragrant

◄ 'Earth Song'
▼ 'Eclair'

'Eclair' — Hybrid Perpetual

The name means 'lightning' in French. Nowadays we would reserve the name for something more dazzling than the dark red of this 'Général Jaqueminot' seedling. No doubt François Lacharme felt it was bright enough in 1883. Perhaps he was thinking of the exceptionally dark crimson flowers 'Eclair' is capable of producing, as dark as thunderclouds lit with lighter flashes … however, you will not see many such unless you pamper this rose a bit. Like so many very dark reds it has not been blessed with all that robust a constitution. The scent is superb. Foliage is a matt mid- to dark green.

'Général Jacqueminot' × unknown
Repeat flowering
Fragrant

'Eclipse' — Large-flowered

Just as well the 1930s are in fashion again, for if ever there was such a thing as an 'Art Deco rose' it would be this Jackson & Perkins masterpiece, created by their hybridist J. H. Nicolas. The deep gold buds are extraordinarily long, and encased in narrow, branching sepals. The fragrant blooms are loosely constructed, the foliage is dark, and it is interesting that this still popular rose first bloomed on the day of an eclipse in 1932, hence its name. Its many awards read like an atlas gazeteer—they include gold medals from Rome, Portland, Bagatelle and the ARS.

'Joanna Hill' × 'Frederico Casas'
Repeat flowering
Fragrant

▲ 'Eclipse'
▼ 'Eddie's Jewel'

'Eddie's Jewel' — Modern Shrub

Raised by the Canadian hybridist Eddie from 'Donald Prior', a Cluster-flowered Rose, crossed with a hybrid of *Rosa moyesii,* 'Eddie's Jewel' is effectively a semi-double version of *R. moyesii,* but without the splendid hips. It is, however, more manageable in growth—to about 2 metres (6 feet) high and a little less in width—and often gives a few autumn, or fall, blooms in compensation. Flowers are a pleasant shade of burgundy-red. Foliage is matt mid-green and the bark is red with few thorns. Prune it only lightly, or you will spoil the pleasant, arching shape of the bush. It was introduced in 1962.

'Donald Prior' × *R. moyesii* hybrid
Repeat flowering

'Edelweiss'
Cluster-flowered
'Snowline'

The names overstate the whiteness of the flowers, which are creamy rather than snowy, but they do warn that this attractive rose is one for cool climates. There it makes a compact bush, its olive-green leaves almost hidden by the clusters of full-petalled, shapely flowers. Where summers are warm and humid, however, it is apt to grow leggy and become shy with its blooms. There is a pleasant, musky scent. 'Edelweiss' was raised in 1970 by Niels Poulsen and introduced by Sam McGredy.

Parentage undisclosed
Repeat flowering
Fragrant

'Eden Rose'
Large-flowered

Following the worldwide success of 'Peace' Francis Meilland could do no wrong. One of the first descendants of 'Peace', 'Eden Rose' of 1950 won the gold medal of the RNRS and wide acclaim for its big, 58-petalled blooms in the style of 'Peace', but richly colored in a remarkable shade of tyrian rose. The 15 centimetre (6 inch) blooms of this vigorous rose are very fragrant and the foliage is a lustrous bright, dark green. The bush version was followed by a climbing sport in 1962, not to be confused with the 1986 'Pierre de Ronsard', sometimes known as 'Eden Rose 85'.

'Peace' × 'Signora'
Repeat flowering
Fragrant

▲ 'Edelweiss'
▶ 'Eden Rose'

'Editor McFarland'
Large-flowered

J. Horace McFarland was a master printer from Harrisburg, Pennsylvania, who in the 1920s and early '30s edited the *Annual of the American Rose Society* and later became president of that organisation. McFarland is remembered

chiefly for his magnum opus, *Modern Roses,* which is to the rose-lover what *Debrett* is to those interested in family lineages. In 1931 France's Charles Mallerin dedicated this rose to him. For years and years, 'Editor McFarland' grew in every garden, a delight in its fine form, intense fragrance, and freedom of bloom. But fashions change and in these days of coral and orange, the deep rose-pink of 'Editor' is not so popular. Foliage is mid-green and leathery.

'Pharisäer' × 'Lallita'
Repeat flowering
Fragrant

▲ 'Edna Walling'
◀ 'Editor McFarland'

'Edna Walling'
Rambler

Edna Walling was a leading designer of gardens and writer of gardening books in Australia during the 1940s and '50s. It brings great prestige to own an Edna Walling garden today, and her many admirers will no doubt rush to plant the rose named in her honor in the late 1980s. Unfortunately, it is only being made available as a weeping standard (which would not have pleased the lady) but it looks to be a very pretty Rambler, with clusters of rose-pink blooms, borne lavishly in spring and more sparingly thereafter, against glossy dark green foliage.

Parentage unknown
Repeat flowering

'Ehigala'
Large-flowered

The Japanese word *ehigala* means 'a pattern or picture of bright flames'. This seems appropriate for this rose, as its basically yellow petals are flamed with coral and pink against glossy green foliage. It was photographed at a flower show in Osaka, and it is a fine example of the new roses being bred in Japan. However, it does not appear to have reached the West as yet and not much is known about it. It is softly fragrant.

Parentage unknown
Repeat flowering

▲'Ehigala'

'Eiffel Tower'
Large-flowered

Brought to perfection by the American team of David Armstrong and Herbert Swim in 1963, this extraordinary rose owes its parentage to 'First Love' and an unnamed seedling from the Armstrong patch. It is double, though not very, with thirty-five petals, and urn-shaped buds even longer than those of 'First Love'. The high-centred blooms may reach 15 centimetres (6 inches) in diameter, and are a.cool medium pink. Very fragrant, they are set off by leathery, semi-glossy foliage on a very tall, upright bush. 'Eiffel Tower' won gold medals in Geneva and Rome.

'First Love' × unnamed seedling
Repeat flowering
Fragrant

'Eldorado Stanford Tea'
Tea

Every great rose garden has a couple of mystery roses—foundlings from old gardens, their original names lost, but too beautiful to forget. Here is one from the Huntington Gardens in San Marino, California. It really is a charming rose, with its perfect form, soft fragrance, delicate creamy color and semi-glossy mid-green foliage. Perhaps it dates from the gold rush days, who knows? When its true name is restored to it, no doubt it will find a wide circle of admirers.

Parentage unknown
Repeat flowering
Fragrant

▲ 'Eiffel Tower'
▼ 'Eldorado Stanford Tea'

'Elegance' — Climber

The name describes it well. It has long, shapely buds and large, wide open blooms, in a soft canary-yellow color, with a delicate fragrance. Although it flowers only in the spring, its season is a long one, and a single plant will give hundreds of perfect, long-stemmed flowers. There are many thorns. Raised by Dr and Mrs Walter Brownell of Long Island in 1937 in their quest for roses that would endure their subarctic winters, it is one of the easiest of yellow roses to grow.

'Glenn Dale' × ('Mary Wallace' × 'Miss Lolita Armour')
Summer flowering
Fragrant

▲ 'Elegance'
▼ 'Elina'

'Elina' — Large-flowered

DICjana
'Peaudouce'

The name to be preferred is 'Elina': 'Peaudouce', even if it is the name the raiser uses, is a brand of babies diapers. That is where the commercial sponsorship of roses can lead! The rose itself is a beauty—large, shapely and delicate in its tones of white and lemon. For a flower so large and pale, it is quite tolerant of wet weather. The bush is strong, with large, dark green, glossy foliage, and is average in height. The fragrance is only slight. 'Elina' was raised by Patrick Dickson and introduced in 1983.

'Nana Mouskouri' × 'Lolita'
Repeat flowering

'Elizabeth Arden' — Large-flowered

It is fitting that a rose of such perfect complexion should bear the name of the lady who dedicated her long life to making women beautiful. The darling of the 1930s, it is not often seen now; more's the pity, as sweetly scented white roses are still rare. The blooms are large and of most perfect form, and the stems long and almost thornless. But the grey-green leaves may need protection against mildew, and the bushes, which are only moderately sized, are inclined to be short-lived. It was introduced in 1929 and is credited to an Englishman, George Prince. There is another rose from a later date known as 'Elizabeth Arden', a soft pink Cluster-flowered Rose from Tantau, but its correct name is 'Geisha'.

'Edith Part' × 'Mrs Herbert Stevens'
Repeat flowering
Fragrant

'Elizabeth Harkness' — Large-flowered

No doubt when Jack Harkness crossed 'Red Dandy' with 'Piccadilly' he was anticipating something dazzling, so it must have been a surprise when 'Elizabeth Harkness' opened its first pastel-tinted blooms. They are enormous, shapely, and blush-white, with softest tints of apricot and pink at the centre, and fragrant too. The bush is strong and free, with dark leaves, but (like many Harkness roses) it is happiest in a cool climate. It is an ideal rose for a bride to carry on her wedding day, and indeed it was named as a wedding present for the raiser's daughter.

'Red Dandy' × 'Piccadilly'
Repeat flowering
Fragrant

▲ 'Elizabeth Harkness'
▼ 'Elizabeth Arden'

'Elizabeth of Glamis' — Cluster-flowered
MACel
'Irish Beauty'

Perfect in its soft shades of salmon and in its shapeliness from bud until petal fall, 'Elizabeth of Glamis' was the first Cluster-flowered Rose ever to win the RNRS's premier award for fragrance. 'Elizabeth of Glamis' is the very ideal of a beautiful Modern Garden Rose, but alas, its constitution appears to be deteriorating, and it sometimes refuses to flourish for no apparent reason. Foliage is a semi-glossy olive-green, tinted red when young. Raised by Sam McGredy and introduced in 1964, it was the first rose to be granted copyright protection in Britain. Elizabeth of Glamis is that expert rosarian, the Queen Mother. A beauty in her day, though not an Irish one, Her Majesty descends from an ancient Scottish family.

'Spartan' × 'Highlight'
Repeat flowering
Fragrant

▲ 'Elveshörn'
◀ 'Elizabeth of Glamis'
▼ 'Elmshorn'

'Elmshorn' — Modern Shrub
The small cherry-pink, scentless flowers of 'Elmshorn' may not be very exciting, but they are carried in distinctive conical trusses, and a specimen shrub in full flower in summer and autumn (or fall) is a colorful sight. It grows about head high, and is outstandingly tough and easy to grow. Foliage is light green, wrinkled and very resistant to disease. It was raised by Wilhelm Kordes and came out in 1950. It is named in honor of the town where the Kordes firm has its headquarters.

'Hamburg' × 'Verdun'
Repeat flowering

'Elveshörn' — Cluster-flowered
KORbotaf

Merit does not always translate into popularity. This rose is one of the toughest and easiest to grow of the 'Patio Roses', flourishing everywhere and smothering itself all season with elegant sprays of neatly formed flowers. Its faults in the public eye are: the name, easily confused with the much larger 'Elmshorn' (Reimer Kordes ought to have known better); the lack of gloss on the dark foliage; the lack of perfume; and the color of the flowers. Their brilliant cerise is uniform and unfading, but outside Germany, where the rose was raised in 1985, most people find it garish, and refuse to buy it, which is a pity.

'The Fairy' × unnamed seedling
Repeat flowering
Fragrant

'Emanuel'   English Rose

With this name, David Austin has not sought biblical connections, but chosen to honor David and Elizabeth Emanuel, the English couturiers, best known for designing the wedding dress of the Princess of Wales. Appropriately, the rose has ruffled flowers, taffeta-like in texture, blending shades of peach, pink and cream. They are fragrant and borne in profusion all season, but alas, the bush, which has glossy mid-green leaves, is a bit liable to black spot. 'Emanuel' was introduced in 1985.

Parentage undisclosed
Repeat flowering
Fragrant

▲ 'Emanuel'

'Emeraude d'Or'   Large-flowered

It was a source of speculation when this rose was introduced whether the curiously shaped petals, picoteed in gold and raspberry pink, would be the beginning of something new, but there is no evidence that it ever caught the public fancy, and it has not been seen in ages. It is still listed in several prestigious American publications, so it must still be available somewhere. No parentage was ever recorded. A 1965 creation of the French rose-breeding concern of Delbard-Chabet, 'Emeraude d'Or' displayed its splendid colors a couple of years later for my camera at Paris's Jardins de Bagatelle. Foliage is a glossy green.

Parentage undisclosed
Repeat flowering

▲ 'Emeraude d'Or'
▼ 'Emotion'

'Emotion'   Hybrid Perpetual

If this name were to be bestowed on a rose today, chances are that it would be one of brilliant, if not shocking, color. The nineteenth century had other ideas, 'Emotion' is a soft, romantic flower in palest pink. The scent is soft and romantic too, and the pale green foliage provides a suitably understated setting for the shapely blooms. There were in fact two roses of the name, one from Guillot in 1862, and the other from Fontaine in 1879. It appears our rose is the latter. If so, it was sometimes known as 'Alice Fontaine'. The bush is not large, and deserves the best of cultivation.

Parentage unknown
Repeat flowering
Fragrant

'Empress Joséphine'
Gallica

Rosa francofurtana, R. turbinata, 'Frankfurt Rose'
The flowers are large for an Old Garden Rose, the papery petals blending light and deep pink, with shadings and veinings of mauve and violet. There is not much fragrance unfortunately. The bush is short and compact, practically thornless, and with smooth, greyish leaves, all of which indicates hybrid ancestry. It is thought that the parents might have been *R. gallica* and *R. cinnamomea*, but no one knows who created it, or just when in the early nineteenth century it was given the name to honor the most famous rosarian in history.

Possibly *R. gallica* × *R. cinnamomea*
Summer flowering

▲ 'Empress Joséphine'
► 'English Holiday'

'Ena Harkness'
Large-flowered

With famous parents like Kordes's 'Crimson Glory' and McGredy's vivid scarlet 'Southport', it is no wonder that 'Ena Harkness' acquired such a glorious red color. The plant is of strong, upright growth, with leathery olive-green foliage, and the blooms high centred, fully double and oh how splendidly fragrant! The whole package was put together by the English amateur raiser Albert Norman (a diamond cutter by trade) and introduced in 1946 by the Harkness Company. Almost half a century later, and 'Ena Harkness' still remains 'a crimson-scarlet standby' in a cool-climate rose garden, flowering freely all season. Feed it well, or the flower stalks will be weak.

'Crimson Glory' × 'Southport'
Repeat flowering
Fragrant

▲ 'Ena Harkness'

'English Holiday'
Cluster-flowered

Moderately fragrant, the yellow and salmon-pink flowers of 'English Holiday' are fairly large and shapely, though their rather tight clusters have been criticised. In cool climates the foliage is a very dark glossy green and the plant blooms well. In warmer climates its growth is on the tall side and black spot can be a problem. Raised by Jack Harkness and introduced in 1977, 'English Holiday' is a pleasant, sunny rose.

'Bobby Dazzler' × 'Goldbonnet'
Repeat flowering
Fragrant

'English Miss'
Cluster-flowered

The lady of the title is the raiser's three-year-old daughter, Sallyanne Pawsey. She has a most dainty rose to her honor: the blush-pink blooms are regularly shaped like small camellias and softly fragrant. Nothing delicate about the plant though: it is strong and compact with glossy dark foliage. 'English Miss' was raised by Roger Pawsey of Cant's of Colchester and introduced in 1977.

'Dearest' × 'Sweet Repose'
Repeat flowering
Fragrant

'Eos'
Modern Shrub

'Eos' seems to be variable in color. Its name, honoring the goddess of the dawn, is thought justified in Britain by the coral colors of its flowers, but in warmer climates the smallish semi-double blooms are usually a more ordinary crimson. It makes a huge shrub, to 4 metres (13 feet) tall and 3 metres (10 feet) wide with lightish green foliage. It is well worth finding a place for it in a large garden, where, for three weeks or so in late spring it will be a fountain of bright color. It is credited to the Canadian breeder Eddie, who introduced it in 1950.

R. moyesii × 'Magnifica'
Summer flowering

▲ 'Eos'
▼ 'English Miss'

'Epidor'
DELepi

Large-flowered

Not much known or grown away from Europe, the Georges Delbard creation 'Epidor' has remained popular on its home territory, particularly in France. A pure deep yellow, with thirty-five petals, it was introduced in 1981, the result of a cross between unnamed seedlings from an all-French set of ancestors. The flowers are large, as would be expected from a descendant of 'Peace', but unfortunately light on fragrance. The growth is bushy, the foliage large, medium green and of matt texture. Its only recorded award is a gold medal at the Roseto di Roma, but its color is enough to brighten your day.

('Peace' × 'Marcelle Gret') × ('Vélizy' × 'Jean de la Lune')
Repeat flowering

'Erfurt'
Modern Shrub

Though introduced as long ago as 1939, 'Erfurt' is still one of the most admired of the Modern Shrub Roses. It makes a bushy plant, the arching stems taking time to build up to their full stature of 2 metres (6 feet). The young leaves are bronze, maturing to deep green, and the wide open flowers are clear pink, paling to white around the yellow stamens. They are of large Cluster-flowered Rose size, and richly musk-scented. It was raised by Germany's Wilhelm Kordes.

'Eva' × 'Reveil Dijonnais'
Repeat flowering
Fragrant

► 'Escapade'
▼ 'Erfurt'

'Escapade'
HARpade

Cluster-flowered

Though 'Escapade' has been hailed as one of the great Modern Garden Roses, it has never become a best-seller. Its flowers are almost single in a soft color, neither pink nor mauve, paling around the stamens. The plant is tall and bears clusters of fragrant blooms against glossy light green foliage. Plant it for its charm, or add a bush or two to a collection of Old Garden Roses to give flowers after they have finished. Jack Harkness raised it in 1967.

'Pink Parfait' × 'Baby Faurax'
Repeat flowering
Fragrant

◄ 'Epidor'

'Esmeralda'　　　　Large-flowered
KORmalda
'Keepsake'

Reimer Kordes has not revealed the complete parentage of this 1981 introduction. Like one of its parents, it is bushy, with dark foliage and stout thorns, and has a great reputation for disease resistance. Fragrance can only be described as moderate, but the forty petals reflex beautifully, and the color is a clear deep pink with lighter tints and gold at the flower's heart. The blooms are large and often come in threes. A real beauty!

Seedling × 'Red Planet'
Repeat flowering

'Ethel Austin'　　　　Cluster-flowered
FRYmestin

Raised by Fryer's in 1984, this rose features lolly-pink, shapely flowers of medium size in small clusters on a sturdy bush against large semi-glossy mid-green foliage. It is fragrant too. Rose lovers seem not to have taken much notice of it and it is now rather rare. It was named for a well-known English retailer of children's clothes.

'Pink Parfait' × 'Red Gold'
Repeat flowering
Fragrant

◀ 'Esmeralda'
▼ 'Ethel Austin'

'Etoile de Hollande' Large-flowered

'Etoile de Hollande' is well described by that old catchphrase 'an oldie but a goodie', for it first swept the world in 1919 when it was introduced by the Dutch hybridists H. A. Verschuren & Sons, and it still has many enthusiastic admirers. The forty or so petals are somewhat reflexed and make up a large and elegant flower of deep velvet-crimson, with all the fragrance of its ancestor *Rosa damascena*. The soft-textured leaden green leaves are inclined to have serrated edges. Do not prune it too hard, and look out for the excellent climbing sport.

'General MacArthur' × 'Hadley'
Repeat flowering
Fragrant

'Etude' Large-flowered Climber

It is not often that a raiser puts out two roses from the same parentage in the same year, but that is what Walter Gregory did in 1965, with 'Pink Perpétue' and 'Etude'. 'Pink Perpétue' is the one that has held public favor, but do not overlook 'Etude'. Its mid-sized coral-pink flowers are lightly scented and come in profusion in summer and intermittently later on. The plant is of comfortable, not too enthusiastic, vigor and the foliage is a glossy light green.

'Danse du Feu' × 'New Dawn'
Repeat flowering
Fragrant

▲ 'Eugénie Guinnoisseau'
◄ 'Etoile de Hollande'

'Eugénie Guinnoisseau' Moss

There is not much moss on the buds, but the flowers of this rose are very attractive—of good size for an Old Garden Rose, cupped in form, and a pleasant blend of mallow-pink fading to mauve. And they are borne repeatedly, on a tall, almost thornless bush. The foliage is dark and rather glossy. This is evidently a rose with much China Rose blood. Scent is very good. 'Eugénie Guinnoisseau' was introduced by Guinnoisseau in 1864. There is another rose, also a repeat-flowering Moss in mauve-pink, called 'Impératrice Eugénie'; it is unlikely this is the same rose.

Parentage unknown
Repeat flowering
Fragrant

'Europeana' Cluster-flowered

There are now so many red Cluster-flowered Roses being brought onto the market that a rose has to be pretty good to hold its popularity as long as 'Europeana' has. Its virtues are its rather low growth and also the prodigality with which it produces its dark crimson blooms against dark bronze-green foliage, tinted red when young. Its faults are minor: a slight tendency to mildew and a habit of making flower clusters so enormous that the stems flop under their weight. Raised by the Dutch breeder George de Ruiter, it was introduced in Europe in 1963 but not until 1968 in the United States, when it won the AARS award.

'Ruth Leuwerik' × 'Rosemary Rose'
Repeat flowering

◄ 'Etude'
▼ 'Europeana'

'Eurorose' Cluster-flowered

This rather pleasant yellow rose tends to crop up more in the parentages of more recent roses than it does in gardens nowadays. Perhaps its parentage tells why. 'Zorina' has been more prolific as a parent of greenhouse roses than of garden roses. 'Eurorose', which sometimes flushes its yellow flowers with red, has passed good characters to its descendants. Foliage is a glossy dark green. It was raised in Northern Ireland by Patrick Dickson and introduced in 1973.

'Zorina' × 'Red Gold'
Repeat flowering

▲ 'Eurorose'
▶ 'Eutin'

'Eutin' Cluster-flowered

'Hoosier Glory'
Like its sister seedling 'Orange Triumph', 'Eutin' was once seen in just about every garden, not so much for the beauty of its individual flowers, which are a rather dull crimson and scentless, as for its unfailing willingness to produce them, in enormous clusters, without needing any special care. Foliage is a dark green and leathery. Despite the occasional touch of mildew, it is a great survivor, and one often sees plants thirty years old or more still adding color to otherwise shabby gardens. It came from Wilhelm Kordes in 1940.

'Eva' × 'Solarium'
Repeat flowering

'Eva' Hybrid Musk

No one seems to love this rose. To most eyes its growth is a bit stiff, and the carmine-red flowers, paler at the centres, are strident and scentless. But Wilhelm Kordes was not breeding for elegance, rather for vigor and hardiness, characters which this 1933 child

of 'Robin Hood' and 'J. C. Thornton' has in abundance. It has passed these qualities on to its many descendants among the Modern Shrubs, the Cluster-flowered Roses, the best of which often 'wear the "Eva" family crest' as one American authority puts it, and even the Large-flowered Roses. Most of the vermilion roses trace back to it too. Foliage is a dark green and matt.

'Robin Hood' × 'J. C. Thornton'
Repeat flowering

▲ 'Eva'
▼ 'Evangeline'

'Evangeline' Rambler

'Evangeline' is probably a better rose than the ubiquitous 'Dorothy Perkins'. It is just as graceful in its growth, and its candy-pink flowers make just as good a display against dark green leathery foliage, with the bonus of sweet fragrance and much less mildew. But the flowers are single, and that has cost it popularity. Like 'Dorothy Perkins' it makes an elegant weeping standard, and flowers late, but there is no repeat bloom. It was raised by Walsh, the Rambler specialist, and introduced in 1906.

Rosa wichuraiana × 'Crimson Rambler'
Summer flowering
Fragrant

'Evelyn Fison' Cluster-flowered

MACev
'Irish Wonder'

'Evelyn Fison' was one of the first truly scarlet roses to hold its color until the petals fall, without going purple. It is still well worth a second look, as the nicely formed flowers are rich and brilliant without screaming it out loud. The bush is sturdy, with abundant dark

green, glossy foliage. It is an excellent rose for cutting too, though it lacks scent and is often accused of closing up shop rather early in the autumn, or fall. The name honors the wife of a prominent English supplier of garden needs, a friend of Sam McGredy, who introduced 'Evelyn Fison' in 1962.

'Moulin Rouge' × 'Korona'
Repeat flowering

'Evening Star' Cluster-flowered

In the cool climates which it prefers, this is one of the most beautiful of white roses, its lemon-white flowers holding perfect form until their petals drop. They are at their loveliest in the autumn or fall when they often take on a hint of palest green; scent is only light. Foliage is dark green and leathery and prone to black spot. 'Evening Star' is not happy in a sultry climate, often simply refusing to grow. It was raised in 1974 by Bill Warriner of Jackson & Perkins, from two other Jackson & Perkins roses.

'White Masterpiece' × 'Saratoga'
Repeat flowering

'Everest' Hybrid Perpetual

'Everest' is one of the last Hybrid Perpetuals, having been raised in 1927 by the great English amateur raiser Walter Easlea. It deserves more attention than it gets, for the flowers are large, high-centred, shapely and fragrant, though they are not really snowy but tinted with lemon towards their centres. Foliage is light green and the bush is compact, like a Large-flowered Rose rather than a typical sprawling Hybrid Perpetual. Indeed this rose's only fault is its dislike of wet weather.

'Candeur Lyonnaise' × 'Madame Caristie Martel'
Repeat flowering
Fragrant

◄ 'Evelyn Fison'
► 'Everest'
▼ 'Evening Star'

▲ 'Excelsa'
◄ 'Everest Double Fragrance'

'Everest Double Fragrance' — Cluster-flowered

Peter Beales of Norfolk, one of England's leading growers of old-fashioned roses, is a prolific author of rose books but less prolific in raising new roses. This is one of his best, though its popularity has not been helped by its cumbersome name. The bush is tall, the foliage glossy, and the flowers among the most fragrant of all of the Cluster-flowered Roses. They are a nice soft pink, usually tinted with coral, and grow paler as they age. 'Everest Double Fragrance' was introduced in 1979.

'Dearest' × 'Elizabeth of Glamis'
Repeat flowering
Fragrant

'Excellenz von Schubert' — Cluster-flowered

When Peter Lambert introduced this rose in 1909, Cluster-flowered Roses had not been thought of. So he classed it and several similar seedlings in a group he named 'Lambertianas' after himself. 'Excellenz von Schubert' is a compact, mid-sized rose with vividly dark green foliage against which the big sprays of bright pink flowers show up very prettily. It is repeat-flowering and very easy to grow. It merits revival as a 'Landscape Rose', despite its lack of scent.

'Madame Norbert Lavavasseur' × 'Frau Karl Druschki'
Repeat flowering

'Excelsa' — Rambler
'Red Dorothy Perkins'

Although it is always described as being crimson, 'Excelsa' is a rather pale crimson; 'cerise' would perhaps be a better description. As the ruffled, rather shapeless blooms age they fade, and at a distance the effect is deep pink. Foliage is a glossy dark green. When M. H. Walsh introduced it in 1909 he gave no details of its parentage, and it is generally assumed to be a sport of 'Dorothy Perkins', the best known of all Ramblers. Certainly it is, apart from its color, identical, even down to the mildew. Like its parent, 'Excelsa' is often seen surviving in the ruins of old gardens.

Sport from 'Dorothy Perkins'
Summer flowering

'Eyepaint' — Cluster-flowered
MACeye
'Tapis Persan'

Almost a Shrub Rose in its vigor, 'Eyepaint' makes a mass of bright color that puts a geranium to shame. The flowers are small, but they come in enormous clusters, and though their brilliant scarlet and gold dulls a bit with age, this does not detract from the massed effect. Another bonus is that the sprays of flowers are very long lasting in water. You will have to keep an eye out for black spot on the very glossy mid-green leaves. 'Eyepaint' was a nickname that Sam McGredy gave to this rose when he was still trying it out, and it stuck when it was introduced in 1975.

Unnamed seedling × 'Picasso'
Repeat flowering

▲ 'Eyepaint'
◄ 'Excellenz von Schubert'

'F. J. Grootendorst'   Hybrid Rugosa

This is the rose everyone loves to hate. The little flowers in their large bunches are rather pretty with their deeply fringed petals, and the bush flowers freely all season. Not in its favor is its lack of scent, and the dull red of the flowers makes the pale green foliage look starved. Happily, there are two much prettier sports in pink and white—'Pink Grootendorst' and 'White Grootendorst'. You will find them in this book. F. J. Grootendorst of Boskoop in Holland was the nurseryman who introduced it in 1918; it was actually raised by a gentleman called de Gooey.

Rosa rugosa × unknown Polyantha Rose
Repeat flowering

▲ 'Fantin-Latour'

▲ 'F. J. Grootendorst'
► 'Fairy Changeling'

'Fairy Changeling'   Ground Cover
HARnumerous

'Fairy Changeling' is reminiscent of 'The Fairy' (one of its parents). The little flowers, in big clusters on a short, spreading bush, are a strange melange of colors: some are pink, either dark or pale, while others can be shades of mauve or magenta against small dark green, glossy leaves. Altogether quite a conversation piece, and a very pretty rose for the front of a collection of Old Garden Roses, where it will hide any bare legs and provide flowers after the Old Garden Roses are over. It was raised by Jack Harkness in 1980. Alas, there is virtually no scent.

'The Fairy' × 'Yesterday'
Repeat flowering

'Fantin-Latour'   Centifolia

This is one of the all-time great roses! Its flowers are perfectly formed in the Old Garden Rose fashion, with intense fragrance and a delightful shade of soft pink. It needs good soil to make a head-high bush, its branches arching under the weight of the abundant blooms, borne over a long summer season only, against broad dark green, smooth foliage. Little is known about its history; it was rediscovered and christened by the English rosarian Graham Stuart Thomas, who points out that it is not a pure-bred Centifolia, despite its official classification. Henri Fantin-Latour was the great nineteenth-century French painter of flowers.

Parentage unknown
Summer flowering
Fragrant

'Fashion'   Cluster-flowered

Winner of the AARS award in 1950, 'Fashion' was one of Eugene Boerner's greatest triumphs. There had been salmon-pink roses before, but none so bright and unfading. There had been Cluster-flowered Roses with good-sized, shapely blooms, but none so striking. It has proved a most important parent, appearing somewhere in the family tree of just about all the coral-colored roses, and most of the Cluster-flowered Roses that followed it. It is still worth growing for its color and long season of bloom. Foliage is olive-green and prone to rust. It was introduced in 1949 by Jackson & Perkins.

'Pinocchio' × 'Crimson Glory'
Repeat flowering

'Fashionette'   Cluster-flowered

When raiser Eugene Boerner introduced 'Fashionette' in 1952, many rosarians thought it an improvement on its parent 'Fashion'. The flowers had more petals, and were of more perfect form; the color was softer and more subtle, and the perfume was stronger. Indeed this was one of the first Cluster-flowered Roses that justified being described as fragrant. The public did not agree, preferring the brighter color of 'Fashion'. 'Fashionette' is not easy to find now, but it remains one of the more stylish of the coral-pink Cluster-flowered Roses. The perfume is rich and sweet, the foliage dark and rarely afflicted by its parent's bugbear, rust.

'Fashion' × unnamed seedling
Repeat flowering
Fragrant

▲ 'Fashionette'

▲ 'Felicia'
◄ 'Fashion'
► 'Félicité et Perpétue'

'Felicia'   Hybrid Musk

The buds are a blend of coral and apricot, opening to loose, semi-double, informal flowers in blush with tints of peach and a lovely sweet fragrance. Like all the Hybrid Musks, 'Felicia' can be kept to Bush Rose size by firm pruning, when it would pass for a Cluster-flowered Rose of exceptional elegance. Treated more gently it will make a branching shrub, head-high and rather wider, with good bold dark green foliage to set off the many sprays of bloom. It was introduced by Joseph Pemberton in 1928. Give it time to show its beauty.

'Trier' × 'Ophelia'
Repeat flowering
Fragrant

'Félicité et Perpétue'   Rambler

Do not be confused by the name: 'Félicité et Perpétue' is not perpetual flowering. It seems that the raiser, M. Jacques, gardener to the Duke of Orléans, wanted to honor the Virgin Martyrs Perpetua and Felicity. They may consider themselves honored indeed, for this descendant of *Rosa sempervirens* has been regarded as one of the best of all Ramblers ever since its introduction in 1827. It is practically evergreen, its dark leaves, plum colored in youth, quite vanishing under the sprays of perfect rosettes late in the rose season. They are softly fragrant. In 1879, it produced a sport, 'Little White Pet', a small bush which is indeed perpetually in bloom.

Parentage unknown
Summer flowering
Fragrant

'Félicité Parmentier' — Alba

Its compact habit, its beautiful grey-green foliage, and the shapeliness of its sweetly scented flowers, their petals exquisitely layered and folded, make 'Félicité Parmentier' one of the most desirable of the Old Garden Roses. It is usually described as pale pink, but in a hot climate the blooms fade to blush-white almost as soon as they open. The bush grows to no more than 1 metre (3 feet) tall. Foliage is grey-green and handsome. The Parmentiers were a family prominent in French horticulture at the time this rose was introduced, about 1834, but the details of its raiser and parents are forgotten.

Parentage unknown
Summer flowering
Fragrant

▲ 'Félicité Parmentier'
▼ 'Ferdy'

'Ferdinand Pichard' — Hybrid Perpetual

It is a matter of choice whether this exuberantly striped rose belongs with the Hybrid Perpetuals (the official classification) or with the Bourbons. This is not a typical sprawling, cabbage-like Hybrid Perpetual, but a daintier, compact bush with light green leaves and cupped and fragrant blooms in pale pink, boldly striped with crimson and purple. It repeats its bloom very well. It was raised in 1921 by a gentleman called Tanne who perhaps felt that at that late date Bourbons were too old-fashioned to sell. Do not overlook it.

Parentage unknown
Repeat flowering
Fragrant

'Ferdy' — Modern Shrub

KEItoli
'Hanami-gawa'

Ignore the official classification of Climbing Miniature, 'Ferdy' is really a Modern Shrub Rose. It grows into an arching, weeping bush about 1.5 metres (5 feet) tall and wide, covering itself several times through the season with innumerable clusters of miniature flowers in a bright, some would say shrill, shade of coral, against mid-green, matt foliage. It is a dazzler; try planting a small group at the top of a retaining wall where its weeping habit will show to advantage. Do not bother with pruning, but allow it a couple of years to settle in and do its stuff. It was raised in 1984 in Japan by Seizo Suzuki, from a Climbing Miniature 'Petite Folie', and is being distributed elsewhere by Meilland's Universal Rose Selection. No scent.

'Petite Folie' × unnamed Climber
Repeat flowering

'Fervid' — Cluster-flowered

The almost-single flowers have distinctively crinkled petals and the scarlet flowers keep their orange glow no matter what the weather. The bush is tall, with dark, glossy green leaves, and

◄ 'Ferdinand Pichard'
▼ 'Fervid'

it flowers long into the autumn, or fall. 'Fervid' is said to be one of the most reliable of roses in sandy soils, which few roses enjoy, and it is surprising to see it so rarely listed. It was introduced in 1960 by E. B. LeGrice, that English raiser of out-of-the-ordinary roses.

'Pimpernel' × 'Korona'
Repeat flowering

'Fiesta' — Large-flowered

'Fiesta' was introduced by Armstrong Nurseries in 1940. It is a sport of 'The Queen Alexandra Rose' which is also an immediate ancestor of 'Peace'. In 'Fiesta' the bicolor arrangement of vermilion and gold of 'Queen Alexandra' is altered to a striped pattern, both unusual and decorative. Often the red veers towards regal purple. The bush is moderately strong, with glossy green leaves.

Sport from 'The Queen Alexandra Rose'
Repeat flowering
Fragrant

▲ 'Fiesta'
▼ 'Fimbriata'

'Fimbriata' — Hybrid Rugosa

Rosa rugosa dianthiflora, 'Phoebe's Frilled Pink'

There are few things more charming than a spray of 'Fimbriata', its little palest pink flowers softly scented, their petals serrated exactly like those of a carnation; however, it is not a rose to grow for a show in the garden. The 1.5 metre (5 foot) bush does bloom all season, but never in any great quantity, and it needs the best cultivation to show anything like the real Hybrid Rugosa exuberance. Foliage is light green and wrinkled. There will be occasional hips in autumn, or fall. A rose for connoisseurs, it was raised by M. Morlet of Avon in France and introduced in 1894.

R. rugosa × 'Madame Alfred Carrière'
Repeat flowering
Fragrant

'Fire King' — Cluster-flowered

MEIkans

Although 'Fire King' won the AARS award in 1960, many people think it is a little outclassed now, citing its increasing fondness for mildew, its rather leggy growth, and the way its brilliant scarlet blooms are apt to be disfigured by blackish edges to the petals. In its day it was a sensational rose, and if you see it in good form you can understand why it still has admirers: it can still put on a dazzling show. The foliage is dark green and leathery. Though almost scentless, it is a fine rose for cutting. It was a Meilland introduction of 1959.

'Moulin Rouge' × 'Fashion'
Repeat flowering

'Firecracker' — Cluster-flowered

When Jackson & Perkins chose the name for this 1955 introduction, the catalogue writers went distinctly over the top about it. 'Scarlet, shading to gold!' They said. It is actually a vivid cerise pink, with just a touch of yellow around the red and gold stamens. The old flowers soften markedly in tone. This is nevertheless one of the best Cluster-flowered Roses for making a bright show in the garden, the compact bushes with their matt-green leaves flowering very heavily all season. For so lightly built a flower, it lasts very well in the vase. Eugene Boerner was the raiser.

'Pinocchio' seedling × 'Numa Fay' seedling
Repeat flowering

▲ 'First Edition'
◀ 'Fire King'
▼ 'Firecracker'

'First Edition' — Cluster-flowered

DELtep
'Arnaud Delbard'

The wide outer petals and shorter inner ones give the flowers of this 1977 AARS winner unusual form, very like the dwarf Gumpo Azalea 'Balsaminiflora', which is similar in its sparkling coral-rose color too. The rose is an erratic performer: in cooler climates it is compact and floriferous; in sultry climates it sulks. Foliage is glossy and mid-green. Perhaps Georges Delbard, the raiser, will favor us with a second edition, with similar charming flowers on a sturdier plant. 'First Edition' came out in 1976.

Unnamed seedling × unnamed seedling
Repeat flowering

'First Love'
Large-flowered

It is not surprising to find that 'First Love' was a parent of 'Eiffel Tower' as it has the same exceptionally long elegant buds. 'First Love' has a smaller flower with fewer petals, and despite its being much admired for the delicacy of its pale, two-toned pink, 'Eiffel Tower' is the better rose, as it is much more fragrant. The foliage is a leathery mid-green. 'First Love' is an earlier (1951) creation by Herbert Swim for the Armstrong stable. Often claimed to be thornless, it is, alas, no such thing!

'Charlotte Armstrong' × 'Show Girl'
Repeat flowering

▲ 'First Love'
▼ 'First Prize'

'First Prize'
Large-flowered

For its lovely, high-centred blooms, 'First Prize' certainly deserves a first prize, and wins them regularly at rose shows in America; it also has the AARS award and the American Rose Society's gold medal to its credit. It was bred by Eugene Boerner for Jackson & Perkins and introduced in 1970. The plant is vigorous and upright. The huge flowers are a blend of soft rose pinks and it is fragrant. The blooms are touched with old ivory at their centres, and the foliage is dark green and leathery.

'Enchantment' × 'Golden Masterpiece'
Repeat flowering
Fragrant

'Flamenco'
Cluster-flowered

A 1959 introduction, 'Flamenco' was one of Sam McGredy's first, marking the return of the McGredy firm to the new rose business after a long absence. The rose world seems to have regarded it as merely a taste of things to come, and even the McGredy catalogue no longer lists it. It is a rose for cool climates, like that of Portland, Oregon, where it was photographed, and where it makes a cheerful display with its coral-pink blooms, lit with touches of yellow and orange. Foliage is dark olive-green and leathery.

'Tantau's Triumph' × 'Spartan'
Repeat flowering

'Flaming Beauty'
Large-flowered

Fragrance may be important in a rose, but it is not everything. Despite being almost scentless, 'Flaming Beauty' was the first rose to win an award at the American Rose Centre's Trial Ground in 1975, the year of its introduction. Bred by Joseph Winchell, it bears big, exhibition-style flowers in flaming red-orange and yellow on a bushy plant with matt green foliage. Grow it not for scent but for its exciting color.

'First Prize' × 'Piccadilly'
Repeat flowering

▲ 'Flammentanz'
◄ 'Flamenco'
▼ 'Flaming Beauty'

'Flammentanz'
Large-flowered Climber
'Flame Dance'

It is unusual for one of Wilhelm Kordes's 'Kordesii' hybrids to be summer flowering only, but such is 'Flammentanz' of 1955. It does, however, make a most gorgeous display in its season, the plants covering themselves in clusters of medium-sized flame-red flowers, and it is said to be one of the most cold-resistant of climbing roses. Foliage is a dark leathery green. Do not expect it to make a very large plant and do not confuse 'Flammentanz' with its contemporary, 'Danse du Feu'.

Rosa eglanteria hybrid × *R. kordesii*
Summer flowering

'Fleur Cowles' — Cluster-flowered

Named for a well-known American writer, 'Fleur Cowles' has appropriately feminine blossoms—blush-white and cream, full petalled and informal, and fragrant as well. They are of medium size, 8 centimetres (3 inches) and come on a dark-leafed bush. Like most pale roses it is easily damaged by rain and shows its best in a sunny climate. It was raised by the English nurseryman Walter Gregory in 1972, and is a seedling of 'Pink Parfait', the other parent being unknown.

'Pink Parfait' × unknown
Repeat flowering
Fragrant

▲ 'Fleur Cowles'
▶ 'Florence Mary Morse'
▼ 'Fleurette'

'Fleurette' — Ground Cover

INTerette
'Flavia'

The Interplant Company of Leersum in Holland is going in for Ground Cover Roses in a big way; there is evidently a demand for them in Europe to brighten up the dreariness of motorways and the like. 'Fleurette' is one of their nicer ones, introduced in 1978. The light pink single blooms have Wild Rose charm and are borne in clusters all season on a spreading, glossy-leafed bush, dense enough to be an effective ground cover. If a few weeds do get through, Interplant claim that it will not be too painful removing them, as 'Fleurette' has very few thorns.

'Yesterday' × unnamed seedling
Repeat flowering

'Florence Mary Morse' — Cluster-flowered

Quite tall, almost a Shrub Rose in fact, 'Florence Mary Morse' has sprays of informal flowers in clear scarlet, which dull only slightly with age. The dark olive-green, leathery foliage is red tinted when young. The rose's faults are lack of scent and a rather long gap between its flushes of bloom. Plant it in a mixed border with suitable perennials to point up its dazzling color and mask its leggy stems. The lady for whom it was named was a member of one of Britain's leading rose-growing families, friends of Wilhelm Kordes who introduced the rose back in 1951. Nurseries sometimes misspell her name 'Florence May'.

'Baby Château' × 'Magnifica'
Repeat flowering

▲ 'Florian'
▼ 'Climbing Florian'

'Florian' — Cluster-flowered

MEIlaur
'Tender Night'

The flat, vaguely camellia-like flowers of this rose are almost the size of a Large-flowered Rose and are borne in small clusters on a tall bush with dark, matt green leaves. They are only slightly fragrant, but good for cutting. It is a Meilland introduction of 1971, still quite widely grown in France but hardly at all elsewhere.

'Tamango' × ('Fire King' × 'Banzai')
Repeat flowering

'Florian, Climbing' — Cluster-flowered Climber

MEIlursar
'Climbing Tender Night'

This is a good climber, of manageable vigor and good repeat-blooming. It bears slightly fragrant, reasonably large flowers in clusters. Their color is a medium red, sometimes with overtones of scarlet. Foliage is a dark, matt green. The original bush form was raised by

Meilland in 1971 but the climbing sport that Meillands introduced in 1976 seems to have eclipsed it in popularity.

'Tamango' × ('Fire King' × 'Banzai')
Repeat flowering

'Flower Carpet'
Ground Cover
NOAtram

The catalogues promise that 'Flower Carpet' has glossy, evergreen, disease-proof leaves and pink, fragrant blooms just about all year, and needs less maintenance than grass. Time will tell. First impressions are that here is a Rambler like 'Excelsa' turned into a smallish, procumbent bush. The leaves are Rambler-like and glossy green and the sprays of little flowers are bright pink and carry some fragrance. They drop cleanly and repeat quickly. 'Flower Carpet' was introduced by Noack in 1990.

Parentage undisclosed
Repeat flowering

'Folklore'
Large-flowered

This rose has an international background. Raised by Reimer Kordes in Germany, it was introduced in 1977 by the Italian firm of Vittorio Barni. It is a very double rose, with forty-four petals and much fragrance. Long, pointed orange buds open to large, high-centred blooms of a slightly paler shade, set off by glossy green foliage. It grows into a very large bush and flowers freely.

'Fragrant Cloud' × unnamed seedling
Repeat flowering
Fragrant

'Folksinger'
Modern Shrub

The late Griffith Buck's rose-breeding programme, carried out under the auspices of Iowa State University, had as its aim the production of roses that would be disease-resistant, easy to grow, and able to put up with the bit-

▲ 'Flower Carpet'
▼ 'Folksinger'

terly cold winters of the United States Mid-West. They mostly resemble the modern Bush Roses in habit and with the same pruning would blend happily with them, though most would be on the tall side. Such a rose is the 1984 'Folksinger', which bears large, loosely formed flowers in shades of peach and yellow. They come in small clusters all season and are pleasingly fragrant. The foliage is a dark, leathery green.

'Carefree Beauty' × 'Friesia'
Repeat flowering
Fragrant

'Fornarina'
Gallica

Individually, the flowers of 'Fornarina' are not particularly exciting, just two-tone pink and fragrant, but they are borne very freely on a compact bush, with dark green leaves, so she makes quite a show in her season. In 1826, when this rose was raised, European art was more completely influenced by the style of Raphael than ever before (or since), so it was timely to name a rose after Raphael's mistress, the celebrated beauty nicknamed La Fornarina, 'The Baker's Daughter'.

Parentage unknown
Repeat flowering
Fragrant

'Foster's Melbourne Cup'
Cluster-flowered
MACmouhoo
'Wellington Cup'

Forget the horses and the gamblers, let alone the crowd drinking Melbourne's famous lager. Think rather of ladies in the Members Enclosure showing off their new dresses and pretty hats. The

▲ 'Folklore'
▶ 'Fornarina'

rose is just as pretty, all cream and blush ruffles, set off by dense, glossy green foliage, bronze when young and olive-green at maturity. The flowers are quite large, nicely scented, and the bush compact and floriferous. It was introduced by Sam McGredy in 1990 and looks a winner.

'Sexy Rexy' × 'Pot o' Gold'
Repeat flowering
Fragrant

'Fountain' — Modern Shrub
'Fontaine', 'Red Prince'

The name 'Fountain' does not call to mind a red rose. Perhaps that is why this very good Modern Shrub Rose has not become as popular as it deserves. The fact that it is virtually a Large-flowered Rose, with shapely, velvety flowers, strongly fragrant, carried all season on a sturdy, head-high shrub with leathery, dark green leaves, makes it all the more desirable. The RNRS saw its merits in 1970, the year of its introduction, and gave it their top award. The raiser was Mathias Tantau.

Parentage undisclosed
Repeat flowering
Fragrant

'Fragrant Cloud' — Large-flowered
TANellis
'Duftwolke', 'Nuage Parfumée'

For many years after its introduction by the German raiser Mathias Tantau, this was the world's best-selling rose. The name is very apt, as it is outstandingly fragrant. The flowers are brick-red and the foliage is a dark olive-green, tinted red when young. Introduced in Europe in 1963, it was not brought to the United States (by Jackson & Perkins) until 1968. Its many awards include the gold medals of the RNRS and Portland,

as well as the rarely awarded James Alexander Gamble Medal for fragrance.

Unnamed seedling × 'Prima Ballerina'
Repeat flowering
Fragrant

'Fragrant Delight' — Cluster-flowered

The name promises perfume, and the coral and salmon flowers, shot with apricot, deliver it. With its upright habit, dark green foliage, and huge sprays of nicely shaped flowers, it is a highly regarded bedding rose in Britain, where it was bred, but it does not seem to enjoy hotter climates. It came from the Wisbech Plant Farm in 1978.

'Chanelle' × 'Whisky Mac'
Repeat flowering
Fragrant

▲ 'Fountain'
◄ 'Foster's Melbourne Cup'

▲ 'Fragrant Cloud'   ▼ 'Fragrant Delight'

THE ROSE IN AMERICA

It is said that Columbus's sailors, on the point of mutiny after weeks of sailing into the unknown, were given the courage to go on by the sight of a floating rose branch that showed them that land was near.

Whether or not this is a true story, there were certainly many roses awaiting them in the New World. Some twenty species are native to North America, among them such beautiful roses as *Rosa virginiana*, *R. californica* and *R. setigera*. The pioneers reported that the Indians transplanted bushes from the wild to adorn their villages and some of the settlers followed suit, the native roses mingling happily in their gardens with roses brought from Europe.

That was in what is now the eastern United States. To the south, in present-day Mexico, the Aztecs practised horticulture as sophisticated as that of Europe, if not more so. Curiously, the rose does not appear to have been a favorite in their gardens. Perhaps the few species native to Mexico just did not suit the Aztec taste for the flamboyant the way the dahlia, the African Marigold or the zinnia did, but at least it was spared being used in the service of the bloodthirsty Aztec gods.

With Christianity, the rose came to Mexico. The most revered shrine in all of the Americas, that of Our Lady of Guadeloupe, was founded in 1521 on a spot which it is said the Virgin Mary marked as her own by miraculously covering it with a growth of roses, and today roses are just as cherished in Mexican gardens as they are everywhere.

The early colonists of the United States needed no divine example, for they brought the English passion for flowers with them. Washington and Jefferson are only the most prominent of a number of colonial gardeners whose gardens are preserved today; both carried on extensive correspondence with fellow enthusiasts in Europe and many a new plant blossomed for the first time in America in the gardens of Mount Vernon or Monticello. It was a two-way traffic— American plants like phlox, clarkias and magnolias enjoyed quite a vogue in Europe towards the end of the eighteenth century.

Jefferson, who once wrote that 'the greatest service that can be rendered to any country is to add a useful plant to its culture' no doubt took an interest in the Rose Garden of the White House, though he did not actually plant it—it dates from 1800 during John Adams's presidency. Neither large nor, as rose gardens go, especially interesting, it is the most famous rose garden in America, visited by an endless list of the world's distinguished and powerful. Not that most of the vistors go to see the roses!

There are many splendid rose gardens in both the United States and Canada where one can feast one's senses on roses to one's heart's content. Most interesting, perhaps, are the 24 test gardens of the All-America Rose Selections (AARS), where the new roses are tested for two years before they are introduced. The roses which the panel of judges decide are the best of the year are given the coveted AARS award, which virtually guarantees sales (and many dollars) to the fortunate hybridists. Roses which receive the AARS award account for some 18 million of the 40-odd million rosebushes sold each year in the United States. It is no wonder, for they include such all-time greats as 'Peace', 'Super Star' and 'Queen Elizabeth'.

That a preponderance of the winners should be American is no reflection on the impartiality of the judges; American hybridists are some of the most skilful in the world. Even the British take notice when a new rose appears from the hand of American experts, and by international consent, a new rose must be registered with the American Rose Society (ARS) for its name to be valid.

▲ *The famous International Rose Gardens in Washington Park in Portland, Oregon, occupy a fine site with extensive views over the city. For many years it was the policy of the city government to plant rosebushes along the streets, gaining Portland the title of the Rose City.*

▶ *The United States led the world in the granting of royalties to the creators of new and improved varieties of plants who hitherto had to practise their art for love and little money. 'New Dawn', introduced in 1931, holds Plant Patent No. 1.*

▲ The climate of many parts of North America is often extreme indeed, and roses need to be tough to survive. Here 'American Pillar' climbs up the walls of the second oldest house on Long Island, flourishing despite freezing Atlantic gales and sub-zero winters. It owes much of its hardiness to the native Rosa setigera.

▲ It says much for the popularity of 'La France' in turn-of-the-century American gardens that a California orange-grower was able to use its name as a brand name without confusing the public. California has given way to Florida as the source of America's oranges, but the rose still holds sway there; most of America's hybridists are California-based.

Founded in 1899, the ARS is neither the oldest nor the largest rose society—those distinctions belong to Britain's Royal National Rose Society—but it is one of the world's most dedicated. In addition to maintaining the registers of new roses (which it publishes in its *Annual* and from time to time in the rose-lover's bible, *Modern Roses*), it maintains one of the world's largest rose gardens at Shreveport, Louisiana, and acts as a clearing-house for knowledge and research about roses. Its 20 000 members are well served, I think—and they are not all the rose-lovers of America, for there are also many smaller local societies and groups dedicated to such specialised enjoyments as Old Roses and Miniatures.

You can tell much about people by the symbols they choose for themselves. Several American States have chosen roses: best known are the Cherokee Rose of Georgia, the Prairie Rose of North Dakota, and 'American Beauty', the official flower of the District of Columbia. New York simply bears 'the rose', and now the whole United States has followed suit, choosing the rose as the national flower. Is it not a hopeful sign when the most powerful nation on earth, whose ferocious eagle has traditionally offered the arrows of war as well as the olive branch of peace, should choose the rose of love?

▲ This is the miraculous apparition of the Virgin of Guadeloupe, patron of Mexico, as depicted in a fresco. Shops throughout the country sell small shrines of the Virgin, often decorated with plastic roses—which may inspire devotion in the faithful but induces shudders in the aesthete.

◄ The Wild Roses of North America are second to none in beauty. Here is the Prairie Rose, Rosa setigera, depicted by the great American naturalist and artist John James Audubon (1785–1851) in his Birds of America. The bird perching in the branches is the Seaside Finch.

'Fragrant Hour'
Large-flowered

One of a dozen or so Modern Garden Roses whose names promise fragrance, 'Fragrant Hour' was developed by New Zealand's Sam McGredy in 1963. High-pointed buds open to 10 centimetre (4 inch) blooms possessing wonderful fragrance, above light green foliage. The color is a remarkable bronze-pink. A gold medal was awarded in 1978.

'Arthur Bell' × ('Spartan' × 'Grand Gala')
Repeat flowering
Fragrant

▲ 'Francis E. Lester'
◄ 'Fragrant Hour'
▼ 'Francis Dubreuil'

▲ 'Fragrant Plum'

'Fragrant Plum'
Large-flowered

AROplumi

Usually described as 'deep purple-rose', the flowers are really a deep pink with overtones of lilac. As they age they become deeper and more pink. But it is a handsome rose nevertheless, large, shapely, and intensely fragrant. It succeeds best in a warm climate where it makes a strong bush with glossy green foliage. Give it a pale yellow or blush-pink rose for contrast. It is a 1988 introduction from Armstrong Nurseries.

'Shocking Blue' × ('Blue Nile' × 'Ivory Tower')
Repeat flowering
Fragrant

'Francis Dubreuil'
Tea

The Tea Roses mostly went in for delicate tones, and the intense velvety crimson of 'Francis Dubreuil' is something quite exceptional. No wonder the raiser named it after himself! As rich and splendid in color as any Large-flowered Rose, it deserves a high place among red roses for warm climates. Like most Teas it is shy of cold. A little shade will help the flowers hold color in hot weather. Foliage is dark green and rather glossy. Francis Dubreuil was a tailor who turned his hand to rose-breeding, and the grandfather of Francis Meilland, the raiser of 'Peace'. He introduced his eponymous rose in 1894.

Parentage unknown
Repeat flowering
Fragrant

'Francis E. Lester'
Rambler

This is an outstanding rose, capable of making a wide, lax shrub or clambering to about 4 metres (13 feet) over a support, which it will smother in mid-summer with its richly perfumed flowers. These are single, shapely and pale pink. The young foliage is maroon, maturing to a dark glossy green. It came from the Lester Rose gardens in California in 1946.

'Kathleen' × unknown
Summer flowering
Fragrant

'François Foucard'
Rambler

Preserved for many years at the Roseraie de l'Haÿ and now finding its way back into the catalogues, 'François Foucard' has, for a Rambler, large, full-petalled flowers in a pleasing shade of lemon-yellow. It is fragrant, often bearing flowers after its main early

▲ 'François Foucard'

touched with yellow at their hearts and pass to a softer shade as they age. They are full of petals and quartered, and sweetly fragrant too. There is a grand display in early summer with scattered flowers to follow, and the foliage is a glossy, dark green. It is not as resistant to mildew, however, as most of the Barbier roses, and it is apt to get a bit bare at the base. Plant something in front. It was introduced in 1906.

Rosa wichuraiana (or *R. luciae*) × 'Madame Laurette Messimy'
Repeat flowering
Fragrant

▲ 'Frank Naylor'
▼ 'Franklin Englemann'

summer display, and is endowed with glossy, dark green foliage. It was introduced in 1900 by Barbier et Cie who declared its parentage as *Rosa wichuraiana* × 'L'Idéal', a coral-red Tea Rose; but there is some evidence that M. Barbier raised his Ramblers not from the Japanese *R. wichuraiana* but from its Chinese counterpart, *R. luciae*.

R. wichuraiana × 'L'Idéal'
Summer flowering
Fragrant

'Frank Naylor' Modern Shrub

This rose makes a head-high shrub, covered all season with sprays of smallish, almost single flowers in an unusual tone of dusky crimson with gold around the stamens. Young foliage is plum tinted, and matures to a dark greyish green. Major-General Naylor was sometime President of the Royal National Rose Society and his namesake rose was introduced in 1978 by Jack Harkness. Harkness has raised some other very attractive roses from it.

(['Orange Sensation' × 'Allgold'] × ['Little Lady' × 'Lilac Charm']) × (['Blue Moon' × 'Magenta'] × ['Cläre Grammerstorf' × 'Frühlingsmorgen'])
Repeat flowering
Fragrant

'François Juranville' Rambler

Another of the Large-flowered Ramblers raised by Barbier et Cie, 'François Juranville' features coral-pink flowers that are

'Franklin Englemann' Cluster-flowered

Named, apparently, for a German rose-grower, this is an Irish-raised rose, from Patrick Dickson in 1970. It has blood-red flowers, like small Large-flowered Roses in size and form, in small clusters (but great numbers of them) on a tall, rather open bush with glossy dark green leaves. It lacks scent, which has told against its wider popularity, but it is a fine garden rose and proving useful as a parent. Herr Englemann has had to endure the indignity of having his name misspelt as Engelmann when the rose was registered; it is given here with the correct spelling.

'Heidelberg' × ('Schlössers Brilliant' × unnamed seedling)
Repeat flowering

◀ 'François Juranville'

'Frau Dagmar Hartopp'   Hybrid Rugosa
'Fru Dagmar Hastrup'

Call it by either version of its name (or just, affectionately, 'Frau Dagmar'), this is perhaps the best of all the Hybrid Rugosas for a small garden. The blooms are single, sweetly fragrant, and a most attractive shade of pale cool pink. The later flowers are accompanied by deep crimson hips, which go perfectly with them. At the very end of the season there are autumn, or fall, plum tints in the rich green, wrinkled foliage. What more could one ask of a small shrub? It seems it came from Denmark in about 1914; no one is sure.

Parentage unknown
Repeat flowering
Fragrant

▲ 'Frau Dagmar Hartopp'
▼ 'Frau Karl Druschki'

'Frau Karl Druschki'   Large-flowered
'Schneekönigin', 'Snow Queen', 'Reine des Neiges', 'White American Beauty'

On its introduction by Peter Lambert in 1901, 'Frau Karl Druschki' was hailed as the finest white rose yet. Over ninety years later, many people award it the title still, citing the statuesque beauty of the huge, high-centred blooms, and the freedom with which they are borne on big, light green, easy-to-grow bushes. They forgive the lack of scent. Frau Karl Druschki was the wife of the President of the German Rose Society.

'Merveille de Lyon' × 'Madame Caroline Testout'
Repeat flowering

'Fred Edmunds'   Large-flowered
'L'Arlesienne'

Oregon nurseryman Fred Edmunds seems to have stolen some of the glory from the Meilland family, who first called this lovely rose 'L'Arlesienne' (after Bizet's opera) in 1943. It is a loosely decorative rose of twenty-five petals, opening in cupped form from long, pointed buds. The coppery orange blooms, up to 13 centimetres (5 inches) in diameter, develop a strong fragrance that helped to earn the Portland gold medal in 1942 and the AARS award in 1944. The bush has an open habit and healthy glossy foliage.

'Duquesa de Peneranda' × 'Marie Claire'
Repeat flowering
Fragrant

'Fred Loads'   Modern Shrub

This is a Modern Shrub Rose for rose-lovers who appreciate bright colors in lavish quantity. Like a gigantic Cluster-flowered Rose in habit, 'Fred Loads' dazzles with great sprays of semi-double, lightly scented flowers in coral-orange, not unlike those of 'Super Star' in tone. Foliage is dark green and lush, and the plant grows very strongly. The plant is vigorous and upright in habit. It needs something shorter to be planted in front of it as most of the blooms come at the top of the bush. Named for a leading British writer on gardening, it was raised by the English amateur raiser Holmes and introduced in 1968. There is a striped sport from 'Fred Loads' called 'Festival Fanfare'.

'Dorothy Wheatcroft' × 'Orange Sensation'
Repeat flowering

▼ 'Fred Edmunds'

tinted with palest apricot; always they are of perfect exhibition form. They are rather large and the clusters small, but there is nothing delicate about the plant, which is strong and bushy. One might cavil about the lack of scent, and wish the small dark green leaves a bit larger. Raised by Bill Warriner of Jackson & Perkins, it is an excellent cut flower, as are its parents.

'Bridal Pink' × 'Dr Verhage'
Repeat flowering

'Frensham' Cluster-flowered

In cool climates 'Frensham' has long been an outstanding rose—taller than head high and completely covered with clusters of warm crimson flowers against dark green, matt foliage. Then, in the 1960s, cries of 'deterioration' and 'mildew' were heard, and 'Frensham' fell from favor. It seems that in recent years the mildew problem is lessening, heralding, one hopes, a revival of popularity for this lovely rose. Raised in 1946 by that remarkable English amateur breeder Albert Norman, its only fault is the faintness of its perfume.

Unnamed seedling × 'Crimson Glory'
Repeat flowering

▲ 'Fred Loads'
▼ 'Freedom'

'Freedom' Large-flowered

DICjem

You do not really need to know that 'Freedom' won the RNRS gold medal in 1983, though that is proof of its great performance over a number of years. Suffice to say that its flowers are absolutely gorgeous! What a dazzling chrome yellow! And it stays that way until the flowers actually fall. It was raised by Pat Dickson of the old Northern Ireland rose-breeding family. It is a neat plant, dense, bushy, and not too tall, freely blooming (though the flowers are by no means big) and clad in glossy green foliage.

('Eurorose' × 'Typhoon') × 'Bright Smile'
Repeat flowering
Fragrant

'French Lace' Cluster-flowered

JAClace

What an appropriate name for this 1982 AARS winner: its flowers are almost exactly the écru color of the best Vincennes lace! Often they are

▲ 'Frensham'
▼ 'French Lace'

▲ 'Friendship'
▼ 'Friesia'

'Friendship' Large-flowered
LINrick

California's Bob Linquist raised this beauty for the Conard-Pyle Company of Pennsylvania in 1978. Not surprisingly from its parentage, it is richly fragrant. Tinted a rich raspberry pink, the twenty-eight petals form a huge, cupped flower, sometimes 15 centimetres (6 inches) across. Foliage is a dark green and the bush is vigorous. It almost goes without saying that it received the AARS award for 1979.

'Fragrant Cloud' × 'Maria Callas'
Repeat flowering
Fragrant

'Friesia' Cluster-flowered
KORresia
'Sunprite'

By whichever name you know it, this is one of the outstanding yellow roses anywhere, its color clear and almost unfading, its flowers neatly formed, carried in large, well-spaced clusters, and fragrant too. It might have been nice if the young leaves had a tint of bronze, but they are unusually healthy, dark green and shiny. It was introduced by Reimer Kordes in 1977. Friesia (Friesland) is a province of the Low Countries, famous for dairying. This was one of the first roses to be given a 'codename', and the RNRS in Britain insists on using it. 'Sunprite', the American name, is most apt.

Unnamed seedling × 'Spanish Sun'
Repeat flowering
Fragrant

'Fritz Nobis' Modern Shrub

Raised by Wilhelm Kordes in 1940, 'Fritz Nobis' grows about 2 metres (6 feet) tall and wide, with broad dark green foliage (and plenty of it) and, in summer, large tender pink flowers open deliciously fragrant from shapely buds. Every twig seems to bloom. The effect is as flowery as any shrub you could think of. As a bonus, there are fat dark red hips, which last well into the late autumn, or fall.

'Joanna Hill' × 'Magnifica'
Summer flowering
Fragrant

'Frontier Twirl' Modern Shrub

This Griffith Buck rose is very much in the Large-flowered Rose mould, and is indeed sometimes classed as such. It is certainly not a very large Modern Shrub, for all its bushiness and disease resistance. The flowers are exceptional, blending coral-orange and gold, nicely shapely, and fragrant as well. The foliage is bronze in youth, maturing deep green and glossy. It was introduced in 1984.

'La Sevillana' × 'Just Joey'
Repeat flowering
Fragrant

▲ 'Fritz Nobis'
▼ 'Frühlingsanfang'

'Frühlingsanfang' Modern Shrub
'Spring's Awakening'

About fifty years ago, Wilhelm Kordes created a series of roses from forms of *Rosa pimpinellifolia* and various Large-flowered Roses, giving them names celebrating the spring (*frühling*)—and appropriately too, as they are all very early in their flowering. 'Frühlingsanfang' is a *very* large, luxuriant shrub—expect it to touch 3 metres (10 feet) in width and be very nearly as tall—with soft green leaves and showers of single flowers, off-white and slightly scented; maroon hips follow. Plant the rose where it can preside over a wild part of the garden.

'Joanna Hill' × *R. pimpinellifolia* 'Grandiflora'
Summer flowering

◄ 'Frontier Twirl'

'Frühlingsgold' — Modern Shrub
'Spring Gold'

The soft yellow flowers of 'Frühlingsgold' are seen everywhere in Germany—in gardens, in parks, even in those little spaces for planting that turn up in the centres of cities. This is a tribute to the beauty of this 1937 Kordes creation; few late spring shrubs are more beautiful or fragrant. It is also a tribute to its toughness and ability to flourish with minimal care. It is an arching shrub to about 2.5 metres (8 feet), elegant even in its spininess. After the spring flowering there will be later blooms if the season is kind. Foliage is light green.

'Joanna Hill' × *Rosa pimpinellifolia* 'Hispida'
Spring flowering
Fragrant

▲ 'Frühlingsgold'
▼ 'Frühlingsmorgen'

'Frühlingsmorgen' — Modern Shrub
'Spring Morning'

The elegance of growth of 'Frühlingsgold' is attenuated into gawkiness in 'Frühlingsmorgen'; you really need to plant a few together in a clump. Then the branches will interlace, and, among bluish green foliage, bear clusters of some of the loveliest single roses of all, their pink melting to primrose around the maroon stamens. They are fragrant, with an odd medicine-chest kind of scent. Although this 1941 Kordes creation is usually credited with being repeat-flowering, do not expect more than a very few autumn, or fall, flowers. There will be hips, though.

('E. G. Hill' × 'Katherine Kordes') × *Rosa pimpinellifolia* 'Grandiflora'
Spring flowering
Fragrant

'Frühlingszauber' — Modern Shrub
'Spring Magic'

This 1942 Kordes creation comes from the same cross as 'Frühlingsmorgen', but has never achieved the popularity of its sister. It is not as good a plant, being very spindly and leggy, and the semi-double flowers lack the elegance of the single ones of 'Frühlingsmorgen'. They are bright and cheerful in cerise-pink and yellow, and make a splash of color in spring with a few hips to follow later. Foliage is dark green.

('E. G. Hill' × 'Katherine Kordes') × *Rosa pimpinellifolia* 'Grandiflora'
Spring flowering
Fragrant

'Fruité' — Cluster-flowered
MEIfructoz
'Fruitee'

A Meilland introduction of 1985, 'Fruité' brings fruit-salad colors to the low-growing Cluster-flowered Roses. The flowers combine brilliance with subtlety, starting out yellow and gradually becoming flushed with salmon and brick-red, in pleasing contrast to the glossy green leaves. It may not have topped the international hit parade, but it is well thought of in Australia, and it looked stunning in Japan where it was photographed. Little scent, alas.

Parentage undisclosed
Repeat flowering

▲ 'Fruité'
◀ 'Frühlingszauber'
▼ 'Fugue'

'Fugue' — Large-flowered Climber
MEItam

Alain Meilland raised quite a few roses with musical names. There were the Large-flowered Roses 'Symphonie' and 'Allegro', the Cluster-flowered Roses 'Concerto' and 'Sarabande', the Miniature 'Minuetto', and 'Fugue', introduced in 1958 and one of the best dark red Large-flowered Climbers in warm climates, where it grows strongly. The mid-sized flowers, in sprays of five to eight, are borne in a great mass in spring and then intermittently. One hears mutterings about mildew and poor color from cold areas. Foliage is dark green and glossy. 'Fugue' has much of the velvety color of 'Guinée', but, alas, little of its fragrance.

'Alain' × 'Guinée'
Repeat flowering

'Futura'
Large-flowered

'Futura' has a big, bold flower in fashionable orange, scented and carried on a sturdy bush with light green glossy leaves. Bill Warriner raised it and introduced it in 1975.

Unnamed seedling × unnamed seedling
Repeat flowering
Fragrant

▲ 'Futura'
▼ 'Fyvie Castle'

► 'Gabriella'

'Fyvie Castle'
Large-flowered

COCkamber
'Amberlight'

Do not confuse the LeGrice Cluster-flowered Rose 'Amberlight' of 1962 with this 1985 creation from Alec Cocker of Aberdeen. 'Fyvie Castle' has a real fruit salad blend of pastel colors—apricot, amber, pale pink and gold—in its large, well-formed, fragrant blooms of thirty-five petals. As befits such a blend of colors the rose has a very mixed parentage. It has a neat, compact habit of growth, glossy green foliage and really good resistance to disease. Its awards include the Gold Star of the Pacific in New Zealand and

the Silver Plate at Baden-Baden. The notable Renaissance pile of Fyvie Castle stands near the Cocker nursery.

('Sunblest' × ['Sabine' × Dr A. J. Verhage']) × 'Silver Jubilee'
Repeat flowering
Fragrant

'Gabriella'
Cluster-flowered

BERgme

You are much more likely to see this dark orange-red rose in the florist's shop than in the garden, for it is not a very good garden rose. It is an outstanding grower in the florist's greenhouse, and one of the world's leading varieties for that purpose. Borne on long, thin stems (the small clusters are usually disbudded), the flowers can last two weeks in water. Like most such roses they are quite without perfume. Foliage is a leathery olive-green. A sport of 'Mercedes', it was discovered by Lars Berggren, a Swedish cut-rose grower, and introduced by Kordes in 1977.

Sport from 'Mercedes'
Repeat flowering

'Gallant'
Cluster-flowered

When 'Gallant' came out in 1968, it was praised for its shapely orange-red flowers, its disease resistance, its abundant flowering, as well as its moderate fragrance, but it appears to have since dropped out of sight! Perhaps it just is not distinctive enough to stand out in the crowd of orange-red roses that compete for admiration (and sales) in the catalogues. Foliage is pale green and glossy. It was raised by Dickson's.

'Super Star' × 'Barbeque'
Repeat flowering
Fragrant

'Gallivarda'
Large-flowered

Although this extraordinary Large-flowered Rose is officially described as 'red with yellow reverse', it looks more like a preview of the brown and ochre colors of more recent years. A Reimer Kordes creation, it was introduced in 1977. The buds of 'Gallivarda' are long and pointed, unfurling to high-centred blooms, to 10 centimetres (4 inches), with thirty-four petals. The bush is vigorous and upright with masses of glossy green foliage.

'Königin der Rosen' × 'Vienna Charm'
Repeat flowering

'Garden Party'
Large-flowered

Now here is a worthy descendant of 'Peace'! Long buds open to huge flared blossoms of twenty-eight petals in ivory and palest pink—the 'Peace' colors but more delicate. Fragrance is surprisingly strong, the grey-green foliage the perfect complement. A well deserved AARS award in 1960 was accompanied by a gold medal in Paris.

'Charlotte Armstrong' × 'Peace'
Repeat flowering
Fragrant

▲ 'Gallivarda'
▼ 'Gallant'

▲ 'Gärtendirektor Otto Linne'
◄ 'Garden Party'
▼ 'Gärtenzauber 84'

'Garnette' Cluster-flowered

There is a whole group of popular cut-flower roses called 'Garnette Roses'—'Pink Garnette', 'Golden Garnette', 'Deep Pink Garnette' and so on—but the original 'Garnette' is a dull red Cluster-flowered Rose introduced by Mathias Tantau in 1951. Florists planted it by the millions in their greenhouses, for as a cut flower it is practically indestructible. It can be grown out of doors in a hot climate, though it will need constant spraying for mildew—leave it to the florists. Most of the tribe are completely scentless. Foliage is dark green and dull.

('Rosenelfe' × 'Eva') × 'Heros'
Repeat flowering

▲ 'Garnette'

'Gärtendirektor Otto Linne' Modern Shrub

'Otto Linne'

Despite its cumbersomely Germanic name, this 1934 Modern Shrub Rose from Peter Lambert (of 'Frau Karl Druschki' fame) has had a recent revival in America. It deserves it, too, with its compact habit, handsome leathery green leaves and constant production of big sprays of deep pink pompoms. It is a little like a double-flowered version of 'Ballerina'. Which you choose depends on whether you like double or single flowers. Alas, there is not much scent.

'Robin Hood' × 'Rudolph Kluis'
Repeat flowering

'Gärtenzauber 84' Cluster-flowered

KORnacho

Gärtenzauber translates as 'garden magic'. It is a catchy name, and you can understand why Reimer Kordes decided to reuse it for this 1984 introduction when sales of the original 'Gärtenzauber', another red Cluster-flowered Rose raised by his father Wilhelm in the late 1950s, fell off. The current version is the sort of rose that sells very well in Germany to park superintendents; it is a tallish bush, easy to grow and making a splash of bright color without too much attention. Foliage is dark green and glossy. Never mind that the individual flowers are scentless and rather ordinary.

(Unnamed seedling × 'Tornado') × 'Chorus'
Repeat flowering

'Gay Princess'
Cluster-flowered

This rose won the AARS award in 1967 and it really is first-rate. It is strong, healthy and lavish with its shell-pink flowers even in the hottest, muggiest weather. They are excellent for cutting, holding their perfect form for days, their delicate color showing very well in artificial light, their fragrance less

elusive than in the garden. Raised by Eugene Boerner it can be called a Large-flowered Rose or a Cluster-flowered Rose at your pleasure; the flowers are quite large, the clusters small. Foliage is dark green and leathery.

'Spartan' × 'The Farmer's Wife'
Repeat flowering
Fragrant

'Geisha'
Cluster-flowered
'Pink Elizabeth Arden'

One of the loveliest of pink roses, with a soft color set off by dark stamens and darkish green, matt foliage, its delicate fragrance, its large perfectly spaced clusters, and its reliable growth, 'Geisha' has never been as popular as it deserves to be. When Mathias Tantau introduced it in 1964, he wanted to call it 'Elizabeth Arden', but there was already a white Large-flowered Rose of that name. 'Pink Elizabeth Arden' was not really apt, as the two roses do not resemble each other at all, so 'Geisha' it became. Then Sam McGredy introduced a yellow rose 'Geisha Girl' in that same year, and the now thoroughly confused public reacted by not buying either!

Parentage undisclosed
Repeat flowering
Fragrant

'Gene Boerner'
Cluster-flowered

This 1969 AARS winner was named by Jackson & Perkins in memory of their Director of Research, the raiser of so

many beautiful roses, who died in 1966. Mid-pink, it rather resembles 'Queen Elizabeth' in color and in being a tall, sturdy bush, though the flowers are somewhat shapelier. It is generally regarded as being not quite as good; the old flowers are apt to go spotty, and it is not nearly as robust and indestructible a plant. Yet, for all the odiousness of the comparison, 'Gene Boerner' is a good rose, and gives a long-lasting cut flower. Foliage is a glossy mid-green. Fragrance is only light. It was introduced in 1968.

'Ginger' × ('Ma Perkins × 'Garnette Supreme')
Repeat flowering

▲ 'Gene Boerner'
◄ 'Gay Princess'
▼ 'Geisha'

'Général Galliéni'   Tea

The American Rose Society classes the color of 'Géneral Galliéni' as a 'red blend', which is very apt, as it is not a straight red but a blend of salmon, red and cream. Usually the red swamps the other colors, but in cool weather the effect is a mixture of apricot and red. The buds are shapely, the open flowers less so; they are fragrant, and in a frost-free climate appear all year. Foliage is olive-green. In life, the general was the first French Governor-General of Madagascar; his rose was raised by Gilbert Nabonnand and introduced in 1899.

'Souvenir de Thérèse Levet' × 'Reine Emma des Pays-Bas'
Repeat flowering
Fragrant

▼ 'Général Galliéni'

'Général Jacqueminot'   Hybrid Perpetual

'General Jack', 'The Jack Rose', 'Richard Smith', 'La Brillante', 'Mrs Cleveland', 'Triomphe d'Amiens'

'Général Jacqueminot' is one of the all-time great studs of the rose world: just about every red rose we have, and many of the others, trace back to it. I wonder if M. Jacqueminot himself, a veteran of Napoleon's wars and an old man by the time his rose came out in 1858, had so large a progeny? 'General Jack' is still worth growing: it makes a tall, slightly leggy bush, flowering freely in spring and repeating well if it is fed and watered, but watch out for mildew. Foliage is a glossy, rich mid-green. There is some dispute whether the credit for its raising goes to a M. Roussel or his gardener, M. Rousselet, and just what its parents were.

Probably 'Gloire des Rosomanes' × unknown
Repeat flowering
Fragrant

'Général Schablikine'   Tea

'Général Schablikine' has always enjoyed a reputation for being a reliable Tea for cool climates. It certainly is a vigorous, free-flowering rose, but even in its heyday (it came out in 1878) it was looked down on by the flower-show fanatics for the quartered form that disqualifies it from the show bench. The coral-red blooms are borne in abundance on stronger stems than are usual among the Teas. It is not very fragrant. The foliage is a glossy dark green. General Schablikine was presumably a hero of the Crimean War, and had achieved elder statesman status by the time Gilbert Nabonnand named the rose.

Parentage unknown
Repeat flowering

▲ 'Général Jacqueminot'
▼ 'Général Schablikine'

THE ROSE IN THE SOUTHERN HEMISPHERE

There are no wild roses native to the southern hemisphere; they arrived with European settlement. In Australia, the date is fixed precisely at 1788. The First Fleet brought with it plants for the new colony at Botany Bay and while the emphasis, naturally enough, was on fruit trees and vegetables, a rosebush or two found their way aboard also. These would have been picked up on the way, at the nurseries in Cape Town; roses had been flourishing at the Cape for a couple of centuries, and South African gardeners prided themselves then, as they still do, on having only the best and most up-to-date varieties.

While the problems of establishing a new home in a very strange land were great, the settlers, or more likely their wives, for the flower garden was very much the lady's department, passed cuttings around, which quickly took root and flourished in the virgin soil and mild climate. 'Nature is so kind in New South Wales,' wrote one visitor, 'that you have only to tickle her with a hoe and she laughs with a harvest,' and the colonists delighted in the profusion of flowers which at home were cosseted conservatory plants for the rich: geraniums, fuchsias and the Banksian Rose, which flourished so mightily that the erroneous belief grew up that this plant was native to Australia. (Incidentally, Australia's 'native rose' is not a rose but *Boronia serrulata*, a distant cousin of the orange.)

The commonest roses in New South Wales appear to have been the China Roses, which flower all year on the east coast of Australia. The two most common were the small crimson one still locally known as 'Lady Brisbane', after the wife of an early governor, and the 'common monthly rose', 'Old Blush', said to have been introduced by the father of the wool industry, John Macarthur. It still grows at his old homestead, Elizabeth Farm, near Sydney.

The story in New Zealand is the same, favorite roses being brought out by the pioneers and then passed around between friends. As in Australia, it was not long before prosperity created openings for nurserymen willing to take the trouble to import the newest varieties, a cumbersome business in the days before air transport or even speedy and reliable steamships. No doubt colonial rose-lovers awaited the latest novelties from Europe eagerly, as they do now, for several nurserymen imported them, and it did not take long for a meritorious new rose to establish itself in Australian and New Zealand gardens. 'Cloth of Gold', 'General Jacqueminot', 'La France' and 'Catherine Mermet' are the familiar roses of the nineteenth century.

For a long time, the traffic in roses was one way, from north to south. Then, the climbing sport of 'Souvenir de la Malmaison', for many years more popular than the original bush, was discovered in a Sydney garden in 1893 and sent in triumph to Europe. It was not until early in the twentieth century, however, when Alister Clark began hybridizing, that roses of any significance were raised in Australia.

Famous too for his daffodils, then a rather new field for the plant breeder, Clark lived in Victoria, a little outside Melbourne. He raised conventional Large-flowered Roses aplenty, among them the still-excellent 'Sunny South' of 1919, but he is best remembered for his first and second generation hybrids of the Burmese Tea Rose, *Rosa gigantea*. The best known are 'Nancy Hayward' and 'Lorraine Lee', indispensable items of furnishing

◄ *An old cottage near Cooma in the Australian Alps is completely smothered in roses, which flourish despite the cold, dry climate.*

▲ *It is often said that roses grow better in New Zealand than anywhere else in the world. These, in an Auckland front garden, uphold the reputation of their country.*

▼ The rose garden at the Botanic Gardens of Adelaide has always been thought of as one of the most attractive in Australia. It is of a kind popular in the mid-nineteenth century but rarely seen today: an oval space, focused on a central fountain and surrounded by a pergola on which climbing roses grow. The roses themselves are replanted every few years to keep the collection up to date, but the layout has changed little in a hundred years.

in any Australian garden for over forty years, for the generosity with which they will bear their warm-colored flowers right through the winter. Alas, they have inherited their progenitor's dislike of cold, but where winters are mild they are unique. They would be sensational in California.

Other Aussie rose-lovers tried their hand at hybridizing too, with pleasing results: Patrick Grant in the 1920s ('Golden Dawn') and Frank Reithmuller in the 1950s ('Titian', 'Carabella'); More recently, Pat Stevens of New Zealand has tried his hand too ('Big Purple').

The 'Down Under' market is not a very big one, and it has been more profitable for rose-growers to import their new roses. At least it had until 1972, when Sam McGredy, fed up with the undeclared civil war in Northern Ireland, shifted his business, lock, stock and barrel, to New Zealand. Now some of the finest of new roses are coming from the southern hemisphere.

Some years ago, two South African Large-flowered Roses made a bit of a splash: the red 'Salvo' and the pink blend 'Rina Herholdt', named for the raiser's wife. There has been little since; South Africa's political isolation cannot have helped her rosarians to make their mark on the world. Yet they are many, and there are active rose societies and fine rose gardens there. Let us hope that soon the rest of the world will recognise them better.

Indeed, all over the hemisphere, in South Africa, in South America, in Australasia, there are rose-lovers and roses. The New Zealanders boast that the rose grows better for them than anyone (and they may just be right!) and the Australians that they grow the biggest roses. This may be shades of old colonial 'skiting', or perhaps just embarrassment that there are no wild roses, but, truly, the rose knows no such competitiveness. Whether she blooms in June or at Christmas, whether she asks her devotees to sharpen their secateurs in January or July, the beauty of the rose is just the same.

Like the emigrants whose homesickness she assuaged, she has come to stay.

◀ Alister Clark was a property-owner in what was then rural Victoria and is now part of the outskirts of Melbourne. Clark was famous for his daffodils as well as his roses. 'Mabel Taylor', with its pale pink trumpet, is one of his that is still popular.

◀ This is Alister Clark's 'Lorraine Lee'. For many years it was Australia's favorite rose. It is said that the raiser, to demonstrate its ability to flower all year, exhibited blooms cut from the same plant every month for twenty months. Alas, its warm color and soft scent have rarely been seen overseas, as it is very sensitive to cold.

▲ 'Queen Elizabeth' is a favorite in the Republic of South Africa, and indeed it is everywhere. Here its clear pink sets off the elegant Cape Dutch house of leading garden writer Una van der Spuy.

'Georg Arends' — Hybrid Perpetual

A leading catalogue once suggested that if you bought this rose you should rename it after the prettiest lady of your acquaintance. One must protest: firstly, there is enough confusion from renaming already, and secondly, why not name a rose for a man? Especially when he was one of the leading German nurserymen of his day. 'Georg Arends' is one of the loveliest of pink roses, blending the qualities of famous parents. The bush is tall and sturdy, the flowers shapely, delicately colored, large and fragrant. Foliage is a leathery mid-green. It was raised by a Herr Hinner in 1910.

'Frau Karl Druschki' × 'La France'
Repeat flowering
Fragrant

▲ 'Georg Arends'
► 'Georgetown Noisette'
▼ 'Georges Vibert'

'Georges Vibert' — Gallica

The ruffled flowers are small but very prettily striped in assorted shades of pink and mauve, and they are fragrant too. The bush is compact and upright, with the typical Gallica leaves, but perhaps more thorns than usual for the group. Georges Vibert was presumably a member of the family of J.-P. Vibert, the rose-breeder of Angers. It was very gracious of M. Robert, as a rival, to dedicate this rose to him—but perhaps the two families were connected by marriage. The year was 1853.

Parentage unknown
Spring flowering
Fragrant

'Georgetown Noisette' — Noisette

This rose apparently came to the Huntington collection from Georgetown in the District of Columbia. 'Georgetown Noisette' is only a provisional name. It looks very pretty in its peachy tone, with its ruffled flowers, and it also has fragrance. Foliage is a glossy green. Like most of its class, it is a Climber, though rather a modest one. Whatever its real ancient name might be, why not adopt 'Georgetown Noisette' officially?

Parentage unknown
Repeat flowering
Fragrant

'Geraldine' — Cluster-flowered
PEAhaze

'Orange' is a much abused word in the rosarian's lexicon, having been pressed into duty to describe roses whose red petals are even the slightest bit on the scarlet side of crimson. 'Geraldine' is 'true' orange blended with lemon. The flowers are shapely, carried on a compact, lush-leafed bush, and last well in the vase. It was raised by the Devon rosarian Colin Pearce, named for his wife and introduced in 1984.

Unnamed seedling × unnamed seedling
Repeat flowering

▲ 'Geraldine'
▼ 'Geranium'

'Geranium' — Modern Shrub

'Geranium' could have been placed with the Wild Roses, as it is not a hybrid but a selected form of *Rosa moyesii*, but it has to be propagated like any garden rose from budding or cuttings to retain its character. Selected at the Royal Horticultural Society's garden at Wisley in 1938, it is probably the best of several named forms of *R. moyesii* for the average garden; it is much less gawky in habit; its hips are just magnificent; and the flowers are a fine bright red, though rather lighter and less vinous than the wild species itself. It is still a big shrub: expect it to grow to 2 metres (6 feet) high and wide. It has dainty, medium green, dull foliage.

Selected form of *R. moyesii*
Spring flowering

'Geranium Red' Cluster-flowered

With its multitude of petals, ruffled and quartered, 'Geranium Red' is reminiscent of an Old Garden Rose. In modern dress, though, for the color is an intense deep orange-red, brilliant without being strident, and becoming darker with age. Foliage is a dark, leathery olive-green, tinted red when young. Few catalogues list it nowadays (though it can be found) and it is well worth seeking out for its unusual beauty and its intense, spicy fragrance. It will repay the best of care. Raised by Eugene Boerner in 1947 it is important historically, for it was the parent of 'Spartan', and through it has transmitted fragrance and compact habit to many of the most desirable of today's Cluster-flowered Roses.

'Crimson Glory' × unnamed seedling
Repeat flowering
Fragrant

▲ 'Geranium Red'
▼ 'Gertrude Jekyll'

'Gertrud Schweitzer' Large-flowered

This large and fragrant rose, of a rare apricot-orange tint, was unveiled in Germany by the team of Reimer Kordes and the Horstmann family. 'Gertrud Schweitzer' has long buds which open to large flowers against dark green foliage. It grows very well in New Zealand, where it was photographed in the beautiful Christchurch gardens at Mona Vale.

'Königin der Rosen' × unnamed seedling
Repeat flowering
Fragrant

▲ 'Gertrud Schweitzer'
▶ 'Gina'
▼ 'Ghislaine de Féligonde'

'Gertrude Jekyll' English Rose
AUSbord

'Gertrude Jekyll' is one of the largest flowered of the David Austin 'English Roses', its deep shocking pink blooms as large as any old Hybrid Perpetual. It is powerfully fragrant too. The bush is upright, to about 1.5 metres (5 feet), with mid-green leaves. It does repeat its bloom, but will benefit from encouragement to do so. It was introduced in 1986. Miss Jekyll was one of the most influential figures in English gardening in the twentieth century, and a lover of Old Garden Roses.

'The Wife of Bath' × 'Comte de Chambord'
Repeat flowering
Fragrant

'Ghislaine de Féligonde' Large Rambler

Pronounce the lady's name as 'Elaine de Féligonde' and you have got over the main obstacle to the revival of this rose, its awkward Flemish name. It is rarely seen these days, but it is one of the most charming Ramblers, with the added bonus that it sometimes bears a second crop of flowers. The fat little buds are quite a strong yellow, but they open to the palest cream with pink tints. Foliage is a glossy green and resistant to mildew. It was raised by the French firm of E. Turbat et Cie and introduced in 1916. 'Ghislaine de Féligonde' is of fairly restrained vigor.

'Goldfinch' × unknown
Repeat flowering

'Gina' Cluster-flowered

While this is primarily a greenhouse cutting rose, it gives quite a good account of itself in the garden. The bushes, with dark green foliage, are well adorned with blood-red blooms in small clusters. They hold their color exceptionally well, but they tend to be rather small outside the greenhouse, and there is no scent to speak of. It is pretty, but perhaps it is best left to the cut flower growers; there are so many fine red garden roses. It was introduced by Reimer Kordes in 1989.

Parentage undisclosed
Repeat flowering

'Ginger Rogers'
Large-flowered

'Salmon Charm'

Apart from Fred Astaire, the only thing missing from this rose is any suggestion of ginger color; despite its official description of 'orange blend' it is in fact a rather blowsy salmon-pink from edge to edge. However, it was not named for its color, but to commemorate Miss Rogers's appearance on the London stage in 1969. Raised by Sam McGredy, it is a tall grower with light green foliage and large thirty-petalled flowers with, yes, a touch of ginger in the fragrance.

'Super Star' × 'Miss Ireland'
Repeat flowering
Fragrant

▲ 'Ginger Rogers'
▼ 'Gingersnap'

'Gingersnap'
Cluster-flowered

'Apricot Prince', 'Prince Abricot'

'Apricot Queen' won the AARS award in 1940, 'Apricot Nectar' in 1965. In 1978, it was the turn of 'Apricot Prince', a creation of Delbards, the French raisers. The two earlier winners are roses of delicate coloring, whereas the new one is brilliant in orange and gold. Perhaps it was to emphasise this difference that Armstrong Nurseries decided to rechristen it 'Gingersnap'. It is a successful rose in warm climates, less so in muggy ones, at its best making a vigorous upright bush bearing many clusters of 10 centimetre (4 inch), lightly fragrant flowers. It has glossy dark green foliage.

('Zambra' × ['Orange Triumph' × 'Floradora']) × ('Jean de la Lune' × ['Spartan' × 'Mandrina'])
Repeat flowering

'Givenchy'
Large-flowered

AROdousna

'Paris Pink'

In the garden, 'Givenchy' is a deep cyclamen pink, lighter on the reverse. Indoors, it opens paler, with the deeper color around the edge. Like its parent 'Double Delight', it needs the sun on its petals for the strong color to develop. The blooms are large, full-petalled and fragrant, borne on an upright, bushy plant with dark green foliage. Raised by Jack Christensen, it was introduced by Armstrong Nurseries in 1985. Hubert de Givenchy is one of Paris's leading couturiers and makers of perfume.

'Gingersnap' × 'Double Delight'
Repeat flowering
Fragrant

'Glenara'
Large-flowered Climber

This 1951 Australian creation must have been a particular favorite of Alister Clark's, for he named it after his Victorian home, 'Glenara'. It is a charming rose, its flowers large and loosely shapely from long buds, in a pleasing shade of rose-pink. They are

▲ 'Glenara'
▶ 'Glenfiddich'
▼ 'Givenchy'

borne freely in early summer, with the odd flower to follow up. Growth is moderate, and it is traditionally grown on a pillar. Foliage is dark green, leathery and large.

Parentage unknown
Repeat flowering

'Glenfiddich'
Cluster-flowered

Deep old gold to amber—the color of a fine malt whisky in fact—'Glenfiddich' bears smallish clusters of shapely 10 centimetre (4 inch) blooms on an upright plant with glossy green leaves. The color makes it very popular, but, despite its sensitivity to severe frosts, it looks its best in cool climates. Hot sun bleaches the flowers to a rather ordinary lemon-yellow. It is a child of the Scotch whisky country, being a creation of Alex Cocker of Aberdeen, who introduced it in 1978.

'Arthur Bell' × ('Circus' × 'Sabine')
Repeat flowering
Fragrant

'Gloire de Chédane Guinnoisseau'
Hybrid Perpetual

The extraordinary mouthful of a name becomes a bit more comprehensible when you learn that the raisers were Messrs Chédane & Pajotin and that there was also a rose-growing family called Guinnoisseau. At a guess, this 1907 'Gloire de Ducher' seedling celebrates a marriage in the family or, less romantically, a business partnership. It is a handsome rose, crimson, shapely and sweetly fragrant. It is not generous with its repeat flowering and its long shoots are best pegged down. It has broad, dull, dark green foliage. Mind the mildew. In its day, it was a leading exhibition rose.

Parentage unknown
Repeat flowering
Fragrant

'Gloire de Dijon'
Noisette
'Old Glory'

In its Victorian heyday, 'Gloire de Dijon' was regarded as the very best of all Climbing Roses, growing with abandon even in light shade. But alas, its vigor has declined, and it can some-

▲ 'Gloire de Dijon'

times be difficult to establish now. Give it the very best of everything, for the flowers are marvellous—great quartered cabbages in soft buff-yellow with tints of mustard and apricot, and richly fragrant. They are borne throughout the season, on strong stems for cutting. It has broad, mid-green, semi-glossy foliage. It was raised by Jacotot of Dijon and introduced in 1853.

Unknown Tea Rose × 'Souvenir de la Malmaison'
Repeat flowering
Fragrant

▲ 'Gloire de Guilan'
◄ 'Gloire de Chédane Guinnoisseau'

'Gloire de Guilan'
Damask

The formal date of introduction is 1949, but this is in fact an ancient rose, brought from Persia in the years between the two world wars by the English garden writer, Nancy Lindsay. She tells us that in Persia it is used for the making of Attar of Roses, and we can well believe it, for the flowers are quite exceptionally fragrant. They are a lovely clear shade of pink, cupped when young but opening flat. They are borne in profusion over foliage which Miss Lindsay describes most aptly as 'mint-green'. 'Gloire de Guilan' is rather sprawling in habit.

Parentage unknown
Summer flowering
Fragrant

'Gloire des Mousseux'
Moss
'Madame Alboni'

The 'Glory of the Mosses' in truth! 'Gloire des Mousseux' has the largest flowers among the mosses—as large as many of the Large-flowered Roses. They open from beautifully mossed buds to clear pink flowers, fading a

little but holding their rich fragrance. The bush is erect, tallish, and well clad with pale green leaves. It was raised by M. Laffay of Bellevue in 1852.

Parentage unknown
Summer flowering
Fragrant

▲ 'Gloire des Mousseux'
▼ 'Gloire des Rosomanes'

'Gloire des Rosomanes'
Bourbon
'Ragged Robin'

Credited to J.-P. Vibert, the official date being 1825, 'Gloire des Rosomanes' is one of the earliest Bourbon Roses, and lurks unsuspected in many American gardens, where it has been used as an understock. It is recommended sometimes as a good rose for hedging, a job that it does well in warm climates like California, though perhaps the tall plants are not quite bushy enough. They do make a bright show of crimson for most of the rose season, and there is some fragrance. *Rosomane* is one of those French words that does not quite translate into English—it means someone crazy about roses.

Parentage unknown
Repeat flowering

'Glory of Edzell' *Modern Shrub*

'Glory of Edzell' is usually classed as a Scotch Rose (*Rosa pimpinellifolia*) but whereas most of the Scotch Roses make compact, even dwarf bushes, this one will happily grow more than head high. It wreathes its spiny branches in spring with single, clear pink flowers; a few dark hips follow in autumn or fall. Foliage is ferny and matt green. Its vigor suggests it might be a hybrid, but with what no one knows. Indeed, none of the authorities admits to knowing much about this pretty rose.

Parentage unknown
Spring flowering
Fragrant

▲ 'Glory of Edzell'
▼ 'Godfrey Winn'

'Godfrey Winn' *Large-flowered*
'Milas de Fortecruiba'

Originally (in 1968) the Spanish raiser Pedro Dot had named this rose 'Milas de Fortecruiba' to honor a Spanish celebrity, and it may not have ever bloomed outside of Spain if it had not been for the well-developed sense of hype of bewhiskered English rosarian Harry Wheatcroft, who snapped up the rights to it and enlisted the enthusiasm of the British radio personality Godfrey Winn. Alas, for all that, the globular, very fragrant mauve blooms are not much heard of these days—like their namesake. Foliage is dark green and quite leathery.

Parentage undisclosed
Repeat flowering
Fragrant

'Gold Badge' *Cluster-flowered*
MEIgronuri
'Gold Bunny'

Most of the world calls it 'Gold Bunny', but the United States name 'Gold Badge' is the officially registered name (unless one uses the unpronounceable codename). However you call it, it is an excellent rose, the flowers fairly large—up to 8 centimetres (3 inches) across—the clear lemon yellow color untinted and unfading, and the fairly low-growing bush very free with its blooms. Foliage is dark green and glossy. It is best in a warm climate; it does not seem to have found the high favor in foggy Britain (where it is accused of susceptibility to black spot) that it has found elsewhere. It is a Meil-land introduction of 1978.

'Rusticana' × ('Charleston' × 'Allgold')
Repeat flowering

▲ 'Gold Badge'
▼ 'Gold Medal'

'Gold Medal' *Large-flowered*
AROyequeli

This superb example of growing gold came to us from Jack Christensen and Armstrong Nurseries in 1982. The deep golden yellow is alloyed with copper at the centre of the flower, which opens flat from the pointed buds. The light fragrance reminds one distinctly of tea; growth is tall and bushy; and the foliage is a glossy green. It is a very fine rose for warm climates.

'Yellow Pages' × ('Granada' × 'Garden Party')
Repeat flowering
Fragrant

'Gold Star'
Large-flowered

CANdide
'Point de Jours'

'Gold Star' is a beautiful rose, with large shapely blooms in deep yellow, and broad, olive-green foliage. Its only fault appears to be rather mediocre fragrance. It can be used as a stunning standard rose.

'Yellow Pages' × 'Dr A. J. Verhage'
Repeat flowering

▲ 'Golden Dawn'

'Golden Chersonese'
Modern Shrub

E. F. Allen, the RNRS's scientific advisor, must have been delighted in 1963 when he saw 'Golden Chersonese' flower in his Suffolk garden, for it showed that he had realised his aim of combining the ferny daintiness and dazzling yellow of the temperamental *Rosa ecae* with the larger flowers, more graceful growth, and better temper of 'Canary Bird'. In its spring season, no flowering shrub is more gorgeous or fragrant, and it is more than presentable later despite there being no hips. Foliage is ferny and dark green. Chersonese was the Greek name for the place now known better as Gallipoli. The Golden Chersonese was apparently a legendary place of wealth and beauty.

R. ecae × 'Canary Bird'
Spring flowering
Fragrant

'Golden Dawn'
Large-flowered

'Golden' is hardly the word: the full-petalled flowers of 'Golden Dawn' are in fact a soft, pale yellow, sometimes blushed with pink on the outer petals. They are very nicely scented and carried on a bushy plant which is not too tall. The leaves are a distinctive greyish green. Sometimes the early flowers are spoilt by split centres, but usually the blooms are as large and shapely as anyone could desire. For many years one of the leading yellow roses in Europe (until 'Peace' came along to steal its thunder), 'Golden Dawn' is of Australian origin, raised by Sydney's Patrick Grant and introduced in 1929.

'Elegante' × 'Ethel Somerset'
Repeat flowering
Fragrant

▼ 'Golden Chersonese'

'Golden Dawn, Climbing'
Large-flowered Climber

The original Large-flowered Rose was raised by Patrick Grant of Sydney in 1929. It was very popular all over the world for many years and is still worth growing. The climbing version that appeared a few years later has retained its popularity better in the face of the newer yellows. The large, shapely flowers in pale yellow (they are hardly 'golden') are very beautiful and fragrant. Foliage is greyish green and usually healthy, but do not expect much in the way of an autumn, or fall, display unless you feed and water the plant well after the first blooming.

Sport from 'Golden Dawn'
Repeat flowering
Fragrant

▲ 'Gold Star'
▼ 'Climbing Golden Dawn'

'Golden Days' Large-flowered
RUgold

'Golden Days', developed by the Dutch grower Ghijs de Ruiter, is described in the reference books as deep yellow in color. It was much paler in tone when it was photographed in British Columbia's Butchart Gardens. Yet somehow the 'golden days' of heady youth seem suited to the pale, radiant shade of gold. It is a faintly fragrant rose, with shapely blooms of thirty-five petals, standing out well against the large, medium green leaves.

'Peer Gynt' × unnamed seedling
Repeat flowering

▲ 'Golden Days'
▼ 'Golden Delight'

'Golden Delight' Cluster-flowered

'Golden Delight', though somewhat overshadowed by its sister-seedling 'Allgold', is still one of the best yellow cluster-flowered Roses from the 1950s. It is more full of petals than 'Allgold', but it is a paler color, and not quite so vigorous and easy to grow. It scores over its rival in the fragrance department though, and many rose-lovers prefer it. Foliage is dark green and glossy. It was raised by E. B. LeGrice and introduced in 1956.

'Goldilocks' × 'Ellinor LeGrice'
Repeat flowering
Fragrant

'Golden Giant' Large-flowered
KORbi
'Goldrausch', 'Fièvre d'Or'

Although it was German-raised (by Reimer Kordes in 1960), 'Golden Giant' seems to be most in favor in the warm climates of India and Australia these days. It takes after its pollen parent 'Buccaneer' in being a real giant of a bush, towering over other plants in the rose garden, in its matt green foliage and in its clear, bright yellow flowers. The blooms are large—to 12 centimetres (5 inches) or more—and are moderately fragrant. It won the gold medal of the RNRS in 1960.

('Condesa de Sastago' × 'Walter Bentley') × 'Buccaneer'
Repeat flowering
Fragrant

'Golden Gloves' Cluster-flowered

The Golden Gloves award is one of the highest in amateur boxing, which ought to suggest that 'Golden Gloves' is a pretty hardy sort of rose. It is still too new to say. Bear Creek Nurseries registered it in 1991, but it is only just now finding its way into the catalogues. It looks pretty good: the plant bushy and well clad in bright green leaves, the flowers, in smallish clusters, bright yellow, shapely like small Large-flowered Roses. There is some scent.

('Friesia' × 'Katherine Loker') × 'Gingersnap'
Repeat flowering
Fragrant

▲ 'Golden Gloves'
▼ 'Golden Giant'

'Golden Holstein'
English Rose

KORtickel

'Kordes Rose Golden Holstein'

Back in 1939, Wilhelm Kordes named a red Cluster-flowered Rose 'Holstein' after the province of Germany where he lived. It is appropriate that his son Reimer should bestow the name 'Golden Holstein' on another rose. It has just the same wide open, semi-double flowers, but here they are deep and dazzling yellow, a splendid sight against the dark foliage. For a rose raised in 1989, this is going against the fashion, which calls for small, exhibition form flowers. The big clusters of blooms are a splendid sight, backed up by dark green foliage. This is an easy-to-grow bush. Scent is moderate.

Parentage undisclosed
Repeat flowering

▲ 'Golden Jubilee'
◄ 'Golden Holstein'

'Golden Jewel'
Cluster-flowered

'Goldjuwel', 'Bijou d'Or'

Another yellow Cluster-flowered Rose of the 1950s, well regarded in its day but seldom seen now, 'Golden Jewel' makes a rather tall, spreading bush and it bears globular canary-yellow flowers in rather open clusters. Unfortunately the rich color fades as the flowers open, and there have been some mutterings in recent years about black spot. Foliage is dark green and glossy. There is not much fragrance, and with the arrival of the scented yellow Cluster-flowered Roses in recent years, 'Golden Jewel' has been quietly put aside. It was raised by Mathias Tantau and introduced in 1959.

'Goldilocks' × 'Masquerade'
Repeat flowering

'Golden Jubilee'
Large-flowered

COCagold

You might occasionally come across 'Golden Jubilee', a Large-flowered Rose raised by the American grower Jacobus in 1948, but the current holder of the name, pictured here, is a 1981 introduction from Alec Cocker of Aberdeen, who dedicated it to all long and happily married couples. (The American Rose Society prefers us to use the codename 'COCagold' to save confusion.) It is a handsome, medium yellow bloom of

▲ 'Golden Jewel'
► 'Golden Masterpiece'

twenty-nine or thirty petals, exhaling the fragrance of tea, and set off by glossy green foliage.

'Peer Gynt' × 'Gay Gordons'
Repeat flowering
Fragrant

'Golden Masterpiece'
Large-flowered

Raised by Eugene Boerner and introduced by Jackson & Perkins in 1954, this was one of the most desirable of yellow roses in the 1950s, and has proved an important parent of yellow Large-flowered Roses since. In cool cloudy weather it can indeed be the splendid color you see in the picture, but sunshine brings it out primrose rather than gold. Never mind, the huge

blooms, full of ruffled petals and softly fragrant, are still spectacular. If only the tall, glossy-leafed bush were a little more generous with them. In humid climates you may need to spray against black spot.

'Mandalay' × 'Spek's Yellow'
Repeat flowering
Fragrant

'Golden Ophelia' Large-flowered

In 1912, the English hybridist William Paul selected a chance seedling to bear the name 'Ophelia'. It became one of the most famous roses of all time, and in the Colchester nursery of Benjamin Cant & Sons it added to its lustre by producing, in 1918, 'Golden Ophelia', a seedling not a sport, in pale creamy yellow, deepening at the centre. It was awarded the RNRS gold medal, and became a world favorite, especially with the greenhouse growers. Foliage is a dark glossy green, but there is little of the 'Ophelia' scent.

'Ophelia' × unknown
Repeat flowering

▲ 'Golden Ophelia'
▼ 'Golden Queen'

'Golden Queen' Large-flowered
KORgitte

Bred in Germany (by Reimer Kordes) 'Golden Queen' seems to have found its home away from home in New Zealand, where it was awarded a gold medal in 1984, and has since been stocked by every one of that country's major rose nurseries. Its color is classed in the United States as 'orange blend'. It was photographed in Christchurch in 1990, where it seemed more like an orange and *pink* blend—but then some roses do vary very much in their colors from climate to climate. Foliage is dark green and glossy.

Parentage undisclosed
Repeat flowering

'Golden Showers' Climber

This 1957 AARS winner is one of the most popular of all yellow roses. True, the brilliant daffodil-yellow of the long buds is rather fleeting, and the wide, ruffled blooms are quite pale around their maroon stamens, but they still look stunning on long, almost black stems against the dark, shining green foliage. 'Golden Showers' takes a year or two to settle in and start climbing, and even then it is only of moderate vigor. It always looks the picture of smartness and good health. Raised by Dr Walter Lammerts, it was introduced in 1956.

'Charlotte Armstrong' × 'Captain Thomas'
Repeat flowering

'Golden Slippers' Cluster-flowered

It is surprising how sometimes two raisers in different countries will come up with something quite new at the same time. In the same year, 1961, that Gordon von Abrams in Oregon brought out 'Golden Slippers', Alain Meilland introduced the rather similar 'Zambra'. Both had a new color—clear, pale orange, with lemon on the reverse—both had glossy green foliage, and both were well received ('Golden Slippers' won the AARS award in 1962). Though 'Golden Slippers' still has its admirers, it is 'Zambra' that proved able to transmit its new color to improved descendants and so is better remembered.

'Goldilocks' × unnamed seedling
Repeat flowering
Fragrant

▲ 'Golden Slippers'
▼ 'Golden Showers'

'Golden State'
Large-flowered

One of Francis Meilland's early successes, 'Golden State' won the 1937 gold medal in Portland, where it was photographed fifty-three years later. It seems to have changed color during this time, for it is definitely not deep yellow, as it was described in its youth. It is now almost cream, opening from pink-tinted buds. The foliage is still healthy, a glossy dark green, and the flowers are large and cupped. The 'Golden State' is California; Meilland named this rose with an eye to the American market. Do not confuse this rose with a later rose of the same name.

'Souvenir de Claudius Pernet' ×
'Charles P. Kilham' seedling
Repeat flowering

'Golden Times'
Large-flowered

Kordes's 'Golden Times' (with code-name KORtimes) is one of the current favorites with the growers whose greenhouses supply the florists shops. Introduced in 1976, it is not much of a garden rose. The rose described and pictured here is the prior (and therefore legitimate) holder of the name, a much larger flower raised in 1970 by Alec Cocker and distributed by Wheatcroft Brothers. It has little fragrance, but the forty-petalled blooms can be 12 centimetres (5 inches) wide and stand out against a mass of glossy green foliage.

'Fragrant Cloud' × 'Golden Splendour'
Repeat flowering

'Golden Wings'
Modern Shrub

Any person who writes about the rose will, sooner or later, end up consulting Roy Shepherd's *History of the Rose*; and anyone who loves roses will, sooner or later, end up falling in love with 'Golden Wings', the only one of his

▲ 'Golden State'   ▼ 'Golden Times'

◄ 'Golden Wings'

rose creations still commonly met with. It is one of the most outstanding of all Modern Shrub Roses: continuous in its flowering, delicious in its scent and golden colour, and perfect in its form, though the flowers are not always perfectly single. Sometimes they indulge in an extra petal or two. Foliage is a dark glossy green and the plant is head high, upright and bushy. It was introduced in 1954.

'Roy Ormiston' × 'Soeur Thérèse'
Repeat flowering
Fragrant

'Goldfinch'
Rambler

This was an attempt (by William Paul in 1907) to raise a yellow Rambler. The little fat buds are a rich, deep color, which will hold quite well indoors, but in the sunshine they quickly fade to cream and then to white. The effect is still pleasing, and 'Goldfinch' can be a good choice for a position where a flat white would be too stark. It is sweetly scented, and almost thornless, with glossy green foliage. There is only the one annual burst of flowers.

'Hélèni' × unknown
Summer flowering
Fragrant

'Goldmarie 84' — Cluster-flowered
KORfalt
'Gold Marie'

The original 'Gold Marie' was a deep yellow Cluster-flowered Rose with slight scent, ruffled flowers and the bad habit of becoming blotched with red as the flowers aged. Its 1984 replacement from Reimer Kordes answers the same description, except that the red is simply a flush on the backs of the outside petals, which retain their clear color until they drop. The bush is more compact, the foliage a paler green. The original 'Gold Marie' apparently played no part in the creation of the new one.

(['Arthur Bell' × 'Zorina'] × ['Honeymoon' × 'Dr A. J. Verhage']) × (seedling × 'Friesia')
Repeat flowering

'Grace Darling' — Large-flowered

The heroine of many an English schoolboy was the fifteen-year-old lighthouse-keeper's daughter, Grace Darling, who rescued the passengers from a shipwreck on the English coast. That was in 1838. In 1884, one of those schoolboys, the now grown-up Henry Bennett, paid homage to her with this exquisite cream and pink rose, one of the earlier Large-flowered Roses to win popularity. It still retains it to a remarkable degree—it is seen from Sydney to Vancouver to the Isle of Guernsey (itself the scene of several notable shipwrecks). The bush is medium sized, but very free and continuous in bloom, and the flowers are well scented. The amount of cream and pink in the blend varies considerably. Foliage is bright green.

Parentage unknown
Repeat flowering
Fragrant

▲ 'Grace Darling'
◄ 'Goldfinch'

'Grace de Monaco' — Large-flowered
MEImit

As beautiful as the Hollywood star who became a real-life princess, 'Grace de Monaco' was named by Francis Meilland in 1956 as a wedding present. It bears gorgeous, 'Peace'-like blooms in softest pink, as sweetly perfumed as a star should be. The plant is vigorous though not tall, with glossy green foliage, not always as free from black spot as it might be, and few thorns. Plant it in the company of the later, and equally lovely, 'Princess de Monaco'.

'Peace' × 'Michèle Meilland'
Repeat flowering
Fragrant

◄ 'Goldmarie 84'

'Graceland' — Large-flowered
JACel

Jackson & Perkins' star hybridist, Bill Warriner, knew he had a winner with 'Graceland'. It is described as exceptionally profuse in its flowering, though the bright yellow flowers are quite scentless. It has dark leathery green foliage. 'Graceland' was named after Elvis Presley's home. It was introduced in 1988 and won The Hague gold medal and the AARS award in 1988.

Parentage undisclosed
Repeat flowering

▲ 'Graceland'
▼ 'Grace de Monaco'

▲ 'Graham Thomas'
► 'Granada'

'Graham Thomas'
AUSmas
English Rose

Graham Stuart Thomas has been one of the leading figures in the revival of interest in the Old Garden Roses, on which he is arguably the world's leading authority. He has frequently lamented the rarity of the ochre-yellow of such Old Garden Roses as 'Lady Hillingdon' among the Moderns. It is appropriate that David Austin has dedicated this 1983 English Rose to him, for ochre-yellow is its color. The flowers are like a Bourbon in their cupped formation and fine fragrance. With its bushy growth and continuous bloom it is one of the best of the 'English' series. Foliage is mid-green.

Seedling × ('Charles Austin' × 'Iceberg' seedling)
Repeat flowering
Fragrant

'Granada'
'Donatella'
Large-flowered

Fragrance and beautiful coloring—a blend of red, pink and yellow—are the most striking features of this beautiful rose, winner of the 1964 AARS award and the Gamble Medal for fragrance in 1968. What is not so clear is its aristocratic pedigree. Its mother, 'Tiffany', and its grandmother, 'Charlotte Armstrong', were also AARS winners. Raised by California's Bob Lindquist, 'Granada' is officially classified as a Large-flowered Rose, but should really be thought of as a Cluster-flowered Rose, albeit a large one, as it often blooms several together on long stems. Altogether a gorgeous rose, but watch the mildew in cool climates! Foliage is olive-green and leathery.

'Tiffany' × 'Cavalcade'
Repeat flowering
Fragrant

'Grand Hotel'
Large-flowered Climber

So mixed is the parentage of Modern Garden Roses that the results of a particular cross can be difficult to predict. Sam McGredy, seeking the huge, fire-red flowers of 'Schlössers Brilliant' on a sturdier plant crossed it with the Modern Shrub Rose 'Heidelberg' and got 'Uncle Walter' in 1963. It was so vigorous that it was reclassified as a Modern Shrub—and as the plant matured the flowers shrank to middling size. Try again, thought Sam, and in 1972, the same cross produced 'Grand Hotel'. The flowers are what was hoped for—large, brilliantly red and shapely. But this time the plant is an out-and-out climber. Grow it for exhibition; it repeats quite well. Foliage is dark green and susceptible to black spot.

'Schlössers Brilliant' × 'Heidelberg'
Repeat flowering

'Grand Masterpiece'
Large-flowered

When a firm as respected as Jackson & Perkins nominates a single rose as 'Rose of the Year', you can be assured it is pretty good—like this memorable 1984 creation from Bill Warriner. It is a true masterpiece of the breeder's art, for its large, 13 centimetre (5 inch), classic and high-centred blooms, carried on exceptionally long stems, for its freedom and continuity of bloom, and for its luminous red color that does not fade as the flowers age. Its only fault is that fragrance is only so-so. The foliage is a mid-green.

Unnamed seedling × 'Tonight'
Repeat flowering

▲ 'Grand Hotel'
► 'Grand Masterpiece'

'Grand Siècle'
Large-flowered

DELagram

English-speaking rosarians have never paid the attention they should to the creations of the French breeders André Chabert and Pierre Delbard. Just look at the picture of 'Grand Siècle'. What a grand century it would be if more roses like this were introduced! First placed before the public in 1977, the flowers of 'Grand Siècle' are of remarkable coloring—pastel pink with touches of cream—beautiful shape, and good size. The fragrance is light, the bushes strongly branching with mid-green foliage.

(['Queen Elizabeth' × 'Provence'] × ['Michèle Meilland' × 'Bayadère']) × (['Voeux de Bonheur' × 'Meimet'] × ['Peace' × 'Dr Debat'])
Repeat flowering

▲ 'Grand Siècle'
▼ 'Grande Amore'

'Grande Amore'
Large-flowered

KORliegra
'Kordes Rose Grande Amore'

This flaming crimson velvet bloom with its long-lasting fragrance is Reimer Kordes's 1968 interpretation of a grand passion. Herr Kordes has not registered its parentage, but that is perhaps of minor importance. What is of note is that it is in every sense a *good* rose. The classic, urn-shaped buds open to exhibition-quality blooms which are borne freely and in quick succession on a compact plant with dusky, leathery green foliage. Give it the best of cultivation—it deserves it!

Parentage undisclosed
Repeat flowering

'Grande Duchesse Charlotte'
Large-flowered

Fame is as fleeting in the world of roses as elsewhere: around the end of World War II the constant winner of gold medals was 'Grande Duchesse Charlotte', raised by Ketten Brothers of the tiny duchy of Luxembourg and named, patriotically, for their then ruler. Alas, it is now but a memory, like the grand lady herself. Which is a pity, as there has never been a rose quite like it: long buds open to huge, twenty-five-petalled blooms in a unique shade of hot red, and foliage is a glossy green. It still survives in collections of AARS winners (it won in 1943), and the nursery trade should revive it.

Parentage unknown
Repeat flowering

'Grand'mère Jenny'
Large-flowered

'Peace' is known as 'Madame A. Meilland' in France in honor of the mother of the raiser, Francis Meilland. 'Grand'mère Jenny', a seedling of 'Peace' and not unlike it in color, takes the family history back a generation, to the raiser's grandmother. It is a smaller, looser flower than its parent (twenty-three petals against forty-three), the yellow and pink tones more pronounced, the scent stronger, and the bush more slender in habit, with dark glossy green foliage. Some people find it more refined and elegant. It was raised in 1950 and of course is adorned with gold medals—from the RNRS and Rome.

'Peace' × ('Julien Potin' × 'Sensation')
Repeat flowering
Fragrant

▲ 'Grande Duchesse Charlotte'

'Grandpa Dickson'
Large-flowered

'Irish Gold'

Pale yellow, with a hint of lime in cool weather and even more than a hint of salmon-pink in hot, the flowers of 'Grandpa Dickson' are very large, full and of perfect exhibition form but only slightly fragrant. The foliage is a glossy green and the wood is rather soft and

▲ 'Grand'mère Jenny'
▼ 'Grandpa Dickson'

very prickly. The bushes are apt to be on the small side and short-lived, and for all its beauty, 'Grandpa Dickson' is really only for the exhibitor. It prefers a cool climate, sulking where summers are hot and humid. The name honors the raiser's father, Alex Dickson, himself a famous breeder of roses, as were his father and grandfather before him. It is called 'Irish Gold' in America. Introduced by Patrick Dickson in 1966, it won the President's International Trophy and the Golden Rose of The Hague in that year.

('Kordes' Perfecta' × 'Governador Braga da Cruz') × 'Piccadilly'
Repeat flowering

'Green Fire' — Cluster-flowered

Sometimes, in cool weather, there is a touch of green in the heart of these flowers, but most days 'Green Fire' appears clear yellow. The 8 centimetre (3 inch) flowers have thirteen petals, and open to show golden stamens. The shrub has glossy green foliage and is bushy. The whole effect is rather like a slightly paler but larger-flowered 'Allgold'. It came from Herbert Swim in California in 1958. An attractive warm-climate rose, 'Green Fire' has been elbowed out of the catalogues by the growing numbers of newer, exhibition-shaped Cluster-flowered Roses.

'Goldilocks' × unnamed seedling
Repeat flowering

'Greensleeves' — Cluster-flowered
HARlenten

The old Green Rose ('Viridiflora') does not have real flowers, just a cluster of leafy growths. However, 'Greensleeves' really does bloom pale green, opening from pink buds. To see them at their

best, cut the sprays just before the flowers are fully blown. The color will develop perfectly in the vase and the blooms last for days. In the garden they are apt to go spotty and blotchy. The plant is on the leggy side, with dark green foliage needing protection from black spot, and there is no fragrance, but this 1980 creation from Jack Harkness is an indispensable rose for the flower arranger.

('Rudolph Timm' × 'Arthur Bell') × (['Pascali' × 'Elizabeth of Glamis'] × ['Sabine' × 'Violette Dot'])
Repeat flowering

'Greensleeves, Climbing' — Cluster-flowered

For all its unusual beauty, the original bush form of 'Greensleeves' can sometimes be unreliable. If you fancy its unique coloring but have had no success with it, then try the climbing sport, which, though not very rampant, can usually be relied on for quite good follow-up flowerings after its main summer display.

Sport from 'Greensleeves'
Repeat flowering

▲ 'Greensleeves'
◀ 'Green Fire'
▼ 'Climbing Greensleeves'

fragrant. Foliage is glossy green and the plant is bushy, with straight, smooth stems for the flower arranger. Raised by E. B. LeGrice, it was introduced in 1975.

'Brownie' × 'News'
Repeat flowering
Fragrant

'Grootendorst Supreme'　Hybrid Rugosa

This is a sport from 'F. J. Grootendorst' which some people prefer to the original, as the flowers are a much more attractive shade of dark garnet-red. They are just as prettily fringed, but they are a shade smaller, and most growers report that it is not as vigorous and easily grown as its parent. 'Grootendorst Supreme' was introduced by F. J. Grootendorst and Sons in 1936. Like its parent it is scentless.

Sport from 'F. J. Grootendorst'
Repeat flowering

▼ 'Grootendorst Supreme'

'Gros Choux d'Hollande'　Bourbon

Its name is very unromantic, translating literally as 'Great Dutch Cabbage'. Little is known about the rose. It is sometimes classed as a Bourbon and sometimes as a Centifolia. It is, however, a very handsome rose, with lush green leaves, and big, rose-pink blooms full of fragrance and symmetrically arranged petals. The bush is fairly compact and upright, with little of the Centifolia floppiness. Some authorities claim it as repeat flowering, but do not count on it. Usually the lavish summer display is all.

Parentage unknown
Summer flowering
Fragrant

▲ 'Gros Choux d'Hollande'
▼ 'Grüss an Aachen'

'Grüss an Aachen'　Cluster-flowered

How to classify this old and famous rose, a cross between a Hybrid Perpetual and a Polyantha? Prune it as a Cluster-flowered Rose and it can be used as a bedding rose. Or you might prefer to go lightly with the shears and allow it to make a smallish Shrub, like one of the 'English Roses'. But do not forgo the pleasure of its pearly pink and cream flowers, full petalled like an Old Garden Rose and quite deliciously fragrant. The foliage is leaden green. It came from a German raiser, Herr Geduldig, in 1909. He named it in tribute to the ancient cathedral city, the imperial capital of Charlemagne.

'Frau Karl Druschki' × 'Franz Deegen'
Repeat flowering
Fragrant

▼ 'Grey Dawn'

'Grey Dawn'　Large-flowered

Is this unique rose a Cluster-flowered Rose? Or is it a Large-flowered Rose? It depends on which catalogue you are reading. Whatever it is, it is a beautiful rose, officially classed as a mauve blend. In actuality it appears rather as if a grey shadow is cast over tints of palest pink and gold. The blooms have forty-five petals, are of medium size, and lightly

'Grüss an Teplitz' — Bourbon
'Virginia R. Coxe'

This is one of those roses that some people adore while others cannot quite understand the fuss. It makes a tall rather rangy bush, which you can train to a pillar or prune back to about 1.5 metres (5 feet). The blooms are deep crimson, borne in nodding clusters of half a dozen or so, and richly fragrant. It is happiest in a warm climate, when it is constantly in bloom, but watch out for mildew! Foliage is dark leaden green, tinted bronze-red when young. Of wildly mixed ancestry, it seems best grouped with the Bourbons, but it is a late arrival, coming from a Hungarian breeder, Geschwind, in 1897.

('Sir Joseph Paxton' × 'Fellemberg') × ('Papa Gontier' × 'Gloire de Rosomanes')
Repeat flowering
Fragrant

'Guinée' — Large-flowered Climber

There is no color more desired in roses than the deepest of velvety reds, but none that the rose seems less willing to offer. Few of the darkest red roses are really good 'doers'. 'Guinée' is one, perhaps the most reliable of them. At its best there are few roses to match its lovely form, sweet scent, and almost-black coloring, but it is only of fairly modest vigor, and unless you treat it well there will be no repeat flowers. It has olive-green foliage. It was a 1938 triumph for Charles Mallerin. The name is intended to suggest Darkest Africa, not golden guineas!

'Souvenir de Claudius Denoyel' × 'Ami Quinard'
Repeat flowering
Fragrant

'Guy Laroche' — Large-flowered
DELricos
'Gorgeous George', 'La Tour d'Argent'

This rose, which came from Delbard of Paris in 1985, is a beauty, except for one minor fault: if the petals were longer, they would show off the contrast of their deep red upper sides and sharp white reverses so much better when the bloom opens. They are symmetrically arranged, come on long stems and have just a faint touch of fragrance. The bush is medium in height, with dark green leaves.

Unnamed seedling × ('Michèle Meilland' × 'Carla')
Repeat flowering

▲ 'Guy Laroche'
◄ 'Grüss an Teplitz'
► 'Hamburger Phoenix'
▼ 'Guinée'

'Hamburger Phoenix' — Large-flowered Climber

Forget meat on buns, the name 'Hamburger Phoenix' honors the resurgence of the city of Hamburg, reduced almost to ashes in World War II. The raiser, Wilhelm Kordes, has noted his aston-ishment at how quickly this 1954 introduction displaced the old favorite 'Paul's Scarlet' from his customers' orders. Possibly the name 'Paul's Scarlet' sounds as awkward to a German ear as 'Hamburger Phoenix' does to us. If you think of Kordes's rose as a reliably repeat-blooming 'Paul's Scarlet', still more brilliant red in color, you will not have a bad picture of it. Foliage is dark green and glossy.

Rosa kordesii × an unnamed seedling
Repeat flowering

'Hana-Gasa' — Large-flowered Climber

The Japanese dictionary gives the definition of *hanagasa* as 'the flower of society'; this is close enough to the meaning of the name of this rose, raised by Seizo Suzuki in 1978. The coral-red flowers are large for a Cluster-flowered Rose, and open rather flat and ruffled from the long buds. They are a little reminiscent of 'Fragrant Cloud', though they are more orange in tone and have nowhere near the fragrance of that rose—but then, few roses do. Foliage is large and light green.

('Hawaii' × unnamed seedling) × 'Miss Ireland'
Repeat flowering
Fragrant

▲ 'Hana-Yume'
► 'Handel'

'Hana-Yume' Large-flowered

Nothing is more frustrating than to see a beautiful new rose at a flower show and not be able to find out anything about it. I was much taken with this pastel-pink, softly fragrant rose at the rose show in Osaka, Japan, a couple of years ago, but it is not listed in any of the Japanese catalogues that I consulted. All I can tell you is that it is quite new, was indeed raised in Japan, and that its name signifies 'a flower in a dream'—beautifully apt for a rose of such delicacy. Foliage is leathery, not dream-like at all.

Parentage undisclosed
Repeat flowering
Fragrant

'Handel' Cluster-flowered Climber

Sam McGredy has said that of all the fine roses he has raised, 'Handel' is his favorite. It is easy to see why: it is a very pretty and distinctive rose. It is white with a touch of cream at the centre and a piping of hot pink around the outside of each petal. The flowers are not all that large—the size of a Cluster-flowered Rose—nor are they scented, but you can not have everything! The olive-green glossy-leafed plant takes its time to build up its branches—you could not call it rampageous—and also to settle down to flowering freely. Be patient! It was introduced in 1965.

'Columbine' × 'Heidelberg'
Repeat flowering

'Hans Christian Andersen' Cluster-flowered

POULander
'America's Choice', 'H. C. Andersen'
One would think that the author of the immortal fairy tales was sufficiently liked in America that there was no need to remove his name from a rose for the American market. There are many red Cluster-flowered Roses, but this fairly new one looks to be one of the best of them. The color is clear blood-red without the hardness that spoils some others and it holds clean until the petals drop. The semi-double blooms are neatly shaped and show their stamens, and the bush is well clad with most handsome bronze-tinted foliage. It is of Danish origin, from Pernille Olesen (née Poulsen), and was introduced in 1986.

Parentage undisclosed
Repeat flowering

'Hansa' Hybrid Rugosa

How you rate this Hybrid Rugosa will depend very much on the severity of your winters. In places like Central Europe or the Mid-West of the United States (where it was raised in 1905 by Schaum of Iowa) it is much admired for its extreme hardiness and its double flowers of purple-red. In milder places its legginess of habit (unusual in a Hybrid Rugosa) and its habit of fading cost it admirers. Foliage is bright green and wrinkled. It flowers quite freely all season, and is sweetly fragrant.

Parentage unknown
Repeat flowering
Fragrant

▲ 'Hansa'
▼ 'Hans Christian Andersen'

▲ 'Hana-Gasa'

'Hansestadt Bremen' Cluster-flowered

Perhaps the recent interest in Modern Garden Roses with Old Garden Rose style flowers will lead to a revival of interest in this unfairly neglected rose, raised by Wilhelm Kordes in 1960. It makes a tall bush adorned with very dark green foliage and huge trusses of rose-pink blooms, each one with fifty symmetrically disposed petals. It is one of the very last roses to shut down its display in the autumn, or fall. Lack of scent is its only fault. It is named in honor of the historic port city of Bremen, in the Middle Ages one of the most powerful republics in Europe.

'Eva' × 'Fanal'
Repeat flowering

▲ 'Hansestadt Bremen'
► 'Happy'
▼ 'Happiness'

'Happiness' Large-flowered
'Rouge Meilland'

As the world's favorite crimson flower-shop rose for over twenty years, 'Rouge Meilland' must have made a fortune for the Meilland family. No wonder they recycled the name after the patent (and the royalties!) finished. It will save confusion if we all agree to use the American name 'Happiness' for the 1948 original, which is still around, its flat, thirty-eight-petalled flowers as warm and unfading a color as ever, the stems as long, the bush as tall. Foliage is dark sage-green. Like all greenhouse roses, it needs a warm climate to grow well out of doors, and there is little scent.

('Rome Glory' × 'Tassin') × ('Chas P. Kilham' × ['Chas P. Kilham' × 'Capichine Chambard'])
Repeat flowering

'Happy' Polyantha
'Alberich'

In 1954, the Dutch hybridist de Ruiter brought out a series of dwarf roses that he called 'Compacta Roses', seven of them named for the Seven Dwarfs (but none for Snow White!). They are mostly dull reds and pinks. Some say 'Happy' is the only one worth growing: it bears as many small crimson flowers as can be crammed onto the bush, but they are scentless; foliage is a dull green. All are derived from 'Robin Hood', and were originally christened in German: 'Geisebrecht', 'Degenhard', 'Burkhard' and so on. Neither true Miniatures nor Polyanthas, they are now largely ignored.

Parentage undisclosed
Repeat flowering

'Happy Wanderer' Cluster-flowered

Scarlet, each smallish bloom lit up by golden stamens, the flowers of 'Happy Wanderer' certainly create a cheerful show. The rose is far from wandering, however: the dark-leafed bush stays quite compact. Sam McGredy, who introduced it in 1972, must be regretting having used the name. It would

▲ 'Happy Wanderer'

be ideal for one of the new ground-covering roses. It is not widely available these days. It was photographed in India and is available in Switzerland too, so it ought to do well under a wide range of climates.

Unnamed seedling × 'Marlena'
Repeat flowering

'Harison's Yellow' — Shrub
Rosa harisonii

You would be hard put to find a rosebush growing on the Lower West Side of Manhattan these days, but that is where 'Harison's Yellow' originated in 1830, on what was then Mr Harison's suburban estate. You see it all over America, lingering in pioneer gardens long after the pioneers, and even their houses, have vanished. It is very pretty: a neat, tallish bush, covered in spring with cupped, soft yellow blooms with golden stamens against dainty mid-green foliage. You can distinguish 'Harison's Yellow' at once from its British sibling, 'Williams' Yellow', by the stamens—'Williams' Yellow' has green carpels instead.

R. spinosissima × R. foetida
Spring flowering
Fragrant

▼ 'Harison's Yellow'

▲ 'Harmonie'
▶ 'Harry Wheatcroft'

'Harmonie' — Large-flowered
KORtember

Raised by Reimer Kordes and introduced in 1981, this rich salmon bloom inherits good fragrance from its parent 'Fragrant Cloud'. Its blooms may be rather short on petals (only twenty in number) but they open high-centred from long, elegant buds and are set off by lightly polished green foliage. Its good qualities won 'Harmonie' the Baden-Baden gold medal in the year of its introduction.

'Fragrant Cloud' × 'Uwe Seeler'
Repeat flowering
Fragrant

'Harry Wheatcroft' — Large-flowered
'Caribia', 'Harry'

As flamboyant as the bewhiskered rose-lover and nurseryman for whom it is named (and on whose nursery it arose as a sport of 'Piccadilly' in 1972), 'Harry Wheatcroft' now blooms in his memory—he died in 1975. It is striped in scarlet and gold, and has the same large flowers and glossy green foliage of 'Piccadilly'. From his base in Nottingham, Harry Wheatcroft travelled the world seeking new roses to introduce to rose-lovers in the United Kingdom; he used often to misquote Thomas Gray: 'Full many a flower is born to blush unseen—but not if I can help it!'

Sport from 'Piccadilly'
Repeat flowering

'Headliner' — Large-flowered
JACtu

Appropriately named, 'Headliner' is an eye-catching rose, centred in white with a deep pink picotee edging, rather in the manner of the older 'Perfecta' but more sharp in its contrast. It bears large, exhibition-style flowers of forty petals, though without much fragrance. The bush is strong and upright, with medium green foliage. Do not confuse this rose with 'Headline', a yellow Large-flowered Rose raised in Australia a few years ago. 'Headliner' was raised by Bill Warriner for Jackson & Perkins and introduced in 1985.

'Love' × 'Color Magic'
Repeat flowering

▶ 'Headliner'

'Heat Wave' — Cluster-flowered

'Madame Paula Guisez'

Raised by Herbert Swim in 1958, 'Heat Wave' was one of the earliest of the hot-colored Cluster-flowered Roses, still capable of making a sultry display with clusters of full-petalled, 10 centimetre (4 inch) flowers. Despite its name, it is not at its best in hot weather, when the color rapidly becomes dull and harsh. The bush is strong with olive-green leaves. Like many of its color group, it has little scent.

Unnamed seedling × 'Roundelay'
Repeat flowering

'Hebe's Lip' — Damask

Rosa damascena rubrotincta, 'Reine Blanche', 'Margined Lip'

A compact bush, for a Damask, bearing some of the most charming blooms among the Old Garden Roses: almost single, creamy white with a crimson margin to the petals, as though a goddess had been putting on her lipstick. Foliage is a fresh green. It follows up its rather short summer season with pretty hips. Despite the proliferation of its names—often a sign of a long history— 'Hebe's Lip' is a relative newcomer. It was raised by William Paul in 1912.

Possibly *R. damascena* × *R. eglanteria*
Summer flowering

'Heidesommer' — Ground Cover

KORlins

The breeders of Ground Cover Roses have a way to go before they achieve plants that can challenge *Hypericum calycinum* or the creeping junipers in usefulness. The roses are still deciduous (which means winter weeds can grow among their branches) and thorny (which makes them a trial to pull out). But Reimer Kordes's 'Heidesommer' comes as close as any yet to the ideal, making a low, spreading bush densely clad with dark green, shining leaves against which the clusters of little white flowers positively sparkle. They appear all season, and have an elusive scent. It was introduced in 1985.

'The Fairy' × unnamed seedling
Repeat flowering
Fragrant

'Heinrich Münch' — Hybrid Perpetual

'Heinrich Münch' suffers from the fault that costs so many of the Hybrid Perpetuals popularity nowadays: it is not at all perpetual. Indeed, it is decidedly shy with its autumn, or fall, blooms unless it is generously encouraged with watering and fertiliser. Do not begrudge it, for the flowers are gorgeous: immense scented cabbages in a beautifully clear and luminous shade of pink against large semi-glossy green foliage. A good one would cause quite an upset among the modern Large-flowered Roses on an exhibition bench. It came to use from W. Hinner in 1911, and is named for the nurseryman who introduced it.

'Frau Karl Druschki' × ('Caroline Testout' × 'Mrs W. J. Grant')
Repeat flowering
Fragrant

'Heinrich Schultheis' — Hybrid Perpetual

Why that doyen of English rose-breeders Henry Bennett should have named this 1882 creation for Herr Schultheis is hard to say—Meinherr certainly seems foreign among such company as 'Her Majesty', 'Grace Darling' and 'Lady Mary Fitzwilliam'. But the name seems apt, for this is very much a man's rose, brilliant pink in tone, well filled with petals, and enormous. It must have been the pride of many a Victorian exhibitor. It is very pleasing to record that the blooms are fragrant, the bush is strong, with large, semi-glossy green foliage, and the flowers come early and late.

'Mabel Morrison' × 'E. Y. Teas'
Repeat flowering
Fragrant

▲ 'Helen Traubel'
◀ 'Heinrich Schultheis'

'Heirloom' Large-flowered

Another stunner from Jackson & Perkins' Bill Warriner, and, like many a family heirloom, one with a bit of mystery about its provenance. Mr Warriner has only stated that it is a cross of unnamed seedlings, leaving us to guess where its most unusual and distinctive deep lilac color came from. Never mind, it is a rose to treasure for its distinctive color, its elegantly long, pointed buds, its strong fragrance, and its bushy, reliable growth. Foliage is leaden green. It was introduced in 1972.

Unnamed seedling × unnamed seedling
Repeat flowering
Fragrant

'Helen Traubel' Large-flowered

Barely double with only twenty-three petals (though they form long buds and elegant open blooms), 'Helen Traubel' is a star, even among the many famous roses from the garden of Californian Herbert Swim. It is of lovely coloring, a luminous blend of pink and apricot, and fragrant too. The bush is tallish, with matt, leathery green leaves and slender stems, and is easy to grow in just about any climate. But a rose named for a celebrated opera star must be allowed a touch of temperament: 'Helen Traubel' is said to be difficult to propagate. It won the AARS award in 1952.

'Charlotte Armstrong' × 'Glowing Sunset'
Repeat flowering
Fragrant

'Helmut Schmidt' Large-flowered
KORbelma
'Simba', 'Goldsmith'

The name of the great German statesman is appropriate for this noble rose. Reimer Kordes created it in 1979, using the pollen of an unnamed seedling on his own 'New Day', introduced only a couple of years before. This is one of the very best yellow roses. The Belgian and Swiss judges certainly thought so when they awarded it gold medals in 1979. The plant is handsome, upright and bushy, and the flowers are shapely and sweetly fragrant. Foliage is a matt dark green.

'New Day' × unnamed seedling
Repeat flowering
Fragrant

◀ 'Heirloom'

'Henri Fouquier' Gallica
'Cocard Majestueuse'

The bush is a bit lax (for a Gallica) but almost thornless, and the flowers are handsome, their rich pink (fading to mauve-pink) petals evenly arranged. It is a good garden rose, responding well to a little bit of extra attention. Foliage is mid-green and smooth. The records of its raiser and parentage are lost. The alternative (but now unused) name means 'Majestic Rosette'.

Parentage unknown
Summer flowering
Fragrant

▲ 'Helmut Schmidt'
▼ 'Henri Fouquier'

'Henri Martin'   Moss
'Red Moss'

This is not, despite its alternative name, a dark red rose, but rather that color that is so common among roses which might be called red or deepest pink at the beholder's whim. It is a lovely,

fragrant rose, elegant in habit with neat dark green foliage, though it is true that there is not a great deal of moss on the buds. It was raised by Laffay and introduced in 1852, and named for the popular historian, one of the circle that promoted the gift of the Statue of Liberty from France to America.

Parentage unknown
Summer flowering
Fragrant

'Henry Nevard'   Hybrid Perpetual

Although 'Henry Nevard' is usually described as dark red, it is not as deep and rich as, say, 'Crimson Glory'. Perhaps it is more accurate to call it bright

▲ 'Henry Nevard'
◄ 'Henri Martin'

crimson. The blooms are large, sometimes very large, and nicely formed. They hold both their bright color and sweet fragrance very well in hot weather. The bush is more compact than usual for a Hybrid Perpetual, and the dark leathery green foliage is resistant to black spot. It is English-bred, by Frank Cant in 1924, a late date for a new Hybrid Perpetual to be introduced.

Parentage unknown
Repeat flowering
Fragrant

'Heritage'   English Rose
AUSblush

David Austin has nominated 'Heritage' as perhaps his favorite of all his English Roses, for its perfect Old Garden Rose

form, its delicate tones of pink and its strong fragrance. The flowers are certainly lovely, and the well-branched, 1.5 metre (5 foot) bush with small, dark green, semi-glossy leaves is excellent, flowering freely all season. It was introduced in 1984.

Unnamed seedling × ('Wife of Bath' × 'Iceberg')
Repeat flowering
Fragrant

'Hermosa'   China
'Armosa', 'Setina', 'Melanie Lamarié, 'Madame Neumann'

'Hermosa' is usually attributed to the obscure French breeder Marcheseau, the date being 1841, but several breeders claimed it, giving it names of their choice. It is thought to be a seedling of 'Old Blush', which it rather resembles, except that it is not so tall (rarely more than knee height), is fuller of petals, and has more lilac in its pink. It is just as free with its flowers from early to late, and in the nineteenth century was considered the best choice among roses for a low hedge. But there is no scent to speak of. Foliage is a dark bluish green and semi-glossy.

Parentage unknown
Repeat flowering

▲ 'Hermosa'
◄ 'Heritage'

'Hero'   English Rose
AUShero

It is a pity that 'Hero' is such a leggy grower—though you can get over its legginess by planting it in a group or using it as a small climber—for its flowers are very pretty, deeply cup shaped, fragrant and a lovely shade of clear pink. It is unusual among the David Austin roses in its gawkiness; most of them make shapely bushes. Foliage is mid-green and semi-glossy. It was introduced in 1982. Hero was, confusingly to modern ears, the *girl* for whom the Greek hero Leander swam the Hellespont.

'The Prioress' × unnamed seedling
Repeat flowering
Fragrant

▲ 'Hiawatha'
▼ 'Hero'

'Hiawatha'   Rambler

Raised by American breeder Walsh in 1904, 'Hiawatha' makes a big show, late in the season, of single flowers in carmine with white centres. It is rather like 'American Pillar', but brighter in color and not so vigorous. Foliage is rich green and leathery. For many years it was one of the most popular of Ramblers, but is less seen nowadays; its scentlessness is against it. Mr Walsh specialised in Ramblers. In 1905, he gave 'Hiawatha' the obvious companion, 'Minehaha', which is rather like 'Dorothy Perkins'.

'Crimson Rambler' × 'Paul's Carmine Pillar'

Summer flowering

'High Esteem'   Large-flowering

Peterson & Deering (the distributors of this large, exhibition-style rose) certainly showed their faith in the product when they named it 'High Esteem' and proceeded to charge $10 a plant, an unheard of price back in 1961. It is a huge bloom, shapely and fragrant, in an attractive medium pink with a silvery reverse, but the compact plant, with leathery green leaves, is not all that free flowering. Grow it only for the show bench! The raiser was Gordon Von Abrams.

('Charlotte Armstrong' × 'Madame Henri Guillot') × ('Multnomah' × 'Charles Mallerin')
Repeat flowering
Fragrant

▲ 'High Esteem'
▼ 'Highdownensis'

'Highdownensis'   Modern Shrub

Sir Frederick Stern will probably be best remembered as the prime author of the *Code of Nomenclature for Cultivated Plants*—and thus the man who put the names of roses into quotation marks—

but he made one of England's great gardens, Highdown in Essex. There he selected this exceptionally fine form of *Rosa moyesii*, notable for the dark burgundy color of its blooms, and its habit, compact and bushy without the usual *R. moyesii* gawkiness. Foliage is a dark coppery green. It is spring flowering only, but with splendid hips. It is a big grower, to 4 metres (13 feet) tall.

Selected form of *R. moyesii*
Spring flowering

'Hippolyte' — Gallica

'Hippolyte' is tall for a Gallica, sometimes growing head high, and the leaves, dark green and smooth, indicate some foreign blood. The flowers are

among the most perfectly formed in soft violet shades and fragrant. They are not at all large, but come in graceful sprays, which often arch gracefully. This is another old beauty whose pedigree has been lost. Do not confuse her with a very ordinary carmine Hybrid Perpetual, 'Hippolyte Jamain', which is occasionally met with.

Parentage unknown
Summer flowering
Fragrant

'Hiroshima's Children' — Cluster-flowered
HARmark

This name commemorates forty years of devotion by Dr Tomin Hamada to the victims of the atomic attacks of World War II on Japan. This is one of the loveliest of all the exhibition-style Cluster-flowered Roses, its 9 centi-

metre (3½ inch) flowers, in their small clusters, exquisite in their perfect form. The flowers are combined shades of cream and pale coral, the blend varying with the season. Lightly scented, 'Hiroshima's Children' is a delightful rose for cutting, but some say that it is not a terribly easy rose to grow to perfection. The bush is of open habit and the foliage is matt green. It was raised by Jack Harkness and introduced in 1985.

Parentage undisclosed
Repeat flowering

◄ 'Hoagy Carmichael'

'Hoagy Carmichael' — Large-flowered

The rose-red, perfumed flower in the picture is an exhibitor's dream. It is frustrating to be able to tell you nothing about it. I photographed it in America a couple of years ago, but have never been able to find any reference to where it might be available, or what its family tree is. I am not even sure whether it dates from the late 1940s, when the real-life Mr Carmichael was delighting the lovers of big-band music, or whether it is brand new. The foliage is mid-green and rather leathery.

Parentage unknown
Repeat flowering
Fragrant

◄ 'Hippolyte'
▼ 'Hiroshima's Children'

'Hobby' Cluster-flowered

Not often seen now, though it was only raised in 1955, 'Hobby' is a generous contributor of color to the garden with its sprays of deep rose-pink to coral flowers. The bush is upright, and the foliage dark green. There is not much scent, and current taste finds the individual blooms rather uninteresting. 'Hobby' was introduced by Mathias Tantau of Germany.

('Schweizergrüss' × 'Red Favourite') × 'Käthe Divigneau'
Repeat flowering

▶ 'Holtermann's Gold'
▼ 'Hobby'

'Holtermann's Gold' Large-flowered
AROyeht

Of American origin (from Armstrong Nurseries) this rose was named by the Sydney Church of England Grammar School, one of New South Wales's leading schools, to celebrate its centenary in 1989; Bernhard Holtermann, who gave the school the land on which it stands, made his fortune in the Australian gold rushes. Appropriately, the rose is brilliant, unfading yellow, its blooms large, well formed and very well scented. The bush is of average height, with glossy green foliage and good resistance to black spot.

('Friesia' × 'Katherine Loker') × 'Gingersnap'
Repeat flowering
Fragrant

▲ 'Homère'

'Homère' — Tea
'The Cape Buttonhole Rose'

Like Homer's poems, the rose named after him by Moreau & Robert in 1858 seems everlasting. Some of the oldest rosebushes in the world are 'Homère'. Even in Britain's cool climate it endures, for it is the hardiest of the Teas. It is a real beauty: variable in color, as many Teas are, but always a delight with its blends of cream and rose-pink, its ruffled petals, and its fine fragrance. The bush is strong, not over tall, 1 metre (3 feet) or so, with dark glossy green foliage and has few (but stout) thorns. Expect 'Homère' to bloom heavily all season.

Parentage unknown
Repeat flowering
Fragrant

'Honey Chile' — Cluster-flowered
Patricia Wylie, of 'Roses of Yesterday and Today' in California, speaks very highly of this rose. Raised by the American rosarian and writer Richard Thomson, it is rather like a shorter growing version of 'Queen Elizabeth' though the flowers are a softer pink, with more

salmon to them. It seems to be a good healthy grower too, and would be a good choice if you find 'Queen Elizabeth' too tall for your garden. Foliage is dark green. Lightly fragrant, it was introduced in 1964.

'Fashion' × 'Queen Elizabeth'
Repeat flowering

'Honey Favorite' — Large-flowered
Introduced by Gordon Von Abrams in 1962, this is a sport from the same raiser's 'Pink Favorite' of 1956. It shares its parents glossy, disease-free leaves, good form and preference for a cool climate, but scores, in the opinion of many, for delicacy of color. The name promises a tone of yellow or at least apricot, but in fact 'Honey Favorite' is a soft pink, with just a little touch of primrose at the heart of the flower. Scent is only slight, alas, but it is a good rose, undeservedly neglected.

Sport from 'Pink Favorite'
Repeat flowering

▲ 'Honey Favorite'
◄ 'Honey Chile'
▼ 'Honor'

▲ 'Honey Flow'

'Honey Flow' — Cluster-flowered
Raised by Australia's Frank Reithmuller in 1958, 'Honey Flow' is very like his more popular 'Cara Bella' in its light green bush, iron constitution, and huge sprays of single blooms which are white with just a hint of pink. 'Cara Bella' is a more positive color, though still pale, and so is more popular, but 'Honey Flow' scores in having the stronger perfume. It really does smell of honey.

Parentage unknown
Repeat flowering
Fragrant

'Honor' — Large-flowered
JAColite
'Michele Torr'

Second alphabetically of the three roses with which Bill Warriner and Jackson & Perkins swept the AARS awards in 1980—'Love', 'Honor', and 'Cherish'. 'Honor' has the largest size flowers, in white with just a hint of lemon at the centre. With only twenty-three petals they just qualify as double. The buds are long and pointed, the foliage unusually dark green and scent is only slight. Warriner has left us to speculate about the parentage, but there is no doubt about the quality of the rose. It has also garnered the Portland gold medal and the United States Rose of the Year award.

Parentage undisclosed
Repeat flowering

'Honorine de Brabant'   Bourbon

Many of the Bourbons are refined to the point of daintiness, but this one is on the bold side, with large broad light green leaves and good-sized blooms that open wide to show stripes and pencillings of violet and mauve over pale pink. It is a tall grower, and can be used either as a large shrub or trained as a pillar rose. It flowers lavishly in spring and quite well thereafter. There is much fragrance and few thorns. Who Honorine de Brabant was is now a mystery, nor does anyone know the raiser's name or the exact date of this excellent rose, possibly from around the 1840s.

Parentage unknown
Repeat flowering
Fragrant

▲ 'Honorine de Brabant'

'Hot Chocolate'   Cluster-flowered

1986 was something of an *annus mirabilis* for amateur rose-breeders in New Zealand—Pat Stevens brought out 'Big Purple', and his colleague J. W. Simpson introduced 'Hot Chocolate'. Both were brand new colors, one purple, the other a deep rich orange, so dark that it can be described fairly as a velvet brown. The color, as with so many unusually toned roses, is best in the cool weather at either end of the season; hot summer pales it into ordinariness. Foliage is leathery, the growth acceptable, but perfume is only slight.

Parentage undisclosed
Repeat flowering

'Ice White'   Cluster-flowered
'Vision Blanc'

At first sight, 'Ice White' looks rather like 'Iceberg', at present the world's best-selling white rose. What Sam McGredy was hoping for when he introduced it in 1966 was a shorter, more manageable version of 'Iceberg', and he has certainly achieved that. What is astonishing is how it came about—all of its parents are orange-toned. Foliage is glossy, a little darker than 'Iceberg'; scent is only faint.

'Madame Léon Cuny' × ('Orange Sweetheart' × 'Tantau's Triumph')
Repeat flowering

▲ 'Ice White'
▼ 'Hot Chocolate'

'Iceberg'   Cluster-flowered
KORbin
'Schneewittchen', 'Fée des Neiges'

Everywhere roses are grown, 'Iceberg' is a best-seller, and deservedly so. It makes a tall bush, with clean light

green leaves, and covers itself all season with large and small clusters of nicely shaped blooms. They are fragrant but not always stark white; cool weather often brings out a touch of pale pink. It was introduced by Reimer Kordes in 1958. There is a splendid climbing version, and the bush is a very good choice for growing as a standard.

'Robin Hood' × 'Virgo'
Repeat flowering
Fragrant

'Iced Ginger' Large-flowered

If there is one thing the Irish agree on, on both sides of the border, it is a good rose. There was never any doubt that in 'Iced Ginger' Pat Dickson of County Down had a world-beater. Not a big rose, and cursed with an ungainly bush, it is nevertheless enchanting in its blends of pink and copper, and sweetly fragrant. Foliage is broad and olive-green but susceptible to black spot. It often flowers in clusters, and is thus sometimes listed as a Cluster-flowered Rose. It was introduced in 1971.

'Anne Watkins' × unnamed seedling
Repeat flowering
Fragrant

▲ 'Iceberg'
▼ 'Iced Ginger'

'Iced Parfait' Cluster-flowered

The great English hybridist Albert Norman once said that the genes of Modern Garden Roses are such a mixed-up lot that the laws of heredity are more a consolation in explaining the failure of a cross than in predicting success. Sister Mary Xavier of Launceston in Tasmania must have had some help from above, because her cross between 'Pink Parfait' and 'Iceberg', introduced in 1972, came

out just as one would expect. The picture tells all! The blooms are a blend of very pale pinks, set against the light green foliage. 'Iced Parfait' has inherited its parents' reliability too. Sister Mary would feel a spiritual bond with Mr Norman. She is said to grow the finest bushes of his 'Ena Harkness' in the world.

'Pink Parfait' × 'Iceberg'
Repeat flowering
Fragrant

▲ 'Iced Parfait'

'Immortal Juno'
English Rose

The raiser, David Austin, has dropped this 1983 English Rose from his own catalogue due to the flowers' inability to stand up to rain, but in dry climates it is much admired. The flowers are large, sometimes very large, beautifully shaped in the Old Garden Rose style, and a lovely shade of warm pink. They are fragrant, the bush strong and foliage is mid-green and smooth. The reason for drawing attention to the goddess's immortality is that there are already at least two other roses called 'Juno'.

Parentage undisclosed
Repeat flowering
Fragrant

▶ 'Impatient'
▼ 'Immortal Juno'

'Impatient'
Cluster-flowered

JACdew

This 1984 AARS winner seems to be little known outside the United States, but is widely grown there. At first sight it is just another bright orange-red Cluster-flowered Rose, but it is a strong plant with dark green foliage and the flowers are given subtlety by the touch of yellow at the petal bases. They are about 8 centimetres (3 inches) across, shapely, and carried in small clusters. There is little scent, and the branches are wickedly thorny, a cause of impatience to its admirers. It was raised by Bill Warriner of Jackson & Perkins.

'America' × unnamed seedling
Repeat flowering

▲ 'Independence'
▼ 'Indica Alba'

'Independence'
Cluster-flowered

'Kordes Sondermeldung', 'Geranium', 'Reina Elisenda'

Rose-lovers today would be disinclined to give 'Independence' high standing among the multitude of scarlet-to-orange roses. Certainly, it is sometimes rather slow with its repeat flowering, but the bush is strong, and the color of the young flowers is still extraordinary against leathery dark green foliage, purplish when young. It was the first time a rose of such coloring had ever been seen and no previous Cluster-flowered Rose had such large and shapely flowers. No wonder Wilhelm Kordes called it 'Sondermeldung', his 'Special Announcement'. The year was 1950. Its own descendants are innumerable.

'Baby Chateau' × 'Crimson Glory'
Repeat flowering

'Indica Alba'
China

In their day, the China Roses tended to be red or pink, and it seems that white varieties were always very rare. They are even rarer now, so it is worth recording this one, which was photographed in the garden of the tomb of I'timad-ud-Daula at Agra, its label reading *Rosa indica alba*. Not much is known about the rose but it grows to a compact bush, with white flowers, and the mid-green foliage seems a bit coarse for a China Rose. What a disappointment if it is actually an imposter!

Parentage unknown
Repeat flowering

▲ 'Ingrid Bergman'

'Ingrid Bergman' Large-flowered
POUlman

One of the great award-winners in recent rose history, 'Ingrid Bergman' has won gold medals at Belfast in 1985, Madrid in 1986 and The Hague in 1987. It was raised by Niels Poulsen of Denmark and introduced in 1983. He named it for a fellow Scandinavian, who was something of an award-winner herself. The double, deep red blooms are of perfect form and backed by glossy dark green leaves, but its parent 'Precious Platinum' has not endowed it with much fragrance. The Poulsen family are working on their red roses—watch out for some more beauties!

'Precious Platinum' × unnamed seedling
Repeat flowering

'Inner Wheel' Cluster-flowered
FRYjasso

These dainty flowers are most unusual in their two-tone color, blending pale candy-pink with coral, and the sprays of bloom are borne on a low bushy plant with good dark green foliage. There is not much scent, but since its 1985 introduction 'Inner Wheel' has been well received as a decorative garden rose. Named in honor of the Association of Rotarian's Ladies, a worldwide community service group, it was raised and introduced by Fryer's Nurseries of Cheshire.

'Pink Parfait' × 'Picasso'
Repeat flowering

'Innoxa Femille' Large-flowered
HARprincely

The British like to think of themselves as above crass commercialism, but the British rose-breeders certainly went in for it in a big way in the early 1980s, actively seeking commercial sponsors for their roses. The idea was that the sponsor would use the rose in its own advertising, to everyone's profit. Witness the very clumsily named 'Innoxa Femille' which was sponsored by a cosmetics company. The dark crimson flowers are well formed and the bush is vigorous and resistant to mildew, with dark leathery green leaves and distinctive double prickles. Only slightly fragrant, it was raised by Jack Harkness and introduced in 1983.

'Red Planet' × 'Eroica'
Repeat flowering

▲ 'Innoxa Femille'
▼ 'Inner Wheel'

'International Herald Tribune' Cluster-flowered
HARquantrum
'Viorita', 'Violetta'

With its low growth and sprays of little, shapeless flowers, like a Polyantha, 'International Herald Tribune' would look decidedly old hat if it were not for its deep violet color, a novelty in a Modern Garden Rose, and its pleasant scent. Foliage is a semi-glossy dark green. It is quite a good grower, for all its shortness, given a sunny spot where the sun can light it up. The name honors the newspaper. The raiser was Jack Harkness who introduced it in 1985.

Unnamed seedling × (['Orange Sensation' × 'Allgold'] × *Rosa californica*)
Repeat flowering
Fragrant

'Intervilles' Cluster-flowered Climber
The roses introduced in the 1950s and '60s by the French raiser Marcel Robichon have never been much seen outside France, and few remain in the catalogues now. Perhaps Robichon just

▲ 'International Herald Tribune'
▼ 'Intervilles'

never had the publicity machine that some of the big raisers like Meilland have. Anyway, here is one of them, a pleasing repeat-flowering Climber, not overly vigorous, with glossy green leaves and clusters of scarlet flowers. 'Intervilles' suffers from lack of scent, but always makes a colorful show. It was introduced in 1964.

Parentage undisclosed
Repeat flowering

▲ 'Intrigue'

'Intrigue'   Cluster-flowered
JACum

In the old days, 'Intrigue' would probably have been classed as a decorative Large-flowered Rose, for its clusters are small, and its flowers large and loose in structure. They are fragrant, borne on long stems for cutting, and are indeed intriguing in color—deep magenta, paling only slightly as they age. The bush is average in height, with dark plum-tinted leaves. Do not confuse this 1984 introduction from Jackson & Perkins, with Kordes's 1978 red Cluster-flowered Rose codename KORlech. You will find that one here too, under its original name 'Lavaglut'.

'White Masterpiece' × 'Heirloom'
Repeat flowering
Fragrant

'Invincible'   Cluster-flowered
RUnatru
'Fennica'

This dark crimson rose, a 1982 introduction from de Ruiter of Holland, does not seem to have established itself in Australia, but is much admired else-

where. The flowers are fairly large, 10 centimetres (4 inches), carried in sprays on good stems for cutting, and last well in a vase. The tall bush is compact, unlike some red Cluster-flowered Roses, and mildew (the curse of roses of this color) is not a problem. The foliage is a dark bronze-green. Australians are missing out on an excellent rose.

'Rubella' × 'National Trust'
Repeat flowering

▲ 'Invincible'
▼ 'Ipsilanté'

'Ipsilanté'   Gallica
The stems are more prickly than most Gallicas, and the dark green foliage not as finely cut as usual, but the flowers are quite superb: beautifully quartered, sweetly fragrant, and of softest lilac-pink. It was highly regarded in its day (the date of introduction is given as 1821, though the raiser is forgotten), and deserves more attention today.

Parentage unknown
Summer flowering
Fragrant

'Irene of Denmark'   Cluster-flowered
'Irene von Dänemarck'

Until 'Iceberg' came along, 'Irene of Denmark' was widely regarded as the best white Cluster-flowered Rose, and it is still a good choice if 'Iceberg' is too tall for you. The flowers are smallish, but full of petals and fragrance, and the compact plant is strong, healthy and floriferous, with bright green leaves. It was raised by the Danish pioneer of Cluster-flowered Roses, Svend Poulsen, in 1948. It blends Polyantha, Noisette, and Large-flowered Rose in its heritage.

'Orléans Rose' × ('Madame Plantier' × 'Edina')
Repeat flowering
Fragrant

▲ 'Irene of Denmark'
▼ 'Irish Elegance'

'Irish Elegance'   Large-flowered
During the reign of King Edward VII there was a vogue in Britain for single-flowered Hybrid Teas (now known as Large-flowered Roses). 'Irish Elegance' is an earlier example from 1901 raised by Alex Dickson, better known for his

huge, many-petalled exhibition roses. It is a beauty, its long buds opening to wide, softly fragrant blossoms in soft tea-rose-yellow, just faintly brushed with pink. 'Bronze', the old catalogues said, and that's not a bad description. The bush is tall, the foliage semi-glossy.

Parentage unknown
Repeat flowering
Fragrant

'Irish Fireflame'
Large-flowered

Another of Alex Dickson's singles, and a lovely companion to 'Irish Elegance'. Add 'Mrs Oakley Fisher' and 'Dainty Bess' and you have a delightful quartet for a period garden. The buds of 'Irish Fireflame' are indeed like brilliant scarlet flames, but they open to soft coral-pink. Of all the group, it is the most fragrant. The glossy-leafed bush is compact and free, the blooms coming in large clusters. Alas, Dickson's had a fire in their offices in 1921 and the records of the breeding of their roses up to then were all destroyed.

Parentage unknown
Repeat flowering
Fragrant

▲ 'Irish Fireflame'
▶ 'Iskra'
▼ 'Isabelle de France'

'Isabelle de France'
Large-flowered

An uncommon Large-flowered Rose dating from 1956, 'Isabelle de France' is treasured by those who grow it, but it rarely appears in a catalogue these days. The long, elegant buds are of unusual coloring, a vermilion-scarlet with almost black tips to the petals, and are long lasting. The growth is vigorous, but perhaps its slightness of fragrance and proneness to black spot have told against it. Foliage is leathery green. It was raised by Charles Mallerin and introduced in 1956.

'Peace' × ('Madame Joseph Perraud' × 'Opera')
Repeat flowering

'Iskra'
Cluster-flowered Climber

MEIhati
'Sparkling Scarlet'

Perhaps better known as 'Sparkling Scarlet', which describes its color exactly, 'Iskra' bears clusters of Cluster-flowered Rose style flowers on a rather bushy climbing plant, well clothed in large, semi-glossy green leaves. It is not overly vigorous, but repeats its bloom very well and makes quite a splash of color in the garden. It is a nice surprise to find the flowers fragrant, unusually so for a rose of this color. It was raised by Meilland and introduced in 1970.

'Danse des Sylphes' × 'Zambra'
Repeat flowering
Fragrant

▲ 'Ispahan'

'Ispahan'
Damask

'Rose d'Isfahan', 'Pompon des Princes'

One of the most garden-worthy of the Old French Roses, both for its long flowering season, just about the longest of any once-blooming rose, and the clear softness of its color, which at first sight might be dismissed as just plain pink. Loosely shapely buds open to flowers that are richly scented, and borne in almost Cluster-flowered Rose clusters on a bushy, upright bush, about 1.5 metres (5 feet) tall. It has glossy, mid-green foliage. Ispahan is the former capital of Persia, known for the beauty of its architecture, its carpets and its roses, though whether this was one of them no one is sure.

Parentage unknown
Summer flowering
Fragrant

▲ 'Ivory Fashion'
▼ 'Ivory Tower'

'Ita Buttrose'
Large-flowered

AROuule

Named for one of Australia's leading journalists, honored for her work for charity, 'Ita Buttrose' blends femininity and strength in its colors, which are a blend of peach and coral, deeper at the petal edges. Carried on long stems, the blooms are of fine exhibition form and lightly fragrant. Foliage is light green, the growth bushy. It is of American origin, having been raised by Jack Christensen in 1984.

('Camelot' × 'First Prize') × 'Gingersnap'
Repeat flowering

► 'Jack Frost'
▼ 'Ita Buttrose'

'Ivory Fashion'
Cluster-flowered

Eugene Boerner must have got a bit of a surprise when the marriage of two salmon roses gave birth to an ivory-white one. It would have been a very pleasant surprise, for 'Ivory Fashion' proved good enough to win the 1959 AARS award. In cool weather there are subtle hints of amber and palest pink. In all weather the flowers are elegant and shapely, the open blooms crowned by their crimson anthers, and there is fragrance as well. For all its elegance, it is an erratic performer, sometimes bushy and full of dark greyish green foliage, sometimes inclined to be straggling in its growth and shy with its flowers, but no one who has grown it once will willingly do without it again.

'Sonata' × 'Fashion'
Repeat flowering
Fragrant

'Ivory Tower'
Large-flowered

Raised by Reimer Kordes, but apparently now the property of America's Armstrong Nurseries, this upright-growing Large-flowered Rose is one for connoisseurs. Its ivory-white is not a best-selling color in the rose world, but in this case it is saved from monotony by shadings of light pink and palest yellow. The long buds open to very fragrant 35-petalled flowers, 14 centimetres (5½ inches) wide, and long lasting both on the bush and when cut. Foliage is dark glossy green and corrugated. It was introduced in 1979.

'Königin der Rosen' × 'King's Ransom'
Repeat flowering
Fragrant

'Jack Frost'
Large-flowered

Officially this is classsed as a Cluster-flowered Rose, but that probably will not bother most people. You see 'Jack Frost' more often in the flower shops, disbudded to carry a single, shapely

flower to each long stem, than in the garden. Fairly well scented, it is one of the more widely grown white greenhouse roses, especially in America where it was introduced in 1962 by Robert Jelly. Its introducers, the E. G. Hill Company, have been growing greenhouse roses since before World War I. 'Jack Frost' is unusual among such roses in having a reasonable degree of fragrance. Leaves are dark green.

'Garnette' × unnamed seedling
Repeat flowering
Fragrant

'Jacques Cartier' Portland
'Marquise Boccella'

It seems that the great French explorer is to be dethroned. Someone has decided that the rose which we have all been admiring under his name is not the 1868 Moreau & Robert introduction, but an 1842 introduction from

▲ 'Jacques Cartier'
▼ 'Jadis'

Desprez of Angers called 'Marquise Boccella'. Let us leave the pundits to argue, and continue to enjoy the pretty pink blooms, ruffled and fluted (but not serrated) like a carnation, the compact vigor of the bush, and the abundant green foliage. Scent is only moderate, but the autumn, or fall, blooms are especially abundant.

'Baronne Prévost' × 'Portland Rose'
Repeat flowering
Fragrant

'Jadis' Large-flowered
'Fragrant Memory'

Jadis is French, and means 'the old days', but this is an American rose raised by Bill Warriner for Jackson & Perkins in 1974, and later re-introduced by them as 'Fragrant Memory', for the benefit of those whose French is a little shaky. Either name is appropriate, for in its exquisite color—lilac washed over rose-pink—and intense perfume, 'Jadis' is indeed evocative of the Old Garden Roses. But the form is modern, full petalled and high centred, and the bush upright with large, leathery green leaves. You might have to watch out for mildew, something which it inherits from both its parents.

'Chrysler Imperial' × 'Virgo'
Repeat flowering
Fragrant

'James Mason' Modern Shrub

A lot of people do not know this, but the well-known star of such movie classics as *The Man in Grey* was a keen admirer of roses. It was a delight when

Peter Beales introduced 'James Mason', the crimson rose, in the year of the great actor's death, 1982. Its interesting parentage makes it three parts Gallica. The flowers are fragrant, and brilliant blood-red. The foliage is mid-green and luxuriant, sometimes so much so that the flowers hide among it.

'Scarlet Fire' × 'Tuscany Superb'
Summer flowering
Fragrant

'James Mitchell' Moss

No one remembers who James Mitchell was, but his rose was raised by Eugène Verdier in 1861. It is an odd choice to bear a man's name, the powder pink flowers flushed with lilac being on the dainty side, and prettily shaped. The buds are nicely mossy and the flowers fragrant. The arching bush can smother itself with them in its late spring season. It has neat dark green foliage

▲ 'James Mitchell'
▼ 'James Mason'

and is usually the first of the Moss Roses in bloom.

Parentage unknown
Summer flowering
Fragrant

▲ 'Jan Spek'

'Jan Spek'   Cluster-flowered

Jan Spek is known to every rose-lover through 'Spek's Yellow', the leading yellow rose of the 1950s and '60s; and though it was not of his own raising—he only made it popular—it is fitting that the rose that bears his own name should be golden yellow too. The buds are often brushed with red, but this vanishes from the open flowers, which are 8 centimetres (3 inches) across and carried in large clusters on a dark-leafed plant of fashionably low growth. 'Jan Spek' was a tribute by Sam McGredy to an old friend and colleague. It was introduced in 1966.

'Cläre Grammerstorf' × 'Doctor Faust'
Repeat flowering

'Japonica'   Moss
'Moussu de Japon' Mousseux du Japan'

The books all say that this is the mossiest of all Moss Roses, the moss not growing simply on the buds but also on the stems and even on the leaves. Perhaps so, but it seems to need the very best of cultivation and a cool climate for this to happen. It is often no more mossy than most other Mosses. There are more attractive flowers in the group than this one's rather small, semi-double flowers of magenta-pink. Despite its name, it appears to be of French origin. It seems to be unheard of in Japan.

Parentage unknown
Summer flowering
Fragrant

▲ 'Jaquenetta'
▼ 'Japonica'

'Jaquenetta'   Cluster-flowered

David Austin has decided that 'Jaquenetta', despite its being a seedling of 'Charles Austin', is not really entitled to be called an English Rose, and should be a Cluster-flowered Rose. It is actually quite a good rose, strong and healthy, and bearing good clusters of refined and fragrant blooms. They are pale peach, informally shaped, showing their stamens, against mid-green foliage. It was introduced in 1983.

'Charles Austin' seedling
Repeat flowering
Fragrant

'Jardins de Bagatelle'   Large-flowered
MEImafris

The 1986 creation of one of the world's leading rose hybridists, Marie-Louisette Meilland, 'Jardins de Bagatelle' is a wonderfully feminine bloom in palest cream,

flushed with delicate pink and yellow, and sweetly fragrant too. The bush is sturdy with broad glossy green foliage. The Palace of Bagatelle in Paris, built by the Comte d'Artois, owes its inspiration to Queen Marie-Antoinette. It is in its beautiful gardens that the famous competition for new roses is held each year. It seems a pity that 'Jardins de Bagatelle' has not won the gold medal there, but it does have gold medals from Geneva and the RNRS in England.

Parentage undisclosed
Repeat flowering
Fragrant

▲ 'Jardins de Bagatelle'
▼ 'Jawahar'

'Jawahar'   Large-flowered

The velvety, scented 'Jawahar' is a creation of the Indian Department of Crops and Agriculture, introduced in 1980. The blooms are large and high centred, borne usually in clusters of three to six; they are a perfect creamy white. The vigorous, bushy plant is notable for strange brown prickles and light green glossy foliage.

'Sweet Afton' × 'Delhi Princess'
Repeat flowering
Fragrant

THE SEARCH FOR THE BLUE ROSE

The early Dutch discoverers of Australia were greeted with derision back home when they reported black swans in New Holland. Had they found blue roses, however, they would have not only been believed but thought to have discovered a new Eden! It is odd, how humans have always dreamed of blue roses. In all the centuries when there were no yellow roses, or flame ones, no one seemed to miss them. Blue roses were the dream. Legend is full of them: a blue rose plays a major role in Rimsky-Korsakov's fairy-tale opera *Sadko*, and we read in the *Arabian Nights* of magicians who turn roses blue, usually in return for the favors of some virtuous maiden. The thirteenth-century Arabian botanist Ibn el-Awam listed a blue rose among those in his garden, though nobody has seen it since; modern scholars have concluded that it was probably the blue form of *Hibiscus syriacus*, the Rose of Sharon.

Human nature being what it is, gardeners have hankered after a blue rose, and nurserymen have been only too willing to oblige. The fact that the roses in question have, at best, turned out to be mauve has not stopped them—as long ago as the beginning of the nineteenth century an 'azure' rose was announced as having just arrived from China. Great was the disappointment when it flowered crimson! Perhaps it was just an innocent mistake in translating the Chinese label—classical Chinese has no word for 'blue'.

In fact, there are many purple and lilac roses among the old roses—'Cardinal de Richelieu', 'Reine des Violettes', 'Belle Poitevine', to name but a few—and in 1909 the Rambler 'Veilchenblau' appeared with the, by now, customary fanfare.

As the flowers fade, they sometimes turn a clear lilac—probably this is the closest to blue that any rose yet comes. Recently there have been some Large-flowered Roses in lilac tones, but names such as 'Blue Moon', 'Shocking Blue' or 'Azure Sea' have been, shall we say, rather optimistic, however lovely the roses themselves may be. Real blue seems as elusive as ever.

Every child who has ever played with a paint box knows that red plus blue equals purple. Surely, if the hybridists could eliminate the red from the purple roses, blue would remain? The answer from the botanists is a stern 'No!' They tell us that the pigment that makes flowers blue, *delphinidin*, is absent from the rose, and indeed from all its relatives in the

▲ *The 'blue rose of the Arabs' is almost certainly* Hibiscus syriacus, *often called (though it is unrelated to the rose) the Rose of Sharon.*

▲ *A tantalising thought for rose-breeders: the intense blue of the cornflower is due to the same pigment that makes the rose red.*

▶ *'Veilchenblau', trumpeted when it was new as the long-desired blue rose, is still the closest to blue of any—but only when it is old, faded, and grown in the shade.*

Rosaceae too. The mauve roses look that way because of the breakdown of the red pigment *cyanidin* in combination with tannins. Which makes sense—who has not seen a red or pink rose slowly turn purplish with age? The modern mauves often have a greyish or even brownish cast—'sullied colours' as the great Irish hybridist Alexander Dickson called them. So it seems that our purple and lilac roses are just reds and pinks suffering from premature old age, and no amount of crossing them will make them any bluer than they are.

Of course, there is always the million-to-one chance that a mutation will produce a delphinidin-bearing rose, just as a chance mutation some sixty years ago gave the rose the scarlet pigment *pelargonidin* which is responsible for the color of such roses as 'Independence', 'Super Star' or 'Alexander'—but do not hold your breath waiting for it. It is frustrating to find that not all blue flowers, however, owe their color to delphinidin; the brilliantly pure blue of the cornflower is due to the same cyanidin pigment that makes the rose red. Indeed, the name cyanidin comes from the Greek for blue. Cyanidin can be either red or blue, depending on the acidity or alkalinity of the flower's sap and the various sugars with which it combines; so, as there are both pink and crimson cornflowers, it seems that to gain a blue rose, all we have to do is persuade the rose to arrange its sap accordingly.

All we have to do! That is a bigger task than its sounds, for the conditions within the flower are controlled by the DNA in the rose's chromosomes, and interfering with them has not been something that, short of magic, we have been able to do.

The advent of gene-splicing (or recombinant DNA technology as it is more properly known) may change all that. Genetic engineering has certainly had some spectacular triumphs—the engineering of the bacterium *Escherischia coli* to create a strain that excretes human insulin has given relief to millions of diabetics. The rose, however, is a much more complex organism than a simple bacterium, and the difficulties of manipulating its genes are formidable.

Nevertheless, an Australian company has taken up the challenge, attempting to graft the blue gene of the petunia onto the rose. Recently they announced that they had found the petunia gene, and were hoping that shortly they would be able to persuade the rose to accept it. Maybe by the time that you read this, they will have succeeded. It is a colossally expensive operation, but the financial rewards of success will be very great. The rose is the world's favorite flower; millions are sold each day in flower shops, and when (and if) the blue rose arrives, the florists will be able to ask their own price for it. No doubt its creators will have patented their invention, and will reap a huge, well-earned reward in royalties.

And law suits too, I fancy. The present plant patent laws that most countries have allow the breeder of a new variety of plant to claim royalties for a number of years on each plant sold, but they do not cover the offspring from hybridization of that variety. The Meilland family made bags of money from the 'Peace' rose, for instance, but a rose bred from 'Peace' by another hybridist (such as Herbert Swim's 'Garden Party'

or Kordes's 'Karl Herbst') will bring them nothing. When the blue rose arrives, it will more than likely be able to pass on its new gene and breed blue-flowered offspring, conceivably better and more profitable than the original. As present laws stand the patent would only refer to the original blue rose, and not to subsequent ones bred from it. Will the courts hold that the gene itself is patented, so that the royalties will go to the original company from the breeder of any new blue rose that carries it? And will the public be allowed to take cuttings for their own gardens for free, as the present plant patent laws in most countries allow? What a pity it would be if the rose, whose destiny has been to increase the happiness of humans, should, by acquiring a new beauty, become the cause of acrimony and bitterness.

◀ *'Blue Moon' is the most popular of the mauve roses, but its name promises much more than it delivers; it is really a pinkish lilac color.*

▼ *It is possible to dye white roses blue by cutting them and standing them in blue dye or ink, but the result is as artificial as these moulded and painted decorations in the Weissblauen Rosen Restaurant in Munich.*

▼ *The non-existence of blue roses has not stopped artists from imagining what they might look like. These, in inlaid marble, are in India.*

◀ *Purple roses have been with us for a long time: 'Cardinal de Richelieu' dates from 1840.*

'Jazz Fest'
Cluster-flowered

The name suggests the early 1970s, and indeed 'Jazz Fest' is an Armstrong introduction of 1971. It is a cheerful rose, splashing its cerise-red clusters over a tallish bush with leathery green leaves. There is little scent, but the flowers are carried on long stems for cutting, and their long buds are quite elegant. 'Jazz Fest' is seen at its best in a warm climate.

'Pink Parfait' × 'Garnette'
Repeat flowering

▲ 'Jazz Fest'
▼ 'Jean de Tilleux'

'Jean de Tilleux'
Large-flowered

Sometimes a new rose will come from distinguished parents but seem to combine the wrong features. 'Jean de Tilleux', from California's Joseph Winchell in 1980, has inherited a good plant and nicely shaped flower from the dark red 'King of Hearts', but it has failed to acquire the many petals and sweet scent of 'Golden Masterpiece'. Still, it is an attractive, long-budded flower in strawberry-pink fading to lavender, and the foliage is lush and dark green.

'King of Hearts' × 'Golden Masterpiece'
Repeat flowering

▲ 'Jean Ducher'

'Jean Ducher'
Tea

Compared with Modern Garden Roses in the same peach-pink to apricot color range, their tones intensified by descent from 'Persian Yellow', the nodding blooms of 'Jean Ducher' may seem pallid. It is a good example, however, of the refinement and delicacy that Victorian rose-lovers so admired. Not that there is anything languishing about the plant, which is one of the hardiest of the Teas, bearing its scented flowers in great abundance for most of the year. Foliage is narrow and bronze-green, tinted plum when young. The name commemorates a member of the long-lived Ducher family, rose-breeders for a century. It was introduced some time in the early 1880s.

Parentage unknown
Repeat flowering
Fragrant

'Jennifer Hart'
Large-flowered

Only in California could a rose be named after a fictional character in a hit TV series, and that is where 'Jennifer Hart' was raised. The perpetrators of the gimmick were Armstrong Nurseries in 1982. It is quite an attractive rose, though, with high-centred blooms of rich ruby-red and sweet tea fragrance, borne on a medium-height, bushy plant with mid-green, semi-glossy foliage. The raisers were Swim & Christensen.

'Pink Parfait' × 'Yuletide'
Repeat flowering

'Jenny Duval'
Gallica

There is an argument going on at present among Old Garden Rose fanciers about the identity of this rose. Some, bolstered by the lack of mention of 'Jenny Duval' in the old rose books, say it is the same as 'Président de Sèze'; others that it is quite different. It is worth the fuss, for it is one of the most remarkably colored roses in existence. It usually opens pale lilac, but as the flowers expand they are apt to take on every shade of purple, magenta, pink and violet that you can think of, all in the same flower, and all quite separate but without stripes or blotches. It is scented and it has been known to make a show of autumn, or fall, foliage. It probably dates from some time in the early nineteenth century.

Parentage unknown
Summer flowering
Fragrant

▲ 'Jenny Duval'
▼ 'Jennifer Hart'

▲ 'Jessie Matthews'
► 'Joaquina Munez'

'Jessie Matthews' — Large-flowered
BEEje

The attractive delicate blooms of 'Jessie Matthews' are more likely to display themselves in clusters in the style of a Cluster-flowered Rose. Individually they are quite large and have thirty-five petals in pale yellow with picotee edges in warm pink. It was introduced in 1982 by Bees Ltd in memory of the charming star of English musical comedy, who lived in Australia for some years. The plant is dense and bushy, the foliage light green in color. A rose of such charm deserves to be, like Jessie's theme song, 'Evergreen'.

'Ernest H. Morse' × 'Rosanella'
Repeat flowering

'Joaquina Munez' — Large-flowered
This is like one of those beautiful mysterious women all dressed in red who appear in novels. She was photographed in the Orient (in Delhi) and has never been seen again, nor does anyone know anything about her. Is she Spanish, Portuguese, or indeed, Indian by birth? And how old is she? Does it matter—'Joaquina Munez' is content merely to open her shapely, scarlet blooms above her glossy green foliage in the Indian sunshine. This rose was probably introduced in the 1960s.

Parentage unknown
Repeat flowering

'Jocelyn' — Cluster-flowered
This is a rose more for the flower arranger than the garden, for its matt mahogany and purple tones do not show up well in the garden, and in hot weather it is apt simply to be deep pink. It is a reasonably healthy grower, however, with attractive dark green leaves. Borne in small clusters, the blossoms are full of petals, though one could wish they were full of fragrance also. Try it in the cutting garden and in arrangements with russet and grey-green leaves. It was a 1972 introduction from E. B. LeGrice, a specialist in the unusual.

Parentage undisclosed
Repeat flowering

▲ 'Jockey'

'Jockey' — Cluster-flowered
'Horrido'

What a strange name Mathias Tantau gave this rose. At least the English name 'Jockey' is appropriate, for like most riders of racehorses the rose is short in stature. Its flowers are blood-red, of only a few petals but carried in quite large clusters, and it has a good reputation as a bedding rose. Foliage is dark green and glossy. Its curious names and lack of fragrance have not helped its popularity, and though it was only introduced in 1963, it is not often seen now.

Parentage undisclosed
Repeat flowering

▲ 'John F. Kennedy'
◄ 'Jocelyn'

'John F. Kennedy' — Large-flowered
When, after President Kennedy's tragic death, Jackson & Perkins offered to name a rose in his memory, Mrs Kennedy requested that it be a white one. Jackson & Perkins had a real beauty for her, with majestic blooms nearly 14 centimetres (5½ inches) across, high

centred and shapely, with a unique touch of lime-green at the flower's heart. It is fragrant too, and the bush is strong, with leathery green disease-resistant leaves, but it is tender in cold climates, and needs good soil to give of its best. It was raised by Eugene Boerner and released in 1965.

Unnamed seedling × 'White Queen'
Repeat flowering
Fragrant

'Johnnie Walker'   Large-flowered

'Arthur Bell', 'Glenfiddich', 'Johnnie Walker'—the Scotch whisky drinker could plant quite a big bed with roses named for his favorite tipple! 'Johnnie Walker' is the newest of the three, yellow like the others, but a difficult color to describe. Buff? Apricot gold? Or just the clear amber of a very fine whisky? There are only twenty petals, but they build up into a large and beautifully formed bloom, lavishly endowed with fragrance. The bush is compact, and the leaves are mid-green. Introduced in 1982, it was raised by Gareth Fryer of Knutsford in Cheshire, one of England's leading rose-growers.

'Sunblest' × ('Arthur Bell' × 'Belle Blonde')
Repeat flowering
Fragrant

'Jolly Roger'   Cluster-flowered

There were in the 1930s a group of roses bearing pirate names—'Captain Kidd', 'Doubloons' and 'Long John Silver' among them—all hybrids of *Rosa setigera* raised by M. H. Horvath of Ohio. 'Jolly Roger' is not one of them, however, but a Cluster-flowered Rose of 1973 from Armstrong Nurseries. It has jolly orange-red flowers, semi-double, scarcely fragrant, in clusters on a low bush with wrinkled green leaves. It has not seized the lasting admiration of rose-lovers and is little grown now. It was photographed in the Huntington Gardens in California, where it was in fine form.

'Spartan' × 'Angelique'
Repeat flowering

◄ 'Johnnie Walker'
▼ 'Jolly Roger'

▼ 'Josephine Bruce'

▲ 'Joseph Guy'

'Joseph Guy'   Cluster-flowered
'Lafayette'

One of the earliest Cluster-flowered Roses—or Hybrid Polyanthas as they were called then—'Joseph Guy' was raised by the French firm of Auguste Nonin et Fils in 1921. Introduced to the United States in 1924 as 'Lafayette', it became very popular there. These days it is really only a historical item, its carmine-red flowers looking dull beside more modern Cluster-flowered Roses. Foliage is a glossy green. Better to grow its two sports, the pink 'Distinction' and the pure white 'Frau Dagmar Späth', both of which you can see in this book.

' Rödhätte' × 'Richmond'
Repeat flowering

'Josephine Bruce'   Large-flowered

Introduced as long ago as 1949, and often criticised for its sprawling growth and fondness for mildew, 'Josephine Bruce' is still much admired. The attraction is the color of the flowers: few red roses are so deep and velvety. There are only twenty-four petals, but they make up a big high-centred flower that opens slowly. Foliage is a dark olive-green. Some people claim that it is intensely fragrant; others find its scent only slight. Perhaps, as happened with 'Ena Harkness', there are two strains of 'Josephine Bruce'. The raisers were Bees of Chester in the United Kingdom.

'Crimson Glory' × 'Madge Whipp' or 'Jane Thornton'
Repeat flowering

'Joseph's Coat' — Cluster-flowered Climber

There are several climbers in the 'Masquerade' colors of yellow turning red, including a climbing sport of 'Masquerade' itself, but many people think of 'Joseph's Coat', raised by Herbert Swim in 1964, as the best of them. True, it is not very rampant (with careful pruning it can be grown as a large shrub) and it rarely makes a great mass of color, but there seem to be at least a few blooms all season, and they are prettily shaped and clear in their colors. Foliage is mid-green and glossy, tinted reddish when young. Joseph, in the Old Testament story, had a coat of many colors, and the name is appropriate for the rose.

'Buccaneer' × 'Circus'
Repeat flowering

'Joybells' — Cluster-flowered

In the shape of its two-toned pink, nicely perfumed flowers, this rose is a model for breeders to follow. Flowers are completely regular and imbricated like a formal double camellia. Nothing could be more attractive for a flower displayed several together. ('English Miss' is another, newer, rose of the same shape.) The plant is strong, with glossy green leaves, the variety's only fault being that its branches are excessively thorny. There is also a red and yellow Large-flowered Rose called 'Joybells', raised by Kordes. Do not confuse it with our present subject, which was a 1961 creation of the English raiser Herbert Robinson.

Unnamed seedling × 'Fashion'
Repeat flowering
Fragrant

'Joyfulness' — Cluster-flowered
'Frohsinn'

Better known these days under its German name ('Joyfulness' is a translation), this rose bears wide, 'Grandiflora' style flowers in a blend of peach and coral. Lightly scented, they open from long, elegant buds. It is a rose very much to the American taste, and it is a little surprising it has not found more favor there. Perhaps its rather leggy growth and the susceptibility of its glossy green leaves to black spot have been against it. Where it does well it is a lovely rose for cutting. It is a 1961 introduction from Mathias Tantau, who has also favored us with 'Frohsinn 82'.

'Horstman's Jubläumsrose' × 'Circus'
Repeat flowering

'Jubilee 150' — Cluster-flowered
MEIclaux
'Pigalle'

There is already a 'Pigalle', a dark red and cream Large-flowered Rose introduced by Meilland in 1946, so this rose is listed by the name given on its introduction to Australia in 1986, the sesquicentenary of South Australia, one of Australia's States. It is a festive blend of yellow and red—the colors of that State—with a good deal of orange thrown in. The foliage is dark red in its youth, becoming dark emerald-green, and the plant is on the tall side, and rather thorny. Unfortunately, 'Jubilee 150' has no fragrance. It was originally a Meilland introduction also.

'Prince Igor' × 'King's Ransom' seedling
Repeat flowering

'Judy Garland'
HARking
Cluster-flowered

The flowers open deep yellow, and, as they develop, a band of orange-red appears at the edge of each petal, gradually spreading over the entire surface like a curtain being slowly drawn across a stage. Large and shapely, with thirty-five petals, they come in small clusters on an upright bush, and are lovely for cutting, as they hold their form until they drop. It has dark green, glossy foliage. Raised in England by Jack Harkness, 'Judy Garland' has been very well received overseas, particularly in Japan and in India. It was introduced in 1978, and named in memory of the great and tragic star.

(['Super Star' × 'Circus'] × ['Sabine' × 'Circus']) × 'Pineapple Poll'
Repeat flowering

▲ 'Judy Garland'

'Julia's Rose'
Large-flowered

Very aptly named for the doyenne of flower arrangers, Julia Clements, 'Julia's Rose' hit the world of floral art like a stroke of lightning when the Wisbech Plant Farm introduced it in 1976. Its color is unique, an indescribable blend of *café au lait* and lavender, and its stems are long and smooth. The foliage is olive-green, red tinted when young. This is a rose for the rose enthusiast, needing protection from disease. The beautiful color only develops fully in cool weather; at the height of summer it is just pale pink. Alas, little of the scent of 'Blue Moon' has been passed on.

'Blue Moon' × 'Dr A. J. Verhage'
Repeat flowering

'Julie Delbard'
DELjuli
Cluster-flowered

You do not often see this rose outside France, but it is well liked there for its very pretty pink and apricot flowers and its compact growth. It seems to be at its best in the sunny climate of the south, where it was photographed. Despite its lack of perfume it is an excellent, long-lasting rose for cutting. Foliage is olive-green, tinted red when young. 'Julie Delbard' is an introduction from Georges Delbard, who raised it and introduced it in 1976.

('Zambra' × ['Orange Triumph' × 'Floradora']) × (['Orléans Rose' × 'Goldilocks'] × ['Bettina' × 'Henri Mallerin'])
Repeat flowering

▲ 'Julie Delbard'

'Julien Potin'
'Golden Pernet'
Large-flowered

Raised by Joseph Pernet-Ducher in 1924, 'Julien Potin' was one of the first so-called 'Pernetianas' (a term reserved for the early yellow Large-flowered Roses) to be a reliable garden rose, though rosarians of the day found it gave its best blooms on the side shoots. Winner of the gold medal in Portland, it is still worth growing in a cool, dry climate, for its primrose-yellow blooms are large and perfectly formed, and the foliage is glossy green. It was named for a leading French horticulturist, famous for his work with orchids, especially *Potinara*.

'Souvenir de Claudius Pernet' × unnamed
Repeat flowering
Fragrant

▲ 'Julien Potin'
▼ 'Julia's Rose'

▲ 'Julishka'

'Julishka'   Cluster-flowered
TANjuka

There is nothing whatever the matter with 'Julishka'. It is a strong very easy-to-grow rose, very free with its brilliant red flowers in clusters. The dark green young foliage is handsome too. True, there is little scent, and the bush is inclined to flop a bit, but these are minor criticisms. So why is it not seen more often? The answer seems to be that there are so *many* bright red cluster roses that 'Julishka' just does not stand out in the crowd. It is a 1976 introduction from Mathias Tantau. The dark green foliage and floppy stems suggest 'Europeana' as a parent.

Parentage undisclosed
Repeat flowering

'Just Joey'   Large-flowered

The Essex city of Colchester is famous in history as the seat of the warrior queen Boadicea, but for the past ninety years it has been famous for its roses too, especially a long succession of beauties from the old firm of Benjamin Cant & Sons. Star among them all, perhaps, is 'Just Joey', raised by Roger Pawsey and named in affectionate tribute to his wife. The bush is only moderate in size, but the richly scented flowers, with their distinctive frilled petals, can be enormous, and they are of unique color, a blend of coppery shades with apricot. It has broad, olive-green foliage. 'Just Joey' was introduced in 1973.

'Fragrant Cloud' × 'Dr A. J. Verhage'
Repeat flowering
Fragrant

'Kabuki'   Large-flowered
MEIgold
'Golden Prince'

'Kabuki' is sometimes claimed (though not by the raiser, Marie-Louisette Meilland, who knows better) to be superior to 'Peace'. It is not. Sure, the flowers are nearly as big as those of 'Peace'; the foliage is just as glossy and handsome; and the buds are longer and slimmer. But their deep gold fades rapidly as the flower opens, and they lack the touches of pink that make 'Peace' so lovely, even when it is pale. It is usually not so free with its blooms either. Still, it is a handsome rose. It was introduced in 1968.

('Monte Carlo' × 'Bettina') × ('Peace' × 'Soraya')
Repeat flowering
Fragrant

'Kalahari'   Large-flowered

It may seem a surprise to us amateurs to find that a salmon-pink rose like 'Kalahari' descends from a brace of red ancestors, two of them climbers, but the genes of the rose have many a trick up their sleeve and a master hybridist like Sam McGredy is ready to make use of them. The result is a tall-growing bush, with fairly large, shapely blooms, long-lasting but with little fragrance. It is a good rose for making a show in the garden, for it is free blooming and healthy. Foliage is a dark glossy green. 'Kalahari' was introduced in 1971.

'Uncle Walter' × ('Hamburger Phoenix' × 'Danse du feu')
Repeat flowering

▲ 'Kabuki'
◄ 'Just Joey'
▼ 'Kalahari'

▲ 'Karlsruhe'

▲ 'Kambala'
▼ 'Kanoe'

'Kambala' — Large-flowered
AROheddo

Raised in America by Armstrong Nurseries, 'Kambala' honors one of Sydney's more prominent schools for young ladies, Kambala College. Its well-scented blooms are deep yellow, shaded with old gold at the centre. They are large and shapely, the bush upright. The foliage is medium green and leathery. Popular in Australia, where it was introduced in 1988, it was apparently never introduced in America.

'Gingersnap' × 'Brandy'
Repeat flowering

'Kanoe' — Large-flowered

When this rose was photographed in Japan a couple of years ago, the growers said that it was introduced in 1939. If this is correct, then the Japanese breeders were then far in advance of the West, where Large-flowered Roses with the same stunning

▼ 'Karl Herbst'

coloring as 'Kanoe'—clear orange and gold—only became available forty-five years later. It is hard to imagine, World War II or no, that such a magnificent flower—large, shapely, and utterly novel—would have escaped the notice of the rest of the world. Foliage is dark green and glossy. There is no information on this rose in English; perhaps when it arrives in the West we shall know more. The name apparently honors Prince Kanoye, younger brother of the late Emperor Hirohito.

Parentage unknown
Repeat flowering

'Karl Herbst' — Large-flowered
'Red Peace', 'The Old Bull'

Herr Herbst was Wilhelm Kordes's right-hand man for many years; however, the name 'Red Peace' seems more appropriate for these huge, fire-red flowers. Even more appropriate is the nickname given by the hybridists, 'The Old Bull'. The pollen of Karl Herbst is potent indeed, and its descendants are

legion—'Perfecta', 'Piccadilly', 'Silver Lining', 'Maria Callas', 'Königin der Rosen', 'Red Devil', 'Grandpa Dickson' — all big, shapely roses. It is as a stud that 'Karl Herbst' will be remembered, for it is a difficult grower, and the blooms are only perfect in autumn, or fall. Foliage is dark green. 'Karl Herbst' was introduced in 1950 and it was awarded the RNRS gold medal in the same year.

'Peace' × 'Independence'
Repeat flowering

'Karlsruhe' — Cluster-flowered Climber

Wilhelm Kordes never disclosed the parentage of 'Karlsruhe', which he introduced in 1957, but it is safe to say that it was bred from *Rosa kordesii*, the fertile seedling from 'Max Graf' which was given the status of a 'hybrid species' and which Herr Kordes used extensively as a parent of cold-tolerant, repeat-flowering climbers. This one makes a moderate-growing plant, with shiny mid-green leaves and deep pink flowers, filled with petals (if not with fragrance) in the Old Garden Rose style. It makes a great show in summer and a lesser one in autumn, or fall. The city of Karlsruhe, founded in 1715, is near Heidelberg, and has been rebuilt after almost total destruction in World War II.

R. kordesii × unknown
Repeat flowering

'Katherine Kordes' — Large-flowered

Wilhelm Kordes has said that 'Katherine Kordes' (one of his early successes introduced in 1929) turned out in the end to be merely a step on the road that led to 'Crimson Glory', its grandchild. The rose world seems to have

agreed with him, for it is rarely cata-logued now. Yet one occasionally comes across a plant in an old garden, bearing shapely, high-centred blooms in almost-red deep pink. Its only faults are that it is not a true, deep red, and it lacks scent. Foliage is dull green.

('Willowmere' × 'Sensation') × 'Madame Caroline Testout'
Repeat flowering

'Katherine Loker'   Cluster-flowered

Both this rose's parents are best known as greenhouse roses, and it seems their offspring 'Katherine Loker' is also best as a greenhouse florist's rose, except in very warm climates. The bright yellow flowers are shapely and long lasting, and the plant appears strong. Foliage is a dark leathery green. This rose is worth a second look. Scent is only slight. It is a 1978 introduction from Herbert Swim and Jack Christensen.

'Zorina' × 'Dr A. J. Verhage'
Repeat flowering

'Kathleen'   Hybrid Musk

'Kathleen' can be thought of as a sister to 'Ballerina'. It has similar large clus-ters of small single flowers, but it is a slightly bigger, more sprawling shrub, and the almost-white blooms, opening from pink buds, are sweetly fragrant of musk. Its admirers (and there are many) compare them to apple blossoms. The

◀ 'Katherine Kordes'

▲ 'Kathleen'
◀ 'Katherine Loker'
▼ 'Kathleen Harrop'

flowers are followed, without prejudice to the later blooms, by sprays of orange hips, and the sight of both together is very pretty indeed. Foliage is dark green. 'Kathleen' is another Pemberton creation, introduced in 1922.

'Daphne' × 'Perle des Jardins'
Repeat flowering
Fragrant

'Kathleen Harrop'   Climbing Bourbon

A 1919 introduction from Alexander Dickson & Sons of Ireland, 'Kathleen Harrop' is a sport from 'Zéphyrine Drouhin', and like its parent, is a Climber, thornless, repeat-flowering, and most strongly fragrant. It differs in being slightly less vigorous and in its much softer color, which is mid-pink with slightly deeper tones on the reverse. Foliage is matt green and su-sceptible to mildew. 'Kathleen Harrop' has always been overshadowed by its celebrated parent, but it is a most lovely rose. Try planting mother and daughter together; their colors are in perfect harmony.

Sport from 'Zephyrine Drouhin'
Repeat flowering
Fragrant

THE ROSE IN INDIA

It is said that Brahma the Creator, wishing to endow the goddess Lakshmi with loveliness beyond that of any other being, gathered the essence of a myriad of roses and bestowed it upon her. It may seem ungrateful after that for her to adopt the lotus and not the rose as her favorite emblem, but perhaps she was being considerate towards her worshippers, for the rose is difficult to grow in most of Hindu India. The climate is too tropical and sweltering, though Wild Roses grow in the Himalayas.

It was not until the advent of Islam and especially the rise of the Moghul emperors in the early sixteenth century that the rose came into its own in Indian gardens. Babur, the founder of the dynasty, seems not to have been overly enchanted by the land he had conquered. In a famous passage in his diaries he laments, among other things, the scarcity of beautiful gardens in Hindustan and the ignorance of Indian gardeners. A keen and knowledgeable gardener himself, he set about raising standards, establishing gardens in the Persian manner throughout his domains. To furnish them, he brought many trees and flowers from Persia and Ferghana; cypresses and almonds, pomegranates and roses. Just what roses they were, no one seems to remember, but they may well have included the Damask Rose (*Rosa damascena*), which is a native of the Middle East. Always prized for its fragrance, it is still the most important source of Attar of Roses.

Thereby hangs a tale. It seems Babur's grandson Jahangir (another great gardener) was boating one day with his empress, the beautiful and clever Nur Jahan, on a lake in one of the royal gardens. Such was the luxury of the Moghul court that the entire surface of the water had been floated with fresh roses. The empress, noticing that the flowers were making the water oily, scooped some of the oil up. It proved to be powerfully scented of roses. Thus was attar of roses invented, and the delighted emperor showered riches and honor on his wife for her discovery. Our source for the story is impeccable: Jahangir's own autobiography. Apparently he was unaware that attar had already been made in Persia for over a hundred years.

Nur Jahan's niece, Arjumand Begum, is known to history as Mumtaz Mahal, she to whose memory Jahangir's son Shah Jahan built the Taj Mahal at Agra. Surely no monument ever raised by man is lovelier than this. Among the flowers that bloom in marble on its walls you will find roses. The gardens of the Taj used to be famous for living roses too, but they were not much in evidence when I was there last. A little to the north, however, at Delhi, the Indian Rose Society has a garden adorned with some of the most beautiful roses I have ever seen. The portraits of some of these are shown in this book. The summer heat of the Indian plains is such that the roses there tend to go into a state of shock, and, most unusually, these flowers are at their best in winter. Many of the latest European and American roses do well, and they are joined by some real beauties bred for the local conditions, notably by Dr P. B. Pal. Among them are such beauties as 'Princess of India' and 'Rajah Surendra Singh'. I should think a warm welcome awaits them should they be introduced to the West. It is also a delight to find such gallant old timers as 'Crimson Glory' and 'Marechal Niel', which Dr Pal considers to be still the best Climbing Roses for hot Indian conditions.

Further away to the north, roses abound in the Vale of Kashmir, and they are grown there commercially for export to the flower shops of Europe. Babur and Nur Jahan would approve. Surely they would be delighted by the roses at the great Moghul gardens of the Shalimar and the Nishat Bagh. Here came, 2300 years ago, the armies of Alexander the Great, and East met West for the first time. Is it fanciful to imagine that those two goddesses of beauty, Aphrodite and Lakshmi, each associated with the rose, linger still in the beauty and fragrance of flowers?

▲ *Indian architecture has always been rich in decoration; these roses adorn the palace of the Turkish Sultana at Fatehpur Sikri, built by the Moghul Emperor Akbar in the Hindu style.*

▲ *Many a beautiful rose has been bred in India in recent years, but few of these are known in other countries. This one is 'Delhi Princess', raised by Dr Pal of Delhi in 1968, but apparently no longer catalogued anywhere.*

◄ The climate of the Indian plains is such that roses there reverse their usual seasons, resting during the summer heat and blooming during the cooler days of winter. These are in the gardens of the Rashtrapati Bhavan in Delhi, the great palace built by Sir Edwin Lutyens in the 1920s for the British Viceroy and now the official residence of the president of India.

▲ Set in a beautiful garden, the Taj Mahal is itself adorned with the flowers of an empire, among them these sensitively carved roses.

◄ No status conscious Maharajah felt his palace complete without a suite of silver-plated furniture. With the reduction in princely fortunes since Independence, pieces like this side chair with its all-over pattern of rose buds often appear in salesrooms and antique shops.

▲ I like to think that the lady in this Indian miniature is none other than the Empress Nur Jahan, but the strictness of purdah in the Moghul court has deprived us of an authentic likeness of her. No mere artist would have been allowed to look upon her unveiled face.

◄ Rosa moschata, a native of the Middle East and Kashmir, is said to be the rose used by Nur Jahan to invent attar of roses. It is powerfully fragrant.

▲ The Nishat Bagh is on the shores of Lake Dal in Kashmir. Often called the most beautiful garden in the world, it has been famous for its roses for centuries. Alas, they were not in bloom when I was there.

► The great statesman of modern India Jawaharlal Nehru loved roses and wore one in his buttonhole whenever they were in season. This is one of the last photographs of him, taken only a few weeks before his death in 1964.

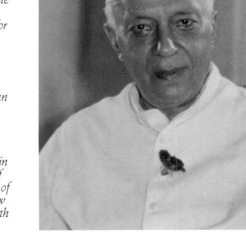

'Keith Kirsten'
Cluster-flowered

This rose is named in honor of one of South Africa's leading nurserymen. It is as bright and cheerful as he is, with its clusters of orange-scarlet, unfading blooms, growing against the lush, dark green foliage. It was raised in Germany by Mathias Tantau, but you will only find it in South Africa, where it was introduced in 1991. Herr Tantau has not revealed the parents, even to Keith!

Parentage undisclosed
Repeat flowering

▲ 'Keith Kirsten'
▼ 'Kentucky Derby'

'Kentucky Derby'
Large-flowered

When Armstrong Nurseries introduced 'Kentucky Derby' back in 1972, many rosarians thought that it was just another red rose—good, but not out of the ordinary. Time has shown it better than that, at least in warm climates. The bush has proved reliable and easy to grow and the flowers are of consistent standard. They are nicely formed, quite large, and their rich color does not fade. Foliage is large, mid-green and leathery.

The only demerit is lack of fragrance. The raiser was David Armstrong.

'John S. Armstrong' × 'Grand Slam'
Repeat flowering

'Kerry Gold'
Cluster-flowered

Introduced by Pat Dickson in 1976, 'Kerry Gold' still looks pretty good, with its flowers of deep yellow, often set off by splashes of red on the outside petals against dark green foliage. The clusters are large and the bush is compact and healthy. This rose likes a cool climate. It is losing popularity in the face of competition from the many more recent yellow Cluster-flowered Roses, many of which surpass 'Kerry Gold' in scent. Despite what many experts claim, if there is a choice of fragrant roses in a particular color, the most sweetly scented will be the better seller.

'Circus' × 'Allgold'
Repeat flowering

'Kerryman'
Cluster-flowered

The Irish tell Kerryman jokes the way the rest of the world tell Irish and Polish jokes; but there is nothing ludicrous about this rose, a 1971 Sam McGredy introduction. It bears quite large 10 centimetre (4 inch) flowers in a blend of pinks with salmon, shapely and in nicely spaced clusters, and there is a soft fragrance. The bush is of medium height, but alas, the shiny, dark green foliage is apt to get black spot. Treat the rose kindly! It is a sister seedling of 'Molly McGredy'.

'Paddy McGredy' × ('Madame Léon Cuny' × 'Columbine')
Repeat flowering
Fragrant

'Kijune'
Large-flowered

The name of this Japanese rose means 'pledge of allegiance'. This seems an odd name for a rose which changes color. 'Kijune' opens bright yellow with slight touches of red, but as the flower ages it becomes entirely red. This is familiar enough among the Cluster-flowered Roses ('Masquerade' is the prototype), but rare in a Large-flowered Rose. Foliage is glossy green. 'Kijune' would be a great hit if it were introduced to the West. The growers give a date 1935, which is hard to believe; 'Masquerade' did not arrive until 1949.

Parentage unknown
Repeat flowering

▲ 'Kerry Gold'
▼ 'Kerryman'

▼ 'Kijune'

▲ 'Kirsten'
◄ 'Kim'

'Kirsten'
Cluster-flowered

POULkir

'Kirsten' is probably intended as Poulsen's answer to Kordes's very successful 'Antique Silk'—it is much the same ecru color, with perhaps a bit more apricot at the centre. The blooms are not large, but very prettily formed, and they open very slowly in the vase, lasting for at least ten days. Foliage is a glossy green. It is basically a greenhouse rose for the florists, who are finding it very useful for wedding bouquets, but it also grows quite well in the garden. It is not as tall a bush as its rival. Poulsen introduced it in 1991, its parentage unrevealed. Do not confuse it with 'Kirsten Poulsen', a deep pink Poulsen Cluster-flowered Rose of 1924.

Parentage undisclosed
Repeat flowering

'Kim'
Cluster-flowered

There are not many yellow dwarf Cluster-flowered Roses—'Patio Roses' as they have been known—and 'Kim' is as nice as any. Its flowers are shapely and astonishingly large for so small a plant; they are often brushed with pink, and last very well in water. Foliage is small, matt and light green. There is some scent. Plant it as an edging to taller roses, to mask bare legs, or as a pot-plant. Named in memory of Master Kim Mulford, it was raised by Jack Harkness and introduced in 1973.

('Orange Sensation' × 'Allgold') × 'Elizabeth of Glamis'
Repeat flowering

▼ 'King's Ransom' (yellow), with 'Virgo'
► 'Kiss'

'King's Ransom'
Large-flowered

Exhibitors are inclined to criticise 'King's Ransom' for floppiness in the open bloom, but its long buds are elegant indeed (fit companions, in the arrangement pictured here, for the shapely 'Virgo'). The name might imply a deeper color than it is, but it is still a beautiful, luminous yellow and it fades but little in the sun. The bush is sturdy and upright, the light green leaves glossy and resistant to black spot, though not always to mildew. Winner of the 1962 AARS award, it was for many years the leading yellow garden rose, a triumph for its raiser Dennison Morey and for Jackson & Perkins.

'Golden Masterpiece' × 'Lydia'
Repeat flowering
Fragrant

'Kiss'
Cluster-flowered

KORokis
'Kordes Rose Kiss'

Primarily a cut-flower variety, 'Kiss' is one of those Cluster-flowered Roses where the individual blooms in the cluster often have stems long enough to be cut separately; or, should the florist choose, the blooms can be treated as a small bouquet on the one stem. Individually, the flowers are not very large, but they are very shapely indeed and last a long time in the vase. Their color is pale salmon-pink, softer and more delicate than 'Sonia', which 'Kiss' is

evidently intended to rival. The bush is tall, with dark green leaves, and very prolific. Scent is only slight. Reimer Kordes introduced it in 1988.

Parentage undisclosed
Repeat flowering

'Kiss of Fire'   Large-flowered

Jean Gaujard's aptly named 'Kiss of Fire' was introduced in 1960, but it seems to be catalogued only in Canada these days. The blooms are large and shapely, in golden yellow, with a brushing of flame around the petal edges, and the foliage is handsomely glossy. If it will grow in both hot India, where it was photographed, and cold Canada, then it should do well just about anywhere. It is somewhat reminiscent of 'Peace' and 'Double Delight', two favorite roses.

Parentage unknown
Repeat flowering

'Kitty Kininmonth'   Large-flowered Climber

For many years one of the most popular of Alister Clark's hybrids of *Rosa gigantea*, 'Kitty Kininmonth' is not so often seen these days. Inevitably it is compared to the same raiser's 'Lorraine Lee', and though it does not make such a gorgeous display, the individual blooms are possibly finer, although not in such a distinctive shade of pink. Foliage is dark green and wrinkled. It is fragrant too and like all the group it is a rampant grower. It resents prolonged frost. Introduced in 1922, it was named, like so many of Clark's roses, for one of his relatives.

R. gigantea × unnamed seedling
Repeat flowering
Fragrant

'Königin der Rosen'   Large-flowered
'Colour Wonder'

The 'queen of roses' enthused Reimer Kordes when he introduced this rose in 1964. It made a big impression in Europe, but not elsewhere. Sure, the flowers were shapely and lovely in color—coral with cream on the

▲ 'Kiss of Fire'
◄ 'Kitty Kininmonth'
▼ 'Königin der Rosen'

reverse—but the bushes were dumpy and shy-blooming. Under glass it is a different story, and it has proved an ideal greenhouse rose, the bushes free flowering, and the blooms, with their thick, short petals, long-lasting and easy for the florist to handle. Foliage is a glossy bronze-green, with plum tints when young. It has transmitted those good qualities to many fine offspring. It is itself a cross between two beauties and it has inherited their prickliness.

'Super Star' × 'Perfecta'
Repeat flowering

'Königin von Dänemark'   Alba
'Reine de Denmarck', 'Queen of Denmark', 'Naissance de Venus'

The most richly colored of the Alba Roses, 'Königin von Dänemark' opens brilliant pink, growing paler by the time the flowers are fully open, and they are most perfectly quartered. In its day, it was a leading exhibition rose. Fragrance is superb, but the plant is inclined to be tall and leggy. The foliage has a distinct glaucous tone to set off the flowers. 'Königin von Dänemark' was raised by James Booth and introduced in 1826. The Booth nursery was in Schleswig-Holstein, then part of Denmark but now in Germany.

'Maiden's Blush' × unknown
Summer flowering
Fragrant

▲ 'Königin von Dänemark'

'Kordes Perfecta'   Large-flowered

KORdlu
'Perfecta'

When it is grown well, this rose lives up to its name—it is indeed perfection. The blooms are huge, their seventy petals arranged with breathtaking symmetry. The color is meltingly lovely—cream, heavily overlaid with cyclamen pink—and the blooms are fragrant. Alas, such perfection is only usual in the autumn, or fall, and then only in warm, dry weather; rain soon ruins everything. The bush is lush in growth and the foliage is very dark green and glossy, with plum tints when young. This is not an easy rose to grow; only exhibitors should grow it. But they can hardly do without it. It was raised by Wilhelm Kordes in 1957.

'Spek's Yellow' × 'Karl Herbst'
Repeat flowering
Fragrant

'Korona'   Cluster-flowered

For years, 'Korona' was the leading orange-red rose, and it is by no means a back number yet. The flowers are as dazzling as ever, though they do tend to dull with age, and the growth is tall and healthy, with flowers abundantly borne in great clusters. Foliage is a matt olive-green. If you except its lack of scent, its only other faults are its occasional slowness in repeating bloom, and the informal shape of the individual flowers, a bit old-fashioned in these days of perfectly formed Cluster-flowered Roses. 'Korona' was a 1956 triumph for Wilhelm Kordes.

'Obergärtner Wiebicke' × 'Independence'
Repeat flowering

'Kronenbourg'   Large-flowered

'Flaming Peace'

When raiser Sam McGredy introduced 'Kronenbourg' in 1965, some British judges of new roses sniffed that it had all the qualities desired in a fine rose except a beautiful color. The flower starts out life in flaming scarlet and gold, but always finishes dull purple with cream on the reverse against shiny dark green leaves. Sam describes it as 'claret and traminer', which is hardly apt for a rose named for his favorite beer! A sport from 'Peace', it is said that he gave the nursery worker who discovered it a bonus, which the lad spent, not on beer, but on a motorbike. Some find it more fragrant than 'Peace'.

Sport from 'Peace'
Repeat flowering

▲ 'Kronenbourg'
◄ 'Kordes Perfecta'
▼ 'Korona'

'La France' Large-flowered

No patriotic Frenchman would give a name like this to a rose unless it was sensational, and back in 1867, 'La France' certainly was. It was the first of a new class, the Large-flowered Roses (Hybrid Teas as they were then known), combining the grace and elegance of the Teas with the vigor and hardiness of the Hybrid Perpetuals. The exquisite, soft pink flowers of 'La France', full of petals and the sweetest perfume, captivate everyone still. Foliage is mid-green and semi-glossy.

Probably 'Madame Victor Verdier' × 'Madame Bravy'
Repeat flowering
Fragrant

▲ 'La France'
▼ 'La Jolla'

'La Jolla' Large-flowered

The 65-petalled 'La Jolla' is a splendid rose for a hot dry climate. The picture was taken in the gardens of the Indian Rose Society in Delhi. The blooms are very large, sometimes too large and heavy for the slim stems, and shapely. They blend pink with cream and gold towards the centre, all overlaid with deeper veining. The bush is upright, with ample, dark green leaves. Raised by Herbert Swim and introduced in 1964, it is named for the Californian town whose inhabitants pronounce it 'La Hoya'.

'Charlotte Armstrong' × 'Contrast'
Repeat flowering
Fragrant

'La Passionata' Large-flowered

DELup
'Betsy Ross'

A bevy of high-powered ladies gave their names to the creation of this lovely Delbard rose of 1968. La Passionata herself was a heroine of the Spanish Civil War, and 'Betsy Ross' was a revolutionary hero too, the creator of the American flag (the 'Stars and Stripes'). The parents of the rose were stunning ladies too. The flowers are large, dark red and shapely against leathery green foliage. What a pity there is so little perfume.

'Gloria di Roma' × ('La Vaudoise' × 'Divine')
Repeat flowering

'La Reine Victoria' Bourbon

'Reine'

It is intriguing that the rose named for Queen Victoria should not only be French-raised (by Joseph Schwartz of Lyon in 1872) but a member of a class named for the French royal family. 'La Reine Victoria' suggests the lady in her youth rather than plump middle age, for the blooms are of a dainty perfection with their shell-shaped petals and soft rose-pink color, like a rose on a Victorian teacup. It has a beautiful fragrance and blooms throughout the season, but it must have the best of cultivation to show its full beauty. Foliage is light green and smooth.

Parentage unknown
Repeat flowering
Fragrant

'La Ville de Bruxelles' Damask

If you want to see what a perfect flower in the Old French style looks like, this rose can be relied on to produce many of them—immaculately quartered, deliciously fragrant and a rich unshaded pink. They are large too, for a Damask, often reaching 13 centimetres (5 inches) across. Alas, the slender branches often bow under the weight of the blooms. Foliage is light green and plentiful. La Ville de Bruxelles is the Belgian capital, but the rose came from J.-P. Vibert of Paris, in 1849.

Parentage unknown
Repeat flowering
Fragrant

▲ 'La Ville de Bruxelles'
◄ 'La Passionata'
▼ 'La Reine Victoria'

'Lady'
Large-flowered

Bred from Georges Delbard's lavender 'Song of Paris' using the pollen of Swim's pastel pink 'Royal Highness', the romantically named 'Lady' is a delightful pink rose in the manner of the beauties of the 1920s, its thirty-five petals slightly deeper on the reverse. The bush is pure 1980s—compact, with strong mid-green foliage—and both parents have contributed their fragrance. 'Lady' came out in 1980, from Herbert Swim's old partner O. L. Weeks.

'Song of Paris' × 'Royal Highness'
Repeat flowering
Fragrant

▲ 'Lady'
▼ 'Lady Brisbane'

'Lady Brisbane'
China

'Cramoisi Supérieur', 'Agrippina'

The pundits will probably throw up their hands at the listing of a rose under a name known not to be authentic—but the rose in the picture *is* the one commonly known in Australia as 'Lady Brisbane', and it is by no means certain that it is 'Cramoisi Supérieur' in colonial dress. It is a typical crimson China, making a dainty low bush, charmingly adorned all year with sprays of little crimson flowers. Their outer petals often show white streaks, a 'fault' inherited by many a red Modern Garden Rose. Foliage is small, dark green, with plum tints when young. 'Cramoisi Supérieur' was raised by the French raiser Coquereau and introduced in 1832. It is not known when it came to Australia.

Parentage unknown
Repeat flowering

'Lady Curzon'
Modern Shrub

Another Modern Shrub Rose which is vigorous enough to train as a Climber, 'Lady Curzon', left to itself, will mound up its prickly branches into a bush much wider than tall. In early summer it covers itself for several weeks with highly fragrant, single flowers in a pleasing shade of mid-pink with just a hint of salmon. Foliage is mid-green, glossy and wrinkled. It would look stunning if allowed to trail among upright blue flowers like delphiniums or campanulas. 'Lady Curzon' was raised in 1901 by the British nurseryman Turner and named for the then wife of the Viceroy of India.

Rosa macrantha × *R. rugosa rubra*
Summer flowering
Fragrant

'Lady Godiva'
Rambler

Introduced by William Paul in 1908, 'Lady Godiva' is a sport of 'Dorothy Perkins', described in the catalogues of the day as, would you believe it, 'flesh colored'. Apart from its color, which many people preferred to the original, it is exactly the same. You do not often see it now, and it is mainly remembered for being the parent of the very popular Polyantha 'The Fairy', which, although it is supposed to be a 'Lady Godiva' sport, looks nothing like it. Foliage is small, dark green and glossy.

Sport from 'Dorothy Perkins'
Summer flowering

▲ 'Lady Godiva'
◄ 'Lady Curzon'
▼ 'Lady Hillingdon'

'Lady Hillingdon'
Tea

Elegant is the word for this rose, the most popular of the Teas for its hardiness, its delicious tea fragrance, and the perfect way in which the plum-colored young leaves set off the slim and shapely yellow flowers. The leaves mature to dark purplish green. Good as the bush is, it is in the climbing form that 'Lady Hillingdon' is most often seen—and with good reason, because it is the most continuously flowering Climbing Rose there is. Give it a sheltered wall in cold climates, for it is not all that hardy. The bush came out in 1910, from the English firm of Lowe & Shawyer. The climbing sport came from Hicks in 1917.

'Papa Gontier' × 'Madame Hoste'
Repeat flowering
Fragrant

'Lady Huntingfield' Large-flowered

The roses from Australian hybridist Alister Clark are suddenly right back in fashion, along with anything else of the romantic, old-fashioned persuasion. There is nothing old-fashioned about this one, however. Its blends of apricot and yellow are right up to date, though it was introduced back in 1937! It is a sturdy plant and the flowers are large, shapely and deliciously fragrant against dark green, glossy foliage. In Australia, Victorian and South Australian nurseries carry it—and perhaps it will soon be admired elsewhere in the world.

Parentage unknown
Repeat flowering
Fragrant

▲ 'Lady Huntingfield'
▼ 'Lady Rose'

'Lady Mary Fitzwilliam' Large-flowered

Named for a grand-daughter of King William IV, 'Lady Mary Fitzwilliam' was raised by Henry Bennett in 1882. It was greeted with derision: 'A weaker and more unsatisfactory grower it would be impossible to find,' sneered one writer of the day. However, it is one of the most important ancestors of Modern Garden Roses, and it is still a lovely, fragrant bloom in soft pink. Foliage is pale green and matt. Beware of impostors—the lovely 'Mrs Wakefield Christie-Miller' is sometimes sold as 'Lady Mary Fitzwilliam'.

'Devoniensis' × 'Victor Verdier'
Repeat flowering
Fragrant

'Lady Meilland' Large-flowered
MEIalsonite

Why has this lovely rose not found favor in the United States? It is firmly entrenched in the catalogues in countries as far apart as Australia, France, New Zealand, South Africa and Italy, and it won quite a few awards on its introduction in 1982. The flowers are a delight, soft coral in color, large in size, beautifully shaped, and fragrant as well. They come on long, straight stems for cutting, on tall bushes with shiny dark green foliage. It is from Meilland of course, and though the parentage is undeclared it is a safe bet that its ancestors are Meilland roses too.

Parentage undisclosed
Repeat flowering
Fragrant

▲ 'Lady Mary Fitzwilliam'
▼ 'Lady Meilland'

'Lady Rose' Large-flowered
KORlady
'Kordes Rose Lady Rose'

Reimer Kordes might have named 'Lady Rose' after a real-life lady, or maybe he just wanted to draw our attention to the fact that there is something that is very feminine in the big, shapely, sweetly scented flowers, despite the brightness of their orange-pink color. There is certainly nothing delicate about the bush, which is on the tall side and rudely healthy, with dark glossy green foliage. 'Lady Rose' won the Belfast gold medal in 1981, the year it was introduced.

Unnamed seedling × 'Träumerei'
Repeat flowering
Fragrant

'Lady Seton' Large-flowered

Free flowering, very fragrant, and a fine garden rose, 'Lady Seton' is also excellent for cutting, something that must have delighted its namesake—'Lady Seton' is the married name of Julia Clements, England's leading flower arranger for many years. Clear rose pink, with just a suggestion of salmon, the flowers are large and of thirty-five petals, and the bush is tallish, with mid-green, semi-glossy foliage. Introduced in 1966 by Sam McGredy, it won several awards for its fragrance, which is just as much a delight after a quarter of a century.

'Ma Perkins' × 'Mischief'
Repeat flowering
Fragrant

sports inherit. Foliage is leaden green. 'Lady Sylvia' was a great favorite in Britain. From its introduction by William Stevens in 1926 until the mid-1960s, if you bought a bunch of pink roses at Covent Garden, the chances are that it would have been 'Lady Sylvia'. Today it will be 'Sonia', but she has not her predecessor's sweetness either of color or scent.

Sport from 'Madame Butterfly'
Repeat flowering
Fragrant

'Lagerfeld' Large-flowered
ARAqueli
'Starlight'

How does one name a series of new roses to tempt the public to buy them as a set? Armstrong Nurseries hit on one newsworthy answer in 1985, with a trio named for Paris couturiers—their 'French collection' of 'Givenchy', 'Lanvin' and 'Lagerfeld' (Meilland had already taken the most famous, 'Christian Dior'). 'Lagerfeld', a Jack Christensen creation, is, appropriately, one of the most stylish of the 'blue' Large-flowered Roses, its pale mauve flowers large, shapely, and fragrant, and its bush as strong as any of them, with leaden green foliage. As a bonus, the autumn, or fall, flowers are followed by large orange hips.

'Blue Nile' × ('Ivory Tower' × 'Angel Face')
Repeat flowering
Fragrant

'Lancôme' Large-flowered
DELboip

One of the leading greenhouse roses (it will bloom in winter at much lower temperatures than many) the deep pink 'Lancôme' is not one of Armstrong's 'French Collection', but a 1973 creation of the French raiser Georges Delbard. Its parentage is distinguished, if complex, and the blooms are large, high centred and long lasting, but, alas, without fragrance. Foliage is dark green.

('Dr Albert Schweitzer' × ['Michèle Meilland' × 'Bayadère']) × ('Meimet' × 'Présent Filial')
Repeat flowering

▲ 'Lady Seton'
▼ 'Lady Sylvia'

▲ 'Lancôme'
▼ 'Lagerfeld'

'Lady Sylvia' Large-flowered
One of the loveliest of all pink roses, 'Lady Sylvia' is a sport from 'Madame Butterfly', which in turn is a sport from 'Ophelia'. 'Lady Sylvia' bears all the good qualities of 'Ophelia'—the perfect form, fine fragrance, and iron-tough constitution that all of the 'Ophelia'

'Lanvin' — Large-flowered
AROlemo

Raised by Jack Christensen in 1975, 'Lanvin' is one of the series that Armstrong Nurseries named for Paris couturiers—their 'French Collection'. It is a vigorous Bush Rose, bearing large, stylish blooms in a medium yellow which holds well in the sun. A pleasing rose for cutting, as the stems are long and slim, it has virtually no fragrance, but then the clear yellows, as a rule, are not noteworthy in this respect. Foliage is dark green, tinted red and semi-glossy. Introduced in 1985, exhibitors should find it worth adding to their collections.

Unnamed seedling × 'Katherine Loker'
Repeat flowering

▲ 'Lanvin'
▼ 'Laura'

'Las Vegas' — Large-flowered
KORgane

The glitzy colors of red and gold certainly suit a rose named for America's gambling and showbiz paradise, but it is a German rose, from Kordes in 1981, and its parents are German too. The glossy green foliage and brown prickles form an effective background to the dazzling blooms, which, unusually for a bicolored rose, are very fragrant. They often come three to a stem. And to complete the picture, the rose won a gold medal in Geneva—a long way indeed from Las Vegas!

'Ludwigshafen am Rhein' × 'Feuerzauber'
Repeat flowering
Fragrant

'Laura' — Large-flowered
MEIdragelac
'Laura 81'

The codename 'MEIdragelac' is the official one, but most people will find that unpronounceable and so prefer 'Laura'. The flowers are very handsome, large, full petalled, and a gentle blend of salmon and cream. They are lightly fragrant, and sometimes come several together. Foliage is fresh green, semi-glossy.

('Pharaoh' × 'Königin der Rosen') × (['Suspense' × 'Suspense'] × 'King's Ransom')
Repeat flowering

▲ 'Las Vegas'
▼ 'Lavaglut'

'Lavaglut' — Cluster-flowered
KORlech
'Lava Glow', 'Intrigue'

This is one of the best of the red Cluster-flowered Roses, its color dark and smouldering, its flowers attractively camellia shaped, the plant compact and floriferous. Many roses of this color tend to scorch in hot sun, but not this one! The dark shiny green foliage does have the fault of susceptibility to black spot, and thus the rose needs a sunny, dry climate to do its best. It is a Reimer Kordes introduction of 1978. The German name, meaning 'Lava fire',

worry. Strong in growth, to 10 metres (30 feet) high and wide on a wall, it bears large, deliciously fragrant golden yellow flowers in profusion early in the season and intermittently afterwards. They only have about fifteen petals, but are most elegantly formed. Foliage is bright green and glossy. This rose has a complicated history. Originally raised in about 1920 by Joseph Pernet-Ducher, it was bought up by Major Lawrence Johnston for his famous garden at Hidcote Manor, from which it was finally introduced to the world in 1948.

'Madame Eugène Verdier' × 'Persian Yellow'
Repeat flowering
Fragrant

▲ 'Lawrence Johnston'
▼ 'Lavender Pinocchio'

▲ 'Lavender Lassie'

is most appropriate; calling it 'Intrigue' confuses it with the excellent purple American rose of that name.

'Grüss an Bayern' × unnamed seedling
Repeat flowering

'Lavender Lassie' Hybrid Musk

Herr Wilhelm Kordes, who raised this rose in 1960, described this rose as a Hybrid Musk. Many people think it is not quite shrubby enough to be thus described. It is more like a tall and sprawling Cluster-flowered Rose; and the flowers are hardly lavender. Rather they are rose-pink, with just a hint of mauve, at least in warm climates (apparently it is more mauve in Germany). However, 'Lavender Lassie' is a very attractive rose, tough and easy to grow, and bears its clusters of many-petalled and strongly fragrant blooms with freedom all season. Foliage is dull green.

'Hamburg' × 'Madame Norbert Lavavasseur'
Repeat flowering
Fragrant

'Lavender Pinocchio' Cluster-flowered

This was the first of the mauve Cluster-flowered Roses to be introduced and in many ways is still the best. The rather odd name makes sense when you realize that the rose is intended as a lavender version of the popular 'Pinocchio' ('Rosenmärchen'). The color is not a straight lavender, but pleasingly mixed with *café au lait* tones; the flowers have a pleasant shape and good fragrance, and the rather short bush is as robust as any of the mauve roses, with matt green leaves. Bred by Eugene Boerner, it was introduced by Jackson & Perkins in 1948.

'Pinocchio' × 'Grey Pearl'
Repeat flowering
Fragrant

'Lawrence Johnston' Large-flowered Climber
'Hidcote Yellow'

This is one of the outstanding Climbing Roses, at least where black spot is not a

'Le Rêve' Large-flowered

Of two rather similar sister seedlings, Joseph Pernet-Ducher chose to introduce 'Le Rêve' as the golden yellow rose of his dreams in 1923. It was not until twenty-five years later that the other came out as 'Lawrence Johnston', to eclipse its sister in popularity. A little smaller in flower and paler in color, 'Le Rêve' is still a most attractive rose, very fragrant, strong in growth, and bearing great quantities of flowers early in the season, against dark shiny green foliage. It is possibly a little more resistant to black spot, but it rarely flowers after its big display.

'Madame Eugène Verdier' × 'Persian Yellow'
Repeat flowering
Fragrant

'Le Rouge et le Noir' Large-flowered
DELcart

Stendahl's eerie novel about the Vatican is probably less well known these days than the red and black of the roulette wheel, but either source for the name suggests the dramatic beauty of this rose raised by Georges Delbard of Paris. The petals are such a deep (though vivid) shade of cardinal red that they often have a black sheen to them. It is reputed to be a very reliable performer. It has dark green leaves, with red tints in its youth.

Parentage undisclosed
Repeat flowering
Fragrant

▶ 'Léda'
▼ 'Le Rêve'

▲ 'Le Rouge et le Noir'

▼ 'Leander'

'Leander' English Rose
AUSlea

David Austin has been criticized for bringing too many of his English Roses onto the market, and some of them *are* rather alike. 'Leander' is a case in point, as it is very like its parent 'Charles Austin'. It has slightly smaller flowers, however, and is a much larger grower, to 2.5 metres (8 feet) tall. The apricot yellow of the flowers is very unusual among the big Shrub Roses. The blooms are borne in wide sprays, and make a fine sight in early summer, but there are not as many to follow as one might like. Foliage is mid-green and smooth. Named for the lover of Hero, it was introduced in 1982.

'Charles Austin' × unnamed seedling
Repeat flowering
Fragrant

'Léda' Damask
'Painted Damask'

There are two forms of this early nineteenth-century rose, just about identical except for color. The English prefer the white one, the tips of its petals stained with carmine, hence the nickname, 'Painted Damask'. The French prefer the pink, on whose petals the carmine stains are less conspicuous. Most books illustrate the English form. So, just to be different, this book shows you the French. Both are luxuriant growers, given good treatment, with lush, dark green leaves. Naturally they are splendidly fragrant. Leda was the maiden seduced by Zeus (disguised as a swan, of all things). One of the children of the union was the beautiful and disastrous Helen of Troy.

Parentage unknown
Summer flowering
Fragrant

'Lemon Honey' Cluster-flowered
DICkindle

Although this is an Irish-bred rose, by Pat Dickson, it appears to be available only in New Zealand. The rest of us are missing out on a most attractive flower: it is large enough to pass for a Large-flowered Rose, shapely, softly scented, and of lovely pastel coloring—a pale lemon yellow and cream. The bush appears to be healthy, with dark green foliage. 'Lemon Honey' came out in 1986.

Parentage undisclosed
Repeat flowering
Fragrant

▲ 'Lemon Honey'
▼ 'Len Turner'

'Len Turner' Cluster-flowered
DICjeep
'Daydream'

This really is a distinctive rose with its red and white flowers, carried in clusters on a very bushy plant, with dark glossy green foliage. It is a splendid rose for cutting, though the stems are not very long. You might try mixing it

in a bowl with the climber 'Handel' of similar coloring but a different flower shape. Forget the name 'Daydream', which has been used several times before, and remember the sterling service of Len Turner, secretary to the RNRS for nearly twenty years. His rose is a 1984 Dickson creation.

'Mullard Jubilee' × 'Eyepaint'
Repeat flowering
Fragrant

▶ 'Léonie Lamesch'
▼ 'Leverkusen'

'Léonie Lamesch' Polyantha

Fräulein Lamesch was the daughter of a well-known German nurseryman, and became the wife of Peter Lambert, remembered by rosarians as the raiser of 'Frau Karl Druschki'. This rose, which he dedicated to his wife, is not a typical Polyantha. The bushes are a bit taller, though still on the short side, and the individual flowers a bit larger. They are a charming blend of creamy yellow and copper tones, due to the influence of Tea Rose ancestry. The foliage is rich green and soft. 'Léonie Lamesch' came out in 1899; it is still well worth growing.

'Aglaia' × 'Kleiner Alfred'
Repeat flowering

'Leverkusen' Cluster-flowered Climber

This is a very handsome rose indeed—well clad with glossy green foliage and bearing large, pale yellow blooms in sprays in summer and autumn, or fall; they are scented too. It is not overvigorous, and makes a fine pillar rose or sprawling shrub. It is especially fine in cool climates. It was introduced in 1954 by Wilhelm Kordes and named for a small town near Cologne.

Rosa kordesii × 'Golden Glow'
Repeat flowering
Fragrant

'Lilac Charm' — Cluster-flowered

A rose for favored climates, as it objects to cold and rain, but a charming one indeed, its single flowers of palest mauve set off by crimson stamens and an elusive fragrance. It is not a very strong grower, needing the best of care, but it flowers quite freely against dull dark green foliage. Cut it young: the color is richer indoors. It was introduced by E. B. LeGrice in 1961. In 1968, LeGrice introduced 'Silver Charm'. Bred from 'Lilac Charm', it is very like it. Some people find it a stronger grower.

'Lavender Pinocchio' × seedling from *Rosa californica*
Repeat flowering
Fragrant

'Lilac Dawn' — Cluster-flowered

Despite its fragrance and its mauve flowers being a rather richer tone than is usual, 'Lilac Dawn' seems to have dropped out of the catalogues, perhaps because its flowers, which are often more pink than mauve, just are not 'blue' enough. Foliage is a leathery light green. It was a 1964 introduction from Swim and Weeks.

'Lavender Pinocchio' × 'Frolic'
Repeat flowering
Fragrant

'Lilac Time' — Large-flowered

Ever since there have been hybridists creating roses, they have been playing games on a hopeful public with names that suggest that the rose in question is blue, or at least purple. Take 'Lilac Time', for example. All that you usually see in the rose is a sort of off-pink. Still, it is a pretty rose, informally shaped, with thirty-three petals and a sweet fragrance. The plant is strong and free with dull light green foliage. It was introduced by Sam McGredy in 1956.

'Golden Dawn' × 'Luis Brinas'
Repeat flowering
Fragrant

'Lili Marlene' — Cluster-flowered

KORlima
'Lili Marleen'

Everywhere you go in Europe, you will see this rose, in great beds at the public parks, in smaller ones at the service station, in twos and threes in front gardens. Everywhere it will be making an eye-catching splash of red. Foliage is dark leathery green and the bush is of average height, sending up its clusters with abandon. Though the flowers are neither large nor scented, they are a real, true red, with no purple or orange in it. It is as memorable as the song for which it was named. One of Reimer Kordes's early successes, it was introduced in 1958.

('Our Princess' × 'Rudolph Timm') × 'Ama'
Repeat flowering

▲ 'Lilac Charm'
▼ 'Lilac Dawn'

▲ 'Lilac Time'
▼ 'Lili Marlene'

'Lincoln Cathedral' Large-flowered
GLAnlin

Mr G. W. T. Langdale of Lincoln certainly believes in supporting his local cathedral, for he named his new rose after it. Introduced in 1983, and winning the RNRS gold medal in that year, it was the only rose Mr Langdale had developed up to that time. It is a large, exhibition flower with twenty-eight petals in a blend of pink and apricot; foliage is lush and glossy green, as you would expect from the parentage.

'Silver Jubilee' × 'Troika'
Repeat flowering

'Lissy Horstmann' Large-flowered

'Lissy Horstmann' might be a little short on petals, only twenty-five, but everything else about it is first rate— the glowing crimson color, the long buds, the strong, upright bush, and, above all, the intense perfume. Foliage is a dark matt green. A fine rose for cutting, it was raised in 1943 by Mathias Tantau senior, the father of the raiser of 'Super Star'. It likes a warm climate.

'Hadley' × 'Heros'
Repeat flowering
Fragrant

▲ 'Lincoln Cathedral'
▼ 'Lissy Horstmann'

'Lilian Austin' English Rose

You can bet that when a raiser names a rose for his mother, he regards it highly. So it is no surprise that 'Lilian Austin' is one of the most desirable of David Austin's English Roses, with big, full-petalled blooms in soft salmon-pink, with plenty of fragrance. The bush is compact, free with its flowers, and the glossy green foliage is ample and healthy. It was introduced in 1973.

'Aloha' × 'The Yeoman'
Repeat flowering
Fragrant

'Limelight' Large-flowered
KORikon
'Golden Medallion'

In cool weather, the young flowers sometimes show a suggestion of lime green, but usually this 1984 Reimer Kordes production is a straight yellow, deep and brilliant. It is a very good yellow rose too, especially for a humid summer climate, the foliage being dark, glossy and disease-resistant. The large,

▲ 'Lilian Austin'
▼ 'Limelight'

shapely blooms are freely borne. Ignore the name 'Golden Medallion', which invites confusion with the American roses 'Medallion' and 'Gold Medal'.

'Peach Melba' × unnamed
Repeat flowering
Fragrant

'Little Darling'
Cluster-flowered

Though 'Little Darling' has never achieved elsewhere the popularity it enjoys in the United States, it is a reliable and most attractive rose. Its salmon-pink and gold flowers are very prettily shaped, and are carried in good clusters all the season, exuding a spicy fragrance. The bush, though not especially tall, is shrubby and spreading, the foliage leathery green and healthy. It can be used as a moderate-sized shrub in a mixed planting or as 1 metre (3 feet) tall flowering hedge. Raised by Carl Duehrsen and introduced in 1956, it has been much used as a parent by American hybridists.

'Captain Thomas' × ('Baby Chateau' × 'Fashion')
Repeat flowering
Fragrant

▲ 'Little Darling'
► 'Little Purple'

'Little Purple'
Cluster-flowered

'Little Purple' is not exactly a Cluster-flowered version of the New Zealand-raised 'Big Purple'. Its small, perfectly formed blooms are more reminiscent of 'Paradise', but in richer dress of deep lilac with burgundy-red edges to the petals. There is fragrance too, and it would be a very pretty rose to introduce to a mixed planting of roses and perennials, giving Old Garden Rose tones throughout the season. Foliage is dark and leaden green, rather like that of 'Paradise'. It was introduced by California's Bear Creek Nurseries in 1991.

Probably sport from 'Félicité et Perpétue'
Repeat flowering
Fragrant

'Liverpool Echo'
Cluster-flowered

Another rose that is perhaps more suited to cool climates than hot, 'Liverpool Echo' bears beautifully spaced clusters of soft salmon-pink flowers, their many petals beautifully arranged, on a bushy, average-height plant with dark green leaves. The perfection of its clusters makes it very popular with exhibitors, but it is also well-liked as a garden rose. Named for the British newspaper, it was raised in Northern Ireland by Sam McGredy and introduced in 1971.

('Little Darling' × 'Goldilocks') × 'München'
Repeat flowering

'Living Fire'
Large-flowered

The flowers of 'Living Fire' are not very large, but they are nicely shaped, vivid in their orange-red color, and rich with fragrance. The foliage is a particularly dark green, setting them off very well. It was raised by Walter Gregory of Nottingham, and introduced in 1972. Do not confuse it with 'Living', a rose of similar color from Herbert Swim in the late 1950s.

'Super Star' × unnamed seedling
Repeat flowering
Fragrant

▲ 'Liverpool Echo'
▼ 'Living Fire'

'Lolita' — Large-flowered
KORlita
'Litaka'

In Vladimir Nabokov's novel *Lolita*, Humbert Humbert had a rather prickly time with a young lady, and perhaps this influenced Reimer Kordes when he named this rose after her in 1973. It is very prickly, like most seedlings from 'Königin der Rosen'. Everyone loves the flowers, with their radiant blends of apricot and gold, their perfect form, and their seductive fragrance. Foliage is dark green and glossy.

'Königin der Rosen' × unnamed seedling
Repeat flowering
Fragrant

▲ 'Lolita'
▼ 'Lorraine Lee'

'Lord Penzance' — Hybrid Sweet Briar

Attracted by the fragrant leaves of the Sweet Briar *(Rosa rubiginosa)*, Lord Penzance crossed it with garden roses in a big way. He brought out no fewer than fourteen Hybrid Sweet Briar Roses in 1894–95. They are effectively Sweet Briars but with brighter colored flowers and, like their parent, are mostly large, scrambling shrubs suitable only for the most informal of gardens. Most were raised from various Hybrid Perpetuals and given the names of heroines from Walter Scott novels; but two were raised from yellow roses and these the noble lord named for himself and his lady. They are more modest in habit, their foliage is fragrant, and they are salmon-pink and gold for his Lordship, pale yellow for 'Lady Penzance'.

R. rubiginosa × 'Harison's Yellow'
Summer flowering
Fragrant

'L'Oréal Trophy' — Large-flowered
HARlexis

This 1982 sport from 'Alexander' resembles it in its vigorous, tall plant, its tendency to produce petals with scalloped edges, and its preference for a cool climate. In hot areas the flowers are apt to be undersized. The color is a pale orange, almost apricot, as against the vivid scarlet of 'Alexander'. Foliage is dark glossy green. Holder of gold

▲ 'Lord Penzance'
▼ 'L'Oréal Trophy'

medals from Bagatelle, Portland and Courtrai in Belgium, 'L'Oréal Trophy' was bred by Jack Harkness and sponsored by a cosmetics manufacturer.

Sport from 'Alexander'
Repeat flowering

'Lorraine Lee' — Large-flowered Climber

Perhaps the best known Australian-raised rose, 'Lorraine Lee' was released by Alister Clark in 1924 and named for a distant cousin visiting from England. Alas, the lady could have had no joy from her rose at home: it needs a hot summer if it is to bear its shapely, long-budded flowers. They are not all that large, but they are softly fragrant and a lovely shade of coral with a glow of gold at their hearts. The original is a Bush Rose, but it is the climbing version of 'Lorraine Lee' that we almost always see, covered in flowers even in winter. Foliage is rich green and glossy.

(*Rosa gigantea* × 'Jessie Clark') × 'Captain Millet'
Repeat flowering
Fragrant

'Los Angeles Beautiful' — Cluster-flowered

For the size of its flowers and the vigor of its growth, 'Los Angeles Beautiful' is sometimes classed as a 'Grandiflora' in the United States, where it was raised by Dr Walter Lammerts. The flowers are rather like those of its parent 'Queen Elizabeth' in size and shape. They derive their prettily blended tones of yellow and coral from the other parent, 'Rumba'. Unfortunately neither parent was able to give them any perfume. The bush has leathery green leaves, and though this 1964 introduction is rarely seen now, it is still worth planting in warm climates—like that of Los Angeles.

'Queen Elizabeth' × 'Rumba'
Repeat flowering

▲ 'Los Angeles Beautiful'
▼ 'Louis Philippe'

'Lotte Gunthardt' — Large-flowered

The thought of ninety petals is enough to set an exhibitor slavering, but he or she would probably be disappointed in 'Lotte Gunthardt', for in this case quantity is not allied to show quality. The blooms open in a confused and informal way and the color is one of those tints between red and orange that some people find garish. Still, the rose has its admirers, among them the distinguished Swiss flower painter for whom it is named. Foliage is dark green and glossy. 'Lotte Gunthardt' was introduced in 1964.

'Queen Elizabeth' × 'Bravo'
Repeat flowering

'Louis Philippe' — China
'Louis Philippe d'Angers'

There were two roses of this name, one from Eugène Hardy in 1824, the other from a M. Guérin ten years later. It is thought to be Guérin's rose that we have today. It makes a rather sparsely leafed bush similar to a small-growing Cluster-flowered Rose. Foliage is a glossy mid-green. It bears, throughout the season, clusters of loosely formed 8 centimetre (3 inch) flowers in deep pink to crimson, sometimes with a purple overcast but almost always markedly paler at the petal edges, as though someone had bleached them. It needs extra care in cultivation to show its true colors.

Parentage unknown
Repeat flowering

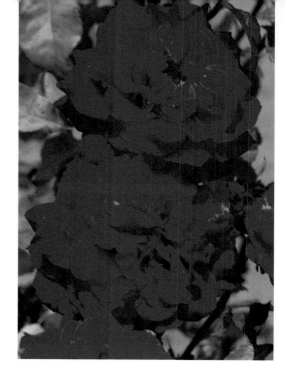

▲ 'Lotte Gunthardt'
▼ 'Louise Odier'

'Louise Odier' — Bourbon

One of the most elegant of pink roses, 'Louise Odier' bears blooms so perfect in their symmetry that they have often been compared to camellias, in a lovely shade of warm pink suffused with lilac and exhaling a beautiful perfume. The bush is sturdy, on the tall side, with healthy bright green leaves—it would make a good hedging plant—and it flowers as continually as a modern Bush Rose. It is also tolerant of shady situations. It came from M. Margottin, the French raiser, few of whose roses are grown today, in 1851.

Parentage unknown
Repeat flowering
Fragrant

of their roses in honor of their 150th birthday, you can be sure it will be worth growing. It seems that commercial considerations took over, as the star of 1986 was rechristened 'Lovely Lady' to entice a public ignorant of rose history. Under either of its names it is a delightful rose, shapely, of soft coral and salmon-pink coloring, and full of the fragrance that so many Modern Garden Roses miss out on. It is a bushy plant with glossy mid-green foliage.

'Silver Jubilee' × ('Eurorose' × Anabell')
Repeat flowering
Fragrant

'Loving Memory' Large-flowered
KORgund
'Burgund 81', 'Red Cedar'
Popular in Europe where it originated, and admired in Australia too, 'Loving Memory' has not taken off elsewhere. Perhaps the variety of its names has put people off. It is a very fine flower for exhibition, the blooms large and high centred and glowing red, and the plant sturdy, with glossy green foliage. Lack of scent is a serious demerit in a red rose, and there is little to offer here. It was raised by Reimer Kordes and introduced in 1981.

Unnamed seedling × seedling from 'Red Planet'
Repeat flowering

▲ 'Lovely Lady'
▼ 'Loving Memory'

'Love' Large-flowered
JACtwin
Jackson & Perkins may be one of the oldest rose-growers in the United States, but even they were not old-fashioned enough to call their trio of 1980 AARS winners 'Love', 'Honor' and 'Obey'—the third is 'Cherish'. 'Love', classed as a 'Grandiflora' by some in the United States, is a little short in growth for that class. Most would be content to have it as a Large-flowered Rose. It is a nice rose, its medium-sized flowers shapely and distinctive in their crimson and white bicoloring. Unlike many bicolors, the contrast holds for the life of the flower. Foliage is dark green and leathery.

Unnamed seedling × 'Red Gold'
Repeat flowering

'Love Story' Large-flowered
TANvery
Mathias Tantau named this rose to cash in on the success of the hit movie *Love Story*, which was released a couple of years before the rose was introduced in 1975. The well-formed flowers are

▲ 'Love'
▼ 'Love Story'

orange, the bush is strong with glossy foliage, and there is no fragrance, which is rather unromantic!

Parentage undisclosed
Repeat flowering

'Lovely Lady' Large-flowered
DICjubell
'Dickson's Jubilee'
When a firm like Dickson's names one

'Ludwigshafen am Rhein'
Cluster-flowered

KORludwig

What makes this rose unusual is the form of the cluster. Each of the half a dozen or so flowers is provided with a stem that is long enough for cutting. The blossoms themselves are fragrant, of Large-flowered Rose size and shape, and deep pink with a strong overtone of coral that becomes more pronounced as they age. The foliage is a soft green color. Ludwigshafen, a town in Germany on the opposite bank of the Rhine from Mannheim, was founded in 1843 by Ludwig I, the father of the mad castle-building King Ludwig. The rose was raised by Reimer Kordes and introduced in 1975. Several similar roses have been introduced in the United States as 'Flora-Teas', a classification the rest of the world has not found useful.

Unnamed seedling × 'Pink Puff'
Repeat flowering
Fragrant

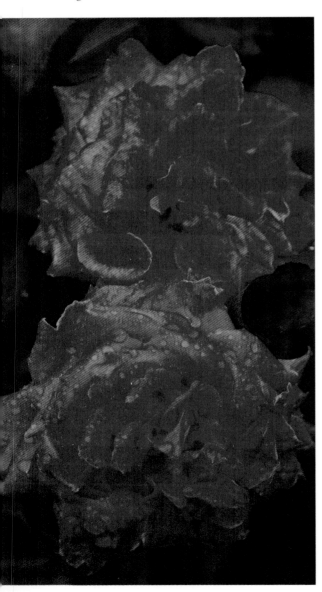

'Luis Brinas'
Large-flowered

The name of Pedro Dot (1885–1976), Spain's master hybridist, is not seen in the catalogues as often as some others these days, but his roses are generally still worth a second look. Take 'Luis Brinas' as an example. Its coppery buds, long and elegant, open to orange and coral blooms, set off against shiny green foliage. The flowers are deliciously fragrant too. Its only fault is a decided preference for sunny climates; in humidity it gets black spot. It was introduced in 1934.

'Madame Butterfly' × 'Frederico Casas'
Repeat flowering
Fragrant

▲ 'Luis Brinas'

'Lutèce'
Large-flowered

Nothing could commemorate Paris, the City of Light, more appropriately than the exquisite 'Lutèce', whose soft pink petals open wide to reveal stamens of purple and gold, all set off by especially handsome glossy green foliage. It was raised by the Parisian hybridist Lathulle,

'Lustige'
Large-flowered

'Lukor', 'Jolly'

The German world *lustige* does not convey the overtones of the English 'lusty'—'Die Lustige Witwe' is the Merry Widow of Franz Lehar's famous operetta. There is certainly something lusty about the plant of this rose, which is a tall, bushy grower with large leathery, glossy foliage, and something very merry about the flowers, brightly beautiful in their coppery red color, fine shape and fascinating fragrance. It was raised by Reimer Kordes in 1973, from two favorite roses. Oddly enough, the Americans use the German name rather than 'Jolly'.

'Peace' × 'Brandenberg'
Repeat flowering
Fragrant

▲ 'Ludwigshafen am Rhein'
▶ 'Lustige'

▲ 'Lutèce'
◄ 'Lyon Rose'

slightly fragrant, and the bush is of moderate growth, with matt green foliage. It was raised by Jack Harkness in 1978; the name apparently honors his grand-daughter. Harkness tells that he had decided not to market this rose, and that when the RNRS gave it an award, he had to ask them for bud wood so that it might be introduced.

'Pink Parfait' × 'Nevada'
Repeat flowering

▲ 'Lysbeth-Victoria'
▼ 'Ma Perkins'

who seems to have had a sense of history, and introduced in 1965. Lutetia was the name of his home town and district of Paris, back in the days of Roman Gaul.

Parentage undisclosed
Repeat flowering

'Lyon Rose' Large-flowered
'The Lyons Rose'

For his success in creating yellow roses, Joseph Pernet-Ducher won the nickname, the Wizard of Lyon, and his roses the title 'Pernetiana', though they are now classified with the Large-flowered Roses. 'Lyon Rose' of 1908 was one of his triumphs, not yellow this time, but a then-new blend of shrimp-pink and coral, its blooms globular and full petalled, with a rather sharp scent inherited from the 'Persian Yellow'. Despite its only moderate vigor and susceptibility to black spot, its color won it the Bagatelle gold medal in 1909 and great popularity. Foliage is dark green and shiny.

'Madame Melanie Soupert' × 'Soleil d'Or'
Repeat flowering
Fragrant

'Lysbeth-Victoria' Cluster-flowered
'Lysbeth-Victoria' bears pale salmon-pink flowers, rather like those of 'Nevada', in large clusters. They are

'Ma Perkins' Cluster-flowered
Novelty is no criterion of excellence. 'Ma Perkins', though raised by Eugene Boerner in 1952, remains one of the best pink Cluster-flowered Roses, its flowers as shapely and fragrant as ever, its blend of pale peach and coral as appealing. The plant is compact and easily grown, though you might sometimes have to guard against mildew, and the dark, matt green foliage is a lovely foil to the

delicate flowers. It never makes a great mass of bloom, but from one end of the season to the other there always seem to be a few exquisite flowers to admire. It was named after a popular broadcaster, no relation to the Perkins family of Jackson & Perkins.

'Red Radiance' × 'Fashion'
Repeat flowering
Fragrant

► 'Madame Abel Chatenay'
▼ 'McGredy's Yellow'

'McGredy's Yellow' — Large-flowered

'Every flower, large or small, of perfect form' proclaimed McGredy's catalogue back in 1934, announcing their new 'McGredy's Yellow'. They then go on to describe it as buttercup-yellow, a considerable exaggeration. Light lemon yellow would be more accurate in cool climates; in hot, the color could be very pale indeed. Foliage is bronze-green. Alas, the rose has deteriorated with age and it takes real skill now to grow it to perfection. The raiser was the father of the present Sam McGredy.

('Mrs Charles Lamplough' × 'Queen Alexandra') × 'J. B. Clark'
Repeat flowering

'Madam President' — Cluster-flowered

Pleasingly formal in shape, the pale pink flowers of 'Madam President' are nearly as large as a Large-flowered Rose. They preside on a bushy plant over dark green leaves. The color of the flower varies in depth with the season, often blending in a hint of peach or rose. Fragrance is only slight. Raised by Sam McGredy and introduced in 1975, its name honors the New Zealand Country Women's Association.

Unnamed seedling × 'Handel'
Repeat flowering

'Madame Abel Chatenay' — Large-flowered

Every rose-lover has some great favorite from childhood. Mine is 'Madame Abel Chatenay', which I vividly remember growing in my mother's garden in Hobart in the early 1930s. The foliage is bronze and its flowers are a delight, in their blend of soft pinks that rose-lovers called 'chatenay-pink'. Raised by Joseph Pernet-Ducher in 1897, it became a great favorite with the greenhouse growers, and just before World War I it was estimated that two out of three roses sold in British flower shops were 'Chatenay'. Its only fault is that the bushes are short lived.

'Dr Grill' × 'Victor Verdier'
Repeat flowering
Fragrant

'Madame Alfred Carrière' — Noisette

For all that it came out in 1879 (from Joseph Schwartz of Lyon), 'Madame Alfred Carrière' can still claim to be the first choice among white Climbing Roses. True, its blooms are not perfectly white, but tinted with blush at their hearts, yet they look white in the mass, and there are masses of them all season. The plant is vigorous but manageable, the foliage is light green and usually disease-free, and there is plenty of fragrance. What more could one want? It does not like hot dry winds which can bring thrips.

Parentage unknown
Repeat flowering
Fragrant

▲ 'Madame Alfred Carrière'
▼ 'Madam President'

'Madame Berkeley' — Tea

Like so many of the Teas, 'Madame Berkeley' changes the color of her dress with the seasons, sometimes preferring a blend of pinks, at others adding touches of gold. One of the freest blooming of the Teas, it is a fine garden plant in a warm climate, though the individual blooms are not especially shapely and only moderately fragrant.

The glossy green foliage is red tinted when young. 'Madame Berkeley' was introduced by the French raiser Pierre Bernaix in 1899.

Parentage unknown
Repeat flowering

'Madame Butterfly'   Large-flowered

One of the world's favorite roses in the years between the wars was the creamy pink, and sweetly fragrant 'Madame Butterfly', a sport from William Paul's 'Ophelia', discovered in 1916 in the nurseries of E. G. Hill & Company of Indiana. Hill's were soon growing it by the millions, and its blooms filled silver rose bowls everywhere. A few years later came a climbing sport, and history repeated itself—there was hardly a fence or pergola in the civilized world not adorned with 'Madame Butterfly'. It is no period piece, however, as it

remains one of the loveliest and most reliable pale pink roses. Foliage is dark green and matt.

Sport from 'Ophelia'
Repeat flowering
Fragrant

◄ 'Madame Berkeley'
▼ 'Madame Caroline Testout'

'Madame Caroline   Large-flowered
Testout'

For many years, it is said, you could not go very far in Portland, Oregon, without encountering 'Madame Caroline Testout'. It was planted in thousands all along the city's streets, and won Portland the title of America's Rose City. It was another triumph for Joseph Pernet-Ducher of Lyon, who had raised it in 1890 and named it for a Paris fashion

designer. Appropriately, it is described as 'satin-pink', the perfect color for 1890. The plant is strong and long lived, and there is an excellent climbing sport too. Foliage is rich green and smooth. It was photographed in Osaka on the occasion of its centenary, looking as radiant as ever.

'Madame de Tartas' × 'Lady Mary Fitzwilliam'
Repeat flowering
Fragrant

'Madame Caroline   Large-flowered Climber
Testout, Climbing'

Pernet-Ducher's grand dame of 1890 is splendid in its climbing version. A little stiff in its growth perhaps, and inclined to get bare at the base, but generous

▲ 'Climbing Madame Caroline Testout'
▼ 'Madame Butterfly'

with its candy-pink cabbages, both in the summer and later. Do not plant it on a red brick wall where it will clash.

Sport from 'Madame Caroline Testout'
Repeat flowering
Fragrant

'Madame Charles Meurice'

Hybrid Perpetual

Here is another museum piece from the Roseraie de l'Haÿ, this time with big, quartered blooms in deep pink. They are fragrant, though not overwhelmingly so. Foliage is mid-green. This is the sort of flower the Victorian exhibitor desired, as big and overstuffed with petals as possible. Modern taste finds roses like this blowsy, and catalogues find room only for those that make a great display in the garden, which 'Madame Charles Meurice' never does—she bears but a handful of flowers. The breeder and date are unknown, but it probably dates from the late nineteenth century.

Parentage unknown
Repeat flowering

▲ 'Madame Charles Meurice'
▼ 'Madame Charles Sauvage'

'Madame Charles Sauvage'

Large flowered

'Mississippi'

You do not see this rose of 1949 very often these days, but like all of Charles Mallerin's roses, it is a distinctive and lovely flower, full and shapely in a beautiful blend of gold and apricot. Some find it deliciously fragrant; others disagree, and the reference books will usually ignore the matter, implying scentlessness. It is a rose for favored climates though; in humid weather it takes black spot very easily.

'Julien Potin' × 'Orange Nassau'
Repeat flowering
Fragrant

'Madame Chédane-Guinnoisseau'

Tea

Not one of the better known of the Teas these days, probably because it is a little tender, 'Madame Chédane-Guinnoisseau' is worth planting in a mild climate. It makes a big bush, with slender wood and finely cut, dark green, glossy foliage characteristic of the Teas, and it is a non-stop producer of loosely double, fragrant blooms. The long buds sometimes justify the raiser's claim of 'canary-yellow', but usually they are paler, and the open blooms rapidly pass to ivory. Raised by the French raiser Louis Lévêque and introduced in 1880, this is a rose of delicate charm.

'Safrano' × unknown
Repeat flowering
Fragrant

▲ 'Madame Chédane-Guinnoisseau'
▼ 'Madame de Brunel'

'Madame de Brunel'

Hybrid Perpetual

'Madame de Brunel' was photographed some years ago at the Roseraie de l'Haÿ, that museum of old roses. Not much is known about the rose, but by the look of its flowers, ruffled in Old Garden Rose style, it is probably one of the earlier Hybrid Perpetuals. The bushes are filled with soft pink blossoms, quite large and fragrant and the foliage is bright green and large. The great engineer Isambard Kingdom Brunel was of French stock; perhaps the rose was named in honor of his mother, Lady Brunel.

Parentage unknown
Repeat flowering
Fragrant

▲ 'Madame de la Roche-Lambert'
► 'Madame Edouard Herriot'

'Madame de la Roche-Lambert'

Moss

The crimson buds are enclosed in long feathery sepals, well covered with dark moss, and the open flowers are full of symmetrically arranged petals, carmine with flushes of lilac. They are nicely fragrant, and borne quite freely on a compact bush, of around 1.5 metres (5 feet) in height, with fine lush green foliage. The main display is in early summer, but there are quite often bonus flowers to follow. M. Robert introduced this rose in 1851.

Parentage unknown
Repeat flowering
Fragrant

'Madame de Sancy de Parabère'

Boursault

'Virginian Lass'

It is a matter of taste whether you include the first 'de' in this rose's full title, and a matter of dispute whether she was raised by the Nantes firm of A. Bonnet & Fils in 1874 or earlier. It is beyond dispute, however, that this is a most unusual rose. A shrubby Climber, it is one of the earliest roses to bloom, covering itself with large flowers in clear pink, against glossy olive-green foliage. Their form is unique: within a circle of large outer petals nestles a bunch of smaller ones, in what is known as an 'anemone centre'. It is a common sight among camellias, but not among roses. Alas, there is little scent, and the display is once a year only. There are no thorns.

Parentage unknown
Summer flowering

'Madame de Watteville'

Tea

'Madame de Watteville' is officially described as lemon-yellow with pink on the petal edges, but like most of the Teas it varies very much with the season. The flower in the picture was photographed in mid-winter (like many Teas it will flower all year long in a mild climate) and the cool weather had paled it almost to cream. It was still lovely, and sweetly fragrant. It is a moderate-sized, slim-wooded bush with dark glossy green leaves. Credit for its raising is given to Guillot Fils in 1883.

Parentage unknown
Repeat flowering
Fragrant

'Madame Edouard Herriot'

Large-flowered

'The Daily Mail Rose'

'Madame Edouard Herriot' created a double sensation in 1912. Firstly for its altogether new color, flame paling to coral pink, and secondly for winning the £1000 prize offered by the London *Daily Mail* for a new rose to bear the newspaper's name. The raiser, Joseph Pernet-Ducher, had already named it for the wife of the man who shortly after became the prime minister of France. Supported by the RNRS, Pernet-Ducher kept his prize, and the rose its original name. It is best grown as a Climber these days, and its loosely semi-double blooms, glossy green foliage and zig-zag branches are as distinctive as ever.

'Madame Caroline Testout' × seedling from 'Soleil d'Or'
Repeat flowering
Fragrant

◄ 'Madame de Sancy de Parabère'
► 'Madame de Watteville'

'Madame Ernest Calvat' — Bourbon

'Madame Ernest Calvat', introduced by the widow Schwartz in 1888, is a sport from 'Madame Isaac Pereire', and like its parent can be trained to a pillar or grown as a large shrub. While richly fragrant like its parent, it differs in its color, flesh pink with deeper shadings. The wonderful plum tonings of the young growth, which mature to bright green, provide a perfect setting for the great blowsy flowers. It needs good soil to be seen at its best, when it is one of the great Victorian roses.

Sport from 'Madame Isaac Pereire'
Repeat flowering
Fragrant

▲ 'Madame Ernest Calvat'
▼ 'Madame G. Forest Golcombet'

'Madame G. Forest Golcombet' — Large-flowered

This glowing rose, 'Madame G. Forest Golcombet', appears to be the earliest rose from Francis Meilland, who raised 'Peace'. That is its only claim to fame, as no modern catalogue, including Meilland's, lists it. Launched in 1928, it is nearly double, bright deep pink in color, and strongly fragrant. Foliage is dull green and prone to mildew.

Parentage unknown
Repeat flowering
Fragrant

'Madame Georges Delbard' — Large-flowered
DELandel

American growers of cut flowers are concerned at the way Colombians are now flooding their market with roses. Georges Delbard of Paris is pleased, no doubt, because his velvet-red 'Madame Georges Delbard' is a favorite among the Colombians. Introduced in 1980, it has the reputation of being one of the relatively few greenhouse roses that does well in the garden. The bush is upright, with handsome, medium green foliage, but unfortunately the flowers have missed out on fragrance.

'Super Star' × 'Samourai'
Repeat flowering

'Madame Hardy' — Damask

It is the dream of every rose-breeder to dedicate a beautiful rose to the woman he loves. It was the privilege of Eugène Hardy, back in 1832, to honor his wife with one of the most beautiful roses of all. There is no doubt that in its perfect whiteness and soft, sweet fragrance, 'Madame Hardy' is altogether irresistible. The bush is inclined to flop; discreet staking is usually needed. This laxity of habit, the coarsely toothed dark green leaves, and the feathery, pine-scented sepals all suggest that it is not a pure-bred Damask. *Rosa centifolia* may have contributed to its beauty.

Parentage unknown
Summer flowering
Fragrant

▲ 'Madame Hardy'
◄ 'Madame Georges Delbard'
▼ 'Madame Isaac Pereire'

'Madame Isaac Pereire' — Bourbon

'Madame Isaac Pereire' is claimed to be the most powerfully fragrant of all roses and the scent of the great cabbage blooms is certainly delicious. Their color might not appeal to modern tastes, it is a shocking pink, heavily overlaid with magenta, needing careful placement in the garden. The bush is strong enough to train as a pillar, and it flowers repeatedly. It needs the best of everything if it is to perform properly. Foliage is bright green. The lady honored by M. Garçon of Rouen in 1881 was the wife of a Parisian banker.

Parentage unknown
Repeat flowering
Fragrant

'Madame Joseph Perraud' Large-flowered
'Sunburst'

On Joseph Pernet-Ducher's death in 1928, his business passed on to Jean Gaujard, who released 'Madame Joseph Perraud' in 1934. Some people think it was in fact one of the last creations of the 'Wizard of Lyon'. It was popular for some years in America as 'Sunburst', but like so many of the early yellow Large-flowered Roses it is best in a warm dry climate where black spot is not a problem. The foliage is a glossy green and the flowers handsome in shape. Their old gold color is lightly touched with salmon. It was raised from Pernet-Ducher's stock.

'Julien Potin' × unnamed seedling
Repeat flowering
Fragrant

'Madame Knorr' Portland

The real-life Mme Knorr is now an enigma. Verdier introduced her rose in 1855. It is a pretty flower, soft pink without much in the way of lilac, nicely quartered, and very fragrant, against matt green foliage. It is usually slighted as one of the less bushy and compact of the Portlands, but this is a bit unfair. Expect it to grow a little more than a metre (3 feet) tall and wide.

Parentage unknown
Repeat flowering
Fragrant

'Madame Léon Cuny' Large-flowered

From Jean Gaujard in 1960, 'Madame Léon Cuny' is one of those roses that can be called a Large-flowered or Cluster-flowered Rose at pleasure. Its medium-sized blooms come both singly and in clusters. They are shapely, in deep pink with white on the petal backs, and the bronze-foliaged bush is upright and very healthy. Being a cross between 'Peace' and an unnamed seedling, it figures more in the stud books than in gardens nowadays. Sam Mc-Gredy has used it as the parent of several Cluster-flowered Roses, such as 'Violet Carson' and 'Molly McGredy'.

'Peace' × unnamed seedling
Repeat flowering

▲ 'Madame Léon Cuny'
◄ 'Madame Joseph Perraud'
▼ 'Madame Knorr'

'Madame Louis Laperrière' Large-flowered

The English might well counter Napoleon's remark that they are a nation of shopkeepers with the idea that France is full of rose-breeders, all naming their creations after their wives! Let us not begrudge Mme Laperrière of Chesnes her modicum of fame, however. Her rose is regarded in Europe as one of the better velvety red roses, in the manner of 'Etoile de Hollande'. Her husband raised it in 1951 and it won the Bagatelle gold medal. It has beautiful fragrance, and does best in cool climates. Foliage is mid-green and leathery.

'Crimson Glory' × unnamed seedling
Repeat flowering
Fragrant

▲ 'Madame Louis Laperrière'
▼ 'Madame Louis Lévêque'

'Madame Louis Lévêque' Moss

Opinions vary about this rose, some people finding it gorgeous and others coarse, lacking a decent growth of moss (which is true) and overblown. I incline to the former camp, for the flowers of 'Madame Louis Lévêque' are magnificent at their best, great confections of pale pink washed with lilac, and fragrant as well. The bush gives many late flowers, at least as many as most Hybrid Perpetuals do. They do not like wet weather. Foliage is matt green. The Lévêque family is as prominent now in French horticulture as it was in 1874, when this rose came out.

Parentage unknown
Repeat flowering
Fragrant

'Madame Nicholas Aussel'

Large-flowered

This is another rose of the 1930s that is rarely seen today. It was photographed in the collection at the Portland Rose Garden. 'Madame Nicholas Aussel' was introduced by the Pernet-Ducher/ Gaujard establishment in Lyon in 1930. M. Pernet-Ducher probably saw it as an improved 'Madame Eduard Herriot' as it has much the same coral color, with larger blooms (those in Portland were enormous), a few more petals and a very strong perfume. The bush is erect and clad in glossy dark green leaves, said to be more resistant to black spot than most 'Pernetianas', as they were once known.

Parentage undisclosed
Repeat flowering
Fragrant

▲ 'Madame Nicholas Aussel'

'Madame Norbert Lavavasseur'

Polyantha

'Red Baby Rambler'

Lavavasseur et Fils introduced 'Madame Norbert' in 1903. The Americans, who were unable to accept the name, rechristened it 'Red Baby Rambler', which is fair enough, as its bunches of little crimson flowers, which 'blue' drastically with age, are like those of a Rambler. The bush, however, is compact, 40 centimetres (16 inches) high or so, flowering all season, against matt green foliage. The rose is of particular note as the parent of 'Orléans Rose', from which most of the popular Polyanthas were sports.

'Crimson Rambler' × 'Gloire des Polyantha'
Repeat flowering

'Madame Pierre Oger'

Bourbon

It does not often happen among roses that a sport becomes more popular than its parent, but here is one instance. Lovely as the rose-pink of 'La Reine Victoria' is, it looks ordinary beside 'Madame Pierre Oger', which is the most exquisite of palest rose-pinks, blushing deeper where the sun strikes the flowers, giving them a translucent delicacy. In all other respects it quite resembles its parent; they look well growing together. 'Madame Pierre Oger' was the mother of the discoverer, M. A. Oger of Caen in Normandy. The rose was introduced by Verdier in 1878.

Sport from 'La Reine Victoria'
Repeat flowering
Fragrant

◄ 'Madame Norbert Lavavasseur'
▼ 'Madame Pierre Oger'

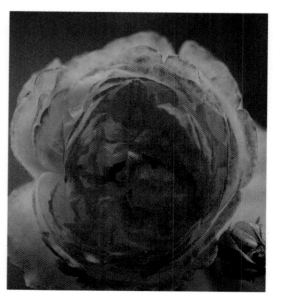

'Madame Plantier' Noisette

'Noisette' is the traditional classification, as the breeding is supposed to be a Damask by *Rosa moschata,* but this rose is really best thought of as an unusually long-limbed and rather lax-growing Damask. Vita Sackville-West put these long branches to good use at Sissinghurst by training them into the lower branches of her apple trees, creating an effect that she described as crinolines of white flowers. Individually, the blooms are well filled with petals and shapely, their whiteness warmed in a cool season with hints of creamy pink. The fragrance is first-rate, but the blooms come only in summer. Foliage is a light greyish green.

Possibly *R. damascena* × *R. moschata*
Summer flowering
Fragrant

'Madame Wagram, Comtesse de Turenne' Tea

Nobody gives 'Madame Wagram' her full title any more, and it would be snobbish to insist on the dignity of 'Comtesse de Turenne'. It is an easy-going rose, growing strongly, if somewhat unevenly, and bearing huge flowers in shades of pink and salmon, against dark glossy green foliage. The flowers are shapely enough for show and would give many a Large-flowered Rose a run for its money. Indeed it is often classed as a Large-flowered Rose. Knowing its parentage would help decide, but M. Bernaix chose not to reveal it when he introduced 'Madame Wagram' in 1895.

Parentage undisclosed
Repeat flowering
Fragrant

▲ 'Madame Wagram, Comtesse de Turenne'
▼ 'Madame Victor Dimitriou'

▲ 'Madame Plantier'

'Madame Victor Dimitriou' Large-flowered

The pattern of deep pink shading to cream and gold at the petal base is not an uncommon one in Modern Garden Roses. Look at 'Handel', 'Perfecta', and 'Len Turner', for instance, and at 'Madame Victor Dimitriou'. France is the only country where this Delbard creation of 1966 is still listed. The blooms are double, fragrant and cup shaped, set off by purple-tinted foliage, and, naturally, there is scent.

Parentage undisclosed
Repeat flowering
Fragrant

'Madame Zöetmans' — Damask

'Madame Zöetmans' is rather like 'Madame Hardy' and came out at the same time (in 1830). In its day, its admirers thought it superior, but in the years since it has been rather eclipsed by its rival. Do not overlook it though. It is still a beauty, with perfectly formed, scented flowers, their whiteness warmed with hints of pink; and the plant is strong and free with its blooms. Foliage is mid-green and rough. The raiser's name has been variously given as Marchet and Marest.

Parentage unknown
Summer flowering
Fragrant

▲ 'Madame Zöetmans'

'Madras' — Large-flowered

It is most frustrating for those of us who follow form when a rose-breeder tells us that the parentage of his latest creation is 'seedling × seedling'. This is the case with 'Madras', introduced by Bill Warriner in 1981. The blooms are stunning, wherever they came from, perfect in form, rich in fragrance, and gorgeous in their deep, glowing pink with suggestions of purple at the petal edges and gold at the base. The foliage is both leathery green and abundant. 'Madras' should have become popular, but some ten years later, it seems to have vanished from the catalogues.

Unnamed seedling × unnamed seedling
Repeat flowering
Fragrant

'Magenta' — Cluster-flowered
'Kordes Magenta'

A strong and prolific grower, almost a Shrub Rose—it will grow 2 metres (6 feet) tall if lightly pruned—'Magenta' bears sweetly fragrant blooms of Old Garden Rose form and petallage. The name suggests the color, on the border between pink and mauve, though it is much gentler than the magenta dye is apt to be in fabrics and 1960s wallpapers. Plant it in a mixed border, with suitable perennials to mask its bare lower stems. Foliage is broad, dark green and leathery. It came from Wilhelm Kordes in 1954.

Unnamed seedling × 'Lavender Pinocchio'
Repeat flowering
Fragrant

▶ 'Magenta'
▼ 'Madras'

'Magic Mountain' — Cluster-flowered

Hardly mountainous in its growth—indeed the bushes are on the low side—'Magic Mountain' has generous clusters of quite large, full-petalled flowers blending yellow and red, the red taking over the bloom as the flower ages. Its chief claim to fame among hordes of similarly hued roses is that it is more fragrant than most. Foliage is dark green, glossy and leathery. It is an Armstrong Nurseries introduction of 1973, a period when Thomas Mann's novel of the same name was enjoying renewed popularity.

'The Texan' × 'Circus'
Repeat flowering
Fragrant

▶ 'Maid of Honor'
▼ 'Magic Mountain'

'Mahina 81' — Large-flowered

Not all of Francis Meilland's roses repeated the sensational success of 'Peace'. One such was 'Mahina' of 1956, a lovely flower in apricot and pink, raised from 'Peace' and 'Fred Edmunds'. It never caught the public fancy, and after Francis's tragic death from cancer in 1958, his family decided to try again. The rose is a beauty, with great, sumptuous flowers, silken as peonies and fragrant too. Foliage is dark green. It was photographed in Kyoto a couple of years ago, but it seems not to have caught the fancy of the rest of the world.

'Peace' × 'Fred Edmunds'
Repeat flowering
Fragrant

▶ 'Mahina 81'

'Maid of Honor' — Large-flowered

One expects a maid of honor to be feminine and fragrant, and 'Maid of Honor' certainly lives up to expectations with shapely, sweetly scented blooms in pale yellow shading to delicate pink. The bush is no swooning maiden though. It is tall and upright, with bold, leathery green foliage. It is the creation of a relatively small concern, the Von C. Weddle family of New Albany, Indiana, who introduced it in 1981.

'Folklore' × unnamed seedling
Repeat flowering
Fragrant

'Maiden's Blush'

Alba

Rosa alba regalis, 'Cuisse de Nymphe', 'La Royale', 'La Virginale', 'Incarnata'

Alas, I have had no success with this lovely rose! It grows well enough, making a 2 metre (6 feet) bush with fine greyish foliage, and covers itself with buds, but in my warm climate they rarely open before they are ruined by thrips. Where thrips are not a worry, it is an exquisite rose, the ruffled flowers of sweetest fragrance and the loveliest flesh-pink. 'Virginal' describes them well. The rose dates from the fifteenth century or earlier.

Parentage unknown
Summer flowering
Fragrant

▲ 'Maiden's Blush'
▼ 'Maigold'

'Maigold'

Large-flowered Climber

'Maigold' is another of those accommodating roses that can be grown either as a climber or a large shrub. Either way it is a delight, with exceptionally handsome, luxuriant green foliage as well as marvellous flowers, semi-double, richly fragrant, in old gold. It has inherited the *R. pimpinellifolia* habit of early blooming, but do not expect more than the occasional flower after the gorgeous spring display. It was introduced by Wilhelm Kordes in 1953.

'Poulsen's Pink' × 'Frühlingstag'
Spring flowering
Fragrant

'Malaga'

Large-flowered Climber

Deep coral-pink, 'Malaga' bears its blooms on and off all season on a shortish climber with glossy green leaves. So far so ordinary, but the nice thing about this 1971 Sam McGredy creation is its really excellent fragrance, a quality not overly abundant among the repeat-flowering modern Climbers. Foliage is glossy and dark green. It was named for the Spanish resort.

('Hamburger Phoenix' × 'Danse du Feu') × 'Copenhagen'
Repeat flowering
Fragrant

'Malicorne'

Large-flowered

DELmator
'Beverly Hills'

Beverly Hills is where Hollywood stars live. Malicorne is where M. Delbard has his nursery in France. 'Malicorne' is one of Delbard's greatest successes, though at first sight it appears to be just another medium-sized orange-red rose. Its great secret is that it will open its flowers in a cooler greenhouse than any other rose. Its flowers can also be cut younger than any other, yet still open perfectly and last for days. Foliage is bright green and glossy. Like most greenhouse roses, it is an indifferent performer in the garden. It was introduced in 1981.

('Zambra' × 'Orange Sensation') × ('Zambra' × ['Orange Triumph' × 'Floradora'])
Repeat flowering

'Manou Meilland'

Large-flowered

MEItuliman

All stars must start to shine sometime. In the case of 'Manou Meilland', one of the Meilland family's most successful roses of recent years, that was in 1979. 'Manou' is the family nickname for Marie-Louisette Meilland, and you know that when a rose bears the name of a family member, the Meillands are pretty proud of it. Well they might be, for the rose is a stunner: large, shapely,

▲ 'Malaga'
▼ 'Malicorne'

▼ 'Manou Meilland'

growing deep pink, and borne freely on a healthy bush. Foliage is dark green and leathery. Lack of fragrance is its only fault.

('Baronne Edmond de Rothschild' × 'Baronne Edmond de Rothschild') × ('Ma Fille' × 'Love Song')
Repeat flowering

'Manuela' — Large-flowered

Mathias Tantau's 'Manuela' of 1968 would seem to bear out the rose-growers' belief that deep-pink roses are difficult to sell. It has never been popular outside Germany and the United Kingdom, where it was championed by the late Harry Wheatcroft. Yet it is a very good rose, its color enlivened by a hint of salmon, its flowers large and high centred, and the bush vigorous and well clad with leathery green leaves. Perhaps it was just not novel enough?

Parentage undisclosed
Repeat flowering
Fragrant

'Manx Queen' — Cluster-flowered
'Isle of Man'

Long one of the leading yellow-flushed-red Cluster-flowered Roses, 'Manx Queen' has rather lost popularity in the face of many newcomers, but it is still a pretty rose, bearing its flowers freely on compact, dark-leafed bushes. Individually the blooms are perhaps not very exciting, being somewhat shapeless and scentless. Its virtue is as a giver of bright color. It is a 1963 Dickson creation.

'Shepherd's Delight' × 'Circus'
Repeat flowering

▲ 'Manuela'
◄ 'Manx Queen'
► 'Marbrée'

'Marbrée' — Portland

Marbrée, meaning 'marbled', seems a bit unimaginative as a name for a rose. It is not all that appropriate either, as the flower is not marbled but delicately spotted with palest pink on a deeper pink ground. This is a most unusual pattern, and the loosely semi-double flowers, with their golden stamens, show it off nicely. Unfortunately, there is little fragrance, but the bush, taller than most of the Portlands, is reliable in its repeat blooming, and the smooth, pointed olive-green foliage is good. The raisers, Robert & Moreau, must have been at a loss for words in 1858.

Parentage unknown
Repeat flowering

'Marchioness of Londonderry'
Hybrid Perpetual

Exhibitors always pant after the newest roses with which to dazzle the judges. Here is one which has been sensational since 1893. A fine bloom of 'Marchioness of Londonderry' can be up to 20 centimetres (8 inches) wide, but it is saved from vulgarity and coarseness by its perfect, high-centred form and the delicacy of its palest pink and flesh tones. It is fragrant too. The bush is tall, a trifle leggy perhaps, and responds well to generous treatment. Foliage is large and matt green. It was raised by Alexander Dickson II and named for a patron and neighbor.

Parentage unknown
Repeat flowering
Fragrant

'Maréchal Davoust'
Moss

In life, Davoust was one of Napoleon's senior officers. His rose befits his rank, being a bold flower in shades of strong pink with suffusions of lilac, nicely scented. The moss is dark green, the bush compact and free with its flowers, though it does not repeat. The smooth foliage is mid-green. It was raised by M. Robert of Angers in 1853.

Parentage unknown
Summer flowering
Fragrant

'Maréchal Niel'
Noisette

This rose was raised in 1864 by Joseph Pradel of Lyon and named in honor of Adolphe Niel who earned his Marshal's baton at the Battle of Solferino. No yellow rose quite so fine had been seen before, and it remains one of the loveliest: soft and pure in color, perfect in form and deliciously fragrant. It made M. Pradel a rich man. It is very tender and a large, heated greenhouse is needed to grow it in cold climates. A bunch of 'Maréchal Niel' from the florist was always the epitome of luxury. In a frost-free climate, it will adorn a wall with pale green foliage and great nodding blooms the color of butter for most of the year.

Seedling from 'Cloth of Gold'
Repeat flowering
Fragrant

▲ 'Maréchal Davoust'
▼ 'Marchioness of Londonderry'

'Margaret Merril'
Cluster-flowered

HARkuly

For all its popularity in Britain, this rose has not been a hit in Australia, probably because it prefers cooler climates. Where it flourishes it is one of the loveliest of roses, its flowers perfectly formed and very sweetly fragrant, their whiteness warmed with a faint pink glow. Give it the best of everything. Foliage is dark green and glossy, sometimes susceptible to black spot. Raised by Jack Harkness in 1977, it is named for Margaret Merril, the fictitious beauty adviser for the Oil of Ulan company.

('Rudolph Timm' × 'Dedication') × 'Pascali'
Repeat flowering
Fragrant

▲ 'Margaret Merril'
◄ 'Maréchal Niel'
► 'Marguerite Hilling'

'Marguerite Hilling'
Hybrid Perpetual

'Pink Nevada'

Pink sports of the blush-white 'Nevada', one of the most widely admired of all Shrub Roses, have occurred in several places, but the honor of naming and introducing the first one fell to Thomas Hilling in 1959. 'Marguerite Hilling' has all the good qualities of its parent, making a large, graceful and very flowery shrub, but the color of the blooms is a beautiful cool pink, paling gradually to white in the centre. It is suitable also trained to a pillar, grown as a climber or planted to make a hedge. Like 'Nevada' it needs regular removal of the old branches to maintain its youthful vigor and beauty. Foliage is pale green.

Sport from 'Nevada'
Repeat flowering
Fragrant

THE ROSE IN CHINA

The nursery trade is not notorious for creating millionaires. The nurseryman must measure his satisfaction in terms of the delight his plants bring rather than just accumulating dollars. Considered thus, the late eighteenth-century proprietors of the Fa Tee Nurseries in Canton (Kwangdong) must rank as the most successful nurserymen ever, for their plants not only gave delight, they created a revolution in gardening half a world away.

European gardeners at this time were keen to taste the prodigious floral richness of China, which they had glimpsed in the decorations of screens, porcelains and furniture, and there can scarcely have been a visiting captain, whether his prime objective was tea, silk or porcelain, who did not bring orders for new and exciting plants. The Qing Government, however, restricted 'foreign devils' to the port of Canton, and that meant that their plant-hunting had to be confined to the local nursery.

The local nursery was the Fa Tee, or 'Flowery Land'. It must have been quite an establishment, for from it came chrysanthemums, deciduous magnolias, *Camellia reticulata*, tree peonies, Indian azaleas, the Tiger Lily and yet other plants without which we cannot imagine our gardens today.

Their selection of roses does not appear to have been very large: the yellow and white Banksian Roses; possibly some of the early pale garden forms of *Rosa multiflora* like 'Cathayensis'; the red and pink China Roses, 'Slater's Crimson' and 'Old Blush'; and Tea-scented Roses, 'Hume's Blush' and 'Parks's Yellow'. These last four are perhaps the most important ancestral roses of all, for they brought true dark crimson color, (relatively) smooth and prickle-free stems, the long-budded flower shape we love so much today, and, above all, the priceless gift of repeat flowering.

The modern rose is the daughter of the roses of the Fa Tee Nursery. Where the Fa Tee got them we do not know. It is certain that the China Roses are of high antiquity, for we see roses very like our 'Old Blush' painted on Chinese screens and porcelain many hundreds of years old. The English geneticist C. C. Hurst speculated that they were originally bred from *R. gigantea*, a great Climber from the South of China, and the rare and elusive wild *R. chinensis*, only very recently run to ground in the remote far western provinces. All we can really say for certain is that they were the creation of unknown Chinese gardeners at some unknown time. When, after the Opium Wars, travel in the Chinese empire became easier, other garden roses found their way to the West. Late in the nineteenth century such a wealth of rose species was discovered in the mountain provinces of Western China that many botanists regard the area as the homeland and cradle of the rose. These include such beauties as *R. moyesii*, *R. hugonis*, *R. setipoda* and the Himalayan Musks.

The Chinese are much more relaxed about gardening than the Japanese, and flowers feature more prominently in their gardens than they do in the austere, religion-saturated gardens of Japan, but even so, the rose has never played the leading role in China that it has in the West. Perhaps the superstition that its

▲ *In 1797, Lord Macartney headed a British diplomatic mission to the Chinese court. The Chinese disliked his manners, and Macartney returned to London not having won any of the trade concessions for which the British had hoped. He was not quite empty-handed, however, as in his baggage were plants of* Rosa bracteata, *known ever since as the Macartney Rose.*

▶ *Fine porcelain is so identified with the Chinese that the English-speaking world has called it simply 'china'. This is a rare and little-known type, a covered cup from a service made exclusively for the Qing Dynasty Empress Cu Xi, and , it is said, designed by her.*

well ahead of us in discovering the benefits of giving children rose-hip syrup.

The gardeners of the Fa Tee would be amazed at the modern Western roses they could now see growing in the grounds of the Temple of Heaven in Beijing, yet how proud they would be to know that they were the children of their own roses, sent to foreign lands all those years ago and now returning to the land of their ancestors.

▲ *Chinese painters divide their subject matter into three broad categories: people, landscape, and flowers and birds. Workers in the decorative arts follow their lead. Pieces decorated with people and landscapes may look merely quaint to Western eyes (and indeed Chinese connoisseurs are apt to dismiss them as vulgar) but who can resist the charm of a piece like this carved panel in gilded wood?*

◀ *The roses of the Fa Tee had two great disadvantages in the eyes of Western gardeners—only mild fragrance and intolerance of the cold. So it is not surprising that they soon fell from popularity in the face of their 'improved' descendants, surviving (in the West) only in the most favored gardens. This is Redouté's portrait of 'Slater's Crimson', long thought lost but now rediscovered in Bermuda.*

thorns might bring prickly discord into the house where roses are brought has played a part; perhaps their delicate beauty has seemed tame beside the gorgeous Tree Peony, the 'king of flowers', and the chrysanthemum; or was it that the China Roses possessed only relatively mild scent? European poets universally praise the rose as much for its fragrance as for its beauty and see it as an emblem of womanhood; Chinese painter-poets (male chauvinists to a man!) preferred to focus on plants like the pine and bamboo, which embodied masculine virtues.

Not that that stopped gardeners from cultivating and developing their roses. There is a book written in the Sung Dynasty which describes some forty different roses. Europe at that time, during the twelfth and thirteenth centuries, could with difficulty gather only half a dozen.

Modern China loves all flowers. The old Chinese roses are still grown, and works of art and decoration featuring them are still being made as beautifully as ever. *R. rugosa*, native to China as well as Japan, is still grown in fields to supply flowers to distill into wine (as intoxicating as delicious, it is said) and to flavor cakes and tea, some of which occasionally reaches our local gourmet shops. It seems the Chinese were

▶ *The tradition of decorating furniture with flowers delicately rendered in lacquer has a two-thousand-year history. This cabinet is brand new, and the roses look like modern Large-flowered Roses, not ancient China Roses. At its feet, another of the Empress Dowager's pieces, a flower pot this time.*

'Maria Callas'
MEIdaud
'Miss All-American Beauty'

Large-flowered

Unlike the great diva for whom it was named, 'Maria Callas' is not at all temperamental. One of the easiest of the exhibition-style roses to grow, it bears enormous, brilliant pink, highly fragrant flowers with great freedom. Foliage is large, dark green and leathery. Like Miss Callas, who was half-Greek, it is

▲ 'Maria Callas'
► 'Mariandel'
▼ 'Climbing Maria Callas'

no real all-American. It was raised in France, by Alain Meilland. It did, however, win the AARS award in 1968, three years after it came out in Europe.

'Chrysler Imperial' × 'Karl Herbst'
Repeat flowering
Fragrant

'Maria Callas, Climbing'
'Climbing Miss All-American Beauty'

Large-flowered Climber

There is something luxurious about a great rosebush full of huge, scented roses. The way to have it is to plant the climbing version of one of the bigger Large-flowered Roses. None is better than 'Climbing Maria Callas', which, though a little stiff in growth, will give cadenzas of the same huge, fragrant flowers that the bush does. The autumn, or fall, encores are dependent on lavish fertilizer and water after the first bloom.

Sport from 'Maria Callas'
Repeat flowering
Fragrant

'Mariandel'
KORpeahn
'The Times Rose', 'Carl Philip', 'Christian IV'

Cluster-flowered

What a multiplicity of names! They indicate the success, or at least the enthusiasm, with which this fairly new rose is being marketed everywhere. It is even in growth, with dark, mahogany-tinted foliage to set off the blazing red flowers, fuller petalled and more interesting individually than many such roses bred for the impact of their massed color. There is not much in the way of perfume, though. 'Mariandel' was raised by Reimer Kordes in 1987.

Parentage unknown
Repeat flowering

'Marie-Claire, Climbing'
Large-flowered Climber

You do not see the original, bush version of 'Marie-Claire', a Meilland introduction of 1944, these days, but the

Climber is worth seeking out for the beauty of its softly fragrant golden-yellow flowers and its slender growth. Foliage is olive-green. You are unlikely to see the rose, however, except in France, where *Marie-Claire* is a popular women's magazine.

Sport from 'Marie-Claire'
Repeat flowering
Fragrant

'Marie d'Orléans'
Tea

An 1883 introduction from Gilbert Nabonnand, and named for a lady of the cadet branch of the old French royal house, 'Marie d'Orléans' appears to be living in the dignified retirement of historic rose collections these days. She should go back out into the wider society of rose gardens; her fragrant, prettily quartered blooms in shades of salmon-pink and coral would find her many new admirers. Foliage is bronze-green. Her behavior in the garden, and whether she shrinks from the cold, I cannot say.

Parentage unknown
Repeat flowering
Fragrant

▲ 'Climbing Marie Claire'
▼ 'Marie d'Orléans'

'Marie Louise' — Damask

History has thought it rather tactless for the gardeners at Malmaison (the Empress Joséphine's house) to dedicate a rose to Napoleon's second wife in 1813, while the divorced Empress Joséphine was still in charge of the garden! Clear pink and fragrant, 'Marie Louise' bears some of the largest blooms among the Old French Roses. They are indeed so large and full of petals that, without the assistance of a supporting stake, the slender Damask branches usually fail to hold them up, and they end up spattered with mud. Perhaps it was Joséphine herself who suggested the name, in barbed courtesy. Foliage is light green and matt.

Parentage unknown
Summer flowering
Fragrant

▲ 'Marie Louise'

'Marie van Houtte' — Tea

The van Houttes were a family of Belgian nurserymen who were famous for the Golden Elm, *Ulmus* 'Vanhouttiana'. 'Marie van Houtte' was introduced by Claude Ducher in 1871 and is still regarded as one of the best of all the Teas, for its hardiness, its vigorous growth, its perfect form and the sweet scent of its blooms. There appear to be two strains about: one in yellow and pink, in the manner of 'Peace'; the other, the one in the picture, much paler in lemon-white and blush. Both are lovely. Foliage is rich green and leathery, with plum tints when young.

'Madame de Tartas' × 'Madame Falcot'
Repeat flowering
Fragrant

▲ 'Marijke Koopman'
▼ 'Marie van Houtte'

'Marijke Koopman' — Large-flowered

The long-stemmed beauties in our picture are just the sort of rose a flower arranger dreams of. They were developed by a slightly unfamiliar name in rose-breeding circles, Gareth Fryer of Knutsford, Cheshire. Fryer knows how to keep mum about a good thing, and has never released the parentage of this rose. The long, pointed buds that open to irregularly scalloped petals, suggest the influence of 'Dr A. J. Verhage'. The color is a bright, medium pink with a touch of gold at the base. The bush is strong, the fragrance just fine. Foliage is dark and leathery. The rose was named in memory of the daughter of a friend of Fryer, who was killed in a car crash.

Parentage undisclosed
Repeat flowering
Fragrant

'Marina'
RinaKOR — Cluster-flowered

It is hard to say whether this 1981 AARS winner was named for the heroine of Shakespeare's *Pericles* or the boat harbors so filled with status in modern life. It is a desirable rose, despite its somewhat thorny branches, for its shapely flowers of salmon-orange, lit with gold, and its handsomely bronze-tinted foliage. It holds its shape and color well, on the plant or as a cut flower. Introduced by Reimer Kordes in 1974, it was not introduced to the United States until later, hence the date of the AARS award.

Unnamed seedling × 'Königin der Rosen'
Repeat flowering
Fragrant

'Marita'
Cluster-flowered

This little-known rose is nonetheless very distinctive, with its petals quilled almost like a cactus dahlia. They are a warm salmon-pink with touches of gold, and carried on a tall open-growing bush. There is no scent. It was introduced by John Mattock, the Oxford rose-grower, in 1961.

'Masquerade' × 'Serenade'
Repeat flowering

'Marjorie Fair'
Modern Shrub

'Red Ballerina'

The alternative name is not in honor of Soviet dancers, but alludes to the similarity of 'Marjorie Fair' to its popular parent 'Ballerina'. It makes an easy-care, lavish-flowering bush with great sprays of single flowers all season, but it has not proved as popular as 'Ballerina'; the carmine and white flowers lack delicacy. The small foliage is bright green. It was introduced by Jack Harkness in 1978. The fair Marjorie was a friend of the raiser.

'Ballerina' × 'Baby Faurax'
Repeat flowering

'Marjory Palmer'
Cluster-flowered

One of the more notable Australian-bred roses, raised by Alister Clark in 1936, 'Marjory Palmer' was one of the most popular Cluster-flowered Roses for many years, holding its own against highly publicised introductions from other countries. It is still a good rose, endowed with excellent glossy green foliage, and bearing its blooms very freely, in large and small clusters. They are not shapely, and their deep rose-pink color is no longer fashionable. The rose may yet prove of use to a modern hybridist looking for fresh blood.

'Jersey Beauty' × unknown
Repeat flowering
Fragrant

▲ 'Marjory Palmer'
◄ 'Marjorie Fair'
▼ 'Marlena'

▲ 'Marina'
► 'Marita'

'Marlena' Cluster-flowered

'Marlena' was introduced in 1964, so is an old lady as Modern Garden roses go, but some people think that it is still the best of all the red Cluster-flowered Roses. It is most certainly outstanding among the low growers, the bushes smothering themselves with flowers of an especially fine color, dark red yet brilliant. Foliage is dark green and glossy. It was raised by Reimer Kordes and apparently the name is a tribute to that great star Marlene Dietrich, who was awarded the red ribbon of the Legion of Honor for her work for Free France in World War II. 'Marlena' was awarded gold medals from Baden-Baden in 1962 and Belfast in 1966.

'Gertrud Westphal' × 'Lili Marlene'
Repeat flowering

▲ 'Marmalade'
► 'Mary Guthrie'

'Marmalade' Large-flowered

'Marmalade' by name, marmalade in color; the long, pointed buds open to thirty-petalled blooms in bright orange with yellow on the reverse. Fragrance is reminiscent of tea. The bush is upright, the foliage large and dark green. It was raised in 1977 by Herb Swim and Arnie Ellis, from two American roses.

'Arlene Francis' × 'Bewitched'
Repeat flowering
Fragrant

'Martha Rice' Cluster-flowered

This rose stood out in California's Huntington Botanic Gardens a few years ago, its dark-leafed bushes well adorned with clusters of medium-sized, shapely blooms in warm deep pink. The rose world does not seem to

▲ 'Martha Rice'

have taken 'Martha Rice' to its bosom, however, as no nursery anywhere lists it. It was introduced in 1970.

Parentage undisclosed
Repeat flowering

'Mary Guthrie' Cluster-flowered

This rose is another one of Alister Clark's seedlings from 'Jersey Beauty', introduced in 1929. It always looks charming, its five-petalled rose-pink flowers and neat growth suggestive of a China Rose. It is healthy and easy to grow and the small foliage is bright green and very glossy. There should be a place for it in modern gardens.

'Jersey Beauty' × unknown
Repeat flowering
Fragrant

'Mary MacKillop' Cluster-flowered

Mother Mary MacKillop dedicated her life to educating children in Australia's outback, and her reward is that she is set to become Saint Mary of the Cross, Australia's first saint. The rose dedicated to her is a charmer, with fragrant shell-pink blooms with deeper touches. Perfectly formed, they are of medium size and are borne in clusters of up to half a dozen on a sturdy, glossy-leafed bush. Raised in California by Armstrong, it was introduced in 1989.

Parentage undisclosed
Repeat flowering
Fragrant

'Mary Queen of Scots' Scotch

Legend has it that this very pretty rose was brought from France to Scotland by the beautiful and tragic lady whose name it bears. Experts pour cold water on that romantic story, saying 'probably late nineteenth century'. Grow it

▲ 'Mary Queen of Scots'
◄ 'Mary MacKillop'

for sentiment or just for the beauty of its little scented flowers in parma violet and lilac, borne in spring-time profusion on a neat, dwarfish bush. Like most of the Scotch Roses, its mid-green leaves turn plum and russet in autumn, or fall, and it prefers a cool climate. It is popular in Ireland.

Parentage unknown
Spring flowering
Fragrant

▲ 'Mary Rose'
▼ 'Masquerade'

'Mary Rose'
AUSmary

English Rose

David Austin has written that 'Mary Rose' comes close to his ideal in the breeding of his English Roses. It has much of the charm of an Old Garden Rose, with the reliable repeat-flowering habit of a Modern Garden Rose. Unfortunately, the rose-pink flowers do not have any perfume, but they *are* very lovely. The bush is sturdy and not too large, and it flowers freely all season. A bush in full bloom is quite a feature in a mixed planting. Foliage is mid-green and matt. It was introduced in 1983, the year that Henry VIII's ship *Mary Rose* was raised from the sea.

'The Wife of Bath' × 'The Miller'
Repeat flowering

'Masquerade'

Cluster-flowered

Rose-growers today are apt to dwell on the faults of 'Masquerade': the spottiness of the dying flowers, the dull, dark olive-green foliage and the lack of perfume. It is difficult to remember the sensation it created when Jackson & Perkins introduced it back in 1949. It

▲ 'Climbing Masquerade'

was a first—a rose that opened bright yellow, and then gradually turned salmon-pink, then red. There are many roses like 'Masquerade' today, most indeed descended from it, but for a bright show in the garden, 'Masquerade' can still hold its own. It was raised by Eugene Boerner.

'Goldilocks' × 'Holiday'
Repeat flowering

▲ 'Master Hugh'

'Masquerade, Climbing' — Cluster-flowered Climber

The climbing version of 'Masquerade', which came out in 1958, is still the most vigorous of the multicolored climbers for jazzing up the front of a house. It can look spectacular in full bloom, but there is only very rarely an autumn, or fall, performance.

Sport from 'Masquerade'
Summer flowering

'Master Hugh' — Modern Shrub

Strictly speaking, 'Master Hugh' ought to be listed among the Wild Roses, as it is raised from seed of *Rosa macrophylla* collected in the wild in China. However, it is so much more splendid than most forms of the species that it has been propagated as a cultivar. The bush is big, to nearly 3 metres (10 feet) tall and wide, with mid-green foliage, and the flowers large and elegant, with five large soft pink petals. They are followed by most splendid hips and preceded by young shoots covered with a greyish bloom like hoar frost. It was introduced in 1966 by Maurice Mason.

Seedling from *R. macrophylla*
Spring flowering
Fragrant

'Matangi' — Cluster-flowered
MACman

Sam McGredy's 'Hand-painted Roses' are often more curious than beautiful. 'Matangi' is a rose of real distinction and character, its basic vermilion color softened and brightened by the palest pink with which the petals are so liberally brushed. The flowers are very nicely shaped too, borne in abundance on a strong plant with small dark green foliage. The only fault is the lack of pronounced fragrance. Introduced in 1974, the name is Maori, and comes from the title of a song of friendship.

Unnamed seedling × 'Picasso'
Repeat flowering

'Matthias Meilland' — Cluster-flowered
MEIfolio

Yet another bright, bright red Cluster-flowered Rose with smallish flowers and no scent. It has its admirers for its low, bushy growth and general air of neatness; among them the raiser, Alain Meilland, who named it for his son. Meilland is not in the habit of naming roses for members of the family unless he thinks they are pretty good. Foliage is mid-green. 'Matthias Meilland' was introduced in 1985 in France, 1988 in the United States.

Parentage undisclosed
Repeat flowering

▲ 'Matthias Meilland'
◄ 'Matangi'

'Medallion' — Large-flowered

Everything about Jackson & Perkins's 1973 'Medallion' is king-size. The plant is tall, the foliage big and leathery, and the flowers enormous. Too large, really, for their slender stems. After a shower of rain they hang their heads and you have to lift them up to appreciate their delightful light apricot color and soft fragrance. Raised by Bill Warriner, it won the AARS award in 1973.

'South Seas' × 'King's Ransom'
Repeat flowering
Fragrant

▲ 'Max Graf'

▲ 'Medallion'
▼ 'Meg'

'Max Graf' — Ground Cover

James H. Bowdich of Connecticut appears to have no other roses to his credit, and he can hardly have made his fortune from this 1919 introduction. 'Max Graf' was grown by few nurserymen then. Now Ground Covers are fashionable, and 'Max Graf' is admired for its shiny foliage and dense, trailing habit. Its only fault is its spring only flowering season, though the single, rose-pink blossoms appear for many weeks then. Yet Mr Bowdich will be remembered as long as roses are grown, for 'Max Graf', in the hands of Wilhelm Kordes, gave rise to the highly cold- and disease-resistant *Rosa kordesii*, which, married to the Modern Garden Roses, has brought forth both the excellent 'Kordesii' Climbers and an evolving race of disease-resistant Bush Roses.

R. rugosa × *R. wichuraiana*
Spring flowering

'Meg' — Large-flowered Climber

This rose is rather stiff and thorny in its growth, so that it can be a most uncomfortable rose to prune and train; it is not very fragrant, and, despite what the books will tell you, it is stingy with its repeat blooms. Nonetheless, 'Meg' is one of the most admired of modern Climbing Roses for the sheer elegance of its peach-toned flowers, opening wide from their long buds to show their crimson stamens. Foliage is dark green and glossy. It is best trained to a tripod or given some support and allowed to make a vast and spreading shrub. It was introduced by an otherwise unknown English raiser called Gosset in 1954.

'Paul's Lemon Pillar' × 'Madame Butterfly'
Repeat flowering
Fragrant

'Maxima' — Alba

Rosa alba maxima, 'Great Double White', 'White Rose of York', 'Cheshire Rose', 'Jacobite Rose'

This is an ancient rose indeed, probably dating from the Middle Ages. It makes a tall, bushy and almost indestructible plant with sage-green leaves, and, in late spring, has showers of scented flowers, palest pink in the bud but opening pure white. Where it grows well it is magnificent, an asset to a cottage-garden mix of old-fashioned flowers. It is thought to be of British origin, and is associated both with the House of York and with Bonnie Prince Charlie, whose adherents chose white roses as their emblem.

Parentage unknown
Late-spring flowering
Fragrant

▲ 'Maxima'

'Megiddo' — Cluster-flowered

Megiddo is in Palestine, and was the scene of two famous battles: one, around 1470 BC, when the Pharaoh Thutmose III vanquished the Hittites; and another in 1918 AD when the British under Lord Allenby defeated the Turks. It is a safe guess that it was the latter victory that is commemorated by this fiery rose, raised by Gandy's Roses of Leicestershire. 'Megiddo' has a great reputation for freedom of bloom, which is no doubt why it remains popular, despite being introduced in 1970, which in the highly competitive world of scarlet Cluster-flowered Rose breeding seems nearly as long ago as ancient Egypt! 'Megiddo' bears large sprays of bright scarlet flowers on a strong growing, upright plant with large olive-green, matt foliage. Gandy's raised it from two Georges Delbard roses.

'Coup de Foudre' × 'Saint-Agaro'
Repeat flowering

▲ 'Megiddo'
▼ 'Melanie Soupert'

▲ 'Memoriam'
▼ 'Memento'

'Melanie Soupert'   Tea

The lady in real life was a member of the great French nursery family (the firm was called Soupert et Notting), and Joseph Pernet-Ducher honored her in 1905 with his 'Madame Melanie Soupert', one of his sensational golden roses. This one is a Tea, far from sensational in its delicate shades of pale pink with the occasional suggestion of apricot, but a very pretty rose nonetheless. Foliage is dark green. It was introduced in 1881 and does not seem to be available anymore. This is one for the specialist grower.

Parentage unknown
Repeat flowering

'Memento'   Cluster-flowered
DICbar

In Britain, where 'Memento' was bred, it is regarded as one of the very best of all bedding roses. Its habit is neat, its foliage is sage-green, handsome and disease resistant and its clusters are perfectly spaced and borne abundantly, whatever the weather. The rest of the world has largely ignored it. Even in Britain its admirers are likely to wish it was more popular, blaming its somewhat indeterminate color, neither red, deep pink, nor truly coral. Whatever, I find it bright and cheerful. It is a 1978 introduction from Patrick Dickson.

'Bangor' × 'Anabell'
Repeat flowering

'Memoriam'   Large-flowered

I can't understand why the American Rose Society should classify 'Memoriam' as white; in Australia it is pink. Very pale, certainly, but definitely pink nonetheless. I have never seen it make a big bush, but it is indispensable for the exhibitor, as the softly scented flowers are very large and of most perfect form, with about forty-five petals. It was introduced in 1962 by the American raiser Gordon von Abrams and named in memory of his wife. It dislikes wet weather. Foliage is dark green and leathery.

('Blanche Mallerin' × 'Peace') × ('Peace' × 'Frau Karl Druschki')
Repeat flowering
Fragrant

'Mercedes'   Cluster-flowered
MerKOR

In the garden, 'Mercedes' is just another scarlet rose, its flowers

shapely, their color bright, the plants upright, and the foliage dark green and leathery. In a greenhouse it is a different story: there it has few rivals for its freedom of flowering, its length of stem, or its ability to last and last when it is cut. For years it has been one of the roses most commonly met with in florists' shops. Mercedes is a common girl's name in Europe, and this 1974 Reimer Kordes creation has nothing to do with German motor cars. It is quite without scent.

'Anabell' × unnamed seedling
Repeat flowering

▲ 'Mercedes'

'Merci'　Cluster-flowered

Despite its name, this is an American rose, from Bill Warriner of Jackson & Perkins. It is highly regarded in the United States for its vigor, resistance to disease and freedom of bloom, but it has not been seen much elsewhere. Perhaps it is the color of the flowers, which are a medium shade of crimson. Europe and Australia tend to like red Cluster-flowered Roses to be dark or flaming. Fond of warm climates, it looks its best in California. Foliage is dark green and leathery. 'Merci' was introduced in 1976.

Parentage undisclosed
Repeat flowering

'Mermaid'　Large-flowered Climber

Like the mermaids of legend, this 'Mermaid' is indeed an alluring beauty, but like them, is not easy to live with. The trouble is its prodigious vigor; the brittle, viciously thorny branches are difficult to train. If you have the room

to give it its head, there is no climbing plant more beautiful. The shining foliage is more or less evergreen, and the huge, perfect flowers are single, softly scented, and of palest yellow crowned with great bosses of amber stamens which remain in beauty after the petals fall. It was introduced in 1918 by William Paul.

Rosa bracteata × unknown Tea Rose
Repeat flowering
Fragrant

▲ 'Merci'
▼ 'Merveille de la Brie'

'Merveille de la Brie'　Rambler

Most of us associate Brie with the cheese rather than the town in France from which it, and this Rambler, comes. It may be a surprise to discover that 'Merveille de la Brie' is not cream but bright cherry-red. It is one of the highlights of the collection of Ramblers at

the Roseraie de l'Haÿ, but most of us will have to go there to enjoy it, as it is currently only available from one French nursery that specializes in obscure Old Garden Roses. Foliage is small and glossy. I do not know its breeder or date of introduction.

Parentage unknown
Summer flowering

'Message'　Large-flowered
MEIban
'White Knight'

'Message' is worth looking at for its perfect form, its sparkling whiteness, sometimes with just a hint of cream, and its strong growth, provided that mildew is not a problem. Its foliage is dark green. Fragrance is only slight. 'Message' is the name bestowed by its raiser, Francis Meilland, in 1957, but under 'White Knight' it won the AARS award in 1958.

('Virgo' × 'Peace') × 'Virgo'
Repeat flowering

▲ 'Mermaid'
▼ 'Message'

'Mevrouw van Straaten van Nes'

Cluster-flowered

'Van Nes', 'Mrs van Nes', 'Permanent Wave', 'L'Indéfrisable', 'Duchess of Windsor'

Under which of its many names you know it, you will have no difficulty in recognizing this rose. Its rather tight bunches of deep cerise pink flowers with their frilly petals are unmistakable. It is not so much a rose for making a display in the garden as for cutting, when the flowers can be admired in close-up. There is very little scent. Foliage is dark green and glossy. This rose was introduced by the brothers Leenders, well-known Dutch rose breeders of the period.

Sport from 'Else Poulsen'
Repeat flowering

'Michèle Meilland'

Large-flowered

Another 'family rose' from Meilland, this one, introduced in 1947, honoring Francis Meilland's daughter. It is the perfect rose for cutting, with its long, thornless, plum-colored stems and its gracefully built 23-petalled flowers. They are of most charming coloring: softest pale pink touched with apricot and, occasionally, just a hint of lilac. The plant is strong and healthy with dark green foliage. Light fragrance is the only demerit.

'Joanna Hill' × 'Peace'
Repeat flowering

'Michelle Joy'

Large-flowered

'Michelle Joy' should please the exhibitor for the fine symmetry of its flowers, which vary in color with the season. Sometimes they are quite a

▶ 'Michèle Meilland'
▼ 'Michelle Joy'

pale shade of coral-pink, at other times much deeper. The bush is strong and free with its blooms and the dark green foliage is glossy. It appears likely to do best in a warm climate. Raised by Jack Christensen in California, it was named in memory of Michelle Joy Cowley of Queensland. Mr Christensen does not seem to have introduced it in the

▲ 'Mevrouw van Straaten van Nes'

United States, probably because exhibitors in America would prefer a longer, slimmer bud and more fragrance.

Unnamed seedling × 'Shreveport'
Repeat flowering

THE ROSE IN JAPAN

People in the West think of Japan as a land of flower-lovers. And indeed it is: the picture of Madame Butterfly gathering cherry blossoms to celebrate her lover's return is not far from the truth. Even the rising sun of the national flag has been interpreted as a chrysanthemum, best-loved of all Japanese flowers and the especial emblem of the Emperor.

The Japanese islands are abundantly rich in wild flowers: azaleas, peonies, the Japanese Iris, wisteria, lilies, camellias, plum and cherry blossoms and the chrysanthemum. We see them everywhere, displayed in what are possibly the world's most refined flower arrangements, which the samurai of old did not disdain to create, and featured in Japanese works of art of all kinds.

Roses are rare in Japan. There are several native to Japan, among them *Rosa multiflora*, *R. wichuraiana* and *R. rugosa*, all of which have given rise to beautiful garden roses in the West. At home, however, they have been admired only mildly. True, there are fine old illustrated books on *bara* and *ibara*, as the rose is known in Japanese, but roses are scarcely ever to be seen in the great classical gardens, and they are not numbered among the noble flowers which scholars cultivated and wrote poems about.

admiration for all things European and American really extended to the well-upholstered Hybrid Perpetuals of the time; even with such traditional flowers as the peony and the camellia the Japanese prefer more lightly built and graceful cultivars than the Chinese do.

The advent of the more elegant Large-flowered Roses helped the rose to find wider acceptance, but it was still a long way from challenging the traditional favorites, and the Second World War and its hysterical rejection of all things Western might have brought the rose into eclipse.

That that did not happen is, according to Seizo Suzuki, Japan's foremost rosarian, due to the introduction of Francis Meilland's wonderful 'Peace'. Here was a rose after the Japanese heart, its huge flowers wide and ruffled, its foliage handsome. If the peony was the king of flowers (as the Chinese held), then here, surely, was the queen.

The Japan Rose Society held its first national rose show in Tokyo in 1948, and interest in roses has grown ever since. The rose now ranks third in popularity in the flower shops, after the chrysanthemum and that other Westerner, the carnation, but if the present trends continue, the rose will soon be rivalling the chrysanthemum.

It cannot be said that Japan has the ideal climate for the

◀ *Rosa rugosa is always known in the West as the Japanese Rose, but it grows wild in Korea and northern China as well, often within sight and spray of the sea. The name Ramanas Rose, sometimes still encountered in books, is a garbled version of the Japanese name.*

▶ *'Hanamigawa', known in the West as 'Ferdy', is one of the most exciting new developments in rose-breeding.*

The rose does not lend itself well to the austere traditional garden, which calls for evergreens and subtle seasonal change within a tightly disciplined design. It is just too flimsy and wayward in growth, and rather too eye-catching in flower. One suspects, in fact, that the Japanese considered *bara* rather vulgar; it is not surprising that two of the earliest of their garden roses to reach the West, 'Seven Sisters' and the mildew-ridden 'Crimson Rambler', are said to have been found in the gardens of what are politely known as 'houses of joy'.

Japan had had the refined China and Tea Roses from China for a thousand years before the West did, but it was not until the opening of Japan to Western influence with the Meiji Restoration that roses came into favor. Not that the new

Modern Garden Rose: her soils tend to be acid and the summers hot and sweltering. Yet roses are grown to great perfection there; to go to one of the great flower shows in places like Osaka is to be overwhelmed by color and fragrance. All the latest roses from overseas are to be seen, but the Japanese hybridists are creating some beautiful flowers of their own. Leader of the group is Suzuki-san himself; his 'Olympic Torch' and 'Mikado' have won honors overseas, and now he has come up with something quite new, a wonderful everblooming Shrub Rose with fountain-like growth and myriads of coral-pink flowers. He calls it 'Hanamigawa', which means 'looking at cherry blossoms by the river'; in the West it has the more abrupt name of 'Ferdy'.

► *The gardens of the Zen temple of Ryoanji in Kyoto. In a style of garden as austere and disciplined as this, the rose, with its wayward growth and showy flowers, has no place.*

'Hanamigawa' builds on a new line of breeding by a colleague, Dr Toru Onodera, who created quite a stir a few years ago with his 'Nozomi', a delightful creeping rose which is the forerunner of the current Ground Cover Roses. Between them, they are harbingers of something new and exciting in roses.

From the Japanese *Rosa multiflora* has come, after nearly a hundred years, the modern Cluster-flowered Roses, and from *R. wichuraiana* and *R. rugosa* some of the finest Climbers and Shrub Roses. Who knows what transformations in the rose-world the roses of Japan will bring next?

▲ *In the West the aim of a maker of artificial flowers is to deceive the viewer into thinking they are real, but Japanese craftsmen see them more as works of sculpture, and delight in making them out of such materials as ivory, tortoiseshell or glass. I saw these stunning blooms at a flower show in Kyoto. They are a triumph of the silversmith's art.*

▲ *Roses have not been a major motif in Japanese art for all its preoccupation with flowers. Their present-day popularity is reflected in much contemporary design, such as this superb silk intended for an obi, the sash worn around a kimono.*

► *'Diamonji' is appropriately named for the great fireworks festival held each year at the Diamon temple near Osaka. Raised in 1981, this Large-flowered Rose seems not to have found its way into Western gardens.*

My thanks to Peter Okumoto for his dedicated research and assistance.

▲ 'Mikado'
► 'Milkmaid'
▼ 'Milestone'

'Mikado' Large-flowered
'Koh-sai'

Gilbert and Sullivan's character may have been a villain rather than a king of beauty, but his name is both Oriental and familiar to Western ears, just right for a Japanese rose (from Seizo Suzuki) destined for the Western market. The *Koh-sai* name is Japanese for 'harmonious friendship', which is appropriate too. The rose has won success in the West, in the form of the 1988 AARS award. Blooms are large, to 12 centimetres (5 inches), well formed and of brilliant red with yellow on the reverse and at the centre. The dark green foliage is glossy. There is little scent, but disease resistance is exceptional.

Parentage undisclosed
Repeat flowering

'Milestone' Large-flowered

Bill Warriner's 1988 'Milestone' is spectacular; the colorings of its forty-five petals are almost three dimensional. They are basically a dense medium red, silvery on the reverses and shading lighter towards the centre, the whole show darkening with age, just what one would expect from its parentage. The foliage is large, medium green and half-glossy. Scent is only slight.

'Sunfire' × 'Spellbinder'
Repeat flowering

'Milkmaid' Noisette

For many years the trellis around the rose garden at the botanic gardens in Adelaide, South Australia, was adorned by the rich green leaves and fragrant blooms of this vigorous Climber. It is an Australian rose, from Alister Clark in 1925, and is a lovely soft egg-yolk-yellow, rapidly paling to milk-white. It is not quite as continuous as its parent, though it does offer plenty of sprays of flowers after its spring crop.

'Crépuscule' × unnamed seedling
Repeat flowering
Fragrant

'Milrose' Cluster-flowered
DELbir

This 1965 introduction from Georges Delbard has been a best-seller, but it is still in the catalogues, especially in France. The soft candy-pink flowers are borne abundantly and are well set off by the mid-green foliage. There is not much scent, but 'Milrose' would be a good choice if you want a rose in this currently rather unfashionable color. You might have to watch out for mildew. It comes from distinguished old parents.

'Orléans Rose' × ('Français' × 'Joseph Guy')
Repeat flowering

'Minuette' Cluster-flowered
LAMinuette
'La Minuette', 'Sweetheart'

I often see this rose at my local florist's, and more than once have brought home a bunch so that I could take its portrait. It was in Canada that I finally managed to capture on film 'Minuette's' shapely flowers, their white petals daintily rimmed in cherry-red. They are not over-large and, like most florists' roses,

have little scent. Foliage is dark green and glossy. 'Minuette' came from Walter Lammerts in 1969. Do not confuse it with either the red Miniature 'Minuetto' ('Darling Flame') or with 'Cécile Brünner', also called 'The Sweetheart Rose'.

'Peace' × 'Rumba'
Repeat flowering

▲ 'Milrose'
▼ 'Minuette'

'Miriam'
Cluster-flowered

MACsupacat

The book of Exodus talks about Miriam the Prophetess taking a timbrel in her hand and dancing, which is certainly a picture suggestive of the bright cheerfulness of this rose. 'Miriam' was, however, more prosaically, yet more affectionately, named for a lady of Sam

▲ 'Miriam'
► 'Miss Edith Cavell'

McGredy's acquaintance. In the garden the shapely blooms can be a very bright combination of gold and carmine. Cut them young for the house and they open to the more delicate tones you see in the picture. It is still new, being introduced in 1992, but it is very promising. Foliage is dark green and glossy.

'Sexy Rexy' × 'Yabadabadoo'
Repeat flowering

'Miss Edith Cavell'
Polyantha

'Edith Cavell', 'Nurse Edith Cavell'

Launched by Gerrit de Ruiter in 1917 as a memorial to England's martyr nurse executed by the Germans, its little flowers are dark, velvety red. It was regarded as much the best red rose in the Polyantha class. Foliage is a dull dark green. Such are the vagaries of fashion that it proved almost impossible, a few years ago, to locate plants to grow on the lady's grave. It was a sport from 'Orléans Rose', and de Ruiter created speed records in propagating it: eighteen months after its discovery, he had grown 80 000 plants! There was a cream Large-flowered Rose called 'Edith Cavell' also. It appears to be extinct.

Sport from 'Orléans Rose'
Repeat flowering

'Miss France'
Large-flowered

'Pretty Girl'

What would our present-day roses be like if Meilland's 'Peace' and Kordes's 'Independence' had not been available to the hybridists? Half of them would not exist at all. Here is one that unites the heritage of both—Jean Gaujard's creation, introduced in 1955. Its long buds are coral-red, opening to informal, decorative blooms in a softer shade of coral-pink, well set off by bronze foliage and a nice fragrance. Fragrance gives it a position above Meilland's brighter but otherwise similar 'Jolie Madame' of 1958.

'Peace' × 'Independence'
Repeat flowering
Fragrant

'Miss Ireland'
Large-flowered

MACir

Never a great success in Australia, as it prefers a cool climate, 'Miss Ireland', introduced in 1961, has had a long and

successful life, which must be a source of great satisfaction to its raiser, Sam McGredy. The large blooms, up to 13 centimetres (5 inches) wide, are bicolored in rich salmon and cream, fully double with thirty-seven petals and wonderfully fragrant. The plant is bushy which makes it an excellent bedding rose, with polished dark green foliage.

'Tzigane' × 'Independence'
Repeat flowering
Fragrant

▲ 'Miss France'
▼ 'Miss Ireland'

'Miss Rowena Thom' Large-flowered

Rose-growers are mortal like the rest of us, but their roses have a degree of immortality. The Montecito partnership of Howard and Smith brought out many beautiful roses from before World War I until the early 1960s. Rose-lovers still remember the satin-pink 'The Doctor' (1936), the coral-pink 'Los Angeles' (1916), the golden 'Fred Howard' (1950)

and the fiery 'Miss Rowena Thom' from 1927. Her very fragrant blooms are large and shapely, their color a brilliant rose, overlaid with mauve and washed gold at the centre. The bush is sturdy, like those of its parents, and the foliage is mid-green and leathery.

'Radiance' × 'Los Angeles'
Repeat flowering
Fragrant

'Mission Bells' Large-flowered

For many years one of the most popular roses, 'Mission Bells' was raised by Theodore Morris and introduced by Germain's of Los Angeles in 1946. It

began to lose ground to brighter colored, more exciting roses in the 1970s. It is so easy to grow, especially in humid climates, that a revival should be considered. The reward will be large, warm pink blooms, opening informal and deliciously fragrant from long, pointed buds, and long, almost thornless stems. Foliage is dark green and soft.

'Mrs Sam McGredy' × 'Mälar-Ros'
Repeat flowering
Fragrant

'Mister Chips' Large-flowered

James Hilton's lovable schoolmaster Mr Chips from the classic movie, starring Robert Donat, might not have been Irish, but the rose certainly is, raised by Patrick Dickson in 1970. It is rather like 'Peace' in color, but richer in light yellow shaded with orange and cerise, all trimmed with raspberry-pink. The form is closer to the exhibition ideal, with high centre and reflexing petals. The foliage is a dark glossy green.

'Grandpa Dickson' × 'Miss Ireland'
Repeat flowering

▲ 'Mister Chips'
◄ 'Mission Bells'
► 'Modern Art'

'Mister Lincoln' Large-flowered

This winner of the 1964 AARS awards has been one of the world's favorite red roses for nearly thirty years. Sure, the English may sniff about mildew and 'blueing', but if you give 'Mister Lincoln' a reasonable amount of sunshine, the plant will be as tall and clean as the great man in whose memory it is named, and the color will be perfect, deep and velvety. The urn-shaped buds open rather

▲ 'Mister Lincoln'
◄ 'Miss Rowena Thom'

flat, but what is that to set beside the pleasure of cutting armloads of long-stemmed, richly fragrant beauties from each bush? Foliage is leathery, matt and dark green. All credit to Herbert Swim and O. L. Weeks who raised it.

'Chrysler Imperial' × 'Charles Mallerin'
Repeat flowering
Fragrant

'Modern Art' Large-flowered

POUlart
'Prince de Monaco'

'Hand-painted Roses' are no longer Sam McGredy's exclusive property. Here is one from Pernille Poulsen, the fourth generation of the Poulsen family to grow roses. It is a safe guess that the McGredy strain is in the two unnamed seedlings that gave rise to 'Modern Art' in 1983. Its blooms are full-sized Large-

flowered Roses, shapely, high centred and in orange-red with white reverses. The deeper 'brushmarks' are most evident in a cool climate. Foliage is clean and dark green, the growth bushy.

Unnamed seedling × unnamed seedling
Repeat flowering

▲ 'Mojave'
▼ 'Molde'

'Mojave' — Large-flowered

In the 1950s, 'Charlotte Armstrong' × 'Signora' was one of Herbert Swim's favorites. It yielded 'Sutter's Gold' as well as this brilliant rose, introduced in 1954. Long buds in deep, pure orange open rather loosely to a large bloom in apricot, orange and red, the rich colors of a desert sunset. (Pronounce the name as 'Mohavee' in the Californian manner.) The blooms are very fragrant, the foliage is gleaming. Its special qualities won 'Mojave' the Geneva gold medal in 1953, and the AARS award in 1954.

'Charlotte Armstrong' × 'Signora'
Repeat flowering
Fragrant

'Molde' — Cluster-flowered
'Mistigri'

I do not know enough German to explain the name, but I do know that it is not pronounced 'Mouldy' as it usually is by English speakers, who are therefore turned off the rose. They

▲ 'Molly McGredy'
▼ 'Mon Cheri'

should not be: it is a good, low-growing bush, and it bears its bright scarlet flowers with freedom; against the dark green leaves they make quite a splash of color. 'Molde' was introduced in 1964 by Mathias Tantau. I suspect 'Gertrud Westphal', the prolific mother of low-growers, has a place in this rose's parentage.

Parentage undisclosed
Repeat flowering

'Molly McGredy' — Cluster-flowered
MACmo

High awards from the expert judges do not always translate into adoration from the public. Sam McGredy considered this rose good enough to name for his sister, and the RNRS gave it its top award in 1969, the year of its introduction. The deep pink and white is not the favorite color of most rose buyers, however, no matter how shapely the flowers and perfect the bush. Lack of strong perfume has not helped either, but it is indeed a very good rose. Foliage is dark green and glossy.

'Paddy McGredy' × ('Madame Léon Cuny' × 'Columbine')
Repeat flowering

'Mon Cheri' — Large-flowered
AROcher

Rather resembling a deeper-colored 'Double Delight', 'Mon Cheri' is in fact descended from that rose. It shows its

parentage in the semi-glossy mid-green foliage, and in the way the high-centred blooms, which start out medium pink lit with yellow at the petal bases, gradually become suffused with dark red, but not in its scent, which is only moderate. The bush is of medium height and upright, and the AARS award was bestowed in 1982. Armstrong's introduced it in 1981.

('White Satin' × 'Bewitched') × 'Double Delight'
Repeat flowering

▶ 'Moonlight'
▼ 'Monsieur Tillier'

'Monsieur Tillier' Tea
'Archiduc Joseph'

There is doubt about the identity of this rose, credited to Pierre Bernaix in 1891, some claiming that it is actually Nabonnand's 'Archiduc Joseph'. Under either name it is an outstanding and easily grown rose for a warm-climate, its abundant blooms opening quartered and fragrant from plump buds. They are a blend of warm colors, but the overall impression is of coral-pink,

softly touched with magenta, an unusual and attractive combination. The olive-green foliage sets it off well, and the bush is upright and compact.

Parentage unknown
Repeat flowering
Fragrant

'Montezuma' Large-flowered

Long eclipsed by its more brilliant rival 'Super Star', 'Montezuma' is enjoying a well-deserved return to popularity for its unique coral color and extraordinary vigor. It does have faults: no scent and an intolerance of extreme conditions, either rain or burning sunshine. Foliage is sage-green, leathery and semi-glossy. Originally classed as a 'Grandiflora', it was raised by Herbert Swim, introduced in 1956, and won gold medals in England, Switzerland and Portland, but, surprisingly, not the AARS award. In the tragedy of the Spanish invasions of Mexico, history often forgets that the Emperor Montezuma was one of the all-time great gardeners.

'Fandango' × 'Floradora'
Repeat flowering

'Moonlight' Hybrid Musk

This rose has sprays of creamy flowers set against dark green foliage; there is sometimes a hint of peaches in the cream in warm climates. 'Moonlight' is really best treated as a Climber, its long branches needing severe pruning to keep it as a Shrub. It is surprising that it is not seen more often, as there is a dearth of reliably repeat-flowering climbing roses in its color range, which is more flattering to a house than stark white. Introduced in 1913 it was one of the first of the Hybrid Musks created by the Reverend Joseph Pemberton.

'Trier' × 'Sulphurea'
Repeat flowering
Fragrant

'Moonsprite' Cluster-flowered

This very pretty rose, one of the most fragrant of all the Cluster-flowered Roses, was rather neglected when it came out in 1956, despite winning several major awards. The raiser's name, Herbert Swim, ought to have made the rose world take more notice. It looks as

◀ 'Montezuma'
▼ 'Moonsprite'

though 'Moonsprite' is finally due for recognition, as its growth is fashionably short and compact, and its flowers filled with petals, almost in the Old Garden Rose style. Its color is the cool cream and pale gold of the rising moon. Foliage is leathery, semi-glossy and dark green.

'Sutter's Gold' × 'Ondine'
Repeat flowering
Fragrant

▲ 'Moth'
▼ 'Morgengruss'

'Morgengruss'   Cluster-flowered Climber
'Morning Greeting'

Many of Wilhelm Kordes's *Rosa kordesii* Climbers come in the strong colors that sell so well in Germany. 'Morgengruss' is an exception. Long, shapely buds open to ruffled blooms, not overlarge but carried in graceful sprays, in all the pale pinks and corals of the sunrise. They are fragrant too, and borne freely all season on strong though not rampageous plants with dark, glossy green foliage. Introduced in 1962, it is a rose

that deserves wider attention than it gets. It has a reputation for hardiness.

Parentage undisclosed
Repeat flowering
Fragrant

'Moth'   English Rose

This is a rather pretty David Austin rose, its petals wide and fluttering as befits its name. The name does not come from the insect that eats holes in sweaters but from one of the fairies who attend Titania in *A Midsummer Night's Dream*. The bush is compact for a Shrub Rose and the soft pink flowers settle on it like a flight of butterflies. Foliage is soft green, the flowers fragrant.

Parentage undisclosed
Repeat flowering
Fragrant

'Moulin Rouge'   Cluster-flowered

Raised by Meilland and introduced to much praise in 1952, 'Moulin Rouge' is a prolific bearer of smallish, brilliant red flowers in large clusters. The foliage is olive-green and glossy. In 1958, Bob Linquist in California introduced 'Elsinore', from 'Floradora' × 'Pinocchio', which is a prolific bearer of smallish, brilliant red flowers in large clusters. The million to one chance had happened! Two raisers, each in different countries, using different parents, had created identical roses. These days they are all labelled 'Moulin Rouge', but if you buy a plant in America it just *might* be 'Elsinore'.

'Alain' × 'Orange Triumph'
Repeat flowering

▲ 'Moulin Rouge'
▶ 'Mountbatten'

▲ 'Mount Shasta'

'Mount Shasta'   Large-flowered

'Mount Shasta' is tall and bushy, with distinctive greyish leaves, but it does not bear its large, high-centred blooms freely enough to avoid being upstaged by 'Pascali', another white seedling of 'Queen Elizabeth' that came out at the same time. It came from Herbert Swim and O. L. Weeks in 1963.

'Queen Elizabeth' × 'Blanche Mallerin'
Repeat flowering
Fragrant

'Mountbatten'   Cluster-flowered
HARmantelle

Very tall and vigorous, 'Mountbatten' is a good choice for the back of the rose bed or for bringing a splash of soft yellow to the mixed border. It does not usually produce large clusters of bloom, but the individual flowers in their small sprays are quite big, nicely formed and softly scented. Foliage is olive-green and leathery. 'Mountbatten' would make an appropriate companion

for 'Alexander' and, like it, honors the memory of a notable British serviceman. The patriotic raiser of both was Jack Harkness, who introduced 'Mountbatten' in 1982.

'Peer Gynt' × [('Anne Cocker' × 'Arthur Bell') × 'Southampton']
Repeat flowering
Fragrant

'Mrs Anthony Waterer'   Hybrid Rugosa

Introduced in 1898 by the great British nursery John Waterer & Sons, 'Mrs Anthony Waterer' has always been admired for the clarity of its crimson, its elegantly cupped form and its intense fragrance. Do not be carried away by its Hybrid Rugosa classification. Its *Rosa rugosa* blood is a little far back and it is, in effect, a vigorous (and thorny) Hybrid Perpetual. Grow it in the same way, pegging down the long shoots, and do not expect the autumn, or fall, display to be as lavish as the main, early summer display. Foliage is bright green and quilted.

'Général Jacqueminot' × unnamed Hybrid Rugosa
Repeat flowering
Fragrant

'Mrs Charles Frederick Worth'   Hybrid Rugosa

Charles Frederick Worth, though an Englishman, was the leading Paris couturier of the late nineteenth century, his clothes coveted by everyone from the Empress Eugénie to the girls in the new department stores. He died in 1898, nine years after the rose was introduced. It is credited to a gentleman

▲ 'Mrs Anthony Waterer'
▶ 'Mrs F. W. Flight'

named Worth. This may be a coincidence or perhaps Charles Worth, like Caroline Testout a few years later, may have used the rose to promote his own business. It is a fairly typical Hybrid Rugosa, with sturdy growth and large, informally double blooms in cool pink.

Parentage unknown
Repeat flowering
Fragrant

'Mrs Dudley Cross'   Tea

Sometimes the 'Mrs' is dropped from the name. This was a leading exhibition rose in its day, for the flowers are enormous and full-petalled, in straw-yellow with shadings of apricot and pink, the pink being more obvious in the autumn, or fall. They are not

borne all that freely, and the plant is not very tolerant of cold. Foliage is glossy green and the stems are thornless. Presumably its English raiser, William Paul, who introduced it in 1907, grew it in a greenhouse. If you garden in a warm climate and relish the idea of occasional sensational flowers, you might like to try 'Mrs Dudley Cross'. It is not very fragrant, however.

Parentage unknown
Repeat flowering

'Mrs F. W. Flight'   Cluster-flowered

Rather uncommon these days, you can still see 'Mrs F. W. Flight' in old hedgerows in South Africa and it looks stunning at the Roseraie de l'Haÿ, on the trellises there. Raised by Cutbush in 1905, it is very much in the 'Dorothy Perkins' mould, with big trusses of ruffled, mid-pink flowers late in the season. The dark green, shiny foliage does not seem as addicted to mildew as 'Dorothy', which is a point in its favor.

'Crimson Rambler' × unknown
Summer flowering

▲ 'Mrs Charles Frederick Worth'
▶ 'Mrs Dudley Cross'

'Mrs Henry Bowles' — Large-flowered

One of the most popular exhibition roses of the 1920s, '30s and '40s, 'Mrs Henry Bowles' is rarely seen today, though some exhibitors still grow it for old times' sake. Its faults are a decline in vigor and the susceptibility of its dark green, glossy leaves to black spot, but it is still capable of producing the occasional show flower—large, high centred, and brilliant pink. Raised by Benjamin Cant and introduced in 1921, it was named for the wife of a well-known English gardener of the day.

'Lady Pirrie' × 'Gorgeous'
Repeat flowering

▲ 'Mrs Henry Bowles'

'Mrs John Laing' — Hybrid Perpetual

Ever since Henry Bennett brought out this rose in 1887, rosarians have been singing her praises, led by Dean Hole: 'Not only in vigor, constancy, and abundance, but in form and features—Beauty's Queen!' All one can add to *that* is, that after a hundred years the bush remains vigorous and free with its flowers, which are as enchanting as ever—large and full without being in the least blowsy, distinctive in their cool pink with just a hint of lilac, and sweetly fragrant. Foliage is light green. 'Mrs John Laing' features in the breeding of some quite recent roses.

'François Michelon' × unknown
Repeat flowering
Fragrant

'Mrs Maud Alston' — Cluster-flowered

I found this rose in the garden of Alister Clark's roses that is being created at Carrick Hill, Adelaide, South Australia, where it looked charming, with its old-fashioned fluffy pink flowers and shiny green leaves. Clark's biographer seems to have missed it, and I can find no more about it. It is a mystery rose.

Parentage unknown
Repeat flowering

'Mrs Miniver' — Large-flowered

'Souvenir de Louis Simon' was the name bestowed by the French raiser Chambard in 1942, but the huge success during the war of the movie *Mrs Miniver* suggested there be a 'Mrs Miniver' rose, and Jackson & Perkins obliged. They rechristened 'Souvénir de Louis Simon' with great success. A lightweight double of twenty-five petals, opening from long buds to show its stamens, it is brilliant crimson and very fragrant, the bush compact with soft green leaves. It is something of a rarity these days.

Parentage undisclosed
Repeat flowering
Fragrant

◄ 'Mrs John Laing'
▼ 'Mrs Miniver'

▲ 'Mrs Maud Alston'
▼ 'Mrs Oakley Fisher'

'Mrs Oakley Fisher' — Large-flowered

'Mrs Oakley Fisher' is one of the most delightful of all the delightful single-flowered Large-flowered Roses that were fashionable in the 1920s. The buds are deep orange, opening to apricot-yellow flowers that are quite fragrant. The bush is vigorous, usually blooming in clusters, and the foliage dark green. The raisers were Cants of Colchester, in 1921.

Parentage unknown
Repeat flowering
Fragrant

▲ 'Mrs Paul'
► 'Mrs Pierre S. Du Pont'

'Mrs Paul' — Bourbon

In 1863 the great English rosarian William Paul dedicated a crimson rose, 'Mrs William Paul', to his wife. It is rarely encountered now, and William's son George was less formal when his turn came in 1891; his wife's rose is simply 'Mrs Paul'. It is a seedling of 'Madame Isaac Pereire', resembling it in its tall, almost climbing branches, its bright green leaves, and its sweetly scented, rather blowsy flowers. They are palest blush pink, as opposed to the brash deep shade of 'Madame Pereire' or the rosy pink of her sport 'Madame Ernest Calvat'. The three roses look splendid together, but do not expect the individual blooms of 'Mrs Paul' to be quite up to the standard of the other two except in the autumn, or fall.

'Madame Isaac Pereire' × unknown
Repeat flowering
Fragrant

'Mrs Pierre S. Du Pont' — Large-flowered

One of the leading yellow roses for many years, and being best in a warm climate, 'Mrs Pierre S. Du Pont' appropriately honors an American lady of French descent, for it was raised by a Frenchman, Charles Mallerin, and was sold in its tens of thousands by an American, Robert Pyle of Conard-Pyle, starting in 1929. The blooms are clear golden yellow, fading lighter, fragrant and of forty petals. The plant is quite bushy and the foliage glossy. Its health and clear color earned it the 1929 Bagatelle gold medal.

('Ophelia' × 'Rayon d'Or') × ('Ophelia' × ['Constance' × 'Souvenir de Claudius Pernet'])
Repeat flowering
Fragrant

'Mrs Reynolds Hole' — Tea

Samuel Reynolds Hole, Dean of Rochester, was one of the great nineteenth-century evangelists of the rose, writing extensively about his beloved flower and lending his hand to the formation of the RNRS, still the largest and most influential rose society in the world. Alex Dickson dedicated a 'silvery rose', a Large-flowered Rose, to him in 1904 ('Dean Hole'). It took the French gallantry of the Nabonnand brothers in 1907 to commemorate his wife. 'Mrs Reynolds Hole' is pink also, and as buxom as a Victorian matron. The bush is sturdy, the dark green foliage is glossy and abundant.

Parentage unknown
Repeat flowering
Fragrant

'Mrs Sam McGredy' — Large-flowered

It is said that when Sam McGredy III decided to name a rose for his wife, she rejected his choice and insisted instead on a rose he was not even considering introducing. 'Mrs Sam McGredy', introduced in 1929, turned out to be one of the all-time greats. Its young foliage is perhaps the most richly purple of any rose, maturing to bronze-green, and the young flower a still unique color of copper-red, paling to salmon-pink as the huge, shapely blooms open. It is fragrant too. If only it were a stronger grower!

('Donald McDonald' × 'Golden Emblem') × (seedling × 'Queen Alexandra')
Repeat flowering
Fragrant

▲ 'Mrs Sam McGredy'
◄ 'Mrs Reynolds Hole'

'Mrs Sam McGredy, Climbing' — Large-flowered Climber

'Mrs Sam McGredy' was never all that robust a bush, and is now best enjoyed in its climbing version. This still retains its vigor, is unusually generous with its repeat flowering and, of course, it has the wonderful color and fragrance of 'Mrs Sam McGredy'. A warm, dry climate suits it best.

Sport from 'Mrs Sam McGredy'
Repeat flowering
Fragrant

▲ 'Climbing Mrs Sam McGredy'
▼ 'Mrs Wakefield Christie-Miller'

'Mrs Wakefield Christie-Miller' Large-flowered

They do not name them like that any more! It is probably nearer true that modern owners of such names are apt to say, 'Oh, do call me Fiona'. There was no such informality in 1909, when Sam McGredy II introduced 'Mrs Wakefield Christie-Miller' to the public. Her recent revival was originally due to her having masqueraded for a while as the long-lost 'Lady Mary Fitzwilliam'. She is a delight in her own right, the large, fragrant, two-toned pink blooms just like the kind you see on Edwardian chintzes. The growth is moderate, and some pampering will be appreciated. Foliage is light green and leathery.

Parentage unknown
Repeat flowering
Fragrant

'Mullard Jubilee' Large-flowered
'Electron'

Sam McGredy has recorded that when, in 1970, the Mullard Electronics Company offered him the then unheard of fee of £10 000 for the naming rights on a new rose, they insisted that it be a world-beater; nothing less would do. They got 'Mullard Jubilee' which won just about every award there was: from the RNRS in 1969, The Hague in 1970, Belfast in 1972, and, under its American name 'Electron', the AARS award for 1973. The flower's color is one you either love or hate: electric deep pink. Foliage is dark green and leathery.

'Paddy McGredy' × 'Prima Ballerina'
Repeat flowering
Fragrant

'Mutabilis' China
Rosa chinensis mutabilis, 'Tipo Ideale'

The origins of this wonderful rose are something of a mystery. It was introduced by Henri Correvon, the Swiss botanist, in 1932, having been presented to him by Prince Borromeo forty years before. Whether it originated in the prince's great gardens at Isola Bella or in China no one knows. Its slim stems build up to a densely leafy bush, 3 metres (10 feet) tall and wide if left unpruned, a third of those dimensions if pruned firmly. However large, it covers itself with sprays of single blooms like butterflies. They open Tea

▲ 'Mullard Jubilee'
▼ 'Mutabilis'

Rose yellow but pass to pink, carmine and crimson. There is no other rose quite like it. The dark green, finely cut foliage is plum colored in its youth.

Parentage unknown
Repeat flowering

▼ 'Nancy Hayward'

'Nancy Hayward' Large-flowered Climber

One of the first plants that I put into my present garden was a 'Nancy Hayward' to climb up and over the first floor balcony railings, and it has been a pleasure ever since to look out and see the railings wreathed from end to end with big single roses in strawberry-red fading to carmine. The show starts in winter and by mid-winter stops the traffic regularly. It is repeated several times until the autumn, or fall. The flowers last very well in the vase, and its only fault is lack of perfume. The mid-green foliage and growth betray its descent from *Rosa gigantea*. Like most *R. gigantea* hybrids it is rather tender. Alister Clark introduced it in 1937.

'Jessie Clark' × unknown
Repeat flowering

▲ 'Nancy Steen'

▲ 'Neelambari'

brilliant, its form excellent, and its compact bush easy to grow and prolific in bloom. Nonetheless, it is one of the best red roses for bedding and has dark, leathery green foliage. No doubt it has found its way into many gardens looked after by the National Trust—a body founded in England in 1895 to care for the nation's heritage—and in the gardens of the National Trusts that have followed it everywhere. It was raised by Sam McGredy in 1970. Bad Neuheim is a famous spa in Germany, and it is appropriate that this rose grows very well there.

'Evelyn Fison' × 'King of Hearts'
Repeat flowering

'Nancy Steen' — Cluster-flowered

Very strong in its growth, and sometimes classed as a Modern Shrub Rose, 'Nancy Steen' bears abundant blooms, large, shapely and fragrant, in a delicate blend of pink and cream. The glossy foliage is bronze-green and leathery. Raised in New Zealand, it honors one of that country's most notable rose-growers, who worked to revive interest in the Old Garden Roses. Credited to G. C. Sherwood, it is of mixed breeding.

'Pink Parfait' × ('Ophelia' × 'Parkdirektor Riggers')
Repeat flowering
Fragrant

'National Trust' — Large-flowered
'Bad Neuheim'

If 'National Trust' had scent, it would be the near-perfect red rose, its color

'National Velvet' — Large-flowered
BURalp

Elizabeth Taylor made her debut in the movie about a young English girl who, disguised as a jockey, won the Grand National in 1944, but it was not until 1988 that Larry Burks of Tyler, Texas, raised the rose which he named to commemorate the event. Appropriately the flowers are velvet-red, opening loose and informal, the way some camellias do. The glossy green foliage is like a camellia too. There is not enough scent to be remarkable. Tyler sometimes calls itself the rose capital of the world, because many of the big American wholesale rose-growers have their nurseries there.

Parentage undisclosed
Repeat flowering

'Neelambari' — Cluster-flowered

Photographed in New Delhi some years ago, this rose showed promise of being one of the very best mauve roses, its flowers of good size and form, the color lively, the foliage dark green and glossy. If a rose can do well in the extreme climate of the Indian plains, it should do well in most places. It was raised by the Indian Agricultural Research Institute and introduced in 1975. The official description held by the ARS has it as 'deep red'. Someone seems to have crossed wires.

'Blue Moon' × 'Africa Star'
Repeat flowering

'Neelum' — Large-flowered

The Indian Agricultural Research Institute has for some years now been breeding roses especially for Indian conditions, and the gardens of the Indian Rose Society in Delhi display some splendid roses as a result. It seems a pity that the rest of the world

▲ 'National Velvet'
◄ 'National Trust'
► 'Neelum'

ignores them. 'Neelum' is typical: it is a large, shapely bloom in silvery pink, with a heady perfume and dark green, glossy foliage. The name is that of an Indian river.

Parentage unknown
Repeat flowering
Fragrant

▼ 'Neue Revue'

'Neue Revue' Large-flowered
KORrev
'News Review'
It is odd that Reimer Kordes introduced 'Neue Revue' in 1962, but held back its parent, 'Königin der Rosen' until 1964.

'Neue Revue' shows its parentage in its thorniness and its glossy, dark green leaves, but also in the soft wood that it inherits from its grandfather 'Perfecta', which makes it a rather unreliable performer. This is a pity, as the blooms can be sensational—large, perfectly formed, richly blending gold, pink and red with touches of coral, and, unusually for such a dazzler, very fragrant. The name honors a widely read and respected German magazine.

'Königin der Rosen' × unknown
Repeat flowering
Fragrant

'Nevada' Modern Shrub
One of the best loved of all the Modern Shrub Roses, 'Nevada' makes a tall, bushy plant, its arching branches wreathed in early summer with big, wide open blooms in pink so pale it passes for white at a short distance. The foliage is pale green with many leaflets. Rarely without flowers until late autumn, or fall, 'Nevada' comes as close as any rose to uniting the grace of a Wild Rose with the flowers and repeat flowering of a Modern Garden Rose. The raiser, Pedro Dot, registered it in 1927 as 'La Giralda' × *Rosa moyesii*, but the pundits have disputed that ever since. It has been suggested that it derives from *R. pimpinellifolia*.

'La Giralda' × *R. moyesii*
Repeat flowering

'Neville Chamberlain' Large-flowered
The British Prime Minister Neville Chamberlain was one of the few politicians who did anything to try to save Belgium from being overrun by the Nazis, so it is fitting that this rose should have been dedicated to him by Belgium's leading rosarian, Louis Lens, in 1940. This would have upset any Nazis who noticed flowers! It bears large, well-shaped blooms in a more delicate color than either parent—softest salmon pink, with a hint of orange at the centre. The foliage is dark green and glossy. A rose for cool climates, it won the Portland gold medal in 1944.

'Charles P. Kilham' × 'Mrs Sam McGredy'
Repeat flowering

'New Daily Mail' Cluster-flowered
'Pussta'
'Madame Edouard Herriot' was introduced in 1912—look her up to see how she became known as the 'Daily Mail Rose'. Then, in 1929, came the crimson Large-flowered Rose, 'Daily Mail Scented', and finally in 1972, Mathias

▲ 'Neville Chamberlain'
◄ 'Nevada'

▲ 'New Daily Mail'
► 'New Day'
▼ 'New Dawn'

Tantau brought out this one, 'New Daily Mail'. It is nothing like either of its predecessors, being a rather large-flowered Cluster-flowered Rose, bright red and scentless. It is quite a good rose, on the tall side and free with its bloom. Foliage is dark green.

'Letkis' × 'Walzertraum'
Repeat flowering

'New Dawn'   Large-flowered Climber
'Everblooming Dr Van Fleet'
'New Dawn', introduced in 1930, is often claimed to be the first repeat-flowering Climbing Rose. This is not true, as many of the Noisettes and Bourbon Climbers flower all season.

They do not like cold, however. 'New Dawn' is a cold hardy rose. It has proved able to transmit its repeat flowering to many lovely descendants. It will reach 6 metres (20 feet) or so on a wall, but is lovely, too, just allowed to grow as a large shrub. Foliage is dark green and glossy. A sport of the once-blooming but otherwise identical 'Dr Van Fleet', it arose in the Connecticut nurseries of a firm named Dreer. It holds the first plant patent issued in the United States.

Sport from 'Dr Van Fleet'
Repeat flowering
Fragrant

'New Day'   Large-flowered
KORgold
'Mabella'
Call it by either name—'New Day' is the officially registered one, 'Mabella' the one the greenhouse growers use—this is one of the outstanding yellow roses, and a great exception to the rule that first-rate greenhouse roses are second-rate in the garden. It is a particularly reliable bush, even in the hot, humid or cold climates that so many yellow roses dislike, and the flowers are large, shapely, brilliant in color, and seemingly immune to weather damage. Foliage is dark green and glossy. It was raised by Reimer Kordes in 1977, from two very much older yellow roses.

'Arlene Francis' × 'Roselandia'
Repeat flowering
Fragrant

'New Year'   Large-flowered
MACnewye
'Arcadian'
'New Year' is a 1982 'Grandiflora' from Sam McGredy. It does not seem to be

▲ 'News'
▼ 'New Year'

on the way to being a worldwide hit, despite winning the 1987 AARS award. The flowers are a delightful blend of clear orange and yellow, and are large and shapely. They have only twenty petals, and some say that they open too quickly in hot weather. The bush is tall and shrubby, with dark green foliage, and it flowers freely enough that the quick-opening can be forgiven.

'Mary Sumner' × unnamed seedling
Repeat flowering
Fragrant

'News'   Cluster-flowered
LEGnews
Although it is always classed as a Cluster-flowered Rose, had 'News' come

▲ 'Niagara Pride'

out earlier than it did, it would probably have been classed as a decorative Large-flowered Rose, for its flowers, though they do come in clusters, are quite large and open wide from long buds. The color is very distinctive: a bright magenta-purple, redder in the bud and softening with age. The rose is fragrant too, and a good grower, with olive-green foliage. It has the enviable characteristic of performing well in poor soils and is also suitable for growing in pots. It can also be planted as a hedge. A very desirable rose, it was raised by E. B. LeGrice, and introduced in 1968.

'Lilac Charm' × 'Tuscany Superb'
Repeat flowering
Fragrant

'Niagara Pride' Large-flowered

Released by one of Canada's leading rose-growers, Carl Pallek of Ontario, in 1982, 'Niagara Pride' is officially described as 'orange blend', but it is really a salmon-pink, with cerise towards the petal edges. That is how it was in Vancouver's Butchart Gardens anyway, where it was photographed. The flowers are shapely, the plant bushy and glossy-leafed. Fragrance is only moderate.

Parentage undisclosed
Repeat flowering

'Nicole' Cluster-flowered
KORicole

White, sometimes with a golden light in the depths, the petals are edged with a distinct band of cherry-pink. There are thirty-five of them, building up a nicely shaped flower with a little fragrance. The foliage is dark green and the plant is strong. 'Nicole' was raised by Reimer

Kordes and introduced in 1975. It is not widely grown, but it is a good rose for cutting, and perhaps more people should try it. Do not confuse it with 'Nicola', a deep pink Cluster-flowered Rose from Gandy's, introduced in 1980, or with a red Large-flowered Rose from France, 'Nicole Debrosse'.

Unnamed seedling × 'Bordure Rose'
Repeat flowering

'Niphétos' Tea

The name is mock Classical Greek for 'snowy', and indeed 'Niphétos' reigned as the purest of white roses from its introduction by Bougère in 1843 until 'Frau Karl Druschki' came along in 1900. It was a great favorite with the nineteenth-century florists, who grew it in glasshouses (it dislikes both cold and wet) and wired its weak stems to

▲ 'Nicole'

hold the flowers up. To modern eyes the open blooms are floppy, but the buds are as long and elegant as anyone could desire. The foliage is pale green. There is a rampant climbing sport.

Parentage unknown
Repeat flowering
Fragrant

'Nitouche' Cluster-flowered

'Nitouche' was a disappointment when it was introduced to Australia; its delicately blended peach and coral tones seemed just wishy-washy and the bush not very strong. Perhaps it just needs the cool climate of Denmark where it was raised. When I saw it a couple of years ago in cooler New Zealand, I did not recognize it. The flowers were large, shapely, most attractive in color, and the dark green and glossy-leafed

▼ 'Niphétos'

▲ 'Nitouche'
► 'Norwich Gold'

bush showed all signs of health and vigor. 'Nitouche' was introduced by Niels Poulsen in 1974.

Unnamed seedling × 'Whisky Mac'
Repeat flowering

'Norma'   Large-flowered

Norma was the Druid priestess whose encounters with the Romans form the story line of Bellini's opera *Norma*. The rose is a large, brilliant red Large-flowered Rose from Jean Gaujard in 1976. If the books are to be believed, it is a cross between a William Paul Hybrid Perpetual of 1894, called 'Clio', and one of Gaujard's earlier red Large-flowered Roses, 'Credo', parents a world apart. 'Norma' is fragrant and sturdy in growth, with large matt green leaves. It has not been publicized much, but it must have many admirers, as quite a few nurseries around the world list it.

'Clio' × 'Credo'
Repeat flowering
Fragrant

'Norwich Castle'   Cluster-flowered

Tallish, upright bushes bear dark green, shiny leaves and slightly fragrant, pleasantly shapely flowers. The English rose-grower and writer, Peter Beales,

▼ 'Norma'

who raised it describes it as being of the color of an excellent beer! It was introduced in 1980. The great Norman castle—now a museum—dominates the East Anglian capital of Norwich. Whether it can be seen from Mr Beales's nursery nearby I do not know.

('Whisky Mac' × 'Arthur Bell') × 'Bettina'
Repeat flowering

'Norwich Gold'   Modern Shrub

The parentage of this 1962 Kordes introduction has not been registered, but it is probably derived from *Rosa kordesii*. It has the characteristic glossy dark green foliage and tendency to climb, but it is decidedly bushy in habit and makes quite a satisfactory shrub. The flowers appear all season, and are of shaggy form, opening from buds in the Large-flowered Rose style. They are not really gold but a blend of salmon and yellow. Fragrance is fine but not outstanding.

Parentage undisclosed
Repeat flowering
Fragrant

◄ 'Norwich Castle'

'Nur Mahal' — Hybrid Musk

Nur Mahal, the all-powerful wife of the Emperor Jahangir of India is credited in legend (and in her husband's diary) with the discovery of Attar of Roses, which is no doubt why Joseph Pemberton dedicated this rose to her memory three hundred years later, in 1923. Ironically, this is one of the least fragrant of his Hybrid Musks. A very pleasing rose, it makes a bushy plant, which can be kept to Bush Rose size with a little pruning. Given its head it will make a 1.5 metre (5 foot) shrub. The foliage of 'Nur Mahal' is dark green and leathery.

'Château de Clos Vougeot' × unnamed seedling
Repeat flowering
Fragrant

▲ 'Nur Mahal'
▼ 'Nymphenburg'

'Nymphenburg' — Modern Shrub

The palace and the gardens of the Nymphenburg just on the outskirts of Munich are a German tourist attraction. The rose is worthy of the name. Its fat buds open to mid-sized flowers, of beautifully ruffed shape, with a delicious fragrance, and in exquisite shades of salmon, peach and gold. They are borne all season in large and small clusters. The shrub is large, but open and lax in habit. Many of its admirers prefer to see it trained as a pillar rose. Foliage is olive-green, glossy and lightly rugose. It was introduced by Wilhelm Kordes in 1954.

'Sangerhausen' × 'Sunmist'
Repeat flowering
Fragrant

'Oeillet Flamand' — Gallica

The French name means 'Flemish carnation'. There seems to be doubt as to whether this is the rose that Vibert raised and introduced in 1845, but its flowers are like carnations in their ruffled fullness, as the name suggests they should be. They are striped in pink, purple and white, the exact proportion of the three colors varying from year to year. Sometimes the overall effect is quite dark, as in the picture, with the striping a subtle two-tone effect. At other times the picture is more of dark stripes on a pale ground. The growth is typical Gallica: compact, but not too thorny; foliage is mid-green and rough.

Parentage unknown
Fragrant

'Oeillet Panachée' — Moss
'Striped Moss'

This rose, which came from Charles Verdier in 1888, its parents unrecorded, is not seen very often. There are probably better striped roses, but this one does add the charm of brownish moss. The blooms are fragrant, though not especially large, and the bush is a dainty affair to about 1 metre (3 feet) or so tall. Foliage is mid-green and smooth.

Parentage unknown
Summer flowering
Fragrant

▲ 'Oeillet Panachée'
▼ 'Oeillet Flamand'

'Officinalis' — Gallica
Rosa gallica officinalis, 'Apothecary's Rose', 'Red Rose of Lancaster', 'Rose of Provins', 'Double French Rose', 'Red Damask'

The most remarkable character of this rose is not evident at first sight. Its flowers, not especially fragrant on the

bush, become intensely so when they are dried. It is thus the pre-eminent choice for the various medicinal and culinary uses to which the rose is put. If you find an antique recipe that calls simply for 'red Rofes', this is the one they mean. It is also a very worthy garden plant, compact, almost thornless, and producing enormous numbers of informal blooms of Cluster-flowered Rose size, carmine with golden stamens. Foliage is mid-green and rough.

Parentage unknown
Summer flowering
Fragrant

'Oklahoma' — Large-flowered

The black rose seems to be as much desired by some people as the elusive blue one. 'Oklahoma' is about as close to black as they come. Sometimes its crimson is so dark you do not notice the flowers until you are standing right next to the bush. The blooms are large and globular, sometimes too much so for shapeliness, and richly fragrant. The dark green foliage is leathery. 'Oklahoma' needs a temperate climate—the flowers scorch in hot areas and turn magenta in cold. It is a very tall grower. It was raised by Herbert Swim and O. L. Weeks in 1963. The name is apt: 'Oklahoma' actually means 'the red man's land'.

'Chrysler Imperial' × 'Charles Mallerin'
Repeat flowering
Fragrant

'Olala' — Cluster-flowered
'Oh La La'

Oh la la indeed. When Maurice Chevalier was making the phrase a catchword for the 1950s, this rose was one of the most eye catching in the garden. On a tall bush, with dark green and leathery leaves, it bears great clusters of brilliant red flowers with lighter centres. Only slightly fragrant, it can still make quite a show. It was raised by Mathias Tantau and introduced in 1956.

'Fanal' × 'Crimson Glory'
Repeat flowering

▲ 'Olala'
◄ 'Officinalis'
► 'Old Blush'
▼ 'Oklahoma'

'Old Blush' — China
'Parson's Pink China', 'Monthly Rose', 'Last Rose of Summer'

'Blush' usually suggests a very pale pink rose, but 'Old Blush' is a mid-pink, though it does, as many of the China Roses do, blush deeper with age. The flowers are not overlarge, 8 centimetres (3 inches) or so, but they are softly fragrant, and borne in great abundance from spring to autumn, or fall. The bush is tallish and slender, with narrow, pointed, mid-green leaves. Introduced from China in 1793, it is one of the most important of all roses historically. It is safe to say that all the repeat-flowering Modern Garden Roses descend from 'Old Blush'. Yet it is no superannuated dowager, but one of the most desirable of roses still; no cottage garden is complete without it.

Parentage unknown
Repeat flowering
Fragrant

'Old Dick's Apricot Rambler' — Rambler

Just about any collection of Old Garden Roses will contain one or two rescued from some local garden and flowering away quite untroubled by the head-scratching going on all around it while the experts try to find out what its name is. Here is one from the Botanic

Gardens at Mount Lofty near Adelaide, South Australia. It is a glossy-leafed Rambler with small clusters of scented flowers in a lovely and unusual shade of deep apricot-yellow, paling to cream in the sun. It gives some repeat bloom. It will probably turn out to be one of M. Barbier's hybrids of *Rosa luciae*.

Parentage unknown
Summer flowering
Fragrant

▲ 'Old Dick's Apricot Rambler'
▼ 'Old Master'

'Old Master'   Cluster-flowered
MACesp
You can either see 'Old Master' as a white rose with a great splash of red on the upper surface of each petal or as a red rose with white reverse, border and edge; either way it is very striking. The foliage is dark green and glossy, the growth free and the flowers scentless.

This was one of the first of Sam McGredy's 'Hand-painted Roses', and it was introduced in 1974. Its ancestry is complicated indeed. As one famous rosarian has said, the genealogies of the Old Testament are simpler!

(['Evelyn Fison' × {'Tantau's Triumph' × *Rosa macrophylla coryana*}] × ['Hamburger Phoenix' × 'Danse du Feu']) × ('Evelyn Fison' × ['Orange Sweetheart' × 'Fruhlingsmorgen'])
Repeat flowering

'Oldtimer'   Large-flowered
KORoi
'Coppertone', 'Old Time'
To class 'Oldtimer' as 'yellow blend' is throwing in the towel. The rarely used name 'Coppertone' describes it very well. It is a sort of coppery tan color, with orange highlights. The blooms are

▲ 'Oldtimer'
▼ 'Olé'

very large, with slightly reflexed petals and the foliage is mid-green and glossy. Reimer Kordes has not revealed the parentage, but it is evident that he intended this 1966 introduction as an improvement on his sensational 1963 'Vienna Charm'. They are certainly alike. Most people, however, find 'Old-timer' a little easier to grow and the plants longer lived.

Parentage undisclosed
Repeat flowering
Fragrant

'Olé'   Cluster-flowered
This 1964 'Grandiflora', which comes from Armstrong Nurseries, California, may equally well be regarded as a decorative Large-flowered Rose, for its flowers are informal and ruffled, and of good size, 10 centimetres (4 inches) or more. They are borne on a shortish plant and in clusters, so most often it is classed with the Cluster-flowered Roses. There is only moderate scent, but the color is stunning: brilliant warm crimson with a distinct overlay of orange. Like its parents, it is best in a warm climate, where it has proved resistant to mildew. Foliage is olive-green and glossy. One would not think that people would confuse *Olé!* a Spanish phrase of public rejoicing, with the more intimate French *Oh la la!*, but the two roses are sometimes confused.

'Roundelay' × 'El Capitan'
Repeat flowering
Fragrant

'Olympiad' Large-flowered
MACauk

Adopted as the official flower of the 1984 Los Angeles Olympics, this rose came to California from New Zealand, where it was raised by Sam McGredy. It is a medal winner in its own right, winning the 1984 AARS award. The blooms are large, well shaped if a trifle flat, and brilliant unfading red. The plant is exceptionally sturdy and easy to grow, with disease-resistant olive-green foliage. Lack of fragrance is its only demerit. Do not confuse this one with an earlier 'Olympiad', raised in 1931 by Pernet-Ducher and known as 'Madame Raymond Gaujard' also. It was a red blend.

'Red Planet' × 'Pharaoh'
Repeat flowering

'Olympic Torch' Large-flowered
'Seika'

Seizo Suzuki made a most spectacular debut in the world of international rose-breeding in 1966 with this large and shapely rose. Literally meaning 'sacred fire', *seika* is the Japanese name for the Olympic torch, so in both languages the rose honors Japan's hosting of the Olympic Games at Tokyo. Fittingly, each bloom combines the Japanese national colors, red and white, with just a touch of Olympic gold at the flower's heart. The bush is strong and upright, with polished green leaves. It performs best in warm climates. There is not much fragrance.

'Rose Gaujard' × 'Crimson Glory'
Repeat flowering

'Omar Khayyám' Damask

'My grave', wrote Omar Khayyám, 'shall be in a place where the breeze shall scatter rose petals upon it.' It was so; a rose grows on the poet's grave to this day. A hundred years ago, seeds were taken from the rose to the grave

◀ 'Olympiad'
▼ 'Omar Khayyám'

▲ 'Ondella'
▶ 'Ophelia'
▼ 'Olympic Torch'

of the translator of *The Rubaiyat*, Edward Fitzgerald, and it is this rose from Fitzgerald's grave that has been propagated and introduced as 'Omar Khayyám'. It is a typical Damask, with soft green leaves and abundant summer flowers in clear pink. Not a first rate bloom, perhaps, but one full of history, sentiment and fragrance. Orange-red hips follow the flowers.

Parentage unknown
Summer flowering
Fragrant

'Ondella' Large-flowered
MEIvanama

One does not often see 'Ondella' as a garden rose, it is essentially a greenhouse variety. Raised by Meilland in 1979, it is in the same orange-red color range as the firm's earlier smash hit 'Baccarà', but it has not proved nearly so successful. It appears to be available only from one nursery in Australia and one in India. The blooms are quite large and shapely, but there is little scent. Foliage is dark green and shiny, with red tints in its youth.

('Elegy' × 'Arturo Toscanini') × ('Peace' × 'Demain')
Repeat flowering

'Ophelia' Large-flowered

'Ophelia' turned up as a foundling at the English nursery of William Paul in 1912. For a couple of years it was ignored, but by the 1920s it had become a favorite. 'The Queen Mother of

Roses' it was called, for it not only produced no less than thirty-six sports, including such beauties as 'Madame Butterfly' and 'Lady Sylvia', it was used by every hybridist to create yet more beautiful roses. It remains as lovely as always, its medium-sized blooms of blush-white exquisitely formed and very fragrant. The bush is as easy as ever to grow, with dark green, leathery foliage. The climbing sport is exceptionally fine too.

Parentage unknown
Repeat flowering
Fragrant

'Orana Gold'   Large-flowered
MACerupt

This rather new (1990) rose from Sam McGredy is not really gold in color, rather a bright blend of yellow, orange and red, softening to coral-pink and yellow as the flowers open. They are only of medium size, but they make a bright show against glossy red-tinted foliage. Scent, alas, is only slight, but it is an excellent rose for cutting, with the stems long and straight and the blooms long lasting.

'Freude' × 'Sunblest'
Repeat flowering

'Orange Juice'   Cluster-flowered
AROraju
'Lady Glencora'

This is one of those in-between roses with large, exhibition-form flowers in fairly small clusters. The color is officially described as 'clear orange', but it varies a bit. Sometimes it is exactly the color of orange juice, at others there is a good deal of yellow in it. There is

not much fragrance, but the plant seems good, with dark green foliage and unusual bright red thorns. It is a 1986 Jack Christensen creation for Armstrong nurseries.

'Katherine Loker' × 'Gingersnap'
Repeat flowering
Fragrant

'Orange Triumph'   Cluster-flowered

Within a few years of its introduction in 1937 by William Kordes, 'Orange Triumph' became one of the world's most widely grown roses, both in gardens and greenhouses. No wonder; for it was, and remains, one of the easiest of all roses to grow, the compact, shiny-leafed bush bearing masses of bright little flowers all season. They can not honestly be described as orange; they are bright geranium-red. There is no scent, but the long sprays last an astonishingly long time, on the plant or in the vase.

'Eva' × 'Solarium'
Repeat flowering

▲ 'Orangeade'
◄ 'Orana Gold'
▼ 'Orange Triumph'

▼ 'Orange Juice'

'Orangeade'   Cluster-flowered

When Sam McGredy introduced this rose in 1959, it created quite a sensation. 'Orangeade' remains one of the best of the dazzling roses. Its orange-red color is less unusual now than it was then, but the grace of its clusters of almost-single flowers remains unique, and the glossy-leafed, thorny plant as strong as ever. Try it in a mixed planting with 'Cocorico' and 'Sarabande', which are not unlike it but much more red.

They will flatter the orange tones in 'Orangeade' and together the effect will smoulder. 'Orangeade' won the RNRS gold medal in 1959.

'Orange Sweetheart' × 'Independence'
Repeat flowering

'Oregold' — Large-flowered
'Miss Harp', 'Silhouette', 'Annaliese Rothenberger'

Not a rose for places with muggy summers, when it is apt to go into shock and refuse to grow, 'Oregold', winner of the 1975 AARS award, is a gorgeous sight where conditions suit it. The blooms are then large, high centred, and a glorious deep buttercup-yellow, with a light fragrance. The foliage is dark green and glossy. 'Oregold' was raised by Germany's Mathias Tantau.

'Piccadilly' × 'Königin der Rosen'
Repeat flowering
Fragrant

'Orient Express' — Large-flowered
The great popularity of 'Whisky Mac' from Mathias Tantau has sent hybridists searching for a similarly beautiful old-gold flower on a less temperamental plant. One of the contenders is Christopher Wheatcroft's 1978 'Orient Express'. It is a good, reliable grower, and the blooms are lovely, high-centred and fragrant, but they are a deeper color than 'Whisky Mac', more of an orange tone, with yellow on the reverse. The foliage is bronze-green. It was named for the famous train that takes travellers from Paris to Venice in absolute luxury.

'Sunblest' × unnamed seedling
Repeat flowering
Fragrant

▲ 'Orient Express'
◀ 'Oregold'

'Oriental Charm' — Large-flowered
Lovers of single roses should clamor now for the re-introduction of 'Oriental Charm', despite its faintly twee name, for it is a beauty. It is not quite single, having a few petals beyond the canonical five, but the color is rich and unusual—orange-red, heavily veined with crimson, and set off by golden stamens. The glossy-leafed bush is tall and free-blooming, the blooms slightly fragrant and excellent for cutting. It was raised, from very mixed ancestry, by Carl Duehrsen of the United States.

('Charlotte Armstrong' × 'Grüss an Teplitz') × ('Madame Butterfly' × 'Floradora')
Repeat flowering

'Othello' — English Rose
AUSlo

Aptly named for Shakespeare's Moor, 'Othello' is one of the darkest of the David Austin roses, its big, well-filled flowers reminiscent of the dark red Hybrid Perpetuals. They vary in color, from light to deep crimson, frequently adding an overlay of purple. It is, as one expects of a red rose, richly fragrant. The bush is strong and upright to about 1.5 metres (5 feet), its faults being an abundance of thorns and that bane of dark red roses, a need for protection from mildew. The foliage is mid-green and leathery. It was introduced in 1986.

'Lilian Austin' × 'The Squire'
Repeat flowering
Fragrant

▲ 'Oriental Charm'
▼ 'Othello'

◄ 'Paddy McGredy'

repeats quite well if it is cosseted a bit, and is fragrant. The stripes are in pink over crimson. Foliage is matt green.

Possibly a sport from 'Rose du Roi'
Repeat flowering
Fragrant

▲ 'Panachée de Lyon'
▼ 'Paloma'

'Paddy McGredy' — Cluster-flowered
MACpa

Sam McGredy has written that when this rose was still unnamed, it was suggested he call it 'New Look', as it was just about the first Cluster-flowered Rose to have flowers of exhibition form on a not-too-tall bush. When it came out in 1962 it bore the name of Sam's younger sister, 'Paddy McGredy'. The flowers are a deep coral-rose, almost red, and make a bright show when in full flush, as they almost cover the plant. Foliage is a leathery olive-green. There are few flowers in between the peak flowerings, and the color tends to bleach in hot weather. This is definitely a cool-climate rose.

'Spartan' × 'Tzigane'
Repeat flowering
Fragrant

'Paddy Stevens' — Large-flowered
MACcratalak

At first sight, 'Paddy Stevens' looks to be a straight coral-rose, much in the manner of the old (and always lovely) 'Mission Bells', but it is really a blend of bright pinks with coral and gold. Large and shapely, the flowers are scented pleasantly. Foliage is dark and glossy, and the bush has a reputation for freedom of flower. It is still new, having been introduced by Sam McGredy only in 1990, but if it lives up to its promise, it should become very popular.

'Solitaire' × unnamed seedling
Repeat flowering
Fragrant

'Paloma' — Large-flowered

Paloma is Spanish for 'dove', an appropriate name for this elegant rose, whose large, white, high-centred blooms open to show red stamens against grey-green foliage. It was raised by Herbert Swim and O. L. Weeks and introduced in 1968 after Swim had set up in partnership with Weeks under the name Swim & Weeks Wholesale Rose Growers.

'Mount Shasta' × 'Message'
Repeat flowering

'Panachée de Lyon' — Portland

Why M. Dubreuil should single out this rose as the 'Striped Rose from Lyon', when there were other raisers there contributing striped roses also, is hard to fathom. He was late on the scene, also, for 'Panachée de Lyon' did not come out until 1895. It is thought to be a sport of 'Rose du Roi', the prototype if not the ancestor of the Portlands and Hybrid Perpetuals, and a rare rose indeed now. Like it, 'Panachée de Lyon' is a short but rather thin bush, which

'Pandemonium' — Cluster-flowered
MACpandem

Although 'Pandemonium' is classed officially as a Cluster-flowered Rose, it is really better thought of as a Shrub. It might even be classed as a Hybrid Musk, as along with the tall, arching growth it has the musk scent, if not powerfully. None of the Hybrid Musks of the Reverend Pemberton, however, has the extraordinary color of this 1987 Sam McGredy creation. Its flowers are dazzlingly striped in orange and yellow and the bronze-tinted foliage sets them off perfectly.

Parentage undisclosed
Repeat flowering
Fragrant

◄ 'Paddy Stevens'

▲ 'Pandemonium'
▼ 'Pania'

scent, but as I saw it in New Zealand a couple of years ago, all the makings of a fine, colorful garden rose, its twenty or so petals holding their ruffled shape until they drop. Tantau has not told us the parentage, but at a guess 'Fragrant Cloud' must appear somewhere in this rose's family tree.

Parentage undisclosed
Repeat flowering

'Papa Meilland' Large-flowered
MEIsar

Great publicity attended the introduction of 'Papa Meilland' in 1963. We were promised nothing less than the finest red rose ever. At its best, 'Papa Meilland' is indeed glorious, its blooms dark and velvety, with a wonderful fragrance. In cool climates, however, like Britain's, the bush is a mildew-smothered runt, and in very hot places the flowers can scorch. Foliage is leathery, leaden green and matt. It still has enough ardent admirers for the 1988 World Rose Convention to declare it 'the world's favorite rose'. It was raised by Alain Meilland and named in tribute to his grandfather.

'Chrysler Imperial' × 'Charles Mallerin'
Repeat flowering
Fragrant

'Papageno' Large-flowered
MACgoofy

'Papageno' is one of the most attractive of the modern striped roses, the irregularity of the off-white stripes only serving to point up the perfect sculp-

▲ 'Papageno'

▲ 'Paola'
▼ 'Papa Meilland'

'Pania' Large-flowered

Named in honor of a heroine of Maori legend, 'Pania', bred in Ireland and released in 1968, marks the beginning of Sam McGredy's love affair with New Zealand, where he has now lived since 1972. Slightly fragrant, the blooms blend delicate salmon-pink and cream with deeper shadings towards the petal edges, and the bush is healthy and full of bloom. Foliage is a leathery green.

'Paddy McGredy' × ('Perfecta' × 'Montezuma')
Repeat flowering

'Paola' Large-flowered
TANaloap

With this 1982 introduction, Mathias Tantau shows yet again how well plum-tinted foliage shows off a deep but bright red rose. 'Paola' has little

tured shape and warm crimson of its flowers. Bred from a Large-flowered Rose and a Miniature and classed as a Large-flowered Rose, it grows more like a Hybrid Perpetual or Bourbon, with long, limber branches that can be pegged down in the Victorian manner. Papageno was the eccentric birdcatcher in *The Magic Flute*, Mozart's fairytale for adults. The rose, from Sam McGredy, was introduced in 1989.

Parentage undisclosed
Repeat flowering
Fragrant

'Paprika'
TANprik

Cluster-flowered

The color of 'Paprika' *is* rather like that of the hot spice from which it takes its name—a bright scarlet red. Often there is a curious purple suffusion at the centre of the flowers, which makes the effect in the garden all the hotter. There is no scent, and the flowers, while fairly large, 8–9 centimetres (3–3½ inches) or so, are unfashionably semi-double. The plant is bushy, the foliage is olive-green, glossy and leathery, and the flowers very resistant to bad weather. It was introduced in 1958 by Mathias Tantau, and awarded the RNRS gold medal in 1959 and the Golden Rose of The Hague in 1961. It deserves to be seen around for a good while yet.

'Märchenland' × 'Schweizergrüss'
Repeat flowering

▲ 'Paprika'

'Parade'

Large-flowered Climber

Raised by Gene Boerner for Jackson & Perkins in 1953, 'Parade' makes a cheerful display with its biggish, informal blooms of deep strong pink. They are

► 'Parkdirektor Riggers'
▼ 'Parade'

pleasingly fragrant and come on long stems for cutting, which is unusual in a Climber. It repeats its bloom very well, though not very continuously. There is apt to be a flowerless period between flushes, but that is the case with many Climbers. They rarely bloom as continuously as the best Bush Roses do. Foliage is glossy green. The plant grows quite well in the shade.

'New Dawn' seedling × 'Climbing World's Fair'
Repeat flowering
Fragrant

'Paradise'
WEzip
'Burning Sky'

Large-flowered

'Paradise' is as dramatic in color as a set for a grand opera. Each of its twenty-eight lavender petals is bordered in ruby-red. True, the contrast fades as the flower ages, but when the large and shapely bloom is at its best, there is nothing quite like it. It is a tall and easily grown bush, doing well everywhere. Foliage is a dark grey-green. It was raised by O. L. Weeks and introduced in 1977. It won the AARS award for 1979.

'Swarthmore' × unnamed seedling
Repeat flowering
Fragrant

'Paraglider'

Modern Shrub

Roses in the apricot to orange color range of 'Paraglider' do not usually have outstanding health, so it is nice to see this 1984 Griffith Buck introduction praised for its hardiness and good habits. Certainly the flowers are attractive, large and shapely. It does not appear to be a very large shrub and, with careful pruning, it could fit into a bed of Large-flowered Roses. The leathery foliage is dark green, tinted copper.

('Country Dancer' × 'Carefree Beauty') × 'Alexander'
Repeat flowering

'Parkdirektor Riggers'

Cluster-flowered Climber

The name of the worthy Herr Riggers has not inspired English-speaking gardeners to rush to buy his rose, and you do not often see it outside Germany. But there it is regarded as one of the best of the repeat-flowering Climbers, vigorous enough for a pergola, and con-

▲ 'Paradise'
▼ 'Paraglider'

stantly displaying clusters of brilliant red, clustered flowers. The foliage is healthy, but the rose has only slight fragrance. It was introduced in 1957 by Wilhelm Kordes.

Rosa kordesii × 'Our Princess'
Repeat flowering

'Parure d'Or' Large-flowered
DELmir

A 'parure' is the name for a suite of matching jewelry—necklace, earrings, maybe a tiara—such as the celebrated one set with emeralds that belonged to the Empress Joséphine. 'Parure d'Or', the rose, adorns itself with sprays of lovely golden yellow flowers touched with red and orange, against dark green leaves. It varies in the number of petals, sometimes being almost single and at others quite double. It came from Delbard-Chabert in 1968 and won the Bagatelle gold medal in the same year.

('Queen Elizabeth' × 'Provence') × ('Sultane' seedling × 'Madame Joseph Perraud')
Repeat flowering

'Pascali' Large-flowered
LENip

When it was introduced in 1963, 'Pascali' created something of a mild sensation in the rose world, by winning an award in every competition for new roses in Europe. This is most unusual, especially for a white rose. It then went on to win the 1969 AARS award. It is firmly established as the world's favorite white Large-flowered Rose, a triumph for its Belgian breeder Louis Lens. True, the blooms are not very large, and they have a hint of cream at the centre, but they are of most perfect form, stand up to wet weather, and are borne in profusion on a tall, healthy bush as you would expect from its parentage. Foliage is dark green and leathery.

'Queen Elizabeth' × 'White Butterfly'
Repeat flowering

'Patricia' Cluster-flowered
KORpatri
'Kordes Rose Patricia'

Modern Roses 9, the Bible of those who seek knowledge of the ancestors of roses, states that 'Patricia' is a sport from 'Elizabeth of Glamis'. No doubt that is correct; and so here we have a sport which was content not merely to change the color of the flowers (to a richer salmon-pink, which is paler on the reverse), but their shape (the petals reflex more sharply); the foliage, which is broader and a deeper green; and the habit of the bush, which is taller and more upright. The perfume, although pleasing, is not quite as good. Though Reimer Kordes has marketed this 1972 introduction mainly as a greenhouse

▲ 'Parure d'Or'
► 'Patrician'
▼ 'Pascali'

▼ 'Patricia'

rose, it performs well as a garden rose in warm climates. It was awarded the 1979 gold medal at Orléans.

Sport from 'Elizabeth of Glamis'
Repeat flowering
Fragrant

'Patrician' Large-flowered

There are a few parents that turn up again and again, among them 'Fragrant Cloud' and 'Chrysler Imperial'. Here we have, from Bill Warriner in 1977, the two getting together once again. The parentage of 'Patrician' is given as 'Fragrant Cloud' × 'Proud Land', and 'Proud Land' is a seedling of 'Chrysler Imperial'. The result is a tall, upright bush with large, very fragrant blooms. The official description is 'cardinal-red' and for once it is exactly right. Foliage is dark red and large.

'Fragrant Cloud' × 'Proud Land'
Repeat flowering
Fragrant

'Paul Crampel' Polyantha

'Paul Crampel' can justifiably be called 'geranium-red'. Its small flowers in their big bunches are exactly the color of the scarlet geraniums, also called 'Paul Crampel', that feature every summer in front of Buckingham Palace. They are both named after the nurseryman who introduced the geranium, which came first. The rose was introduced in 1930. It is a sport of 'Superb', itself one of the many sports of 'Orléans Rose'. 'Gloria

▼ 'Paul Crampel'

Mundi' is similar, perhaps with a touch more orange. 'Paul Crampel' has small dull green leaves.

Sport from 'Superb'
Repeat flowering

'Paul Neyron'   Hybrid Perpetual

Until 'Peace' came along, 'Paul Neyron' held, unchallenged, the heavyweight title—the 'Largest Rose in the World'. When aided by good soil and lavish manuring, it can still be a knockout, the fat buds opening flat, filled with petals, and 20 centimetres (8 inches) or more across. Their rich pink color is so distinctive that the color 'neyron rose' has become part of the gardener's vocabulary. The bush is tall and flowers both freely and repeatedly against rich green foliage. It was raised by A. Levet in 1869. If you remember gigantic roses like pink cabbages in your grandmother's garden, they were almost certainly this one.

'Victor Verdier' × 'Anna de Diesbach'
Repeat flowering
Fragrant

'Paul Ricault'   Centifolia

Although this rose, introduced by a Frenchman named Portemer in 1845, is usually classed as a Centifolia, its smooth green leaves and relatively few thorns betray its China Rose ancestry, and it is perhaps best classed as a once-flowering Bourbon. There are, however, no grounds for doubt over the flowers, which are superb—big, full of most symmetrically arranged petals, and sweetly fragrant. In its summer season, the arching bush is fairly loaded with rose-pink blooms.

Parentage unknown
Summer flowering
Fragrant

'Paul Transon'   Rambler

Soft coral-pink, flat, full of petals, and delightfully fragrant, the flowers of 'Paul Transon' cluster very effectively against dark, shiny green foliage which is copper-tinted when young. They are produced in great abundance during summer, and if you feed and water it generously after the flowers fade, there will be quite a good display to follow. Like most of the seedlings of *Rosa luciae* raised by Barbier et Cie, it needs little pruning apart from the occasional removal of the oldest branches. The date of introduction was 1901.

R. luciae × 'L'Idéal'
Repeat flowering
Fragrant

◀ 'Paul Neyron'
▼ 'Paul Transon'

▶ 'Paul's Lemon Pillar'
▼ 'Paul Ricault'

'Paulii'   Ground Cover
Rosa rugosa repens alba

Though this rose is usually credited to the English hybridist William Paul, of 'Paul's Scarlet' fame, there is doubt about its origin. It appears to be a cross

▲ 'Paulii'

between *R. rugosa* and *R. arvensis*. Its admirers think it one of the best Ground Cover Roses, pointing to its vigor and splendid show of scented white roses in summer. One famous rosarian, on the other hand, has described it as being like a thicket of blackberries, only less pretty and without delicious fruit! (Certainly it is viciously thorny.) Foliage is light green and wrinkled. There is a pink version, 'Paulii Rosea', which everyone admires. It is less overwhelmingly vigorous than the original.

R. arvensis × *R. rugosa*
Summer flowering
Fragrant

'Paul's Lemon Pillar'   Large-flowered Climber

'Paul's Lemon Pillar' is a desirable Climbing Rose, making a great summer display of huge, shapely creamy white flowers, suffused with lemon, and

deliciously scented. It follows up with pleasing hips in autumn, or fall. It is usually rather more than pillar-sized. Foliage is large and dark green. William Paul introduced it in 1916.

'Frau Karl Druschki' × 'Maréchal Niel'
Summer flowering
Fragrant

'Paul's Scarlet Climber'
Cluster-flowered Climber

Despite the competition from many of the more recent, repeat-flowering red Climbers, 'Paul's Scarlet' remains one of the most popular. True, it does not produce many blooms after its great summer display, but it is of manageable size and is one of the easiest roses to grow. 'Scarlet' exaggerates its beautiful color, better described as blood-red, without any hint of purple. Unfortunately, it is only very mildly scented. Foliage is mid-green and squarish. It was raised by William Paul and introduced in 1916. It is a wonderful rose for cottage-garden plantings, its color going with just about anything.

'Paul's Carmine Pillar' × 'Rêve d'Or'
Summer flowering

'Peace'
Large-flowered

'Madame A. Meilland', 'Gioia', 'Gloria Dei'

Legend has it that the exiled Duke of Windsor, visiting Francis Meilland's nursery near Lyon, was the first to be shown a yet unnamed new rose, its huge flowers blending yellow and pale pink, its dark green foliage large and shining, its vigor prodigious. 'It is,' he said, 'undoubtedly the most beautiful rose in the world.' That was in 1939, and with the confusion of World War II, the new rose appeared under several names—'Madame A. Meilland' in France, in honor of Francis Meilland's late mother, 'Gioia' in Italy, 'Gloria Dei' in Germany, and everywhere else, as 'Peace'. The world echoed the Duke: 'Peace' won every award there was, and remains the world's favorite rose. It needs protection against black spot in humid climates.

(['George Dickson' × 'Souvenir de Claudius Pernet'] × ['Joanna Hill' × 'Chas P. Kilham']) × 'Margaret McGredy'
Repeat flowering

'Peace, Climbing'   Large-flowered Climber
'Climbing Madame A. Meilland'

'Peace' can be quite magnificent in its climbing version. Enormously vigorous, this sport bears the same beautiful glossy foliage, and the flowers, though perhaps a trifle less enormous than on the bush, are every bit as lovely. It must have a warm climate to flower well. In Britain it is a failure, giving leaves and rarely a flower. Place it carefully, for the branches are heavy and stiff, and do not expect too much in the way of autumn, or fall, blooms, although there will be some.

Sport from 'Peace'
Repeat flowering

▲ 'Peach Melba'
◄ 'Climbing Peace'

'Peach Melba'   Cluster-flowered
KORita
'Gitte'

To judge by its recorded ancestors, raiser Reimer Kordes probably intended 'Peach Melba' to be a greenhouse rose, but it is well regarded in America as a rose for the garden. Despite its brilliantly toned ancestry, it is a delicate blend of apricot and pale pink, the blooms large and fragrant, against dark olive-green foliage. The plant is bushy and upright. It was introduced in 1978.

('Fragrant Cloud' × 'Peer Gynt') × (['Dr A. J. Verhage' × 'Königin der Rosen'] × 'Zorina')
Repeat flowering
Fragrant

'Peachblow'   Large-flowered

'Peachblow' is the subtle, pinkish glaze that you can see on priceless Chinese porcelain, and the name suggests the delicacy and charm of this old-timer, raised by L. B. Coddrington of New Jersey in 1942. The blooms are nicely shaped, in shades of softest salmon and peach with yellow lights, and scent is delicate and sweet. Foliage is glossy and dark green.

'Madame Butterfly' × unnamed seedling
Repeat flowering
Fragrant

'Pearl'   Rambler

Some years ago, *Rosa multiflora* enjoyed quite a vogue in the United States as a 'living crash barrier' along highways, where it made a thicket dense enough to catch a car that ran off the road, and as a 'living fence' or clipped hedge in gardens. For all its importance as an understock and as an ancestor of the modern Cluster-flowered Roses, it is hardly one of the more gorgeous rose species. If you fancy trying it, you would be best to choose a form selected for its appearance. 'Pearl' is as good as any. Its blooms and hips are larger than usual, and quite attractive in their season. Foliage is light green.

Selected form of *R. multiflora*
Summer flowering
Fragrant

▲ 'Peachblow'
▼ 'Pearl'

▲ 'Pearl Drift'

'Peggy Lee' — Large-flowered

This is a splendid sport from 'Century Two'. It occurred in the garden of John R. Feizel, in Evansville, Illinois, and was distributed by Armstrong Nurseries in 1983. It resembles its parent in good habit, and its shapely, scented blooms. They are in one of Miss Lee's favorite colors: soft pale pink. Foliage is glossy and olive-green.

Sport from 'Century Two'
Repeat flowering
Fragrant

'Pearl Drift' — Ground Cover
LEGgab

From its parents, one might expect 'Pearl Drift' to be a rampageous Climber, but it is in fact a metre (3 foot) tall, spreading shrub, much favored by those who grow roses for ground cover. If it has not inherited its parents' vigor, it has got their health and beauty. The semi-double blooms in palest pearly pink are really charming, and fragrant too. Foliage is dark green and flossy, with red tints. It was introduced in 1980, having been raised by E. B. LeGrice, who aroused the envy of fellow hybridists by succeeding in breeding from the practically sterile 'Mermaid'.

'Mermaid' × 'New Dawn'
Repeat flowering
Fragrant

'Peer Gynt' — Large-flowered
KORol

Reimer Kordes must have had Grieg's popular music in mind rather than Ibsen's weirdly gloomy play when he named this deep yellow rose in 1968. It is popular in Europe, but in a warm and humid climate it does not do very well. The blooms are large, very full of petals, and open flat. Warm weather brings a touch of coral-pink to the petal edges. The foliage is olive-green and leathery. It has itself been much used for breeding. It won the Belfast gold medal in 1970. Fragrance is delicate.

'Königin der Rosen' × 'Golden Giant'
Repeat flowering

▲ 'Peggy Lee'
▼ 'Peer Gynt'

'Perfume Delight' — Large-flowered

The perfume of 'Perfume Delight' is very variable; sometimes it is rich and sweet, sometimes, in hot weather, only faint. It is a big, nicely shaped flower, in vivid deep pink with overtones of purple against dark green, glossy foliage. It is a delight for flower arrangers as the stems are long. Raised by O. L. Weeks for Jackson & Perkins, it won the AARS award for 1974.

'Peace' × (['Happiness' × 'Chrysler Imperial'] × 'El Capitan')
Repeat flowering
Fragrant

▲ 'Perfect Moment'
▼ 'Perfume Delight'

'Penelope' — Hybrid Musk

Like most of the Hybrid Musks from the Reverend Mr Pemberton, 'Penelope' can be either disciplined into a Cluster-flowered Rose sized bush or (more attractively) trimmed only lightly. Its branches are well clad with dark green foliage, and the flowers are borne in huge abundance in early summer, after which 'Penelope' is often inclined to take a nap before the autumn, or fall, flowers appear. The blooms are then succeeded by beautiful salmon-pink hips. There are many who regard this 1924 seedling of 'Ophelia' as one of the most satisfying of all Shrub Roses.

'Ophelia' × 'Trier'
Repeat flowering
Fragrant

▲ 'Penelope'
▼ 'Perdita'

'Perdita' — English Rose

This 1983 David Austin creation looks more like a bushy Cluster-flowered Rose than an English Rose. In any case it is a very pretty rose, with small clusters of cupped flowers in pale peach-pink, and it is pleasingly fragrant. Growing to only about a metre (3 feet), it would be a good choice in a mixed bed with perennials. Foliage is dark green. It is named for the heroine of Shakespeare's *The Winter's Tale*.

'The Friar' × (unnamed seedling × 'Iceberg')
Repeat flowering
Fragrant

'Perfect Moment' — Large-flowered

KORwilma
'Jack Dayson'

This 1990 introduction from Reimer Kordes certainly stands out in the crowd. Each petal is half golden yellow and half tangerine-red, and the blooms are large and of perfect form, against dark green leathery foliage. Roses of such startling color are not always of strong constitution, so it is good to hear that the AARS judges gave 'Perfect Moment' high marks for disease resistance and winter hardiness when they gave it their award for 1989. Scent is quite good.

'New Day' × unnamed seedling
Repeat flowering
Fragrant

▲ 'Persian Yellow'

◄ 'Pergolèse'
▲ 'Pernille Poulsen'

'Pergolèse' — Portland

I have not grown this rose myself, so cannot speak from intimacy (though I do enjoy Signor Pergolesi's music), but whenever I have met with it in collections of Old Garden Roses it seemed to me an especially attractive pink, usually heavily flushed with lilac and paling as the flowers age. I cannot understand why so many books insist that it is crimson, unless the writers have been fixated on the deeper color of the half open buds. However you describe it, 'Pergolèse' is a first-rate Old Garden Rose, compact in habit, and as free with its shapely, perfumed blooms in autumn, or fall, as in spring. Foliage is mid-green and smooth. It was introduced by Morcau in 1860.

Parentage unknown
Repeat flowering
Fragrant

'Perle d'Or' — Cluster-flowered

'Perle d'Or' is sometimes called the yellow 'Cécile Brünner', but is actually rather a soft peaches-and-cream color. It does resemble 'Cécile Brünner' in its sprays of small, exquisitely perfect buds, carried throughout the season. It is quite as distinctive and lovely, and just as easy to grow. It is beautifully perfumed, even more so than 'Cécile Brünner'. Foliage is rich green. It came to us from Francis Dubreuil in 1883. Perhaps if modern breeders would like to try similar crosses, we might have more of these delightful beauties.

Unnamed polyantha × 'Madame Falcot'
Repeat flowering
Fragrant

'Pernille Poulsen' — Cluster-flowered

The coral-pink flowers tend to open quickly and turn pale with age, but they have a little fragrance, and are among the first of the Modern Garden Roses to bloom in the spring, a foretaste of pleasures to follow. The bush is of average height, with mid-green foliage. Raised by Niels Poulsen and introduced in 1965, 'Pernille Poulsen' bears the name of his eldest daughter, now a notable hybridist herself.

'Ma Perkins' × 'Columbine'
Repeat flowering
Fragrant

'Persian Yellow' — Shrub
Rosa foetida persiana

The story goes that the 'Persian Yellow' was brought to England by the diplomat Sir Henry Willcocks in 1837 and presented to the Royal Horticultural Society in London. It created a great sensation, plants being sold for as many guineas as ordinary roses fetched shillings. It remains the deepest yellow of all double roses and, though spring flowering only, is well worth growing in dry climates where its notorious fondness for black spot can be thwarted. Not pure-bred *R. foetida*, it is thought to be the offspring of a marriage with a Damask Rose. Expect it to grow about 1.5 metres (5 feet) tall.

Parentage unknown
Spring flowering
Fragrant

▲ 'Petaluma Powderpuff'
◄ 'Perle d'Or'

'Petaluma Powderpuff' — Tea

This is yet another Old Garden Rose that has survived in anonymity in California's sunny climate to be preserved and studied at the Huntington Gardens. It is certainly a pretty flower in pastel shades of pink and peach, has a pleasing tea fragrance, and is a reliable performer in the garden. Foliage is dark green. Let us hope its true name is soon found so it can resume its place in modern gardens.

Parentage unknown
Repeat flowering
Fragrant

'Peter Frankenfeld' — Large-flowered

Reimer Kordes is apparently a follower of show business, and fond of dedicating roses, such as 'Peter Frankenfeld', to entertainers he admires. Named in tribute to the German comedian, to be sure, it does them both proud. The blooms are large, of perfect exhibition form, and of deep rose-pink, against olive-green semi-glossy foliage. It is only mildly fragrant, but it is one of the most reliable and free blooming of exhibition-style roses. It has been a real winner since 1966 and it does especially well in rather difficult humid climates.

Parentage undisclosed
Repeat flowering

▲ 'Peter Frankenfeld'
▼ 'Petite de Hollande'

'Petite de Hollande' — Centifolia

Rosa centifolia minor, 'Petite Junon de Hollande', 'Pomon des Dames'

While it is scarcely a Miniature, the 'Little Dutch Rose' is indeed a smaller edition of the 'Rose des Peintres', R. *centifolia*. The flowers are of the same exquisite form and clear pink; the coarsely toothed foliage a similar soft green; the bush shorter and bushier, and very free with its flowers. The only thing about it that is not reduced is the perfume. Graham Thomas, the English lover of Old Garden Roses, describes it as one of the very best Centifolias to grow where space is limited. It dates from 1838.

Parentage unknown
Summer flowering
Fragrant

▲ 'Petite Lisette'

'Petite Lisette' — Damask

A Vibert introduction of 1817, 'Petite Lisette' is almost a Miniature Rose. The bush is only a metre (3 feet) tall and the leaves and the flowers, 2.5 centimetre (1 inch) pompoms, are about half the normal size. The whole plant is of diminutive charm, the flowers cool pink and beautifully fragrant, with mid-green, matt foliage. It is a fine rose for the front of a border of Old Garden Roses or for a mixed planting.

Parentage unknown
Summer flowering
Fragrant

'Pfälzer Gold' — Large-flowered

TANalzergo

The official description of this 1981 introduction from Mathias Tantau has it as 'deep yellow', but whenever I have seen it the shapely blooms have been lemon-yellow, with the outer petals paler from the sunshine. It is a most attractive and unusual effect. The bush is tall, upright and glossy leafed, and the flowers are long lasting in the vase. They are quite scentless, however.

Parentage undisclosed
Repeat flowering

▲ 'Phoenix'
▼ 'Pfälzer Gold'

'Phoenix' — Large-flowered

'Phoenix' has double, high-centred blooms, light cerise in color, and heavily fragrant. The bush is vigorous and the foliage is olive-green and glossy. Raised by Herbert Swim and introduced by Armstrong Nurseries in 1973, it is named for the capital city of Arizona, its sponsor.

'Manitou' × 'Grand Slam'
Repeat flowering
Fragrant

THE ROSE IN MUSIC

Music by its nature is an art that depicts emotions rather than things, but that has never stopped musicians over the years celebrating the silent beauty of the rose, both in their songs and in the accoutrements of their profession. Flowers garlanded the heads of Greek singers; even now, a singer is presented with flowers after the performance; and it is said that Dame Joan Sutherland, that diva of divas, never sang without a red rose in her dressing room for inspiration.

The fashion nowadays is for musical instruments to be severely plain, but in centuries past decoration was lavished on them. Violas de gamba were painted with roses, as were lutes and zithers, and the circular hole in their soundboards was usually filled with delicate filigree in fine wood or ivory and known as the 'rose'. You see it still in the guitar, though nowadays it is usually left empty; harpsichord makers still fit theirs with a gilded angel guarding the maker's initials and surround it with garlands of painted flowers, pre-eminently roses.

In the tragic movie *The Rose*, the overworked and insecure pop singer of the title (played by another red-headed diva, Bette Midler) took the flower as her emblem, painted it on her private jet and displayed it in neon lights at her concerts; and one of the current favorites among rock bands is the group Guns and Roses, whose name symbolises the mixture of aggressiveness and tenderness that characterises their music.

They take their place in a long line of musical characters identified with the flower, from the lady addressed by Josquin des Pres in the fifteenth century as 'O Rosa Bella' to the 'Yellow Rose of Texas', 'the sweetest darkie Texas ever knew'. The identity of her rose has set rose-lovers guessing; 'Harison's Yellow' is the favorite candidate.

There is no doubt, however, of the identity of Thomas Moore's 'The Last Rose of Summer', that poignant song of the transience of beauty and love: it was inspired by a bush of 'Old Blush' flowering in November in a garden near Dublin. And it is a safe guess that the florist in the 1960s hit answered the request for 'Some Red Roses for a Blue Lady' with 'Happiness' ('Rouge Meilland'), the leading red florist's rose of the day. What might Johann Strauss's 'Roses of the South' have been? Flower-shop roses imported from Italy? Or, more romantically, 'Kazanlik', brought from the attar fields of Bulgaria, at that time part of the Austrian Empire? Sophisticated flowers at any rate. The blooms that Brahms (in his 'Sapphic Ode') remembers gathering with his beloved from the hedgerow would have been simple wildflowers, redolent of the sweetness of remembered love, and all the more poignant for Brahms, who was a life-long bachelor.

Bizet does not say what the flower was that Carmen gave Don José to inflame his passion, but most producers of the opera *Carmen* have cast a red rose, the flower of love and desire, in the role. It has become an essential part of the way most people visualise the faithless gypsy—all chalk white skin, red lips and green eyes, her raven black hair framed in a black lace mantilla, the red rose held between her teeth as she dances.

◄ *The custom of presenting roses to one's beloved (or at least to a lady one fancies) has been celebrated endlessly by Tin Pan Alley in songs from 'Only a Rose' to 'Red Roses for a Blue Lady'.*

► *'The Presentation of the Rose', from Der Rosenkavalier, as realized by the Australian Opera, starring Suzanne Johnston as Oktavian and Joanna Cole as Sophie.*

► Gustav Mahler was a composer who found answers in the beauty of the rose.

The rose that the young Oktavian carries in the title role of *Der Rosenkavalier*, the 'Knight of the Rose', is an artificial one, made of silver—and he presents it to his beloved Sophie on behalf of someone else. It is not true that such roses were the usual token of betrothal in Vienna at that time; Richard Strauss and his librettist Hugo Von Hoffmenstal invented the custom for the sake of their bitter-sweet opera, first performed in 1911. In the end, true love triumphs over the artifices of society: the promise of the silver rose is real for Oktavian and Sophie.

I have no doubt that the roses of which Susanna sings in the last act of Mozart's *Marriage of Figaro* were real, for the scene takes place in a garden— 'Come, my darling, don't delay and I will crown your brow with roses'—and the melody is of such tenderness and perfect beauty that opera-lovers have always referred to 'Deh veni, non tardar' as the 'Rose Aria'.

At the end of Purcell's *Dido and Aeneas*, Dido, abandoned by the glory-seeking Aeneas, dies of unrequited love, and cupids appear from Elysium to scatter the rose of love over her. 'Soft and tender as her heart', goes the chorus in a melody that breaks down into sobs and silence.

Love and death were themes that haunted Gustav Mahler all his life, and he gives voice to them in his Second Symphony, written from 1888 to 1895. It opens with a mighty funeral dirge, asking, 'Why have you lived and suffered? Is it all a huge, frightful joke?' It is not until the fourth movement that the contralto enters, to invoke the rose—'O little red rose'—and to be answered with the sublime music of the Resurrection—'I shall die, but only to live, to rise again.' And where else could he find his answer but in the rose, its thorns the pain of mankind, its flowers glowing with the light of heaven?

◄ *'Crown me and in your sacred grove I'll sing': Greek singers used to be crowned with garlands of roses such as this one depicted by Redouté. It is the frontispiece to his great book* Les Roses.

▲ *The eighteenth-century tradition of painting the soundboards of harpsichords with flowers has been beautifully revived in this instrument by the Sydney maker Carey Beebe. The gilded angel who occupies the sound hole (itself known as the 'rose') is garlanded in flowers painted by Diana Ford.*

producing them in large numbers. Foliage is dark green and glossy. Alas, its vigor seems to be declining, and it is not often seen now.

Parentage undisclosed
Repeat flowering
Fragrant

▲ 'Picture'
▼ 'Pierre de Ronsard'

'Picasso' · Cluster-flowered
MACpic

It seems that Sam McGredy initially started raising seedlings from the Shrub Rose 'Frühlingsmorgen' for the sake of its hardiness and disease resistance. But he soon discovered that it was able to transmit to modern roses the marbled and variegated colors of its ancestor, *Rosa pimpinellifolia*. The result was what he has called his 'Hand-painted Roses'. 'Picasso', which came out in 1971, was the first of them. Though its foliage is dull and the flowers small and scentless, the mixture of pink, red and white on each petal can be very striking.

'Marlena' × ('Evelyn Fison' × ['Frühlingsmorgen' × 'Orange Sweetheart'])
Repeat flowering

'Piccadilly' · Large-flowered

Raised by Sam McGredy and introduced in 1960, 'Piccadilly' soon gained the reputation of being the most reliable of the red and yellow bicolors—much to the embarrassment of the London judges who, noting that it was too lightly built for exhibition, did not give it a gold medal. It did win in Rome and Madrid, however. There is a big planting of these scarlet and gold roses not far from Piccadilly Circus in London, in front of Wren's Church of St James. Foliage is dark green and glossy, with red tints in its youth.

'McGredy's Yellow' × 'Karl Herbst'
Repeat flowering

'Picotee' · Cluster-flowered

In horticulture, a picotee is a carnation with a white or cream flower more or less heavily edged with red or pink.

▲ 'Picasso'
◀ 'Piccadilly'
▼ 'Picotee'

Although 'Picotee', the rose, hardly has enough petals to pass for a carnation, it does have the characteristic color pattern, in white and pink. Foliage is dark green and glossy. Raised by Frank Raffel of Stockton, California, it has not been widely distributed. It looked most attractive in Pasadena's Huntington Gardens where it was photographed. The Huntington people say it performs well. It was introduced in 1960.

'Little Darling' × 'Gertrude Raffel'
Repeat flowering

'Picture' · Large-flowered

The story goes that Sam McGredy III, father of the present Sam, having sent one of his new seedlings to the RNRS's trial ground, decided not to introduce it after all. He threw out his plants, and then had to ask for his own rose back when the judges gave it top prize! Introduced in 1932 as 'Picture', it was for a long time one of the most widely loved pink roses, for its soft color warmed with salmon, its perfect shape, and its delicate scent. The flowers are not large, but it made up for that by

'Pierre de Ronsard' · Large-flowered Climber
MEIviolin
'Eden Rose 88'

Best known for his romantic sonnets, France's 'prince of poets' was a keen gardener, and it is appropriate that he be commemorated in a rose. 'Pierre de Ronsard' bears large, softly fragrant blooms, full of petals like an old Tea Rose, pale pink, deepening markedly in the centre. The plant is of pillar-rose vigor, and can also be used as a free-standing shrub. Almost thornless, it has good, lush, bright green, glossy foliage and blooms freely and repeatedly. It is a 1987 Meilland introduction.

Parentage undisclosed
Repeat flowering
Fragrant

▲ 'Pimlico '81'
► 'Pink-a-Boo'

'Pimlico '81'   Cluster-flowered
MEIdurajan
'Pimlico'

One would expect a rose called after one of London's riverside suburbs to be English-raised and sold in that country. In fact this is a French rose, from Meilland, and despite winning a gold medal in Belfast in 1983, it now seems to be available only in France. It is quite a good red Cluster-flowered Rose, its flowers wide and bright, its foliage dark green and glossy. It was introduced in 1980 and won the Belfast gold medal in 1983.

('Tamango' × 'Fidelio') × ('Charleston' × 'Lili Marlene')
Repeat flowering

'Piñata'   Cluster-flowered Climber
'Piñata' is in fact Japanese, despite its Spanish (or rather, Californian) name. It was introduced in the United States by Jackson & Perkins, but was raised by Seizo Suzuki in 1978. It is one of the most dazzling of the modern climbers, covering itself several times each season with sprays of blooms in blends of yellow and scarlet, the scarlet taking over as they age. The plant is not too vigorous, and has plenty of olive-green leaves. There is little scent, as is so often the case with brilliantly colored flowers.

Parentage undisclosed
Repeat flowering

'Pink-a-Boo'   Cluster-flowered
Another rose which is disappearing from the catalogues, 'Pink-a-Boo' has full-petalled, and good-sized flowers, which are rose-pink, sometimes shaded with salmon. It is also fragrant. The plant seems sturdy and the foliage is leathery. Perhaps it is just another victim of the old being pushed out for the new and 'improved'. It was raised by Eugene Boerner and introduced in 1960.

'Spartan' × 'Pink Garnette'
Repeat flowering
Fragrant

'Pink Chiffon'   Cluster-flowered
The palest of pinks, the flowers of 'Pink Chiffon' are filled with silky petals, almost in the Old Garden Rose style. They are sweetly fragrant, and carried in good sized clusters on a rather low, spreading bush with dark green foliage. It needs a dry climate, for the delicate blossoms are easily damaged by rain. This is one of the great modern roses; the flowers are irresistible. It was raised by Eugene Boerner and introduced by Jackson & Perkins in 1956.

'Fashion' × 'Fantasia'
Repeat flowering
Fragrant

'Pink Favorite'   Large-flowered
'Pink Favorite' is best grown in cool climates. Where summers are hot, the blooms tend to be on the small side and their already dark pink deepens into hardness, assorting oddly with the dark green, highly polished foliage. The foliage is outstandingly resistant to fungus diseases, so this is a good rose to grow where they are troublesome. In cool

▲ 'Pink Chiffon'
▼ 'Piñata'

autumn, or fall. Foliage is bright green and quilted, with a tendency to look pallid. Like all the Hybrid Rugosas, it is an easy rose to grow. It is scentless. Pronounce the name 'Grote-en-dorst', in the Dutch fashion.

Sport from 'F. J. Grootendorst'
Repeat flowering

▲ 'Pink Grootendorst'
◄ 'Pink Favorite'

'Pink Panther'   Large-flowered
MEIcapinal

The cartoon character indelibly associated with the late Peter Sellers looks rather fetching in two shades of candy-pink, but Meilland's rose is a uniform coral-pink, with the attractive habit of going deeper with age instead of fading. The flowers can be enormous. They start out high centred, opening rather flat. The bush is tallish, with splendidly glossy green foliage, and it flowers with freedom for such a big rose. Sadly, there is no perfume at all. 'Pink Panther' was introduced in 1981.

'Meigurami' × 'Meinaregi'
Repeat flowering

◄ 'Pink Garnette'
▼ 'Pink Panther'

climates the blooms are superlative. It was raised by Gordon Von Abrams and introduced in 1956. There is virtually no scent.

'Juno' × ('George Arends' × 'New Dawn')
Repeat flowering

'Pink Garnette'   Cluster-flowered

This is a pink sport of 'Garnette', introduced by Jackson & Perkins in 1951. Like its parent, it has clusters of small, scentless flowers, notable for lasting forever in the vase no matter how the florist treats them. It is not much of a garden rose, being subject to mildew. There are several pink sports from 'Garnette', which vary in their precise colors. Foliage is dark green and dull.

Sport from 'Garnette'
Repeat flowering

'Pink Grootendorst'   Hybrid Rugosa

A sport from 'F. J. Grootendorst', introduced in 1923, 'Pink Grootendorst' is the most popular of the fringe-petalled Grootendorst roses. The flowers are a pretty shade of candy-pink, with just a hint of salmon, and the sturdy, chest-high bush is rarely without a cluster or two from spring until late in the

'Pink Parfait' — Cluster-flowered

Perfectly formed, these 8 centimetre (3 inch) blooms are a confection of soft pinks, growing paler towards the centre, where they are often touched with apricot and cream. They have a soft fruity fragrance, and come very freely in small and biggish clusters on a medium-sized, even-growing bush with mid-green leaves and elegantly thin, almost thornless, stems. No rose is perfect and 'Pink Parfait' has the fault of its color bleaching in hot weather. Cut it young, or plant it where there will be a little afternoon shade. It is still one of the loveliest pink roses ever raised. One of Herbert Swim's greatest triumphs, it was introduced in 1961, to be honored with both the AARS award and the gold medal of the RNRS.

'First Love' × 'Pinocchio'
Repeat flowering
Fragrant

'Pink Peace' — Large-flowered
MEIbil

Why Francis Meilland, or his United States agent, Robert Pyle, should have given this 1959 introduction such a name escapes most people, for it resembles its grandparent 'Peace' not in the least. It is, however, a very good rose, the tall, matt-foliaged bushes easy to grow and flowering with great freedom. The blooms can be huge, if a little loosely formed, and they are intensely fragrant. 'Dusty pink' the catalogues say, and there is indeed something muted in their deep color, each petal showing a very narrow edge of paler pink. A rose for warm climates, 'Pink Peace' remains very popular in the United States.

('Peace' × 'Monique') × ('Peace' × 'Mrs John Laing')
Repeat flowering
Fragrant

'Pink Perpétue' — Cluster-flowered Climber

Introduced in 1965, 'Pink Perpétue' was one of the first of the modern repeat-flowering, not too vigorous Climbers to become widely popular. It is strange how long it took gardeners generally to latch onto them. It remains a good one, reliable in its repeat flowering and lavish with its clusters of bloom, nicely fragrant, in a pleasing shade of bright rose-pink, against light green, glossy foliage. It was raised by the English nurseryman Walter Gregory. The rather odd English-French name is meant to recall 'Félicité et Perpétue'.

'Danse du Feu' × 'New Dawn'
Repeat flowering
Fragrant

'Pink Pillar' — Modern Shrub

The name does not do it justice. The loosely informal blooms with their scalloped petals blend every shade of pink, coral and apricot, and they have a pleasing fragrance too. But it is apt in warning that the growth is really too lax to make a satisfactory shrub; train 'Pink Pillar' as a pillar or a moderate climber. Like most of the roses from Mr and Mrs Brownell of Long Island, this 1940 introduction has the reputation of being extremely resistant to cold winters.

Parentage unknown
Repeat flowering
Fragrant

▲ 'Pink Peace'
▼ 'Pink Perpétue'

▲ 'Pink Parfait'
▼ 'Pink Pillar'

'Pink Rosette' — Cluster-flowered

Raised by a gentleman called Krebs and introduced in 1948 by the California firm of Howard & Smith, 'Pink Rosette' must be due for a revival. Its very low, 'Patio Rose' growth is in fashion, and so should be the prim, almost artificial arrangement of its petals, like a candy-pink milliner's rose designed for a party hat. The foliage is leathery and dark green, the flowers slightly fragrant.

Parentage unknown
Repeat flowering

'Pinkie, Climbing'   Cluster-flowered Climber

The original 'Pinkie', which won the 1948 AARS award, is still a desirable 'Patio Rose' (as some would call it), with very dwarf growth and clusters of small candy-pink flowers. The little-known climbing sport is quite wonderful. It is of manageable vigor, and covers itself with sweetly fragrant flowers all season against bright green, glossy foliage. Few Climbing Roses of any kind bloom so constantly. The original came from Herbert Swim in 1947, a seedling of 'China Doll'. *Pinkie*, starring Jeanne Crain, was a hit movie of the day.

Sport from 'Pinkie'
Repeat flowering
Fragrant

▲ 'Climbing Pinkie'
▼ 'Pink Rosette'

▲ 'Piroshka'

'Piroshka'   Large-flowered
TANpika

This rose, launched by Mathias Tantau in 1972, does not seem to be very widely grown. Perhaps its name, awkward to an English ear, and the fact that it is an 'ordinary' pink has held it back. However, it is a very good rose, strong growing and shapely, and with perfectly satisfactory fragrance. Foliage is a leathery green.

'Fragrant Cloud' × 'Dr A. J. Verhage'
Repeat flowering
Fragrant

'Playboy'   Cluster-flowered
'Cheerio'

The scarlet and gold, almost single flowers are quite large and come in well-spaced clusters, but there is only a little fragrance. They certainly make a bright display, and the plant is strong, with dark green foliage. Perhaps the name 'Playboy' was sponsored by the magazine, or maybe it is just a tribute to the gaiety of the rose. It seems to

have turned off the British—this 1976 introduction from Cocker of Aberdeen is currently much more popular in America than at home.

'City of Leeds' × ('Chanelle' × 'Piccadilly')
Repeat flowering

'Playgirl'   Cluster-flowered
MORplag

'Playgirl' is a very feminine, though hardly demure, flower in bright pink. Its five petals make up a shapely bloom, carried usually in sprays of five or so. It was raised by Ralph Moore in California in 1986. It has little scent, but is free flowering, upright in growth, and not very thorny. Foliage is mid-green and semi-glossy.

'Playboy' × 'Angel Face'
Repeat flowering

▲ 'Playgirl'
▼ 'Playboy'

'Pleasure' Cluster-flowered
JACpif

'Pleasure' won the 1990 AARS award for Jackson & Perkins. It shows every promise of being one of the very best pink Cluster-flowered Roses, its flowers ruffled and the color warm, shot with coral and salmon. In the United States it is being praised for its strong resistance to mildew and rust, and for its abundant flowering. There is not much in the way of fragrance. Foliage is mid-green.

Unnamed seedling × 'Intrigue'
Repeat flowering

▲ 'Pleasure'
▼ 'Plentiful'

'Plentiful' Cluster-flowered
Bright rose-pink, the flowers are filled with petals and lightly quartered in the Old Garden Rose manner. They come in large clusters on a vigorous upright bush, with bright green glossy foliage. They make a generous display. They are not of Old Garden Rose fragrance,

however. Raised by E. B. LeGrice and introduced in 1961, 'Plentiful' has never been a real best-seller, but is unlikely to disappear, it has many admirers.

Parentage undisclosed
Repeat flowering

'Pluto' Cluster-flowered
'Hurdy Gurdy'

'Pluto', a 1986 introduction from Sam McGredy, seems to have had a short career—no one lists it now. Perhaps the nursery people just did not know what to make of it. By the size of its dark green, shiny leaves and flowers, it should be a Miniature, but it makes an ordinary-sized, rather prickly, bush. The boldly striped blooms in deep garnet-red and white always attract attention in my garden. Perhaps a few enterprising rose-growers should take it up again.

'Matangi' × 'Stars 'n' Stripes'
Repeat flowering

'Polo Club' Cluster-flowered
AROtigny

'Polo Club', which came from Jack Christensen of Armstrong's in 1986, could hardly be mistaken for any other, and it is surprising that it is not more widely grown. The petals are an unusual spoon shape; there are about twenty-five of them, making up a prettily shaped flower. The color is striking: each brilliant yellow petal is edged in red, and the pattern holds without the red taking over as the flower ages. The tall, glossy-leafed bushes give their mid-sized blooms in small clusters all season.

'Gingersnap' × 'Young Quinn'
Repeat flowering

▼ 'Polo Club'

▲ 'Pluto'
▼ 'Polynesian Sunset'

'Polynesian Sunset' Large-flowered
In Polynesia the sunset is usually deep rose, passing to lilac—nothing like this 1965 rose from Eugene Boerner. Perhaps the coral tone of the flowers creates the association with Polynesia. The blooms are not of classic form, but they are decorative and abundantly borne on a good bush, with leathery green foliage. There is good fragrance.

'Diamond Jubilee' × 'Hawaii'
Repeat flowering
Fragrant

'Ponderosa' Cluster-flowered
KORpon

This is one of those roses whose value is in the profuse display of bright color it gives in the garden rather than the beauty of its individual blooms, which, for all their sharp orange-red color, are smallish and scentless, against very dark green foliage, with red tints in its growth. Flowers are borne in abundance, on a conveniently dwarf bush, not unlike that of its parent 'Marlena'. It is not quite so easy to grow as that rose, though. A 1970 introduction from Reimer Kordes, 'Ponderosa' is still popular in Germany, but less so elsewhere these days.

Unnamed seedling × 'Marlena'
Repeat flowering

▲ 'Ponderosa'

'Portrait' Large-flowered
MEYpink
'Stephanie de Monaco'

Every rose-lover dabbling in the art of hybridization dreams of raising a prize-winner. Imagine the thrill it must have been for Carl Meyer to hear that his 'Portrait' was the first amateur-raised rose to win the coveted AARS award in 1962. He deserved it—this is a lovely rose in two tones of pink, shapely, fragrant, and a very good grower. Foliage is dark green and leathery. The recipe for success was deceptively simple: cross two excellent roses.

'Pink Parfait' × 'Pink Peace'
Repeat flowering
Fragrant

'Pot o' Gold' Large-flowered
DICdivine

In Ireland, it is said that if you can catch a leprechaun he has to give you a pot of gold for his freedom. Rose-lovers do not have to wait for the elusive Wee Folk, they can have the joy of this golden rose from Pat Dickson. Its blooms are mid-sized, usually coming in threes, of bright color, good form and fragrance. The bush is spreading and healthy. The leaves are mid-green. Pat Dickson introduced it in 1980.

'Eurorose' × 'Whisky Mac'
Repeat flowering
Fragrant

▲ 'Pot o' Gold'
▼ 'Portrait'

▲ 'Poulsen's Bedder'
▼ 'Pounder Star'

'Poulsen's Bedder' Cluster-flowered
'Poulsen's Grupperose'

This is a lovely rose, with its nicely formed sprays of flowers, ruffled, slightly scented, and tinted a lovely shade of powder-pink. By current standards it would not be called a good bedding rose; though it flowers freely enough, its growth is too tall. Foliage is olive-green. Svend Poulsen introduced his 'Grupperose' in 1948.

'Orléans Rose' × 'Talisman'
Repeat flowering

'Pounder Star' Large-flowered
MACnic
'Karma'

The flowers are medium red and open wide from long, pointed buds. There are only twenty petals, but they hold long enough for this to be a good exhibition rose. The bush is compact, the foliage is dark green and the fragrance is spicy. It was introduced in 1982 by Sam McGredy.

'John Waterer' × 'Kalahari'
Repeat flowering
Fragrant

'Prairie Fire'
Modern Shrub

This is a bright red Shrub Rose of considerable vigor. Raised at the University of Minnesota, 'Prairie Fire' has apparently inherited its wild parent's exceptional resistance to disease and frost. Foliage is olive-green and glossy.

'Red Rocket' × *Rosa arkansana*
Repeat flowering

resisting the mildew that plagues red roses. The color holds without blueing, in all climates. All one could wish for is more perfume. Dickson's introduced it in 1974. Do not confuse it with a much older 'Red Star', the parent of some of the earliest Cluster-flowered Roses.

'Red Planet' × 'Franklin Englemann'
Repeat flowering

▲ 'President Herbert Hoover'
▼ 'President Chaussé'

'President Chaussé'
Large-flowered

'Mark Sullivan'

This rose needs dry summer air to give its softly fragrant flowers, in an indescribably lovely blend of gold all veined and shaded with scarlet. As the blooms age, the color softens and takes on pearly subtlety. The bush is on the short side, the foliage dark green and highly polished. If only Charles Mallerin, who introduced it in 1942, had been able to endow it with a loathing for black spot! In a warm humid climate black spot makes it impossible to grow.

'Luis Brinas' × 'Brasier'
Repeat flowering
Fragrant

▲ 'Prairie Fire'
▼ 'Precious Platinum'

multi-branched plant that their customers expect. This is no sign of weakness, for it makes an exceptionally tall, healthy bush, with sparse dark green, leathery foliage. The flowers are a splendid melange of orange, pink and gold, opening paler, very large, and with a strong, spicy fragrance, One of the classic Large-flowered Roses, it is still popular in Australia, where Mr Hoover spent some time as a young mining engineer.

'Sensation' × 'Souvenir de Claudius Pernet'
Repeat flowering
Fragrant

'President Leopold Senghor'
Large-flowered

MEIluminac

This is a splendid dark and handsome red rose. Its long buds open cupped and fragrant, the plant is bushy and its dark green foliage is glossy. It was raised in 1979 by Marie-Louisette Meilland from a veritable tribe of unnamed seedlings, each the result of self-pollinating an earlier Meilland red rose. The name honors the great African statesman.

'Precious Platinum'
Large-flowered

'Opa Pötschke', 'Red Star'

'Precious Platinum' may seem an odd name for a red rose, but Pat Dickson was loath to miss out on the sponsorship of a firm of refiners of precious metals. It is one of the best of all red roses. The flowers are large, of beautiful form and color, and the bush is well clad in glossy green foliage,

'President Herbert Hoover'
Large-flowered

'President Hoover'

The politicians of his day were not very fond of President Hoover, blaming him, unfairly, as it now appears, for the Great Depression and forcing his resignation from office. Nurserymen are not fond of the rose that L. B. Coddrington named for him in 1930. Their complaint is that it rarely makes the kind of

▲ 'President Leopold Senghor'

([{'Samourai' × 'Samourai'} × {'Crimson Wave' × 'Crimson Wave'}] × ['Pharaoh' × 'Pharaoh']) × ('Pharaoh' × 'Pharaoh')
Repeat flowering
Fragrant

'Pretty Jessica'   English Rose

This is almost a dwarf version of a David Austin English Rose, growing to less than 1 metre (3 feet). It has real Old Garden Rose style flowers: they are globular, with full petals and sweet scent, and in the old-fashioned soft pink that has no hint of salmon. The raiser finds the mid-green foliage a little sparse, which is a fair criticism, if a minor one. 'Pretty Jessica' was introduced in 1983. David Austin named it for Portia's confidante in Shakespeare's *The Merchant of Venice*.

Unnamed seedling × 'The Wife of Bath'
Repeat flowering
Fragrant

'Prima Ballerina'   Large-flowered
'Première Ballerine'

'Prima Ballerina' was a slow starter. When Mathias Tantau introduced it in 1957, it was obvious it was a beautiful flower—large, of most elegant form, intensely fragrant, and of a lively deep pink. Foliage is light green and leathery. It took the rose-buying public some years to realize what a star performer it really was and start queuing up at the box office. Surprisingly, it has never been a best-seller in America, although it is in the style of the roses Herbert Swim was raising there to such acclaim in the 1950s.

Unnamed seedling × 'Peace'
Repeat flowering
Fragrant

▲ 'Prima Donna'
◄ 'Pretty Jessica'

'Prima Donna'   Large-flowered
TOBone

Everyone knows that a prima donna is the leading lady in an opera, and that a prima ballerina does not sing. Compare the pictures of this rose and 'Prima Ballerina' however, and you would think they came out of the same production. 'Prima Donna' has a few more petals, but they are more loosely arranged. It does not have the finishing touch of fragrance, however. Foliage is mid-green and semi-glossy. It was raised in Japan where Takeshi Shirakawa introduced it in 1983. It is primarily a greenhouse rose.

(Unnamed seedling × 'Happiness') × 'Prominent'
Repeat flowering

▲ 'Prima Ballerina'
▼ 'Primevère'

'Primevère'   Rambler
'Primrose'

No doubt in crossing *Rosa wichuraiana* (or *R. luciae*) with the vivid yellow Large-flowered Rose 'Constance', M. Barbier was hoping for a deep yellow Rambler. It was not to be: 'Primevère' is a color best described by its other name, 'Primrose'. The flowers are quite fragrant, nicely formed in the Large-flowered mould, and the foliage is shining green. It is of moderate vigor. Just occasionally there will be a few repeat blooms. This is one of the latest of the Barbier ramblers, introduced in 1929.

R. luciae × 'Constance'
Summer flowering
Fragrant

THE EMPRESS JOSÉPHINE AND HER ROSES

Nowadays a florist is a person who makes a living selling flowers in a shop, but in the eighteenth century this was not so. Then, a florist was an amateur dedicated to growing, to impossible standards of perfection, one of a very small number of 'florist's flowers'. These included the tulip, the carnation, the auricula, and the ranunculus, but not the rose, which was a flower for the gardener and the poet rather than the hobbyist. Its pre-eminence today is due, more than to anyone else, to the Empress Joséphine.

She was born Marie-Josèphe Rose Tacher de la Pagerie in 1753. Legend says that while she was still a child on the West Indian island of Martinique an elderly Negro seeress predicted that both she and a playmate would become queens. This must have seemed a remote prospect for Joséphine when at the age of sixteen she was married off to the Vicomte de Beauharnais. Her friend Aimé de Rivery did indeed, after a string of adventures that read like the plot of some grand opera, become the Sultana of Turkey.

In the meantime, Joséphine's loveless marriage produced two children, Eugène and Hortense. Then, Vicomte de Beauharnais became embroiled in the politics of the French Revolution and ended up on the guillotine in 1794, a fate his Vicomtesse was lucky to escape. Despite the revenues of the Beauharnais estates, Joséphine was reduced, so the malicious gossip of the day had it, to living by her charms.

Though no great beauty, she was one of those women who fascinate every man they meet. Among her admirers was the young Napoleon Bonaparte, still a mere artillery expert, but already destined for greatness. He fell passionately in love with her and, perhaps more for security than for love, she consented to marry him in 1796.

In 1798, they bought the undistinguished Château de la Malmaison near Paris for their country residence. While her husband's military and political career carried him to ever greater glory, culminating in his coronation as Emperor of the French in 1804, Joséphine redecorated La Malmaison from top to bottom in exquisite, and extravagant, taste and transformed its gardens into the envy of Europe.

She was no Louis XIV, interested only in terraces and fountains as a backdrop for imperial pomp, but a genuine and knowledgeable lover of plants. Malmaison became a leading centre of botanical research, and Empress Joséphine financed expeditions to go far beyond her husband's empire to bring back rarities for the collections there.

It is said that she introduced over two hundred new plants to France, among them the dahlia, the Chilean Bell-flower, named in her honor *Lapageria rosea*, and the still rare *Brunsvigia josephinae* from South Africa, as charming (and as temperamental!) as the lady herself. The leading botanists of the day studied and classified them, and on hand to record them all for

▲ *Napoleon presiding over his wife's garden.*

▶ *The empress herself, from a cameo. Contemporaries praised her perfect figure, her musical voice, and her superb mind. Josephine's perfect taste in everything from clothes to furniture to gardens set the style for the whole of Europe, and she was also a connoisseur of works of art.*

▶ *A centaur in bronze in the Malmaison garden. The rose is 'Vendôme', a Modern Garden Rose, but one of which Joséphine would surely have approved.*

▲ *The Château de la Malmaison today. Its curious name, the 'House of Evil', is the subject of several legends: that in Merovingian days it was the seat of a lord so libidinous that the virtue of no maiden in the district was safe; that a later lord was notable for his abominable cruelty; and that late in the Middle Ages it was the site of a hospital for lepers. None of which seems relevant to the elegant eighteenth-century house that Joséphine knew.*

▲ *Redouté's portrait of* Rosa frankofurtana, *the rose now always known as 'Empress Joséphine'. It is a beautiful rose, well worthy of the proud name.*

◄ *'Souvenir de la Malmaison' is not one of Joséphine's, but a creation of 1843. Legend has it that the Grand Duke Michael of Russia, disappointed that there were no roses remaining at Malmaison, named it in her memory.*

science was the greatest flower painter of them all, Pierre Joseph Redouté.

Joséphine's great love, however, was the flower whose name she bore, the rose. She set out to grow every variety in existence. Her gardeners, led by a Scot, Hewartson, created new ones, and eventually the rose garden at Malmaison boasted more than two hundred and fifty varieties. Quite an achievement, when one remembers that only fifty years before even Linnaeus could only muster twenty. They were grown, if Redouté's magnificent portraits are anything to go by, to hitherto unknown perfection. What exciting days they must have been for lovers of the rose, as the ancient roses of China began to arrive and to transform the roses of the West beyond recognition. It was to Malmaison that they came. Despite the bitter war raging between England and France for the domination of Europe, ships carrying Joséphine's roses were allowed through the Royal Navy's stern blockade of the French ports, by order, it is said, of the Prince Regent himself. Truly, the beauty of the rose does transcend earthly politics.

Alas, politics intruded on Joséphine's life. Unable to bear Napoleon a son, she was divorced for reasons of state in 1809. Theirs had been a stormy marriage. There is no doubt, how-ever that he loved and respected her to the last, through the bitter days of the collapse of the empire. She lived out her life in dignified retirement among her beloved flowers, dying at Malmaison in 1814.

Redouté's great book *Les Roses* finally came out in 1817, dedicated not, as history might wish, to Joséphine's memory, but to a lady of the newly restored Bourbon monarchy. Such are the realities of politics and patronage. The world remembers the roses as hers, however. It was she who first revealed to gardeners their infinite variety and established the rose as a universal favorite—a position it has never lost.

Hortense, by then the Queen of the Belgians, inherited Malmaison. After several changes of ownership it passed to the French State. The château itself survives, open to the public and filled with treasures, a monument both to Joséphine and to Napoleon. The estate has been much curtailed, however, and lovely as the gardens still are, their full glory is but a memory.

The rose lives on, of course, and all lovers of beauty owe a debt of gratitude to the girl from Martinique. Many of her favorites are grown still—there is a collection at the Roseraie de l'Haÿ—and those who would can drink deep of their beauty and perhaps muse upon the fate of empires.

'Prince Camille de Rohan'
Hybrid Perpetual

'La Rosière', 'Souvenir d'Auguste Rivoire'

The flowers of this 1861 introduction from Eugène Verdier are not very large: their stalks tend to be weak, and unless it is given the best of soil and cultivation, the plant is inclined to be weak and afflicted with rust. So why then has 'Prince Camille de Rohan' survived? For the sake of its fragrance and its ravishing color: deep, deep red shaded with maroon. In this respect there are few roses to equal it, and rosarians continue to pamper it. When it is happy, it flowers abundantly in both summer and autumn, or fall. Foliage is dull green.

Probably 'Général Jacqueminot' × 'Géant des Batailles'
Repeat flowering
Fragrant

▲ 'Prince Camille de Rohan'
▼ 'Prince Igor'

'Prince Igor'
Cluster-flowered

MEIhigor
'Frenzy'

The flowers are fragrant and of good shape, and excellent in color. They are real orange, with yellow on the reverse, passing to orange-red as they age. The plant is bushy, the foliage light green and matt. You rarely see a bush of 'Prince Igor', rather it is the excellent climbing sport that holds the public. The original was a Meilland introduction of 1970. *Prince Igor*, the opera, was the masterpiece of Alexander Borodin, known in the West mainly for the Polovtsian Dances in Act II.

('Sarabande' × 'Dany Robin') × 'Zambra'
Repeat flowering
Fragrant

'Prince Tango'
Large-flowered

A rose does not have to be all that ancient to survive only in the great public collections. To judge by its appearance, 'Prince Tango' is a fairly new variety, not older than about 1950. It has disappeared completely from the catalogues, has been dropped from all the reference books, and this picture, taken at the Jardins de Bagatelle some years ago, may well be its last mention. Perhaps, indeed, its raiser entered it in the Concours des Roses de Bagatelle and, when it did not win, did not even introduce it. Foliage is light green.

Parentage unknown
Repeat flowering

'Princess Alice'
Cluster-flowered

HARtanna
'Zonta Rose', 'Brite Lites'

The individual flowers are not very large, but they are nicely shaped and arranged in unusually large clusters, carried on long stems for cutting. The plant is tall and upright, the foliage dark green. It is another rose that gives its excellent best in a cooler climate. It was raised in England by Jack Harkness and introduced in 1985. Princess Alice, Duchess of Gloucester, is apparently a very keen gardener.

'Judy Garland' × 'Anne Harkness'
Repeat flowering

▲ 'Princess Alice'
▼ 'Prince Tango'

▲ 'Princess Margaret of England'

'Princess Margaret of England'   Large-flowered
MEllista
'Princess Margaret', 'Princesse Margaret d'Angleterre'

Her Majesty's younger sister is Princess Margaret Rose, and the temptation to name a rose for her was irresistible. Benjamin Cant first did in 1932, when the lady was but a wee child. Our present rose is a Meilland creation of 1968. It resembles 'Queen Elizabeth' in color, though the blooms are larger, of classic Large-flowered shape, and the bush is not so tall. Scent is slight. Foliage is leaden green and leathery. The rose is the daughter of 'Queen Elizabeth'.

'Queen Elizabeth' × ('Peace' × 'Michèle Meilland')
Repeat flowering

'Princess Michael of Kent'   Cluster-flowered
HARlightly

In real life, the glamorous princess is strikingly tall, but the rose is short and compact. Its flowers are large and shapely in brilliant yellow, and often single. The variety could pass for a Large-flowered Rose. Scent is moderate, the foliage dark green, glossy and healthy. At least it is so in Britain and in Oregon. How 'Princess Michael of Kent' fares in hotter and sunnier climates, I have not seen. It was raised by Jack Harkness and introduced in 1981.

'Manx Queen' × 'Alexander'
Repeat flowering

'Princess Michiko'   Cluster-flowered

When Dickson's of Hawlmark introduced this rose in 1966 and named it in honor of the then Crown Princess, now the Empress, of Japan, one of Britain's leading rosarians was moved to express the hope that rust was not a problem in that country, for the sake of diplomacy! Its proneness to rust is this rose's great fault, but all else is good news: the strong growth, the bushy habit, and the extraordinary brilliance of the flowers, still the most dazzling of the orange-red group, and not dulled by the carmine flush in the old blooms. It does, indeed, grow very well in Japan. Foliage is mid-green and glossy.

'Spartan' × 'Circus'
Repeat flowering

'Princess of India'   Large-flowered
'Indian Princess'

You are more likely to find this rose catalogued as 'Indian Princess', but the officially registered 'Princess of India' makes it clear that it is not a Red Indian lady commemorated in its beauty. The flowers are, however, strawberry-red, deeper on the outer petals, and they are highly fragrant. It is indeed a rose of Indian origin, raised by Delhi's Dr B. P. Pal and introduced in 1980. Both its parents can take mildew, so it is pleasing to find that 'Princess of India' has a reputation for being resistant to the disease. Foliage is dark green and smooth.

'Super Star' × 'Granada'
Repeat flowering
Fragrant

▲ 'Princess Michiko'
▼ 'Princesse de Monaco'

'Princesse de Monaco'   Large-flowered
MEImagerimic
'Grace Kelly', 'Preference'

One of the world's favorite roses, it is as beautiful and elegant as the lady herself was. The blooms are large, shapely and fragrant, and the bush is easy to grow and has glossy dark green leaves. The color is exquisitely delicate, from white to ivory, shading to warm pink at the edges. It holds until the petals drop. Francis Meilland raised 'Grace de Monaco' back in 1955. This one is from his widow, Marie-Louisette, in 1981.

'Ambassador' × 'Peace'
Repeat flowering
Fragrant

◄ 'Princess Michael of Kent'
► 'Princess of India'

'Princesse de Sagan' China

This is an old variety that has been lost and rediscovered but has not yet been widely distributed again. It was raised by Francis Dubreuil, the grandfather of Francis Meilland, in 1887 from unrecorded parents. As photographed at the Osaka Flower Show a couple of years ago, it looks to be less dainty than many of the crimson Chinas, and thus possibly not as purebred and aristocratic as its namesake. The crimson color is very fine, and it is a bushy and free-blooming plant, with dark green foliage.

Parentage unknown
Repeat flowering

▲ 'Princesse de Sagan'
► 'Pristine'
▼ 'Priscilla Burton'

'Priscilla Burton' Cluster-flowered
MACrat

Raiser Sam McGredy has described his 'Priscilla Burton' as 'something of a chameleon', and it does vary remarkably in its colors. At its best it is an indescribable blend of light and dark pinks with white, but it can also come straight pale pink or mix a great deal of red into its complexion. The plant, though, is uniformly vigorous and healthy, and the foliage is dark green. Introduced in 1978 'Priscilla Burton' was named for the wife of the chairman of the British garden products firm Fison's.

'Old Master' × unnamed seedling
Repeat flowering

'Pristine' Large-flowered
JACpico

Fragrance is an elusive thing to describe, but at least most of us can tell whether a rose is fragrant or not. 'Pristine' is an anomaly. It won the Edland Medal, the premier British award for fragrance, but many people find it almost scentless. Even Bill Warriner, who raised it, describes the scent as 'light'. Everyone agrees on the beauty of the flowers, with their sculptured petals and ethereal coloring, and on the sturdiness and reliability of the bush. Foliage is dark green and glossy. Jackson & Perkins introduced it in 1978.

'White Masterpiece' × 'First Prize'
Repeat flowering

'Prominent' Cluster-flowered
KORp
'Korp'

The flowers are large and shapely, though the clusters are small, and the bush is tall and floriferous. The color is such that the rose is indeed prominent in the garden—a hot orange-red, in the style of 'Alexander' or 'Super Star'. It holds very well, too, without fading or going purple, and there is some scent. Foliage is olive-green. It was raised by Reimer Kordes and introduced in 1971. It did not find its way to the United States until 1977, when it was introduced and adorned with the AARS award.

'Königin der Rosen' × 'Zorina'
Repeat flowering

▲ 'Prominent'

'Promise' Large-flowered
'Poesie'

In real life, a promise comes before the ceremony at which you vow to 'love, honor and cherish' and so it was in Jackson & Perkins' catalogues. 'Promise' was introduced in 1976, and was later followed by the 'Love', 'Honor' and 'Cherish' trio of AARS winners in 1980. 'Promise' has not proved as popular as they have, but it is quite a good rose, with very large blooms of fine, high-centred form, in a pleasing light pink with a touch of coral to it. The bush is strong, a little on the tall side perhaps. Foliage is dark green and glossy and scent is, well, just a promise.

'South Seas' × 'Peace'
Repeat flowering

'Prosperity' Hybrid Musk

The bush is more upright and compact than most of Pemberton's Hybrid Musks. You do not get the effect of branches bending under the weight of blooms that is so much a part of the charm of, say, 'Penelope'. There are plenty of flowers, pure white rosettes in great bunches, and they are sweetly scented. The foliage is an unusually brilliant green, so the whole picture is smart and fresh-looking all season. 'Prosperity' was introduced in 1919. There is a very similar 'Pink Prosperity', differing mainly in its warm pink color, but less popular than the original.

'Marie-Jeanne' × 'Perle des Jardins'
Repeat flowering
Fragrant

▲ 'Promise'

▲ 'Proud Titania'

'Proud Titania'   English Rose
AUStania

This rose is named for Shakespeare's fairy queen. The blooms are full and quartered in the Old Garden Rose manner, white with just a hint of peach at the centre, and fragrant. They are borne repeatedly on a compact, 1 metre (3 feet) tall bush with medium green, semi-glossy foliage. This is one of the smaller among David Austin's English Roses. It was introduced in 1983.

Unnamed seedling × unnamed seedling
Repeat flowering

▲ 'Purple Splendour'

green, but there is little scent. It was raised by E. B. LeGrice and introduced in 1976. It was one of his last successes—he died in 1977.

'News' × 'Overture'
Repeat flowering

▲ 'Prosperity'
► 'Prospero'

'Prospero'   English Rose
AUSpero

Even the raiser admits that this is a difficult rose to grow, lacking vigor, as so often the very dark roses do. If you would like a bit of a challenge, the mid-sized deep crimson and purple blooms are beautifully quartered, borne repeatedly and richly fragrant. Foliage is dark green and matt. It needs the best of everything. It was raised by David Austin and introduced in 1982.

'The Knight' × 'Château de Clos Vougeot'
Repeat flowering
Fragrant

'Purple Splendour'   Cluster-flowered
'News' brought the rich purple of the Old Garden Roses into the Moderns. 'Purple Splendour' presents it in a yet clearer and deeper shade, and the flowers are both smaller and fuller of petals. It is in fact a more conventional Cluster-flowered Rose than 'News', from which it was bred, but has never been quite so popular, perhaps for that very reason. It is a good rose, its plant strong and upright, and the foliage matt

▲ 'Quatre Saisons Blanc Mousseux'
▶ 'Queen Elizabeth'

'Quatre Saisons Blanc Mousseux' — Moss

Rosa damascena bifera alba muscosa, 'Perpetual White Moss'

If you cannot cope with the cumbersome French name, by all means use the English, remembering that both are grossly exaggerated. Like the 'Rose à Quatre Saisons' from which it sported, both gaining moss and changing color on the way, the 'Perpetual White Moss' only gives a skimpy display to follow its summer crop. A cluster of blooms can, however, be very pretty, their silky whiteness set off by the brownish and rough-textured moss. Growth and the greyish green, downy foliage are just like its parent and the fragrance is just as good.

Sport from 'Rose à Quatre Saisons'
Repeat flowering
Fragrant

'Queen Adelaide' — Large-flowered
MEIvildo
'Yves Piaget'

Here Marie-Louisette Meilland has tried to bring to a modern Large-flowered Rose some of the full-petalled style of the Old Garden Roses of Queen Adelaide's day. The blooms are certainly full-petalled and globular in a lovely deep shade of Old Garden Rose pink, paling as they age. The plant is thoroughly modern, however—bushy, upright, and with large, glossy, dark green foliage, not, alas, always as free of black spot as it might be. It was introduced in 1983.

('Pharaoh' × 'Peace') × ('Chrysler Imperial' × 'Charles Mallerin')
Repeat flowering
Fragrant

'Queen Elizabeth' — Cluster-flowered
'The Queen Elizabeth Rose'

The WFRS, in 1980, declared 'Queen Elizabeth' the world's best rose. It is a little too tall for some. The outrageous height of the bush is a result of the enormous vitality of the variety—'Queen Elizabeth' seems to flourish anywhere. Long, high-centred buds open to large blooms of clear, bright pink, produced in clusters. Foliage is dark green, glossy and leathery. The archetype of the American 'Grandifloras', it was raised in 1954 by California's Walter Lammerts and won just about every top award, including the AARS award. Lammerts' British agent Harry Wheatcroft suggested dedicating it to the young Queen of England.

'Charlotte Armstrong' × 'Floradora'
Repeat flowering

◀ 'Queen Adelaide'
▼ 'Queen Margarethe'

'Queen Margarethe' — Cluster-flowered

Another of the currently popular 'Patio Roses', 'Queen Margarethe' is classed as a Cluster-flowered Rose, but it is really more like a rather enlarged Miniature, growing to about 80 centimetres (30 inches), with glossy dark green leaves and perfectly formed flowers in proportion. The blooms are the prettiest shade of pale pink and delicately scented. It was raised in 1991 by the Poulsen company and named in honor of the Queen of Denmark, which suggests that its Danish raiser must think very highly of it.

Parentage unknown
Repeat flowering
Fragrant

'Radox Bouquet'
Cluster-flowered

HARmusky

'Rosika'

Richly fragrant (though hardly of bath salts!) the flowers of 'Radox Bouquet' are softly pink and full-petalled, almost, though not quite, in the Old Garden Rose style. The bush is modern, rather upright, and well-clothed in shiny leaves. Raised in England by Jack Harkness in 1980, it is highly regarded there. It is probably happiest in a cool climate.

('Alec's Red' × 'Piccadilly') × ('Southampton' × ['Cläre Grämmerstorf' × 'Frühlingsmorgen'])

Repeat flowering

Fragrant

'Raja Surendra Singh of Nalagarh'
Large-flowered

A rose of suitably oriental splendor, 'Raja Surendra Singh of Nalagarh' sets its magnificent apricot to gold blooms off against deep, olive-green, plum-tinted foliage. It opens well in hot weather, and also in cool nights—the peak blooming season for roses on the Indian plains is winter. It is an Indian-raised rose and is not available elsewhere, more is the pity.

Parentage undisclosed

Repeat flowering

'Ralph's Creeper'
Ground Cover

This is not named after just any old Ralph, but after Ralph Moore, California's master of the Miniatures. It is, in fact, one of his seedlings, though it is not a Miniature but a Ground Cover. The leaves are glossy and very dark indeed, the better to set off the blooms in brilliant scarlet and gold which are Cluster-flowered Rose size. Scent is only faint. I have no details of the parentage, but as Mr Moore rarely releases the by-products of his search for better Miniatures, I should think he is rather taken by this one. So am I.

Parentage undisclosed

Repeat flowering

◄ 'Radox Bouquet'
▼ 'Ralph's Creeper'

'Ramona'
Cluster-flowered

'Red Cherokee'

A sport of the 'Pink Cherokee' which occurred in the California nursery of Diterich & Turner in 1913, 'Ramona' is exactly like its parent except for its much deeper color. It is not quite red—cerise would be a better description—with the petals a more muted tint on their reverses. It flowers early and long, with the occasional flower in the autumn, or fall. Like all the 'Cherokee' roses, it dislikes extreme cold. Foliage is dark green and polished.

Sport from 'Pink Cherokee'

Repeat flowering

Fragrant

◄ 'Raja Surendra Singh of Nalagarh'

▲ 'Raspberry Ice'

'Raspberry Ice'
Cluster-flowered

KORtabris

'Tabris'

Although this rose was raised by Reimer Kordes and was introduced in 1986, the Kordes's catalogue does not list it. Presumably he must have sold it to another firm to distribute, or else, as occasionally happens one of his agents thought more highly of its pink and white flowers and bushy habit than the raiser did. Foliage is dull green and semi-glossy. The name 'Raspberry Ice' was aimed at the American market, but the Americans call it 'Tabris', after the city in Iran from which the fine Tabriz carpets come. As the rose has not been officially registered under either name, there are no details of its parentage available.

Parentage unknown

Repeat flowering

▼ 'Ramona'

'Raubritter'
Modern Shrub

'Raubritter' is one of the most popular of the Modern Shrub Roses, both for its unusual cascading habit and for its unique flowers. These are on the small side, but come in lovely bunches, and are of most unusual form, the shell-shaped petals making a perfect pale pink sphere. They are extremely long lasting, both individually and as a total display on the bush. It will eventually spread to more than 2 metres (6 feet) wide, but is rarely more than a metre (3 feet) tall. Watch it for black spot, and do not expect much in the way of scent. Foliage is pale green, matt and leathery. It was raised by that master of the unusual, Wilhelm Kordes, and he introduced it in 1936.

'Daisy Hill' × 'Solarium'
Repeat flowering

▲ 'Raubritter'
▼ 'Red Coat'

'Raymond Chenault'
Large-flowered Climber

Yet another repeat-flowering Climber short enough in growth to be equally well treated as a Shrub Rose, 'Raymond Chenault' has glossy dark green foliage and brilliant red flowers with a hint of scarlet, lit up further by its yellow stamens. It is not especially fragrant, but pleasantly so. The name honors a French nurseryman, a colleague of the raiser, Wilhelm Kordes. It was introduced in 1960.

Rosa kordesii × 'Montezuma'
Repeat flowering

'Red and White Delight'
Cluster-flowered

'Peppermint Twist'

This is one of the nicest of the recent spate of striped roses, its colors clear and definite without being too gaudy, and the medium-sized blooms, borne in clusters of half a dozen or so, opening wide from long buds, the better to show off the contrast of clear crimson and white. The plant is bushy, upright and tends to be rather tall. Foliage is mid-green and semi-glossy. There is scent, though not as a prime attraction. Raised by Jack Christensen at Armstrong's in the United States, 'Red and White Delight' was introduced in 1991. The name invites confusion with both 'Double Delight' and 'White Delight', unfortunately.

'Pinstripe' × 'Maestro'
Repeat flowering

'Red Coat'
English Rose

'Redcoat'

'Red Coat' is a single-flowered English Rose, and it could just as well be classed simply as a Modern Shrub, along with, for example, Kordes's so-called 'Park Roses', which it resembles. It makes a head-high shrub with light pruning. Disciplined a bit more it can be treated as a tallish Bush Rose. Either way it makes quite a show all season, the slightly scented blooms covering the bush. They are quite large, and open bright red, rapidly passing to a softer shade, against dark green matt foliage. David Austin, the raiser, thinks highly of 'Red Coat' as a flowering hedge, and as such it is a kind of updated 'Gloire des Rosomanes'. It was introduced in 1973.

'Parade' × unnamed seedling
Repeat flowering

▲ 'Raymond Chenault'
▼ 'Red and White Delight'

'Red Cushion'
Cluster-flowered

This 1966 Armstrong Nurseries introduction seems to have dropped out of circulation in its home country, but it is still very well liked in Japan, where it was photographed, for its resistance to mildew. The name might suggest a 'Patio Rose', but it is in fact a Cluster-flowered Rose of about average height, bearing clusters of open flowers, their blood-red color set off by the golden stamens and by the dark glossy green foliage. There is little scent, but the flowers are long lasting in water. It was raised by David Armstrong.

'Circus' × 'Ruby Lips'
Repeat flowering

▲ 'Red Cushion'
▼ 'Red Devil'

▲ 'Red Gold'

'Red Gold'   Cluster-flowered
DICor
'Rouge et Or'

The young flowers are very shapely, carried in handsome trusses of strong yellow sharply edged with red. The plant is tall, with dark green foliage. 'Red Gold' can be sensational. It was the first British-raised rose to win the AARS award (in 1971) for over twenty years. The flowers, unfortunately, age very badly, fading and going blotchy, and the foliage gets black spot in humid climates. It was from Dickson in 1971.

(['Karl Herbst' × 'Masquerade'] × 'Dr Faust') × 'Piccadilly'
Repeat flowering

'Red Glory'   Cluster-flowered
Although officially a Cluster-flowered Rose, 'Red Glory' grows big enough to be used as a Shrub Rose. Despite its name, it is not red, but a blend of red and deep pink. The semi-double, ruffled flowers are very pretty, though not very fragrant. If they are not removed when they fade there will be bunches of hips in autumn, or fall. Foliage is leathery and semi-glossy. It was raised by Herbert Swim and introduced in 1958, specifically as a rose for hedges. The idea of breeding roses for their value to landscape designers has recently been taken up with a vengeance, notably by Meilland in France.

'Gay Lady' × ('Pinocchio' × 'Floradora')
Repeat flowering

'Red Masterpiece'   Large-flowered
This 1974 rose from Bill Warriner would be just about perfect, except it is fussy about climate. Where summers are cool or humid it gets mildew and does not open its flowers properly. Give it a decent amount of sunshine and there is no better red rose. The blooms are large and high centred, their color rich and velvety and their perfume outstanding. The bush is tall and clad with dark green foliage.

('Siren' × 'Chrysler Imperial') × ('Carrousel' × 'Chrysler Imperial')
Repeat flowering
Fragrant

'Red Devil'   Large-flowered
DICam
'Coeur d'Amour'

Named by the raiser Pat Dickson for the men of his old RAF Squadron, 'Red Devil' is a wonderful red rose, strong in growth, rudely healthy and capable of giving huge, exhibition style blooms with freedom and without cosseting. It is very fragrant too. It has two faults however: the brilliant color is only medium crimson rather than the deep velvety tone that everyone loves; and it is intolerant of prolonged rain on the flowers. Neither of these should stop anyone from growing it. It was introduced in 1967 and has been adorned with a string of medals.

'Silver Lining' × 'Prima Ballerina' seedling
Repeat flowering
Fragrant

◄ 'Red Glory'
▼ 'Red Masterpiece'

'Red Planet' Large-flowered

The blooms are superb in shape and color, a rich if not very deep crimson, and the foliage is mid-green, polished and very healthy. The plant is, however, rather shy with its handsome blooms, and fragrance, while there is some, is not as memorable as that of its parent 'Red Devil'. In short, this is an exhibitor's rose. It was raised by Pat Dickson of Northern Ireland and introduced in 1969. It won the highest honors in England.

'Red Devil' × unnamed seedling
Repeat flowering
Fragrant

'Red Radiance' Large-flowered

The flowers are deep, glowing cerise-pink, and it is an exaggeration to call them red. However, they are certainly much deeper and richer than the pale, two-toned pink flowers of 'Radiance', from which 'Red Radiance' is a sport. Present-day rose-lovers do not care for the rather dull green leaves or the cabbage-like incurving form of the flowers. For many years, though, 'Radiance' (introduced in 1904 by John Cook of Baltimore) and 'Red Radiance', which came along in 1916, were the best-selling roses in the United States, thanks to their cast-iron constitutions, lavish bloom and fine fragrance. Old-fashioned they may be, but they remain among the easiest of all Large-flowered Roses to grow.

Sport from 'Radiance'
Repeat flowering
Fragrant

► 'Red Success'
▼ 'Red Radiance'

▲ 'Red Planet'

'Red Success' Large-flowered
MEIrodium

Had Meilland introduced 'Red Success' in 1956 instead of 1976, it would probably have been called 'Orange Success', for the red does lean very strongly towards orange. The outer petals are usually a darker shade than the inner, and the whole flower tends to go darker and redder with age. There are about thirty-five petals, beautifully symmetrically arranged, making it a fine show rose. There is little scent, but the bushes are tall and free flowering, and the olive-green leaves blend well with the flowers. Warm climates are definitely preferred.

Parentage undisclosed
Repeat flowering

'Regensberg' Cluster-flowered
MACyoumis
'Young Mistress', 'Buffalo Bill'

It would not be quite accurate to call this rose 'shocking pink', even though it is one of the most eye-catching roses in the garden. The brilliant pink is in fact splashed and washed over a lighter ground, which shows through here and there. The petals are edged white and the flowers have a white eye, with yellow stamens. This is one of Sam McGredy's 'Hand-painted Roses', and one of the very best of them, for the flowers are large, to 11 centimetres (4½ inches) across, shapely, double, with twenty-one petals, moderate fragrance, and carried in abundance, on a very dwarf but healthy bush of 'Patio Rose' type. Foliage is bright green and glossy. Introduced in 1979, it was the first rose that Sam McGredy raised in New Zealand after his move there from Northern Ireland. The name is a compliment to the flower painter Lotte Gunthardt, who already had a rose named for her. Regensberg in Switzerland is her home town.

'Geoff Boycott' × 'Old Master'
Repeat flowering
Fragrant

► 'Regensberg'

▲ 'Retro'
◄ 'Reine des Mousseuses'

'Reine des Mousseuses' — Moss

I do not know much about this rose, which I saw in a South Australian collection. I understand it dates from 1860. But I like the full, well-scented flowers, their bright pink petals beautifully arranged, and the mossy buds. The plant is perhaps bushier than some Mosses and the dark green foliage is pleasant. It deserves wider distribution.

Parentage unknown
Summer flowering
Fragrant

'Reine des Violettes' — Hybrid Perpetual

Officially classed as a Hybrid Perpetual since its introduction by Mille-Mallet in 1860, 'Reine des Violettes' would be better placed among the Bourbons, both for its slender, thornless branches, and for its moderately sized flowers, flat and quartered like a Gallica Rose. Its colors are pure Gallica too, wonderful blends of mauve and purple, sometimes soft and delicate, at others startling, and always beautifully set off by the smooth grey-green leaves. There is fragrance. Give it the best of everything; it needs and deserves it.

Parentage unknown
Repeat flowering
Fragrant

'Renae' — Cluster-flowered Climber

Introduced in 1954, 'Renae' is an unexpected offshoot of the raiser Ralph Moore's search for beautiful Miniatures. To all intents, it is a repeat-flowering Rambler, with very flexible branches and bunches of small, pale pink, well-scented blooms on and off all season. It is reminiscent of a more elegant 'Dorothy Perkins', without the mildew. It makes a first-rate weeping standard. Do not expect it to grow as large as the old 'Dorothy'-type Ramblers.

'Etoile Luisante' × 'Sierra Snowstorm'
Repeat flowering
Fragrant

'Retro' — Cluster-flowered

MEIbalans

Introduced in 1980, this is another of Meilland's 'Landscape Roses', making a moderately sized but very tough bush and bearing clusters of full-petalled salmon-pink flowers all season. It is a pretty rose with bright green foliage. It is unfortunate that it was introduced just before 'Bonica' whose success has rather overshadowed it.

Parentage undisclosed
Repeat flowering

'Rêve d'Or' — Noisette

'Golden Chain'

Rêve d'or is French for 'golden dream'. The rose, however, is a soft, buttery yellow with tints of peach. It is a very lovely rose, climbing strongly enough to adorn the front of a house with glossy, dark green leaves, tinted with copper in their youth, and many sprays of richly scented, frilly blooms, opening to around 10 centimetres (4 inches) from pointed buds. It likes warmth and needs a sheltered spot in cool climates. Flowers come all season. Mme Ducher introduced it in 1869 and nine years later it produced a sport, 'William Allen Richardson', which starts out life much

▶ 'Renae'
▼ 'Reine des Violettes'

▼ 'Rêve d'Or'

deeper, almost orange, before fading out completely. 'Rêve d'Or' is much nicer all round.

Parentage unknown
Repeat flowering
Fragrant

▲ 'Riverview'

'Ringlet'
Large-flowered Climber

Although this Alister Clark creation of 1922 is officially classed as a Large-flowered Climber, its flowers are more like those of a Cluster-flowered Rose, being only of medium size and borne in sprays. They are very pretty, almost single, their white petals touched with pink and lilac at the edges, and they are fragrant. The plant is strong, and you can expect some repeat bloom. Foliage is small and mid-green. 'Ringlet' would be a an appropriate choice for a quiet color scheme, especially in a 1920s style garden, if you were looking for something a little unusual.

'Ernest Morel' × 'Betty Berkeley'
Repeat flowering
Fragrant

▲ 'Ringlet'
▼ 'Risqué'

'Ripples'
Cluster-flowered

One of the lesser-known mauve roses, and one of the most desirable, 'Ripples' bears 9 centimetre (3½ inch) flowers in a deeper shade of mauve than most, with attractively ruffled and fluted petals and a powerful fragrance. The bush is upright; the foliage is light green, but unfortunately rather prone to mildew. It is a little reminiscent of 'Angel Face', which came out at about the same time, but the flowers are larger and less inclined to turn pink with age. 'Ripples' is a 1971 introduction from England's E. B. LeGrice.

('Tantau's Surprise' × 'Marjorie LeGrice') × (unnamed seedling × 'Africa Star')
Repeat flowering
Fragrant

▶ 'Rob Roy'
▼ 'Ripples'

'Risqué'
Large-flowered

'Risqué' holds its tomato-red color well, without fading or going magenta, and the foliage is dark green and medium in size. 'Risqué' makes an excellent garden rose. The blooms open very prettily to show yellow stamens. Fragrance is only slight. 'Risqué' was raised by O. L. Weeks and introduced by him in 1985.

Parentage undisclosed
Repeat flowering

'Riverview'
Large-flowered

'The Riverview Centenary Rose'

Dark red roses are always expected to be highly scented; in this respect 'Riverview' is a disappointment. In other respects it is a good rose, its petals velvety, the blooms large and high centred, and the plant strong, with dull green foliage. The flower is very long lasting, sufficiently so that it has been grown for the florists' trade. It was raised by Armstrong Nurseries, introduced in 1980 and named to mark the centenary of St Ignatius' College in Sydney, familiarly known as Riverview from its position above the Lane Cove River where regattas are held each year.

'Cara Mia' × ('Night and Day' × 'Plain Talk')
Repeat flowering

'Rob Roy'
Cluster-flowered

Long shapely buds open to rather loose flowers, carried in small trusses on a tall and healthy bush. The greatest asset of the rose is its warm crimson color, rich and velvety, and its greatest drawbacks are its only slight fragrance and its preference for a cool climate. Foliage is dark green and leathery. An Alex Cocker introduction of 1970, it was named, patriotically, for Sir Walter Scott's legendary hero.

'Evelyn Fison' × 'Wendy Cussons'
Repeat flowering

'Robert le Diable'   Centifolia

'Robert le Diable' may not be one of the better Old Garden Roses for the garden, as the bush is both lax and spindly. Its flowers are extraordinary, however; formed in the Old Garden Rose style, they display an astonishing range of quite sombre colors—crimson, purple, dove-grey and violet. The centre of the flower is often green. Scent is good, though not overpoweringly so. Foliage is a matt soft green. Its raiser and date of origin are unknown, but it is a safe guess that it came out about 1831, when Giacomo Meyerbeer's opera, *Robert le Diable,* was the sensation of Paris.

Parentage unknown
Summer flowering
Fragrant

'Robin Hood'   Hybrid Musk

'Robin Hood' was raised by Joseph Pemberton in 1927, and has never been one of the more ardently admired of his

Hybrid Musks: its rather stiff growth and lack of scent have told against it. The cherry-red to carmine flowers are colorful enough, though, and it has been a noteworthy parent, giving rise to 'Eva', and its line, and to 'Iceberg'. Perhaps breeders should take another look at it. Foliage is dark green on a bushy plant.

Unnamed seedling × 'Miss Edith Cavell'
Repeat flowering

◄ 'Robert le Diable'
▼ 'Robusta'

'Robusta'   Modern Shrub
KORgosa
'Kordes Robusta'

Most hybrids of *Rosa rugosa* tend to take strongly after it, but this 1979 Kordes introduction shows its *R. rugosa* ancestry chiefly in its prickliness and the leathery quality of its dark green leaves. Otherwise it is a fairly typical (and good) Modern Shrub Rose, raising upright branches to about head high, crowned with trusses of brilliant red, single flowers all through the season. Alas, there is little of the clove-like *R. rugosa* fragrance.

R. rugosa regeliana × unknown
Repeat flowering

◄ 'Robin Hood'

'Rocky'   Modern Shrub
MACkepa
'Blushing Maid'

This 1979 rose from Sam McGredy honors the Sylvester Stallone movies. Derived from Sam's 'Hand-painted Rose' breeding line, it is effectively an overgrown Cluster-flowered Rose, bearing its clusters of shapely flowers all season on a tall bush with dark green foliage.

'Liverpool Echo' × ('Evelyn Fison' × ['Orange Sensation' × 'Frühlingsmorgen'])
Repeat flowering

▼ 'Rocky'

▲ 'Rödhätte'

'Rödhätte' Cluster-flowered
'Little Red Riding Hood'

Most people would not give this rose a second glance today. Its flowers are on the small side, scentless, and a plain shade of red, with the plant having dull green leaves and more mildew than is acceptable. It is a historic rose, however, being the first of the Hybrid Polyanthas, or Cluster-flowered Roses as they are called now. Dines Poulsen introduced it in 1917. His aim in crossing a Large-flowered Rose with a Polyantha was to encourage hardiness for his very cold Danish climate. The Poulsen firm is still in business, with many fine roses to its credit.

'Madame Norbert Lavavasseur' × 'Richmond'
Repeat flowering

'Roger Lambelin' Hybrid Perpetual
This is one of those roses you either love, finding its dark crimson flowers deckle-edged in white quite unusual and beautiful, or you hate, thinking it

bizarre and unhealthy looking. Perhaps people in the latter camp have just never seen a good flower, for, like 'Prince Camille de Rohan' from which it sported in 1890, it is not an easy rose to grow, needing good rich soil and protection from any diseases that may be about. Foliage is mid-green and dull. If it likes you, it flowers repeatedly and fairly freely. The introducer was Joseph Schwartz of Lyon.

Sport from 'Prince Camille de Rohan'
Repeat flowering
Fragrant

'Roman Holiday' Cluster-flowered
LINro

Although it won the AARS award in 1967, the year after its introduction, 'Roman Holiday' has dropped out of the catalogues. This is a shame as it still looks pretty good, its compact plants, with dark green, glossy leaves still flaunting clusters of blooms in a festive blend of red and orange with flashes of gold. They are fragrant too. Admittedly, it was never as good in cold and humid climates. Raised by Bob Lindquist, it was introduced in 1966.

('Pinkie' × 'Independence') × 'Circus'
Repeat flowering
Fragrant

'Ronningii' Tea
'Angel's Camp'

Here is yet another old Tea Rose preserved at the Huntington Gardens in San Marino, its shapely, softly fragrant blooms reminiscent of a paler-toned 'President Herbert Hoover' in shades of peach and rose. Foliage is semi-glossy and dark green. There must be many old Teas surviving in old gardens in mild places like California, South Africa and Australia, giving a good account of

◀ 'Roger Lambelin'
▼ 'Ronningii'

themselves despite neglect, or perhaps because of it. Teas dislike any but the lightest pruning, and will shrink from the overzealous gardener's secateurs.

Parentage unknown
Repeat flowering
Fragrant

▲ 'Roman Holiday'
▼ 'Rosabell'

'Rosabell' Cluster-flowered
COCceleste

'Rosabell' looks to be a charmer, with large sprays of smallish flowers, full petalled and neatly formed, in a lovely shade of soft pink. The bush is low growing, with glossy green leaves, and the effect is like an updated Polyantha. This is a new trend, away from the large-flowered Cluster-flowered Roses, with exhibition-type flowers. It is an Alec Cocker introduction of 1988. There is not a great deal of fragrance.

Unnamed seedling × 'Darling Flame'
Repeat flowering

'Rosamunde' Cluster-flowered
KORmunde

Do not confuse this with 'Rosa Mundi' (*Rosa gallica versicolor*). 'Rosamunde' is not striped nor particularly old, having been raised by Reimer Kordes in 1971. It is not seen very often, but it is a charming rose, with clusters of nicely shaped flowers in clear candy-pink, against leathery green foliage. It seems to be a very easy rose to grow, flourishing in gardens where other roses will suffer from neglect. Fragrance is only moderate. The name was never registered.

Parentage undisclosed
Repeat flowering

'Rosarium Uetersen' Large-flowered Climber
KORtersen

This was raised by Reimer Kordes, introduced in 1977 and named for a rose garden with which he is associated. This rose bears large, 10 centimetre (4 inch) coral-pink flowers in small clusters. They are fragrant and usually loosely quartered. Growth is strong, to about 3 or 4 metres (10–13 feet) and, like most of the seedlings of *Rosa kordesii*, it is resistant to both cold and mildew. Foliage is dark and glossy.

R. kordesii × 'Karlsrühe'
Repeat flowering
Fragrant

'Rose à Quatre Saisons' Damask
Rosa damascena bifera, 'Four Seasons Rose', 'Autumn Damask', 'Alexandrian Rose'

The title 'Four Seasons' is a great exaggeration, whether it be expressed in

▲ 'Rosamunde'
► 'Rose d'Amour'
▼ 'Rose à Quatre Saisons'

▼ 'Rosarium Uetersen'

English or in French, but in the days before the truly everblooming China Roses the willingness of this rose to give some flowers (though not very many) after its first crop made it much prized. Nowadays it seems rather ordinary. It is leggy in growth, with pale green foliage, and not very distinguished in its plain pink color or its shapeliness of bloom. It is, however, very richly fragrant. No one knows its origin; speculation that it might have been referred to in one of Virgil's poems is simple fantasy.

Parentage unknown
Repeat flowering
Fragrant

'Rose d'Amour' Modern Shrub
Rosa virginiana plena, 'St Mark's Rose'

Much confusion surrounds this lovely rose. To begin with, it is not a double form of *R. virginiana* but a hybrid whose origins are a matter of guesswork. In addition to the names noted above, it has also been called *R. rapa*, *R. lucida plena*, and 'Rose d'Orsay', all, it seems, in error. That one of Redouté's most popular plates, of a wild Gallica Rose, is labelled *Rose d'Amour*, and that there is a Large-flowered Rose carrying the name also (from Gaujard in 1936) scarcely helps. Our rose can hardly be described as large, but rather as the epitome of daintiness, its exquisite buds opening to lightly fragrant, semi-double blooms. Their precise tone of pink varies with the weather, but is always cool and pleasing. The tall, glossy-leafed bush is not really repeat flowering, but as it starts very late in summer and continues long in blooms, there will often be some autumn, or fall, flowers.

Possibly *R. virginiana* × *R. carolina*
Late-summer flowering

▲ 'Rose de la Reine'

▲ 'Rose Gaujard'

'Rose de la Reine' — Hybrid Perpetual
'La Reine', 'Reine des Français'

Pointed buds open to large globular flowers, full of petals and fragrance. The color is best described simply as rose-pink. The bush is upright, with mid-green foliage, and grows to about a metre (3 feet). It repeats its flowering without needing as much encouragement as some Hybrid Perpetuals do. Raised by Laffay in 1842, it was one of the first of the class, and for many years one of the most popular of all roses. It has been a most famous parent. Few indeed are the later roses that cannot trace their pedigrees to it.

Parentage unknown
Repeat flowering
Fragrant

'Rose de Rescht' — Damask

Despite its fairly recent discovery and reintroduction, by Nancy Lindsay, the well-known English writer, nothing is known about the origin of this rose. It is not a Damask, though it is usually classed as such. It is not a Portland either. It makes a compact bush, with bright green, dense foliage, and it bears its sweetly scented flowers, cerise becoming flushed and shaded with magenta, in several flushes through the season. It is one of the best Old Garden Roses for the modern garden, almost as prolific and continuous as a Cluster-flowered Rose, at least while it is young. Old bushes need severe discipline at pruning time or they get lazy.

Parentage unknown
Repeat flowering
Fragrant

▲ 'Rose du Roi'

'Rose du Roi' — Hybrid Perpetual
'Crimson Perpetual'

This is one of the most important of historical roses, the progenitor of the Hybrid Perpetuals and thus of their descendants, the Large-flowered Roses. It is evidently suffering from old age, as it needs good cultivation in order to grow well and bear, throughout the season, its fragrant crimson blooms. The bush is on the short side and foliage is small and dark green. It was raised in the gardens of the Palace of Saint-Cloud, and legend has it that the director resigned when its patriotic raiser, Souchet, dedicated the new rose to the king rather than to him. It was introduced in 1816.

Parentage unknown
Repeat flowering
Fragrant

◄ 'Rose de Rescht'
► 'Rose Hannes'

'Rose Gaujard' — Large-flowered

'M. Jean Gaujard thought so highly of this rose that he named it after himself.' So says one of the most respected of rose books, with more than a trace of cattiness. Gaujard's confidence was not misplaced: when 'Rose Gaujard' is indeed at its best, you will have people knocking at the door to ask the name of that wonderful cyclamen pink and white rose. Some blooms will fall short of that standard, but fortunately 'Rose Gaujard' grows strongly and flowers lavishly. Foliage is glossy and bright green. Gaujard did himself the honor in 1957. Scent is only light.

'Peace' × seedling from 'Opéra'
Repeat flowering

'Rose Hannes' — Large-flowered

Do not confuse this one with 'Hanne', a Danish-raised deep red rose of 1959 with a good reputation in cold climates. Despite its Nordic-sounding name, 'Rose Hannes' is an English rose from Christopher Wheatcroft. The flowers are a delight in their fragrance and delicate tones of white and gold. The blooms are large, the form perfect and foliage is glossy and mid-green. 'Rose Hannes' is little seen outside the United Kingdom. Even there, it is regarded as essentially a show rose.

Parentage undisclosed
Repeat flowering
Fragrant

'Rose-Marie Viaud' — Rambler

Introduced by the otherwise unknown French rosarian named Igoult in 1924, 'Rose-Marie Viaud' is a seedling from 'Veilchenblau' and resembles its parent in its thornlessness and glossy dark green leaves. Many people consider it superior, for its little flowers are more double and richer in color. They open purple and fade through every pretty shade of lilac and mauve. Growing both roses is a good idea, for 'Rose Marie Viaud' does not start blooming until 'Veilchenblau' is nearly finished. Do not confuse it with 'Rose Marie', a pink Large-flowered Rose from the 1920s.

'Veilchenblau' × unknown
Summer flowering

'Rose of Tralee' — Cluster-flowered

Sam McGredy has written of his surprise that no one had ever thought to create a rose to celebrate the old Irish song, 'The Rose of Tralee'. He made good the omission in 1964 with this coral-pink Cluster-flowered Rose. Its large flowers, some 8–10 centimetres (3–4 inches) wide, are borne in small

▲ 'Rose of Tralee'
▼ 'Rose Parade'

clusters. As you might expect from its parentage, it is a tall, shrubby bush, with dark green leaves. One could wish for more luxuriant foliage; as it is the plant is inclined to look a bit leggy. Fragrance is not very pronounced, but it is an attractive rose.

'Leverkusen' × 'Korona'
Repeat flowering

'Rose Parade' — Cluster-flowered

Pasadena's famous Rose Parade takes place on New Year's Day, a time of year when, even in southern California, there will not be many roses in bloom, except in greenhouses. 'Rose Parade', the rose, can be expected to cover itself from one end of the normal season to the other with clusters of full-petalled bright pink roses. They are also sweetly fragrant. The bush is compact and the large glossy leaves are unusually resistant to disease. It is regarded in the United States as one of the very best pink roses for making a splash of color in the garden. This 1975 AARS winner was raised by Benjamin Williams of Maryland. It is the best known of several roses he is credited with.

'Sumatra' × 'Queen Elizabeth'
Repeat flowering
Fragrant

'Rose Queen' — Large-flowered

I like this rose, introduced by Germains of Los Angeles in 1962, but I seem to be in a minority. It never won any awards and is found in very few catalogues these days. Its blooms are very large, of excellent high-centred form, and they are delightfully fragrant. They look splendid against the dark green foliage. This rose is no relation to Kordes's

'Königin der Rosen', which might be translated as 'Rose Queen'.

'Chrysler Imperial' × unnamed seedling
Repeat flowering
Fragrant

◀ 'Rose-Marie Viaud'
▼ 'Rosemary Rose'

'Rosemary Rose' — Cluster-flowered

It is interesting how the perceptions of gardeners change. When 'Rosemary Rose' came out in 1954, its full-petalled flowers were described as being flat like zinnias. Now a resemblance to the quartered Old Garden Roses is more likely to be noticed. Either way, they are very pretty, somewhat scented, and carried in large clusters. Their color is that typical Old Garden Rose color which can be described as either deep pink or a light crimson. The dark green leaves are strikingly red when young, an attractive character passed on to its descendants, but watch that they are

▼ 'Rose Queen'

not disfigured with mildew. It was raised by the Dutch grower de Ruiter. The name honors the daughter of his English agent, Walter Gregory.

Unnamed seedling × 'Grüss an Teplitz'
Repeat flowering
Fragrant

'Rosenelfe'   Cluster-flowered
'Rose Elf'

This was the first Cluster-flowered Rose with flowers like miniature Large-flowered Roses, and it remains one of the loveliest of them, its 6 centimetre (2½ inch) flowers individually of perfect form, the cluster beautifully spaced and arranged. The color is clear pink, without a hint of hardness, and it is also fragrant. The plant is on the low side, nicely clad in dark green leaves. It may mildew occasionally, but that is its only fault. It was raised by Wilhelm Kordes and introduced in 1936.

'Else Poulsen' × 'Sir Basil McFarland'
Repeat flowering
Fragrant

'Rosenresli'   Modern Shrub
KOResli

'Rosenresli' is officially a Shrub Rose, but its glossy-leafed branches are quite long and are limber enough for it to be trained as a Climber or pillar rose. Its flowers are very attractive, lightly built in what used to be called the 'decorative' manner, soft salmon-pink with lights of gold, and fragrant. It is a little reminiscent of that old favorite 'Shot Silk', but with more coral in the color. No doubt Reimer Kordes, who raised 'Rosenresli' in 1985, would be pleased by that comparison.

Parentage undisclosed
Repeat flowering
Fragrant

▶ 'Rosy Cheeks'
▼ 'Rosenresli'

▲ 'Rosenelfe'
▶ 'Roseraie de l'Haÿ'

'Roseraie de l'Haÿ'   Hybrid Rugosa

It is not clear whether this rose, which apparently originated at the great rose garden whose name it bears, was a seedling or a sport of a wild form of *Rosa rugosa*, but it is an outstanding bloom. The plant is as lush and leafy as one could wish, with all the hardiness and resistance to disease for which *R. rugosa* is famous, and the flowers, opening large and informal from long, shapely buds, are borne all season. They are deep purple-crimson and fragrant. The foliage is light green and rugose. The rose's only omission is the lack of hips. The later displays are more abundant if you are generous with watering during hot weather. Propagated by hybridist Cochet-Cochet.

Seedling or sport from unknown hybrid of *R. rugosa*
Repeat flowering
Fragrant

'Rosy Cheeks'   Large-flowered

Anderson's Rose Nurseries are an Aberdeen firm with the laudable habit of only cataloguing roses with good fragrance. Naturally, one would expect a rose of their own introduction to be beautifully scented, and 'Rosy Cheeks' does not disappoint. The blooms are very large indeed, some 18 centimetres (7 inches) across, of perfect exhibition form (thirty-five petals) and a pleasing shade of cerise with yellow on the reverse. Foliage is glossy. It was introduced in 1975. Like its pollen parent, 'Grandpa Dickson', it is happiest in a coolish climate.

'Beauty of Festival' × 'Grandpa Dickson'
Repeat flowering
Fragrant

'Rosy Cushion'
Modern Shrub
INTerall

Interplant of Holland are marketing this as a Ground Cover Rose. In fact it is not dense enough in growth for this purpose. The low, spreading shrub, with dark green, glossy leaves, does become a mound of pretty single pink and cream flowers several times each season, so the name 'Rosy Cushion' is apt enough. There is little scent. It came out in 1979.

'Yesterday' × unnamed seedling
Repeat flowering

▶ 'Rosy Cushion'

▲ 'Royal Albert Hall'
▼ 'Royal Dane'

'Royal Albert Hall'
Large-flowered

London's great concert hall is built in dark red bricks adorned with yellow terracotta and crowned with a green copper dome. It is not surprising that the rose that honors it is a bicolor in red and yellow, with bright green leaves. A creation of Alec Cocker of Aberdeen, it is a big flower of fine exhibition form, good fragrance and good performance in the garden.

'Fragrant Cloud' × 'Postillion'
Repeat flowering
Fragrant

'Royal Dane'
Large-flowered
'Troika'

This rose looks good from the minute it starts to grow in spring. The young foliage is plum-red and brilliantly glossy, maturing to dark green. It flowers early too, the blooms large and richly fragrant, in a melange of orange and copper with touches of cerise. It grows best, and is most richly colored, in cool climates.

('Super Star' × ['Baccarà' × 'Princess Astrid']) × 'Hanne'
Repeat flowering
Fragrant

▲ 'Royal Gold'

'Royal Gold' — Large-flowered Climber

If you want to grow a deep, deep yellow rose for exhibition, then this is it. It is pleasantly fragrant too. Plant it only if you have a warm dry climate, for it languishes and takes black spot where summers are humid and where winters are cold it is apt to be frosted. In warm climates 'Royal Gold' makes a strong pillar rose, flowering quite freely all season, the beautiful color being well set off by slightly grey-toned glossy foliage. It was raised by Dennison Morey for Jackson & Perkins and introduced in 1957.

'Climbing Goldilocks' × 'Lydia'
Repeat flowering
Fragrant

'Royal Highness' — Large-flowered
'Königliche Hoheit'

This is a rose for a sunny climate; rain damages its silken petals. That is the only reservation. 'Royal Highness', the winner of the 1963 AARS award, is one of the great roses of the 1960s. Carried on long, almost thornless stems, the blooms are large, of most perfect high-centred form, and the most beautiful pale luminous pink, ethereal without being at all wishy-washy. It is fragrant too. The plant is bushy, of average height, with splendid glossy foliage. It was a triumph for Herbert Swim and O. L. Weeks.

'Virgo' × 'Peace'
Repeat flowering
Fragrant

'Royal Romance' — Large-flowered
RULis
'Liselle'

The Dutch raiser de Ruiter preferred to call his rose 'Liselle', but when Fryer's introduced it to the United Kingdom, it became 'Royal Romance' in honor of the Duke and Duchess of York. Its peach and titian flowers echoed the color of the duchess's hair. They are of good size, excellent shape (thirty-five petals) and fragrant, showing up well against dark bronze-green foliage; de Ruiter originally introduced it in 1980.

'Whisky Mac' × 'Matador'
Repeat flowering
Fragrant

▲ 'Royal Romance'
▼ 'Royal Highness'

'Royal Sunset' — Large-flowered Climber

After the acclaim that greeted 'Royal Gold' in 1957, Jackson & Perkins introduced several more 'Royal' Climbers of Doctor Morey's breeding. 'Royal Sunset' of 1960 is probably the best. 'Sunset' describes the copper, flame and apricot colors well, though they are usually soft

rather than blazing, and the blooms are large and shapely. Foliage is leathery. Like 'Royal Gold', it is not a rose for humid climates. It has some of its pollen parent's fine fragrance.

'Sungold' × 'Sutter's Gold'
Repeat flowering
Fragrant

'Royal William' — Large-flowered
KORzaun
'Duftzauber '84', 'Fragrant Charm'

This rose was introduced in 1983, when Britain was celebrating the birth of Prince William. The Palace apparently did not approve the name, as the rose industry tells us 'Royal William' commemorates the tricentenary of the Glorious Revolution of 1688. It is a fine red rose, dark, velvety and fragrant, borne on strong, bushy plants, with dark green, semi-glossy foliage. The blooms vary with the season; at their best they are large and shapely. It was raised by Reimer Kordes. The German name, 'Duftzauber '84', originally used for a lighter red Kordes rose of 1969, means 'scented magic'.

'Feuerzauber' × unnamed seedling
Repeat flowering
Fragrant

▲ 'Royal Sunset'
▼ 'Royal William'

'Rozette Delizy' — Tea

One of the newest of the Teas, 'Rozette Delizy' was introduced by the brothers Nabonnand in 1922. It is a lovely, free-blooming rose, its flowers not large enough for exhibition but long and elegant in the bud and colorful in blends of cream, pale yellow and pink. They are fragrant too, and the dark green foliage, which is plum tinted in its youth, is lusher than that of many Teas.

'Général Galliéni' × 'Comtesse Riza du Parc'
Repeat flowering
Fragrant

▲ 'Rozette Delizy'
▶ 'Rubens'

'Rubaiyat' — Large-flowered

The color on the border between pink and red, like a Ceylon ruby, is one that nature must think suits the rose, for there are many that wear it. One of the very best is 'Rubaiyat', raised by the father of the present Sam McGredy in 1946. The blooms are large and long-budded, opening wide and decorative. The plants are tall and strong, with dark green leathery foliage, and they bloom generously all season. It won the AARS award for 1947.

('McGredy's Scarlet' × 'Mrs Sam McGredy') × seedling from 'Sir Basil McFarland'
Repeat flowering
Fragrant

'Rubens' — Tea

The great painter is always known for the glowing brilliance of his reds and for the plump voluptuousness of his naked ladies. Moreau & Robert, in 1859, chose a flower in what was in those days described as 'flesh color'. The blending of pale pinks with ivory and cream is exceptionally lovely, and the flowers are shapely and endowed with the true Tea fragrance. 'Rubens', however, is one of the lesser known Teas these days, due to its lack of hardiness. Gardeners in mild climates should not overlook it. Foliage is bright green and smooth.

Parentage unknown
Repeat flowering
Fragrant

'Rumba' — Cluster-flowered
'Rhumba'

If only 'Rumba' would shed its dead flowers, it would be an ideal garden rose. Its neat little blooms are carried in huge clusters; the bush is compact and glossy; and the reddish young leaves and very dark green mature ones make a perfect background for the bright colors of the flowers. They start out yellow, rapidly becoming flushed with orange and red, and look as attractive in the vase as in the garden. There are so many that dead-heading is quite a job, and you will need to keep an eye out for black spot in humid climates. 'Rumba' is a 1958 Poulsen introduction.

'Masquerade' × ('Poulsen's Bedder' × 'Floradora')
Repeat flowering

▲ 'Rumba'
◀ 'Rubaiyat'

'Ruskin'
'John Ruskin' Hybrid Rugosa

'Ruskin' does not really conform to the Rugosa norm of large but bushy growth. It makes branches 3–4 metres (10–13 feet) long, which are densely thorny and well clad with strong light green, rugose foliage, and is best used as a pillar rose—to be trained while wearing stout gloves! At their best, the flowers are extraordinary great cabbages of deep crimson flushed with purple, their scent memorable. Do not count on it, however: more often they are just ordinary. It does not repeat its flowering very well. Named in honor of the great Victorian writer on art, it was introduced by Van Fleet in 1928.

'Souvenir de Pierre Leperdrieux' × 'Victor Hugo'
Repeat flowering
Fragrant

▲ 'Ruskin'

'Russeliana'
Rambler

'Russell's Cottage Rose', 'Scarlet Grevillea', 'Souvenir de la Bataille de Marengo', 'Old Spanish Rose'

The Grevilleas are a group of shrubs, native to Australia, to which no rose bears the slightest resemblance. It seems that the name 'Scarlet Grevillea' arises from this rose having been introduced from the Far East about 1840 by Sir Charles Greville. If he was responsible, he was guilty of false advertising, for 'Russeliana' is hardly scarlet but a deep magenta-pink, fading to a much softer, dusty color as the flowers age. The plant is one of the strongest of ramblers, with coarse mid-green foliage, and the flowers are scented. Some say that it derives from *Rosa multiflora*;

R. rugosa and *R. setigera* have both been suggested as more likely ancestors. It is a great survivor in difficult conditions.

Parentage unknown
Summer flowering
Fragrant

'Rusticana'
Cluster-flowered

MEIléna
'Poppy Flash'

This rose is one of the nicer of the 'screaming orange' Cluster-flowered Roses, the flowers being lightened by a touch of gold. They go redder as they age, so a bush in full bloom displays subtly varied colors against its mid-green leaves. Individually the blooms are nicely shaped, but it is as a giver of color in the garden that 'Rusticana' is notable. The growth is both strong and even, and there is an excellent climbing sport available. Meilland raised it and introduced it in 1971. Scent is not a strong point.

('Dany Robin' × 'Fire King') × ('Alain' × 'Mutabilis')
Repeat flowering

'Rusticana, Climbing'
Cluster-flowered

'Climbing Poppy Flash'

The climbing sport of 'Rusticana' is one of the better hot-colored climbers, being both brilliant and subtle in its mixed colorings. Repeat flowering is quite good.

Sport from 'Rusticana'
Repeat flowering

'Saarbrücken'
Modern Shrub

Another of Wilhelm Kordes's 'Park Roses', 'Saarbrücken' makes a bushy plant to 2 metres (6 feet) tall and bears smallish flowers in large trusses. They have little scent, but are a brilliant shade of red, often with an overlay of

▲ 'Rusticana'
▼ 'Climbing Rusticana'

scarlet, and are borne repeatedly. In its season, it makes quite a splash of color. The foliage is dark green and leathery. Saarbrücken is near Frankfurt, and noted for its parks and gardens. Its rose was introduced in 1959.

Parentage undisclosed
Repeat flowering

◄ 'Russeliana'
▼ 'Saarbrücken'

'Sabrina'
Large-flowered

MEIgandor

Sabrina was a blonde bombshell of the 1950s, and in 1960 Alain Meilland dedicated a big crimson and gold rose to her. You do not see it much now, which is a pity, as the gaudiness is offset by fine fragrance. In 1977 the Meilland firm re-used the name. The new 'Sabrina' is essentially a greenhouse rose, with shapely, long-lasting blooms in a shade described as apricot-orange. It is very long lasting in the vase, but scentless and only reliable as a garden rose in warm climates. Foliage is rich green and glossy, with plum tints in the young growth.

Unnamed seedling × unnamed seedling
Repeat flowering

'Salet'
Moss

Most writers on the Old Garden Roses are inclined to be disparaging about 'Salet', and it is true that there are classier roses available and that the buds are not particularly mossy. Yet the clear bright pink blooms, ruffled and fragrant, do have considerable charm, and they are borne in great abundance throughout the season. This is by far the most reliably repeat flowering of the Moss Roses. The bush is Cluster-flowered size, with few thorns and pale green leaves. An 1854 creation of François Lacharme of Lyon, it has recently been used in the breeding of modern Moss Roses.

Parentage unknown
Repeat flowering
Fragrant

'Sally Holmes'
Modern Shrub

'Sally Holmes' is a much admired rose for the great beauty of its almost single, ivory-white flowers, large and slightly fragrant. They are borne sometimes in huge, tightly packed clusters. Sometimes the clusters are smaller and more widely spaced, which shows off the beauty of the flowers to better advantage. Some thinning of the buds in the larger trusses can improve the effect. Foliage is dark green and glossy. It was raised by an English amateur hybridist called Holmes and introduced in 1976. Expect it to grow to just under 2 metres (6 feet) tall and to be densely bushy.

'Ivory Fashion' × 'Ballerina'
Repeat flowering

◀ 'Sabrina'
▼ 'Sally Holmes'

▶ 'Samba'
▼ 'Salet'

▲ 'Salmon Sorbet'

'Salmon Sorbet'
Cluster-flowered

A very pretty striped rose from Bear Creek Nurseries in California, 'Salmon Sorbet' displays its coral and white blooms, usually with a few stripes of pale pink thrown in, in small clusters on a lowish, compact bush. The size of the bush is a great asset, making it easier to place the rose in the garden and arrange companion plantings that it will not upstage. Scent is a pleasing bonus in this 1991 introduction. Foliage is dark green and leathery.

Parentage undisclosed
Repeat flowering
Fragrant

'Samba'
Cluster-flowered

KORcapas

Reimer Kordes has not registered the parentage of 'Samba', a 1964 introduction, but from the look of the rose, and the name, it is probably a seedling of 'Rumba'. It is very like 'Rumba' in its colors—yellow going orange and red—but the flowers are a little larger and the clusters smaller. The Kordes catalogue claims it to be superior for

▲ 'San Francisco'

growing under glass as a cut flower. This would seem to be its main use, as it is rarely seen as a garden rose. Foliage is glossy.

Parentage undisclosed
Repeat flowering

'Samourai' — Large-flowered
MEIelec
'Scarlet Knight'
To name a rose for Japan's knights of old is not as odd as it might seem, for many of the samurai passed their time between heroic deeds cultivating flowers, especially the Higo camellias. 'Scarlet Knight' is apt too, for the big completely flat flowers are pure scarlet, taking on velvety, darker tones in the sun. The bush is sturdy, of average height, and despite a slight tendency to mildew, a very reliable performer. The handsome foliage is bright green and leathery. 'Samourai' was introduced by Alain Meilland in 1968 and won the AARS award that year. There is only a faint scent.

'Happiness' × 'Independence'
Repeat flowering

► 'Sander's White'
▼ 'Samourai'

'San Francisco' — Large-flowered
This rose was photographed in the public rose gardens in Oakland, across the bay from its namesake city. The large flowers are usually borne in clusters, to 10–13 centimetres (4–5 inches) across, opening sometimes high-centred, sometimes cupped, from ovoid buds and giving a stronger fragrance than is usual from roses of its bright red color. The bushes are strong and healthy, with dark green, leathery foliage. 'San Francisco' was raised in 1952 by Dr Walter Lammerts and introduced in 1952.

'Dean Collins' × 'Independence'
Repeat flowering
Fragrant

'Sander's White' — Rambler
'Sander's White Rambler'
Since its introduction in 1912, 'Sander's White' has generally been accepted as the very best white Rambler. So it should. It is not unmanageably vigorous, its leaves are dark green, glossy and healthy, and the small flowers are pure in tone and fragrant as well. It makes a perfect weeping standard, and is a good choice for a pergola, the flowers hanging down so that you can see them. It flowers late, and does not repeat. Its origin is unknown. It was introduced by the famous firm of orchid growers, Messrs Sander of St Albans, who apparently had no idea where they got it from.

Parentage undisclosed
Summer flowering
Fragrant

'Sangria'
Cluster-flowered

MEIestho

The name dates this rose, for sangria, a Spanish drink blending red wine and fruit juice, was a fad of the 1960s. It is rare now, and so is the rose, a Meilland introduction of 1966. This is a colorful garden rose, with large trusses of smallish, semi-double flowers with ruffled petals and little fragrance. The color was officially described as orange-red, but it actually blends red with orange and so the name was appropriate. Foliage is dark green.

'Fire King' × ('Happiness' × 'Independence')
Repeat flowering

 'Sangria'
▼ 'Santa Fé'

'Sanguinea'
China

'Miss Lowe's Variety', 'Bengal Rose', 'La Sarguine', 'Bengal Cramoisi Double'

Most of the reference books accept 'Sanguinea' and 'Miss Lowe's Variety' as being the same, though some consider that 'Sanguinea' is rather larger and has darker crimson flowers. It is single-flowered, not very fragrant, and bears small clusters of flowers from spring to first frost. The centre of the flower is white. Like most of the China Roses it blooms all year in a frost-free climate. The bush is about the size of a modern Bush Rose, with pale green foliage, which has red tints in its youth. It is thought to be a sport from 'Slater's Crimson China', the original Crimson China with double flowers, long believed extinct, but now rediscovered.

Sport from 'Slater's Crimson China'
Repeat flowering

'Santa Catalina'
Large-flowered Climber

From a cross of the deep pink Cluster-flowered Rose 'Paddy McGredy' and the red Modern Shrub Rose 'Heidelberg', one would expect a dark toned rose. Sam McGredy must have been surprised when 'Santa Catalina' turned out to be pale pink, with just the occasional deeper flush, and that it was a Climber as well, though a shrubby one. It blooms well all season; the flowers are almost of Large-flowered Rose size and fragrant; and the foliage is notably dark green and glossy. Some find the foliage too glossy and think it is inclined to upstage the delicate tones of the flowers.

'Paddy McGredy' × 'Heidelberg'
Fragrant

'Santa Fé'
Cluster-flowered

'All the health and vigor of its mother "Super Star" and the charming grace of its father "Mischief",' enthused the McGredy catalogue when Sam introduced 'Santa Fé' in 1967. Regrettably, it has not inherited the beautiful luminosity of color of either of its parents, however: it is a rather bland shade of deep salmon-pink. It is a good grower, nevertheless, with leathery, bronze-green leaves, and the flowers are large and quite shapely enough for exhibition. It likes a cool climate. There is no fragrance.

'Super Star' × 'Mischief'
Repeat flowering

▲ 'Sanguinea'
▼ 'Santa Catalina'

▼ 'Santa Maria'

'Santa Maria'
Cluster-flowered

The Columbus quincentennial might create a revival of interest in this 1969 McGredy creation, but where will the marketing people buy their plants of 'Santa Maria'? It has disappeared from the world's catalogues. If they do find it, they will be rewarded by masses of bright orange-red flowers, borne on compact bushes with dark green foliage, maroon-tinted in its youth.

'Evelyn Fison' × ('Ma Perkins' × 'Moulin Rouge')
Repeat flowering

▲ 'Sarah Arnot'
▼ 'Sarabande'

'Sarah Arnot' — Large-flowered

Hailed in Britain when it was first introduced in 1956 as one of the most perfect Large-flowered Roses since the war, 'Sarah Arnot' has never found the same favor elsewhere, possibly because it inherits from 'Ena Harkness' a preference for cool climates. At its best it is indeed a lovely rose, large, shapely and fragrant, and a beautiful shade of rose-pink. The plant is bushy, with handsome green foliage. The raiser was D. W. Croll of Aberdeen. The RNRS bestowed its gold medal in 1956.

'Ena Harkness' × 'Peace'
Repeat flowering
Fragrant

'Sarah Van Fleet' — Hybrid Rugosa

Although 'Sarah Van Fleet' is as bushy as can be, it grows very tall, to 3 metres (6 feet), and it is not always clad with foliage to the base. Plant it at the back of the border, with other things in front to hide its legs, and you can enjoy the bronze young leaves, which mature light green, and the masses of loosely double, scented blooms in pale, cool pink. Though some authorities dispute the stated parentage, it looks to be halfway between the two types, and has inherited much of the Rugosa habit and toughness. The raiser was Walter Van Fleet, the year of introduction, 1926. It flowers all season.

Rosa rugosa × 'My Maryland'
Repeat flowering
Fragrant

'Saratoga' — Cluster-flowered

The AARS winner for 1964, and for a while one of the most popular white roses, 'Saratoga' has been losing ground in recent years to 'Iceberg'. But it

▲ 'Sarah Van Fleet'
▼ 'Saratoga'

'Sarabande' — Cluster-flowered

MEIhand, MEIrabande

This is one of the great Meilland roses, notable for its flaming scarlet color, its healthy and even growth, its resistance to disease, and its abundant flowering. It was raised in 1957 and won the AARS in 1960, but the rise of the Cluster-flowered Roses having exhibition-style flowers since then has robbed it of popularity, for its flowers are almost single. They are very elegant, open slowly and last well in the vase. Foliage is mid-green and semi-glossy. The Sarabande is an old Spanish dance.

'Cocorico' × 'Moulin Rouge'
Repeat flowering

remains a desirable rose, less robust than 'Iceberg' perhaps, but with larger individual blooms, shapely, fragrant, and often brushed with cream in the bud. Foliage is mid-green, glossy and leathery. Raised by Eugene Boerner, it was introduced by Jackson & Perkins in 1963. Saratoga is a town in the Hudson Valley, the site of a famous engagement in the American War of Independence, and also the town where the raiser spent his holidays.

'White Bouquet' × 'Princess White'
Repeat flowering
Fragrant

'Satchmo' Cluster-flowered

Although Sam McGredy considers that his 'Satchmo' (1971) has been superseded by its seedling 'Trumpeter' (1977), also named in honor of the great jazz musician Louis Armstrong, this older rose still has plenty of admirers for its bright scarlet color, its shapely clusters and its freedom of bloom. It is a compact and healthy grower, with bright green, shiny foliage, plum tinted in its youth. Its faults, admittedly minor, are a tendency for the old flowers to darken unevenly and a certain slowness in repeat flowering. There is not much in the way of fragrance.

'Evelyn Fison' × 'Diamant'
Repeat flowering

▶ 'Scarlet Queen Elizabeth'

▲ 'Scarlet Fire'
◀ 'Satchmo'

'Scarlet Fire' Gallica
'Scharlachglut'

The admirers of 'Scarlet Fire' enthuse over the exciting summer display of dazzling velvet-red blooms, large and perfect in their five-petalled symmetry. Its detractors point out that it is a very large and thorny shrub, at least 2.5 metres (8 feet) each way, that there is little scent and that the space it occupies could be given to two or three more compact, and repeat-flowering, Modern Shrub Roses. It all depends on how much garden room you have. Foliage is ashen green. A Wilhelm Kordes introduction of 1952, it has fine hips.

'Alika' × 'Poinsettia'
Summer flowering

'Scarlet Queen Elizabeth' Cluster-flowered

'That's just what it is,' burbled the catalogues in 1963, 'the wonderful "Queen Elizabeth" in red.' Well, that is what it is not. It is certainly as vigorous and easy to grow, but where 'Queen Elizabeth' is upright, 'Scarlet Queen Elizabeth' is lax in growth. The orange-red flowers are smaller and shapeless. They look well,

however, against bronze-green leaves that retain the mahogany tint of youth well into old age. Though quite scentless, this is a good rose for a position where you want a really hot-colored shrub. It was raised by Patrick Dickson.

Seedling from 'Korona' × 'Queen Elizabeth'
Repeat flowering

'Scherzo' Cluster-flowered
MEIpuma

The truly bicolored Cluster-flowered Roses, as distinct from the many blends, have not been popular, perhaps because the contrast between the upper and lower surfaces of the petals is not so well displayed as in a large flower, and is lost in a cluster of fully opened blooms. 'Molly McGredy', in pink and white, and 'Scherzo', in orange-red and white, are the best of them. 'Scherzo' is a very good rose, its individual flowers shapely, though not

▲ 'Scherzo'

fragrant, and carried in abundance on an upright, bushy plant, with dark green foliage, plum tinted in its youth. It was raised by Marie-Louisette Meilland and introduced in 1971.

'Tamango' × 'Prince Igor'
Repeat flowering

'Schneelicht' Hybrid Rugosa

David Austin, with his 'English Roses', had a nineteenth-century forerunner in the Hungarian Geschwind of Karpona, who raised a series of *Rosa rugosa* × *R. multiflora* hybrids which he called 'Hungarian Roses'. 'Schneelicht', meaning 'snow light', of 1894 is the only one you are likely to see today. It is a great mounding bush with dark green, rugose foliage and sprays of large single flowers in early summer. It can be used as a tallish ground cover, over an area about 3 metres (10 feet) square, or it can be trained to make a thorny hedge.

R. rugosa × unknown Musk Rose
Repeat flowering
Fragrant

'Schneezwerg' Hybrid Rugosa
'Snow Dwarf'

Do not be misled by the name: this is a tall rose. Pruning will keep it both shorter and compact. It is a very popular shrub with landscape designers in Europe as it combines toughness and hardiness with a long flowering season and a surprising daintiness of appearance. Foliage is a lush bright green and not as rugose as usual. It is best in the autumn, or fall, when the shining white flowers with their golden stamens are accompanied by round orange hips. The smallish, dark leaves turn gold before they fall for the winter. It is credited to Peter Lambert in 1921.

Thought to be *Rosa rugosa* × *R. bracteata*
Repeat flowering
Fragrant

▼ 'Schneezwerg'

▲ 'Schneelicht'
▶ 'Schweizergrüss'

'Schweizer Gold' Large-flowered
'Swiss Gold'

Raised by Reimer Kordes in 1972 and then distributed by Adolph Horstmann, 'Schweizer Gold' combines good high-centred form with long petals, in a large bloom of mid-yellow which deepens towards the centre. Foliage is matt, light green and plentiful, the bush strong. There is quite a good fragrance. This is a rose for cool climates. Baden Baden, where it won the gold medal in 1972, though not one of the colder parts of Germany, is still very cool.

'Königin der Rosen' × 'Peer Gynt'
Repeat flowering
Fragrant

'Schweizergrüss' Cluster-flowered
TANschweigru

'Red Favourite', 'Holländerin', 'Salut à la Suisse'
For many years this was the favorite red Cluster-flowered Rose everywhere, and it is still widely planted, despite the competition from so many newcomers. Individually the blooms are nothing much, being on the small side and scentless, but they are freely borne in large clusters, and hold their strong dark color very well. The plants are

rather tall, with leaden green leaves and many thorns. You need to give them some extra water and fertiliser after bloom or they can be sluggish to repeat. It has been a great success for Mathias Tantau, who raised it and introduced it in 1964.

'Karl Weinhausen' × 'Tantau's Triumph'
Repeat flowering

'Scintillation' Modern Shrub

Raised by David Austin, but not classed among his English Roses, 'Scintillation' is not repeat flowering, but its summer season is unusually long, and the sight of its low, wide bush covered in single blooms is very attractive. They are softly scented, and palest pink, with a distinct lilac flush on the outer petals. It would be tempting to use 'Scintillation' for ground cover but it is not quite dense enough. Allow it to sprawl among other flowers. Foliage is dark green and matt. It was introduced in 1967.

Rosa macrantha × 'Vanity'
Summer flowering

◀ 'Schweizer Gold'
▼ 'Scintillation'

by an American called Schwartz and introduced in 1964. There was another 'Sea Foam', from William Paul in 1919, said to be a seedling of 'Mermaid'.

(['White Dawn' × 'Pinocchio'] × ['White Dawn' × 'Pinocchio']) × ('White Dawn' × 'Pinocchio')
Repeat flowering

'Scorcher' — Large-flowered Climber

The name, however apt it may have seemed to Australian raiser Alister Clark when he bestowed it in 1922, seems a bit exaggerated nowadays by comparison with such scorching colors as those of 'Altissimo' or 'Danse du Feu'. 'Scorcher' is just a deep, strawberry-pink or cherry-red. The bush in full spring bloom (there are, unfortunately, no later flowers) is cheerful enough, and the almost-single flowers are individually quite pretty. Foliage is large, wrinkled and mid-green. Lack of scent is a demerit, which may prevent this rose from regaining popularity even among patriotic Australian gardeners.

Seedling from 'Madame Abel Chatenay'
Spring flowering

'Scotch Yellow' — Scotch

There are in fact several double yellow forms of *Rosa pimpinellifolia* flowering cheerfully away in gardens, oblivious to the confusion over what their proper names might be. 'Scotch Yellow' is really just a flag of convenience. They are all charmers, with the typical neat low growth and fine foliage of all the Scotch Roses, and with smallish, bright yellow flowers in spring. *R. pimpinellifolia* itself does have cream color forms in the wild, but most of the 'Scotch Yellows' are thought to derive their bright color from *R. foetida*.

Forms of *R. pimpinellifolia*
Spring flowering
Fragrant

'Sea Foam' — Ground Cover

'Sea Foam' is usually used as a ground cover. It is a rather short growing Rambler, its branches only being about a metre (3 feet) long—not long enough to be much use for covering a wall, but enough to make a pretty weeping standard. The flowers are Rambler-like, many petalled in bunches. They are white and slightly scented. Unlike most Ramblers, they are borne repeatedly, against small, dark green, glossy foliage. This pretty and useful rose was raised

'Sea Pearl' — Large-flowered

'Flower Girl'

'Sea Pearl' remains popular in Europe, and the ARS rates it highly. It has never really been a hit in Australia, probably because its delicate coral-pink and cream colors bleach under the hot sun. The long, shapely buds open to quite large blooms, usually in clusters of five or so; there is some fragrance; and the bush is tall and strong, with dark green foliage. In the old days it would probably have passed as a decorative Large-flowered Rose, and it is indeed the child of two Large-flowered Roses. It was introduced by Dickson in 1964.

'Kordes Perfecta' × 'Montezuma'
Repeat flowering
Fragrant

▲ 'Sea Foam'
▼ 'Sea Pearl'

▲ 'Scotch Yellow'
◄ 'Scorcher'

'Seagull'
Rambler

From the time of its introduction by the English grower Pritchard in 1907 until the establishment of 'Sander's White' as the public's favorite, 'Seagull' was unquestionably the best white Rambler. It is effectively a double-flowered version of *Rosa multiflora*, with the species' ability to do well in difficult conditions. It has fresh green foliage and a strong, sweet perfume. In its summer season, the vigorous plant covers itself with huge trusses of blooms, their petallage not so full as to hide their almost-orange stamens. It was not derived from a thornless form of *R. multiflora*, however, and there are prickles!

R. multiflora × 'Général Jacqueminot'
Summer flowering
Fragrant

▲ 'Seagull'
▶ 'Seashell'

'Seashell'
Large-flowered

Despite winning the 1976 AARS award, 'Seashell' has been criticized for its susceptibility to black spot. There has been only praise for its blooms, however, which are large and beautifully formed, the petals overlapping with the regularity of the tiles on a roof. The color is lovely, a clear shade of coral-pink, sometimes deeper at the petal edges, lit with gold. There is a slight tea fragrance. The foliage is dark green and glossy. It was created by Reimer Kordes and introduced in 1974.

Unnamed seedling × 'Königin der Rosen'
Repeat flowering

'Serenade'
Large-flowered

The books always describe 'Serenade' as coral-orange, which suggests something in the manner of 'Super Star', but it is really much more delicate than that, a blend of coral-pinks. The blooms are neither large nor full of petals, but they are produced with freedom over a long season, on a sturdy bush with matt green foliage, richly bronzed in its youth. The raiser was Eugene Boerner and Jackson & Perkins introduced it in 1949. You may have to search the catalogues to find it now.

'Sonata' × 'Mrs H. A. Verschuren'
Repeat flowering

'Serratipetala'
China

'Rose Oeillet de Saint Arquey'

The French name suggests that the flowers look like carnations, and indeed they do, with their serrated petals. The color is interesting: the inner petals are candy-pink, the outer ones are dark crimson. These unique blooms are borne in small clusters throughout the season, but never very freely, and the bush is inclined to be scrawny, with glossy dark green leaves. It is definitely a rose for the specialist. There is little scent. Its origin is unknown but it is thought to be French-bred some time early in the twentieth century.

Parentage unknown
Repeat flowering

▲ 'Serenade'
▼ 'Serratipetala'

▲ 'Shades of Pink'

'Shades of Pink' Cluster-flowered

This is a vigorous rose, with fine trusses of bloom and flowers blending several shades of pink. It was raised by a British Columbian rose-lover, George Mander, in 1985. The parentage, 'Robin Hood' crossed with 'Pascali', is not as odd as it might look: Reimer Kordes had crossed 'Robin Hood' with the best white rose of the day back in 1958 and the result was 'Iceberg'. Mander has not quite repeated that triumph, but 'Shades of Pink' is worthy of being better known. Foliage is mid-green and glossy.

'Robin Hood' × 'Pascali'
Repeat flowering

▲ 'Seven Sisters'

'Seven Sisters' Rambler

Rosa multiflora platyphylla

This is an old Oriental rose, thought to have been brought to Europe from Japan in about 1816. The name is probably a translation from the Japanese. There are usually many more than seven blooms in each cluster, and each is different in color. They open almost purple, then fade through pink to white before the petals drop. In the days of its introduction to the West, there were few richly colored climbing roses, and even now when we have so many, a plant of 'Seven Sisters', smothered in softly scented blooms in their varied colors, is a charming sight indeed. Foliage is broad and a lush bright green. Give it a sheltered spot as it is rather sensitive to cold.

Parentage unknown
Summer flowering
Fragrant

'Shady Lady' Cluster-flowered

MEIcaso

This rose has been credited to an Australian amateur gardener by some writers, but Meilland also claims it. In itself it is not all that startling, with sprays of small, scentless flowers in carmine with white in the centre, but it has the almost unique character of being able to grow and flower well in shade. Deane Ross, Meilland's agent in Adelaide, proves the point with a bed sited beneath a willow tree. That was where the picture was taken. Foliage is bright green. It was introduced in 1987.

Parentage unknown
Repeat flowering

'Shannon' Large-flowered

MACnon

It is unclear whether Sam McGredy named this rose after Ireland's longest river or its major airport; either way it is a graceful tribute. Some people consider it superior to its parent 'Queen Elizabeth': the flowers are larger and better formed, and the plant less sky-scraping in habit. The color is not quite the same: there is more salmon in it. Alas, it has no more scent. It is not so

▲ 'Shady Lady'
▼ 'Sexy Rexy'

'Sexy Rexy' Cluster-flowered

MACrexy

Fancy calling an innocently blushing rose like this 'Sexy Rexy'! Forget the name, and admire the perfect symmetry of the flowers, their delicate shell-pink color, their elusive scent and the freedom with which the short, neat bush bears them. Foliage is bright green and glossy with red tints when young. It was introduced in 1984.

'Seaspray' × 'Dreaming'
Repeat flowering
Fragrant

▲ 'Shannon'
▶ 'Sheer Bliss'

'Sheer Elegance' — Large-flowered
TWObe

The American AARS award should guarantee a rose that will do well just about anywhere, but 'Sheer Elegance', the 1989 winner, seems to be establishing a marked preference for cooler climates. Where it does well, it justifies its name—the blooms are shapely indeed, with strongly reflexed petals, in pale rose-pink with the petal edges darkening a little as the flower matures. The bush is strong, with leathery foliage. 'Sheer Elegance' was raised by a new name on the rose-breeding scene, a man named Twomey.

Parentage undisclosed
Repeat flowering

sturdy and adaptable as its parent. Foliage is dark green and leathery. It is definitely a rose for cool climates. Sam McGredy introduced it in 1965.

'Queen Elizabeth' × 'McGredy's Yellow'
Repeat flowering

'Sharon Louise' — Large-flowered

'Sharon Louise' is a good rose that has never got the publicity it should. Introduced in 1969, it still pleases with its regular symmetry, its tender coloring, its delicate fragrance and with its willingness to grow and flower freely, even in a difficult climate. Foliage is dark and leathery. The raiser was an Australian, H. H. Parkes.

'Peace' × 'Virgo'
Repeat flowering
Fragrant

▶ 'Sheer Elegance'
▼ 'Sharon Louise'

'Sheer Bliss' — Large-flowered
JACtro

This winner of the 1987 AARS award is aptly named: the blooms are delightful, whether in their long and elegant youth or when they have opened out to silky looseness. They are of the palest of pale pinks, almost white, but shaded deeper in their hearts, and there is a most pleasing spicy fragrance. The bush is strong and dense, with matt dark green foliage and brown prickles. 'Sheer Bliss' was raised by Bill Warriner and is a lovely rose for cutting and arranging in a silver vase.

'White Masterpiece' × 'Golden Masterpiece'
Repeat flowering
Fragrant

'Sheila's Perfume'
Cluster-flowered

HARsherry

The Sheila in question is an English-woman, the wife of the raiser, John Sheridan. 'Sheila's Perfume' is much praised as one of the few bicolored roses with scent, albeit rather faint. It is not a classic bicolor, rather yellow with a red border. It is a nice rose, however, with large and shapely flowers on an upright bush with handsome plum-tinted dark green leaves. It was introduced by the Harkness firm in 1985.

'Peer Gynt' × seedling from 'Daily Sketch'
Repeat flowering
Fragrant

▲ 'Sheila's Perfume'

'Sherry'
Cluster-flowered

The name is appropriate: the brownish orange flowers are like an *amoroso* sherry in color. The golden stamens save the flowers from dullness in the garden, but this is essentially a rose for the flower arranger. It is a tallish bush, with dark green foliage, but is an erratic performer, sometimes magnificent, at others spindly and shy with its blooms. It is a McGredy introduction of 1960 and is a sister of the better-known 'Orangeade'.

'Independence' × 'Orange Sweetheart'
Repeat flowering

'Shining Hour'
Large-flowered

JACref

It is a little early yet to say whether this 1989 AARS winner will establish itself as one of the top yellow roses, but it certainly looks pretty good so far. There are not many petals, but they make up a shapely bloom, and their unusual pointed form gives the flower

▲ 'Shining Hour'
► 'Shot Silk'

a distinctive outline. It was raised by Bill Warriner, which should give cause for confidence. Foliage is bright green and glossy.

'Sunbright' × 'Sun Flare'
Repeat flowering

'Shocking Blue'
Cluster-flowered

KORblue

The color is shocking indeed, but it is more magenta than blue! The flowers are of fine shape and good size and are very heavily perfumed as well. Disbudded, it is a popular florist's rose. The bush is on the tall side, with shiny, dark green leaves. The rose has the reputation of being both prolific and continuous in flower. It may miss the ethereal touch of such roses as 'Blue Moon', but is a fine rose nevertheless. It was raised by Reimer Kordes and introduced in 1974.

Unnamed seedling × 'Silver Star'
Repeat flowering
Fragrant

► 'Shocking Blue'
▼ 'Sherry'

'Shot Silk'
Large-flowered

Alex Dickson, father of Patrick, was once asked which of his roses was his favorite. The reply was unhesitating: 'Shot Silk', introduced in 1924. The upright bushes are attractive for their shining emerald-green foliage alone, and the many flowers are of great beauty in their neat shape, their brilliant pink underlaid with gold, and their rich fragrance. The climbing sport is still popular and worthwhile.

'Hugh Dickson' × 'Sunstar'
Repeat flowering
Fragrant

'Shot Silk, Climbing' Large-flowered Climber

The climbing version is as good as the bush. It is vigorous enough for the façade of a two-storey house, which it will adorn with beautiful shining foliage and a great display of sweetly fragrant blooms early in the season. Opinions vary regarding its repeat performance, some finding it generous, others niggardly. It does best in a cool climate; heat tends to bleach the color.

Sport from 'Shot Silk'
Repeat flowering
Fragrant

▲ 'Show Girl'
▼ 'Climbing Shot Silk'

'Show Girl' Large-flowered

More like a refined ballerina than a brassy showgirl, this beautiful rose was raised by Walter Lammerts in 1946. Its high-centred, deep rose-pink blooms are buxom enough for exhibition, and heavily fragrant; they are borne on long stems on an upright plant with leathery, mid-green foliage. 'Show Girl' was awarded a gold medal from the ARS, though rather late in the day, in 1988. You may need to watch out for mildew in hot climates.

'Charlotte Armstrong' × 'Crimson Glory'
Repeat flowering
Fragrant

'Showbiz' Cluster-flowered

TANweike
'Ingrid Weibull', 'Bernhard Daneke Rose'
'Showbiz' won the AARS award for 1985 and has been busy building up a reputation as one of the best of all roses for making what a decorator would call 'a strong red statement'. It is a low bush, with dark green, glossy foliage, covering itself with masses of smallish, fluorescent red flowers. It is quick to repeat. It is a little like 'Europeana', but the color is not nearly so dark, nor does it have the striking young foliage. It does appear to be unusually resistant to mildew, the scourge of the red Cluster-flowered Roses. It is a 1981 Mathias Tantau introduction.

Parentage undisclosed
Repeat flowering

'Showoff' Large-flowered

ARowago
'Showoff' was raised in 1986 by Jack Christensen, but it seems to have vanished from the catalogues already. Is it perhaps that Christensen has not yet got around to introducing it? The blooms are as red as can be, with silver blended into the reverses of the thirty-five petals, and they are large, brilliant and shapely, if not very fragrant. The bush is average in height, with dark green leaves. Do not confuse this rose with an earlier 'Show Off', a red climber of 1952.

'Typhoo Tea' × 'Snowfire'
Repeat flowering

▲ 'Showbiz'
▼ 'Showoff'

A GREAT ROSE GARDEN: THE ROSERAIE DE L'HAŸ

Queen Mary's Rose Garden in London; the Parque de Oeste in Madrid; Washington Park in Portland, Oregon; the rose gardens at Sissinghurst Castle and Mottisfont Abbey in the English countryside; and Carrick Hill Gardens and Werribee Park in the very different landscape of Australia. The list could go on for pages, but of all the world's beautiful rose gardens, one of the very best must be the Roseraie de l'Haÿ just outside Paris.

Part of the charm of Roseraie de l'Haÿ is that it is devoted so exclusively to the rose. Here there is none of the artful blending of roses with other flowers such as one sees at, say, Sissinghurst or the Planten and Blumen in Munich; here no other plants are admitted than grass and the neatly clipped box that lines the beds. Everywhere you look there is nothing but a profusion of roses.

In this the garden reflects its creator, Jules Gravereaux, a *roso-mane* (a 'rose maniac') if ever there was one. Having made a fortune as one of the founding partners in Le Bon Marché, the great Parisian department store, Gravereaux retired in 1892 to a country estate at l'Haÿ. His interest in the roses there developed into an all-consuming passion. Not only did he plant them by the thousand, so that by 1900 he had over 3000 varieties, he also collected works of art, books and memorabilia featuring roses. In 1899, he commissioned landscape architect Edouard André to design the garden as we see it today, to be a living museum of all the world's roses.

In this ambition he was consciously following in the footsteps of the Empress Joséphine, to whom he paid tribute by gathering all the roses known to survive from her collection,

197 of them, and planting them in his Malmaison Border, still one of the highlights of the garden.

The fame of the Gravereaux roses was such that in 1914 the inhabitants of l'Haÿ were granted the right to an augmentation of the name. The town is now called l'Haÿ-les-Roses. After M. Gravereaux's death in 1916, the estate passed to his heirs, who sold it to the French State in 1937. It is now looked after, beautifully, by the parks and gardens authorities of the city of Paris.

It is not only lovers of roses who should see the Roseraie de l'Haÿ, for in its perfectly balanced formality it is one of the great examples of the Second Empire style (albeit a few years late) in garden design. Not all that large as French gardens go, covering about 2 hectares (5 acres), it is laid out around a central axis culminating in the famous trellised pavilion which shelters a single statue. From the central pavilion, wings adorned with marble urns spread out to embrace an oval space centred on a pool. With boldness and restraint, the entire structure is covered with a single variety of Rambler, the glowing pink 'Alexandre Girault' being the chosen rose.

From here paths radiate, crossed by others to create secondary vistas and compartments, each of which is planted to show some aspect of the rose's history: the Malmaison borders; a section devoted to Hybrid Perpetuals; one to roses grown for the florists' shops; one for Modern Garden Roses no longer in commerce (you will find several of these among the portraits in this book); and collections of species and Old Garden Roses, as well as the very latest introductions. Everywhere there are Climber Roses and Ramblers, trained on

▲ *The statue is of Cupid, and where should Love be better housed than among roses?*

◄ *The great trellis forms the centrepiece of the garden. It is entirely covered with the Rambler 'Alexandre Girault' whose flowers, blending copper and gold, seem a shimmering pink from a distance. The beds in front contain Modern Garden Roses.*

► *These arches bear some of the most photographed roses in the world. They exemplify the great skill with which this garden has been laid out, for while pergola-shaded paths have been featured in large gardens since the days of the Romans, this series of separate arches shows off roses better than a continuous roof does.*

▲ *The splendid cultivar of Rosa rugosa raised by M. Cochet and named in honor of this garden, 'Roseraie de l'Haÿ'.*

▼ *A collection of French-bred roses that are no longer in commerce is preserved in a small garden of its own. Here may be found such beauties as this one, 'Pièce d'Or', waiting for the day when rose-lovers may again want to plant them.*

pillars, in festoons, garlanding urns and statues, all immaculately groomed, with never a leaf or flower out of place.

The effect of so many roses of all types and colors cheek by jowl could be dazzling and indigestible, but they are flattered both by the firm framework of box hedges which outline the beds and the backdrop of magnificent deciduous trees in the park beyond. Few of us would grow roses so single-mindedly or on such a scale, but this garden points up one great lesson in their use: give them a strong green frame rather than the 'setting' of ill-assorted brickwork, concrete driveway and spotty mixed shrubbery that they so often have in suburban gardens.

Alas, the museum which once displayed a collection of artworks and books featuring roses, the greatest in the world, is no more: thieves broke into the building in 1980 and as yet nothing has been recovered.

If you are lucky enough to be in Paris in June, do not miss seeing the Roseraie: catch the Metro to Bourg-la-reine, and then it is a short bus ride to the gates.

'Shreveport' — Large-flowered

The ARS has its offices in Shreveport, Louisiana, in the midst of gardens that are planted with many thousands of roses. The 'Shreveport' rose, named in its honor, is German-bred by Reimer Kordes. It won the 1982 AARS award as a 'Grandiflora'; the shapely blooms do tend to come in small clusters. They are a blend of orange and salmon-pink, have a light tea fragrance, and are borne on strong but not overly tall bushes, with dark olive-green foliage. It is an excellent rose for cutting.

'Zorina' × 'Uwe Seeler'
Repeat flowering

'Shropshire Lass' — English Rose

In the old days, 'Shropshire Lass' would have been called a 'Hybrid Alba'. Its raiser, David Austin classes it with his English Roses, though it is not repeat flowering. It would make a pleasing companion for his 'Constance Spry'. Like it, it can be grown as a large shrub or a climber, but it is more compact in growth, with lush, mid-green foliage, and the flowers are a trifle smaller and almost single. They are blush-white. Fragrance is sweet, and the plant tough and hardy. In this 1968 creation, Austin honors the English County where he has lived all his life.

'Madame Butterfly' × 'Madame Legras de Saint-Germain'
Summer flowering
Fragrant

'Sierra Glow' — Large-flowered

A blend of sunset-pinks, the thirty-petalled blooms of 'Sierra Glow' open from long buds, and are carried on fine long stems for cutting, on a vigorous and prolific bush, with mid-green, leathery foliage. It was raised by Dr Walter Lammerts, introduced in 1942, and was popular in the United States in the 1950s and early '60s, but you do not often see it now. It came from the same cross, but in the reverse order, that produced Dr Lammerts's epoch-making 'Charlotte Armstrong'.

'Crimson Glory' × 'Soeur Thérèse'
Repeat flowering
Fragrant

▲ 'Shreveport'

▲ 'Shropshire Lass'
▼ 'Sierra Glow'

'Signora Piero Puricelli' — Large-flowered
'Signora'

A most important parent, 'Signora', as she is affectionately known, is still a desirable rose, even if her ability to shake off black spot is not what it used to be. The foliage is dark green, red-tinted and glossy, and the tea-scented blooms open wide to display a splendid blend of red, orange and gold. It was introduced in 1937 by Italy's Domenico Aicardi. In my younger days, two of Signor Aicardi's other roses were very popular: the deep pink 'Gloria di Roma' and the huge, dawn-pink 'Eterna Giovanezza' ('Eternal Youth').

'Julien Potin' × 'Sensation'
Repeat flowering
Fragrant

▲ 'Signora Piero Puricelli'
▼ 'Silent Night'

'Silent Night' — Large-flowered

The name has nothing to do with Christmas carols. Raiser Sam McGredy's sponsor for this 1969 introduction was a British maker of mattresses. The flowers are profuse, large and nicely formed, the color soft yellow tinted pink, and foliage is dark green, with a hint of red when young. 'Silent Night' won the Geneva gold medal in 1969.

'Daily Sketch' × 'Hassan'
Repeat flowering

▲ 'Silk Hat'

▲ 'Silver Lining'
▼ 'Silver Jubilee'

'Silk Hat' — Large-flowered
AROsitha

A gentleman's silk hat is usually black, but this rose is a mixture of American beauty red and cream. This rose was raised by Jack Christensen in 1985 and it is a beauty. The fifty-petalled blooms of exhibition form are produced by a bushy yet upright plant with large, mid-green leaves. The flowers have a good fragrance.

'Night 'n' Day' × 'Plain Talk'
Repeat flowering
Fragrant

'Silver Jubilee' — Large-flowered

In earlier days, there was a pale yellow Large-flowered Rose called 'Silver Jubilee', introduced by Alex Dickson in 1937. The universally admired modern bearer of the name came from another Alexander, Alec Cocker in 1977. Its only fault is lack of scent. The flowers, in a lovely blend of soft pinks, are large, high centred and shapely, and the bush is excellent, compact yet very strong, with luxuriant bright green, glossy foliage. It is strongly disease resistant. These are good habits derived ultimately from the Climber *Rosa kordesii*, which lies in the background of the unnamed seedling that was pollinated by 'Mischief'. Many rosarians consider 'Silver Jubilee' to be the finest Large-flowered Rose since 'Peace'.

(['Highlight' × 'Colour Wonder'] × ['Parkdirektor Riggers' × 'Piccadilly']) × 'Mischief'
Repeat flowering

'Silver Lining' — Large-flowered

The name describes it well, but the color of 'Silver Lining' varies very much with the seasons. Sometimes it is an overall silvery pink, at others much brighter so that it is almost a pink and silver bicolor. But the perfect form is constant and so is the sweet fragrance. (This is an outstanding exhibition rose.) The bush is sturdy, with dark green polished foliage, and for such a large rose flowers very freely. It was raised in 1958 by Alex Dickson and was one of the last triumphs of a long career. In the hands of his son Patrick, 'Silver Lining' has given rise to a fine line of red Large-flowered Roses, from 'Red Devil' to 'Precious Platinum'.

'Karl Herbst' × seedling from 'Eden Rose'
Repeat flowering
Fragrant

▲ 'Silver Moon'
▼ 'Simplicity'

'Silver Moon' — Large-flowered

'The perfect choice,' writes Peter Mallins of Brooklyn Botanic Garden, 'if you want to slipcover a barn with roses.' Indeed it would be, for 'Silver Moon' is one of the most vigorous of all climbing roses, even outgrowing 'Mermaid'. It flowers only in the spring, but is then a lovely sight, with hundreds of ivory flowers shining against the dark green foliage; it is fragrant too. It is not for climates with cold and frosty winters, however. The raiser was American rosarian Dr Walter Van Fleet, who introduced it in 1910.

Thought to be *(Rosa wichuraiana ×*
'Devoniensis') × R. laevigata
Spring flowering
Fragrant

'Simplicity' — Cluster-flowered

JACink

Jackson & Perkins advertise 'Simplicity' as the 'blooming fence' and it is indeed a very even, bushy and free-blooming

Cluster-flowered Rose. Planted a bit closer than normal, it makes a very nice chest-high hedge. The foliage is a rather pale green, the flowers soft pink, very pleasing in the mass, though individually the flowers are neither especially shapely nor fragrant. They are large, to 8–10 centimetres (3–4 inches). Jackson & Perkins claim it does not need careful pruning, just trimming. Bill Warriner raised it for them in 1978, and has followed up with 'White Simplicity' and the ruby-red 'Bloomin' Easy'.

'Iceberg' × unnamed seedling
Repeat flowering

▲ 'Smooth Sailing'
◀ 'Slater's Crimson China'

'Slater's Crimson China'   China
Rosa chinensis semperflorens

It is never easy to be certain of the correct identification of the various crimson China Roses, all rather alike, that survive in various botanic gardens. The rose pictured is almost certainly 'Slater's Crimson China', long believed to be extinct but recently found again in Bermuda. The head-high bush, the dark green leaves, plum-toned in youth, and the small clusters of brilliant crimson flowers do match the descriptions in the reference books, as well as old pictures such as Redouté's. 'Slater's Crimson China' is a rose of commanding importance, for prior to its arrival in England from the Fa Tee Nurseries in the 1790s, there were no true dark red roses in the West, only purple Gallicas. All our true red roses derive their gorgeous color from 'Slater's Crimson China'.

Parentage unknown
Repeat flowering

'Pink Favorite', with their exceptionally pretty coloring of cream and pink like that of 'Little Darling'. Neither parent had much scent to offer. The raiser was one of the lesser-known American hybridists, Harvey Davidson, and he introduced 'Smooth Sailing' in 1977. Foliage is dark green and glossy.

'Little Darling' × 'Pink Favorite'
Repeat flowering

'Snow Ballet'   Modern Shrub

Introduced with a flourish of trumpets in 1977, 'Snow Ballet' seems to be dropping out of the catalogues, which is a pity, as there are not all that many really good white roses for the garden. It makes a spreading shrub, not too tall,

▲ 'Snow Ballet'
▼ 'Smoky'

▲ 'Sir Walter Raleigh'

'Sir Walter Raleigh'   English Rose
AUSpry

David Austin has described 'Sir Walter Raleigh' as the nearest he has been able to come to a repeat-flowering version of 'Constance Spry'. This exaggerates its merits somewhat, as the flowers are nothing like as gorgeous as those of that much admired rose. They are, however, pleasingly formed, sweetly fragrant, and a clear rose-pink with just a hint of coral. The head-high bush, with luxuriant green foliage, certainly does flower throughout the season. Introduced in 1985, it is named to commemorate the tercentenary of the foundation of the American colony of Virginia, in which Sir Walter played a leading role.

'Lilian Austin' × 'Chaucer'
Repeat flowering
Fragrant

'Smoky'   Large-flowered

'Smoky ox-blood red, shaded burgundy', reads the official description, so the name is apt for this Jackson & Perkins introduction of 1968. The name is a familiar one in American folklore. You will either love or hate this rose, with its curious scent of liquorice, but it is quite a good grower and it is sure to be a conversation piece with visitors. The blooms are of good size and form, and foliage is leathery.

Parentage undisclosed
Repeat flowering
Fragrant

'Smooth Sailing'   Large-flowered

'Smooth Sailing' is a rose of interesting breeding. It inherits from its parents a strong and healthy constitution. The blooms, in size and shape, resemble

▲ 'Snowfire'

the foliage is dark green and rather small. The flowers, however, are larger than either parent, being 10 centimetres (4 inches) across, filled with petals and borne throughout the season in small and large clusters. It was raised by a Mr Clayworth and introduced by Harkness & Co.

'Sea Foam' × 'Iceberg'
Repeat flowering

'Snowfire'   Large-flowered

'Snowfire' certainly produces a spectacular flower: large, sometimes enormous, of perfect exhibition form and startling color. The upper surface of the petals is dark red, the underside brilliantly white, the white showing through as a fine white edge to the red. There are mixed reports on the plant, some finding it satisfactory, others complaining that it will not grow strongly and is prone to mil-

▶ 'Soleil'
▼ 'Softly Softly'

dew. It was raised by Reimer Kordes and introduced by Jackson & Perkins in 1977. Foliage is dark green and leathery.

'Schlössers Brilliant' × 'Liberty Bell'
Repeat flowering

'Softly Softly'   Large-flowered
HARkotur
This rose gives Jack Harkness the distinction of being the first to name a rose after a TV series. *Softly, Softly* was certainly very popular at the time the rose came out in 1980. It is one of those roses that can be called a Large-flowered or Cluster-flowered Rose at pleasure. The blooms are not overlarge and tend to be borne in clusters. They are a blend of soft pinks. Foliage is olive-green and leathery.

('White Cockade' × ['Highlight' × 'Colour Wonder']) × ('Parkdirektor Riggers' × 'Piccadilly')
Repeat flowering

'Soldier Boy'   Large-flowered Climber
If you find the popular 'Altissimo' strident but like the idea of a red, single-flowered Climber, take a look at this 1953 LeGrice creation. It is not as free with its later blooms as 'Altissimo', but the color is softer—crimson rather than scarlet—and yellow stamens light the flowers. It is of pillar rose dimensions, but, alas, it has not inherited the sweet fragrance of 'Guinée'. Foliage is glossy and emerald-green. If you fancy a still deeper red single climber, seek out the crimson-maroon 'Sweet Sultan', which is much admired in Britain.

Unnamed seedling × 'Guinée'
Repeat flowering

▲ 'Soldier Boy'

'Soleil'   Cluster-flowered
Not the golden color of the sun at noon, but rather the fiery red it shows at sunset, 'Soleil' displays symmetrical flowers in clusters on a neat and low-growing plant. One would think it would be a fashionable 'Patio Rose', but it came before its time, in 1958. It was raised by Charles Mallerin, the amateur French breeder, every one of whose roses is distinct and beautiful. Foliage is a clear green.

Parentage undisclosed
Repeat flowering

'Soleil d'Or'   Large-flowered
No rose ever created a greater sensation than 'Soleil d'Or' on its first showing in Paris in 1900. The first fruit of Joseph Pernet-Ducher's twenty years of breeding with the mulish 'Persian Yellow', it was not quite the longed-for yellow Bush Rose. (It is rather a blend of yellow and coral-pink.) It was, how-

ever, the start of something new. All the modern yellow roses, and a great many of other colors, descend from it. These days it is best left to the collections of botanic gardens. The flowers may be pretty, but the bush is weak and the glossy, rich green foliage is rather addicted to black spot.

'Antoine Ducher' × 'Persian Yellow'
Repeat flowering
Fragrant

▲ 'Soleil d'Or'
▼ 'Sombreuil'

'Sombreuil' — Climbing Tea
'Mademoiselle de Sombreuil'
Mlle de Sombreuil was a heroine of the French Revolution. The rose named in her memory did not come out until 1850, being raised by a M. Robert. It is a splendid flower, large, bursting with petals, and of delicate tones of cream and white, occasionally with just a hint of pink. The scent is superb. You rarely see the original bush version now. 'Sombreuil' is much more familiar as a Climber. It dislikes cold climates, and appreciates loving care, even in a mild climate. The foliage is medium green and semi-glossy.

Thought to be 'Gigantesque' × unknown
Repeat flowering
Fragrant

'Sonia' — Large-flowered
MEIhelvet
'Sonia Meilland', 'Sweet Promise'
Probably still the most popular greenhouse rose in the world, its salmon-pink blooms seemingly part of the furniture in every florist's window, 'Sonia' also has a very good reputation as a garden rose. However, the plant is very thorny, the stems are much shorter in the garden than in the greenhouse, and in hot climates the blooms fade very much in the summer sunshine. The bush is tall and vigorous, with dark green, glossy foliage, and the flowers are on the small side but very shapely. 'Sonia' must have made a fortune for the Meilland family, who brought it out in 1973.

'Zambra' × ('Baccarà' × 'Message')
Repeat flowering

'Sophie's Perpetual' — China
'Paul's Dresden China'
This is yet another Old Garden Rose that has been brought into popularity after being almost forgotten. How it could have been neglected is hard to explain, for it is a willing grower and bears blooms of great charm, cupped in form and palest pink heavily shaded and flushed deeper, sometimes almost red. The flowers are fragrant, the growth tall enough to be trained to a pillar. Foliage is dark green and the bush has few prickles. The name honors Countess Sophie Benckendorf, who, sometime in the 1920s, planted the rose in the garden from which it was reintroduced by Peter Beales in 1960.

Parentage unknown
Repeat flowering

'Soraya' — Large-flowered
Soraya was the one-time empress of Iran, divorced by the Shah and supplanted by Farah Diba, who also has a rose named for her, 'Kaiserin Farah'. It is a nice irony that while 'Kaiserin Farah' has dropped out of all of the catalogues, 'Soraya' continues to be admired. It is one of the most elegant of all the orange-red Large-flowered Roses, its color smouldering and quite brilliant yet subtle, its form cupped and symmetrical, its plant strong and glossy leafed. Scent is not very strong. It was raised by Francis Meilland and introduced in 1955.

('Peace' × 'Floradora') × 'Grand'mère Jenny'
Repeat flowering

▲ 'Soraya'
◄ 'Sonia'
▼ 'Sophie's Perpetual'

► 'Souvenir d'Elise Vardon'
▼ 'South Seas'

'South Seas'   Large-flowered
'Mers du Sud'

This is a rose that has had mixed receptions in different countries, some people raving about the enormous coral-pink blooms, opening wide and ruffled from urn-shaped buds, others finding them loose and blowsy. The bush is of a size to match, but for all its height and vigor it is sometimes rather shy with its flowers. There is only a little scent. Foliage is broad, dark green and semi-glossy. 'South Seas' was raised by Dr Denison Morey and introduced by Jackson & Perkins in 1962.

'Rapture' × unknown Large-flowered Climber
Repeat flowering

'Southampton'   Cluster-flowered
'Susan Ann'

Soft orange, veering towards apricot and often flushed with coral-red, the flowers of 'Southampton' are pleasantly shapely and carried in moderate-sized clusters. They are fragrant too. The bush is tallish and spreading and the bronze-green, glossy foliage is among the healthiest in the color group. An English-raised rose, from Jack Harkness in 1972, and very well regarded in Britain, 'Southampton' has not fared very well in the hotter climates. The color tends to fade in strong sunshine.

('Ann Elizabeth' × 'Allgold') × 'Yellow Cushion'
Repeat flowering
Fragrant

► 'Southampton'

'Southern Belle'   Large-flowered
The hibiscus 'Southern Belle' is known for its absolutely enormous flowers, but the rose of the same name is only a moderate size, much more suitable for a young lady to wear in her hair while entertaining a gentleman caller on the verandah of some stately mansion. Flowers are deep pink, prettily shaped, and come in small clusters on a bush with semi-glossy foliage. 'Southern Belle' was raised in California by Swim & Ellis and introduced in 1981. There is very little in the way of fragrance.

'Pink Parfait' × 'Phoenix'
Repeat flowering

▼ 'Southern Belle'

'Souvenir d'Elise Vardon'   Tea
Victorian rose-lovers poured extravagant praise on the beauty of this rose, and abuse on its reluctance to produce flowers in any quantity. Perhaps it was just the English climate, for in warmer climates it seems to give a perfectly good account of itself. The flowers are

▲ 'Souvenir de la Malmaison'
▶ 'Souvenir de Madame Leonie Viennot'

lovely in their soft shades of cream, apricot and pink, and in their perfect form. 'Souvenir d'Elise Vardon', raised by Marest of Paris in 1855, was the first rose to display the high-centred, spiral form, with no hint of quartering, that we now accept as the ideal. Foliage is semi-glossy.

Parentage unknown
Repeat flowering
Fragrant

'Souvenir de la Malmaison' — Bourbon
'Queen of Beauty and Fragrance'
Forget the romance of the name, and look at this famous rose objectively. The wide flowers, as large as a Large-flowered Rose, are blush-pink, quartered and fragrant, and really so beautiful that they are a fitting tribute to the Empress Josephine, the first wife of Napoleon Bonaparte. The bush is strong and healthy, with mid-green glossy foliage and it repeats its bloom reliably. The English title is no exaggeration. In warm climates, which it prefers, it is one of the first roses to bloom and the last to finish. It was raised by Jean Beluze of Lyon in 1843. There is an excellent climbing sport, which originated in Australia in 1893.

'Madame Desprez' × unknown Tea Rose
Repeat flowering
Fragrant

'Souvenir de Madame Breuil' — Moss
This rose is quite a charmer, with heavily mossed buds and cup-shaped flowers in deep carmine laced with purple and fading to magenta-pink. The bright green foliage is broad, with a hint of gloss suggesting Bourbon ancestry, and the plant is vigorous and bushy. Not much is known of its origin. It would date from about the 1850s.

Parentage unknown
Repeat flowering
Fragrant

'Souvenir de Madame Leonie Viennot' — Climbing Tea
Refer to her affectionately as 'Madame Leonie', but do not overlook this rose if you need a beautiful and uncommon Climbing Rose. In cold climates she appreciates the warmest wall. Prune her only lightly, if at all, for the finest flowers come from the old wood. The flowers are large, exquisitely long-budded and shapely, in shining blends of salmon and cream. They are richly fragrant too, and borne in profusion all season. The raiser was Andre Bernaix of Lyon, who introduced it in 1898. Foliage is a glossy bronze-green.

Parentage unknown
Repeat flowering
Fragrant

'Souvenir de Philemon Cochet' — Hybrid Rugosa
Introduced in 1899, this rose is a sport from 'Blanc Double de Coubert'. It resembles its parent in everything except in its greatly increased complement of petals. The white flowers are so double that they sometimes open as perfect spheres, something like double hollyhocks. It is not quite as free with its flowers as its parent. Philemon Cochet was the brother of the raiser,

M. P. C. M. Cochet-Cochet. Foliage is light green and rugose.

Sport from 'Blanc Double de Coubert'
Repeat flowering
Fragrant

'Souvenir de Pierre Leperdrieux' — Hybrid Rugosa
It is surprising that this 1895 Hybrid Rugosa is not better known. It has all the group's good habits—the lush, light green, rugose foliage and bushy growth, and the strong clove-like fragrance—and bears large flowers, almost single, with only seven or eight petals, in a pleasant shade of cerise with undertones of purple, the cream stamens lighting up the centres. There are often hips in the autumn, or fall, too.

Parentage unknown
Repeat flowering
Fragrant

▲ 'Souvenir de Pierre Leperdrieux'
▼ 'Souvenir de Philemon Cochet'

◀ 'Souvenir de Madame Breuil'

▲ 'Souvenir de Pierre Vibert'

'Souvenir de Pierre Vibert'
Moss

J.-P. Vibert of Angers was one of the famous early rose-breeders; you will find his famous 'Baronne Prevost', and some others of his, in this book. He flourished in the 1840s and '50s, and the date of 'Souvenir de Pierre Vibert', 1867, is probably about right for his colleagues Moreau & Robert to have dedicated it to his memory. It is the sort of rose he would have been happy to raise, its flowers dark and shapely in shades of crimson and violet, the buds nicely mossed. The bush is only of moderate vigor, but it often gives a few autumn, or fall, blooms. Foliage is lush green and matt.

Parentage unknown
Repeat flowering
Fragrant

'Souvenir de Thérèse Levet'
Tea

Regarded in its day as one of the very best of the red Tea Roses, 'Souvenir de Thérèse Levet', which was raised by A. Levet and introduced in 1886 and obviously named for a member of his family, is not often seen these days. It is not among the hardier of the Teas, and when compared with our many rich and brilliant red roses its muted crimson might seem a trifle dull. It is a good rose, however, shapely and scented, and it flowers quite well all season. In hot weather the color is apt to be a paler, almost cherry-red. Foliage is a glossy dull green.

'Adam' × unknown
Repeat flowering
Fragrant

▲ 'Souvenir du Docteur Jamain'

'Souvenir du Docteur Jamain'
Hybrid Perpetual

This rose is much admired by English lovers of Old Garden Roses, but it does not like hot climates, where the flowers will scorch. Try giving it a little shade in the afternoon, and then you can look forward to large fragrant flowers, not so double that the golden stamens cannot light up the port-wine colors of the petals. It is inclined towards legginess, and needs the best of cultivation to be seen in its full beauty. It was raised by François Lacharme and introduced in 1865. Foliage is mid-green and smooth.

'Charles Lefèbvre' × unknown
Repeat flowering
Fragrant

'Souvenir d'un Ami'
Tea

'Souvenir d'un Ami' was one of the best loved of Tea Roses in the nineteenth century, for the sake of its comparative hardiness and ease of culture, its delicious fragrance, its lovely long buds, and its color, soft pink lit with coral. Foliage is a rich olive-green. The delicate romance of its name, which means 'in memory of a friend' must have charmed many people, and when a Mr Prince of Oxford discovered a white sport, he kept the tradition by calling it 'Souvenir de S. A. Prince' in memory of his wife Sarah. 'Souvenir d'un Ami' was introduced by Bélot-Defougère in 1846.

Parentage unknown
Repeat flowering
Fragrant

'Sparrieshoop'
Modern Shrub

'Sparrieshoop', named for the village where Wilhelm Kordes Söhn have their nurseries, is sufficiently long-limbed that it can be trained as a short climber, but it is also handsome as a big spreading shrub. The young shoots are bronze, the mature leaves dark green and glossy. Sweetly fragrant, the flowers are apple-blossom-pink and come in large clusters all season. They are not quite single, having just one or two extra

▲ 'Souvenir d'un Ami'
▼ 'Souvenir de Thérèse Levet'

▲ 'Spartan'
▼ 'Sparrieshoop'

petals. This charming rose was raised by Kordes and introduced in 1953.

('Baby Château' × 'Else Poulsen') × 'Magnifica'
Repeat flowering
Fragrant

'Spartan'   Cluster-flowered

When Jackson & Perkins introduced 'Spartan' in 1955, they gave it the most elaborate and expensive publicity ever mounted for a new rose, including colored pages in *Time* and the *Saturday Evening Post*. Rumor has it that as 'Spartan' had been pipped for the AARS award, Jackson & Perkins were determined to outsell the winner. With hindsight, perhaps it should have won, for it was, and still is, a stunning rose. The bush is tall and strong, with olive-green, glossy foliage, very red tinted in its youth, producing flowers in great abundance. They are fragrant too, but above all their color was new and sensational—a vivid coral tone, not quite orange, not quite deep enough to be red. It has been a prolific parent.

'Geranium Red' × 'Fashion'
Repeat flowering
Fragrant

'Spek's Centennial'   Cluster-flowered

All rose-lovers know Holland's Jan Spek for his 'Spek's Yellow', but few realise how old his firm is. It has been around for a century, and 'Spek's Centennial', introduced in 1992, is a tribute from Spek's long-time friend and associate, Sam McGredy. This time the rose is not quite yellow, but a blend of yellow and coral, which combine if you look at it

from a little distance to give an unusual effect of burnished bronze. The flowers are medium sized in clusters of half a dozen or so, the stems are long, and the bush is compact with bronze-toned foliage. Too new to be sure of its performance everywhere, 'Spek's Centennial' scores high for distinctiveness.

'Sexy Rexy' × 'Pot o' Gold'
Repeat flowering

'Spek's Yellow'   Large-flowered
'Golden Scepter'

Strangely enough, 'Spek's Yellow' did not win a major award when it was introduced in 1947. Perhaps the judges faulted it for the loose, rather ragged form of its blooms, but the public took it to heart and it became the most popular yellow rose for twenty years. The buds are long and pointed, and the deep, rich yellow pales only a little as the blooms open. They are often borne in clusters, on a very tall open bush with glossy, dark green foliage. Do not try to prune hard for bushiness or it will sulk. Jan Spek of Boskoop was the introducer of the rose. The actual raiser was Hans Verschuren.

'Geheimrat Duisberg' × unnamed seedling
Repeat flowering
Fragrant

▲ 'Spek's Centennial'
▼ 'Spek's Yellow'

ROSE HIPS

I t is the proud boast of rose-lovers that the fruit of the rose is in fact the richest of all known sources of vitamin C. Whether this be so or not, all the authorities, however, agree that, weight for weight, rose hips leave the orange way behind. Not that one would eat them like an orange—there is very little flesh on a hip. Basically it is just a hollow shell, enclosing a bunch of more or less hairy seeds, each of which, a botanist will argue, is an *achene*, the true fruit of the rose. The hip is really only the packaging. In order to eat them, hips must first be cooked and then have the seeds strained off. The resulting puree can then be made into pies (medieval favorites), jam, *sauce eglantine* (a Victorian favorite with venison) or rose-hip syrup, given to British children during World War II at a time when oranges were extremely difficult to obtain.

Pleasant as all these are (they have a distinctive, delicate, sweet-yet-tart flavor), rose hips have only ever played an accessory role at the table. It is for their decorative qualities in the garden that they are admired. Not that people see them often, as we are always urged to prevent them forming on our roses in case they distract the plant from making further flowers.

Most of the repeat-flowering roses need warmth to ripen their fruit properly, a characteristic they inherit along with their repeat flowering from the China Rose, and in cool climates any that are allowed to form by careless gardeners are apt to be

overtaken by the winter. If you live in a mild climate, however, it can be well worth allowing the autumn, or fall, flowers to set seed, just to see what develops. I can vouch for pleasing displays of hips on 'Queen Elizabeth', 'Cara Bella' and 'Orangeade', and no doubt there would be many more. The soft coral-pink hips of 'Penelope' are much praised by English rosarians.

Hybridity and a multiplicity of petals reduce the rose's fertility, so many garden roses do not give much in the way of a display of hips. It has to be admitted anyway that a few hips do not do much to relieve the dowdiness of a Bush Rose, whether Large- or Cluster-flowered, as it approaches dormancy.

To see the beauty that rose hips can bring to the autumn, or fall, and early winter garden, we must turn to the Wild Roses

and their immediate hybrids. These will have hips in profusion, ranging from pea-sized, polished globes of such as *Rosa pisocarpa* to the great scarlet flagons of *R. moyesii* and *R. macrophylla* and their relatives. These are undoubtedly the finest in the genus—and few berry-bearing shrubs can match them—but the orange globes of the Rugosas, like small cherry tomatoes, and the great sprays of coral berries of the Himalayan Musks (*Rosa helenae* is usually given first prize here) are not to be sneezed at either.

The more informal growth of the Wild Roses shows the hips off better than the stiffer habit of the Bush Roses does, and sometimes there will be tinted autumn, or fall, foliage too. True, few roses are up to the standard of *R. virginiana* in this respect, but the clear yellow of the Rugosas is one of their assets; *R. glauca*, already decorative in leaf, goes bronze to set off its dark, copper-red hips; and

many of the Gallicas will assume quite pleasing tints of gold and brown, with hips to crown them. Many other roses will at least touch their drying leaves with russet, to set off the predominantly orange tones of the fruit.

◄ Rosa blanda *is noteworthy for its thornlessness and the earliness with which it bears its pretty pink flowers, but its bright hips are by no means to be despised.*

► *The small black hips characteristic of the Scotch or Burnet Rose (Rosa pimpinellifolia) and its hybrids. They may not be brightly colored, but they have a subtle charm.*

▲ While it is mostly among the Wild Roses that we look for displays of hips, many garden roses can put up a fine show, at least in climates where summers are long enough to ripen them to full color. This is 'Altissimo'.

▲ Rosa virginiana, *in the autumn, or fall, combines showers of round scarlet hips with the brightest tinted foliage of any rose, to make it every bit as striking at the end of the season as when it bears its elegant blossoms in late spring.*

◄ *Were I planning to plant roses to have hips for jam- or syrup-making, my choice would be* Rosa rugosa, *for not only are its hips big and fleshy, but there are often successive crops of them from successive crops of flowers. They look mighty handsome in the garden too. This is* 'Frau Dagmar Hartopp', *with hips of a deeper red than most.*

▲ *Many Wild Roses give generous sprays of hips for cutting. Though taking off the thorns so they will not scratch the flower arranger is a chore, they do last very well in the vase. Here is* Rosa woodsii fendleri *from the United States.*

▲ *Many rose-lovers consider* Rosa moyesii, *and its close relatives, to have the most splendid hips of all. Very fine they are too, but they ripen early. In a hot climate they need to be grown in a lightly shaded position or the sun will scorch them, preventing them from achieving fine color.*

▲ *A study in soft tones:* Rosa sweginzowii *photographed at Kew Gardens in September. For all their charm, few roses will make as brilliant a show in fruit as, say, a pyracantha will; they are for lovers of the dainty and subtle.*

'Spellbinder' — Large-flowered
WARdido

There are conflicting reports about the constitution of this rose, some saying that it is vigorous and healthy, others that it is sickly. So ask how it does in your area before planting it. The flowers are unique, and they deserve the name. Officially described as ivory to crimson, they in fact blend cream, pale yellow, pink and red, all marbled and brocaded together in the manner of a variegated camellia. The flowers open quite flat to complete the resemblance. The breeder was Bill Warriner. Jackson & Perkins introduced it in 1977. Fragrance is only slight. The foliage is dark green, thick textured and distinctively pointed.

'South Seas' × unnamed seedling
Repeat flowering

▲ 'Spellbinder'

'Springfields' — Cluster-flowered
DICband

This 1978 Pat Dickson creation seems to have got lost in the crowd of yellow-orange-red Cluster-flowered Roses of the 1980s. Across the world, there are only two or three nurseries offering 'Springfields'. Its 8 centimetre (3 inch) flowers are shapely, slightly fragrant and vividly colored. The plant is sturdy, with semi-glossy leathery foliage, and if it takes after its parents it should be a very long-lasting cut flower.

'Eurorose' × 'Anabell'
Repeat flowering

'Stadt Den Helder' — Cluster-flowered
INTerhel

'Stadt den Helder' is a fairly typical bright red Cluster-flowered Rose, its flowers slightly fragrant and carried in large clusters. It was raised by the Dutch firm of Interplant and introduced in 1979. It is a rose for very cool climates, such as in Canada. Den Helder is a seaport in Holland, notable for the presence of a naval base, a meteorological observatory, a zoological station and a lighthouse. Foliage is large, dark green and matt.

'Amsterdam' × ('Olala' × 'Diablotin')
Repeat flowering

'Stanwell Perpetual' — Scotch

'Stanwell Perpetual' was introduced in 1838 and apparently arose as a chance seedling in the garden of a man called Lee, who lived in Stanwell, Middlesex. It is thought to be a cross between *Rosa pimpinellifolia* and a Damask Rose, but its ability to repeat its bloom is much greater than either. The sprawling, grey-leafed bush is rarely without at least a few flowers. Delightful they are too: blush pink, full of petals, and softly scented. No rose could be a more charming introduction to the beauty of the Old Garden Roses. Leave the bush to build itself up unpruned, to about chest high.

Possibly *R. damascena bifera* × *R. pimpinellifolia*
Repeat flowering
Fragrant

▲ 'Stadt Den Helder'
▼ 'Stanwell Perpetual''

◄ 'Springfields'

'Starfire' — Large-flowered

'Starfire' is a good example of the sort of rose for which the Americans created the 'Grandiflora' classification. Though its blooms come in clusters, they are too big to pass as Cluster-flowered Roses, and too loose and informal for commercial success as a Large-flowered Rose. It is a very good rose, a worthy winner of the AARS award in 1959. The bush is tall and ruggedly easy to grow, with dark grey-green, glossy foliage. It flowers in great abundance all season, and the blooms are a lovely clear, bright red that holds until the petals drop. They come on

▲ 'Starfire'
▼ 'Stargazer'

▲ 'Sterling Silver'
▼ 'Stephanie Diane'

very long stems for cutting. Raised by Walter Lammerts, 'Starfire' has only one fault, lack of scent.

'Charlotte Armstrong' × ('Charlotte Armstrong' × 'Floradora')
Repeat flowering

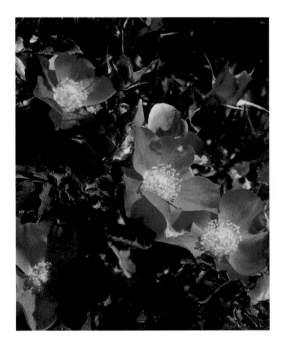

'Stargazer' — Cluster-flowered

'Stargazer' is one of the most charming of the 'dwarf' Cluster-flowered Roses. The 0.5 metre (1 foot 6 inch) tall bush covers itself in season with clusters of little blooms, their color varying with the weather from orange-red to deep pink, but always with a golden star at the centre. Foliage is mid-green. There is little fragrance. It is a 1977 Jack Harkness introduction, and looks best when several bushes are planted rather close together to make a galaxy of stars.

'Marlena' × 'Kim'
Repeat flowering

'Stephanie Diane' — Large-flowered

'Stephanie Diane' is only moderately vigorous, but exhibitors will be very interested in it for the large size and the perfect form of its brilliant flowers. Their color looks especially good under artificial light, and they open very evenly and slowly when cut. It is of good breeding, but it has inherited little of the perfume of 'Fragrant Cloud'. Introduced in 1971 by Bees of Chester, it seems to be popular mainly in the United Kingdom. A cool climate would seem indicated. Foliage is olive-green and leathery.

'Fragrant Cloud' × 'Cassandra'
Repeat flowering

'Sterling Silver' — Large-flowered

Thirty or so years ago Mrs Gladys Fisher had quite a reputation for raising roses of unusual colors. 'Sterling Silver', a sensation when it came out in 1957, is the best known today. Many people think it is still the most exquisite of any mauve rose, but the plant is not even moderately vigorous. If you fall for its pale and luminous color and sweet perfume, be prepared to coddle it. It has been the parent of most of the more recent mauves. Do not confuse it with 'Sterling', a bright pink Large-flowered Rose of 1933, rarely seen now. Foliage is dull leaden green and matt.

Unnamed seedling × 'Peace'
Repeat flowering
Fragrant

'Sue Lawley'
Cluster-flowered
MACspash
'Spanish Shawl'
Here we have yet another of Sam McGredy's 'Hand-painted Roses', this time in bright red, with a pink or cream border and centre. The flowers are not overstuffed with petals, so they show their pattern well, and are carried in clusters of seven or so on a compact bush with heavy dark green foliage. It was bred from several generations of unnamed 'Hand-painted' seedlings, introduced in 1980, and named for a popular British television star on the occasion of the arrival of her first-born.

Unnamed seedling × unnamed seedling
Repeat flowering

'Sue Ryder'
Cluster-flowered
HARlino
This 1983 rose from Jack Harkness has been well-received in Britain, but is hardly known elsewhere. It is really an exhibitor's rose, as it can produce the loveliest sprays of shapely, faintly scented blooms in orange and gold, but it is sometimes rather shy with them. Foliage is mid-green and semi-glossy. It was raised in honor of Lady Ryder and her many years work in assisting the homeless and unfortunate.

'Southampton' × unnamed seedling
Repeat flowering

▶ 'Sue Lawley'
▼ 'Sue Ryder'

'Summer Days'
Large-flowered
Large and high centred, the blooms of 'Summer Days' are a refreshing pale yellow, suggestive of the soft light of an English summer. The flowers are semi-double, with thirty-six petals, and up to 9 centimetres (3½ inches) across. It was introduced by Bees of Chester in the United Kingdom in 1976. The plant is on the tall side, with glossy mid-green foliage and is quite vigorous.

'Fragrant Cloud' × 'Dr A. J. Verhage'
Repeat flowering
Fragrant

▶ 'Summer Days'

▲ 'Summer Rainbow'
◄ 'Summer Dream'
► 'Summer Sunshine'

'Summer Dream' — Large-flowered

JACshe

This was Jackson & Perkins's 1987 Rose of the Year. The large blooms are balanced by the delicacy of their coloring, a blend of soft pinks and peach tones. They are of fine, high-centred form and good, if light, fragrance. The long stems often display two or three blooms together. Foliage is mid-green. The hybridist was Bill Warriner.

'Sunshine' × unnamed seedling
Repeat flowering
Fragrant

'Summer Fashion' — Cluster-flowered

'Arc de Triomphe'

There are quite a few Cluster-flowered Roses that start out yellow and pass to red as they age. Here is one where the colors are in a softer key. 'Summer Fashion' opens pale lemon yellow, fading almost as soon as the flowers are fully blown to ivory white, gradually becoming suffused with soft rose-pink. Borne usually in small clusters, they are nicely formed and fragrant. Foliage is large and mid-green. It was raised by Bill Warriner and introduced by Jackson & Perkins in 1985.

'Precilla' × 'Bridal Pink'
Repeat flowering
Fragrant

'Summer Rainbow' — Large-flowered

'Summer Rainbow' often displays a tint of magenta on the edges of its red, orange and yellow petals. The blooms are large, full petalled and quite shapely enough for exhibition, and look well against dark green, polished foliage. The bushy plant is a little shorter than the average. The raiser was one of the lesser known American names in rose-breeding, Robert G. Jelly of Richmond, Indiana, and he had the rose introduced by the Conard-Pyle Company in 1966.

'Peace' × 'Dawn'
Repeat flowering

'Summer Snow' — Cluster-flowered

It is quite common for a Bush Rose to produce a climbing sport, but it is very rare for the reverse to happen. 'Summer Snow' is one of the rarities. Introduced in 1938 by Jackson & Perkins, it is a sport of 'Climbing Summer Snow', raised by the French firm of Couteau

▲ 'Summer Snow'
◄ 'Summer Fashion'

two years earlier. Until the introduction of 'Iceberg' it was the most popular white Cluster-flowered Rose in the United States. Its slight fondness for mildew proved its undoing. It is still worth considering when you want a low-growing, heavy-blooming white bush, and there is sweet fragrance too. Foliage is bright green and glossy.

Sport from 'Climbing Summer Snow'
Repeat flowering
Fragrant

'Summer Sunshine' — Large-flowered

'Soleil d'Eté'

Raised by Herbert Swim and introduced by Armstrong Nurseries in 1962, 'Summer Sunshine' has long had the solid reputation of being one of the more reliable yellow roses for humid climates where the yellow roses often languish. It is a tendency inherited, way back, from the 'Persian Yellow'. The color of the blooms is exceptionally deep and shining, and fades but little as the bloom ages, but the spent petals often do not drop cleanly. The plant is on the short side, though usually there are plenty of the rather thin branches, with semi-glossy, dark green foliage. Scent is light but pleasant.

'Buccaneer' × 'Lemon Chiffon'
Repeat flowering
Fragrant

'Sun Flare' — Cluster-flowered

JACjem

Rose-breeders like the publicity that a topical name can bring to a new rose, but 1983, the year 'Sun Flare' won the AARS award, was not a notable year for solar activity. It is an appropriate name for the pale, luminous yellow of the 10 centimetre (4 inch) flowers, displayed on a fashionably low and spreading bush in clusters of up to a

▲ 'Sun Flare'
▼ 'Sunblest'

▲ 'Sunday Best'
▼ 'Sundowner'

dozen. There is a pleasant fragrance, officially described as 'liquorice-like', but more suggestive of a nice old vermouth to some. It was a Bill Warriner creation for Jackson & Perkins. Foliage is small and glossy.

'Friesia' × unnamed seedling
Repeat flowering
Fragrant

'Sunblest'   Large-flowered
'Landora'
There are other yellow roses with larger or shapelier blooms, deeper and brighter colors and stronger growth, but 'Sunblest' is still perfectly acceptable in each department. It is a good, reliable rose and very popular. While not outstandingly fragrant, it is pleasingly so, and the clear yellow blooms stand out well. It was raised by Germany's Mathias Tantau in 1973. Gold medals have been awarded in Japan and New Zealand. Foliage is dark emerald-green and glossy.

Unnamed seedling × 'King's Ransom'
Repeat flowering
Fragrant

'Sunday Best'   Large-flowered
At first sight, Alister Clark's 'Sunday Best' looks like an improved version of 'Nancy Hayward'. The single flowers are as large, if not larger, and a more brilliant color, bright red fading to crimson. They are a trifle more fragrant, though that is not saying much. It loses out to its rival in not being as early in bloom and not being repeat flowering. That said, it can be a striking rose, the plant tall and vigorous enough to clad the façade of a two storey house. In its season it makes a splendid display. It came out in 1924. Foliage is pale green and wrinkled.

'Frau Karl Druschki' × unnamed seedling
Repeat flowering

'Sundowner'   Large-flowered
MACcheup
In Australia and New Zealand, a sundowner is an itinerant worker with the bad habit of turning up late in the working day. Sam McGredy has said that he followed the usage of the rest of the world, for whom a sundowner is a refreshing drink after a hard day's work. The name is apt for the sunset colors. The shapely blooms open brilliant coral and gold, passing to salmon-pink and cream. They are sweetly fragrant. The bush is tall, with leathery olive-green foliage. 'Sundowner' won the 1979 AARS award, but you might have to watch for mildew.

'Bond Street' × 'Peer Gynt'
Repeat flowering
Fragrant

'Sunny Honey'   Cluster-flowered
Introduced by Dicksons in 1972, 'Sunny Honey' retains its place in the catalogues only in New Zealand. The flowers are delightful in their blend of peach and yellow, flushed with red on the backs of the petals, and they are fragrant too. Foliage is dark green.

'Happy Event' × 'Elizabeth of Glamis'
Repeat flowering
Fragrant

► 'Sunny Honey'

▲ 'Sunny June'
► 'Sunny South'

'Sunny June'
Modern Shrub

At first sight, 'Sunny June' is so like the better known 'Golden Wings' that more than one nurseryman has muddled them up. 'Sunny June' is really better trained to a pillar or as a short climber, whereas 'Golden Wings' is the better choice as a free-standing shrub, and it is rather more tolerant of cold winters. 'Sunny June' is a shade brighter in tone, but a touch smaller and less fragrant. It has a charming habit of closing up for the night. Foliage is bright green and semi-glossy. The two roses are not related. 'Sunny June' was a creation of Walter Lammerts in 1952.

'Crimson Glory' × 'Captain Thomas'
Repeat flowering

▼ 'Sunrose'

'Sunny South'
Large-flowered

For years one of Australia's favorite roses, 'Sunny South' was raised by Australia's favorite rosarian, Alister Clark, in 1918. Despite its age, it is currently enjoying a revival of popularity. Plant it at the back of the bed, as it is every bit as tall and vigorous as 'Queen Elizabeth'. Some think it a better rose: the blooms are a softer blend of pink and cream and they are splendidly informal. They are fragrant too. The stems are often over 1 metre (3 feet) in length, with rich green leaves.

'Gustav Grünerwald' × 'Betty Berkeley'
Repeat flowering
Fragrant

'Sunrose'
Cluster-flowered

'Sunrose', raised in New Zealand in 1974 by Sam McGredy, has not found favor outside that country, but it looks pretty good there, its flowers shapely, and lightly fragrant; their coral to salmon color is clear and stable. The bushes look strong and healthy, with notably dark green, shining foliage. Per-

haps it does not 'travel well', as a wine-lover would say of his specialty.

Parentage undisclosed
Repeat flowering
Fragrant

'Sunset Jubilee'
Large-flowered

The jubilee in question was that of America's *Sunset* magazine and the rose is appropriately in sunset tones of pink with an undertone of coral. The flowers are high centred, opening to show their stamens, and the bush is described as vigorous with leathery and light green

▼ 'Sunset Jubilee'

▲ 'Sunsilk'
▶ 'Super Star'

foliage. 'Sunset Jubilee', which was raised by Eugene Boerner, was introduced in 1973, but appears to have vanished from the catalogues. Even *Sunset* does not include it in their latest rose book. Fragrance is only slight.

'Kordes Perfecta' × seedling from 'Pink Duchess'
Repeat flowering

'Sunsilk'
Cluster-flowered

With its large and shapely blooms, 'Sunsilk' might pass for a small Large-flowered Rose, but they come in quite adequate clusters. The color is a lovely pale, clear yellow. It is less attention-grabbing than the deeper yellows like 'Friesia' perhaps, but a most useful blending color in the garden and the vase, and one which is surprisingly rare in flowers. Scent is only slight, growth average, the foliage mid-green. Forget about shampoo, and think of sunshine and silky petals instead. 'Sunsilk' was raised by Fryer's Nurseries of Cheshire and introduced in 1974.

'Pink Parfait' × seedling from 'Red Gold'
Repeat flowering

▶ 'Sutter's Gold'
▼ 'Suspense'

'Super Star'
Large-flowered

TANorstar
'Tropicana', 'Orienta'

The new color that 'Super Star' brought to roses in 1960 caused much head-scratching. Was it pure light vermilion, coral-orange or pale scarlet? In fact, it is carmine pink, with a transparent overlay of orange. There have been recent complaints about mildew, but usually the bush is virile and healthy, with dark green, glossy leaves, producing shapely, scented blooms in abundance. Everyone who saw it wanted it. For years it was the world's best-selling rose. Mathias Tantau was the raiser.

Seedling from 'Peace' × seedling from 'Alpine Glow'
Repeat flowering
Fragrant

'Suspense'
Large-flowered

MEIfan

The exhibitors of the day criticized 'Suspense' for its lack of the desired high centre, but it remains one of the best roses for making a real shock of color in the garden. The plants are tall and strong, with large, glossy, dark green leaves, flaunting an abundance of blooms. These are huge, and a dazzling scarlet red with yellow on the reverse and at the centre. Scent is only slight, though. 'Suspense' was introduced by Meilland back in 1960.

'Henri Mallerin' × ('Happiness' × 'Floradora')
Repeat flowering

'Sutter's Gold'
Large-flowered

'Sutter's Gold' demonstrates just how elegance and reliability can outweigh lack of exhibition form. Since it was introduced by Herbert Swim in 1950, adorned with the AARS and other awards, it has been one of the best-loved Modern Garden Roses. True, the gold-touched scarlet of the buds pales in the open blooms, which are only semi-double and rather fleeting in hot weather. Stylish and richly fragrant they are generously given, from early in the season until the end of it. The plant is tall, a bit leggy perhaps, but with very dark green, polished leaves and few thorns. The name commemorates the discovery of gold in California by Frank Sutter a century before.

'Charlotte Armstrong' × 'Signora'
Repeat flowering
Fragrant

pink, with that sheen that rose catalogues love to call 'silvery', and the buds are long, in the manner favored in America. Indeed this is an American rose, from O. L. Weeks in 1983, and it won the AARS award that year. The bush is strong and upright and foliage is dark green.

Unnamed seedling × 'Tiffany'
Repeat flowering
Fragrant

'Sutter's Gold, Climbing' Large-flowered Climber

'Sutter's Gold' has always been loved for its intense fragrance, early flowering, and the sheer elegance of its long buds. The climbing sport retains all of these virtues, and its slender, relatively thorn-free branches make it one of the easiest of the climbing sports to manage in the garden. Its repeat blooming is variable: do not expect too much from it.

Sport from 'Sutter's Gold'
Repeat flowering
Fragrant

'Sweet Afton' Large-flowered

Named for the old Scottish folk song, 'Sweet Afton' is a rose of lyrical beauty. The blooms are of the softest coloring: almost white and blushing pale pink towards the centre, and very sweetly fragrant as well. Form is classic, and the blooms large. The bush is tall and spreading, but apparently susceptible to black spot. Foliage is dark green and glossy. David Armstrong and Herbert Swim share the credit, and the date of introduction was 1964.

('Charlotte Armstrong' × 'Signora') × ('Alice Stern' × 'Ondine')
Repeat flowering
Fragrant

'Sweet Surrender' Large-flowered

A rose with an outrageously romantic name like this had better be fragrant, and 'Sweet Surrender' certainly is that. The color is a tender shade of rose-

▼ 'Sweet Surrender'

'Sweet Vivien' Cluster-flowered

This is a rose of unusual breeding and it is a real charmer. The flowers have just a few petals too many to be quite single, but that does not detract from the freshness of their apple-blossom coloring. Leave the latest blooms on the plants, and they will be followed by large, pear-shaped hips. The plant is low growing, and very bushy, the foliage dark green and quite exceptionally resistant to disease. The perfume is rather faint. 'Sweet Vivien' was introduced in 1961 by Frank Raffel, a rose-grower from Stockton, California. 'Sweet Vivien' has never been as widely distributed as she deserves to be.

'Little Darling' × *Rosa odorata*
Repeat flowering

'Sweetheart' Large-flowered
COCapeer

'Cécile Brünner' is sometimes called 'the Sweetheart Rose', but this Large-

▲ 'Sympathie'
◀ 'Sylvia'
▶ 'Takao'
▼ 'Taihape Sunset'

flowered Rose from Alec Cocker is nothing like it. The blooms are several times as large, rose-pink with yellow at the petal base, and, despite their fifty petals and high centre, not quite so exquisitely perfect in shape. The bush is upright, the foliage is mid-green and large, but it is inclined to shyness of blooming. The fragrance is a notable feature. This is an exhibitor's rose, and one for cool climates.

'Peer Gynt' × ('Fragrant Cloud' × 'Gay Gordons')
Repeat flowering
Fragrant

'Sylvia'　Cluster-flowered
KORlift
'Congratulations'
The raiser, Reimer Kordes, insists that his 'Sylvia' is a Cluster-flowered Rose. Everyone else says no: it is a Large-flowered Rose—and a big one too. Either way, it is one of the loveliest of pink roses, tender in its color (warmed with just a hint of coral), its perfect form and its delightful fragrance. The foliage is olive-green and semi-glossy. The blooms are very freely produced, and it is a well-regarded florist's rose. Congratulations are in order to Kordes, who introduced 'Sylvia' in 1978.

'Carina' × unnamed seedling
Repeat flowering
Fragrant

'Sympathie'　Large-flowered Climber
Most of the Climbers descended from *Rosa kordesii* are like Cluster-flowered Roses in their blooms, but 'Sympathie' is as large as a Large-flowered Rose, shapely, and a beautiful deep crimson. It is fragrant too, and it is surprising that it is not better known. Perhaps its moderate growth, to 3 metres (10 feet) or so, makes it sound weak. It is a

strong and healthy grower, with bright green, glossy foliage, and the repeat bloom is excellent. It was raised by Reimer Kordes and introduced in 1964.

'Wilhelm Hausmann' × 'Don Juan'
Repeat flowering
Fragrant

'Taihape Sunset'　Large-flowered
KORlinde
Reimer Kordes's great friend and colleague Sam McGredy probably named this rose. It is only catalogued in New Zealand, where the name would hardly raise eyebrows or twist tongues the way it might in Germany. The blooms are elegantly shaped, and a dazzling sunset-orange backed with yellow, glowing against dark, purple-toned foliage. Scent is present, though not lavishly. Kordes introduced it in 1987.

Parentage undisclosed
Repeat flowering

'Takao'　Large-flowered
The rose dedicated to Princess Takao by the Japanese raiser Okumoto is a

beauty, with large shapely blooms, whose pointed petals reflex most elegantly. They have the fragrance of a Damask Rose, and start life deep yellow, gradually becoming entirely scarlet. Foliage is medium sized and mid-green. Okumoto-san introduced 'Takao' in 1975. Unfortunately, it appears to be available only in Japan. It would probably make a sensation in the West. Princess Takao was the last member of the Tahitian Royal family.

('Masquerade' × 'Lydia') × ('Montezuma' × 'Miss Ireland')
Repeat flowering
Fragrant

'Talisman'　Large-flowered
In most catalogues today 'Talisman' has given way to its great-grandchild 'Granada' but there are many old rosarians who ask for it still. It remains an easy rose to grow, the bolt-upright bushes bearing their medium-sized rather flat blooms with great freedom. When it came out in 1929, there was

▲ 'Talisman'

nothing quite like its scarlet and gold brilliance, and the Montgomery Rose Company, its raisers, asked and got six times the price of other roses for it. For many years one of the leading florist's roses, it has inherited the tendency of 'Ophelia' to produce sports—no fewer than thirty-nine of them. Foliage is light green and semi-glossy.

'Ophelia' × 'Souvenir de Claudius Pernet'
Repeat flowering
Fragrant

▲ 'Tangerine Tango'

'Tangerine Tango' Cluster-flowered

Not for a hundred years have so many striped roses been released, with Sam McGredy in New Zealand and Armstrong's in California vying in their raising. The older ones arose as sports, but these are deliberately raised, building on Ralph Moore's work with striped Miniatures. If you followed their family trees, you would probably find his 'Stars 'n' Stripes'. 'Tangerine Tango', introduced in 1991 by Armstrong's, is a pretty conventional orange-red rose, except for the amazing white stripes. It has leaden green leaves.

Parentage undisclosed
Repeat flowering

▶ 'Tatjana'

'Tasogare' Cluster-flowered

Tasogare is Japanese for 'in the twilight'. This rose has prettily shaped, fragrant blooms in wide clusters on a spreading bush. It does not seem to be available in the West. It is an unusual shade of mauve, and it seems to be free of the mildew which sometimes troubles roses of this color. It was raised by Moriji Kobayashi and introduced in 1977. Foliage is dark green and glossy.

'Gletscher' × ('Sterling Silver' × 'Gletscher')
Repeat flowering
Fragrant

'Tatjana' Large-flowered

KORtat
'Rosenthal', 'Rosenwunder'
Rosenthal make some delicate bowls and vases which would show this rose off perfectly. There are not many petals, but the buds are quite long and elegant, and the blooms very fragrant. For a red rose, it is very resistant to mildew. Foliage is dark green and dull. It is a Reimer Kordes introduction of 1970.

'Liebezauber' × 'Präsident Dr H. C. Schröder'
Repeat flowering
Fragrant

▲ 'Tasogare'
▼ 'Tausendschön'

'Tausendschön' Rambler

'Thousand Beauties'
'Tausendschön' was raised by the German breeder Schmidt in 1906, and earns its name from the freedom with which, late in the spring, it adorns its thornless branches with clusters of smallish, prettily cup-shaped flowers, against emerald-green, glossy foliage. They open a delicate ice-cream-pink and gradually pass to white. It is notably disease resistant and easy to grow, but is not especially fragrant. In 1914, it gave rise to a sport, 'Echo' ('Baby Tausendschön'), a small, repeat-flowering bush, classed as a Polyantha. In its turn, 'Echo' produced a series of more brightly colored sports, culminating in the orange 'Margo Koster', for very many years popular in California, though rarely seen now.

'Daniel Lacombe' × 'Weisser Herumstreicher'
Summer flowering

▲ 'Tea Rambler'
▶ 'Tequila'

'Tea Rambler'   Rambler

Raised by William Paul in 1904, 'Tea Rambler' was rather overshadowed at the time by the instant popularity accorded 'Dorothy Perkins'. Now it has many admirers, for its soft color, pink with just a hint of salmon, neat shape, and delicate fragrance. The flowers are smallish, but are carried in good-sized clusters, and look well against the slim branches and clean mid-green leaves. The name is appropriate, for the rose does combine the Rambler style with something of the elegance of the Tea Roses, though not, unfortunately, with their repeat flowering.

'Crimson Rambler' × unknown Tea Rose
Summer flowering
Fragrant

'Teeny'   Large-flowered

This rather lovely pink and white rose was photographed several years ago at Los Angeles's Rose Hills Cemetery, where it was one of the highlights of their collection. To judge by the attention it receives in the catalogues, it might as well not exist. The flowers belie the name, being quite large, and the bush is healthy and prolific, with handsome mid-green foliage. It is of

French origin, from a firm called NIRP International. There are no records of its parentage or date of birth.

Parentage unknown
Repeat flowering

'Tequila'   Cluster-flowered
MEIgavasol

At first sight, just another yellow-going-red Cluster-flowered Rose, but it is not quite. The basic color is actually an orange, with yellow at the heart, and the carmine stain that develops as the flower ages never does quite take it over. The effect in the garden is thus of a mixture of orange and coral flowers, set against dark green, red-tinted foliage on an average-height bush. Introduced in 1982 by Marie-Louisette Meilland, it has happily not inherited the fault of 'Rumba' of clinging to its dead flowers.

'Rusticana' × seedling from 'Rumba'
Repeat flowering

'Texas Centennial'   Large-flowered

Just about every garden used to have a bush of 'Texas Centennial', seemingly always adorned with large, strongly fragrant blooms in beautiful blends of pink and strawberry-red. It can still cause a sensation, and like 'President Herbert Hoover', from which it was a sport, it is one of those roses that seems to do well everywhere. Foliage is dark green and semi-glossy. The introducer was A. F. Watkins of the Dixie Rose Nursery. He and his company are long gone, but are remembered for this beautiful rose, introduced in 1935.

Sport from 'President Herbert Hoover'
Fragrant

'Thalia'   Rambler

For many years one of the most popular white Climbers, 'Thalia', introduced by Schmidt and Peter Lambert in 1895, is something of a back number now, for there are many white Ramblers available. A large old plant of 'Thalia', however, in full late spring bloom, its great trusses of creamy flowers set against dark green leaves and exhaling sweet fragrance, can still cause oohs and aahs of delight. It is not repeat flowering, though, and a heavy shower of rain will ruin the display.

Parentage unknown
Spring flowering
Fragrant

▲ 'Texas Centennial'
◀ 'Teeny'
▶ 'Thalia'

▲ 'The Doctor'
▼ 'The Fairy'

'The Doctor'　Large-flowered

'The Doctor' was Dr J. H. Nicolas, the Director of Research for Jackson & Perkins, but the rose was introduced by Howard & Smith—an exemplary courtesy from one raiser to a rival. There are many people still who consider its cool, clear color to be the loveliest of any pink rose. The enormous, high-centred blooms are very fragrant indeed. It is no longer an easy rose to grow, however, needing extra care and protection from disease. Foliage is a soft leaden green. It was introduced in 1939.

'Mrs J. D. Eisele' × 'Los Angeles'
Repeat flowering
Fragrant

'The Fairy'　Polyantha

During all the years the Polyanthas have been out of fashion, 'The Fairy' has retained the affection of rose-lovers. Few roses are easier to grow, and the short but spreading bushes are densely clad in disease-proof dark green, glossy leaves and adorned for most of the year with clusters of neat small flowers in a lovely shade of clear pink. Its only fault is that they fade in hot weather. 'The Fairy' is still one of the very best low-growing roses, and the parent of many of the better Ground Cover Roses. It was introduced by J. A. Bentall in 1932.

Thought to be a sport from 'Lady Godiva'
Repeat flowering

'The Flower Arranger'　Cluster-flowered
FRYjam

An English-raised rose, from Fryer's in 1984. It has not been much grown elsewhere. Its peach and apricot flowers are nicely shaped and borne in well-spaced clusters. They are, as befits a rose named for the silver jubilee of the National Association of Flower Arrangers, fine cut flowers. The bush is upright and bushy, with large, glossy, dark green foliage. Scent is only slight.

Unnamed seedling × unnamed seedling
Repeat flowering

'The Miller'　English Rose

This rose is the first, alphabetically, of a series of David Austin roses named for characters in *The Canterbury Tales*. 'The Miller' bears medium-sized flowers, rose-pink and slightly fragrant, in sprays, like a compromise between a Cluster-flowered and a Bourbon Rose. The bush is head high, but can be held at little over a metre (3 feet) with firm pruning, and it flowers repeatedly. Foliage is mid-green. Introduced in 1970, the rose is surpassed in quality by several of Austin's later introductions. However, its reputation for good performance in difficult conditions earns it a place here.

'Baroness Rothschild' × 'Constance Spry'
Repeat flowering
Fragrant

▲ 'The Flower Arranger'
▼ 'The Miller'

'The Prioress'　English Rose

'The Prioress' makes a rather slender bush with cupped blooms in pearly pink, lightly fragrant and borne repeatedly. It is really more like a Cluster-flowered Rose in its habit than a Shrub. Foliage is mid-green. It was introduced in 1969 by David Austin.

'La Reine Victoria' × unnamed seedling or 'Ma Perkins' × unnamed seedling
Repeat flowering

▼ 'The Prioress'

'The Squire' — English Rose

Very dark red roses are difficult for the raiser to come up with. The color is associated with reluctant growth, as though nature would prefer to do without it. 'The Squire' is one of the few David Austin roses that needs coddling. It will, however, make quite a sturdy, if somewhat leggy, bush, and the deepest crimson colored flowers, perfectly cupped and quartered, are very fragrant. Do not expect them in lavish quantity. Foliage is dark green and rough textured.

'The Knight' × 'Château de Clos Vougeot'
Repeat flowering

▲ 'The Squire'
▶ 'Tiffany'

'The Sun' — Cluster-flowered

'The Sun' was sponsored by and named for Rupert Murdoch's London-based newspaper, but the coral of its flowers *is* suggestive of dawn or sunset. Perhaps more of dawn, as it pales a little with age and the effect en masse is more delicate than an individual, young flower might suggest. Shapely in the bud, the blooms rapidly open wide. They are borne in good clusters on a mid-sized bush of neat habit with glossy, olive-green foliage. There is scent, but not enough to get excited over. Introduced by Sam McGredy in 1973, 'The Sun' is the result of rather mixed breeding.

('Little Darling' × 'Goldilocks') × 'Irish Mist'
Repeat flowering
Fragrant

▶ 'The Sun'

'The Yeoman' — English Rose

This is a lovely rose, with its wide and informal blooms of soft pink, shaded and flushed with apricot, and its strong fragrance. It is not one of the sturdiest of the David Austin roses, needing good care to give of its best. Where it flourishes, it makes a bushy plant to about 1.5 metres (5 feet) tall, flowering very freely in early summer and quite well later. Foliage is mid-green. With regular Cluster-flowered type pruning, it can be used as a bedding rose. It was introduced in 1969.

'Ivory Fashion' × ('Constance Spry' × 'Monique')
Repeat flowering
Fragrant

'Tiffany' — Large-flowered

This 1955 AARS winner from Bob Lindquist is a favorite pink rose. Its cool, silvery color is made luminous by a glow of yellow at the heart, and the long buds open wide and elegant. It is a grandchild of 'Talisman', from which it inherits upright growth, olive-green foliage and delightful fragrance. It is an easy rose to grow, being of sturdy disposition. The ARS gave it the Gamble Medal for fragrance in 1962 and it will

▲ 'The Yeoman'
▼ 'Tiki'

probably be around for many years yet.

'Charlotte Armstrong' × 'Girona'
Repeat flowering
Fragrant

'Tiki' — Cluster-flowered

Slightly fragrant, the flowers of 'Tiki' are fairly large, to 9 centimetres (3½ inches), and shapely. They tend to come in fairly small clusters and the color is a blend of salmon and coral-pink, deeper on the outside of the bloom, paler at the heart, rather in the manner of 'Pink Parfait'. The bush is sturdy and dark green foliage is glossy. 'Tiki' has never been nearly as popular, however, as its sister seedling, 'Violet Carson'. 'Tiki' was named by Sam McGredy on the occasion of his 1964 visit to New Zealand, where he subsequently settled.

'Madame Léon Cuny' × 'Spartan'
Repeat flowering
Fragrant

'Titian'
Modern Shrub

Officially, 'Titian' is a Cluster-flowered Bush Rose. In Australia, where it was raised and introduced in 1950, its vigor is such that it is always grown as a large shrub or trained as a pillar rose. Few roses can outdazzle it when it is in full bloom, covered from top to bottom with large, lightly fragrant flowers. The color is extraordinary: close up they are deep pink, but at a little distance the sun lends them such brilliance that they seem scarlet, and their tone intensifies with age. One of the healthiest and easiest of all roses to grow, it was raised by Frank Riethmuller of Sydney, apparently from the Kordes Shrub Rose strain. Foliage is soft green. A very vigorous climbing sport appeared in Germany in 1964.

Parentage unknown
Repeat flowering

'Tobago'
Cluster-flowered

DELtago

A strong-growing rose that bears really charming, fragrant blooms of apricot-yellow splashed with pink against dark green, semi-glossy foliage. They hold their even tone until they drop without going spotty the way many blended

▲ 'Titian'
▼ 'Tobago'

▲ 'Today'

roses do. It seems to have dropped out of the catalogues these days. It came from Delbard in 1961.

'Avalanche' × ('Zambra' × 'Orange Sensation')
Repeat flowering
Fragrant

'Today'
Large-flowered

MACcompu

'Today' is still a very new rose—Sam McGredy introduced it only in 1990—so perhaps it will improve with age. The flowers, perhaps, are a bit too small to be in proportion with the very strong, tall bush. People made this same complaint about 'Pascali', and it was a great hit. Everything else is good news: the blooms are shapely and long lasting, they hold their bright orange and yellow until they drop, without going red or purple, and they harmonize perfectly with the bronze-green foliage. Scent is quite good.

Unnamed seedling × unnamed seedling
Repeat flowering
Fragrant

▼ 'Torvill and Dean'

▲ 'Tony Jacklin'

'Tony Jacklin'
Cluster-flowered

One of the shapeliest of all the exhibition-style Cluster-flowered Roses, and fragrant too, 'Tony Jacklin' is a lovely soft shade of coral, luminous without being harsh. The clusters are not large, but nicely spaced, and the average-sized bush is strong and healthy, with olive-green semi-glossy foliage. This 1972 McGredy introduction deserves more attention than it gets. Sam McGredy usually gives the details of the breeding, but not in this case. It is named for the popular English golfer.

Parentage undisclosed
Repeat flowering
Fragrant

'Torvill and Dean'
Large-flowered

LANtor

The British team of Jayne Torvill and Christopher Dean skated their way to Olympic gold medals and the adulation of millions. Their rose may not be quite such a medal winner, but it has many admirers for its fine form and the way pink and gold dance together across the petals. The bush is strong and upright, its foliage dark green and glossy. The

fragrance is only slight, unfortunately, and it has inherited a preference for cool climates from its parents. Bees of Chester introduced it in 1984.

'Grandpa Dickson' × 'Alexander'
Repeat flowering

'Touch of Class' Large-flowered
KRIcarlo
'Maréchal le Clerc'
The name is pure American; indeed 'Touch of Class' was the AARS award-winner for 1986. It is, in fact, of French origin, coming from the long-estab-lished Michel Kriloff of Antibes, and in Europe it is just as likely to be found as 'Maréchal le Clerc'. It is a very fine rose, tall, strong, shapely and distinc-tive in its blends of pink and coral, which grow more delicate towards the heart of the flower. Foliage is dark green and semi-glossy. Much prized for exhibition and for cutting, it has two faults: only slight fragrance and a predilection for mildew.

'Micaëla' × ('Queen Elizabeth' × 'Romantica')
Repeat flowering

'Tournament of Roses' Large-flowered
JACient
The blooms are quite large, of fine form, and often come in small clusters, hence its United States classification of

▼ 'Tournament of Roses'

◄ 'Touch of Class'
▼ 'Träumerei'

'Grandiflora'. The color is light pink, deeper on the reverse, reminiscent of 'Madame Abel Chatenay' with a touch of coral, though its scent is nowhere near as strong. The bush is tallish, with glossy green leaves. It was introduced by Bill Warriner and won the 1989 AARS award.

'Impatient' × unnamed seedling
Repeat flowering

'Träumerei' Cluster-flowered
KORrei
'Reikor', 'Reverie'
This relatively little known rose is one of the most outstanding of the larger-flowered Cluster-flowered Roses, its

coral orange flowers shapely, long lasting both on the bush and in the vase, and intensely fragrant. It is a free-blooming and compact bush, with glossy, olive-green foliage. It is a 1974 introduction from Reimer Kordes. Kordes's Australian agent, Roy Rumsey, suggests it as a companion plant for 'Friesia'. 'Träumerei' (or 'Dreaming') is one of the best-loved piano pieces of Robert Schumann.

'Königin der Rosen' × unnamed seedling
Repeat flowering
Fragrant

'Träumland' Cluster-flowered
'Dreamland'
Pink with a hint of coral, 'Träumland' bears slightly scented, open flowers on a low growing bush, not quite as small as, say, 'China Doll', but not much larger. The foliage is leathery, dark green and usually free from disease. It is one of the earliest of the very short-statured Cluster-flowered Roses, having come from Mathias Tantau in 1958. You will usually find it listed under the English version of the name.

'Cinnabar Improved' × 'Fashion'
Repeat flowering

▼ 'Träumland'

'Traviata'
Large-flowered

Verdi's opera *La Traviata* is based on Alexandre Dumas's novel *La Dame aux Camélias* whose heroine sometimes wore a white flower, and sometimes a red one. The rose combines both in a bicolor arrangement, and also adds good fragrance. Growth and mid-green foliage are fine, and it is surprising that this rose, introduced by Alain Meilland in 1962, has not made more of an impact than it has. Fragrant bicolors are not all that common.

'Baccarà' ('Independence' × 'Grand'mère Jenny')
Repeat flowering
Fragrant

▼ 'Traviata'

'Tribute'
Large-flowered

JACrose

'Tribute' gets a demerit for lacking the strong fragrance that one expects from a rose with its bright cerise coloring. Otherwise it is a fine rose, its long buds opening ruffled and informal and the bush of sturdy, upright habit, with large foliage. Bill Warriner was the raiser and it was introduced in 1983 by Jackson & Perkins.

Unnamed seedling × unnamed seedling
Repeat flowering

▲ 'Tricolore de Flandre'
▶ 'Trigintipetala'

'Tricolore de Flandre'
Gallica

Finely striped in both purple and blush, 'Tricolore de Flandre' is much in the mould of 'Camaieux'. It is a little less subtle in its tonings perhaps, but makes up for that by being easier to grow. It has a few more petals too, but this is no great advantage in displaying the stripes. It is sweetly scented, and the plant is compact and rather bushy, with rough-textured, mid-green foliage. The name is a patriotic gesture by the raiser, Louis van Houtte (in 1846). The van Houtte nurseries, in what is now called Belgium, were responsible for introducing many plants as well as roses, best known among them being the Golden Elm, *Ulmus* 'Vanhoutteana'.

Parentage unknown
Summer flowering
Fragrant

'Trier'
Rambler

Introduced by Peter Lambert in 1904, 'Trier' was in its day admired as the most perpetually flowering of Climbing Roses. Nowadays we have many repeat-flowering Climbers, and 'Trier' is remembered chiefly as the progenitor of Joseph Pemberton's Hybrid Musks. Its scented off-white flowers come in bunches all season, and look well against the pale green leaves. It is not really a Rambler: it is decidedly shrubby in growth and needs much encouragement to climb to 2 metres (6 feet). It is believed to be a self-pollinated seedling of the now almost extinct Rambler 'Aglaia'. Trier is the town in Germany, founded by the Romans, where Lambert had his nursery.

Probably 'Aglaia' × 'Aglaia'
Repeat flowering
Fragrant

◀ 'Tribute'

'Trigintipetala'
Damask

Rosa damascena trigintipetala, 'Kazanlik'

Kazanlik is the centre of the Valley of Roses in Bulgaria, where the Attar of Roses comes from; and this is the rose from which it is chiefly made. A very ancient rose, it makes an arching bush with soft, rather pale green leaves and bears flowers in great profusion. They do not usually have quite the thirty petals that the name implies, and they are not especially shapely. Their bland cool pink is restful and charming, however, and the scent is wonderfully intense and sweet. You often find its buds dried in pot-pourri, and they display the elongated receptacle typical of the Damasks very well.

Parentage unknown
Spring flowering
Fragrant

▼ 'Trier'

'Troilus'
English Rose

One of the largest of the David Austin English Roses, this 1983 introduction is capable of producing some sumptuous flowers, huge, full of petals and with fragrance. They are a lovely shade of buff, paler on the outer petals. Often they come in clusters, when the individual blooms are not quite so large.

▲ 'Troilus'
▼ 'Tropique'

'Trumpeter' — Cluster-flowered

Named, like its parent 'Satchmo', in honor of the late Louis Armstrong, 'Trumpeter' is regarded by many people as the very best of the orange-red Cluster-flowered Roses. The flowers are medium sized, neatly formed without being especially shapely, only slightly scented, but they are borne in great abundance, and hold their jazzy color until they drop, without fading, burning, or turning purple. Foliage is mid-green and glossy. It was raised in New Zealand by Sam McGredy and introduced in 1977.

'Satchmo' × unnamed seedling
Repeat flowering

▲ 'Trumpeter'
◄ 'Tuscany'

The bush is moderate in growth, to about 1.2 metres (4 feet), and sturdy, with broad, Large-flowered style mid-green foliage. It is named for the hero of Shakespeare's tragedy of the Trojan War, *Troilus and Cressida*.

('Duchesse de Montebello' × 'Chaucer') × 'Charles Austin'
Repeat flowering
Fragrant

'Tuscany' — Gallica

Often claimed to be of high antiquity, and to be the 'Velvet Rose' described by Gerard in the sixteenth century, 'Tuscany' is one of the very best of all the almost-black roses, its wine-dark blooms set off by golden stamens. The bush is compact and floriferous, with leaden green foliage. Some think this rose is of Italian origin, owing its dark color to *Rosa pendulina*; most think it looks pure-bred *R. gallica*. Its sport, 'Tuscany Superb', is preferred by many to the original. The flowers are larger, the scent is sweeter and the foliage more luxuriant.

Parentage unknown
Summer flowering
Fragrant

'Tropique' — Large-flowered

This is a fine pillar rose, with dark green foliage and clusters of Cluster-flowered style flowers in hot scarlet on and off all season. It suffers in the popularity stakes from being rather like the slightly earlier (1954) 'Danse du Feu', but it holds its color better. Georges Delbard raised it and introduced it in 1956.

Parentage undisclosed
Repeat flowering

'Typhoon' — Large-flowered
'Taifun'

The odds of getting a marketable rose from a batch of seedlings are thousands to one against. How much more they must be against getting two out of the same seed pod. That is what happened to Reimer Kordes in 1972 with 'Adolf Horstmann' and 'Typhoon'. The two are very much alike, 'Typhoon' having less yellow in its copper-gold-pink blend than its sibling. The bush is strong and healthy, with olive-green semi-glossy foliage, and the flowers are so resistant to bad weather that, as Sam McGredy has said, it would take quite a storm to flatten them—hence the name.

'Dr A. J. Verhage' × 'Königin der Rosen'
Repeat flowering
Fragrant

▼ 'Typhoon'

▲ 'Tyriana'

'Tyriana'　　　　Large-flowered

The tyrian purple dye that was so precious in Roman days that it was reserved for the emperors is actually a bright blood-red, but the name survives for a color between red and purple—exactly the color of this rose in fact. It was raised by Meilland in 1963, but has vanished from the catalogues already. It was photographed in the collection of the Roseraie de l'Haÿ near Paris. Its spectacular coloring should have won it enduring fame. Foliage is dark green.

Parentage undisclosed
Repeat flowering
Fragrant

'Uncle Sam'　　　　Large-flowered

'Uncle Sam wants YOU!' the army recruitment posters used to tell young Americans, but it seems American rose-lovers no longer want 'Uncle Sam'. This 1965 creation from Bill Warriner and Jackson & Perkins has disappeared from the catalogues. It is worth recording, however, for its large, long-budded flowers in glowing deep

pink—not the rose-buyer's favorite color, admittedly. The bush is tallish, the foliage deep green and matt but not very luxuriant.

'Charlotte Armstrong' × 'Heart's Desire'
Repeat flowering
Fragrant

'Uncle Walter'　　　　Large-flowered
MACon

'A real man's rose' said Sam McGredy when in 1963 he dedicated 'Uncle Walter' to his Uncle Walter Johnson, who ran the McGredy nurseries after Sam McGredy II's death. It is certainly virile in growth, and it is better regarded as a Shrub Rose than a Bush Rose. Try it as a red companion for 'Queen Elizabeth'. The blood-red blooms are of perfect exhibition form, but they need a cool climate to achieve any size. In Australia they are rarely more than 8 centimetres (3 inches) across. The foliage is glossy, olive-green, with red tints in its youth. The scent is only slight, but the brilliant color is quite unfading.

'Schlössers Brilliant' × 'Heidelberg'
Repeat flowering

▲ 'Uncle Walter'
▼ 'Uncle Sam'

▲ 'Unique Blanche'
▼ 'Vale of Clwydd'

'Unique Blanche'　　　　Centifolia
'Unique', 'Vierge de Cléry', 'White Provence'

'Unique Blanche' is to all intents a white form of *Rosa centifolia*, the 'Rose des Peintres', and closely resembles it in its growth, foliage and shape of flower. Where *R. centifolia* is soft pink, this one is white, opening from pink buds and often retaining a touch of pink on the outermost petals. Foliage is soft green and coarsely toothed. There is sweet fragrance. In the old days 'Unique Blanche' had a reputation for flowering late but then continuing in bloom for an exceptionally long time. It was discovered in 1775, in a cottage garden in Suffolk, and it is said that the nurseryman who discovered it made so much money by it that he sent the original owner a valuable silver cup by way of thanks. How it acquired so many French names is unexplained.

Parentage unknown
Summer flowering
Fragrant

'Vale of Clwydd'　　　　Cluster-flowered
BEEval

This striking rose was photographed at the Chelsea Show in 1984, the year

▲ 'Valerie Swane'

after its introduction by Bees of Chester. It should have had a great future. It seems, however, that it is now only available in India. The flowers combine the bright yellow of its pollen parent, 'Arthur Bell', with the distinctive carmine edge of its seed parent, 'Handel'. Foliage is mid-green and semi-glossy. There is no perfume.

'Arthur Bell' × 'Handel'
Repeat flowering

'Valerie Swane'   Large-flowered

ARObipy
'Crystalline'

The IRA has ruled that 'Valerie Swane' and 'Crystalline' are the same rose. Valerie Swane, one of Australia's foremost rose-growers, said no, and listed them separately in her catalogue. Her rose, she claimed, is more ivory in its whiteness than 'Crystalline', is slightly larger in its blooms, less tall in its growth and, most important, much more fragrant. Nevertheless, they are very alike. Foliage is mid-green. Jack Christensen is given the credit, in 1987.

Parentage unknown
Repeat flowering
Fragrant

'Variegata di Bologna'   Bourbon

This is a latecomer for a Bourbon, having been introduced by an otherwise obscure rosarian called Bonfigioli in 1909. In some ways it is the most striking of all striped roses, the pinkish off-white flowers being lavishly striped with violet. They are well scented too. The bush is tall and arching, with leaden green foliage, and flowers lavishly in spring but sparingly thereafter. It needs rich soil. Starved, it is liable to

take black spot. Occasionally, it reverts to its parent 'Victor Emmanuel', a fine dark violet rose in its own right.

Sport from 'Victor Emmanuel'
Repeat flowering
Fragrant

'Veilchenblau'   Rambler

'Blue Veil', 'Violet Blue', 'Blue Rambler', 'Rosalie'

'Veilchenblau' was introduced in 1909 with loud claims that here at last was the blue rose. Blue it is not: rather the little flowers, in generous clusters, open purple and pass to delicate shades of lilac and mauve, against light green foliage. Hot sun bleaches them into dowdiness, so this is one of the few roses which is best grown in light shade. Its proud raiser, Schmidt of Erfurt, could not have foreseen that, thornless and easily raised from cuttings, it has been used as an understock.

'Crimson Rambler' × 'Errinerung an Brod'
Summer flowering

'Vendôme'   Rambler

It is rather disappointing to find that this cherry-red Rambler, which makes such a delightful backdrop to the statue of the centaur at Malmaison (page 335), has dropped out of the catalogues and disappeared from the reference books, its name recycled for a salmon-pink Cluster-flowered Rose. The original 'Vendôme' still survives in the collection of the Roseraie de L'Haÿ, but if you fancy recreating the Malmaison picture in your own garden, 'Paul's Scarlet' would be a good substitute.

Parentage unknown
Summer flowering

▲ 'Variegata di Bologna'

▲ 'Veilchenblau'
▼ 'Vendôme'

'Versicolor' — Gallica
Rosa gallica versicolor, R. g. variegata, 'Rosa Mundi'

The original striped rose, and in many people's eyes still the best, this is a sport of 'Officinalis' which it exactly resembles except for the carmine and blush stripes and splashes on its petals. Foliage is mid-green and stiff. This rose's beauty and popularity has led to a great deal of romantic nonsense being written about it: how it was brought back from Damascus by a lovesick, and garden-conscious, crusader and dedicated to the 'Fayre Rosamond' (also known as Jane Clifford), the mistress of Henry II. The facts are that it originated in a Norfolk garden in the early years of the seventeenth century.

Sport from 'Officinalis'
Summer flowering
Fragrant

▲ 'Versicolor'

'Via Mala' — Large-flowered
VIAkor

Quite what Reimer Kordes expected from this 1977 cross of his mauve 'Silver Star', rarely seen now, and the bright yellow 'Peer Gynt' is hard to imagine. The result is a most attractive white rose. The blooms are double (thirty-three petals), high centred and shapely, opening from long buds, and the bush is upright with leathery, glossy, dark green leaves. Scent is only slight, and you may find the blooms need protection from prolonged wet weather, a common failing in white roses with their delicate petals. Scent is only slight.

'Silver Star' × 'Peer Gynt'
Repeat flowering

'Vick's Caprice' — Hybrid Perpetual
'Wick's Caprice'

Vick was the gentleman in whose Rochester, New York, garden this rose appeared in 1892 as a sport from pink 'Archduchesse Elisabeth d'Autriche'. It is an upright, not overly tall bush, with large, mid-green leaves and full-petalled flowers, pleasantly fragrant but memorable mainly for their bizarre stripings in lilac-pink, white and carmine. Every bloom is different, and they are borne repeatedly. Its fault is intolerance of wet weather, which makes the flowers 'ball' and refuse to open.

Sport from 'Archduchesse Elisabeth d'Autriche'
Repeat flowering
Fragrant

▲ 'Victor Hugo'

'Victor Hugo' — Large-flowered
MEIvestal
'Senator Burda', 'Spirit of Youth'

The rose illustrated is not Ernest Schwartz's dark red Hybrid Perpetual of 1884, but a newish one from Marie-Louisette Meilland, introduced in 1985. It is as dramatic as the great French writer and patriot himself. The flowers are huge, brilliantly deep in color, and the foliage is mid-green and leathery. It is widely listed in France, but outside that country it is virtually unknown as yet. Scent is good.

Parentage undisclosed
Repeat flowering
Fragrant

▲ 'Via Mala'
▼ 'Vick's Caprice'

▲ 'Vesper'

'Vesper' — Cluster-flowered
In a photograph, this lovely rose might look to be just another salmon-pink flower, but in real life it is a very distinct color that can only be described as a pastel orange. It shows up very well under artificial light, which makes 'Vesper' a desirable rose for cutting, and it flowers well on a sturdy bush, against small, blue-grey foliage. It seems to be a better rose in a cool climate, though; hot sun can fade the flowers so that they really are just a 'nothing' pink. It is a 1966 introduction from E. B. LeGrice.

Parentage undisclosed
Repeat flowering
Fragrant

'Victoriana' — Cluster-flowered

The late E. B. LeGrice had a talent for raising roses in unusual colors, and this, one of his last (it came out in 1977), is one of the most extraordinary of all. The shapely blooms combine deep orange and brown, with distinct flushes of purple. The reverses of the petals are white. They are sweetly scented, and the bush, though not tall, is vigorous enough, with dark olive-green leaves. Flower arrangers are apt to fall in love with it at first sight.

Parentage undisclosed
Repeat flowering
Fragrant

'Vienna Charm' — Large-flowered

KORschprat
'Wiener Charme', 'Charme de Vienne', 'Charming Vienna'

'Vienna Charm' is one of those infuriating roses that is utterly gorgeous, but temperamental to grow. Humidity will cause it to snuffle with black spot and mildew, and cold cuts it back. It is only in a warm, dry climate that you can rely on the tall, lanky bush giving anything like a generous number of its huge blooms in their unique color. The color was well described by the raiser Reimer Kordes as 'somewhere between copper and pure gold'. The buds are long, the open blooms loose, and they are fragrant. Foliage is glossy and dark green. Kordes raised it and introduced it in 1963.

'Golden Sun' × 'Chantré'
Repeat flowering
Fragrant

'Ville d'Angers' — Large-flowered

Introduced in 1929 by Belgian nurseryman Louis Lens (who gave us 'Pascali' thirty-four years later), 'Ville d'Angers' was a very popular rose in its day. Its cerise color was considered clear and bright, its petals were elegantly and regularly arranged, and it was well regarded as a bedding and general garden rose. It has lost popularity, and is now only seen in the collection of rose antiques at the Roseraie de l'Haÿ. It is not particularly fragrant, and compared with the lusty, glossy sturdiness of the post-World-War-II roses raised from 'Peace', its matt-leafed bush is likely to look rather thin.

Parentage undisclosed
Repeat flowering

▲ 'Ville d'Angers'
◄ 'Victoriana'
► 'Violet Carson'

'Violacea' — Gallica

'La Belle Sutane', 'Maheka', 'Cumberland'

Tall, pale-leafed and arching in growth, like a Damask, 'Violacea' flowers early in the season. While it does not stay out as long as some, it is a splendid sight in full bloom, the almost single flowers being deep rich purple, with an almost white zone around the golden stamens. Give it a pale rose, or a clump

▲ 'Violacea'

of something like a campanula, to set off its dark color, and let the experts fight over its origin and age.

Parentage unknown
Summer flowering

'Violet Carson' — Cluster-flowered

MACio

One of the leading characters in 'Coronation Street' was 'that dreadful woman' Ena Sharples, played by Violet Carson, a keen rose-lover away from the cameras. 'Violet Carson', the rose, bears the prettiest flowers imaginable. They are softly fragrant, of perfect form, like miniature exhibition roses, and of gentle soft salmon-pink with cream on the reverse. They come in good-sized clusters on an average-sized bush adorned with dark olive-green, glossy foliage, strikingly plum colored in its youth. A Sam McGredy creation, introduced in 1963, it has a pleasing light fragrance.

'Madame Léon Cuny' × 'Spartan'
Repeat flowering
Fragrant

◄ 'Vienna Charm'

'Virgo' — Large-flowered
'Virgo Liberationem'

For many years after its introduction in 1947, 'Virgo' was *the* white rose, loved for the purity of its color, warmed by just a suggestion of ivory at the heart, and for the supreme elegance of the way in which the shell-shaped petals unfold from the long buds (the open blooms are rather flat). It is a rose that needs good cultivation, however, being only moderately vigorous and rather subject to mildew on its leaden green leaves. Wet weather spots its delicate petals. 'Pascali' may be more reliable, but a vase of perfect blooms of 'Virgo' is loveliness indeed. It is one of the jewels of Charles Mallerin's art as a hybridist.

'Blanche Mallerin' × 'Neige Parfum'
Repeat flowering

▲ 'Virgo'
▼ 'Viridiflora'

'Viridiflora' — China
'Green Rose', 'Monstrosa'

No one seems to know the true origin of the 'Green Rose', but it has been around since the 1830s and looks as though it will find its way into catalogues for years to come. Not because it is any great beauty but because it is so curious. It has no petals, just a bunch of green leaves. In bud it is quite pretty, but the open 6 centimetre (2½ inch) pompoms are apt to be spoiled by maroon blotches. Naturally, there is no scent, but the flowers are very long lasting and useful for arrangements. The bush grows to a metre (3 feet) and flowers all season. Foliage is dark green and glossy.

Parentage unknown
Repeat flowering

'Vision' — Large-flowered
POUloni
'Benoni 75'

There are two roses of this name: one, a pink and gold Large-flowered Rose, came from Pat Dickson in 1967. The rose in the picture is the other one, which was introduced ten years later by Niels Poulsen. It is a pleasing salmon-red rose, best in a cool climate (the twenty-two petals open rather too quickly in hot weather), its warm color well set off by dark green, shiny foliage. The scent from 'Vision', regrettably, is only slight.

Parentage undisclosed
Repeat flowering

'Viva' — Cluster-flowered
This 1974 Jackson & Perkins introduction, raised by Bill Warriner, is no longer as widely grown as it used to be. It is still a handsome rose, its deep, velvet-red blooms almost of Large-flowered Rose size and beautifully formed. It is usually well furnished with bloom and the tallish plants, with dark green, glossy foliage, are healthy. Perhaps its lack of strong fragrance, a quality expected in a rose of its color, has lost it admirers.

Unnamed seedling × unnamed seedling
Repeat flowering

◀ 'Viva'
▼ 'Vogue'

'Vogue' — Cluster-flowered
Legend has it that 'Vogue' sprang from the very same seed pod as 'Fashion', one of Eugene Boerner's most successful roses. It is a very fine rose in its own right, good enough to win the AARS award in 1952. Its flowers are darker than those of 'Fashion'—deep pink with just a touch of coral—but they are more sweetly scented and borne in beautifully spaced clusters on a healthier bush. It is one of the first to show its flowers and the last to finish.

▼ 'Vision'

▲ 'Vol de Nuit'

Foliage is grey-green and glossy. It has given rise to an excellent clear medium pink sport, 'Bazaar'.

'Pinocchio' × 'Crimson Glory'
Repeat flowering
Fragrant

'Vol de Nuit' — Large-flowered
DELrio
'Night Flight'

'Vol de Nuit' is one of the loveliest of the mauve Large-flowered Roses, its color richer than most and it is often warmed with pink. The blooms are of good size and shape; scent is excellent; and the plant is as strong as any of its color. (Many mauves are only of moderate vigor.) Foliage is light green and matt. The name is from the novel by Antoine de Saint-Exupéry, after whom the raiser, Georges Delbard, had already named a mauve rose.

Unnamed seedling × 'Saint-Exupéry'
Repeat flowering
Fragrant

'Voodoo' — Large-flowered
AROmiclea

If you insist on the rare combination of brilliant color and rich fragrance, then 'Voodoo' is for you. Its blend of red, coral and gold stands out in the garden, and the fragrance is excellent, the bush vigorous, with dark green, glossy foliage. If it has a fault, it is that the leaves could be a little bigger. There are also suggestions that it dislikes cool, sunless climates. It was raised in California, under the hand of Jack Christensen. It won the 1988 AARS award.

['Camelot' × ('First Prize' × 'Typhoo Tea')] × 'Lolita'
Repeat flowering
Fragrant

'Waiheke' — Cluster-flowered
MACwaihe
'Waikiki

This is a most handsome rose, its large blooms opening from long and elegant buds. They come both in small clusters and singly on a tall bush, and they are bicolored, in coral with cream reverses to the petals. They are lightly fragrant. Foliage is a glossy, dark green. It was raised by Sam McGredy and introduced in 1987. It looks very promising.

Parentage undisclosed
Repeat flowering

'Wapiti' — Cluster-flowered
MEInagre
'Laurence Olivier'

Introduced in Europe in 1988, this is an interesting rose. Its ruffled flowers are of good size and a most vivid shade of red. They are very freely produced on a bushy, vigorous plant. Foliage is dark green. Whether or not this rose does well in warm climates remains to be seen. It was raised by Marie-Louisette Meilland.

Parentage undisclosed
Repeat flowering

▲ 'Waiheke'
◄ 'Warrawee'

'Warrawee' — Large-flowered

Mrs Harding Fitzhardinge named this rose for the Sydney suburb where she lived and gardened, and for many years it was one of the most popular of pale pink roses in Australia, admired for the Tea Rose delicacy of its flowers and its ability to flourish in the acid, sandy soils of coastal New South Wales. The blooms are high centred and shapely, opening to reveal golden stamens, the petals' delicate shell-pink a shade deeper on the reverse, and they exhale sweet fragrance. Foliage is matt and dull green, and the bush is average in height. Introduced in 1935, it remains a rose of quiet refinement. The old growers maintain it likes fairly hard pruning.

Parentage unknown
Repeat flowering
Fragrant

◄ 'Voodoo'
▼ 'Wapiti'

▲ 'Warrior'
▼ 'Watsoniana'

'Warrior' — Cluster-flowered

This 1977 LeGrice creation has not gained a great deal of publicity, but it is building up a good reputation for its reliability, at least in the cool climates that it apparently prefers. The flowers are neatly formed, borne in large clusters, and look very well against the light green, semi-glossy foliage, purple-tinted when young, which sets off their glowing blood-red color. There is little fragrance, but the blooms last well in the vase, and the plant is bushy.

'City of Belfast' × 'Ronde Endiablée'
Repeat flowering

'Watsoniana' — Shrub

Rosa multiflora watsoniana, 'Bamboo Rose'
'Watsoniana' is often claimed to be a Japanese form of *R. multiflora*, a native of that country, but it seems that in fact

it originated in the garden of a Mr Watson in Albany, New York, and its derivation from *R. multiflora* is by no means certain. It would, however look charming in a Japanese-style garden, with its long, narrow leaflets, often curiously deformed and twisted and mottled in white. It is only quite a small bush, needing a bit of pampering; the small white flowers are scented but otherwise not noteworthy.

Parentage unknown
Repeat flowering
Fragrant

'Wendy Cussons' — Large-flowered

That it has been possible to give the parents of so many of the roses in this book is a tribute to the dedication of their raisers. Keeping track of thousands of seeds and seedlings throughout the development of a new rose is a meticulous and expensive business. Walter Gregory, though one of England's most successful rose nurserymen, frankly admitted that he could not afford to do this, and that although the books give the parents of 'Wendy Cussons' as 'Independence' × 'Eden Rose', he could not guarantee it. No matter, this almost red rose is just about perfect—in a cool climate like Britain's. In warmer areas it grows so vigorously that many flowers come malformed. Foliage is mid-green and leathery.

'Independence' × 'Eden Rose'
Repeat flowering
Fragrant

▲ 'Wendy Cussons'
▼ 'Western Sun'

'Western Sun' — Large-flowered

In 1957, Wilhelm Kordes introduced 'Golden Sun' ('Goldene Sonne'), which was acclaimed for its color, the most luminous yellow of any rose, and deplored for the unreliability of its growth. Svend Poulsen promptly used its pollen on 'Spek's Yellow', and gave us 'Western Sun' in 1965. It has much of 'Golden Sun's' wonderful color, but is a more reliable performer. It remains one of the better very deep yellow roses, even though it does like a bit of pampering. The blooms are large and high centred, the bush on the short side, with dark green, glossy leaves. Scent is not prominent.

'Spek's Yellow' × 'Golden Sun'
Repeat flowering

▲ 'Whisky Mac'
▼ 'White Delight'

'Whisky Mac'   Large-flowered
TANky
'Whisky'

One famous rosarian has described 'Whisky Mac' as the triumph of beauty over commonsense. Everyone grows it, grizzling about its need to be pampered but forgiving it its unreliability for the sake of its wonderful flowers—when they consent to appear. Large, shapely and sweetly perfumed, they are of unique, irresistible and indescribable color: deep gold, burnt orange or the color of a fine malt whisky? Even given the best of everything, the bushes are short lived. Foliage is dark green and glossy. For all its faults, Mathias Tantau must have known it would be a best-seller when he introduced it in 1965.

Parentage undisclosed
Repeat flowering
Fragrant

'White Delight'   Large-flowered
JACglow

Jackson & Perkins's Rose of the Year for 1990 might be better named 'Off-White Delight', for there are distinct

blushes of ivory and coral. The effect is delightful. The blooms are of good size and shape, borne on long straight stems for cutting, and the bush flowers in profusion. Jackson & Perkins claim it is unusually quick to repeat. Foliage is dark green and glossy. Fragrance is only light. Bill Warriner raised it, and is no doubt expecting a great future for it.

'White Masterpiece' × 'Futura'
Repeat flowering

'White Dorothy Perkins'   Rambler
'White Dorothy'

Introduced by the English firm of B. R. Cant & Sons in 1908, this is a sport of the American-raised 'Dorothy Perkins', and exactly like its parent except that the flowers are mostly white. In those days, Ramblers grown in large pots and trained on canes to make pillars of bloom were fashionable decorations for ballrooms and the like, and Cants were among the leading suppliers of them. 'White Dorothy' must have been a pleasant surprise when it appeared in their nursery. Foliage is small, dark green and glossy and has a tendency to develop mildew.

Sport from 'Dorothy Perkins'
Summer flowering

'White Grootendorst'   Hybrid Rugosa
'White Grootendorst' is the newest of the Grootendorst series. It came out in 1962, a sport of 'Pink Grootendorst'. It exactly resembles this rose in its

fringed flowers and its ease of growth and occasionally the half-open flowers will be tinged with palest pink. It is surprising that it has not become as well known as the others in the set. In some ways it is the prettiest, and it would look most attractive planted in tandem with the pink one, maybe as a waist-high hedge, to flower from spring to autumn, or fall. It is just as resistant to extreme cold. Foliage is light green and quilted.

Sport from 'Pink Grootendorst'
Repeat flowering

▲ 'White Grootendorst'
▼ 'White Dorothy Perkins'

▲ 'White Maman Cochet'
▼ 'White Lightnin''

'White Maman Cochet' — Tea

'Maman Cochet' was introduced by S. Cochet in 1893. It is one of the most commonly encountered Tea Roses in America. It is not included here, however, despite its indestructible vigor and perfect form, as there are many other pink Old Garden Roses that outclass it. The white sport, which came from John Cook of Baltimore in 1896, is a different matter. Its creamy blooms, blushed with palest pink in the sun, are really lovely. Do not expect it to endure much rain or cold though, and prune only very lightly. Foliage is dark green, with plum tints, and semi-glossy.

Sport from 'Maman Cochet'
Repeat flowering
Fragrant

'White Mary Rose' — English Rose

This is a sport from David Austin's popular 'Mary Rose'. It certainly seems to be just the same, except for its glistening whiteness, and is a welcome addition to Austin's range. Like its parent, it can be pruned hard for bedding or allowed to grow more freely into quite a large shrub. In either mode it will bear its slightly scented flowers all season. Foliage is mid-green.

Sport from 'Mary Rose'
Repeat flowering

'White Masterpiece' — Large-flowered

'White Masterpiece' gives just about the largest blooms of any white rose, 15 centimetres (6 inches) across, as a matter of course, even more if you pamper it. It should be pampered, for it is not very free with its huge flowers, and hot, humid weather brings on the fungus diseases on the mid-green, glossy leaves. It is really one for the exhibitor, who will be quite enchanted with its perfect form and the delightful greenish glow in the flower's heart. The judges will not be giving points for perfume though. Eugene Boerner was the raiser and he introduced it in 1969.

Unnamed seedling × unnamed seedling
Repeat flowering

▲ 'White Mary Rose'

'White Meidiland' — Ground Cover

MEIcoublan
'Blanc Meillandécor'
Meilland have introduced a series of 'meidiland' roses, designed not so much for home gardens as for landscapers to grow on the verges of roads or in parks. 'White Meidiland', raised in 1987, is perhaps the most attractive. It

'White Lightnin'' — Large-flowered

AROwhit
'White Lightnin'' won the AARS award partly on the strength of its fragrance, which is unusually intense for a pure white rose. It has other good qualities too: the bush is sturdy and reliable, with dark glossy green foliage, and the flowers are borne freely, both one at a time and in small clusters. The thirty petals are most attractively ruffled and the color is clean and clear. The flower is 9–10 centimetres (3½ inches) across. It was raised by Swim and Christensen for Armstrong Nurseries, and was introduced in 1981.

'Angel Face' × 'Misty'
Repeat flowering
Fragrant

▲ 'White Masterpiece'
▶ 'White Meidiland'

makes a densely prostrate, sprawling bush, covering itself several times through the season with clusters of smallish, ivory-white flowers. Foliage is glossy and bright green. Scent is a good point; many of the new Ground Cover Roses lack it. Meilland claim the series need little care, can be pruned with a lawn-mower set high every two or three years, and will put up with people walking on them!

Parentage undisclosed
Repeat flowering
Fragrant

▲ 'White Simplicity'
▼ 'White Sparrieshoop'

▲ 'White Spray'
▼ 'Wienerwald'

'White Simplicity' Cluster-flowered
JACsnow

Bill Warriner scored quite a hit in 1979 with 'Simplicity', designed as an easy-care rose for people with little time for gardening. He followed it up with the red 'Bloomin' Easy' and, in 1990, with 'White Simplicity', to give a more or less matched set in pink, red and white. Some may find the white the nicest of the three; its compact habit, shining foliage and pure white flowers are a little reminiscent of its great-grand-parent 'Iceberg', which was introduced in 1958 by Reimer Kordes.

'Sun Flare' × 'Simplicity'
Repeat flowering

'White Sparrieshoop' Modern Shrub
'Weisse aus Sparrieshoop'

Sports are sometimes more lovely than the roses from which they sprang. For instance, many people prefer 'Chicago Peace' to 'Peace' and 'Madame Pierre Oger' to 'La Reine Victoria'. 'White Sparrieshoop' has not made its mark; the public much prefers Kordes's 1953 pale pink original to his 1962 white version. The white one can be very lovely indeed, but the blooms go pink as they age, and they do not always do so very evenly. Apart from its color, it is the same as its parent, and performs just as well. Foliage is mid-green and glossy.

Sport from 'Sparrieshoop'
Repeat flowering
Fragrant

'White Spray' Cluster-flowered

The incredible popularity of 'Iceberg' has led to other white Cluster-flowered Roses being neglected, despite their merits. This one is a case in point, introduced in 1968 by LeGrice. Compared with 'Iceberg', it is a more compact and upright grower, and the individual blooms are rather larger and more in the Large-flowered Rose mould, with firm petals. They are creamy white in the bud, open snow-white, and are fragrant. They come in small clusters on long stems for cutting. Foliage is mid-green and matt.

Unnamed seedling × 'Iceberg'
Repeat flowering
Fragrant

'Wienerwald' Large-flowered
'Vienna Woods', 'Kordes' Rose Wienerwald'

The blooms, in a warm blend of soft pink and coral, are of perfect exhibition form, with fine fragrance, and they are borne freely on a reliable bush. Foliage is large, dark green and leathery. This rose does not do so well in sunless climates. Reimer Kordes raised it and introduced it in 1974.

'Königin der Rosen' × unnamed seedling
Repeat flowering
Fragrant

'Wife of Bath' — English Rose

One of the shorter growers among David Austin's roses, 'Wife of Bath' rarely tops 1 metre (3 feet) in height, making a twiggy bush filled with small sprays of sweetly fragrant blooms. They open loose and cupped from fat buds to a pretty, old-fashioned color scheme of pale pink with much deeper tones in their centres. It repeats its bloom very well, and has a reputation of being an easy rose to grow. Introduced in 1969 it celebrates the liberated lady of *The Canterbury Tales*.

'Caroline Testout' × ('Ma Perkins' × 'Constance Spry')
Repeat flowering
Fragrant

▲ 'Wife of Bath'
► 'Wilhelm'

'Wilhelm' — Hybrid Musk
'Skyrocket'

'Wilhelm' lacks the graceful arching growth of Pemberton's true Hybrid Musks, and also their rich fragrance. It is a fine, upright shrub, however, capable of making quite a show with its many clusters of smallish, plum-red blooms which fade to lilac. Foliage is large, glossy and leathery. There are pleasing hips to follow when the autumn, or fall, blooms are finished. It needs paler roses to set it off. It is a seedling from the same parents as 'Eva', and came out a year later, in 1934. Kordes named it in honor of both his father and himself.

'Robin Hood' × 'J. C. Thornton'
Repeat flowering

'Will Scarlet' — Hybrid Musk

'Will Scarlet' is a sport of 'Wilhelm', which was discovered by the English rosarian Graham Thomas and introduced in 1950. It is identical to its parent except that it is a little more fragrant and much brighter in color. Foliage is large, glossy and leathery. It is a cheerful red rose, softening in tone as the flowers age. The name connects it with 'Robin Hood', its grandparent.

Sport from 'Wilhelm'
Repeat flowering

▲ 'Will Scarlet'

'William III' Scotch

William of Orange ascended the throne of England in 1688, and it would be delightful to record that his rose dates from that time, but history is not so kind. Although its date of raising is unknown, it is generally attributed to the early nineteenth century when the Scotch Roses were fashionable. It is one of the most distinctive of them, the compact prickly bush covering itself in spring with small double flowers, pale on the underside of the petals, a wonderful purple on top. Black hips follow, and autumn, or fall, usually sees burnished tones in the dying foliage.

Form of *R. pimpinellifolia*
Spring flowering
Fragrant

'William Lobb' Moss

'Old Velvet Moss', 'Duchesse d'Istrie'

This is one of the grand Victorian roses, tall in growth (it is best trained to a pillar) and gorgeous in the colors of its blooms, which open wide and informal to display just about every shade of soft purple, fading to dove-grey and lilac. Foliage is soft green and matt. There is not much moss, but there is much fragrance. Appropriately, it honors one of the great Victorian gardeners, who was responsible for seeking and introducing all kinds of plants, not just roses, to English gardens. It is French bred, from Laffay in 1855.

Parentage unknown
Summer flowering
Fragrant

▲ 'William III'
▼ 'William Lobb'

'William Shakespeare' — English Rose
AUSroyal

This rose exemplifies as well as any other what David Austin has been seeking in his English Roses—flowers of Old Garden Rose style and perfection combined with the continuous and free blooming of the Modern Garden Bush Roses. Its blooms are pure Gallica: flat, immaculately quartered, fragrant and of velvet richness in their blended shades of crimson and purple. The rather thorny bush is about 1.2 metres (4 feet) tall, and upright in habit, the dark green foliage showing much of the Gallica roughness. Introduced in 1987, it is one of Mr Austin's own favorites, named in homage to perhaps the most famous Englishman of all.

'The Squire' × 'Mary Rose'
Repeat flowering
Fragrant

▲ 'William Shakespeare'

glance at the heart of the flowers will tell them apart, for instead of the golden stamens of 'Harison's Yellow', 'Williams' Double Yellow' has green carpels. The raiser was a great pomologist, though whether he actually raised the famous 'Williams' Bon Chretien' pear, known as 'Bartlett' in America, is uncertain.

Rosa foetida × *R. pimpinellifolia*
Spring flowering
Fragrant

'Winchester Cathedral' — English Rose
AUScat

'Winchester Cathedral' was introduced in 1988, the 900th anniversary of the Norman cathedral of Winchester, the cathedral with the longest nave in England. It conforms pretty well to the David Austin style, with full-petalled, quartered blooms and fragrance. In this case they are white, and the shrub is bushy and compact, flowering all season. Foliage is mid-green and lush.

Parentage undisclosed
Repeat flowering
Fragrant

▲ 'Winchester Cathedral'
▼ 'Wini Edmunds'

▲ 'Williams' Double Yellow'

'Williams' Double Yellow' — Scotch
'Prince Charlie's Rose', 'Old Yellow Scotch', 'Lutea Plena'

Raised in 1828 by John Williams from Pitmaston, Worcestershire, 'Williams' Double Yellow' makes a compact, waist-high bush with dark leaves, the usual Scotch Rose profusion of thorns and masses of smallish golden flowers. They hold their color without fading, but one might wish the petals dropped more cleanly. Still, that is only a minor defect in this very hardy, easily grown rose. It is sometimes confused with 'Harison's Yellow', the New-York-raised double yellow Scotch Rose, but a quick

'Wini Edmunds' — Large-flowered
Raised by Sam McGredy and named as a surprise present for the wife of his American agent Fred Edmunds, 'Wini Edmunds' is certainly a striking flower in blood-red with a white reverse. Large and shapely, it would be a fine choice for prizes on the show bench. It was introduced in 1973. From the parentage, it is probably happiest in cool climates. This is fitting, as the Edmunds nursery is in Oregon. Foliage is dark green, glossy and leathery.

'Red Lion' × 'Hanne'
Repeat flowering
Fragrant

'Winifred Coulter' — Cluster-flowered
Introduced in 1962, 'Winifred Coulter' may not be seen much these days, except in California, but it is still a worthy member of the rather small group of bicolored Cluster-flowered Roses. It has a reputation for almost perfect continuity of bloom, and the flowers are an attractive blend of deepest pink and white. They are only slightly scented. There is a climbing sport, which makes quite a show in the Californian spring, and is then nearly as free as the bush. Foliage is dark green and semi-glossy. The raiser, W. H. Kemple, apparently has no other roses

▲ 'Winifred Coulter'
▼ 'Wise Portia'

to his credit, but judging by the parentage of this rose he seems to have been an imaginative man.

'Baby Château' × 'Contrast'
Repeat flowering

'Winning Colours'   Cluster-flowered
TWOwin

Every so often, along comes a new raiser of roses. 'Winning Colours' was introduced in a very limited way in 1989 and marks the debut of the raiser Twomey. If this rose is any indication, he will be a man to watch. It is really best treated as a Large-flowered Rose, as the clusters are rather small. With disbudding it makes a knockout exhibition rose. Its gold and scarlet colors are spectacular. How it will grow in hot climates remains to be seen. It is not outstandingly fragrant. Foliage is dark green and very glossy.

Parentage undisclosed
Repeat flowering

'Wise Portia'   English Rose
AUSport

One of the shorter growers among David Austin's English Roses, rarely touching a metre (3 feet) in height, 'Wise Portia' bears large blooms, filled with petals and fragrance in the Old

Garden Rose manner. They vary a bit with the season. At their best they are rich, deep pink, flushed with purple and mauve. Give it favored treatment to see it at its best. Foliage is mid-green and matt. The very model of wisdom and sagacity, Portia is the heroine of Shakespeare's *The Merchant of Venice.* The rose was introduced in 1982.

'The Knight' × 'Glastonbury'
Repeat flowering
Fragrant

▲ 'Wishing'
▼ 'Winning Colours'

'Wishing'   Cluster-flowered
DICkerfuffle
'Georgie Girl'

Another 'Patio Rose', 'Wishing' is low and compact in its growth, but quite large in the flowers, to 8 centimetres (3 inches) across. They are of Large-flowered form and blend several shades of apricot and pink. There is little scent. Foliage is mid-green and semi-glossy. This Patrick Dickson creation is very popular in the United Kingdom, where it was introduced in 1985.

'Silver Jubilee' × 'Bright Smile'
Repeat flowering

'Woburn Abbey' — Cluster-flowered

Up to 1960, real orange-juice orange was unknown as a rose color, except as a fleeting tint in blends like 'Signora', so it was remarkable when the color suddenly appeared in three new roses: in 'Zambra' (France) and in 'Golden Slippers' (United States), both in 1961, and then in 'Woburn Abbey' a year later. Most rose-lovers quickly decided that 'Woburn Abbey' was the best of them. The plant is the strongest and most disease resistant, with leathery, mid-green, red-tinted, glossy foliage. Much to everyone's surprise, it had been raised by two English gardeners, G. Sidey and A. Cobley, dabbling with a cross that had so far yielded nothing for professional rose-breeders.

'Masquerade' × 'Fashion'
Repeat flowering

▶ 'Wolley-Dod's Rose'
▼ 'Woburn Abbey'

'Wolley-Dod's Rose' — Modern Shrub

Rosa villosa 'Duplex'

A semi-double form or hybrid of the British *R. villosa* (the Apple Rose), this lovely spring-flowering Shrub Rose takes its name from the turn-of-the-century English gardener in whose

garden it apparently originated. It grows to about 2 metres (6 feet) tall and wide. The clear pink flowers (unscented, which is a pity) look very fine against the grey leaves. Large, dark red hips follow before the leaves fall to give it a second season of beauty. Cool climates suit it best.

Parentage unknown
Summer flowering

'Woman and Home' — Large-flowered

The name will seem slightly less sexist when one remembers that the rose was sponsored by the popular English women's magazine. It bears large, regularly shaped blooms on a good bush with dark green, glossy foliage. The color, officially described as orange, is really only so in the young bud. The blooms open in a blended coral pink. Fragrance is only slight. 'Woman and Home' was raised by Walter Gregory

▲ 'Woman and Home'
▶ 'Yabadabadoo'

of Nottingham and introduced in 1976. It seems happiest in an English-style cool climate.

'Apricot Silk' × seedling from 'Piccadilly'
Repeat flowering

'World Peace'   Large-flowered
BURworpe
Raiser Anthony Perry of California has declined to say whether 'World Peace' owes anything to Meilland's 'Peace', or whether the name is just an expression of aspiration and hope. It is a remarkable flower, basically a straw color, but heavily and variably overlaid with a melange of tones from pink to maroon and red, with a bit of gold and coral thrown in. The foliage is dark green and the plant bushy. Fragrance is not this 1987 introduction's strong point.

Parentage undisclosed
Repeat flowering

'Yabadabadoo'   Large-flowered
MACyabba
Fred Flintstone would yell 'yabadabadoo' when something pleased him very much. Sam McGredy is probably trying

▼ 'World Peace'

to tell us that this is a most pleasing rose. Whether the rest of the world has been all that excited about it is hard to say. One does not come across it very often in gardens or in catalogues. Introduced in 1981, it is a good bushy grower, with mid-green, semi-glossy leaves, and the flowers are a lovely shade of deep yellow. They are rather short on petals (twenty) and perfume.

Parentage undisclosed
Repeat flowering

'Yakimour'   Large-flowered
MEIpsilon
Introduced in 1980 by Marie-Louisette Meilland, 'Yakimour' has not been very widely distributed. It just does not seem to have made an impact. It is a very distinctive flower, full and symmetrical in form, in an unusually clear-cut bicolor arrangement of dark red and gold. It seems to be a good grower, too. Foliage is bright green and glossy.

Parentage undisclosed
Repeat flowering

'Yankee Doodle'   Large-flowered
It would be appropriate for 'Yankee Doodle' to be an all-American production, and it is indeed an AARS winner, for 1976. It is in fact a German

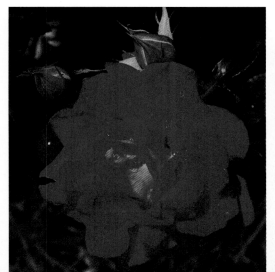

▲ 'Yankee Doodle'

rose, raised by Reimer Kordes. It is a splendidly vigorous plant, easy to grow and resistant to disease. The color of the flowers is admirable, yellow with flushes of peach and carmine. Their shape has rosarians sharply divided, some finding it full-petalled in the Old Garden Rose style; others say it is overstuffed and shapeless. Foliage is light green and glossy. Scent is elusive.

'Königin der Rosen' × 'King's Ransom'
Repeat flowering

'Yellow Butterfly'   Modern Shrub
MORwings
Ralph Moore is best known for his Miniatures, in the breeding of which he has used some unusual parents. He rarely introduces a rose that is not a Miniature. When he does introduce such a rose, you can be sure it is pretty good. 'Yellow Butterfly' is that, though it has not yet achieved wide distribution, as it was only introduced in 1989. It is a sprawling shrub, with glossy leaves and wide-open golden yellow flowers all season. One is reminded of Roy Shepherd's classic 'Golden Wings', and Mr Moore's choice of codename invites the comparison. To my eye, 'Yellow Butterfly' does not suffer by it, which is praise indeed.

Parentage undisclosed
Repeat flowering

◀ 'Yakimour'
▼ 'Yellow Butterfly'

'Yellow Button'

English Rose

Hardly a tall shrub—it rarely touches a metre (3 feet) in height—'Yellow Button' nonetheless has a graceful, arching habit rather than the stiffer, more upright growth of a Bush Rose. The flowers are distinctive: not over-large, borne in small clusters, and full of petals arranged in old-style quarterings. Their color varies: sometimes pale yellow, other times deeper, but the richer tones in the centre are fairly constant. Foliage is a rather light green. Flowering is profuse in early summer and again later. It is a 1975 David Austin introduction.

'Wife of Bath' × 'Chinatown'
Repeat flowering
Fragrant

▼ 'Yellow Button'

'Yellow Charles Austin'

English Rose

At first glance, the name makes little sense, as 'Charles Austin' is itself yellow, albeit a blended yellow with flushes of apricot and pink. This sport is a clear lemon yellow, which some people prefer to the original. Introduced by David Austin in 1979, 'Yellow Charles Austin' resembles the original except in its color, and like it will grow to more than head high. They will both benefit from fairly firm pruning or they will get leggy and repeat flowering will suffer. Foliage is mid-green.

Sport from 'Charles Austin'
Repeat flowering
Fragrant

◀ 'Yellow Charles Austin'
▼ 'Yellow Pages'

'Yellow Pages'

Large-flowered

The Yellow Pages are a worldwide institution, but don't expect to find advertisements on the petals of this rose! Introduced by Sam McGredy in 1972, the blooms of 'Yellow Pages' are deep yellow. Both parents tend to have red flushes on their petal edges; 'Yellow Pages' eliminates these but keeps the fine fragrance of 'Arthur Bell'. It is a good yellow rose for bedding, its only fault being that the dark green, glossy foliage is a bit small.

'Arthur Bell' × 'Peer Gynt'
Repeat flowering
Fragrant

'Yesterday'

Polyantha

'Tapis d'Orient'
Most Polyanthas are period pieces, but this is modern; it was introduced by Jack Harkness in 1974. It is a charmer, making a lowish bush (though it occasionally sends up a shoot or two taller than the rest) and its dainty flowers come in graceful sprays. 'Yesterday' is

(*R. gallica versicolor*), which is a very different rose indeed.

Parentage unknown
Repeat flowering
Fragrant

▲ 'York and Lancaster'
▼ 'Yorkshire Bank'

mid-pink with a suggestion of lilac, and best of all, it is fragrant. Foliage is small, bright green and glossy.

('Phyllis Bide' × 'Shepherds' Delight') × 'Ballerina'
Repeat flowering
Fragrant

'Yolande d'Aragon' Hybrid Perpetual

This rose is one of the earlier Hybrid Perpetuals, raised by Vibert in 1843, and as one might expect the flowers are flat and quartered in the Old French manner. Nicely scented, they vary in their precise tone of pink, being sometimes quite clear rose and at others decidedly washed with mauve. The bush is upright, not too tall, and repeats its bloom reliably. Foliage is mid-green and matt.

Parentage unknown
Repeat flowering
Fragrant

▲ 'Yesterday'
▼ 'Yolande d'Aragon'

'York and Lancaster' Damask

Rosa damascena versicolor, R. d. variegata
The houses of York and Lancaster had white and red roses for their emblems in the Wars of the Roses. 'York and Lancaster' is not red and white, however, but white flecked with pale pink, the blooms sometimes being all of one color or even half and half, but never striped. They are of informal shape, borne in sprays, and fragrant. Foliage is light green and matt. Its origin is unknown, but it is thought to be very old and to be the rose described as 'nor red nor white' by Shakespeare in his Ninety-Ninth Sonnet. 'Versicolor' is the official name, but 'York and Lancaster' is to be preferred for its romance and to avoid confusion with 'Rosa Mundi'

'Yorkshire Bank' Large-flowered

RUtrulo
'True Love'
If ever there was a rose with two weirdly assorted names, it is this one. Who associates romance with a bank? It is a pity that 'Yorkshire Bank' seems to be the most used name, as it really is quite a romantic flower in palest, mother-of-pearl tints of pink and peach. The flowers are large, with thirty-six petals, and are shapely and fragrant. The bush is on the tall side, as one might expect from the parentage. The foliage is bright green. The raiser was Holland's Gijs de Ruiter.

'Pascali' × 'Peer Gynt'
Repeat flowering
Fragrant

'Youki San'
Large-flowered
MEIdona
'Madame Neige'

The two names mean the same thing, but the Japanese seems more romantic than the French. Meilland thinks so too, as it is the registered, official version, even in France. When they brought out 'Youki San' in 1965, it was hailed as the perfect white rose, as indeed the flowers are. They are of most elegant shape, high centred, symmetrical and an unsullied snowy white. They are also very fragrant. The plant lets it down, as it is only of moderate vigor and rather more subject to mildew than it ought to be. Lucky are those whose soil and climate suit it. Foliage is a light grey-green.

'Lady Sylvia' × 'Message'
Repeat flowering
Fragrant

'Young at Heart'
Cluster-flowered

'Young at Heart' is grown exclusively in Australia and New Zealand, where it is sponsored by the National Heart Foundation. In the United States, where it was raised by Armstrong Nurseries, it would be classed as a 'Grandiflora', despite its only average height, as the shapely, high-centred flowers are of medium size and come in clusters as well as singly. Pleasantly fragrant, they are an attractive shade of peach to apricot, sometimes veering towards light pink. The dark green, glossy foliage sets them off well. 'Young at Heart'

was introduced as Australian 'Rose of the Year' in 1989.

Parentage undisclosed
Repeat flowering
Fragrant

▲ 'Youki San'
▼ 'Young at Heart'

'Yvonne Rabier'
Polyantha

So long as roses are grown, and surely that will be forever, rose-lovers will argue about their classification. Take 'Yvonne Rabier' for instance. When Turbat introduced it in 1910 he called it a Polyantha (what else could he call it then?), but now you are just as likely to find it listed as a 'dwarf Cluster-flowered Rose' or 'Patio Rose'. Whatever, it remains a delight, with its glossy, light green leaves and clusters of shapely white flowers, like tiny Large-flowered Roses, and its soft scent. It flowers willingly all season.

Parentage unknown
Repeat flowering
Fragrant

▲ 'Yvonne Rabier'

'Zambra'
Cluster-flowered
MEIalfi

The success of 'Woburn Abbey' has not quite upstaged 'Zambra', which still has many admirers and has proved an important parent. The flowers only have about twelve petals, but they are arranged in beautiful clusters, and their pure orange, lightened with lemon around the stamens, is perfectly set off by glossy, bronze-green foliage. If only it were not so very prone to black spot. Raised in 1961 by Alain Meilland from two unnamed seedlings, it is named after an ancient Spanish dance. Much to

◄ 'Zambra'

▲ 'Zéphyrine Drouhin'
► 'Zorina'

Meilland's embarrassment, apparently, *la zambra* is colloquial in parts of Italy for what in Australia is called a 'dunny'.

('Goldilocks' × 'Fashion') ×
('Goldilocks' × 'Fashion')
Repeat flowering

'Zéphyrine Drouhin'
Cluster-flowered Climber

'The Thornless Rose'
You will find the odd prickle, but 'Zéphyrine Drouhin' is mostly thornless, which makes it first choice for hanging a picket fence with roses, as it will not harm passers-by. Paint the fence white, and it will show up the brilliant cerise of the smallish, clustered blooms, which appear on and off all season and are delightfully fragrant. Do not plant it on a wall; unless it is out in the fresh air it will probably get mildew. Foliage is light green and smooth. It is the only recorded creation of the French raiser Bizot and came out in 1868.

Parentage unknown
Repeat flowering
Fragrant

'Zigeunerknabe'
Bourbon

'Gipsy Boy'
This rose is only a Bourbon by default: the raiser, Peter Lambert, could not think of what else to call it. It is really just a large-growing, spring-flowering Shrub Rose, with prickly stems, coarse, healthy mid-green, matt foliage and

bunches of maroon flowers which have golden stamens. There is very little in the way of fragrance, but this is one of the easiest of all roses to grow, always making a bold splash of color in its season. It came out in 1909.

Probably 'Russeliana' × unknown
Hybrid Rugosa
Summer flowering

'Zorina'
Cluster-flowered

This is one of those roses that you do not see very often these days. Its name will bring back memories of the famous Hollywood ballerina. It has proved a valuable parent, giving its offspring great strength of petal, lovely form and colors unexpectedly delicate considering its own slightly brash coral orange. Perhaps the most distinctive contribution is the shape of its cluster: each flower has a long stem of its own, so that the inflorescence is not so much a bunch as a bouquet. Foliage is dark green and leathery. 'Zorina' was raised by Eugene Boerner and introduced in 1963. Primarily a greenhouse rose, it is fine in the garden in a hot climate.

Seedling from 'Pinocchio' × 'Spartan'
Repeat flowering

▼ 'Zigeunerknabe'

MINIATURE ROSES

MINIATURE ROSES

The Miniature Roses are grouped together partly because they are a very distinct and charming group of roses, partly because people without gardens can still grow them in pots on balconies and in windowboxes and still have the pleasure of the rose, and partly because their tiny scale is apt to be distorted or smothered in reproduction along with their bigger sisters. How often in books does one find a Miniature shown at the same size as some huge Large-flowered Rose?

Even a few years ago, many a rose-lover would have wondered why they were included at all; few took the Miniatures seriously. They might be all right in pots, but not in a real rose garden, and certainly not on the show bench! The very names given to the class—'Fairy Roses', 'Baby Roses', 'Pixie Roses'—suggested frivolity rather than something inspiring real admiration.

Happily, that has changed. Today, no collection of roses is considered complete without at least a few Miniatures. The Miniature classes at rose shows are contested every bit as keenly as any others and several varieties have received high awards, though as yet none has won the coveted All-America Rose Selections award.

Just what is a Miniature Rose? It is, or should be, a perfectly scaled down replica of a Large-flowered Rose, with everything—flowers, stems, foliage and thorns—in perfect proportion. Some are very tiny indeed, but it is the larger Miniatures that usually make the better garden plants. You can plant them in the garden without fear that they will be instantly smothered by any flimsy weed, and their blooms are large enough to show up. They come in every color possible in a rose. Many display the classic high-centred form of the Large-flowered Roses and some grow stems long enough for cutting. In their freedom and almost perfect continuity of bloom, they are second to none. Their only shortcoming is lack of scent; few can honestly be described as more than mildly fragrant.

There are also Climbing Miniatures, their branches usually about 1.5 metres (5 feet) long. For all their prettiness, they can be awkward to place in the garden and their chief value may well prove to be in their contribution to the new race of Ground Cover Roses, many of which have Miniature ancestry. So do many of the 'Dwarf Cluster-flowered Roses', sometimes called 'Patio Roses', and even some of the smaller Shrub Roses. Clearly the story of the Miniature Roses is not yet finished.

All Miniatures descend from 'Rouletii', something of a mystery rose. In the early 1800s, miniature forms of the already diminutive China Roses appeared, introduced, it was said, from Mauritius. They became fashionable pot-plants for decorating windowsills, particularly in Paris, but, the rosarians of the day being more interested in the new and huge Hybrid Perpetuals, the fashion died out. So might the Miniature Roses, had not a Swiss soldier by the name of Roulet discovered a lone survivor on a village windowsill near Geneva at the end of World War I. Its original name lost, it was rechristened 'Rouletii' in his honor, and introduced in 1922.

Pedro Dot in Spain and John De Vink in Holland raised some very pretty seedlings from 'Rouletii'. Then, after World War II, Ralph Moore of Sequoia nursery in California discovered that Miniatures could be crossed with Large-flowered and Cluster-flowered Roses, even with Climbers, without being enlarged too much. It was from this discovery that Miniatures began to take off and new varieties of superlative quality appeared.

Ralph Moore remains the master of the Miniature Rose, and a majority of the varieties on the following pages are his. This is not to decry the contributions of other raisers such as Alain Meilland, the prolific Sam McGredy and Harmon Saville.

'Angelita' — Climbing Miniature
MACangeli
'Snowball'
One of a number of creeping Miniatures for ground cover from Sam McGredy, 'Angelita' (1982) rarely reaches 30 centimetres (12 inches) tall but spreads to several times that. Its white flowers, creamy yellow in the centre and often touched with pink appear over a long season. It looks pretty in a hanging basket. Foliage is light green and dense.

'Moana' × 'Snow Carpet'
Repeat flowering

▲ 'Angelita'
▼ 'Anna Ford'

'Anna Ford' — Miniature
HARpiccolo
This 1980 Jack Harkness introduction was named for the English television star. It takes after the Cluster-flowered side of its parentage, but is quite small enough to be classed as a Miniature. Its eighteen-petalled glowing orange flowers look well growing in containers and won it the highest awards of the RNRS. Foliage is dark green and glossy.

'Southampton' × 'Minuetto'
Repeat flowering

'Baby Diana' — Miniature
SAVadi
Not necessarily related to the elegant Princess of Wales, 'Baby Diana' hails from the United States and the talents of F. Harmon Saville of Nor'East Miniature Roses. An orange bicolor with yellow reverse, it is double and has twenty petals. Growth is bushy; leaves are small and mid-green; the prickles are brown; and fragrance is only moderate.

'Zorina' × ('Sheri Anne' × 'Glenfiddich')
Repeat flowering

'Baby Masquerade' — Miniature
TANba, TANbakede
'Baby Maskarade', 'Baby Carnaval'
Mathias Tantau's 'Baby Masquerade' is virtually a miniature version of its parent. It made rather a sensation when it was introduced in 1956, with its multicolored flowers. They age from yellow to pink and then to crimson. The color effects vary with the season, but the blooms invariably have twenty-three petals. Foliage is dark green and semi-glossy.

'Masquerade' × 'Tom Thumb'
Repeat flowering

▲ 'Baby Masquerade'
► 'Bleunette'

▲ 'Bit o' Sunshine'
◄ 'Baby Diana'

'Bit o' Sunshine' — Miniature
A Miniature Rose from California's Ralph Moore, 'Bit o' Sunshine' has been around since 1956. Like so many of Moore's Miniatures, it is bred from the mysterious 'Zee', regarded by Moore as his prize bloodstock and never released to other breeders. The semi-double, eighteen-petalled flowers of 'Bit o' Sunshine' are of charming informality. Foliage is mid-green.

'Copper Glow' × 'Zee'
Repeat flowering

'Bleunette' — Miniature
RUIblun
'Azulabria', 'Blue Peter'
'Bleunette' is not really blue but lilac-purple. It is a little charmer, raised by Gijs de Ruiter and introduced in 1983. It is one of the smallest of Miniatures. There is little fragrance. It is not the first Miniature to claim to be blue: that was Ralph Moore's 'Mister Bluebird' of 1960, which for its presumptions has vanished from the catalogues. Foliage is light green and semi-glossy.

'Little Flirt' × unnamed seedling
Repeat flowering

▲ 'Cinderella'
▼ 'Colibri '79'

'Boys' Brigade' — Miniature
COCdinkum

'Boys' Brigade' was named to celebrate the centenary of the British youth organization and was raised by Scotland's Anne Cocker, the widow of Alec Cocker, and introduced in 1984. I saw it first at Berlin's Bundesgärtenschau in 1985, and was impressed with the way it starred its bright green foliage with red and white five-petalled blooms in clusters. It would make a good living Christmas decoration for those in the southern hemisphere.

('Minuetto' × 'Saint Alban') × ('Little Flirt' × 'Marlena')
Repeat flowering

'Cinderella' — Miniature
The first Miniature to have a real rosy scent, 'Cinderella' is officially described as white. At the Alpengärten of the Vienna Belvedere, where it was photographed, it was showing quite a range of colors. Introduced in 1955, it is practically free of thorns. The raiser, John de Vink of Boskoop, approaches his nursery by a fairy-tale drawbridge over a canal.

'Cécile Brünner' × 'Tom Thumb'
Repeat flowering
Fragrant

'Cricket' — Miniature
AROket

Raiser of some of the most spectacular Large-flowered Roses in this book, Jack Christensen has shown his versatility with 'Cricket', created for Armstrong's in 1978. It is a glowing little sun in brilliant orange and yellow, shining against very dark green foliage. The flowers are 3 centimetres (1¼ inches) wide and give just a whiff of fragrance.

'Anytime' × ('Zorina' × 'Dr A. J. Verhage')
Repeat flowering

'Centerpiece' — Miniature
SAVapiece

Deep yet bright red and double, with thirty-five petals, 'Centerpiece' develops into a small, semi-glossy bush covered in tiny, high-centred and scentless blooms. It was raised by Harmon Saville and introduced in 1985. The foliage is unusually dark green in tone.

('Sheri Anne' × 'Tamango') × ('Sheri Anne' × ['Yellow Jewel' × 'Tamango'])
Repeat flowering

▲ 'Boys' Brigade'
▼ 'Centerpiece'

'Colibri '79' — Miniature
MEImal

There are two roses called 'Colibri', with old-gold flowers suggestive of the Parisian jewellers for whom they are named. The original came from Meilland in 1958 and won the Golden Rose of The Hague in 1962. The one in the picture is an 'improved' version from Meilland in 1978. They are very similar. Perhaps the new version is just a little more orange in tone, and a trifle bigger. Foliage is dark green and glossy.

Parentage undisclosed
Repeat flowering

'Dorola' — Miniature
MACshana
'Benson & Hedges Special'

Sam McGredy had already named a Large-flowered Rose 'Benson & Hedges Gold' and, to save confusion between the two, the IRA registered the Miniature as 'Dorola'. Under either of its names, this is one of the best yellow Miniatures. Foliage is dark and glossy. It was introduced in 1982.

'Minuetto' × 'New Day'
Repeat flowering
Fragrant

▲ 'Cricket'
▼ 'Dorola'

'Double Joy' Miniature

Ralph Moore, of America's Sequoia Nursery, released this perfect Miniature Rose in 1979. It is a perfectly shaped double flower of thirty-five petals and medium size, to 4 centimetres (1¹/₂ inches) in diameter, and quite fragrant. Foliage is small (even for a Miniature) and glossy, and the plant is bushy.

'Little Darling' × 'New Penny'
Repeat flowering
Fragrant

'Dresden Doll' Miniature

Of the several Miniature Moss Roses raised by Ralph Moore, 'Dresden Doll', introduced in 1975, is perhaps the most charming. The little flowers are perfect replicas of an old-fashioned, full-sized Moss Rose, the scented moss covering the buds and the soft pink flowers loosely double and cupped in the old manner. However, the plant is compact, the foliage glossy, and the perpetual flowering habit is very much in the modern manner. The flowers are fragrant too, if not quite so strongly as an old Moss Rose.

'Fairy Moss' × unnamed Moss Rose seedling
Repeat flowering
Fragrant

▲ 'Double Joy'
▼ 'Dresden Doll'

'Duke Meillandina' Miniature
MEIpinjid
'Classic Sunblaze', 'Duc Meillandina'

Modern Roses 9, the official international register of rose names, prefers the almost unpronounceable codename. The 'Duke Meillandina' I have in my garden is a blend of pink, cream and yellow, rather like 'Magic Carrousel' but in a deeper blend, with more yellow at the base. It is a fairly large flower and bush (for a Miniature), and a long-lasting cut flower. Leaves are dark green, the fragrance slight. Meilland introduced it in 1985.

Sport from 'Orange Meillandina'
Repeat flowering

'Esther's Baby' Miniature
HARkinder

'Esther's Baby' is Jack Harkness's contribution to the hoopla surrounding the first-born of a British media personality in 1979. The bonny baby rose has tiny pointed petals arranged so that the darkest pink ones are at the centre where they frame golden stamens. Foliage is glossy.

('Vera Dalton' × ['Chanelle' × 'Piccadilly']) × 'Little Buckaroo'
Repeat flowering

'Fashion Flame' Miniature

'Fashion Flame' from 1977 is as lovely as any of Ralph Moore's creations. It is an unusual blend of coral-orange with a touch of lavender on the outer petals. The foliage is large and coarse for a Miniature and the small, thirty-five-petalled blooms are nicely fragrant.

'Little Darling' × 'Fire Princess'
Repeat flowering
Fragrant

'Fire Princess' Miniature

Introduced almost a quarter of a century ago, in 1969, 'Fire Princess' remains a fine rose and has been the parent of many distinguished baby roses. It is fiery scarlet and the foliage is small, dark green and glossy with red tints when young; not that you see much of it under the mass of bloom! The plant is dwarf and compact. It is one of Ralph Moore's.

'Baccarà' × 'Eleanor'
Repeat flowering

▲ 'Fire Princess'
◀ 'Duke Meillandina'

▲ 'Esther's Baby'
▼ 'Fashion Flame'

▲ 'Firefly'

'Firefly' — Miniature

MACfrabra

Sam McGredy's Miniature 'Firefly' is not to be confused with a Large-flowered Rose of the same name, which was popular in Australia in the 1920s but rarely seen now. This one came out in 1985. Sam describes it as an 'orange blend', which seems fair enough; the small twenty-petalled blooms have a slight fragrance and the plant is dwarf, bushy with dark and glossy, neat leaves.

'Mary Sumner' × 'Ko's Yellow'
Repeat flowering

'Foxy Lady' — Miniature

AROshrim

This rather adult name, in a group where tradition has suggested names reminiscent of childhood, was bestowed in 1980 by Jack Christensen. The rose really is a beauty, blending salmon and cream in its long-pointed buds and twenty-five-petalled blooms, which are 3 centimetres (1¼ inches) in width, on dwarf bushes with small, neat foliage.

'Ginger Snap' × 'Magic Carrousel'
Repeat flowering

▲ 'Foxy Lady'
► 'Fringette'

'Freegold' — Miniature

MACfeego
'Penelope Keith'

Sam McGredy unveiled this pleasing golden Miniature in 1983. It combines deep yellow with a shade that can only be described as old gold on the petal reverse, and the blooms are perfect Miniatures of exhibition-style Large-flowered Roses. Foliage is small, semi-glossy and light green.

'Seaspray' × 'Dorola'
Repeat flowering
Fragrant

'Fringette' — Miniature

I first saw 'Fringette' in Vienna, in the Belvedere Palace alpine garden, where only the most diminutive of flowers are admitted. Indeed it rarely grows more than 20 centimetres (8 inches) tall and has the tiniest flowers imaginable. They have twenty-five deep pink petals, with the centre of the bloom in white. Foliage is small. It is a 1964 introduction from Ralph Moore.

Unnamed seedling × 'Magic Wand'
Repeat flowering

'Golden Angel' — Miniature

'Golden Angel' has open blooms, which are prettily shaped and have sixty-five petals. They are a clear yellow and fairly fragrant. Foliage is mid-green and semi-glossy, and growth is bushy and short, which may come as a surprise as one parent was the Rambler 'Golden Glow'. Rarely seen now, 'Golden Glow' apparently has the ability to give strength but no size to Miniatures; Moore has used it extensively as a parent.

'Golden Glow' × ('Little Darling' × unnamed seedling)
Repeat flowering

◄ 'Freegold'
▼ 'Golden Angel'

▼ 'Green Diamond'

'Green Diamond' — Miniature

The 'Green Rose' ('Viridiflora') actually has a bunch of leaves in place of petals. Ralph Moore's 1975 'Green Diamond' does have petals, twenty-five of them. They start out pink, but by the time the tiny blooms are open they have turned a soft chartreuse green. The bush is dwarf but upright, with dark green foliage.

Unnamed Polyantha × 'Sheri Anne'
Repeat flowering

▲ 'Green Ice'

'Green Ice' Miniature

Forget the fact that the flowers go green with age—which is a variable habit; sometimes they are quite green, at others only faintly so—this is one of the best white Miniatures, each flower flat and filled with petals like a scaled-down Old Garden Rose. The plant is bushy with shining bright green leaves. It was introduced in 1971 by Ralph Moore.

(*Rosa wichuraiana* × 'Floradora') × 'Jet Trail'
Repeat flowering

'Guletta' Miniature
'Tapis Jaune'

Dutch Hybridist Gijs de Ruiter introduced this rose in 1973; fifteen years later it was still sufficiently well regarded to be featured in a big display at the Berlin Garden Show, where the picture was taken. It makes a neat bush to about 40 centimetres (16 inches) tall, with tiny blooms in bright yellow. They have a pronounced Old Garden Rose fragrance. Foliage is dark green.

'Rosy Jewel' × 'Allgold'
Repeat flowering
Fragrant

'Gypsy Jewel' Miniature

The Miniatures vary in size, from the tiny to those that could pass as small Cluster-flowered Roses. Ralph Moore's 1975 'Gypsy Jewel' is one of the larger ones, making a 60 centimetre (2 foot) tall bush with deep rose-pink flowers, 5 centimetres (2 inches) across. Foliage is dark green.

'Little Darling' × 'Little Buckaroo'
Repeat flowering

▲ 'Hula Girl'
◄ 'Guletta'
► 'Janna'

'Holy Toledo' Miniature
ARObri

Introduced by Jack Christensen and Armstrong Nurseries in 1978, this is one of the most widely admired Miniatures for its wonderful color, its pretty flower shape, its bushy growth and its polished, dark green foliage. It won the ARS's highest award for a Miniature, in 1980.

'Apricot Prince' × 'Magic Carrousel'
Repeat flowering

▼ 'Holy Toledo'

▲ 'Gypsy Jewel'

'Hula Girl' Miniature

Ernest Williams of Mini Roses in Dallas, Texas, released this fine Miniature in 1975. Its shapely double flowers, which have a fine fruity fragrance, are deep orange in bud but open to salmon-pink with a touch of yellow showing beneath. Tallish for the class, 'Hula Girl' won the ARS award for excellence in 1976. Foliage is glossy and quilted.

'Miss Hillcrest' × 'Mabel Dot'
Repeat flowering
Fragrant

'Janna' Miniature

Ralph Moore has often used the Cluster-flowered Rose 'Little Darling' in breeding his Miniatures, and 'Janna', introduced in 1970, has a double dose. The influence of 'Little Darling' shows in the finely shaped bud and bicolored petals in pink and cream. Miniatures like this are a great success with florists. Foliage is olive-green.

'Little Darling' × ('Little Darling' × [*Rosa wichuraiana* × unnamed Miniature])
Repeat flowering

'June Time' Miniature

A true Miniature, 'June Time' bears sprays of little flat pompoms in rose-pink, almost like a tiny Rambler; not surprising, as it is bred, via a string of un-

▲ 'June Time'
▼ 'Kaikoura'

named seedlings, from *Rosa wichuraiana*. It makes a small, compact bush with no tendency to ramble; however, as so often with Miniatures, there is no scent. Foliage is glossy.

(*R. wichuraiana* × 'Floradora') × (['Etoile Luisante' seedling × 'Red Ripples'] × 'Zee')
Repeat flowering

'Kaikoura'   Miniature
MACwalla
'Kaikoura' may sound Japanese, but it is in fact Maori, the name of a place in New Zealand. Introduced by Sam McGredy in 1978, 'Kaikoura' is a dark-foliaged plant, tall for a Miniature, but bearing abundant orange and red blooms all season.

'Anytime' × 'Matangi'
Repeat flowering

'Ko's Yellow'   Miniature
MACkosyel
Sam McGredy named 'Ko's Yellow' in honor of Ko Schuurman, the wife of his colleague Frank Schuurman. It was she who first saw the potential of its classically formed buff-yellow blooms and bushy plant. Foliage is glossy and bright green. It was raised from an unusual breeding line and introduced in 1978.

('New Penny' × 'Bambridge') × ('Border Flame' × 'Manx Queen')
Repeat flowering

'Lady Meillandina'   Miniature
MEIlarco
'Lady Sunblaze', 'Peace Sunblaze'
This is one of the prettiest of the Marie-Louisette Meilland Miniatures, its flowers shapely and delicate in shades of pale pink and peach. 'Peace Sunblaze' is a misleading name: the flowers resemble 'Peace' not in the least. Those who exhibit Miniatures should love it, and it is a very long-lasting cut flower. Foliage is dark and glossy.

Parentage undisclosed
Repeat flowering

'Lemon Delight'   Miniature
There is still no satisfactory full-sized yellow Moss Rose, but there is one among the Miniatures—Ralph Moore's 'Lemon Delight'. A cross between two other Moore mossy Miniatures, it was introduced in 1978 and makes a compact upright bush, with small yellow blooms, opening from long, mossy buds. Foliage is mid-green and glossy. A charmer, and slightly fragrant.

'Fairy Moss' × 'Goldmoss'
Repeat flowering

◀ 'Ko's Yellow'

'Little Artist'   Miniature
MACmanly
'Top Gear'
Introduced in 1978, 'Little Artist' was Sam McGredy's very first 'Hand-painted' Miniature. The bush is compact, if a little tall by Miniature standards, and the semi-double flowers with their bold splashes of red and white make quite a show. Foliage is dark green.

'Eyepaint' × 'Ko's Yellow'
Repeat flowering

▲ 'Little Artist'
▼ 'Lady Meillandina'

▼ 'Lemon Delight'

▲ 'Little Eskimo'
▼ 'Macspice'

▲ 'Magic Carrousel'
▼ 'Mary Marshall'

'Little Eskimo' — Miniature

Whiter than white, 'Little Eskimo' makes a perfect little igloo of dark green leaves and snowy flowers, borne seven or so to a cluster. With the same parentage as 'Green Ice', it was a Ralph Moore introduction of 1978. The foliage has much of *Rosa wichuraiana*'s polish, but the flowers have little of its fragrance.

(*R. wichuraiana* × 'Floradora') × 'Jet Trail'
Repeat flowering

'Macspice' — Miniature
MACspike

The unique 'Macspice' produces its flowers in foot-long, larkspur-like sprays, as many as fifty tiny mauve-pink flowers to the spray. The effect of the spreading arching bush is totally charming. Foliage is bright green. It was a Sam McGredy introduction of 1983.

'Anytime' × 'Gärtendirektor Otto Linne'
Repeat flowering
Fragrant

'Magic Carrousel' — Miniature
MORousel

One of Ralph Moore's greatest successes, 'Magic Carrousel' is admired for the reliability of its growth and the sheer prettiness of its shapely little blooms, each white petal distinctly edged with cerise. Pick a bowl over several days and you will have a multicolored display. It makes a rather leggy bush. Prune it hard. Foliage is dark green and bronze when young.

'Little Darling' × 'Westmont'
Repeat flowering
Fragrant

'Mary Marshall' — Miniature

Though introduced a while ago, in 1970, Ralph Moore's 'Mary Marshall' still holds its place for ease of growth and the daintiness of its long-pointed buds, which open to long-lasting blooms of deep pink with just a touch of coral. Foliage is small, dark and semi-glossy.

'Little Darling' × 'Fairy Princess'
Repeat flowering

'Nozomi' — Climbing Miniature

Officially a Climbing Miniature (it will grow head-high when trained on a wall), 'Nozomi' is more popular as a Ground Cover. It is delightful growing thus, the trailing shoots covered in sprays of little flowers, single and blush-white like apple blossom. Although it does not repeat, and there is no fragrance, this unassuming rose is set to be the most important rose yet raised in Japan, for most of the new class of Ground Cover roses are bred, directly or indirectly, from it. Its raiser, Dr Toru Ondera, may describe himself as 'only an amateur rose-lover', but this 1968 creation assures him a place in the history of the rose.

'Fairy Princess' × 'Sweet Fairy'
Summer flowering

'Ocarina' — Miniature
OcaRU
'Angela Rippon'

An ocarina is a small flute, made of clay and popular with primitive tribes the world over, but when Fryer's of Cheshire introduced this de Ruiter creation to Britain in 1978 they thought it better named for Ms Rippon, the television personality. By either name, the salmon-

▼ 'Nozomi'

▲ 'Ocarina'

flowered style, and the neat bush reaches about 40 centimetres (16 inches) high. Foliage is dark green and glossy.

Unnamed seedling × unnamed seedling
Repeat flowering

◄ 'Over the Rainbow'
▼ 'Peek-a-Boo'

pink blooms of this rose are outstanding. It is the top-rated Miniature almost everywhere. Foliage is dark green.

'Rosy Jewel' × 'Zorina'
Repeat flowering

'Orange Sunblaze'   Miniature
MEIjikatar
'Orange Meillandina'
This is the first of the 'Sunblaze' or 'Meillandina' series, introduced as the 'world's first indoor roses' by Meilland. This claim has proved exaggerated, though they can be brought indoors for a short stay when the flowers are out. It was introduced in 1978. Foliage is matt green and small.

'Parador' × ('Baby Bettina' × 'Mevrouw van Straaten van Nes')
Repeat flowering

'Over the Rainbow'   Miniature
Introduced by Ralph Moore in 1972, 'Over the Rainbow' remains one of the best of the bicolored Miniatures, though purists might find the blooms a trifle large. The bush is upright but compact, and takes kindly to a short spell indoors. Foliage is dark green and leathery. It has a climbing sport with the delightful name of 'Climbing Over the Rainbow'.

'Little Darling' × 'Westmont'
Repeat flowering

'Orange Honey'   Miniature
To see the orange and gold blooms of 'Orange Honey' at their dazzling best, grow it in light shade. It was introduced by Ralph Moore in 1979. The bush is dwarf and spreading, the foliage matt green, and there is fruity fragrance.

'Rumba' × 'Over the Rainbow'
Repeat flowering

▲ 'Orange Honey'
▼ 'Orange Sunblaze''

'Oz Gold'   Miniature
'Oz Gold' was introduced by Sam McGredy in 1984. It really is golden yellow, a brilliant burnished color, with a touch of cerise on the outer petals. Each flower is perfectly formed in the Large-

'Peek-a-Boo'   Miniature
DICgrow
'Brass Ring'
With this fine rose, Pat Dickson has shown us that he is just as good with Miniatures as he is with Large-flowered Roses. It is a little large for the class and is usually listed as a 'Patio Rose'. The copper-apricot flowers are a charming sight, borne in sprays all along the arching branches. Foliage is mid-green and glossy. Introduced in 1981, it is of unusual breeding.

'Memento' × 'Nozomi'
Repeat flowering   ·

'Perla de Montserrat'   Miniature
One of the first Miniatures to become popular, raised by Pedro Dot in 1945, 'Perla de Montserrat' is also one of the tiniest. It has much of its pollen parent's charm in its perfectly shaped little flowers in pearly pink. Each has eighteen

◄ 'Oz Gold'
▼ 'Perla de Montserrat'

▲ 'Pink Star'
◄ 'Petite Folie'

petals and they usually come in small clusters. Foliage is small and mid-green.

'Cécile Brünner' × 'Rouletii'
Repeat flowering

'Petite Folie'　Miniature
MEIherode

'Petite Folie' was the first of a class of roses which look set to become popular in the 1990s—its leaves and flowers are Miniature, but the bush is of Cluster-flowered Rose size. Foliage is mid-green, bronze when young. When it came out in 1968, no one knew quite what to make of it. It was raised by Alain Meilland.

('Dany Robin' × 'Fire King') × ('Cri Cri' × 'Perla de Montserrat')
Repeat flowering

'Pink Cameo'　Climbing Miniature
'Climbing Pink Cameo'

In spite of their charm the Climbing Miniatures have never achieved wide popularity. Ralph Moore's 'Pink Cameo', introduced back in 1954, remains one of the very best. Try twining its 1.5 metre (5 feet) long branches along a low fence, to adorn it all season with petite, soft pink blooms. Foliage is mid-green and coarse.

('Soeur Thérèse' × 'Wilhelm') × 'Zee'
Repeat flowering

▼ 'Pink Cameo'

'Pink Star'　Miniature
INTerpink

'Pink Star' is one of those in-between roses. Its leaves and flowers are like a Miniature, but its growth is spreading and sprawling, which suggests it as a Ground Cover Rose. The blooms are semi-double and light pink, the foliage pale green and semi-glossy. It was introduced by Interplant of Holland in 1978.

'Yesterday' × unnamed seedling
Repeat flowering

'Pink Sunblaze'　Miniature
MEIjidiro
'Pink Meillandina'

Marie-Louisette Meilland's 1980 sport from 'Orange Sunblaze' is exactly the same as the original except that the color is medium rose-pink, centred in gold. Like its parent, it is best as a pot-plant, to be brought indoors for a short stay. Foliage is dark green.

Sport from 'Orange Sunblaze'
Repeat flowering

'Pinstripe'　Miniature
MORpints

It is a safe guess that the unnamed seedling in this rose's parentage derives from 'Stars 'n' Stripes'. Some people consider 'Pinstripe' an improvement. It is just as

prettily striped, in red and white, and the bush is compact with neat, mid-green foliage. There no scent, unfortunately. Ralph Moore introduced it in 1986.

'Pinocchio' × unnamed seedling
Repeat flowering

▲ 'Pompon de Paris'
◄ 'Pink Sunblaze'
▼ 'Pinstripe'

'Pompon de Paris'　Miniature
Some people consider that this Miniature China Rose, introduced in 1839, survived in Switzerland to be reintroduced as 'Rouletii'. Other people think the two are different. Both are in this book, so you can make up your own mind about it. They both have pretty rose-pink flowers, deeper in the bud, all season. The foliage is finely cut and dark green. There is also a charming climbing sport, 'Climbing Pompon de Paris', growing to about 2 metres (6 feet).

Parentage unknown
Repeat flowering

'Popcorn' Miniature

This rose was bred by Dr Denison Morey of Santa Rosa, California. It could not be more appropriately named, with its clusters of fluffy white flowers opening from the butter-tinted buds just like pieces of popcorn. Foliage is small and mid-green. It was introduced in 1973 by Pixie Treasures.

'Katherine Zeimet' × 'Diamond Jewel'
Repeat flowering
Fragrant

'Pride 'n' Joy' Miniature

Released in 1992 by California's Bear Creek Nurseries, this 1992 AARS winner is one of the new breed of rather large Miniatures, making a fine splash of color in the garden from many full-petalled blooms in a melange of copper, orange and salmon-pink, the overall effect being best described as tangerine. The leaves are glossy, russet when the stems are young, and long enough for cutting.

'Chattam Centennial' × 'Prominent'
Repeat flowering
Fragrant

'Red Ace' Miniature

There are two red Miniatures of this name—one, codenamed AmRUda, from de Ruiter of Holland, the other, the one in the picture, from Harmon Saville in 1980. Saville's 'Red Ace' is a shapely Large-flowered Rose in miniature, bright crimson in color, and makes a bushy, compact plant, with fine glossy foliage. AmRUda is a much darker red.

'Rise 'n' Shine' × 'Sheri Anne'
Repeat flowering

'Red Rascal' Miniature
JACbed

The boundary between Miniatures and low-growing Cluster-flowered Roses is pretty vague, with the placement of a rose in one group or the other being pretty much at the whim of the nursery

▲ 'Red Rascal'
◄ 'Popcorn'
► 'Renny'

marketing manager. 'Red Rascal' is often listed as a Cluster-flowered Rose, or a 'Patio Rose', but in fact it is a Miniature, albeit a tall-growing one. The small clusters of blood-red flowers open from ovoid buds to perfect exhibition form, rather like miniature versions of 'Ena Harkness', though without its scent. Foliage is dark greyish green and glossy. Bill Warriner, who introduced it in 1986, has no doubts about its class; he has registered it as a Miniature.

Unnamed seedling × unnamed seedling
Repeat flowering

▲ 'Pride 'n' Joy'
▼ 'Red Ace'

► 'Rise 'n' Shine'

'Renny' Miniature
MOReny

This is one of the larger of Ralph Moore's Miniatures, both in bush and in flower. The purist may prefer to class it as a 'Patio Rose', but either way it is a charmer, its flowers full-petalled and shapely, their softly blended shades of pink and coral refreshing to the eye. The glossy foliage is neat and smart looking. It was introduced in 1989.

Parentage undisclosed
Repeat flowering

'Rise 'n' Shine' Miniature
'Golden Meillandina'

I am not sure how the name 'Golden Meillandina' got attached to this rose, which is not one of Meilland's but instead from Ralph Moore of Sequoia Nursery in California. Introduced in 1977, it is, quite simply, the very best yellow Miniature. Like so many yellow roses, though, it sometimes takes black spot. Foliage is fine and glossy.

'Little Darling' × 'Yellow Magic'
Repeat flowering
Fragrant

▲ 'Robin Redbreast'
▼ 'Rosada'

▲ 'Rouletii'
▼ 'Royal Salute'

'Rouletii'　　　Miniature
Rosa chinensis minima

Discovered growing in a pot on a windowsill in Switzerland, 'Rouletii' was introduced in 1922 by Henri Correvon, who named it for its discoverer, a soldier by the name of Roulet. The ancestor of the modern Miniatures, it is a pure-bred China Rose. It is rather like a scaled-down version of 'Old Blush', with soft rose-pink flowers and neat pointed leaves. There is no scent. Blooming all year, it is not to be neglected just because of its more up-to-date offspring.

Parentage unknown
Repeat flowering

'Robin Redbreast'　　　Miniature
INTerrob

'Robin Redbreast' is better thought of as a 'Patio Rose', being more like a scaled-down Cluster-flowered Rose than a true Miniature. It makes a bush about 50 centimetres (1 foot 6 inches) tall and wide, carrying large clusters of single blooms in bright red with white eyes. The foliage is mid-green and glossy. Introduced by Interplant of Holland, it came out in 1983.

Unnamed seedling × 'Eyepaint'
Repeat flowering

'Rosada'　　　Miniature
'Rosata'

Spain's Pedro Dot was one of the pioneering breeders of Miniatures. He was especially fond of really tiny ones, and 'Rosada' is still one of the smallest of all. Raised in 1950, it makes a 20 centimetre (8 inch) bush, with matching flowers in pale peach edged with pink. Foliage is glossy. There is no fragrance.

'Perla de Alcanada' × 'Rouletii'
Repeat flowering

'Royal Salute'　　　Miniature
MACros
'Rose Baby'

England's Prince William was saluted by two red roses at his birth—the full-sized 'Royal William' and this delightful Miniature from Sam McGredy, introduced in 1982. The bush is compact, the foliage glossy and dark, and the clusters of rosy red flowers so cheerful that all 'Royal Salute' needs is fragrance.

'New Penny' × 'Marlena'
Repeat flowering

'Scarlet Sunblaze'　　　Miniature
MEIcubasi
'Scarlet Meillandina'

It was the Berlin Garden Show of 1985 that convinced me of the value of these slightly larger-growing Miniatures for filling in corners of the garden with color. Prominent in the displays there was 'Scarlet Sunblaze'. The profuse double flowers are scarlet, verging on orange, and the foliage is dark green and bronze-tinted. It had been introduced by Marie-Louisette Meilland in 1980.

'Tamango' × ('Baby Bettina' × 'Mevrouw van Straten van Nes')
Repeat flowering

▲ 'Scarlet Sunblaze'
▼ 'Seaspray'

'Seaspray'　　　Miniature
MACnewing

'Seaspray' is not white, in fact, but palest pink, flushed darker—an exquisite combination. It is also well scented and the plant is bushy, low and spreading, with bright green foliage. Sam McGredy was the raiser, John Mattock of Oxford the introducer, in 1982. Try it as a Ground Cover Rose.

'Moana' × 'Anytime'
Repeat flowering
Fragrant

'Shooting Star' — Miniature

Unusually for a Meilland rose, 'Shooting Star' has no codename, perhaps because the Conard Pyle Company who distributed it in America did not see the need—1972 was early days for the codename system. It is a pretty Miniature, with cupped flowers in light yellow on a compact bush with mid-green leaves.

'Rumba' × ('Dany Robin' × 'Perla de Montserrat')
Repeat flowering

▲ 'Shooting Star'
▼ 'Sno'

'Sno' — Miniature

Ernest Meredith and Margaret Rovinski of Santa Ana, California, are hardly household names in the world of rose-breeding. However, if the pair continue to raise roses as charming as this 1982 creation they may become so. 'Sno' (nurseries sometimes offer it as 'Snow') makes a pretty bush, low but spreading, and for much of the season its light green foliage is fairly covered with many petalled, snow-white flowers, borne in small clusters. They are very fragrant, and if you allowed 'Sno' to overflow a tall container, you would not have to stoop to smell them. It is not quite dense enough for ground cover.

Unnamed seedling × 'Gold Pin'
Repeat flowering
Fragrant

'Softee' — Miniature

This is a pretty bush indeed, with its mid-green foliage and small clusters of creamy white pompoms. Even better is the climbing sport, which flowers all season, and is thornless, so you could train it on a verandah handrail. 'Softee' is yet another beauty from California's master of the Miniature, Ralph Moore, who introduced it in 1982.

Unnamed seedling × unnamed seedling
Repeat flowering
Fragrant

'Starina' — Miniature

MEIgabi

Individually, 'Starina' tops the Miniature popularity polls with its perfectly shaped blooms of brilliant scarlet, its reliable, bushy growth, and its freedom of bloom. Foliage is dark and leathery. Its only fault is that the bushes are sometimes short lived. It was a 1965 triumph for Marie-Louisette Meilland.

('Dany Robin' × 'Fire King') × 'Perla de Montserrat'
Repeat flowering

'Stars 'n' Stripes' — Miniature

Introduced in 1976 by Ralph Moore as his contribution to the United States Bicentennial, 'Stars 'n' Stripes' has been the progenitor of the recent wave of striped roses. In its own right it is a charmer, though some rosarians have been heard to complain that it is shy flowering. It is like a miniature version of 'Versicolor'. The flowers are small and striped in crimson and white. Foliage is mid-green and not very glossy.

'Little Chief' × ('Little Darling' × 'Ferdinand Pichard')
Repeat flowering
Fragrant

'Sunmaid' — Miniature

'Sunmaid' was introduced in 1975 by Hette Spek, son of Jan Spek (of 'Spek's Yellow' fame), and is widely regarded as the best multicolored Miniature, at least by people who live where mildew is not a problem. When it does well, its yellow and orange flowers shine against dark green, glossy leaves.

Parentage undisclosed
Repeat flowering

▲ 'Sunmaid'
◄ 'Softee'

▲ 'Starina'
▼ 'Stars 'n' Stripes'

'Sunny Day'   Miniature
SAVasun

'Sunny Day' has been criticised as shapeless and scentless. It is charming, however, with its cheerful yellow flowers against the glossy dark green foliage. Harmon Saville of Nor'East Miniature Roses introduced it in 1986.

Parentage undisclosed
Repeat flowering

▲ 'Sunny Day'
▼ 'Thunder Cloud'

'Sunspray'   Miniature
AROrasp

This 1981 Miniature from Armstrong Nurseries and Jack Christensen is one of the deepest and most brilliant of all yellow roses. At least it is so in the bud and freshly opened flowers with their distinctive shell-shaped petals. Alas, they fade as they age, and hang on the bush, the flip side, so to speak, of their exceptionally long life. Never mind: just snip the old flowers off, and the glossy-leafed bush will produce plenty more to take their places.

'Gingersnap' × 'Magic Carrousel'
Repeat flowering

'Thunder Cloud'   Miniature

Officially described as simply 'orange-red', this 1979 Ralph Moore creation is more unusual than that. The tiny, full-petalled flowers are indeed orange-red in the bud, but as soon as they are fully open the color clouds over to a marvellous shade, better illustrated than described. It does remind one of a storm cloud at sunset. The bush is compact, with glossy dark green leaves, and there is also a repeat-blooming climbing form. There is no scent, though.

'Little Chief' × 'Fire Princess'
Repeat flowering

'Tom Thumb'   Miniature
'Peon'

'Rouletii' may have been the first of the modern Miniatures, but it was Pedro Dot's 'Peon', rechristened 'Tom Thumb' by Robert Pyle, that caught the public fancy in 1936. It is still worth growing, even if its crimson flowers look a trifle plain beside some of the more glamorous roses of recent years. Foliage is very small and semi-glossy.

'Gloria Mundi' × 'Rouletii'
Repeat flowering

▲ 'Sunspray'
▼ 'Tom Thumb'

'Wanaka'   Miniature
MACinca
'Longleat', 'Young Cole'

Sam McGredy has named 'Wanaka' as his best Miniature, and it is certainly a beauty, the flowers holding their dazzling scarlet without fading. It is indeed so eye-catching that from a little distance one

'Wee Matt' Miniature

Apart from the similarity of names, there is no reason to confuse 'Wee Matt' with 'Wee Man'. It has more petals, sometimes the inner ones being so small that they could better be called petaloids. The flowers are a brighter red than 'Wee Man'. Foliage is broad and mid-green. It makes quite a pleasant Miniature standard, though it would be nice if its unknown raiser (the name is unregistered) had been able to give it some fragrance.

Parentage unknown
Repeat flowering

'Zwergkönig '78' Miniature
'Dwarf King '78'

The original 'Zwergkönig', raised by Wilhelm Kordes in 1954, was the darkest of the Miniatures, its ruffled flowers an almost black-red. The new version, from Kordes's son Reimer in 1978, has the reputation of being stronger and easier to grow. The foliage is dark green, small and neat.

Parentage undisclosed
Repeat flowering

▲ 'Wanaka'
▼ 'Wee Man'

would think one was looking at a geranium rather than a rose. Wanaka is a town in New Zealand. Foliage is glossy. McGredy introduced the rose in 1978.

'Anytime' × 'Trumpeter'
Repeat flowering

'Wee Man' Miniature
'Tapis de Soie', 'Silken Carpet'

The flowers are only of fourteen petals, but they are bright red, set off with golden stamens and specially effective in well-spaced clusters. Foliage is dark and semi-glossy. There is little scent, for this is one of the earlier Miniatures from Sam McGredy, introduced in 1974.

'Little Flirt' × 'Marlena'
Repeat flowering

▲ 'Wee Matt'
▼ 'Yellow Sunblaze'

'Yellow Sunblaze' Miniature
MEItrisical
'Yellow Meillandina'

'Yellow Sunblaze' is a desirable yellow rose, its petals often touched prettily with pink. Foliage is dark and glossy. Like all the other 'Sunblaze' or 'Meillandina' roses it is at its best as a pot-plant.

('Rusticana' × ['Charleston' × 'Allgold']) × 'Gold Coin'
Repeat flowering

'Zwergkönigin '82' Miniature
KORwerk
'Dwarf Queen '82'

The original 'Dwarf King' had a consort, introduced in 1955. The new one has a pink consort also, 'Zwergkönigin '82'. Apart from the color it is similar in all other respects to 'Zwergkönig '78'. It is a Kordes introduction of 1982. The names 'Dwarf King' and 'Dwarf Queen' are not as unimaginative as they might seem—pick up your Grimm's Fairy Tales again and you will see. Our gallery of roses ends in enchantment.

'Korkönig' × 'Sunday Times'
Repeat flowering

▲ 'Zwergkönig '78'
▼ 'Zwergkönigin '82'

THE CULTIVATION OF THE ROSE

THE CULTIVATION OF THE ROSE

To go by the incredibly detailed and long-winded instructions you sometimes find in 'how to grow roses' books, you might think the 'Queen of Flowers' was temperamental and difficult to grow. Happily that is not so. The rose owes its universal popularity as much to its ease of cultivation as to its beauty.

Heaven, to a rose, would be a bed in rich, well-drained soil and a temperate climate, neither hot and sultry nor frigid. Yet the rose is an amazingly adaptable plant, and beautiful roses can be grown just about anywhere—the collection of photographs in this book, taken all over the world, are evidence of that.

Climate

I have seen quite presentable roses in tropical Singapore, and once met a gentleman from Latvia who entertained me with descriptions of how he grew prize-winning blooms in that country's harsh and icy climate; but growing roses in such extremes is a labor of love. Tropical heat and humidity favors fungus diseases at the expense of the rosebushes; and where the temperature falls below 0°F (–18°C) the Teas, Chinas and most Noisettes will need greenhouse cultivation, and even the modern Bush Roses will need protection from the cold in the form of loose soil and/or brushwood heaped over the bases of the plants. Let the temperature fall 15°F further (to –26°C), and only the most cold tolerant roses (the Rugosas, some of the modern shrubs derived from *Rosa pimpinellifolia*, and the toughest of the Wild Roses) will survive.

Perhaps the ideal is a Mediterranean climate where the winter reaches 32°F (0°C) and summer humidity is fairly low. Here all roses will flourish, including the Teas and their relatives (though they will be happiest where it never actually freezes). As so often in gardening, local knowledge and experience is what counts, and a trip to a nearby rose garden or a talk to the neighborhood rose enthusiast will quickly tell you what types of roses grow best in your area.

Wherever you live, sunshine is the first essential. You do occasionally see a rosebush surviving in the shade, but they need at least half the day in sunshine to flourish. Nurserymen grow their plants out in fields open to the sun all day, and far from trees. Being rather greedy itself, the rose does not like other roots sharing its bed.

Soil

It used to be said that roses needed clay, but that is now known not to be true. Most rose lovers nowadays agree that the fine, crumbly loam that suits most plants is the ideal (though if it is on the heavy side, the rose will not mind); but any fertile soil will do, except the sandiest (though even here the Rugosas will thrive) and the swampy. True, *Rosa nitida* and *R. palustris* will put up with wet feet, but few other roses will; and if your soil is poorly drained, the laying of agricultural drains or the building up of raised beds will prove worthwhile.

Whether the soil should be acid or alkaline is a moot point. Most books say 'slightly acid', but I should dispute that. In the course of looking at roses all over the world for this book, it has struck me that the best always seemed to be growing in mildly alkaline soil. Where the soil is sufficiently acid for such plants as camellias and rhododendrons to flourish, I should not hesitate to add lime (in the form of dolomite, for preference) to my rose beds.

Whatever your soil, prepare it generously. As one old rose-grower puts it, 'the rose prefers a rich diet to Cuisine

Roses grow well without protection.

Garden roses need protection against cold; many Wild Roses are hardy.

Too cold for all but the hardiest of Wild Roses.

Roses can be grown but heat and humidity are likely to prove a problem.

Roses can only be grown with irrigation in desert areas; most Wild Roses and many Old Garden Roses will dislike the summer heat.

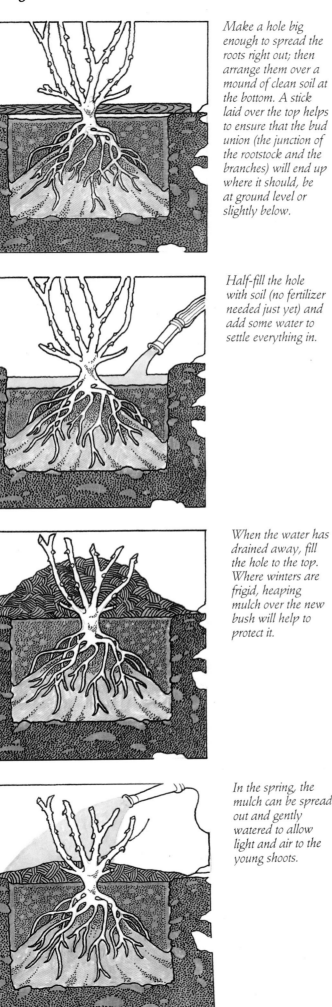

Planting

Make a hole big enough to spread the roots right out; then arrange them over a mound of clean soil at the bottom. A stick laid over the top helps to ensure that the bud union (the junction of the rootstock and the branches) will end up where it should, be at ground level or slightly below.

Half-fill the hole with soil (no fertilizer needed just yet) and add some water to settle everything in.

When the water has drained away, fill the hole to the top. Where winters are frigid, heaping mulch over the new bush will help to protect it.

In the spring, the mulch can be spread out and gently watered to allow light and air to the young shoots.

Minceur'. Cultivate the bed deeply, incorporating as much old manure and compost as you can, and then let it all settle for several weeks before you plant.

Planting

Buy the best plants you can. In the United States, rosebushes are graded for quality, as Grades 1, 1 ½ and 2. Never content yourself with less than Grade 1, even if the price is higher. A runty bush in the nursery is likely to remain so forever. No reliable nurseryman, especially a specialist in roses, would sell a second-grade plant, but a surprising number find their way into chainstores and supermarkets to tempt people who cannot resist a small price tag. When you remember that a rosebush is already two years old when you buy it, roses are not really expensive.

Roses are one of the few plants that are usually sold bare-rooted; that is, the bush is lifted from the ground to be sold without any soil on its roots. There is usually some sort of material like straw or peatmoss packed around them to keep them moist, however. Planting is a trifle more complicated than just tipping an ordinary shrub out of its pot and placing it in a hole, but not much. First, you make a hole wide enough to spread out the roots and deep enough so that the bud union (the point at which the cultivated rose and the wild roots are joined and from which the branches spring) will end up at soil level, more or less. Set it deeper in cold climates, higher in warm ones. Then spread the roots out over a mound of soil at the bottom, fill up a little over halfway with clean soil (no fertilizer, please; it may burn the delicate new roots), and tip in a bucket of water to settle it all in. There should, if your bed has been cultivated to a nicety, be no need to trample on the roots to firm them. When the water has drained away, fill the hole to the top with soil, and, if you like, heap some mulch up around the bush to be spread out later. Naturally, you will not have delayed planting your new purchases and will not have allowed the roots to dry out, carrying the plants in a bucket of water or wrapped in wet hessian.

The best time for planting depends on your climate. It will be some time during the rose's dormancy, and in a mild climate you can plant from late autumn, or fall, until early spring. Where winters are really hard, as in much of the northern United States, it is better to wait until the ground begins to warm up in spring rather than expect a bush with no new roots to endure months of freezing weather. However, trust the reputable growers, you can be sure their plants will be available only at the appropriate planting time.

During the Season

There is usually no need to water a young rosebush until it starts to grow in the spring. During the summer you should not allow roses to dry out, as drought does not encourage growth and flowering. Water deeply and infrequently (the roots go deep), but do try not to get the foliage wet any more than you have to, as wet leaves are an invitation to black spot. A soaker hose, set upside down among the bushes, or a trickle irrigation system, can be most useful. So can mulching the beds with any sort of organic matter that is available—compost, rotted manure, straw, shredded bark, even newspaper. Do not use sawdust, as it consumes nitrogen and can set like cement if it dries out.

A mulch will also help control weeds, which should never be allowed to flourish in rose beds. Not only do they make

Watering

Heaping soil on the downhill side of bushes planted on slopes will help hold water and control erosion. Ground Cover Roses would be the best choice on a slope as steep as this.

Wetting the foliage encourages black spot. One way of avoiding this is to lay a soaker hose upside down between the bushes. Mulch will effectively conceal it.

In dry climates, consider building a rampart of earth about 10 centimetres (4 inches) high around the 'drip line' of each bush, to form a water-holding basin. It is a great saver of water, and the use of a trickle watering system can make further economies.

A watering basin can be filled with mulch (rotted cow manure is ideal) which will not only save water but soft-pedal the crater-like effect of the basins.

you, the gardener, look negligent, they rob the roses of water and nourishment and, by crowding the plants, create the sort of conditions where rose pests and diseases can get started. Pull them out as soon as you see them appearing.

You may well need to spray against insects and fungi, of which there are many that attack roses, but let us deal with that unhappy subject (and it is not so bad) later. See page 447.

Unless you are expecting hips, keep the spent flowers trimmed off to encourage the later ones, but do not take too much foliage. The same applies to cutting blooms for the house. Do not levy too many long-stalked blooms at any one time; always leave at least two leaves on each stem.

Disbudding

It is customary among exhibitors to thin the buds of Large-flowered Roses to one per stem, so that the plant will concentrate its energy into that single perfect bloom; but if you are content to enjoy your roses as they come, there is no need to do it. Similarly, do not bother thinning the shoots in the early spring, in the hope of gaining fewer but gigantic flowers. Leave such tricks to the lovers of exhibition chrysanthemums! Thinning the buds of Cluster-flowered Roses or the Old Garden Roses is unthinkable; their beauty is largely in the multiplicity of their flowers.

PRUNING

The annual job of pruning is not strictly necessary as roses will survive and flower unpruned; wild roses are not pruned, after all. Yet a rose growing in a garden should be pruned each year to keep it youthful and presentable—the management of one of the famous English rose gardens decided some years ago to leave its wild roses quite unpruned and 'natural' but it was not long before the secateurs were reached for.

Pruning is not at all difficult or complicated. Remember the point of it is to keep the bushes young: a rose doesn't make a permanent framework of branches in the way a camellia or hibiscus does, but grows almost like a herbaceous plant. It constantly renews itself by making strong new shoots from the base to take the place of those of former years that have flowered themselves into feebleness. Eventually old branches die; dead wood on a healthy rose bush is no cause for alarm.

So take the job in three stages: first remove dead wood entirely; then any branches that are evidently so old and infirm as to be unable to bear fine flowers, or else just too small and skinny to do so; then shorten the branches that you have decided to retain. How much you shorten depends on climate; you prune harder in frosty places (where, in any case, the decision may be taken out of your hands; you must cut out all frost-damaged wood, no matter how short that leaves the bush) and more lightly in mild ones.

Very hard pruning used to be the fashion, but no longer—current practice is to shorten your retained branches by a third to a half.

Those are the principles. You can follow them pretty closely with the Large- and Cluster-flowered Bush Roses; Shrub Roses, old and new, are trimmed more lightly (if in doubt, just cut out the spent wood and see how the plant behaves). Climbers should not have the not-yet-flowered long canes of the current season shortened except to remove any skinny ends; and many of the Wild Roses merely need tidying—again, just cut out dead and feeble wood. Ramblers

Pruning

The first stage of pruning is to remove dead wood entirely, then any weak branches or those that cross over others to crowd out the centre of the bush.

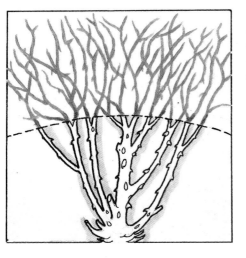

Then shorten the branches you have elected to retain by a third to a half. Go gently in mild climates, harder in cold ones.

Cut just above a growth bud (found where a leaf has joined the stem), leaving no long stub to rot. Make sure your secateurs are sharp and hold them so that the bruised bit of bark is on the part you cut off.

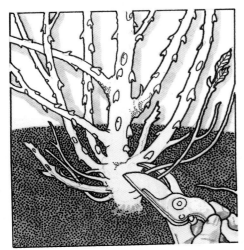

Suckers from the understock should be removed as soon as you notice them. Rip them out; but if they are too established for that, cut them as close to their origin as possible.

Ramblers are the simplest of all roses to prune. Immediately after bloom, cut away all the branches that have just flowered, either to where a new shoot is arising or right to the ground. Simple, but a time-consuming and prickly job!

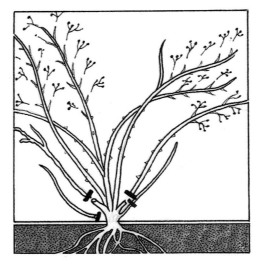

Repeat-blooming Climbers, both Large- and Cluster-flowered, are best pruned in winter. Remove old and worn-out wood, cutting either to a strong young branch or right to the ground. Shorten the strong laterals that bore last year's flowers, and just take out the skinny tips of new canes.

are the simplest of all; few of them produce branches good for more than one flowering, so, immediately the flowers are over, you cut the just-flowered branches right out to make way for the new ones. Simple, but a lot of labor, which is one reason why the group is less popular than it used to be. The once-flowering Old Roses can be pruned in the winter like a Bush Rose, or you can simply trim out the oldest, twiggiest branches just after flowering if you prefer. The Miniatures can be treated with care, judging every cut, or you can just cut them down by half. It seems to make little difference to their performance. Do not fret too much about following the rules exactly—roses are not that easy to kill!

But do make sure your secateurs and pruning saws are really sharp. Blunt tools will tear instead of cutting cleanly, and that will do far more harm to the plant than 'incorrect' pruning. Ask your local rose grower to recommend someone who sharpens secateurs; it is not an easy job.

When you have finished pruning, snip off any old leaves remaining on the bushes, and gather up all the debris and burn it. It is likely to be harboring fungus spores and insect eggs, and is too prickly for the compost heap anyway.

Now, while the mass of thorny branches has been reduced, is the time to get the beds ready for the upcoming season, pulling out any persistent weeds, forking in last year's mulch, and applying a new one. Then you can sit back for a bit and admire the new leaves as they come in all their tones of red, bronze and mint-green, anticipating the flowers they presage.

Cuttings

The best cuttings come from a strong stem that has borne a good flower, preferably from the middle third of its length. Take cuttings either at pruning time or immediately after flowering. Clip off any leaves.

If you are not able to plant your cuttings immediately, roll them up in damp paper so that they do not dry out.

A dip in hormone rooting powder is a help to success, but make sure it is fresh; it loses potency quite quickly.

Traditionally, cuttings are inserted at an angle, but you can set them vertically if you prefer. They go in, into sandy soil, to half their length.

PROPAGATION

Most of us are content to expand our rose collection by buying plants, leaving the nurseryman to do the work of propagating them; but if you plan to go in for roses in a big way—or if you fall in love with an unlabelled or unprocurable rose in a friend's garden—it is nice to know that roses are quite easy to propagate.

The easiest way of all is by layering. You simply bend a branch down to the ground, burying a section of it. A couple of nicks will encourage the new roots, and, if you make your layer sometime shortly after mid-summer, you should be able to sever the new plant from its parent and transplant it the following winter. Naturally, the rose has to have branches limber enough to be bent to the ground, and this limits layering to Climbers, Ramblers, Ground Covers (some of which will, blackberry-like, layer themselves spontaneously) and the laxer Shrub Roses—Bush Roses are usually far too stiff.

The nurseryman gets over the variability of plants grown from cuttings by grafting his roses onto suitable understocks chosen for the vigor of their roots. You and I can follow his example, as budding, the method of choice, is much the easiest of all forms of grafting—Murray Fredericks' diagrams make the procedure plain. Indeed, the hardest part may well be acquiring your understocks; nurserymen are often reluctant to sell them outside the trade.

The best way to obtain roots, therefore, is to buy a plant or two of a suitable variety and take cuttings from it yourself. One of the thornless clones of *Rosa multiflora* would be ideal, but 'Vielchenblau' and 'Gloire de Rosomanes' have their devotees too; and one nurseryman of my acquaintance suggests 'New Dawn', despite its prickliness, as it strikes very easily and makes splendid strong roots. The cuttings are taken in the usual way, in summer, autumn or fall, or winter—except that you must excise all the 'eyes' except the top one (a razor blade will do it), or there will be a lifetime of unwanted suckers.

Plant your cuttings in a nursery bed about half a metre (1 foot 7 inches) apart and, if they were rooted autumn or fall, they should be ready for budding the following summer. The best time is just after the first flowering, when the sap in the understock will be flowing strongly, encouraged by a watering a week or so before you plan to bud, and the buds mature. Follow the diagrams, using a razor blade if you do not have a special budding knife. Just as with cuttings, the bit of leaf stalk you use as a handle will tell you, by dropping away, if the bud is going to take.

There probably will not be much further activity till winter, when you behead the stock entirely just above the bud. It will grow and flower that summer, and the following winter the new plant will be ready for its permanent home.

Standards are made by budding onto exceptionally long rootstocks, setting two buds for symmetry; but I must confess to having never tried it—the very thought of trying to strike cuttings, 1 metre (3 feet 3 inches) long, even of so obliging a plant as *Rosa multiflora*, defeats me.

Budding

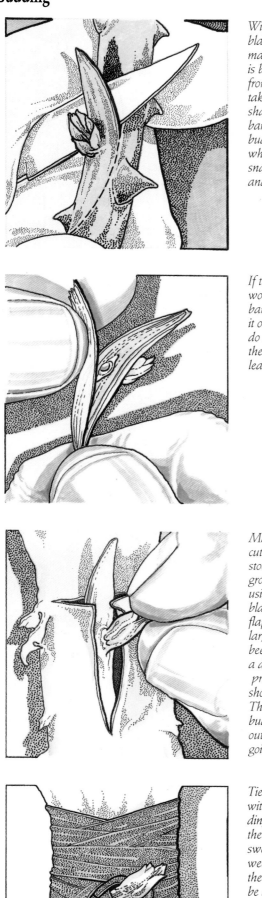

With a razor-sharp blade (the purpose-made budding knife is best) cut the bud from the stem, taking a shield-shaped piece of bark with it. The buds are ready when the thorns snap off easily and cleanly.

If there is a sliver of wood behind the bark, you can snap it out. If you cannot do so without taking the bud with it, leave it in.

Make a T-shaped cut in the bark of the stock just above ground level and using the back of the blade lift back the flaps like a coat collar; if the bed has been well watered a day or two previously this should be easy. Then just slip in the bud. Do not let it dry out while all this is going on.

Tie the bud in place with raffia or budding tape. When the bud begins to swell, after three weeks or so, remove the tape. Raffia can be allowed to rot away in time. Come winter, the stock is cut away to just above the bud, which will grow away in spring.

PESTS AND DISEASES

Queens tend to have enemies; it is one of the problems of queenhood. The Queen of Flowers is no exception—the list of bugs waiting to pounce as soon as the gardener's back is turned seems longer than that for any other flower.

Happily, most are rare, and even the common ones aren't nearly as bad as they sound. Give your bushes a thorough spray immediately pruning has finished—plants, bed and all—to give them a clean start to the season, and you may well be able to dispense with the commonly advocated chore of spraying with a combined insecticide and fungicide every fortnight during the growing season.

Of the insects, chief is the aphid (alias greenfly) which infests many other plants besides roses. Not that you ever see just one—the several species have all achieved the conservative clergyman's dream of reproduction without sex. This enables them to breed in enormous numbers on soft young shoots, sucking out enough sap to cripple them and, more insidiously, spreading viruses. So as soon as you see the advance guard, it is out with the spray gun. Any insecticide will wipe them out, and non-sprayers can try drowning them with repeated jets from the hose.

Thrips is another insect whose damage is caused by its numbers. The individual insect is so tiny as to to be almost invisible, but if they congregate in their hundreds among the rose petals they will soon have them looking like something the cat dragged in. Thrips are most likely to fly when a hot wind is blowing, and they prefer the paler-colored flowers. A systemic insecticide works best.

Scale insects live a sedentary life on the lowest parts of the bush, protecting themselves from their enemies by exuding shields of wax, usually white. They are more damaging than they look, and should either be sprayed with white oil or swabbed with an old brush dripping with methylated spirits, both of which will dissolve the wax and suffocate the insects.

Katydids and other grasshoppers, caterpillars, and several pollen-eating beetles sometimes show an interest in rose bushes, but apart from the bronze Japanese beetle, cursed by American gardeners for its decimation of the flowers, they do little harm and are easily dealt with—if the birds have not already got them—by a squirt of insecticide.

Fungi are more trouble, really, than insects; most roses are liable to fungus attack at some time or other. Once fungi have taken hold, they are more difficult to get rid of; and the gardener has to do it alone: insects are preyed on by other insects like ladybugs and by birds, while fungi appear to have no natural enemies.

The three most dangerous fungi are rust, black spot and mildew. Rust is the most dangerous, and immediately you see it (it looks just as its name implies and usually starts on the underside of the lowest leaves) repeated sprayings with a copper-based fungicide are a matter of urgency. Otherwise the bush will soon be denuded of leaves and maybe even killed. Fortunately, rust is not common.

Black spot ranks next—once the tell-tale fringed black spots appear on a leaf, that leaf is doomed. The fungus can only take hold on damp leaves, which is why you are advised not to wet your bushes when watering, and why black spot is worst in warm, humid climates. The fairly new systemic fungicides have made controlling it easier, but if you live in a humid-summer climate it would be prudent to

Pests and Diseases

Aphids attack many other plants besides roses—here they are on the young shoots of an orange tree. They are themselves under attack by lady-bugs, one of the insects that any wise gardener encourages.

The white rose scale, a much more serious pest than it looks. It is often encountered on old and neglected bushes; removing it is the first step to restoring them to vigor.

Black spot, bane of rose lovers in humid climates. Though there is no garden rose which is immune, there are many which have sufficient resis-tance to flourish with minimum attention from the spray gun.

A bad case of thrips—these flowers of 'Michèle Meilland' are quite ruined.

The most feared of all rose problems, the fatal and incurable wilt virus.

The stems of standard roses can get sunburnt. One solution is to wrap them in tea-tree branches. Old sacking would be just as effective, if less pretty.

The dark red roses are always said to be the most susceptible to mildew, and this bedraggled specimen of 'Deuil de Paul Fontaine' proves the point.

Katydids, which belong to the grasshopper family, have a voracious appetite for blooms—particularly roses. They change color according to their diet.

spray for prevention rather than cure, and that means once a fortnight for the whole growing season. Naturally, if you live in a black spot area you will not give garden room to vari-eties known to be susceptible to the disease. Alas, they include very many of the yellows and blends, which derive both color and susceptibility from *Rosa foetida*.

Mildew is a lesser evil than these, but it can still be devas-tating. It usually strikes the young shoots and is worst in dry weather. A spray or two as soon as it is seen (you will recog-nize the distorted, unhappy look that precedes the grey mildew powder when once you have seen it) should be accompanied by a thorough watering. Keep up the spraying and watering until the symptoms disappear and the new growth is clean.

Fortunately you are unlikely to be troubled by rust, black spot and mildew all at once, but you should still select your rose varieties for their resistance to whichever is the main problem in your area. Then you may be able to get away with only giving a single spray immediately after pruning to start the plants off clean for the new season. Lime sulphur is the traditional stuff for this, and you use it lavishly, spraying bushes, beds and all. If any fungus spore or insect can survive that, it is tough indeed!

Viruses can survive anything, and the only thing to do about the worst of them, the dreaded rose wilt, is to burn the

affected bush as soon as your diagnosis is confirmed, lest the disease spread. In the meantime, sterilize any secateurs that come in contact with it, and wage fierce war on aphids. The picture shows what it looks like. The good news (though no consolation to me!) is that wilt is apparently confined to Aus-tralasia and to Italy, which is why most countries prohibit the importation of rose bushes from there.

Mosaic virus, on the other hand, is universal, and the con-sensus is that it does little harm. You will recognise it by the way it makes yellowish scribbles on the older leaves.

Sprays

I have deliberately refrained from suggesting spray chemicals by name, leaving you to take the advice of the experts at your local garden centre. Remember that both insects and fungi come in slightly different strains from place to place, and that many develop resistance to a particular chemical alarmingly quickly; what is effective here, today, may very well not be so tomorrow, elsewhere.

The chemical companies are always bringing out new products, and so the fashionable rose remedies change quickly. Better products, so they claim. Maybe so, maybe not—but we have come a long way from the days of the Empress Joséphine, whose gardeners used to carefully

▲ *Gardens like the rose garden at Bagatelle might be the epitome of formality, but the use of dwarf hedges to hide the thorny stems of the roses is worth copying. They need not be clipped box, as here; dwarf lavender, santolina, rosemary, or even sage would make a soft frame for the flowers.*

▼ *You do not even have to have a garden! Some years ago, I was admiring the balconies that are such a feature of the old houses of Verona, when, looking up, I saw not a modern Juliet sighing for her Romeo, but a flourishing rosebush in a pot.*

sponge mildew-blighted leaves with vinegar. Make sure you treat all chemicals as the dangerous poisons they are. Use them with circumspection, and store them safely away from children and pets. Follow the directions on the package to the letter; but take the perpetual claims for the safety of chemicals with a grain of salt.

DESIGNING A ROSE GARDEN

'The garden for the rose, not the rose for the garden' was the slogan of that great Victorian writer on roses, Dean Hole. Even now, many rose addicts (and this, surely, is the most addictive of all flowers!) would agree. For them, the design of a rose garden is simply a matter of accommodating and displaying as many of their favorite roses as possible. Lesser plants are relegated to positions too shady for the roses, or admitted with some reluctance to provide flowers outside the rose season.

While in an ordinary-sized suburban garden a purist (or obsessive) approach like this can easily lead to the garden becoming just a rose factory, it can lead to magnificence when carried out on a grand scale. Just take a look at the Roseraie de l'Haÿ or many another public rose garden. Such

▲ *The public, roses-only garden at its finest: Queen Mary's Rose Garden in London's Regent's Park.*

◄ *There is no more flattering dress for a handsome house (or a dull one!) than a climbing rose, which will adorn but never obscure the architecture. Hence at Haddon Hall in Derbyshire, 'Albertine' showers warm pink flowers over the blues and mauves of the stateliest delphiniums I have ever seen.*

▼ *It is possible to adapt the Victorian style to a smaller scale, as in this example in Canada, where Old Garden Roses grow in a cottagey mix with other flowers. An arrangement like this is all the better for some permanent focal point like the sundial. You could use a statue or a pool, even a handsome light fitting, if you preferred.*

gardens tend to formality in design, both because it is impossible anyway to make a collection of rose beds cut out of a lawn, or linked by paved paths, look other than artificial, and also to bring some measure of order and aesthetic unity to what can easily be seen as a shapeless jumble of bushes.

Few of us these days have the space or the money to make rose gardens in this manner, but there is much to learn from them. First is the value of a simple green backdrop for roses. We may not have space for stands of fine trees, but we can at least clad ugly walls, sheds or fences with creepers, and allow groundcovering plants to spill over pavings and driveways. True, there are roses for these purposes, but most roses are too flimsy and shapeless in growth to form the framework of a garden; they are best used to fill in and decorate. The Rugosas are perhaps an exception. Second is the importance of allowing ourselves enough space to move among the roses. No one can admire a rose if they have to duck and weave down a narrow pathway trying to avoid its thorny branches!

Not all of us will want to devote our gardens exclusively to the rose; it may be our favorite flower, but we do not want to forgo the pleasure of the company of so many others. We will espouse a different tradition, one best exemplified by such gardens as that of Claude Monet at Giverney, where roses grow in happy harmony with all sorts of other flowers. It is indeed an older tradition, for the formal, roses-only garden dates only from the time of the Empress Joséphine.

Before then, roses were grown mixed in with other plants; even the 'roseries' of the Middle Ages featured fragrant herbs and plants that we would now consign to the vegetable

▲ Plans for rose gardens, from the Victorian classic William Paul's The Rose Garden, first published in 1848. But where is the house? Maybe a hundred metres away. These were gardens-within-gardens, intended for the adornment of vast country estates and visited by none but the head gardener and his boys except during the rose season.

▲ With their summer-long flowering, Modern Garden Roses are leading candidates for a position by the swimming pool. Here their warm colors shine against the turquoise water, but I wonder whether they should not have been set a little further back? Swimming costumes do not offer much protection against rose prickles these days.

▼ The garden designer's dream: a rose that grows bushy to the ground (no ugly bare stems to camouflage here), and bears good-sized fragrant flowers. I saw it at a German flower show and waited anxiously for it to be introduced; but it never was. Its raisers, Dickson's of Northern Ireland, tell me that they did not find it sufficiently reliable. Let us hope it is a forerunner of things to come.

▲ *What could be more romantic than a canopied seat framed in roses? Here in a Johannesburg garden, 'Climbing Iceberg' shines in an all-white color scheme.*

▶ *Grass paths always look delightful in a rose garden, but they do tend to wear out underfoot, especially in a dry-summer climate. This Natal garden solves the problem neatly with stepping stones. I like the lavish use of grey foliage to set off the warm colors of the roses.*

◀ *'Helen Traubel' flourishing mightily under a regime of very light pruning. A single rosebush like this can light up a basically green garden.*

garden. Some would suggest that the rose should be banished there too. Enjoy the flowers in vases, they say, but leave the scruffy, prickly bushes unvisited among the cabbages and beans. They have a point, but the rose's bad legs can be just as well camouflaged by ornamental plants as by capsicums. Blue flowers like delphiniums and campanulas (and clematis to accompany Climbing Roses on walls) are indispensable, as the rose does not supply that color, but there is no need to confine yourself to them. Think, for instance, of dawn-pink irises with their flaring blooms and sword-like leaves setting off the roundness of a rose of similar hue such as 'Pink Chiffon'; of mahogany day lilies with the coral of 'Alexander' or 'Fragrant Cloud'; of regal lilies rising through the tumbling branches of 'Cardinal de Richelieu' in a blend of color and rich fragrance.

Just remember, when ordering and setting out your roses, to allow sufficient space for the other plants, so that the roses themselves will not be over-crowded.

That is how I would design my rose garden, were I creating one now; and I would go further than that, not even thinking about roses until the permanent elements of the garden: space for sitting out and for children to play; trees for shade; shrubs and climbers to mask unwanted views; paving, steps and paths; had all been allowed for. Only then would I fill in the spaces with roses and their companions. The garden would be satisfying without them; and when the time of roses arrived, it would be glorious indeed.

Claude Monet's garden at Giverney down river from Paris must be the world's favorite garden. Wherever you look, there are roses, attended by a kaleidoscope of beautiful flowers of every kind. They have always been in perfect health whenever I have seen them, giving the lie to those who claim roses must be isolated for their own good.

OTHER MEMBERS OF THE ROSE FAMILY

Living things never evolve in isolation, and the rose is no exception. It heads a very large family of plants which is called Rosaceae by the botanists. The Rosaceae is a distinguished and important family. Native mostly to the temperate zones, it includes many of the world's favorite fruits: the apple, pear, plum, cherry and more, along with some beautiful flowers—not that any rose-lover would admit to any of them rivalling the rose in beauty.

Here are some of them: I think you will agree there are enough plants with a legitimate claim to the royal blood of flowerdom without considering those that have only pretensions to the title, like the Christmas Roses, the Guelder Rose, the Hawaiian Wood Rose and their ilk, none of which is even remotely related to the subject of this book.

Alchemilla
Lady's Mantle
Old-fashioned Lady's Mantles are delightful herbaceous perennials for moist, well-drained soil. They produce masses of lobed leaves resembling those of pelargoniums, but furry. Dainty yellow flowers lack petals and are scarcely larger than a pinhead. They appear in dense trusses throughout summer.

Chaenomeles
Flowering Quince
Dense, spiny shrubs to 2.2 metres (7 feet) tall, and as wide, the Japonicas commence blooming in winter and con-

▲ *Crataegus oxyacantha* cultivar

tinue for months. There are many cultivars, flowering in every shade of pink, red, white and orange. They enjoy full sun and summer moisture, and are hardy down to –10°C (14°F). Remove a third of the oldest stems each year to ensure profuse bloom.

Cotoneaster
Rockspray
These include very hardy evergreen or deciduous shrubs with many garden uses. They are dusted in spring with a covering of tiny flowers, which are followed by autumn, or fall, berries. These are the chief attraction. All Rocksprays grow fast and need well-drained soil.

Crataegus
Hawthorn
The illustrated cultivar of common Hawthorn is but one of perhaps a thousand species of these rose relatives, found principally in North America. They are frost hardy and grown principally for their fruit, ranging in size from currant to small apple in diameter. The masses of spring blossom show the rose relationship best.

◀ *Chaenomeles lagenaria*

Eriobotrya
Loquat
Closely related to apples, pears and quinces, the oriental Loquat is popular in subtropical climates but is out of favor since the discovery that fruitfly larvae can overwinter in the fruit. The evergreen foliage is handsome; the five-petalled flowers are fragrant; and the fruit ripens at various times in winter according to variety.

Heteromeles
Toyon, California Holly
Without California's ubiquitous Toyon, there would not be a Hollywood, for *Heteromeles* was the bright-fruited shrub that attracted settlers in the first place. It can be propagated from seed, cuttings or by layering.

Holodiscus
Ocean Spray
Like *Aruncus* and *Filipendula*, *Holodiscus* is a rose relative without the rose-type flowers. Instead there are arching panicles of tiny white blossom that are reminiscent of breaking waves. These are succeeded by a mass of tiny berries which bring birds for miles.

Malus
Apple, Crabapple

The most popular fruit in cooler climates, fruiting apples ripen from summer on. You are sure to find one you like from among 1000-odd cultivars. Their smaller relatives, the crabapples, are grown for spring blossom in a variety of colors, and clusters of small fruits later.

Neviusia
Snow Wreath

The sole species of *Neviusia* was discovered in Alabama in the mid-nineteenth century. It is closely related to the Japanese *Kerria*, for which it might be mistaken when not in blossom. The flower heads consist of a mass of white stamens gathered in short open cymes.

Photinia
Japanese Photinia

Semideciduous *Photinia* is much used for hedging, where the glossy red foliage is quite eye-catching. In spring the bushes develop flat panicles of tiny white flowers, though their acrid smell is not to everyone's taste. *Photinia* should be pruned regularly to keep growth dense and colorful.

Potentilla
Cinquefoil

No northern hemisphere cool garden would be completely furnished without a few *Potentilla*. They are annual, perennial or shrubby and all have a strong resemblance to roses in their foliage and in their five-petalled flowers. These may be pink, scarlet, maroon, orange, white or yellow.

Prunus

Beyond their passing resemblance to true roses, you must have a really creative imagination to spot the relationship between, say, a Japanese Flowering Cherry and an evergreen Portugal Laurel. *Prunus glandulosa* is the dwarf-flowering Almond Cherry, with pink or white varieties. *Prunus laurocerasus* is an evergreen small tree. *Prunus serrulata*, in incredible variety, is the ornamental Japanese Cherry Blossom, with the green 'Ukon' type particularly desirable in spring. Both spring and autumn, or fall, flowerings can be expected from *Prunus subhirtella*. *Prunus persica* blooms in many colors with flowers that strongly resemble roses.

Pyracantha
Firethorn

The autumn, or fall, fruiting Firethorns, with berries of yellow, scarlet and orange, are among the most spectacular garden shrubs either outdoors or cut as large branches for indoor decoration.

Pyrus
Pear

Pears grow wild in Europe, Asia and Africa, but not in the Americas or Australia. Flowers strongly resemble single roses and, of course, Apples—they all have five petals. Elongated fruits are typical of pears, although some varieties are round.

▲ *Malus* 'Gorgeous' (Crabapple)

Raphiolepis
Yeddo Hawthorn

Raphiolepis can be relied upon for spring display in climates from cold to cool temperate and is hardy down to –9°C (16°F). It will grow close to the sea and is a problem only in very dry areas, unless you can provide semi-shade.

Sorbus
Rowan, Mountain Ash

An important fruit-bearing genus of the rose family are the many species of *Sorbus*, all from cool temperate areas in the northern hemisphere. Relatively tasteless, the fruits are sometimes brewed into a cider-type beverage. *Sorbus* species are mostly tree size.

▲ *Pyrus* 'Williams' Bon Chrétien'
▼ *Potentilla fruticosa*

ROSE TERMINOLOGY

Like most activities and pastimes, rose-growing has evolved its own special jargon, sometimes incomprehensible to the uninitiated. In this book I have tried to use ordinary English, but there are some rose words that merit explanation. Here they are.

AARS Award There are many trial grounds around the world, usually run by local rose societies, where new roses are evaluated and considered for prizes before they are introduced to the public. Examples are those of the Royal National Rose Society at St Albans in England and the International Trial Gardens in Portland, Oregon. Others are in Lyon, Paris (the Parc de Bagatelle), Madrid, Rome, Belfast and New Zealand. Founded in 1939, All-America Rose Selections Inc. differs in existing solely to evaluate new roses (it is not an arm of the American Rose Society) and in maintaining no fewer than twenty-five test gardens all over the United States. Less than 5 per cent of roses tried out win the coveted AARS award, which should guarantee a rose is capable of excellence just about anywhere.

Bicolor Many roses have a different shade of color on the upper and lower surfaces of each petal; often the two colors are sharply contrasted, and the rose is described as, say, 'red with a yellow reverse'. The effect is virtually unique to the rose, and derives from the genes of the Austrian Copper Rose Examples are 'Alleluia' and 'Love' in red and white, and 'Piccadilly' in red and gold. Roses where the two tones are shades of the same color, as in 'La France' or 'Red Devil', would not usually be described as bicolors.

'Piccadilly', a striking bicolor.

Blend A rose with two (sometimes more) colors on each of its petals, but without the front/back contrast of a bicolor. 'Peace', blending yellow and pink, is the classic example of a blend.

Blue, blueing Although catalogue writers are fond of tempting their customers by describing certain roses as 'blue', and even naming them accordingly—as with 'Blue Moon' and 'Azure Sea'—there is no such thing yet. All these roses are some shade of pinkish lavender, a result of the breakdown of the pink pigment cyanidin in combination with tannins. A red or pink rose that is said to 'blue' is one that tends to turn magenta with age. This is a fault, and is more likely to happen (with susceptible varieties) in cold weather, or when the bloom is cut and brought indoors.

Briar Strictly speaking, this term refers to the Dog Rose (*Rosa canina*) and its relatives, including the Sweet Briar and the Austrian Briar. It is often also used loosely for any Wild Rose, especially one that is used as an understock. You sometimes hear it said that a rosebush has 'reverted to briar' when what has happened is that a careless gardener has allowed suckers from the stock to smother the cultivated variety that was budded on to it.

Bud For most of us, a bud is an immature flower that has not yet unfolded its petals, but rose-lovers often use the term to describe a rose until it is about half open. A variety such as 'Eiffel Tower' is praised for the beauty of its long, pointed buds.

Bush Rose An ordinary rosebush, of more or less upright growth, and calling for vigorous pruning each winter, as distinct from a Climber or a Shrub Rose. Strictly speaking, all roses are shrubs, but the term Shrub Rose refers to a rose of more informal growth than a conventional Large-flowered or Cluster-flowered Rose, suitable for including in a shrubbery.

Climbing Rose, Climber Strictly speaking, no rose climbs in the sense that a grape vine or a jasmine does. A Climbing Rose is one that makes shoots of considerable length, suitable for training over a fence or pergola, or into some shrub or tree, in the same way that one might use a true climbing plant. It will need assistance to stay there and not just flop about.

Cultivar This is botanists' jargon, short for 'cultivated variety', and means a variety of plant that has originated in gardens rather than in the wild. I have preferred the less pedantic 'variety', while recognizing that most roses have in fact originated as garden plants, propagated as clones from outstanding individual plants.

Decorative All roses are decorative, but the term is officially used to describe a Large-flowered Rose that is too lightly built to be of use for exhibition. 'Audie Murphy' and 'Piccadilly' are examples.

Double A rose with more than its natural complement of petals, formed at the expense of stamens. For a rose to be described as 'fully double' it needs to have more than thirty (some of the Old Garden Roses can have up to eighty), with the stamens not prominent in the full-blown flower. One with fifteen to twenty, opening to show its stamens, is 'semi-double'.

Rosa multiflora with its five petals, and 'Charles De Mills', one of the most double roses of all.

Exhibition rose A Large-flowered Rose suitable for winning prizes because it conforms to the exhibitor's ideal of a rose 'with an abundance of petals, gracefully and symmetrically arranged around a well-formed centre'. 'Red Devil', 'Perfecta', and 'Peace' are good examples of this type. 'Exhibition varieties', however, are not always very generous with their huge flowers.

The sort of bloom an exhibitor dreams of—'Gold Medal'.

Grandiflora A term coined in America to describe a tall Bush Rose, bearing well-formed, moderately sized blooms in small clusters. 'Queen Elizabeth' is the prototype. In this book, I have preferred to follow the World Federation of Rose Societies' lead and class Grandifloras with the Large-flowered or Cluster-flowered Roses as seems most appropriate in each case.

Ground Cover A rose of prostrate habit, suitable for growing as ground cover (that is, to make a low mat of foliage and flowers and suppress weeds). It must be admitted few roses do the job as well as such plants as the hypericums and the creeping junipers.

Hip The fruit of the rose, produced by any rose whose genes do not make it sterile. The Modern Garden Roses only ripen them into beauty in mild climates. The hips are quite a feature of some roses, such as *Rosa moyesii* and the Rugosas. Rose hips are edible, and can be made into jam, wine and syrup. They are one of the richest known natural sources of vitamin C. Sometimes 'hip' is archaically and pedantically spelt 'hep'.

Miniature A miniature camellia usually bears tiny flowers on a full-sized shrub, but a Miniature Rose is expected to be miniature in growth also, with everything, leaves, stems, flowers and all, reduced in perfect proportion on a bush which grows to about 35 centimetres tall.

Patio Rose A relatively new and unofficial classification, for Cluster-flowered Bush Roses of short growth but full-sized flowers, suitable for decorating patios. 'Europeana' and 'China Doll' are examples.

Pegging down A style of growing roses popular in Victorian days but less often seen now, where the long shoots of Hybrid Perpetuals and Bourbons were bent to the ground and fixed there with wooden pegs, so as to encourage blooms along their whole length. It is still worth doing with these and with such leggy Modern Garden Roses as 'Papageno' or 'Scarlet Queen Elizabeth' if their branches are flexible enough.

Pillar rose A Climbing Rose of moderate vigor, suitable for training up a pillar or verandah post, to make a column of bloom in season. It is an unofficial description rather than an officially recognized class, the vigor of any variety being partly dependent on how well it is grown.

Prickles A botanist will tell you that a 'thorn' is an outgrowth from the wood, like those of a bougainvillea, and that roses do not have thorns, but 'prickles', which are developments of the bark. Be that as it may, the prickles of the rose are still sharp.

Rambler A Climbing Rose, usually bearing small flowers in bunches, with very long and flexible canes. 'Dorothy Perkins' is the classic example. Very few Rambler Roses are repeat flowering. They are sometimes classed with the species that gave them birth, such as *Rosa multiflora, R. sempervirens* and *R. wichuraiana*.

Remontant A rose does not make growth and flower buds all at once the way, say, a hibiscus or petunia does. It grows, makes flowers at the end of the shoots, and then repeats the process as many times as the warm weather allows. It 'rises again', as the French word 'remontant' suggests. I have normally preferred the less concise but easier English phrase 'repeat flowering', and have eschewed such exaggerations as 'continuous' and 'perpetual'. The English translation of the French 'Hybride Remontant' as 'Hybrid Perpetual' considerably overstates the merit of these roses, but we are stuck with it.

Scarlet Strictly, a red with a good deal of orange in it, seen in such varieties as 'Julishka' and 'Fragrant Cloud'. To describe a blood-red rose like 'Olympiad' as scarlet is commercial hype, but nurserymen have been doing it for over a hundred years. True scarlet was unknown until a mutation brought the pigment pelargonidin into the rose's chemistry in the late 1930s.

Seedling In ordinary gardener's language, a baby plant, still in its nursery bed, but in rose parlance it means a new variety, raised from seed of course, that has not yet been named and introduced to commerce. You will often see the phrase 'unnamed seedling' in rose parentages.

Shrub A rose of more informal growth than a conventional Large-flowered or Cluster-flowered Rose. Not all Shrub Roses are of large growth. *Rosa ecae* for instance is quite diminutive in stature.

Single A rose with the five petals of a Wild Rose; garden roses described as single, like 'Sparrieshoop' and 'Lilac Charm' are allowed a couple more.

'Easlea's Golden Rambler', a pillar rose.

Species In botany, a population of plants or animals that have similar characteristics and interbreed freely, such as *Homo sapiens*. Gardeners use the term loosely to refer to any Wild Rose, and sometimes find it confusing that two rather different roses (from their point of view) can be classed as belonging to the same species.

Sport A spontaneous change that leads a rose to produce a branch different from the rest of the bush, and which, when propagated, retains the difference and thus gives rise to a new variety. 'Chicago Peace' is a sport of 'Peace', differing in the color of its flowers; 'Climbing Peace' differs in its climbing habit.

Standard 'Iceberg' raising its flowers aloft over other plants.

Standard A standard is a rose budded on top of a long understock, so as to raise its branches aloft on a single stem, like a floral lollipop. The stem is usually about a metre (3 feet) long; if less, the plant is called a half-standard. Weeping standards have longer stems still, with a Climber or Rambler budded on top in the hope that its branches and flowers will cascade to the ground.

Understock Roses are one of the few common garden plants that are usually grafted, in their case by means of budding onto the roots of a strong Wild Rose, an understock. The junction is called the bud union, and any shoots that arise from below the bud union will be those of the Wild Rose that provided the roots.

Watershoot The soft, watery shoots that arise from the base of a rosebush, and which form the foundation of the new wood for the future. Cherish them, and do not confuse them with suckers from the understock, which should be removed at once.

SOME FAMOUS ROSE BREEDERS

There have been many hundreds of dedicated rose-lovers, both amateur and professional, pursuing the quest for new and more beautiful roses. Some have their name attached to just one or two; others have been more prolific. The following are some of the best known.

Aicardi, Domenico He is Italy's best-known raiser, remembered today for 'Signora Piero Puricelli' (1936), and also for 'Glory of Rome' and 'Eternal Youth' (both from 1937), which were popular with exhibitors until well into the 1960s.

Austin, David A contemporary English rose-breeder. The son of a Norfolk farmer, he has sought to blend the grace and full-petalled flowers of the Old Garden Roses with the brighter colors and repeat flowering of the Moderns in a series of hybrids he calls his 'English Roses'. Many have names taken from the works of Chaucer and Shakespeare.

Armstrong Nurseries A leading American firm, now part of the Bear Creek conglomerate. David Armstrong is responsible for some fine roses such as 'Aquarius' and 'Kentucky Derby', but the firm has also introduced the creations of Herbert Swim, Jack Christensen, and other breeders.

Barbier et Cie An early twentieth-century French firm, based near Orléans and responsible for some fine Ramblers, officially derivatives of *Rosa wichuraiana* but thought by some to have been bred from *R. luciae*; 'Alberic Barbier' and 'Albertine' are best-known.

Bennett, Henry Known as 'the father of the Hybrid Tea'. He was a late nineteenth-century cattle-farmer turned rose-breeder and one of the first to practise controlled hybridization exclusively. 'Lady Mary Fitzwilliam', introduced by him in 1882, is a most important ancestor of Modern Garden Roses; 'Mrs John Laing' is the most popular of his roses today.

Boerner, Eugene S. A mid-twentieth-century American breeder, nicknamed 'Papa Floribunda' for the stream of superlative roses of that type he created as Director of Research for Jackson & Perkins from the mid-1940s until his death in 1966. Among them are 'Masquerade', 'Fashion' and 'Pink Chiffon'. Except for 'Diamond Jubilee' (1947) and the posthumous 'First Prize' (1970), the Large-flowered Roses he created were less ardently admired.

Brownell, Dr and Mrs Walter An American couple who from the 1920s to the late 1950s worked to develop 'sub-zero roses' to withstand the severe winters of their Rhode Island home; 'Elegance' (1937) is their best known rose.

Buck, Dr Griffith J. A contemporary American rose-breeder and Professor of Horticulture at Iowa State University, for which he raised a long series of roses combining grace and fragrance with ease of culture in the extreme climates of the American Mid-West. Among them are 'Amiga Mia' and 'Country Dancer'.

Cant, Benjamin & Co. (now Cant's of Colchester) A hundred-year-old English firm, the raisers of many fine roses during that whole time.

Christensen, Jack A contemporary American breeder, successor to Herbert Swim at Armstrong Nurseries and raiser of such beauties as 'Holy Toledo' and 'Voodoo'.

Clark, Alister An Australian amateur rose-grower, whose creations, from the time of World War I until after World War II, were very popular in his home country. The best known today are the Climbers derived from *Rosa gigantea*, like 'Lorraine Lee' (1924) and 'Nancy Hayward' (1937).

Cochet-Cochet, P. C. M. A leading turn-of-the-century French rosarian, consultant to the formation of the Roseraie de l'Haÿ and noteworthy for many of the best *Rosa rugosa* hybrids, among them 'Roseraie de l'Haÿ' and 'Blanc Double de Coubert'.

Cocker, Alexander A Scottish nurseryman who achieved great success with his first foray into rose-breeding, 'Alec's Red' (1969). He followed it up with many more, notably 'Silver Jubilee' (1977), before his untimely death in 1978. He worked in close co-operation with Jack Harkness.

Delbard, Georges A contemporary French raiser, who is currently specializing in Large-flowered Roses for the cut-flower trade such as 'Lancôme'. He often works in association with André Chabert. Their joint productions ('Gingersnap' is one of these) are credited 'Delbard-Chabert'.

de Ruiter, Gijs A contemporary Dutch rose-breeder who is best known for Cluster-flowered Roses of the quality of 'Europeana'.

Dickson, Alexander, & Sons Sometimes known as Dickson's of Hawlmark or just Dickson's Nursery. It is a Northern Irish family firm founded in 1836. Since 1886, innumerable fine roses have come from the hands of Alex Dickson II ('George Dickson' 1912), Alex III ('Shot Silk', 'Dame Edith Helen', 'Silver Lining') and from the present head of the firm, Patrick Dickson ('Red Devil', 'Disco Dancer', 'Pot O' Gold').

Dot, Pedro A Spanish raiser, celebrated for a long succession of brilliantly colored Large-flowered Roses. He is even more celebrated for 'Nevada', and his pioneering work with Miniatures. Since his death in 1976, his firm has been run by his sons, Simon and Marino.

Dupont, André Superintendent of the Empress Joséphine's rose garden and thought to be the first to cross-fertilize roses artificially. He is commemorated in 'Dupontii'.

Fisher, Gladys A mid-twentieth-century American raiser, who specialised in roses with unusual colors. 'Sterling Silver' (1957) is her best known.

Gaujard, Jean A mid-twentieth-century French raiser. He took over Pernet-Ducher's nursery on the master's death in 1924 and his best known rose is 'Rose Gaujard', named for himself. His other creations are less well known outside France.

Guillot, Père et Fils A nineteenth-century French father and son concern, founded by Pierre (Guillot Père) in 1826. 'Madame Bravy' (1848) is his best known rose, but it is overshadowed by his son Jean-Pierre's 'La France' (1867), 'Catherine Mermet' (1869) and the first Polyantha, 'Mignonette' (1880).

Hardy, Eugène Director of Paris's Jardins de Luxembourg in the 1820s and '30s. He used to give his new roses to friends rather than sell them commercially. As William Paul predicted, 'Madame Hardy' keeps his name famous. 'Bon Silène' and *Hulthemosa hardii* are also examples of his mastery.

Harkness, Jack The English firm of R. Harkness & Co. had been established for many years before Jack Harkness took up hybridizing in 1962. Such roses as 'Escapade', 'Alexander', and the first hybrids of *Rosa persica* since Eugène Hardy's have won Harkness the reputation of being England's foremost rose-breeder today.

Hill There were two American firms of this name, active in the first half of the twentieth century: E. G. Hill, famous for 'Columbia' and 'Madame Butterfly'; and the Joseph Hill company, less notable, though 'Sensation' (1922) proved an important parent. Both of these firms were leading growers of cut roses, and both were headquartered in Richmond, Indiana.

Horvath, Michael A late nineteenth-century American raiser remembered for his pioneering work with *Rosa wichuraiana*, even though not many of the roses themselves are still grown.

Howard, Fred A Californian raiser. His firm, Howard & Smith, were successful raisers of Large-flowered Roses from just before World War I until the late 1950s. His rose 'The Doctor' (1936) was once voted the most beautiful rose in America.

Jackson & Perkins America's largest firm of rose-growers, now part of the Bear Creek conglomerate, itself now owned by the Reynolds Tobacco Company. They have been in business since 1872. 'Dorothy Perkins' (1901), an early success, has been followed by an endless stream of beauties from the hands of J. H. Nicolas, Eugene Boerner and Bill Warriner, as well as from many of the leading European raisers.

W. Kordes Söhn A German firm, founded in 1887. Its international reputation was made by Wilhelm Kordes II, possibly the greatest, certainly the most imaginative, of all rose-breeders, who gave the world 'Crimson Glory', 'Independence', 'Frühlingsmorgen', 'Perfecta', 'Pinocchio', the 'Kordesii Climbers' and many, many others. Since his retirement in 1964 (he died in 1975), the firm has been run by his son, Reimer, creator of 'Iceberg', 'Friesia' and 'Königin der Rosen'.

Lacharme, François A mid-nineteenth century French raiser and a leading creator of Hybrid Perpetuals, Bourbons and Noisettes. 'Boule de Neige' (1867) and 'Souvenir du Docteur Jamain' (1865) are the best known of his roses today.

Lambert, Peter A turn-of-the-century German hybridist, still celebrated for 'Frau Karl Druschki' (1900) and 'Gartendirektor Otto Linne' (1934). He also raised a series of Shrub Roses called 'Lambertianas', and 'Trier', which is an ancestor of most of the Hybrid Musks.

Lammerts, Dr Walter An American (based in California), geneticist and plant-breeder, responsible for introducing the Yunnan cultivars of *Camellia reticulata* to the West and for creating modern cultivars of *Leptospermum*. His roses are also of the highest importance, including 'Charlotte Armstrong' and 'Queen Elizabeth'.

Le Grice, Edward Burton A mid-twentieth-century English raiser whose systematic and careful breeding yielded a long series of Cluster-flowered Roses of unusual distinction, from 'Dainty Maid' (1940) to 'Allgold', 'Lilac Charm', 'News', 'Victoriana' and others in the 1950s until his death in 1977.

Laffay, M. A French raiser from the early and mid-nineteenth century, to whom the early development of the Hybrid Perpetuals is usually attributed. He used to raise seedlings in enormous quantities—a couple of hundred thousand a year.

Leenders, brothers Inter-war Dutch raisers, notable for pink Large-flowered Roses of unusual refinement, the most important of which is 'Comtesse Vandal'.

Lens, Louis Belgium's leading twentieth-century rose-breeder. 'Pascali', a late creation (1963), is his masterpiece.

McGredy, Samuel, & Sons There have been no fewer than four Sam McGredys heading this old Irish firm, founded in 1828. Sam II started raising roses in about 1900, among them 'Queen Alexandra'; Sam III followed in the 1920s and '30s with roses such as 'Mrs Sam McGredy' and 'McGredy's Yellow'. His early death in 1934 led to a hiatus until the present Sam, Sam IV, reached his majority. He has followed 'Orangeade' (1959) with too many beautiful roses to mention. In 1972 he moved his business to New Zealand. It is now called Sam McGredy Roses International.

Mallerin, Charles A French railway engineer, the most celebrated of all amateur raisers of roses. Among his creations are 'Mrs Pierre S. Dupont' (1929), 'Virgo' (1947) and 'Danse du Feu' (1954). He died in 1960.

Meilland, Francis A French hybridist, famous above all as the raiser of 'Peace', which he followed by many others nearly as remarkable. On his early death from cancer in 1958 his firm, officially known as Universal Rose Selections (URS), passed to his son Alain and widow Marie-Louisette, who continue to create notable roses.

Moreau & Robert A mid-nineteenth-century French firm, famous for Moss Roses.

Moore, Ralph S. California's master of the Miniature. Nearly half those in this book have issued from his Sequoia Nurseries. He is still going strong.

Nabonnand, Clement, Gilbert and Pierre French brothers, in the late nineteenth century who specialised in Teas. 'General Schablikine' is their best known.

Norman, Albert He was an English amateur breeder, a diamond setter by trade, who won fame just after World War II with 'Ena Harkness' and 'Frensham'. Later successes included 'Ann Elizabeth', named for his grand-daughter. He died in 1962.

Pal, Dr J. B. Active mainly in the 1960s, Dr Pal has been India's best known rose-breeder, creating such beauties as 'Princess of India'. He has been followed by others, under the auspices of the Indian Rose Society and the Indian Government, but unfortunately few of their productions receive notice outside the subcontinent of India.

Paul, William and George Nineteenth-century English rose-growers, raisers and introducers of new roses from the late 1840s right up to the end of World War I. 'Paul's Scarlet', 'Ophelia' and 'Mermaid' are their three best known.

Pemberton, Reverend Joseph An English rosarian, sometime President of the National Rose Society, and creator in the 1920s of the Hybrid Musks, which are still among the best regarded of Shrub Roses.

Pernet-Ducher, Joseph A French hybridist, dubbed 'the Wizard of Lyon' for his success in marrying *Rosa foetida* to the garden roses, thereby bringing in shades of pure yellow, coral and flame. The strain, which began in 1900 with 'Soleil d'Or', was christened 'Pernetiana' in his honor. He had already made his mark with 'Madame Abel Chatenay', 'Madame Caroline Testout', and 'Cécile Brünner'. He started out by marrying the daughter of the Widow Ducher and inherited her nursery.

Poulsen A Danish firm, founded in 1978. Dines Poulsen raised several good roses in the first years of the twentieth century, but the famous Poulsen is his son Svend, virtual creator of the Cluster-flowered Roses, with such varieties as 'Else Poulsen' and 'Kirsten Poulsen', both introduced in 1924. Under the direction, from the 1960s, of Svend's son Niels, and now of Niels's daughter Pernille and her husband Mogens Olesen, the firm continues to raise splendid roses of all types.

Robinson, Herbert An English raiser, from the late 1930s to the late '50s, of both Large-flowered and Cluster-flowered Roses which are well thought of in the United Kingdom. 'Joybells' is a favorite.

Suzuki, Seizo A contemporary Japanese hybridist, Japan's foremost, and director of the Keisei Rose Research Institute outside Kyoto. He created such outstanding roses as 'Olympic Torch', 'Mikado' and 'Ferdy'.

Swim, Herbert C. An American hybridist, associated for most of his career with Armstrong Nurseries, but for a while working in freelance partnership with O. L. Weeks. They dominated American rose-breeding in the 1950s and '60s with such world-beating roses as 'Sutter's Gold', 'Mister Lincoln', 'Montezuma', 'Pink Parfait' and 'Royal Highness'.

Tantau, Mathias, father and son German rose-raisers. Mathias senior started the firm in 1981, but the son raised it to world fame with such roses as 'Super Star', 'Fragrant Cloud' and many more to follow.

Van Fleet, Dr Walter An American rose-breeder notable for fine Climbing Roses raised in the inter-war years, above all 'New Dawn'. His garden in New Jersey remains a Mecca for rose-lovers.

Vibert, J.-P. A French raiser, whose career spanned the heyday of the Gallicas and their tribe and saw the rise of the Hybrid Perpetuals. Many of the finest Old Garden Roses are attributed to him.

Von Abrams, Gordon A mid-twentieth-century American hybridist, associated with the firm of Peterson and Deering. The use of unusual breeding lines produced such beauties as 'Pink Favorite', 'Memoriam' and 'Golden Slippers'.

ROSES WITH SPECIAL QUALITIES

Some exceptionally fragrant roses

Our sense of smell is not very well developed and its memory is unreliable. All too easily, the rose one smells today eclipses that sniffed a week or a month ago. As with many of our senses, perceptions vary. So here are some roses that always delight me.

'Aotearoa'
'Belle de Crécy'
'Belle Isis'
'Blanc Double de Coubert'
'Blue Moon'
'Bobbie James'
'Buff Beauty'
'Bullata'
'Catherine Mermet'
'Celeste'
'Chrysler Imperial'
'Common Moss'
'Constance Spry'
'Crimson Glory'
'Dame Edith Helen'
'Desprez à Fleur Jaune'
'Diamond Jubilee'
'Dolly Parton'
'Double Delight'
'Eiffel Tower'
'Etoile de Hollande'
'Fantin-Latour'
'Fragrant Cloud'
'Friesia'
'General Jacqueminot'
'Gloire de Dijon'
'Grace de Monaco'
'Jadis'
'La France'
'Lady Hillingdon'
'Lady Mary Fitzwilliam'
'Madame Abel Chatenay'
'Madame Isaac Pereire'
'Maiden's Blush'
'Maréchal Niel'
'Maria Callas'
'Oklahoma'
'Prima Ballerina'
'Prince Camille de Rohan'
'Shocking Blue'
'Souvenir de la Malmaison'
'Sutter's Gold'
'The Doctor'
'Tiffany'
'Troilus'
'Trigintipetala'
'Zéphyrine Drouhin'

Early-flowering Roses

The first flowers of the season (like the first fruits) are always the most exciting; and while the rose season doesn't begin in earnest until spring has turned to summer, you can have roses earlier. Not early enough to go with the daffodils perhaps (unless you bring a couple of Large- or Cluster-flowered Roses into the greenhouse), but well ahead of the main season. Here are a few spring-flowering beauties:

'Altaica'
'Belle Portugaise'
'Cantabrigiensis'
'Golden Chersonese'
'Harison's Yellow'
'Lorraine Lee'
'Nancy Hayward'
Rosa banksiae lutea
R. ecae 'Helen Knight'
R. hugonis
R. laevigata

Most of the Hybrid Rugosas and many of the Scotch (Burnet) Roses are also early flowering.

A little later, heralding the main season, come:
'Albertine'
'Black Boy'
'Frühlingsgold'
'Frühlingsmorgen'
'Lady Hillingdon, Climbing'
'Maigold'
'Mermaid'
'Madame Alfred Carrière'
'Maréchal Niel'
'Paul's Lemon Pillar'
Rosa bracteata
R. sericea pteracantha
R. stellata mirifica
'Souvenir de la Malmaison, Climbing'
'Souvenir de Madame Léonie Viennot'
'Stanwell Perpetual'
'Sutter's Gold' (always the first of the Large-flowered roses to open with me; but much depends on how warm and sunny your garden is!)

Winter-flowering Roses

In frosty climates, the only way to have roses in winter is to grow them under glass; but, in warm-temperate and sub-tropical climates where there will be little or no frost, there are some roses (almost all of China, Tea, or *R. gigantea* derivation) which can be relied on to bloom in mid-winter and on into early spring, if they are given a light pruning and some fertilizer in mid-autumn to encourage them to form a crop of flower buds before the cool weather sets in. The flowering will be best where the plants are given a warm, sheltered spot. These are a few that perform well in southern Australia, and could be expected to do likewise in South Africa, southern California and the gulf states of the USA, or in Bermuda:

'Crépuscule'
'Doctor Grill'
'Duchesse de Brabant'
'General Gallieni'
'Lady Brisbane'
'Jean Ducher'
'Lorraine Lee' (outstanding)
'Mutabilis'
'Nancy Hayward'
'Niphetos'

'Old Blush'
'Roulettii'
'Slater's Crimson China'

Some Roses without Prickles

While the prickles of roses are something that we all get used to, there are situations in the garden where thornlessness is desirable—where a rose is growing along a front fence, for instance, and might injure passers-by. It is not always realized that prickle-free roses do exist; and here are some of them.

'Blush Boursault'
'Dupontii'
'Goldfinch'
'Kathleen Harrop'
'Madame Plantier'
'Madame de Sancy de Parabère'
'Mrs John Laing'
Rosa banksiae lutea
R. blanda;
R. foliolosa
R. gallica
R. multiflora (many forms)
R. pendulina
'Reine des Violettes'
'Rose-Marie Viaud'
'Veilchenblau'
'Zéphyrine Drouhin'

Some Excellent Roses for Cutting

Cut roses are not especially long-lived. A chrysanthemum might last three weeks in the vase, some orchids nearly a month; but a rose that lasts a week is exceptional. The greenhouse-grown roses that you buy at the florist are a special breed (you will find most of the current favorites in this book) and if they are handled carefully should stay fresh for six or seven days; but many a garden rose will live out its full life if you cut it in the cool of the day and stand it in cool, deep water for a few hours before arranging it and bringing it into the living room. Here are some that have given me great pleasure, with reasonably lasting flowers (four or five days) on consistently long stems.

'Alexander'
'Allgold'
'Antique Silk'
'Avon'
'Baccarà'
'Bewitched'
'Bridal Pink'
'Bridal White'
'Brown Velvet'
'Carla'
'Courvoisier'
'Dolly Parton'
'Double Delight'
'Duet'
'Eclipse'

'First Love'
'French Lace'
'Gay Princess'
'Glenfiddich'
'Golden Ophelia'
'Lilac Charm'
'Lissy Horstmann'
'Madame Abel Chatenay'
'Madame Butterfly'
'Malicorne'
'Maria Callas'
'Michèle Meilland'
'Montezuma'
'New Day'
'Olympiad'
'Ophelia'
'Pascali'
'Princess Margaret of England'
'Queen Elizabeth'
'Red Devil'
'Red Radiance'
'Rumba'
'Sonia'
'Starfire'
'Sunny South'
'Touch of Class'
'Virgo'
'Zorina'
Many of the larger-growing Miniatures are wonderful for small vases.

Some Exceptionally Disease-Resistant Roses

The resistance which a rose can mount against any disease is something of a variable quantity; much depends on the soil, climate and situation in which it is growing. The diseases themselves flourish more in some climates than others; and it is not unknown for a variety to begin life highly resistant to disease and lose that resistance gradually over the years. All the roses on this list have given a good account of themselves for me.

'Altissimo'
'Apricot Queen'
'Audie Murphy'
'Ballerina'
'Bonica '82'
'Buccaneer'
'Carabella'
'Cécile Brunner'
'Celeste'
'Comtesse de Cayla'
'Desprez à Fleur Jaune'
'Dortmund'
'Duet'
'Elveshörn'
'Esmeralda'

'Ferdy'
'Fragrant Cloud'
'Friesia'
'Gärtendirektor Otto Linne'
'Gingersnap'
'Golden Wings'
'Hans Christian Andersen'
'Heidesommer'
'Iceberg'
'Julishka'
'Lady Hillingdon'
'Mermaid'
'Mission Bells'
'Monsieur Tillier'
'Montezuma'
'Nancy Hayward'
'Orange Triumph'
'Pascali'
'Paul's Scarlet Climber'
'Queen Elizabeth'
Rosa bracteata
'Silver Jubilee'
'The Fairy'
'Titian'
'Yankee Doodle'
and just about all the Hybrid Rugosas

BIBLIOGRAPHY

The literature of the rose is vast, and I cannot claim to have even seen, let alone read, more than a small sample of it. The following are some rose books that have chanced to be in the bookshops I frequent, and so found their way onto my own shelves. Most have yielded information that has gone into this book, and to their authors I am duly grateful; all are worth the buying and the reading.

Austin, David, *The Heritage of the Rose*, Antique Collectors' Club, London, 1988.

Bassity, Matthew A. R., *The Magic World of Roses*, Hearthside Press, New York, 1966.

Beales, Peter, *Classic Roses*, Collins Harvill, London, 1985.

Beales, Peter, *Twentieth Century Roses*, Collins Harvill, London, 1988.

Coats, Peter, *Pleasures and Treasures: Roses*, Weidenfeld & Nicolson, London, 1962.

Cowles, Fleur, *The Flower Game*, Collins, London, 1983.

De Wolf, Gordon P. (ed), *Taylor's Book of Roses*, Houghton Mifflin, Boston, 1986.

Edwards, Gordon, *Wild and Old Garden Roses*, Readers' Union, Newton Abbot, 1975.

Edwards, John Paul and the editors of *Sunset* Magazine, *How to Grow Roses*, Lane Book Company, Menlo Park, 1960.

Fagan, Gwen, *Roses at the Cape of Good Hope*, Breestradt Publikases, Cape Town, 1988.

Fisher, John, *The Companion to Roses*, Viking, Harmondsworth, 1986.

Gault, S. Millar and Synge, Patrick M., *Dictionary of Roses in Colour*, Ebury and Michael Joseph, London, 1971.

Genders, Roy, *The Rose, A Complete Handbook*, Hale, London, 1965.

Gibson, Michael, *Growing Roses*, Croom Helm, London, 1984.

Gibson, Michael, *The Rose Gardens of England*, Collins, London, 1984.

Gordon, Jean, *The Pageant of the Rose*, Red Rose Publications, Woodstock, 1961.

Gore, Catherine Frances, *The Book of Roses, or The Rose Fancier's Manual*, London, 1838. Facsimile edition, Heyden, London and Philadelphia, 1978.

Griffiths, Trevor, *The Book of Old Roses*, Mermaid/Michael Joseph, London, 1983.

Haring, P. A. (ed.), *Modern Roses 9*, American Rose Society, Shreveport, 1986.

Harkness, Jack, *Roses*, J. M. Dent & Sons, London, 1978.

Harkness, Jack, *The Makers of Heavenly Roses*, Souvenir Press, London, 1985.

Harkness, Peter, *The Photographic Encyclopedia of Roses*, Bramley Books, Godalming, 1991.

Jekyll, Gertrude and Morley, Edward, *Roses for English Gardens*, Country Life, London, 1901.

LeGrice, E. B., *Rose Growing Complete*, Faber and Faber, London, 1965.

Keayes, Ethelyn Emery, *Old Roses*, Macmillan, New York, 1935.

McCann, Sean, *Miniature Roses*, David & Charles, London, 1985.

McFarland, J. Horace, *The Rose in America*, Macmillan, New York, 1923.

McGredy, Sam, *Look to the Rose*, David Bateman, Auckland, 1981.

Malins, Peter and Graff, M. M., *Peter Malins' Rose Book*, Dodd, Mead & Company, New York, 1979.

Mansfield, T. C., *Roses in Colour and Cultivation*, Collins, London, 1943.

Nisbett, Fred J., *Growing Better Roses*, Alfred A. Knopf, New York, 1974.

Nottle, Trevor, *Growing Old-fashioned Roses in Australia and New Zealand*, Kangaroo Press, Sydney, 1983.

Pal, B. P., *The Rose in India*, Indian Council of Agricultural Research, Delhi, (undated).

Park, Bertram, *Collins' Guide to Roses*, Collins, London, 1956.

Park, Bertram, *The World of Roses*, George S. Harrap, London, 1962.

Paul, William, *The Rose Garden*, Sherwood, Gilbert and Piper, London 1848.

Ridge, Antonia, *For Love of a Rose*, Faber and Faber, London, 1963.

Ridge, Antonia, *The Man Who Painted Roses*, Faber and Faber, London, 1974.

Redouté, P. J., *Redouté's Roses*, facsimile of the plates of *Les Roses*, Wellfleet and the Natural History Museum, London, 1990.

Rose, Graham, and King, Peter, *The Love of Roses*, Quiller Press, London, 1990.

Rossi, B. V., *Roses, A Practical and Complete Guide for Amateur Rose Growers*, Robertson & Mullens, Melbourne, (undated).

Shepherd, Roy E., *History of the Rose*, Macmillan, New York, 1954.

Steen, Nancy, *The Charm of Old Roses*, Herbert Jenkins, London, 1966.

Swane, Valerie, *Growing Roses*, Kangaroo Press, Sydney, 1992.

Thomas, A. S., *Better Roses*, Angus & Robertson, Sydney, 1950.

Thomas, Graham Stuart, *The Old Shrub Roses*, J. M. Dent & Sons, London, 1957.

Thomas, Graham Stuart, *Shrub Roses of Today*, J. M. Dent & Sons, London, 1962.

Thomas, Graham Stuart, *Climbing Roses, Old and New*, Phoenix House, London, 1965.

Thomas, Graham Stuart, *A Garden of Roses*, Watercolours by Alfred Parsons, RA, Pavilion Books, London, 1987.

Westrich, Josh, *Old Garden Roses*, Thames and Hudson, New York, 1988.

Young, Norman, *The Complete Rosarian*, St Martin's Press, New York, 1971.

The American Rose Society, the Royal National Rose Society (UK) and the Australian Rose Society all issue Annuals which are full of information and pictures. The rose societies of other countries do so too, but I have not seen them.

Many a rose nursery issues an informative catalogue. Take a look at those of Roses of Yesterday and Today (California); the Keisei Rose Research Institute (Japan); R. Harkness & Co. (UK); Keith Kirsten (South Africa); W. Kordes Sohn (Germany); and Deane Ross (South Australia). There are many, many others. Beverly Dobson in the USA produces an annual list of roses (Bev Dobson's Combined Rose List) available all over the world, which has been my constant companion while this book was being written.

ACKNOWLEDGEMENTS

While a book of favorite roses has been on my writing schedule for nearly forty years, the opportunity to complete it has, up to now, proved elusive. But what might have been an annoyance to my publishers has in the end proved beneficial to the book. Not only have many new and beautiful roses offered their beauty to my camera in the intervening years, but others which had almost vanished from the nurseries have been patiently waiting in my photographic files, to bloom afresh on these pages. Many friends and rose-loving acquaintances, both old and new, have helped bring the chosen roses before my camera, and I am indebted to all of them. They include the following.

In North America
Shirley Beach, Victoria, British Columbia, Canada
Margaret Davis OBE, Montecito, California, USA
Maryanne Green, Santa Barbara, California, USA
Jim Lichtman, Los Angeles, California, USA
Al and Ginny Littau, New York, New York, USA
Ross and Kathleen McWhae, Victoria, British Columbia, Canada
Professor Milton Meyer, Pasadena, California, USA
Patricia Stemler Wiley, Watsonville, California, USA
John Winston, Hollywood, California, USA
David Wittry, Beverly Hills, California, USA

In the United Kingdom
Bridgeman Art Library, London
Bryan and Joanna Burley, Essex
Lucy Burley, London
David Garde, London
Diana Walsh, Hertfordshire

In New Zealand
Sam McGredy, Auckland
Nicole Roucheux, Auckland
Eion Scarrow
Merv Spurway, Christchurch

In South Africa
Nancy Gardiner, Pietermaritzburg
Keith Kirsten, Waterskloof
Una van der Spuy, Stellenbosch

In Australia
John Ballard, Canberra, ACT
Margo Balmain, Adelaide, SA
Rodney Beames, Adelaide, SA
Geoffrey Burnie, Sydney, NSW
Trish and Stephen Clifton, Vermont, Vic.
Brian Donges, Sydney, NSW
Walter Duncan, Watervale, SA
Eddy Graham, Millthorpe, NSW
Philip Grattan, Sydney, NSW
Pamela Jane Harrison, Camden, NSW
Roger Mann, Sydney, NSW
Dean Miller, Adelaide, SA
Rod Nelson, Sydney, NSW
Colin Olson, Coffs Harbour, NSW
Tony Rodd, Sydney, NSW
Ed Ramsay, Sydney, NSW
Deane Ross, Willunga, SA
David Ruston, Renmark, SA
Roy Rumsey, Sydney, NSW
Shirley Stackhouse, Sydney, NSW
Terry Williams, Bungonia, NSW

In Asia
Gloria Barreto, Hong Kong
Peter Okumoto, Kyoto, Japan

In Europe
Mme Rene-Paul Jeanneret, Paris, France
Arnaud de Vinzelles, Paris, France

In addition, I am grateful to the owners, managers and directors of the following gardens, who allow camera-toting members of the public to photograph their roses.

Auckland Botanic Garden, New Zealand
Australian National Rose Garden, Old Parliament House, Canberra, ACT, Australia
Balboa Park, San Diego, California, USA
Bantry House, Cork, Eire
Beechwood, SA, Australia
Berkeley Rose Gardens, University of California, Berkeley, USA
Berlin Stadlich Gartenschau, 1985, Berlin, Germany
Botanic Gardens of Adelaide and Mount Lofty, SA, Australia
Brooklyn Botanic Gardens, New York, USA
Butchart Gardens, Vancouver Island, British Columbia, Canada
Cambridge Botanic Gardens, England
Carrick Hill, Adelaide, SA, Australia
Chateau de Malmaison, Paris, France
Chelsea Flower Show, London, England (several years)
Chelsea Physic Garden, London, England
Christchurch Botanic Gardens, New Zealand
Claude Monet's Garden, Giverney, France
Cloyne Rose Nursery, Cooma, NSW, Australia
Descanso Gardens, Sacramento, California, USA
Glasgow International Garden Festival, 1988, Scotland
Great Dixter, Sussex, England
Haddon Hall, Derbyshire, England
Heronswood Garden, Dromana, Vic., Australia
Hidcote, Gloucestershire, England
Huntingdon Gardens, San Marino, California, USA
Ilnacullin, Garinish, Eire
Indian National Rose Garden, Delhi, India
Irish National Botanic Garden, Glasnevin, Eire
Jardin Botanique, Geneva, Switzerland
Kew Palace, Richmond, Surrey, England
Kyoto Gardens, Kyoto, Japan
La Source, Orleans, France
Lal Bagh, Bangalore, India
Lime Kiln Gardens, Suffolk, England
Los Angeles State and County Aboretum, California, USA
Milton Park, Bowral, NSW, Australia
Mount Usher, Wicklow, Eire
Muckross House, Killarney, Eire
Munich Botanischer Sammlung, Germany
Nishat Bagh, Srinagar, Kashmir, India
Oakland Rose Gardens, Oakland, California, USA
Old Botanic Gardens, Brisbane, Qld, Australia
Orange Botanic Gardens, NSW, Australia
Pacific Coast Botanic Garden, California, USA
Pallant's Hill, Vic., Australia
Parc de Bagatelle, Paris, France
Parc Florale, Paris, France
Parker's Nursery, Sydney, NSW, Australia
Pialligo Nurseries, Canberra, ACT, Australia
Powerscourt, Wicklow, Eire
Queen Mary's Rose Garden, Regent's Park, London, England
Roseraie de l'Haÿ-les-Roses, France
Royal Botanic Garden, Edinburgh, Scotland
Royal Botanic Gardens, Kew, England
Royal Botanic Gardens, Melbourne, Vic., Australia
Royal Botanic Gardens, Sydney, NSW, Australia
Ryoanji, Kyoto, Japan
Saville Garden, Windsor, England
Schönbrunn Palace, Vienna, Austria
Shalimar Bagh, Kashmir, India
Sherringham's Nursery, Sydney, NSW, Australia
Sissinghurst Castle, Kent, England
Strybing Arboretum, San Francisco, USA
Sunset Magazine, Menlo Park, California, USA
Swane's Nurseries, Sydney, NSW, Australia
Syon Park, Middlesex, England
Timoleague House, Cork, Eire
Villa Fiorentina, Cap Ferrat, France
Villa Marlia, Lucca, Italy
Wakehurst Palace, Sussex, England
Wallington National Trust Garden, UK
Washington Park, Portland, Oregon, USA
Wellington Botanic Garden, New Zealand

While the vast bulk of the photographs are my own, the following people were kind enough to lend me transparencies: Branco Gaica, The Australian Opera, Sydney, NSW, Australia; Carey Beebe, The Harpsichord Centre, Sydney, NSW, Australia; Keith Kirsten, Waterskloof, South Africa; Patricia Stemler Wiley, Watsonville, California, USA; Ray Joyce photographed the scattered rose petals and most of the artworks; and Murray Fredericks did the line drawings.

INDEX

Consulting Editor: Roger Mann
Designer: Diane Quick

Captions
Pages 2–3: 'Firecracker'.
Pages 4–5: 'Madame Alfred Carrière' covering a cottage at Sissinghurst Castle.
Pages 14–15: Rosa rubiginosa.
Pages 30–1: 'Gold Marie '84'.
Pages 422–3: 'Little Artist'.

Library of Congress Cataloging-in-Publication Data

Macoboy, Stirling.
    The ultimate rose book : 1,500 roses—antique, modern (including miniature), and wild—all shown in color and selected for their beauty, fragrance, and enduring popularity / by Stirling Macoboy: foreword by Patricia Stemler Wiley.
        p.   cm.
    Includes bibliographical references (p.) and index.
    ISBN 0–8109–3920–7
    1. Roses. 2. Roses—Varieties. 3. Roses—Pictorial works.
  4. Rose culture. I. Title.
  SB411.M345 1993
  635.9'33372—dc20

                                  93–10419
                                  CIP